3rd Edition
INTERCULTURAL
COMMUNICATION

3rd Edition
INTERCULTURAL
COMMUNICATION

A Contextual Approach

JAMES W. NEULIEP
St. Norbert College

SAGE Publications
Thousand Oaks ▪ London ▪ New Delhi

For information:

Sage Publications, Inc.
2455 Teller Road
Thousand Oaks, California 91320
E-mail: order@sagepub.com

Sage Publications Ltd.
1 Oliver's Yard
55 City Road
London EC1Y 1SP
United Kingdom

Sage Publications India Pvt. Ltd.
B-42, Panchsheel Enclave
Post Box 4109
New Delhi 110 017 India

Printed in the United States of America.

Library of Congress Cataloging-in-Publication Data

Neuliep, James William, 1957-.
Intercultural communication : a contextual approach / James W. Neuliep.—3rd ed.
    p. cm.
Includes bibliographical references and index.
ISBN 1-4129-1741-7 (pbk.)
   1. Intercultural communication. 2. Culture. I. Title.
HM1211.N48 2006
303.48′2—dc22

                         2005023033

This book is printed on acid-free paper.

05   06   07   08   09   10 9 8 7 6 5 4 3 2 1

Acquiring Editor:	Todd R. Armstrong
Editorial Assistant:	Deya Saoud
Project Editor:	Astrid Virding
Typesetter:	C&M Digitals (P) Ltd.
Cover Designer:	Michelle Lee

Contents

Preface

Intercultural Communication: A Contextual Approach (3rd ed.) is designed for college-level students taking their first course in intercultural communication. The purpose of the book is to introduce students to some of the fundamental topics, theories, concepts, and themes that are at the center of the study of intercultural communication.

The overall organizational scheme of the book is based on a *contextual model of intercultural communication*. The model represents intercultural communication as the exchange of verbal and nonverbal messages that occurs within the cultural, microcultural, environmental, socio-relational, and perceptual contexts of the interactants. The model is presented in Chapter 1.

The organizational scheme of this new edition remains essentially unchanged from the second edition, but many substantive revisions have been incorporated.

Chapter 1 alerts students to the importance and necessity of intercultural communication in the twenty-first century. Current data from the U.S. Census Bureau are reviewed and point to the growing diversity of the U.S. population, focusing on the growth of the Hispanic population. The chapter continues with extended discussions of the nature of human communication and culture. While reading Chapter 1, students can complete and score the Personal Report of Communication Apprehension (PRCA-24), the Generalized Ethnocentrism scale (GENE), and the Personal Report of Intercultural Communication Apprehension (PRICA). The chapter closes with a delineation of five fundamental assumptions of intercultural communication.

In Chapter 2, culture is defined as an accumulated pattern of values, beliefs, and behaviors shared by an identifiable group of people with a common history and verbal and nonverbal code system. The outer circle of the model of intercultural communication represents the cultural context. This is the largest circle because culture permeates every aspect of the communicative exchange, even the physical geography. All communicative exchanges between persons occur within some culture. The cultural context is the focus of Chapter 2. Well-recognized topics such as individualism-collectivism, high-low context, weak-strong uncertainty avoidance, value orientations, and high-low power distance are discussed. Self-report scales measuring each of these topics are included in the chapter.

The focus of Chapter 3 is the microcultural context. Within most cultures are groups of people that differ in some significant way from the general macro culture. These groups are sometimes called minorities, subcultures, or cocultures. In this book, the term *microculture* is used to refer to those identifiable groups of people that share a set of values, beliefs, and behaviors and that possess a common history and verbal and nonverbal symbol system that is similar to, but systematically varies from, the larger, often dominant cultural milieu. Microcultures can be different from the larger culture in a variety of ways, most often because of race, ethnicity, language, religion, or even because of their behavioral practices. Such microcultures develop their own language for communicating outside of the dominant or majority culture's context or value system. Chapter 3 includes an extended discussion of four U.S. microcultures: Hispanics, African-Americans, Amish, and Hmong.

Chapter 4 focuses on the environmental context. Whereas culture prescribes the overall rules for communication, the environmental context prescribes when and what specific rules apply. The environmental context includes the physical geography, architecture, landscape design, housing, perceptions of privacy, time orientation, and even the climate of a particular culture. These environmental factors play a key role in how people communicate. In this chapter, students are given the opportunity to assess their privacy preferences and their monochronic/polychronic orientations. Chapter 4 includes coverage of the nature of privacy in the United States, with a special focus on the perceptions of privacy among U.S. students.

Chapter 5 focuses on the perceptual contexts of the interactants. The perceptual context refers to the individual characteristics of the interactants, including their cognitions, attitudes, dispositions, and motivations. How an individual gathers, stores, and retrieves information is uniquely human but also culturally influenced. An individual's attitudes about others, including stereotypes, is culturally influenced. Also included in Chapter 5 is a discussion of American racism as a parallel to ethnocentrism.

The socio-relational context is the focus of Chapter 6. Whenever two people come together and interact, they establish some sort of social relationship based on their group memberships. Within such relationships each person assumes a role. Roles prescribe with whom, about what, and how to communicate. Roles vary from culture to culture. For example, in just about every culture there are student and teacher role relationships. How student/teacher roles are defined varies significantly from culture to culture. For example, the U.S. American definition of student varies significantly from the Japanese definition of student. What it means to be a mother or father varies considerably from one culture to another. One's roles prescribe the types of verbal and nonverbal symbols that are exchanged. Chapter 6 contains a discussion of family groups and sex groups. In addition, the contextual model of intercultural communication represents the socio-relational context as defined by the verbal and nonverbal code.

Chapter 7 focuses on the verbal code and human language. Throughout much of the book, cultural *differences* are highlighted. In Chapter 7, however, language is characterized as essentially *human* rather than cultural. Based on the ideas of Noam Chomsky and other contemporary linguists, Chapter 7 points out that regardless of culture, people are born with the capacity for language. Humans are born with universal grammar and, through culture, are exposed to a subset of it that constitutes their particular culture's language (e.g., English, French, and so on). The language of a particular culture is simply a subset of universal language. To be sure, however, culture certainly affects how we use language. Thus, Chapter 7 outlines several styles of language and how they vary across cultures.

Chapter 8 focuses on the nonverbal code. After a discussion of the relationship between the verbal and nonverbal code, seven channels of nonverbal communication are discussed: kinesics, paralanguage, proxemics, haptics, olfactics, physical appearance/dress, and chronemics.

In the section on kinesics, the use of gestures across cultures and an extended discussion of affect displays across cultures is presented. In the coverage of paralanguage, cultural uses of silence and tonal languages are discussed. Cultural variations of space are covered in the section on proxemics. High- and low-contact cultures are the focus of the section on haptics. An extended discussion of olfactics across cultures is presented, and students can assess their perception of smell by completing the Personal Report of Olfactic Perception and Sensitivity (PROPS) scale. The discussion of physical appearance and dress looks at cultural variations in Muslim cultures and Japan, among others. The discussion of chronemics reviews Hall's monochronic/polychronic distinction in addition to a treatment of the use of calendars across cultures. Finally, the chapter closes with a cross-cultural application of Nonverbal Expectancy Violations Theory.

Chapter 9 discusses the development of intercultural relationships. Five factors that affect relationships are the focus of this chapter: uncertainty reduction, intercultural communication apprehension, sociocommunicative style, empathy, and similarity. Each factor is discussed with an emphasis on intercultural relationships. The chapter also includes a discussion of relationship differences among Eastern and Western cultures, marital relationships across cultures, interracial and intercultural relation-ships, arranged marriages, mate selection practices across cultures, and divorce. In this chapter students can complete the Sociocommunicative Style Scale and the Factors in Choosing a Mate instrument and compare their preferences with other cultures.

Chapter 10's focus is intercultural communication in organizations. In this chapter, all of the contexts presented earlier are applied to the organi-zational context. Organizational examples from the cultural, microcultural, environmental, perceptual, and socio-relational contexts have been updated. Because they are three of our largest trade partners, management perspectives in Japan, Germany, and Mexico are highlighted, plus the Middle East. In addition, a model of intercultural conflict, with an emphasis in organizations, is included.

The focus of the revised Chapter 11 is acculturation and culture shock. The central theme of Chapter 11 is the practical aspects of traveling or mov-ing to a new culture. A model of assimilation/acculturation is presented along with factors that influence the acculturation process, such as per-ceived similarity and host culture attitudes. A four-stage "U" model of cul-ture shock is outlined. In addition, the chapter includes a discussion of the "W"-curve model of culture shock. The chapter also includes a variety of self-report inventories to help students prepare for their journeys abroad.

The focus of Chapter 12 is intercultural competence. The model represents intercultural competence as four interdependent components—knowledge, affective, psychomotor, and situational features. A self-assessment instrument is included so that students can assess the knowledge component of the competence model. In addition to the model, a section on intercultural training has been incorporated.

Most chapters contain a number of self-assessment instruments. These are designed so that students can learn about themselves as they learn about important concepts in intercultural communication. The instruments included in the chapters have documented validity and reliability. As in the first edition, most of the chapters in the revised edition of this book contain *intercultural conversations*. These hypothetical scripts illustrate how the various concepts discussed in the chapters manifest themselves in human interaction. Each chapter also includes a summary, glossary of terms, and an extensive reference list.

A number of people have been instrumental in the revision of this book. As in the earlier editions, this book has been strongly influenced by the writing and research of the late William B. Gudykunst. Bill's influence can be seen throughout the book. Gudykunst's substantial contributions to the field remain a strong influence on the way we write and teach about intercultural communication. The editorial and production staff at Sage

Publications deserve much of the credit for what is good in this book. They have been incredibly patient with me and I wish to express my gratitude publicly. My editor, Todd Armstrong, has been extremely supportive of this project. Very special thanks to my assistant editor, Deya Saoud. Deya has been unbelievably tolerant and merciful of my numerous missed deadlines. Thanks also to Astrid Virding, the senior project editor, and Liann Lech, the copy editor, who each spent countless hours on the production of the book. Thanks to Joan E. Aitken (University of Missouri-Kansas City) and to Steven T. McDermott (California Polytechnic State University), the reviewers of the book, whose many suggestions were incorporated into the revision. I appreciate very much your constructive comments and recommendations. Thanks also to Corwin King (Central Washington University), Radda Hegde (New York University), Henry Tkachuk (Concordia College), and Tina Kistler (Santa Barbara City College) for reviewing this second edition, as well as Benjamin Broome (Arizona State University), Donal Carbaugh (University of Massachusetts, Amherst), Wendy V. Chung (Alliant International University), Natalie Dollar (Oregon State University), Daradirek Ekachai (Marquette University), Madeline M. Keaveney (California State University, Chico), Corwin King (Central Washington University), Jaesub Lee (University of Houston), Candice Thomas-Maddox (Ohio University) for their comments on the first edition.

A very special and sincere thank you goes to my students, from whom I have learned a great deal about culture and life. This book has always been about, and for, you.

—J.W.N.

—DePere, WI

CHAPTER 1

The Necessity of Intercultural Communication

". . . the history of our planet has been in great part the history of the mixing of peoples."

—Arthur M. Schlesinger, Jr.[1]

Chapter Objectives

After reading this chapter, you should be able to

1. List and discuss the benefits of intercultural communication.
2. Recognize the increasing racial and ethnic diversity in the U.S. population.
3. Identify and discuss the eight dimensions of communication.
4. Assess your degree of communication apprehension.
5. Define and discuss the nature of culture.
6. Identify and discuss the five contexts of intercultural communication.
7. Discuss the relationship between intercultural communication, uncertainty, and anxiety.
8. Assess your degree of intercultural communication apprehension.
9. Identify and discuss the three fundamental assumptions of intercultural communication.
10. Assess your degree of ethnocentrism.

At the dawn of the twenty-first century, Marshall McLuhan's vision of a *global village* is no longer considered an abstract idea but a virtual certainty. Technological and sociopolitical changes have made the world a smaller planet to inhabit. The technological feasibility of the mass media to bring events from across the globe into our homes, businesses, and schools dramatically reduces the distance between peoples of different cultures and societies. Telecommunication systems link the world via satellites and fiber optics. Supersonic jets carry people from one country to another faster than the speed of sound. Politically, the end of the cold war between the United States and the former Soviet Union has brought decades of partisan tensions to an end. Some countries that were once bitter enemies are now joining forces. Mass migrations force interaction between people of different races, nationalities, and ethnicities. Noted historian and Pulitzer Prize winner Arthur Schlesinger warns us that history tells an ugly story of what happens when people of diverse cultural, ethnic, religious, or linguistic backgrounds converge in one place. Witness the war in the former Yugoslavia. As the stranglehold of ideological repression in Eastern Europe was released, ethnic groups that once lived peacefully within their geopolitical borders now clash and kill one another by the thousands in the name of nationalism and *ethnic cleansing*. The hostility of one group of people against another, *different* group of people is among the most instinctive of human drives. Schlesinger contends that unless a common goal binds diverse people together, tribal hostilities will drive them apart. By replacing the conflict of political ideologies that dominated in the twentieth century, ethnic and racial strife will usher in the new millennium as the explosive issue.[2] Only through intercultural communication can such conflict be managed and reduced. Only by competently and peacefully interacting with others who are different from ourselves can our global village survive.

THE NEED FOR INTERCULTURAL COMMUNICATION

International tensions around the globe, the most noticeable to U.S. Americans in the Middle East, Northern Ireland, and Eastern Europe, are striking examples of the need for effective and competent intercultural communication. Although political in origin, such conflicts are fueled by ethnic and religious differences. Indeed, national conflicts within our own borders, often ignited by racial and ethnic tensions, underscore the necessity for skillful intercultural communication. An international incident with potentially global consequences occurred between The People's Republic of China and the United States, stressing the need for intercultural communication. The incident began on April 1, 2001, when a U.S. Navy surveillance plane collided with a Chinese fighter jet in international airspace over the South China Sea. As a result of the collision, the U.S. plane, an EP-3 electronic warfare and surveillance aircraft, was damaged and nearly crashed. However, because of heroic efforts on the part of the crew, the plane landed safely at a Chinese air base. China reported that its plane was missing and its pilot was presumed dead. The 24-member crew of the U.S. plane was detained by the Chinese military. China and the United States disagreed as to the cause of the collision, each side blaming the other.[3]

In the days and weeks following the incident contentious negotiations took place between Chinese and U.S. officials over the release of the U.S. crew. For their release, China demanded that the United States accept responsibility and apologize for the collision. The United States refused, arguing that the collision was the fault of the Chinese pilot. In the meantime, public pressure was mounting on President Bush to gain the release of the crew. On April 4, then-Secretary of State Colin Powell expressed "regret" over the collision and the disappearance of the Chinese jet pilot. Although Chinese officials acknowledged Powell's statement as a move in the right direction, they insisted that the United States apologize for the incident. On April 8, Vice President Dick Cheney and Colin Powell rejected China's demands for an apology but expressed "sorrow" about the disappearance of the Chinese pilot. They also drafted a letter of sympathy to the pilot's wife. The Chinese continued to demand an apology. On April 10, U.S. officials said that President Bush would be willing to offer, to the Chinese, a letter expressing regret over the incident, including a statement admitting that the U.S. aircraft landed in Chinese territory without seeking permission. The Chinese continued to demand an apology.

Finally, on April 11, the United States issued a letter to the Chinese Foreign Minister asking him to "convey to the Chinese people and to the family of pilot Wang Wei that we are very sorry for their loss." The letter continued, "We are very sorry the entering of China's airspace and the landing did not have verbal clearance." To be sure, the word "apology" did not appear in the letter. But in their announcement of the letter to the Chinese people, Chinese officials chose to translate the double "very sorry" as "shenbiao qianyi," which, in Chinese, means a deep expression of apology or regret, and is an expression not used unless one is admitting wrongdoing and accepting responsibility for it. Based on that letter and the subsequent translation, China agreed to release the 24-member crew. John Pomfret, of the Washington Post Foreign Service, asserted, "In the end, it was a matter of what the United States chose to say and what China chose to hear." Apparently, such delicacies in communication are common during U.S.-China

Table 1.1   Benefits of Intercultural Communication

1. Healthier Communities

2. Increased Commerce

3. Reduced Conflict

4. Personal Growth through Tolerance

negotiations. According to Bates Gill, director of the Center for Northeast Asian Policy Studies at the Brookings Institution, U.S. negotiators often use words such as "acknowledge" that, when translated into Chinese, mean "admit" or "recognize" so that the Chinese can interpret such wordings as an admission of U.S. guilt.[4]

Benefits of Intercultural Communication

Although the challenges of an increasingly diverse world are great, the benefits are even greater. Communicating and establishing relationships with people from different cultures can lead to a whole host of benefits, including healthier communities; increased international, national, and local commerce; reduced conflict; and personal growth through increased tolerance (see Table 1.1).

Joan England argues that genuine community is a condition of togetherness in which people have lowered their defenses and learn to accept and celebrate their differences. England contends that we can no longer define equality as "sameness," but instead must value our differences with others whether they be about race, gender, ethnicity, lifestyle, or even occupation or professional discipline.[5] Healthy communities are made up of individuals working collectively for the benefit of everyone, not just their own group. Through open and honest intercultural communication people can work together to achieve goals that benefit everyone, regardless of group or cultural orientation. According to M. Scott Peck the overall mission of human communication is (or should be) reconciliation. He argues that effective communication can ultimately lower or remove walls and barriers of misunderstanding that separate human beings from one another. Peck states that the rules for community building are the same rules for effective communication. Communication is the foundation of all human relationships. Moreover, argues Peck, the principles of community are applicable to any situation in which two people are gathered together,

Table 1.2   Common Stereotypes

. . . about Blacks	. . . about Whites	. . . about Asians
"They're lazy."	"They think they know everything."	"They're sneaky."
"They live on welfare."	"They're all arrogant."	"They're good at math."
"They like to dance."	"They're all rich."	"I wouldn't trust them."
"They smoke crack."	"They're materialistic."	"They're really shy."

including the global community, in the home, business, or neighborhood. Healthy communities support all community members and strive to understand, appreciate, and acknowledge each member.[6]

Our ability to interact with persons from different cultures both from within and outside our borders has immense economic benefits. According to the U.S. Department of Commerce, the markets that hold the greatest potential for dramatic increases in U.S. exports are Argentina, Brazil, China, India, Mexico, Poland, South Africa, South Korea, Turkey, and ASEAN (The Association of Southeast Asian Nations, which includes Brunei, Indonesia, Malaysia, the Philippines, Singapore, Thailand, and Vietnam). India, for example, offers immense prospects for growth and earning potential in practically all areas of business, especially for small and medium-sized businesses. Only through successful intercultural communication can such business potentials be realized.[7]

Conflict is inevitable; we will never be able to erase it. We can, however, through cooperative intercultural communication, reduce and manage conflict. Often, conflict stems from our inability to see another person's point of view, especially if that person is from a different culture. We develop blatant generalizations about them (which are often incorrect) and mistrust them (see Table 1.2). Such feelings lead to defensive behavior, which fosters conflict. If we can learn to think and act cooperatively by engaging in assertive (not aggressive) and responsive intercultural communication, we can effectively manage and reduce conflict with others.

As you communicate with people from different cultures you learn more about them and their way of life, including their values, history, and habits, and the substance of their personality. As your relationship develops you start to understand them better, perhaps even empathizing with them. One of the things you will learn (eventually) is that although your cultures are different, you have much in common. As humans we all have the same basic desires and needs, we just have different ways of achieving them. As we learn that our way is not the only way, we develop a tolerance for difference. This can be accomplished only when we initiate relationships with people who are different from ourselves.

Diversity in the United States

One need not travel to faraway countries to understand the need for, and experience the benefits of, intercultural communication. Largely because of immigration trends, cultural and ethnic diversity in the United States is a fact of life. Immigrants, in record numbers, are crossing U.S. borders. Nearly 34 million persons living in the United States (i.e., 12 percent) were not U.S. citizens at birth. More than half of these people were born in Latin America.[8]

Every ten years, at the beginning of a new decade, the U.S. Department of Commerce conducts a census. The results of the 2000 census profile the remarkable racial and ethnic diversity that has been a hallmark of American society. From 1990 to 2000 the U.S. population growth of 33 million people was the largest census-to-census increase in American history. As of January 2005, there were approximately 295 million people in the United States. Of these people, nearly 70 percent were White non-Hispanics, 13 percent were Hispanic, 12 percent were Black non-Hispanic, 4 percent were Asian or Pacific Islander, and 1 percent were American Indian.[9]

Overall, from 2000 to 2004 the U.S. population grew 4.3 percent. But different racial and ethnic groups grow at different rates. For example, White non-Hispanics make up nearly 70 percent of the U.S. population today. But Census Bureau data suggest that by the year 2050 non-Hispanic Whites will comprise approximately 53 percent of the population (see Figures 1.1a and 1.1b).[10]

One of the most significant population trends in the United States is the growth of the Hispanic population. The federal government uses the terms Hispanic and Latino interchangeably and classifies Hispanics/Latinos as an ethnic group but not a racial group. According to the U.S. Census Bureau, Hispanics are a heterogeneous group composed of Mexicans, Cubans, Puerto Ricans, persons from Central and South America, and persons of other Hispanic origin. Nearly 80 percent of all Hispanics-Latinos live in the southern or western areas of the United States. In fact, half of all Hispanics in the United States live in two states, California and Texas. But that trend is likely to change in the next decade as the Hispanic population expands geographically. For example, from 1990 to 2000 the Hispanic population of Green Bay, Wisconsin, grew nearly 600 percent.[11]

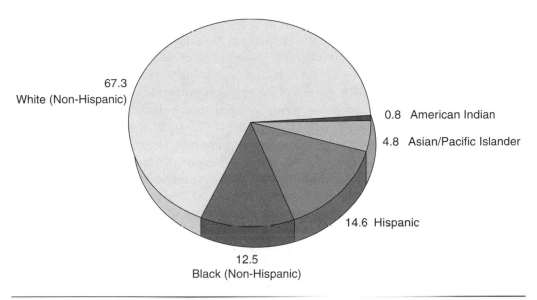

Figure 1.1a   2010 US Population Estimates

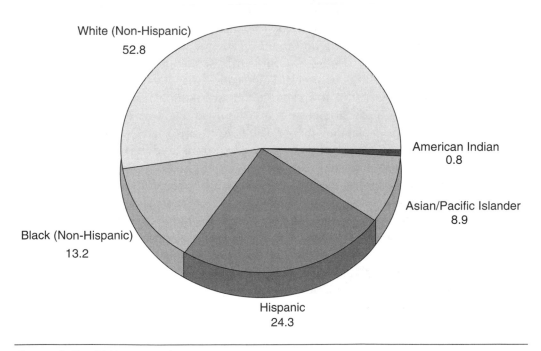

Figure 1.1b   2050 US Population Estimates

African-Americans, now the second largest non-White group, make up just over 12 percent of the total population. Whereas the Hispanic population is projected to grow considerably in the next 25 years, the African-American population is projected to remain relatively stable and increase only 1 percentage point (to 13 percent of the population) by the year 2025. Over half of all Black people live in the South and over half of all Blacks live inside central metropolitan cities.

Persons of Asian descent make up about 4 percent of the population and include persons of Asian Indian, Chinese, Filipino, Japanese, Korean, Vietnamese, and other Asian origins. American Indians and Alaskan Natives comprise just less than 1 percent of the total U.S. population.

In addition to the rapid growth of non-White populations in the United States, another trend is emerging: an increasing number of groups are revitalizing their ethnic traditions and promoting their cultural and ethnic uniqueness through language. Language is a vital part of maintaining one's cultural heritage, and many people become very protective of their native language. For example, in July 2002, in Brown County, Wisconsin, a county with a sizable Hmong and Hispanic community, the county Board of Commissioners made English the official language of its government and called for more spending to promote English fluency. The all-White Brown County board voted 17–8 to approve the measure. "It's saying this is our official language. This is what we believe in, and we should encourage English," said Board Supervisor John Vander Leest. On the other hand, in August 2004, the Texas border town of El Cenizo, whose population is heavily Hispanic, adopted Spanish as its official language. Mayor Rafael Rodriguez said that he and most of the town's residents speak only Spanish. According to Rodriguez, "In past administrations, the meetings were done in English and they did not explain anything." The vote means that town business will be conducted in Spanish, which then will be translated into English for official documents to meet the requirements of Texas law. Rodriguez said the city council's intent was not to usurp English or create divisions, but to make local government more accessible to the town's residents. "What we are looking for is that the people of the community who attend the meetings and who only speak Spanish be able to voice their opinions," Rodriguez said.

Nearly one in five people in the United States (i.e., 47 million) speak a language other than English at home. Of those 47 million, nearly 30 million speak Spanish at home. Ten percent speak an Indo-European language, and about 7 percent speak an Asian or Pacific Islander language. Interestingly, most of the people who speak a language other than English at home report that they speak English very well. When these people are combined with those who speak only English at home, more than 92 percent of the U.S. population has no difficulty speaking English.[12]

Although the United States prides itself on being a nation of immigrants, there is a growing sense of uncertainty, fear, and distrust between different cultural, ethnic, and linguistic groups. These feelings create anxiety that can foster separatism rather than unity. Arthur Schlesinger alerts us that

> a cult of ethnicity has arisen both among non-Anglo whites and among nonwhite minorities to denounce the idea of a melting pot, to challenge the concept of "one people," and to protect, promote, and perpetuate separate ethnic and racial communities.[13]

Many Americans are frustrated, confused, and uncertain about these linguistic and definitional issues. Only through intercultural communication can such uncertainty be reduced. Only when diverse people come together and interact can they unify rather than separate. Unity is impossible without communication. Intercultural communication is a necessity.

Human Communication

Communication is everywhere. Everywhere, every day, people are communicating. Even when they are alone, people are bombarded with communication. Communication Professor Charles Larson estimates that Americans are exposed to more than 5000 persuasive messages every day.[14] Most people would be miserable if they were not allowed to communicate with others. Indeed, solitary confinement is perhaps the worst form of punishment inflicted on humans. Human communication—that is, the ability to symbolize and use language—separates humans from animals. Communication with others is the essence of what it means to be human.

Communication has a profound effect on humans. Through communication people conduct their lives. People define themselves via their communication with others. Communication is the vehicle by which people initiate, maintain, and terminate their relationships with others. Communication is the means by which people influence and persuade others. Through communication, local, regional, national, and international conflicts are managed and resolved.

Ironically, however, communication, and particularly one's *style* of communication, can be the source of many problems. Marriage counselors indicate that a breakdown in communication is the most frequently cited reason for relational dissolution in the United States.[15] A specific kind of communication; that is, public speaking, is one of the most frequently cited fears people have, even more than they fear death.

This book is about the ubiquitous subject labeled communication. Specifically, this is a book about *intercultural* communication; that is, communication between people of different cultures and ethnicities. Throughout the course of this book you will be introduced to a whole host of concepts and theories that explain the process of people of differing cultural backgrounds coming together and exchanging verbal and non-verbal messages. Chapter 1 is designed as an introductory chapter and is divided into three parts. The first part of the chapter outlines and discusses the nature of communication. This part of the chapter will examine communication variables that apply to everyone, regardless of cultural background. The second part outlines and discusses culture. Culture is seen as a paradox; that is, culture is simultaneously a very subtle and clearly defined influence on human thought processes and behavior. The last part of the chapter presents a model of intercultural communication that will serve as the organizing scheme of the rest of this book.

The Nature of Human Communication

Because of its ubiquitous nature communication is very difficult to define. Thirty-five years ago, Frank Dance compiled a list of 98 different definitions of communication.[16] A few years later, Dance and Carl Larson presented a listing of over 125 definitions of communication.[17] If you were to go to your university library and select ten different introductory communication texts, the probability is that each will offer a different definition of communication.[18] Although there are many definitions of communication, these definitions are important because the way people define communication influences how they think and theorize about communication.

Although there is no universally agreed-upon definition of communication, there are certain properties of communication upon which most communication scholars agree describe its nature. Outlined below are eight of these properties along with eight definitions of communication (see also Table 1.3). These definitions come from a variety of scholars with diverse backgrounds in the communication field.

Dimension 1: Process. Almost all communication scholars concur that communication is a process. A process is anything that is ongoing, ever-changing, and continuous. A process does not have a specific beginning or ending point. A process is not static or at rest; it is always moving. The human body is a process; it is always aging. Communication is always developing; it is never still or motionless. There is no exact beginning or ending point of a communication exchange. Although individual *verbal* messages have definite beginning and ending points, the overall process of communication does not. For example, Jose and Juan meet in the hallway and greet each other. Jose says, "What's up, Juan?" and Juan says, "Not much, man." Both Jose's and Juan's verbal messages have exact beginning and ending

Table 1.3   Eight Properties and Definitions of Communication

1. Process	"Communication theory reflects a process point of view . . . you cannot talk about the beginning or the end of communication." (Berlo)[19]
2. Dynamic	"Communication is a transaction among symbol users in which meanings are dynamic, changing as a function of earlier usages and of changes in perceptions and metaperceptions. Common to both meanings is the notion that communication is timebound and irreversible." (Bowers & Bradac)[20]
3. Interactive-Transactive	"Communication occurs when two or more people interact through the exchange of messages." (Goss)[21]
4. Symbolic	"All the symbols of the mind, together with the means of conveying them through space and preserving then in time." (Cooley)[22]
5. Intentional	"Communication has as its central interest those behavioral situations in which a source transmits a message to a receiver(s) with conscious intent to affect the latter's behavior." (Miller)[23]
6. Contextual	"Communication always and inevitably occurs within some context." (Fisher)[24]
7. Ubiquitous	"Communication is the discriminatory response of an organism to a stimulus." (Stevens)[25]
8. Cultural	"Culture is communication . . . communication is culture." (Hall)[26]

points. But to determine exactly when and where their *nonverbal* communication begins and ends is virtually impossible. They may not be verbally communicating with each other, but they are still communicating nonverbally. Even if they walk away from each other they are communicating that they are no longer talking with each other. A process is something that continues to develop and change; it does not stop, nor can it reverse itself. Because communication is irreversible, it affects future communication. How Jose and Juan interact with each other today is very much influenced by how they interacted yesterday, last week, or even years ago. Think about your own relationships with your friends and how what you have said to each other in the past influences what you say today. Imagine the last time you had an argument with your boy/girlfriend, for example. You may have said some things you now regret. Such interaction influences your relationships and how you interact today.

Dimension 2: Dynamic. Inextricably bound to the notion that communication is a process is that communication is dynamic. The terms *process* and *dynamic* are closely related. Part of what makes communication a process is its dynamic nature. Something that is dynamic is considered active and/or forceful. Unfortunately, communication is typically discussed as if it were some physical entity or thing that people can hold or touch. Because communication is a dynamic process, it is impossible to capture its essence in a written definition or graphic model. This problem is not unlike the problem faced by a photographer who tries to capture the dynamic essence of a running horse with a photograph. Certainly the photograph can be very informative about the horse, but the camera cannot make a complete reproduction of the object photographed. The relationship between the fore and hind legs, the beautiful "dynamic" muscular motions cannot be truly represented in a photograph. Hence, any discussion of communication as a dynamic process is subject to the same kind of limitations as the photographer.[27] To fully appreciate the process one must be a part of it or witness it in motion. As a dynamic process communication is flexible, adaptive, and fluid. Communication is a dynamic process and hence is impossible to identically replicate in a picture, drawing, or model.

Dimension 3: Interactive-Transactive. Communication is interactive and transactive because it occurs between people. While some might argue that people can communicate with themselves (what is called *intrapersonal* communication), most scholars believe that interaction between people is a fundamental dimension of communication. Communication requires the *active* participation of two people sending and receiving messages. Active participation means that people are *consciously directing* their messages to someone else.[28] This means that communication is a two-way process, or interactive. Likewise, to say that communication is transactional means that while Jose is sending messages to Juan, Juan is *simultaneously* sending messages to Jose. Juan's eye contact, facial expression, and body language are nonverbal messages to Jose informing him how his message is being received. Each person in an interactional setting simultaneously sends (encodes) and receives (decodes) messages. For example, when you listen to your friends talk about the great party they went to last night, it is obvious to you that they are sending you messages. At the same time they describe the party to you, you are sending messages to them, too. Your eye contact, smiles, and other nonverbal reactions are communicating to them your interest in their story. Hence, both you and your friends are sending and receiving messages at the same time.

Dimension 4: Symbolic. That communication is symbolic is another fundamental assumption guiding most communication scholars. A symbol is an arbitrarily selected and learned stimulus that represents something else. Symbols can be verbal or nonverbal. Symbols are the vehicle by which

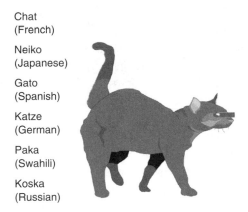

Chat
(French)

Neiko
(Japanese)

Gato
(Spanish)

Katze
(German)

Paka
(Swahili)

Koska
(Russian)

Figure 1.2 Different languages use different codes

the thoughts and ideas of one person can be communicated to another person. Messages are constructed with verbal and nonverbal symbols. Through symbols meanings are transferred between people. Symbols (i.e., words) have no natural relationship with what they represent (they are arbitrarily selected and learned). For example, the verbal symbols "C.A.T." have no natural connection with cute, fuzzy animals that purr and like to be scratched. The symbols "C.A.T." have no meaning in other languages (see Figure 1.2).

Nonverbal symbols are arbitrary as well. Showing someone your upright middle finger may not communicate much in some cultures. Verbal and nonverbal symbols are only meaningful to people who have learned to associate them with what they represent. People can allow just about any symbols they want to represent just about anything they want. For example, you and your friends probably communicate with each other using private symbols that no one else understands. You have your own secret code. You have words, phrases, gestures, and handshakes that only you and your friends know, understand, and use. This allows you to communicate with each other with your own "foreign" language. Drug dealers and users, for example, have an elaborate and highly rule-governed language that allows them to communicate about their illegal activities. In drug language, the phrase "blow a splif" is symbolic code for "smoke a marijuana cigarette."

Any verbal language (e.g., English, Chinese, Russian) is a code made up of symbols. The letters of the English alphabet (e.g., "A, B, C . . .") are a set of symbols that represent sounds. When we combine the individual symbols (e.g., "C + A + T") they become meaningful. By using symbols, people can represent their thoughts and ideas through writing or speaking. Once an idea has been encoded with symbols, it becomes a message. During communication, people encode their thoughts and send them to someone else. The other person listens to the message and translates it; that is, decodes it. When Jose saw Juan he encoded a greeting. Juan decoded (i.e., translated) the message and encoded a response. Interaction, then, is the process of encoding and decoding messages. People who speak different languages are simply using different codes.

Dimension 5: Intentional. Perhaps one of the most debated issues regarding the communication process centers around intentionality. On one side of the debate are those who argue that communication is intentional. On the other side are those who insist that communication can occur unintentionally. Intentional communication exists whenever two or more people consciously engage in interaction with some purpose.[29] For example, if Kyoko says to Akira, "Hey, do you want to go out to eat tonight?" and Akira responds by saying, "Yeah, that sounds like a good idea!" intentional communication has surely taken place.

Unintentional communication may exist, however. For example, at a party, Kyoko thinks that Akira is consciously ignoring her because he interacts with several other people. Kyoko senses that Akira is consciously sending her a message when, in fact, Akira's intention is simply to talk with new friends. Akira is not intentionally ignoring Kyoko but she thinks that he is indeed sending her a message (i.e., a nonverbal message). Since a response has been elicited in Kyoko, some communication scholars argue that communication has occurred.

Three interpretations can be drawn from the above discussion. To many communication scholars intentionality is a central property of the communication process. Others insist that any message interpreted by a person qualifies as communication whether or not the message was intentionally sent. Still others insist that all behavior, intentional or not, is informative and meaningful, and thus is communicative. Thus, whenever a person (e.g., Kyoko in the above example) responds to some stimulus (e.g., Akira talking with other people) communication has occurred. In this book, the type of communication that will be discussed is intentional communication. This book takes the position that intentional communication, either verbal or nonverbal, is more informative than unintentional communication.

Dimension 6: Contextual. Communication is dependent on the context in which it occurs. The effects and outcomes, styles and fashions, and the resulting meaning are all dependent on the context in which the communication occurs. In this book, a context is the cultural, physical, relational, and perceptual environment in which communication occurs. In many ways the context defines the meaning of any messages. For example, the context of the classroom defines the kind of communication that will occur. Most students sit quietly while the professor psychologically stimulates them with a brilliant lecture.

There are essentially four different kinds of context that influence the process of communication: (a) the cultural and microcultural environment, (b) the physical environment, (c) the socio-relational environment, and (d) the perceptual environment. The cultural context includes all of the factors and influences that make up one's culture. This context will be discussed in detail in the next section of this chapter. The physiological context is the actual geographical space or territory in which the communication takes place. For example, communication between Juan and Jose will be different when they are interacting on a busy street in a big city compared to when they are in their university library. The socio-relational environment refers to social roles and group memberships (e.g., demographics). Sex, age, religious affiliation, education level, and economic status affect how one communicates and relates with others. Finally, the perceptual context includes all of the motivations, intentions, and personality traits people bring to the communication event. When you are interacting with your professor about an examination that you just failed, you have a very different set of motivations and intentions from when you are asking someone out on a date.

Dimension 7: Ubiquitous. That communication is ubiquitous simply means that communication is everywhere, done by everyone, all of the time. Humans are constantly bombarded with verbal and nonverbal messages. Wherever one goes there is some communication happening. In fact some scholars in the field of communication argue that it is impossible to not communicate. Paul Watzlawick, Janet Beavin, and Don Jackson have argued that *one cannot not communicate.* The logic of their argument is that (a) behavior has no opposite; one cannot not behave; (b) in an interactional setting, all behavior has informational value and/or message value; it is informative; (c) since behavior is informative, it is communicative; and (d) if behavior is communicative, and one cannot not behave, then one cannot not communicate.[30]

Dimension 8: Cultural. Culture shapes communication and communication is culture bound. People from different cultures communicate differently. The verbal and nonverbal symbols we use to communicate with our friends and families are strongly influenced by our culture. Perhaps the most obvious verbal communication difference between two cultures is language. Even cultures speaking the same language have different meanings for different symbols, however. For example, although English is the dominant language spoken in the United States and England, many words and phrases have different meanings between these two cultures. In England, to "bomb"

Table 1.4   Australian Colloquialisms

Amber Fluid = beer
Bag of Fruit = slang for men's clothing
Barbie = barbeque
Bickie = cookie
Bottler = expression for a person who performs well
Off = to describe rotten food
Tucker = food

an examination is to have performed very well. To have "intercourse" with someone is simply to talk with them. When in London, do not bother to ask for directions to the nearest bathroom or restroom. In England, it is called the "water closet" or the "WC." Australians also speak English, but have a variety of colloquialisms not well understood by persons from the United States (see Table 1.4).

Culture also has a dramatic effect on nonverbal communication. Nonverbal symbols, gestures, and perceptions of personal space and time vary significantly from culture to culture. In the United States, for example, people generally stand about two-and-a-half feet, or an arm's length, away from others when communicating. In many Middle Eastern cultures people stand very close to one another when interacting, especially men (see Figure 1.3). They do this in order to smell each other's breath. In Saudi Arabia, two men walking together are likely to be holding hands as a sign of trust.

Communication, then, is the dynamic process of encoding and decoding verbal and nonverbal messages within a defined cultural, physiological, socio-relational, and perceptual environment. Although many of our messages are sent intentionally, many others, perhaps our nonverbal messages, can unintentionally influence others.

Human Communication Apprehension

Although communication is difficult to define, we know that people begin to communicate at birth and continue communicating throughout their lives. We also know that many people experience fear and anxiety when communicating with others, particularly in situations such as public speaking, class presentations, a first date, or during a job interview. The fear or anxiety people experience when communicating with others is called communication

Figure 1.3   In Middle Eastern cultures, people stay very close to each other when interacting
Source: Copyright © Chris Hondros/Getty Images.

apprehension (CA). In the past thirty-five years a substantial body of research has accumulated regarding the nature and prevalence of communication apprehension. Jim McCroskey, considered the father of the communication apprehension concept, argues that nearly everyone experiences some kind of communication apprehension sometimes, but roughly 1 in 5 adults in the United States suffers from communication apprehension virtually whenever they communicate with others. McCroskey argues that experiencing communication apprehension is normal; that is, all of us experience it occasionally, but it can be a problem for us. McCroskey argues that there are four types of communication apprehension: traitlike, context-based, audience-based, and situational. Traitlike communication apprehension is an enduring general personality predisposition where an individual experiences communication apprehension most of the time across most communication situations. Twenty percent of adults in the United States experience traitlike communication apprehension. Context-based communication apprehension is restricted to a certain generalized context, such as public speaking, group meetings, or job interviews. Persons with context-based communication apprehension experienced anxiety only in certain contexts and not others. Audienced-based communication apprehension is triggered not by the specific context, but by the specific person or audience with whom one is communicating. Hence, persons with audience-based communication apprehension experience anxiety when communicating with strangers, or their superiors. College students with audience-based communication apprehension may experience anxiety when communicating with professors, but not when communicating with other students. Finally, situational-based communication apprehension, experienced by virtually everyone, occurs with the combination of a specific context and a specific audience. For example, students may feel anxious interacting with professors only when they are alone with the professor in the professor's office. At other times, perhaps in the hallways or in the classroom, interacting with the professor may not be a problem.[31] To repeat, virtually everyone experiences communication apprehension at some time. To experience communication apprehension does not mean you are abnormal or sick. What follows is the Personal Report of Communication Apprehension (PRCA-24), a scale designed to measure your degree of communication apprehension. Take a few moments and complete the scale.

SELF-ASSESSMENT 1.1

Directions: This instrument is composed of twenty-four statements concerning your feelings about communicating with other people. Please indicate in the space provided the degree to which each statement applies to you by marking whether you (1) Strongly Agree, (2) Agree, (3) Are Undecided, (4) Disagree, or (5) Strongly Disagree with each statement. There are no right or wrong answers. Many of the statements are similar to other statements. Do not be concerned about this. Work quickly; just record your first impressions.

_____ 1. I dislike participating in group discussions.

_____ 2. Generally, I am comfortable while participating in group discussions.

_____ 3. I am tense and nervous while participating in group discussions.

_____ 4. I like to get involved in group discussions.

_____ 5. Engaging in group discussion with new people makes me tense and nervous.

_____ 6. I am calm and relaxed while participating in group discussions.

_____ 7. Generally, I am nervous when I have to participate in group discussions.

_____ 8. Usually I am calm and relaxed while participating in meetings.

_____ 9. I am very calm and relaxed when I am called upon to express an opinion at a meeting.

_____ 10. I am afraid to express myself at meetings.

_____ 11. Communicating at meetings usually makes me uncomfortable.

_____ 12. I am very relaxed when answering questions at a meeting.

_____ 13. While participating in a conversation with a new acquaintance, I feel very nervous.

_____ 14. I have no fear of speaking up in conversations.

_____ 15. Ordinarily I am very tense and nervous in conversations.

_____ 16. Ordinarily I am very calm and relaxed in conversations.

_____ 17. When conversing with a new acquaintance, I feel very relaxed.

_____ 18. I am afraid to speak up in conversations.

_____ 19. I have no fear of giving a speech.

_____ 20. Certain parts of my body feel very tense and rigid while giving a speech.

_____ 21. I feel relaxed while giving a speech.

_____ 22. My thoughts become confused and jumbled when I am giving a speech.

_____ 23. I face the prospect of giving a speech with confidence.

_____ 24. While giving a speech, I get so nervous I forget facts I really know.

Scoring: The PRCA-24 allows you to compute a total score and four subscores. The total score represents your degree of traitlike CA. Total scores may range from 24 to 120. McCroskey argues that any score above 72 indicates general CA. Scores above 80 indicate a very high level of CA. Scores below 59 indicate a very low level of CA.

Total PRCA Score:

Step 1. Add what you marked for scale items 1, 3, 5, 7, 10, 11, 13, 15, 18, 20, 22, and 24.

Step 2. Add what you marked for scale items 2, 4, 6, 8, 9, 12, 14, 16, 17, 19, 21, and 23.

Step 3. Subtract the score from step 1 from 84 (i.e., 84 minus the score of step 1). Then add the score of step 2 to that total. The sum is your PRCA score.

The subscores indicate your degree of CA across four common contexts: group discussions, meetings, interpersonal conversations, and public speaking. For these scales, a score above 18 is high and a score above 23 is very high.

Subscores for Contexts:

Group Subscore: 18 + scores for items 2, 4, and 6, minus scores for items 1, 3, and 5.

Meeting Subscore: 18 + scores for items 8, 9, and 10, minus scores for items 7, 10, and 11.

Interpersonal Subscore: 18 + scores for items 14, 16, and 17, minus scores for items 13, 15, and 18.

Public Speaking Subscore: 18 + scores for items 19, 21, and 23, minus scores for items 20, 22, and 24.

Source: Copyright James C. McCroskey. Scale used with permission of James C. McCroskey.

The Nature of Culture

Like communication, culture is ubiquitous and has a profound effect on humans. Culture is simultaneously invisible yet pervasive. As we go about our daily lives, we are not overtly conscious of our culture's influence on us. How often have you sat in your dorm room or classroom, for example, and consciously thought about what it means to be an American? As you stand in the lunch line do you say to yourself, "I am acting like an American"? As you sit in your classroom do you say to yourself, "The professor is really acting like an American"? Yet most of your thoughts, emotions, and behaviors are culturally driven. One need only step into a culture different from one's own to feel the immense impact of culture.

Culture has a direct influence on the physical, relational, and perceptual environment. For example, the next time you enter your communication classroom, consider how the room is arranged *physically,* including where you sit and where the professor teaches, the location of the chalkboard, windows, etc. Does the professor lecture from behind a podium? Do the students sit facing the professor? Is the chalkboard used? Next, think about your *relationship* with the professor and the other students in your class. Is the relationship formal or informal? Do you interact with the professor and students about topics other than class material? Would you consider the relationship personal or impersonal? Finally, think about your *perceptual disposition;* that is, your attitudes, motivations, and emotions about the class. Are you happy to be in the class? Do you enjoy attending? Are you nervous when the instructor asks you a question? To a great extent, the answers to these questions are contingent on your culture. The physical arrangement of classrooms, the social relationship between students and teachers, and the perceptual profiles of the students and teachers vary significantly from culture to culture.

Like communication, culture is difficult to define. Australian anthropologist Roger Keesing argues that

> culture does not have some true and sacred and eternal meaning we are trying to discover, but that like other symbols, it means whatever we use it to mean, and that as with other analytical concepts, human users must carve out—and try to partly agree on—a class of natural phenomena it can most strategically label.[32]

Just about everyone has his or her own definition of culture. To be sure, over 40 years ago two well-known anthropologists, Alfred Kroeber and Clyde Kluckhohn, found and examined 300 definitions of culture, none of which was the same.[33]

Perhaps too often people think of culture only in terms of the fine arts, geography, or history. Small towns or rural communities are often accused of having no culture. Yet culture exists everywhere. There is as much culture in Gallup City, New Mexico (population 52), as there is in New York City, New York (population 8,008,278). The two cultures are simply different. Simply put, culture is people.[34]

Although there may not be a universally accepted definition of culture, there are a number of properties of culture upon which most people agree describe its essence. In this book, *culture* is defined as "an accumulated pattern of values, beliefs, and behaviors, shared by an identifiable group of people with a common history and verbal and nonverbal symbol systems."

Accumulated Pattern of Values, Beliefs, and Behaviors. Cultures can be defined by their value and belief systems and by the actions of their members. People who exist in the same culture generally share similar values and beliefs (see Table 1.5). In the United States, for example, individuality is highly valued. An individual's self-interest takes precedence over group interests.

Table 1.5   Values Across Cultures

Saudi Arabia	*Maori (New Zealand)*
Islam	Land
Hospitality	Kinship
Cleanliness	Education
India	*Yemen*
Family Lineage	Islam
Superanatural Guidance	Self-Respect & Honor
Sexual Inequality	Family

Americans believe that people are unique. Moreover, Americans value personal independence. Conversely, in Japan, a collectivistic and homogeneous culture, a sense of groupness and group harmony is valued. Most Japanese see themselves as members of a group first, as individuals second. Where Americans value independence, Japanese value interdependence. Norwegians value conformity. Norwegian children are taught to put the needs of society above their own. Cultural aspects of conformity are embodied in what Norwegians call *Janteloven,* which denotes the fear of individuality and the tendency to stand out in a crowd. Although the Norwegian literacy rate is among the highest in the world, Norwegian schools do not have accelerated programs for gifted and talented students. Norwegians believe that to divide students on intellectual ability would disrupt the social cohesion.[35]

The values of a particular culture lead to a set of expectations and rules prescribing how people should behave in that culture. Although many Americans prefer to think of themselves as unique individuals, most Americans behave in similar ways. Observe the students around you in your classes. Although you may prefer to think that you are very different from your peers, you are really quite similar to them. Most of your peers follow a very similar behavioral pattern to your own. For example, on a day-to-day basis, most of your peers attend classes, take examinations, go to lunch, study, party, and write papers.

Americans share a similar behavioral profile. Most Americans work an average of 40 hours a week, receive some form of payment for their work, and pay some of their earnings in taxes. Most Americans spend their money on homes and cars. Almost every home in the United States has a television. Although Americans view themselves as unique individuals, most of them have very similar behavioral patterns.

An Identifiable Group of People With a Common History. Because the members of a particular culture share similar values, beliefs, and behaviors, they are identifiable as a distinct group. In addition to their shared values, beliefs, and behaviors, the members of a particular culture share a common history. Any culture's past inextricably binds it to the present and guides its future. At the core of any culture are traditions that are passed on to future generations. In many cultures, history is a major component of the formal and informal education systems. To learn a culture's history is to learn that culture's values. One way that children in the United States develop their sense of independence, for example, is by learning about the Declaration of Independence, one of this country's most sacred documents. Elementary school children in Iran, for example, learn of the historical significance regarding the political and religious revolution that took place in their culture in the 1970s and 1980s. Russian children are taught about the arts in Russian history. Russian children are taught about famous Russian composers, including Tchaikovsky, Rachmaninoff, and Stravinsky. The art of the past helps Russians remember their culture and history as they face disruptive social and political crises. Such historical lessons are the glue that binds people.[36]

Verbal and Nonverbal Symbol Systems. One of the most important elements of any culture is its communication system. The verbal and nonverbal symbols with which the members of a culture communicate are culture bound. To see the difference between the verbal codes of any two cultures is easy. The dominant verbal code in the United States is English, whereas the dominant verbal code in Mexico is Spanish. But although two cultures may share the same verbal code, they may have dramatically different verbal styles. Most White Americans, for example, use a very direct, instrumental, personal style when speaking English. Many Native Americans who also speak English use an indirect, impersonal style and may prefer the use of silence as opposed to words.[37]

Nonverbal code systems vary significantly across cultures as well. Nonverbal communication includes the use of body language, gestures, facial expressions, voice, smell, personal and geographical space, time, and artifacts (see Figure 1.4). Body language can communicate a great deal about one's culture. When adults interact with young children in the United States, for example, it is not uncommon for the adult to pat the head of the child. This nonverbal gesture is often seen as a form of endearment and is culturally acceptable. In Thailand, however, where the head is considered the seat of the soul, such a gesture is unacceptable. Belching during or after a meal is viewed by most Americans as rude and impolite, perhaps even disgusting. But in parts of Korea and the Middle East, belching after a meal might be interpreted as a compliment to the cook.[38]

Figure 1.4 Nonverbal communication, including body language, can communicate a great deal about one's culture

Source: Copyright © James Neuliep.

People communicate nonverbally through smell also. Americans, in particular, seem obsessed with the smell of the human body and home environment. Think of all of the products you used this morning before you left for class that were designed to mask the natural scent of your body, including soap, toothpaste, mouthwash, deodorant, and cologne and/or perfume. Persons from other cultures often complain that Americans tend to smell antiseptic.

Microcultural Groups. Within most cultures, groups of people, or *microcultures,* coexist within the mainstream society. Microcultures exist within the broader rules and guidelines of the dominant cultural milieu but are distinct in some way, perhaps racially; linguistically; or via their sexual orientation, age, or even occupation. In some ways, everyone is a member of some microcultural group. Microcultures often may have histories that differ from the dominant cultural group. In many cases microcultural groups are subordinate in some way, perhaps politically or economically. In the United States, Native American tribes might be considered

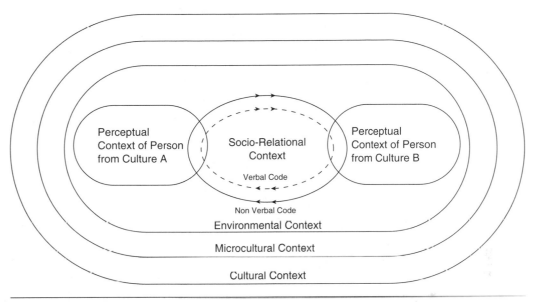

Perceptual Context of Person from Culture A

Socio-Relational Context

Verbal Code

Perceptual Context of Person from Culture B

Non Verbal Code

Environmental Context

Microcultural Context

Cultural Context

Figure 1.5   A contextual model of intercultural communication

microcultures. For example, in addition to their formal education provided by the larger culture, Navaho children informally learn their microculture's history by hearing the traditions of their people.[39]

The Amish of Lancaster County, Pennsylvania, can be considered a microcultural group. Although the Amish are subject to most of the same laws as any other group of citizens, they have unique values and communication systems that differentiate them from mainstream American life. For example, Amish children are exempt from compulsory attendance in public schools after eighth grade. Although almost all Amish speak English, when they interact amongst themselves they speak German. During church services, a form of High German is used. Hence, most Amish of Lancaster County speak three languages.[40]

A Contextual Model of Intercultural Communication

Intercultural communication occurs whenever a minimum of two persons from different cultures or microcultures come together and exchange verbal and nonverbal symbols. A central theme throughout this book is that intercultural communication is contextual. A contextual model of intercultural communication is presented in Figure 1.5.

According to the model, intercultural communication occurs within a variety of contexts, including a cultural, microcultural, environmental, perceptual, and socio-relational context. A context is a complex combination of a variety of factors, including the setting, situation, circumstances, background, and overall framework within which communication occurs. The largest, outer circle of the model represents the cultural context. This is the largest circle because the dominant culture permeates every aspect of the communicative exchange, even the physical geography. All communicative exchanges between persons occur within some culture. In this textbook, the cultural context is the focus of Chapter 2.

The next largest circle in the model is the microcultural context. As mentioned earlier, within most cultures, separate groups of people co-exist. These groups, called microcultures, are in some way different from the larger cultural milieu. Sometimes the difference is ethnicity, race, or language. Often, microcultures are treated differently by the members of the larger culture. Microcultures are the focus of Chapter 3.

The next largest circle in the model is the environmental context. This circle represents the physical geographical location of the interaction. While culture prescribes the overall rules for communication, the physical location indicates when and where the specific rules apply. For example, in the United States there are rules about yelling. Depending on the physical location, yelling can be prohibited or encouraged. In a church, yelling is generally prohibited, whereas at a football game yelling is the preferred method of communicating. The physical environment includes the physical geography, architecture, landscape design, and even the climate of a particular culture. All of these environmental factors play a key role in how people communicate. In this book, the environmental context is discussed in Chapter 4.

The two circles in the model within the socio-relational context represent the perceptual contexts of the individuals interacting. The perceptual context refers to the individual characteristics of the interactants, including their cognitions, attitudes, dispositions, and motivations. How an individual perceives the environment and how he or she gathers, stores, and retrieves information is uniquely human but also culturally influenced. How an individual develops attitudes about others, including stereotypes, changes somewhat from culture to culture. The perceptual context of the individual is the emphasis of Chapter 5.

The circle encompassing the perceptual contexts in the model is the socio-relational context. This refers to the relationship between the interactants. Whenever two people come together and interact they establish a relationship. Within this relationship each person assumes a role. Right now, you are assuming the role of student. The person teaching your communication class is assuming the role of teacher. Roles prescribe how people should behave. Most of the people with whom you interact are related to you via your role as student. The reason you interact with so many professors is because you are a student. What you interact about, that is, the topic of your interaction, is also defined by your role as student. You and your professors interact about courses. How you interact with your professor, that is, the style of talk (e.g., polite language), is also prescribed by your role as student. The language and style of your talk with your professor is probably very different from the language and style of talk you use when you go back to your dorm room and interact with your friends. Probably the last ten people with whom you interacted were directly related to you via your role as student. When you go back to your hometown during semester break and step into the role of son/daughter or brother/sister, you are assuming a different role and your interaction changes accordingly. Your interaction varies as a function of what role you are assuming.

Roles vary from culture to culture. Although in just about every culture there are student and teacher role relationships, how those roles are defined vary significantly. What it means to be a student in the United States is very different from what it means to be a student in Japan. In Japan, for example, students go to school six days a week. Japanese teachers are highly respected and play a very influential role in the Japanese student's life. What it means to be a mother or father varies considerably from one culture to another. In the Masai culture of Kenya, a woman is defined by her fertility. To be defined as a mother in Masai culture, a woman must endure circumcision (i.e., clitoridectomy), an arranged marriage, and wife-beating.[41] One's roles prescribe the types of verbal and nonverbal symbols that are exchanged. In this book, the socio-relational context and role relationships are the focus of Chapter 6.

In the model, the socio-relational context is graphically represented by two circles labeled nonverbal and verbal messages. The nonverbal circle is the larger of the two and is represented by a continuous line. The verbal circle is smaller and is represented as a series of dashes in the shape of a circle. The nonverbal message circle is larger than the verbal message circle because the majority of our communicative behavior is nonverbal. Whether we are using words or not, we are communicating nonverbally through eye contact, body stance, and space. In addition, our nonverbal behavior is ongoing; we cannot not behave. The verbal message circle is a series of dashes in the shape of a circle to represent the *digital* quality of verbal communication.[42] By digital, we mean that, unlike our nonverbal communication, our verbal communication is made up of words that have recognizable and discrete beginning and ending points. A word is like a digit. We can start and stop talking with words. Our nonverbal behavior goes on continuously, however. Chapter 7 concentrates on verbal communication codes and Chapter 8 centers on nonverbal codes.

The general theme of this book, as represented in the model, is that intercultural communication is defined by the interdependence of these various contexts. The perceptual contexts combine to create the socio-relational context, which is defined by the verbal and nonverbal messages sent. The socio-relational context is influenced by the environmental context and defined by the microcultural and cultural contexts. These contexts combine in a complex formula to create the phenomenon of intercultural communication.

Intercultural Communication and Uncertainty

When we interact with someone from a different culture we are faced with a lot of uncertainty. We may not know anything about the person's culture, values, habits, behavior, dress, and so on. We may not know what to say or do in such circumstances. This uncertainty about the other person may make us feel nervous and anxious. Communication theorist Charles Berger contends that the task of interacting with someone from a different culture who may look, act, and communicate differently presents the intercultural communicator with some very complex predictive and explanatory problems. To some extent, to effectively interact with someone from a different culture we must be able to predict how our interaction partner is likely to behave and, based on those predictions, select our appropriate verbal and nonverbal messages.[43]

Berger theorizes that whenever we come together and interact with a stranger, our primary concern is to reduce uncertainty, especially when the other person is someone who we will meet again, provides rewards for us, or behaves in some deviant way. Often, when we are faced with high levels of uncertainty we experience anxiety. In high-uncertainty situations our primary goal is to reduce uncertainty and to increase the predictability about the other. This can be accomplished via specific verbal and nonverbal communication strategies such as question asking and appropriate nonverbal expressiveness.[44]

Some types of communication situations may be more or less anxiety producing than others. For example, Buss argues that situations that are novel, unfamiliar, and/or dissimilar lead to increased anxiety. Those situations containing new, atypical, and/or conspicuously different stimuli are likely to increase our sense of anxiety. Based on this criteria, initial interaction with someone, or interacting with someone from a different culture, may produce heightened anxiety.[45]

Intercultural communication experts William Gudykunst and Young Kim argue that when we interact with people from different cultures, we tend to view them as strangers. Strangers are unknown people who are members of different groups. Anyone entering a relatively unknown or unfamiliar environment falls under the rubric of stranger. Interaction with people from different cultures tends to involve the highest degree of "strangerness" and the lowest degree of familiarity. Thus, there is greater uncertainty in initial interaction with strangers than with people with whom we are familiar. According to Gudykunst and Kim, actual or anticipated interaction with members of different groups (e.g., cultures or ethnic groups different from our own) leads to anxiety.[46]

If we are too anxious about interacting with strangers, we tend to avoid them. Neuliep and McCroskey state that this type of communication anxiety can be labeled intercultural communication apprehension; that is, the fear or anxiety associated with either real or anticipated interaction with people from different groups, especially different cultural or ethnic groups.[47]

Intercultural Communication Apprehension

Successfully interacting with someone from a different culture requires a degree of communication competence. According to Brian Spitzberg, most models of communication competence include a cognitive, affective, and behavioral component. The cognitive component refers to how much one knows about communication. The affective component includes one's motivation to approach or avoid communication. The behavioral component refers to the skills one has to interact competently. An interculturally competent communicator is *motivated* to communicate, *knowledgeable* about how to communicate, and *skilled* in communicating. In addition, an interculturally competent communicator is *sensitive* to the expectations of the context in which communication occurs. Competent communicators interact effectively by adapting messages appropriately to the context. Competent communicators understand the rules, norms, and expectations of the relationship and do not significantly violate them. Communicators are effective to the degree that their goals are accomplished successfully.[48]

According to Neuliep and McCroskey, a person's affective orientation toward intercultural communication involves the individual's degree of motivation to approach or avoid a given intercultural context or person. Communication studies indicate that at least 20 percent of the United States adult population experiences high levels of fear or anxiety even when communicating with members of their own culture. Other studies indicates that 99% of Americans experience communication apprehension at some time in their lives, perhaps during a job interview, a first date, etc. One outcome of communication apprehension is to avoid communication. When people feel anxious about communicating with others they tend to avoid such situations.

Given that intercultural communication may be more anxiety producing than other forms of communication, the number of people suffering from intercultural communication apprehension (ICA) may be considerable. Identifying such individuals may be the first step toward more effective and successful intercultural communication.[49]

In Box 1.2 is an instrument called the Personal Report of Intercultural Communication Apprehension (PRICA). This scale was developed by communication researchers Neuliep and McCroskey. The PRICA is very similar to the Personal Report of Communication Apprehension (PRCA) that you completed earlier in this chapter. The difference between these two scales is that the PRICA assesses your degree of apprehension about communicating with someone from a culture different from yours. After completing each scale you can compare your scores. The PRICA instrument is composed of 14 statements concerning your feelings about communication with people from other cultures. Please indicate in the space provided the degree to which each statement applies to you by marking whether you (1) strongly agree, (2) agree, (3) are undecided, (4) disagree, or (5) strongly disagree with each statement. There are no right or wrong answers and many of the statements are designed to be similar to other statements. Do not be concerned about this. Work quickly and record your first impressions. That you respond to these statements as honestly as possible is very important or else your score will not be valid.

SELF-ASSESSMENT 1.2

Personal Report of Intercultural Communication Apprehension[49]

(1) strongly agree, (2) agree, (3) are undecided, (4) disagree, or (5) strongly disagree

_____ 1. Generally, I am comfortable interacting with a group of people from different cultures.

_____ 2. I am tense and nervous while interacting in group discussions with people from different cultures.

_____ 3. I like to get involved in group discussions with others who are from different cultures.

_____ 4. Engaging in a group discussion with people from different cultures makes me tense and nervous.

_____ 5. I am calm and relaxed when interacting with a group of people who are from different cultures.

_____ 6. While participating in a conversation with a person from a different culture I feel very nervous.

_____ 7. I have no fear of speaking up in a conversation with a person from a different culture.

_____ 8. Ordinarily I am very tense and nervous in conversations with a person from a different culture.

_____ 9. Ordinarily I am very calm and relaxed in conversations with a person from a different culture.

_____ 10. While conversing with a person from a different culture, I feel very relaxed.

_____ 11. I'm afraid to speak up in conversations with a person from a different culture.

_____ 12. I face the prospect of interacting with people from different cultures with confidence.

_____ 13. My thoughts become confused and jumbled when interacting with people from different cultures.

_____ 14. Communicating with people from different cultures makes me feel uncomfortable.

To score the instrument, reverse your original response for items # 2, 4, 6, 8, 11, 13, and 14. For example, for each of these items 1 = 5, 2 = 4, 3 = 3, 4 = 2, and 5 = 1. If your original score for Item #2 was 1, change it to a 5. If your original score for Item #4 was a 2, change it to a 4, etc. After reversing the score for these seven items, then sum all 14 items. Scores cannot be higher than 70 or lower than 14. Higher scores (e.g., 50–70) indicate high intercultural communication apprehension. Low scores (e.g., 14–28) indicate low intercultural communication apprehension.

To the degree to which you answered the items honestly, your score is a fairly reliable and valid assessment of your motivation to approach or avoid intercultural communication. Spitzberg argues that as your motivation increases so does your confidence. As confidence increases, intercultural communication competence also is likely to increase. People who are nervous and tense about interacting with people from different cultures are less likely to approach intercultural communication situations and probably are not confident about encountering new people from different cultures.[50]

Another key component to intercultural competence is knowledge. Communication knowledge refers to the ability to perceive situational variables that influence one's communicative choices and to select behaviors adaptive to those situational variables. Communication knowledge also involves understanding the consequences of enacting behaviors. Knowledgeable communicators have a relatively large repertoire of behavioral strategies for communicating. They are able to perceive how others are responding to their behaviors and refine and adapt their behaviors accordingly. To be interculturally competent communicators need knowledge of other cultures. Hopefully, this book will provide a foundation from which to build your communication knowledge about people from other cultures.

Intercultural communication competence also involves skill; that is, the ability to enact the desired and appropriate behavioral options. Because any given behavior might be judged competent in one culture and incompetent in another, skillful communicators are sensitive to the context in which communication occurs. They choose from their behavioral repertoires the kinds of verbal and nonverbal actions most appropriate for the culture and situation. Empathy, respect, interest in the particular culture, flexibility, and tolerance play key roles in intercultural sensitivity. Skillful intercultural communicators must be willing to modify their behavior as an indication of respect for people of other cultures.[51]

FUNDAMENTAL ASSUMPTIONS ABOUT INTERCULTURAL COMMUNICATION

A central premise of this book is that intercultural communication is a complex combination of the cultural, microcultural, environmental, perceptual, and socio-relational contexts between two people who are encoding and decoding verbal and nonverbal messages. Because of the complexity of this process, a fundamental assumption about intercultural communication is that, during intercultural communication, the message sent *is usually not* the message received.

Assumption #1: During intercultural communication, the message sent is usually not the message received.

Whenever people from different cultures come together and exchange messages, they bring with them a whole host of thoughts, values, emotions, and behaviors that were planted and cultivated by culture. As we have said, intercultural communication is a symbolic activity where the thoughts and ideas of one are encoded into a verbal and/or nonverbal message format, then transmitted through some channel to another person who must decode it, interpret it, and respond to it. This process of encoding, decoding, and interpreting is filled with cultural noise. Noted intercultural communication scholar William Gudykunst has noted that during intercultural communication, culture acts as a filter through which all messages, both verbal and nonverbal, must pass. To this extent, all intercultural exchanges are necessarily, to a greater or lesser extent, charged with ethnocentrism. Hence, during intercultural communication, the message sent is not the message received.[52]

Ethnocentrism refers to the idea that one's own culture is the center of everything, and all other groups (or cultures) are scaled and rated with reference to it. Sociologist W. Sumner argued that ethnocentrism nourishes a group's pride and vanity while looking on outsiders, or outgroups, with contempt.[53] Although culture may mediate the extent to which we experience it, ethnocentrism is thought to be universal. One of the effects of ethnocentrism is that it clouds our perception of others. We have a tendency to judge others, and their communication, based on the standards set by our own culture. Neuliep and McCroskey have argued that the concept of ethnocentrism is essentially descriptive, and not necessarily pejorative. Ethnocentrism may serve a very valuable function when one's ingroup is under attack or threatened. Moreover, ethnocentrism forms the basis for patriotism, group loyalty, and the willingness to sacrifice for one's own group. To be sure, however, ethnocentrism can be problematic. In not looking past their own culture, people see little importance in understanding other cultures. At high levels, ethnocentrism is an obstacle to effective intercultural communication.[54]

Neuliep and McCroskey have developed the GENE scale, which is designed to measure ethnocentrism. The GENE scale and the directions for completing it are presented below.

SELF-ASSESSMENT 1.3

The GENE scale is composed of 22 statements concerning your feelings about your culture and other cultures. In the space provided to the left of each item indicate the degree to which the statement applies to you by marking whether you (5) strongly agree, (4) agree, (3) are neutral, (2) disagree, or (1) strongly disagree with the statement. There are no right or wrong answers. Some of the statements are similar. Remember, everyone experiences some degree of ethnocentrism. Fortunately, as we will see in Chapter 5, ethnocentrism can be managed and reduced. Be honest! Work quickly and record your first response.

1._____ Most other cultures are backward compared to my culture.

2. _____ My culture should be the role model for other cultures.

3. _____ People from other cultures act strange when they come into my culture.

4. _____ Lifestyles in other cultures are just as valid as those in my culture.

5. _____ Other cultures should try to be more like my culture.

6. _____ I'm not interested in the values and customs of other cultures.

7. _____ People in my culture could learn a lot from people of other cultures.

8. _____ Most people from other cultures just don't know what's good for them.

9. _____ I respect the values and customs of other cultures.

10. _____ Other cultures are smart to look up to our culture.

11. _____ Most people would be happier if they lived like people in my culture.

12. _____ I have many friends from other cultures.

13. _____ People in my culture have just about the best lifestyles of anywhere.

14. _____ Lifestyles in other cultures are not as valid as those in my culture.

15. _____ I'm very interested in the values and customs of other cultures.

16. _____ I apply my values when judging people who are different.

17. _____ I see people who are similar to me as virtuous.

18. _____ I do not cooperate with people who are different.

19. _____ Most people in my culture just don't know what is good for them.

20. _____ I do not trust people who are different.

21. _____ I dislike interacting with people from different cultures.

22. _____ I have little respect for the values and customs of other cultures.

To determine your ethnocentrism score, complete the following steps:

Step 1: Add your responses to scale items 4, 7, and 9.

Step 2: Add your responses to scale items 1, 2, 5, 8, 10, 11, 13, 14, 18, 20, 21, and 22.

Step 3: Subtract the sum from Step 1 from 18 (i.e., 18 minus Step 1 sum).

Step 4: Add the results of Step 2 and Step 3. This sum is your generalized ethnocentrism score (note that not all items are used in scoring). Higher scores indicate higher ethnocentrism. Scores above 55 are considered high ethnocentrism.

Assumption #2: Intercultural communication is primarily a nonverbal act between people.

Some foreign language teachers might have us believe that competency in a foreign language is tantamount to effective and successful intercultural communication in the culture that speaks that language. To be sure, proficiency in a foreign language expedites the intercultural communication experience. But intercultural communication is primarily and fundamentally a nonverbal process. The expression of intimacy, power, and status among communicators is typically accomplished nonverbally through paralinguistic cues, proxemics, haptics, oculesics, and olfactics. In Korea, for example, one's hierarchical position is displayed via vocal tone and pitch. When a subordinate takes receipt of an important piece of paper, such as a graded exam from a respected professor, the student grasps it with both hands (not just one), accompanied with a slight nod of the head, and indirect eye contact—all nonverbal signs of deference.

The well-known anthropologist Edward Hall has argued that people from different cultures live in different sensory worlds. Hall claims that people from different cultures engage in a selective screening of sensory information that ultimately leads to different perceptions of experience.[55] Regarding olfactics (smell), most cultures establish norms for acceptable and unacceptable scents associated with the human body. When people fail to fit into the realm of olfactic cultural acceptability, their odor signals others that something is wrong with their physical, emotional, or mental health. In the United States, we are obsessed with masking certain smells, especially those of the human body. In Western and Westernized cultures, body odor is regarded as unpleasant and distasteful, and great efforts are expended in its removal. Many Muslims believe that cleanliness of the body and purity of the soul are related. Muslim women are told to purify themselves after menstruation. Cleanliness is prescribed before and after meals. As we will see in Chapter 8, our nonverbal messages complement, augment, accent, substitute for, and repeat our verbal messages.

Assumption #3: Intercultural communication necessarily involves a clash of communicator style.

In the United States, talk is a highly valued commodity. People are routinely evaluated by their speech. Yet silence—that is, knowing when not to speak—is a fundamental prerequisite for linguistic and cultural competence.[56] The use and interpretation of silence varies dramatically across cultures. In many collectivistic cultures, such as Japan and Korea, silence can carry more meaning than words, especially in the maintenance of intimate relationships. In fact, the Japanese, and some Native American tribes in the United States, believe that the expression of relational intimacy is best accomplished nonverbally. They believe that having to put one's thoughts and emotions into words somehow cheapens and discounts them.

In the United States we value, and employ, a very direct and personal style of verbal communication. Personal pronouns are an essential ingredient to the composition of just about any utterance. Our motto is "Get to the point," "Don't beat around the bush," "Tell it like it is," "Speak your mind." Many cultures, however, prefer an indirect and impersonal communication style. In these cultures, there is no need to articulate every message. True understanding is implicit, coming not from words but from actions in the environment where speakers provide only hints or insinuations. The Chinese say, "One should use the eyes and ears, not the mouth," and "Disaster emanates from careless talk." The Chinese consider the wisest and most trustworthy person as the one who talks the least but the one who listens, watches, and restricts his or her verbal communication.[57]

Assumption #4: Intercultural communication is a group phenomenon experienced by individuals.

Whenever we interact with a person from a different culture we carry with us assumptions and impressions of that other person. The specific verbal and nonverbal messages that we exchange are usually tailored for the person based on those assumptions and impressions. Often, such assumptions and impressions are based on characteristics of the other person by virtue of his or her membership in groups such as his or her culture, race, sex, age, and occupation group. In other words, we have a tendency to see others not as individuals with unique thoughts, ideas, and goals, but rather as an "Asian," or a "woman," or an "old person," or "a cab driver." In other words, we do not see the person, we see the groups to which the person belongs. The problem with this is that group data may not be a reliable source upon which to construct our messages. Because someone belongs to a specific racial, ethnic, sex, or age group does not necessarily mean that he or she takes on the thoughts, behaviors, and attitudes associated with such groups. Thus, the potential for miscommunication is great. During intercultural communication, we have to be mindful that while the person with whom we are interacting is from a different cultural group, he or she is also an individual. Only through intercultural communication can we ever get to know the person as an individual.

Assumption #5: Intercultural communication is a cycle of stress and adaptation.

As mentioned earlier in this chapter, when we come together with a person from a different culture, we may feel uncertain, apprehensive, and anxious. Such feelings are stressful. Hence, sometimes intercultural communication can be stressful. The good news is that we can learn and adapt to such stress and eventually grow. During intercultural communication we have to be mindful that the communication strategies we use with persons with whom we are familiar may not be effective with persons from other cultures. Thus, we have to learn to adapt and adjust our communication style. We have to recognize that we will make mistakes, learn from them, adapt, and move on. A good beginning point is to recognize that people from different cultures are different—not better or worse, but simply different. Once we are able to do this, we can adjust and adapt out verbal and nonverbal messages accordingly and become competent interactants.

CHAPTER SUMMARY

The purpose of this chapter was to emphasize the necessity of intercultural communication and to define and clarify the terms *communication* and *culture*. The first part of this chapter argued that recent technological, political, and sociological advancements have created a global village only dreamed about twenty years ago. While the dream of a global village holds great promise, the reality is that diverse people have diverse opinions, values, and beliefs that clash and too often result in violence. Only though intercultural communication can such conflict be managed and reduced.

The second part of this chapter offered some definitions of communication and culture. Both terms are difficult to define. Communication involves the simultaneous encoding and decoding of verbal and nonverbal messages with someone else within some context. Culture, in part, can be defined as an accumulated pattern of values, beliefs, and behaviors shared by an identifiable group of people with a common history and verbal and nonverbal symbol system. Intercultural communication is essentially contextual. The cultural, microcultural, and environmental contexts surround the communicators, whose socio-relational context is defined by the exchange of verbal and nonverbal messages that are encoded and decoded within each interactant's perceptual context. The final part of this chapter lets you discover something about yourself; in this case, your intercultural communication apprehension. Competent intercultural communicators are willing to approach intercultural situations and are sensitive to the differences in them.

GLOSSARY OF TERMS

Communication Apprehension: The fear or anxiety associated with either real or anticipated communication with another person or group of persons.

Communication: The simultaneous encoding, decoding, and interpretation of verbal and nonverbal messages between people.

Context: The cultural, physical, social, and psychological environment.

Culture: An accumulated pattern of values, beliefs, and behaviors shared by an identifiable group of people with a common history and verbal and nonverbal symbol system.

Dynamic: Something considered active and forceful.

Environmental Context: The physical, geographical location of communication.

Ethnocentrism: The tendency to place one's own group (cultural, ethnic, or religious) in a position of centrality and worth, and to create negative attitudes and behaviors toward other groups.

GENE: Self-report instrument designed to measure generalized ethnocentrism.

Intentionality: During communication, the voluntary and conscious encoding and decoding of messages.

Interactive: A process between two people.

Intercultural Communication: Two persons from different cultures or co- cultures exchanging verbal and nonverbal messages.

Intercultural Communication Apprehensions (ICA): The fear or anxiety associated with either real or anticipated communication with a person from another culture or co-culture.

Microculture: An identifiable group of people coexisting within some dominant cultural context.

Perceptual Context: The attitudes, emotions, and motivations of the persons engaged in communication and how they affect information processing.

Personal Report of Communication Apprehension (PRCA): Self-report instrument designed to measure communication apprehension.

Process: Anything ongoing, ever-changing, and continuous.

Socio-Relational Context: The role relationship between the interactants (i.e., brother/sister).

Symbol: An arbitrarily selected and learned stimulus representing something else.

Transactional: The simultaneous encoding and decoding process during communication.

Uncertainty: The amount of unpredictability during communication.

REFERENCES

1. Schlesinger, A. M. (1993). *The Disuniting of America: Reflections of a Multicultural Society.* New York: Norton (p. 10).
2. Ibid.
3. Pomfret, J. "Resolving Crisis was a Matter of Interpretation." *Washington Post.* (2001, April 12). Quotes of letter taken from page A1; Rupple, D., "Equitable Resolution: Each Side Gained, Lost in US-China Plane Crisis" [online]. Available: http://abcnews.go.com . . . yNews/chinaplanecrisis 010411.html
4. Ibid.
5. England, J. T. (1992). Building community for the 21st century. ERIC Digest. ED347489 [online]. Available: http://www.ed.gov/databases/ERIC_Digests/ed347489.html
6. Peck, M. S. (1987). *The different drum: Community making and peace.* New York: Touchstone.
7. U.S. Department of Commerce. (1998). *Big emerging markets* [online]. Available: http://www.ita.doc.gov/bems/index.html
8. Larsen, L. (2004). *The Foreign-Born Population in the United States.* Current Population Reports, P20–551, U.S. Census Bureau, Washington, DC.
9. Perry, M. J., & Mackun, P. J. (2001). *Population Change and Distribution.* U.S. Department of Commerce, U.S. Census Bureau. Population Projections Program, Population Division, U.S. Census Bureau, Washington, DC. Percentages have been rounded.
10. Population Projections Program, Population Division, U.S. Census Bureau, Washington, DC.
11. Profile of General Demographic Characteristics: 2000. U.S. Census Bureau, Census 2000 Summary File 1, Matrices P1, P3, P4, P8, P9, P12, P13, P17, P18, P19, P20, P23, P27, P28, P33, PCT5, PCT8, PCT11, PCT15, H1, H3, H4, H5, H11, and H12.
12. "Texas Town Adopts Spanish As Official Language," Reuters News Service, August, 2004; "County: English Is Official Language." The Associated Press, July 18, 2002; Shin, H. B., & Bruno, R. (2003). *Language Use and English-Speaking Ability: 2000.* U.S. Department of Commerce. U.S. Census Bureau.
13. Schlesinger, *The Disuniting of America,* (p. 15).
14. Larson, C. U. (2001). *Persuasion: Reception and Responsibility* (9th Ed.). Belmont, CA: Wadsworth, (p. 4).
15. Safran, C. (1979). "Troubles That Pull Couples Apart: A Redbook Report," *Redbook,* 83, 138–141.
16. Dance, F. E. X. (1970). "The 'Concept' of Communication," *Journal of Communication,* 20, 201–210.

17. Dance, F. E. X., & Larson, C. E. (1976). *The Function of Human Communication: A Theoretical Approach.* New York: Holt, Rinehart and Winston.

18. Fisher, B. A. (1978). *Perspectives on Human Communication,* New York: Macmillan.

19. Berlo, D. K. (1960). *The Process of Communication,* New York: Holt, Rinehart and Winston, (p. 24).

20. Bowers, J. W., & Bradac, J. J. (1982). "Issues in Communication Theory: A Metatheoretical Analysis," in *Communication Yearbook 5,* M. Burgoon (Ed.), New Brunswick, NJ: Transaction Books, (p. 3).

21. Goss, B. (1983). *Communication in Everyday Life.* Belmont, CA: Wadsworth.

22. Cooley, C. (1909). *Social Organization.* New York: Scribner, (p. 61).

23. Miller, G. R. (1966). "On Defining Communication: Another Stab," *Journal of Communication,* 16, 92.

24. Fisher, B. A. (1994). *Interpersonal Communication: Pragmatics of Human Relationships.* New York: Random House, (p. 22).

25. Stevens, S. S. (1950). "Introduction: A Definition of Communication," *The Journal of the Acoustical Society of America,* 22, p. 689.

26. Hall, E. T. (1959). *The Silent Language.* New York: Doubleday.

27. Berlo, D. K. (1960). *The Process of Communication,* New York: Holt, Rinehart and Winston, (p. 24).

28. Motley, M. T. (1990). "On Whether One Can(not) Not Communicate: An Examination Via Traditional Communication Postulates," *Western Journal of Communication,* 54, 1–20.

29. Ibid.

30. Watzlawick, P., Beavin, J., & Jackson, D. (1967). *Pragmatics of Human Communication: Patterns, Pathologies, and Paradoxes,* New York: Norton.

31. McCroskey, J. C. (1997). *An Introduction to Rhetorical Communication,* 7th ed. Boston: Allyn and Bacon.

32. Keesing, R. (1974). "Theories of Culture," in B. J. Siegel (Ed.), *Annual Review of Anthropology,* (pp. 73–97). Palo Alto, CA: Annual Reviews.

33. Kroeber, A. I., & Kluckhohn, C. (Eds.), (1954). *Culture: A Critical Review of Concepts and Definitions,* New York: Random House; Seelye, H. N. (1993). *Teaching Culture: Strategies for Intercultural Communication.* Lincolnwood, IL: National Textbook Company.

34. U.S. Census Bureau, (2001). Washington, DC.

35. Yurkovich, D., Pliscott, K., & Halverson, R. (1996). *The Norwegian Culture.* Unpublished student manuscript, St. Norbert College, De Pere, WI; Gayle, A. R., & Knutson, K. P. (1993). "Understanding Cultural Differences: Jenteloven and Social Conformity in Norway," *Et Cetera,* 50, 449.

36. Westfahl, G., Koltz, R., & Manders, A. (1996). *Ethnic Russian Culture and Society.* Unpublished student manuscript, St. Norbert College, De Pere, WI; Resnick, A. (1993). *The Commonwealth of Independent States.* Chicago: Childrens Press.

37. Basso, K. (1990). "To Give Up on Words": Silence in Western Apache Culture. In D. Carbaugh (Ed.), *Cultural Communication and Intercultural Contact,* (pp. 303–320). Hillsdale, NJ: Erlbaum.

38. Axtell, R. (1991). *Gestures: Do's and Taboos of Body Language Around the World.* New York: Wiley.

39. McNeley, J. (1981). *Holy Wind in Navaho Philosophy.* Tucson, AZ: University of Arizona Press.

40. Moellendorf, S., Warsh, H., & Yoshimaru, K. (1996). *The Amish Culture: A Closer Look at the People of Lancaster County.* Unpublished student manuscript, St. Norbert College, De Pere, WI.

41. Vandehey, K., Buerger, C., & Krueger, K. (1996). *Traditional Aspects and Struggles of the Masai Culture.* Unpublished student manuscript, St. Norbert College, DePere, WI; Angeloni, E. (Ed.), (1995). *Mystique of the Masai.* Guilford: Dushkin.

42. Watzlawick et al., *Pragmatics of Human Communication.*

43. Berger, C. R. (1992). "Communicating Under Uncertainty." In W. B. Gudykunst & Y. Y. Kim (Eds.), *Readings on Communicating with Strangers,* (pp. 5–15). New York: McGraw-Hill.

44. Berger, C. R., & Calabrese, R. (1975). "Some Explorations in Initial Interaction and Beyond," *Human Communication Research,* 1, 99–112.

45. Buss, A. H. (1980). *Self-Consciousness and Social Anxiety.* San Francisco, CA: W. H. Freeman & Company Publishers.

46. Gudykunst, W. B., & Kim, Y. Y. (1997). *Communicating with Strangers: An Approach to Intercultural Communication.* New York: McGraw-Hill.

47. Neuliep, J. W., & McCroskey, J. C. (1997). "The Development of Intercultural and Interethnic Communication Apprehension Scales." *Communication Research Reports,* 14, 145–156.

48. Spitzberg, B. H. (1997). "A Model of Intercultural Communication Competence," in L. A. Samovar & R. E. Porter (Eds.), *Intercultural Communication: A Reader,* (8th Edition), (pp. 379–391), Belmont, CA: Wadsworth.

49. Neuliep & McCroskey, "The Development of Intercultural and Interethnic Communication Apprehension Scales."

50. Spitzberg, "A Model of Intercultural Communication Competence," (pp. 347–359).

51. Bhawuk, D. P., & Brislin, R. (1992). "The Measurement of Intercultural Sensitivity Using the Concepts of Individualism and Collectivism." *International Journal of Intercultural Relations,* 16, 413–436.

52. Gudykunst, W. (1997). "Cultural Variability in Communication: An Introduction," *Communication Research,* 24, 327–348.

53. Sumner, W. G. (1906). *Folkways,* Boston: Ginn.

54. Neuliep, J. W., & McCroskey, J. C. (1997). "The Development of a U.S. and Generalized Ethnocentrism Scale," *Communication Research Reports,* 14, 385–398.

55. Hall, E. T. (1959). *The Silent Language,* New York: Doubleday.

56. Braithwaite, C. (1990). "Communicative Silence: A Cross-Cultural Study of Basso's Hypothesis," in *Cultural Communication and Intercultural Contact,* D. Carbaugh (Ed.), Hillsdale, NJ: Erlbaum, (pp. 321–328).

57. Gudykunst, W. B., & Ting-Toomey, S. (1988). "Verbal Communication Styles," in *Culture and Interpersonal Communication,* W. B. Gudykunst and S. Ting-Toomey (Eds.), Newbury Park, CA: Sage, (pp. 427–441).

Cultural Context

CHAPTER 2

The Cultural Context

Culture hides more than it reveals, and strangely enough what it hides, it hides most effectively from its own participants.

—Edward T. Hall[1]

Chapter Objectives

After reading this chapter, you should be able to

1. Compare and contrast individualism and collectivism.

2. Identify some cultures that are individualistic and some that are collectivistic.

3. Compare and contrast high- and low-context cultures.

4. Identify some cultures that are high context and some that are low context.

5. Compare value orientations among cultures.

6. Compare and contrast high and low power distance cultures.

7. Identify some cultures that are high power distance and some that are low power distance.

8. Compare and contrast high and low uncertainty avoidant cultures.

9. Identify some cultures that are weak uncertainty avoidant and some that are strong uncertainty avoidant.

10. Assess your degree of individualism/collectivism, high/low context, and power distance.

The cultural context in which human communication occurs is perhaps the most defining influence on human interaction. Culture provides the overall framework wherein humans learn to organize their thoughts, emotions, and behaviors in relation to their environment. Although people are born into a culture, it is not innate. Culture is learned. Culture teaches one how to *think,* conditions one how to *feel,* and instructs one how to *act,* especially how to *inter-act* with others; in other words, communicate. In many respects the terms *communication* and *culture* can be used interchangeably. The influence of culture on human interaction is paradoxical. As we conduct our daily lives most of us are unaware of our culture. Yet culture influences our every thought, feeling, and action. As the internationally recognized anthropologist Edward Hall asserts in the quote at the beginning of this chapter, culture hides more than it reveals, particularly from its own members.

Australian anthropologist Roger Keesing argues that culture provides people with an implicit theory about how to behave and how to interpret the behavior of others. People from different cultures learn different implicit theories. These theories are learned through socialization. Through socialization individuals learn the dominant values of their particular culture and their self-identities.[2]

Over the past few decades, anthropologists, communication researchers, psychologists, and sociologists have isolated several dimensions of cultural variability that can be used to differentiate cultures. These dimensions are representative of the different implicit cultural theories. This chapter will focus on five dimensions of cultural variability: individualism-collectivism, high-low context, value orientations, power distance, and uncertainty avoidance. Each of these dimensions affects how people communicate.

The five dimensions of cultural variability will be presented along cultural continua. The cultural continua allow for the representation of the dimensions as continuous and varying in magnitude by degree. No culture is purely and absolutely individualistic or collectivistic, for example. Instead, a culture may be more individualistic or more collectivistic than some other culture. Moreover, these cultural dimensions of variability are not opposites; that is, they may coexist in some cultures. In addition, many cultures are in a state of great transition.

Collectivistic cultures might gravitate toward individualism while individualistic cultures adopt collectivistic values. For example, Japan is considered a collectivistic, group-oriented society. However, since the 1950s, Japan has been strongly influenced by Western culture. Many Japanese scholars have observed that the younger generation of Japanese, while still considered collectivistic, are more individualistic than their parents and especially their grandparents.

Likewise, although the United States is considered one of the most individualistic cultures on the planet, many U.S. businesses and corporations employ collectivistic management models in the workplace, focusing on teamwork and cooperation. While reading through this chapter, remember that cultures are not static. Cultures are dynamic, continuously developing, and evolving.

INDIVIDUALISM-COLLECTIVISM

Perhaps the single most studied dimension of cultural variability that is used to compare and contrast cultures and microcultures is individualism-collectivism (see Figure 2.2).

Individualism ◀————————————▶ Collectivism

Figure 2.2

Cultures falling on one side of the continuum are individualistic while those falling toward the other side are collectivistic. Cultures falling at the midpoint might possess both individualistic and collectivistic characteristics. Gayle and Knutson write that Norwegians, for example, possess both individualistic and collectivistic tendencies. Norwegians are taught to put the needs of society above their own and to embrace a classless society. Simultaneously, however, Norwegians value personal independence. While Norwegians conform to social norms, the individual Norwegian rebuffs traditional rules and standards. Norwegians strive for independence yet do not depend on others to recognize their individual achievements. Norwegians believe that they must recognize their own good qualities in order to gain self-esteem.[3]

Perhaps Norway is unusual to the degree that its people carry collectivistic and individualistic tendencies, but regardless of culture, most persons carry to some degree both individualistic and collectivistic tendencies. The difference is that in some cultures individualistic tendencies tend to dominate while in others, collectivistic tendencies dominate.[4]

Harry Triandis, from the University of Illinois, is well known for his work on individualism and collectivism. Triandis writes that in individualistic cultures, emphasis is placed on individuals' goals over group goals. In individualistic cultures social behavior is guided by personal goals, perhaps at the expense of other types of goals. Individualistic cultures stress values that benefit the individual person. The self is promoted because each person is viewed as uniquely endowed and possessing distinctive talent and potential. Individuals are encouraged to pursue and develop their abilities and aptitudes. In many individualistic cultures people are taught to be creative, self-reliant, competitive, and assertive.[5]

Triandis argues that an important ingredient of individualistic cultures is that the individual is emotionally disconnected from ingroups such as the family. Because the individual has been taught to be independent, social control depends more on personal guilt than on shame or other social norms or conformity. Ironically, members of individualist cultures tend to belong to many groups; but their affiliation with them is short-lived. Many of the groups to which an individualist belongs are designed to enhance self-worth. Such groups might include self-help groups, therapy groups, or occupational groups.[6]

Triandis traces the origins of individualism to ancient Greece, where literature (e.g., the *Iliad* and the *Odyssey*) celebrates the accomplishments of individuals. Triandis also notes that ecology (i.e., features of geography, resources, and the history of a society) can shape the level of individualism in a culture. For example, modern, industrial-urban, fast-changing cultures tend to be individualist. In many cases, individualistic cultures are often highly complex and affluent. Complex cultures have heterogeneous populations and economies based on occupational specialization where individuals do different jobs. Cultural complexity also occurs in cultures where people are separated from one another either geographically or through migration patterns. Many individualist cultures have a history of colonization, for example.[7]

Affluence also correlates with individualism. Financial independence means that one may be less dependent on others to satisfy needs. As cultures become more affluent, they tend to become more individualistic. Some scholars even link climate to individualism and collectivism. Cultures in cooler climates tend to be individualistic and cultures in warmer climates tend to be collectivistic. Colder climates are likely to foster and support individual initiative and innovative solutions to problems. Warmer climates render individual achievements less necessary. Many English-speaking Western cultures are considered individualistic (e.g., United States, Canada). Many Western European cultures also are individualistic (e.g., Germany, Switzerland, England).[8]

In contrast, according to Triandis, in collectivistic cultures, group goals have precedence over individual goals. Collectivistic cultures stress values that serve the ingroup by subordinating personal goals for the sake of preserving the ingroup. Collectivistic societies are characterized by extended primary groups such as the family, neighborhood, or occupational group in which members have diffuse mutual obligations and expectations based on their status or rank. In collectivistic cultures people are not seen as isolated individuals. People see themselves as *interdependent* with others (e.g., their ingroup) where responsibility is shared and accountability is collective. A person is seen not as an individual, but as a member of a group.[9]

Triandis points out that while collectivistic cultures stress the importance of the group over the individual, their members tend to belong to fewer groups than persons in individualistic cultures. Unlike the individualist, the collectivist is emotionally connected to the ingroup. A collectivist's values and beliefs are consistent with and reflect those of the ingroup. Moreover, a collectivist's association with his or her ingroups may last a lifetime. In many collectivistic cultures, the primary value is harmony with others. Triandis observes that because group harmony is so highly valued, obedience to and compliance with ingroup pressures is routine. One's behavior is role based, and deviations from the prescribed role are discouraged and often negatively sanctioned. In this sense, a person's behavior is guided more by shame than by personal guilt. A collectivist who stands out from the group disrupts the harmony and may be punished. Most collectivistic cultures value social reciprocity, obligation, dependence, and obedience. But by far, the primary value stressed by many collectivistic cultures is harmony.[10]

Ecological factors can affect the level of collectivism in certain societies. Isolated societies, such as island cultures, tend to be collectivistic. People have very clear ideas about what behaviors are appropriate. People follow the norms of the society closely since they are less likely to be influenced by neighboring cultures. In addition, Triandis believes that collectivism is based on the tenet that collaboration and cooperation ultimately lead to survival. Both collaboration and cooperation require obedience and harmony, which is typically managed and coordinated by someone in charge, such as an authority. Authority, or one's rank in the group, is a salient feature of many collectivistic cultures. Collectivists tend to see each other as hierarchically ranked roles, not individuals. Collectivism can be found in parts of Europe like Southern Italy and rural Greece. Much of Africa, Asia, and Latin America is considered collectivistic (see Table 2.1).[11]

Table 2.1

Individualistic-Oriented Cultures	*Collectivistic-Oriented Cultures*
United States	Guatemala
Australia	Ecuador
Great Britain	Panama
Canada	Venezuela
Netherlands	Colombia
New Zealand	Indonesia
Italy	Pakistan
Belgium	Costa Rica
Denmark	Peru
Sweden	Taiwan
France	South Korea
Ireland	El Salvador
Norway	Thailand

AN INTERCULTURAL CONVERSATION: INDIVIDUALISTIC AND COLLECTIVISTIC CULTURES

In the following exchange, Mr. Patterson, an American manager working in Korea, is meeting with his supervisor, Mr. Wyman, who is also American. The United States is considered an individualistic culture whereas Korea is considered collectivistic. In this scenario, Mr. Patterson reports to Mr. Wyman about some changes he has made within several of his sales teams. Later, Park Young Sam, their Korean counterpart, enters into the dialogue.[12]

Mr. Patterson: *Good morning Mr. Wyman, thanks for meeting with me this morning. As you know, our division has been doing very well this quarter. In fact, our numbers are up across the board.*

Mr. Wyman: *Yes, I've seen your quarterly reports. Nice job!*

Mr. Patterson: *Thanks. In order to recognize their hard work, I've made some changes in our sales teams. I've created team leaders in each group. In our product group, I promoted Lee Young-sam. In the marketing group, I promoted Chun Tae-woo, and in the technology group, I promoted Choi Mino. All of them have been real leaders. I think this idea will really motivate them. In fact, I met with the groups individually and announced the promotions.*

Mr. Wyman: *Good job, Patterson. I can see you're really on top of things. Good work.*

Two Months Later

Mr. Patterson, Mr. Wyman, and Park Young Sam, a Korean manager, are discussing the poor performance of Mr. Patterson's sales teams.

Mr. Wyman: *Well, just look at these dismal results. The numbers for this quarter are way down from last quarter. What's happened?*

Mr. Patterson: *I don't know. Ever since I introduced the team leader concept the groups' productivity has really plummeted. I thought it was a great idea. I guess I chose the wrong people to lead the teams. I'll assign new leaders tomorrow.*

| **Park Young Sam:** | *Well . . . you may select new leaders if you desire, but the men you chose were all very capable. However, by elevating them you made them stand out and disrupted the harmony of each group. In Korea, we all work hard for the group . . . not just one person.* |
| **Mr. Patterson:** | *I guess I should have just left things as they were.* |

Following their individualistic orientations, Mr. Patterson and Mr. Wyman were perfectly comfortable with the idea of creating team leaders within the individual sales groups. However, as Park Young Sam mentions, doing so upset the harmony of the groups, which in turn led to poor performance. In the United States, workers are often motivated by the opportunity for promotion and advancement as this serves the individualistic drive for individual achievement. In collectivistic cultures, however, workers may be motivated by being a part of a cohesive and productive team.

Individualism and collectivism are terms that describe whole cultures. But cultures are not pure. As Triandis notes, members of collectivist cultures may practice individualistic tendencies while members of individualist cultures may value collectivist ideals. Joe Feldhausen notes, for example, that Denmark is a country with both collectivistic and individualistic tendencies. In Denmark, Feldhausen writes, individual freedom is nurtured through a devotion to established traditions and customs. Regarding income and social rank, Danes are staunchly egalitarian. At the same time, however, Danes considered themselves free to be nonconformist and to stand out from the group. In this way, Danes may be at the theoretical midpoint of the individualism and collectivism cultural continuum.[13]

PATTERNS OF INDIVIDUALISM AND COLLECTIVISM ACROSS THE UNITED STATES

Although the United States is considered individualistic, considerable regional variation exists. Because of ecological, historical, and institutional practices, the Deep South is the most collectivistic region of the United States. Defeat in the Civil War, the institution of slavery, relative poverty, and the prominence of religion all contribute to the collectivistic tendencies of the South. In addition, the Southwest, having been settled by Mexican and Spanish populations before White settlers entered the area, is also considered fairly collectivistic. Hawaii, too, has a culture different from that of the rest of the United States with approximately 65 percent of its population coming from Asian cultures. Hence, much of the culture has collectivistic characteristics. Hawaii, too, would be considered collectivistic. On the other hand, the Mountain West and Great Plains is thought to be the most individualistic region in the United States.[14]

In their research Vandello and Cohen created an index of collectivism designed to measure collectivism in different regions of the United States. Their index was composed of eight items, including the percentage of people living alone, percentage of elderly people living alone, percentage of households with grandchildren in them, divorce to marriage ratio, percentage of people with no religious affiliation, average percentage of those voting Libertarian over the past four presidential elections, ratio of people carpooling to work to people living alone, and percentage of people self-employed. Their index showed a general pattern of relative collectivism in the South, particularly in the former slave states, with maximum individualism in the Great Plains and Mountain West. Montana was the most individualistic state and Hawaii was the most collectivistic (see Table 2.2).[15]

Table 2.2

Most Collectivistic States	Most Individualistic States
Hawaii	Montana
Louisiana	Oregon
South Carolina	Nebraska
Mississippi	Wyoming
Maryland	South Dakota
Utah	Colorado
Virginia	North Dakota
Georgia	Washington
California	Kansas
New Jersey	Iowa

Variations of individualism and collectivism can be seen within any culture. No culture is purely, and entirely, individualistic or collectivistic, for example. To account for this phenomenon, Triandis and other cross-cultural researchers distinguish between individualism and collectivism at the *cultural* level and idiocentrism and allocentrism at the individual *psychological* level. Many cross-cultural researchers believe that individualism-collectivism cannot be measured at the cultural level. We should not label entire cultures as individualistic or collectivistic because persons within those cultures may vary considerably. We can, however, measure an individual's degree of individualism-collectivism. When an individual carries individualistic tendencies, we call him or her idiocentric. When an individual carries collectivistic tendencies, we call that person allocentric. Idiocentrism and allocentrism are the individual equivalents of cultural individualism-collectivism. Allocentrics tend to define themselves with reference to social entities (e.g., families, hometowns) more so than do idiocentrics. Allocentrics internalize the norms of the ingroup and enjoy behavior along ingroup expectations. Allocentrics are less likely to be lonely than idiocentrics. The self-esteem of allocentrics tends to be based on getting along with others, compared to idiocentrics, whose self-esteem is often based on getting ahead of others.[16]

William Gudykunst and his colleagues contend that another way to conceptualize individualism-collectivism at the individual level is to focus on self construals; that is, how the individual thinks of him- or herself. How individuals conceive of the self is one of the major determinants of their behavior. People use different construals of the self, including the independent self and the interdependent self. The independent self predominates in individualistic cultures and the interdependent self predominates in collectivistic cultures.[17]

Communication Consequences of Individualism-Collectivism. A given culture's orientation toward individualism or collectivism has important behavioral consequences for that culture's members. Among collectivists, social behavior is guided by the group. Along with group membership come prescribed duties and obligations. Among individualists, social behavior is guided by one's personal attitudes, motivations, and other internal processes. Where individualists are taught to compete, the collectivist learns to cooperate. To be sure, individualistic cultures value and reward successful competition. The United States, for example, is replete with contests and ceremonies that recognize individual accomplishment. People are publicly rewarded for being the most beautiful, thinnest, strongest, fastest, tallest, smartest, youngest, oldest, funniest, or the "best" at whatever one aspires to. Collectivistic cultures, on the other hand, stress harmony and cooperation. Collectivists strive for the approval of the ingroup, which is accomplished not by standing out but by conforming to the group's norm. From the collectivist's perspective an individual who stands out from the group disrupts harmony. In the United States, "the squeaky wheel gets the grease," but in Japan, "the tallest nail gets hammered down."[18]

Markus and Kitayama write that in individualistic cultures how people see themselves privately is how they present themselves publicly. One's intrapersonal concept (e.g., "I am scholarly," "I am trustworthy," "I am principled") is seen in the individualist's public behavior. The collectivist, however, may have an inconsistent public and private self. Collectivists are likely to behave publicly according to the ingroup's norm regardless of their personal attitudes. The collectivist's self-esteem may depend on whether he or she can fit in and be part of a relevant, ongoing relationship with other group members. Collectivists see themselves as interdependent with others.[19]

Triandis maintains that a culture's individualistic or collectivistic orientation will likely affect child-rearing practices. In individualistic cultures, child rearing emphasizes independence, exploration, creativity, and self-reliance. Individualist parents encourage their children to be unique, express themselves, and be independent. The children of individualist parents understand that they are to leave home once they reach a certain age or education level. In fact, it is thought of as odd or unusual if children past the age of 21 or so still live at home with their parents. Though rank order exists in the individualist's family, decisions are often made democratically. In collectivistic cultures, child rearing emphasizes conformity, obedience, security, and reliability. Collectivistic parents teach their children the importance of family lineage and ancestry. Typically the father dominates the collectivist's home, where family rank is often determined by sex and age.[20]

Collectivists are more conscious of ingroup/outgroup distinctions than are individualists. According to Gudykunst and his colleagues, individualists tend to initiate and maintain specific friendships based on desirable qualities of the other person. Collectivists form friendships that are determined by their hierarchical role in society. Collectivists perceive and rate their ingroup friendships as more intimate than do individualists. On the other hand, individualists tend to apply the same value standards to all, whereas collectivists tend to apply different value standards to members of their ingroups and outgroups. For example, collectivists are likely to use the equality norm (i.e., equal distribution of resources) with ingroup members and the equity norm (i.e., unequal distribution of resources) with outgroup members.[21]

Individualism and collectivism are multidimensional. No single attribute is sufficient to classify a person as individualist or collectivist. That one or another culture may be more or less individualistic or collectivistic does not mean that it cannot share with another culture similar values related to other things. As Schwartz notes, wisdom, broad-mindedness, and inner harmony serve both personal and ingroup interests. Cultures that are considered collectivistic may have values that are collective but are not those of the ingroup. For example, equality for all, social justice, preserving the natural environment, and world peace are values that serve the larger cultural milieu and society, not only the ingroup.[22]

Vertical and Horizontal Individualism and Collectivism. While it is clear that individualistic cultures differ from collectivistic cultures, individualistic cultures can, and do, differ from other individualistic cultures. The same can be said of collectivistic cultures. Some individualistic cultures, for example, link self-reliance with competition while other individualistic cultures do not. Some collectivistic cultures emphasize ingroup harmony above all else while other collectivistic cultures do not. To account for some of these finer distinctions among individualistic and collectivistic cultures, Triandis and his colleagues differentiate between vertical and horizontal individualism and collectivism.[23]

According to Singelis, Triandis, Bhawuk, and Gelfand, horizontal individualism is a cultural orientation where an autonomous self is valued, but the individual is more or less equal in status with others. The self is perceived as independent but nevertheless the same as others. Vertical individualism is the cultural orientation where an autonomous self is also valued but the self is seen as different from and perhaps unequal with others. Status and competition are important aspects of this orientation. The United States and France are examples of vertical individualism, whereas Sweden and Austria are examples of horizontal individualism.[24]

Horizontal collectivism is the cultural orientation where the individual sees the self as a member of an ingroup whose members are similar to each other. The self is interdependent and the same as the self of others. Equality is expected and practiced within this orientation. China is probably a good example of horizontal collectivism. Theoretical communism is an example of extreme horizontal collectivism. Vertical collectivism is the cultural orientation in which the individual sees the self as an integral part of the ingroup but the members are different from each other, some having more status than others. The self is interdependent, and inequality within the group is valued. In this orientation serving and sacrifice are important. Japan, India, and rural traditional Greece are examples of vertical collectivism.

Measuring Individualism-Collectivism. Cross-cultural researchers have spent considerable efforts in developing instruments designed to measure one's relative degree of horizontal and vertical individualism-collectivism. Presented below is an instrument designed by Harry Triandis and his colleagues.[25]

SELF-ASSESSMENT 2.1

Below are 32 statements designed to assess your attitudes and beliefs about your-self. There are no right or wrong answers and some of the statements are similar to others. In the space to the left of each item, indicate the degree to which you either strongly agree or strongly disagree. If you are unsure or think that an item does not apply to you, enter a 5 in the blank. In short, use this key:

Strongly Disagree 1   2   3   4   5   6   7   8   9   Strongly Agree

1. _____ I often do "my own thing."

2. _____ One should live one's life independently of others.

3. _____ I like my privacy.

4. _____ I prefer to be direct and forthright when discussing with other people.

5. _____ I am a unique individual.

6. _____ What happens to me is my own doing.

7. _____ When I succeed, it is usually because of my abilities.

8. _____ I enjoy being unique and different from others in many ways.

9. _____ It annoys me when other people perform better than I do.

10. _____ Competition is the law of nature.

11. _____ When another person does better than I do, I get tense and aroused.

12. _____ Without competition it is not possible to have a good society.

13. _____ Winning is everything.

14. _____ It is important that I do my job better than others.

15. _____ I enjoy working in situations involving competition with others.

16. _____ Some people emphasize winning; I'm one of them.

17. _____ The well-being of my co-workers is important to me.

18. _____ If a co-worker were to get a prize, I would feel proud.

19. _____ If a relative were in financial difficulty, I would help within my means.

20. _____ It is important to maintain harmony within my group.

21. _____ I like sharing little things with my neighbors.

22. _____ I feel good when I cooperate with others.

23. _____ My happiness depends very much on the happiness of those around me.

24. _____ To me, pleasure is spending time with others.

25. _____ I would sacrifice an activity I enjoy very much if my family did not approve of it.

26. _____ I would do what pleased my family, even if I detested that activity.

27. _____ Before taking a major trip, I consult with most members of my family and many friends.

28. _____ I usually sacrifice my self-interest for the benefit of my group.

29. _____ Children should be taught to place duty before pleasure.

30. _____ I hate to disagree with others in my group.

31. _____ We should keep our aging parents with us at home.

32. _____ Children should feel honored if their parents receive a distinguished award.

Scoring:

1. Add your responses for items 1 through 8. This is your Horizontal Individualism Score.

2. Add your responses for items 9 through 16. This is your Vertical Individualism Score.

3. Add your responses for items 17 through 24. This is your Horizontal Collectivism Score.

4. Add your responses for items 25 through 32. This is your Vertical Collectivism Score.

Alternative Scoring Method:

1. Add your responses for items 1 through 16. This is your Individualism score.

2. Add your responses for items 17 through 32. This is your Collectivism score.

There are advantages and disadvantages to being an individualist, just as there are to being a collectivist. Neither approach is "better" than the other; they are simply different orientations. The goal is to recognize and understand the differences, thereby increasing your intercultural competence.

To be sure, the individualism-collectivism dimension of cultural variability has been used extensively in describing cultural differences; perhaps too much. Asian cultures, in particular, are often branded as collectivistic. Recently the individualism-collectivism dichotomy has been the subject of criticism. In her analysis of the Chinese, Hui-Ching Chang argues that by describing cultures as only "collectivistic," which focuses on the structure of society, much of the creativity of individual Asian cultures, including very rich histories, has been ignored. As Chang asserts,

> Although it is through the lens of the metaphor "collectivism" that we are allowed to focus on group membership and patterns of relationships in Asian cultures, at the same time, we lose sight of other aspects of delicate cultural reasoning that underlie manifested behavior patterns.[26]

The essence of Chang's argument is that we cannot rely on single metaphorical distinctions such as individualism-collectivism if we really want to accurately describe and ultimately understand other cultures.

THE PANCULTURAL SELF

As mentioned above, in individualistic cultures, emphasis is placed on individual goals over group goals, values that benefit the self are championed, the self is promoted, and individuals are encouraged to pursue and develop their individual abilities and aptitudes. In these cultures people are taught to be creative, self-reliant, competitive, and assertive. The *individual self* is the most fundamental basis for self-definition. In contrast, in collectivistic cultures, group goals have precedence over individual goals, values that serve the ingroup are stressed, and people are not seen as isolated individuals but as interdependent with others. In these cultures the *collective self* is the most fundamental basis of self-definition.

Yet there is a growing body of literature that suggests that the individual self is *pancultural*. That is, that the individual self is more fundamental to self-definition than the collective self *across all cultures*. In other words, people in all cultures strive to maintain and achieve positive self-regard as a primary motivation. Current research suggests that both individualistic and collectivistic cultures sanction and even endorse self-enhancement, but via different means. Collectivism is just another way to promote the self. For example, in individualistic cultures of the West (i.e., United States, Canada, Great Britain) it is accepted and tolerated to show off one's success. In Eastern cultures (Japan, Korea, China) it is accepted and tolerated to expect reciprocity based on seniority. In other words, in both types of cultures, a person's motivations for behavior and self-definition stem primarily from one's personal identity and an independent sense of self. Moreover, research demonstrates that on self-description tasks, people generate more aspects of their individual self than their collective self, regardless of their cultural individualism or collectivism. Some researchers have even suggested that social harmony, a primary value among collectivists, often serves as a means through which to accomplish individual goals. Other researchers have argued that collectivism is explainable not in terms of a fundamentally different cognitive organization of the self, but because it is advantageous to the self in the long run. Still others maintain that in collectivistic cultures individuals may temporarily sacrifice their self-interest for the group as long as they expect to receive rewards from the group eventually. Finally, in both individualistic and collectivistic cultures, self-enhancement is sanctioned through upward mobility, status seeking, and general promotions of the self. In both types of cultures, people engage in strategic efforts to self-enhance.[27] As Gaertner, Sedikides, and Graetz note,

> Given a choice, however, most persons would opt to stay home rather than go to war, save their hard-earned money rather than pay taxes, and relax in the company of their favorite music than engage in community volunteer work. At the same time, most persons would cherish the protection of the group when attacked individually, seek the financial support of the group when experiencing individual financial troubles, and call on the aid of the community in times of individual disaster. The individual self is the primary basis for self-definition.[28]

HIGH- AND LOW-CONTEXT COMMUNICATION

Human communication is dependent on the context in which it occurs. In addition to the verbal and nonverbal codes that are exchanged between interactants, the salient features of a communicative context include the cultural, physical, socio-relational, and perceptual environments (see Table 2.3). The cultural context includes, among myriad other variables, such features as

Table 2.3

Contextual Features

Culture (race, language)		
Physical Environment (office, church)	→ **Communication Decisions** →	**Message**
Social Relationship (superior/subordinate)		
Psychology (attitudes, emotions)	Verbal Choices	
	Nonverbal Choices	

individualism and collectivism. The physical environment includes the actual geographical location of the interaction (e.g., office, classroom, bedroom). The socio-relational environment encompasses the relationship between the interactants (e.g., superior/subordinate, teacher/student, husband/wife). The perceptual environment consists of the attitudes, motivations, and cognitive dispositions of the interactants. Each of these environments provides a wealth of information to the interactants about how to communicate. *The degree to which interactants focus on these contexts while communicating varies considerably from culture to culture.*

Depending on contextual features present during communication, some persons choose to focus more on the verbal codes than on the nonverbal elements while others will actively monitor the nonverbal elements of the context. Edward Hall describes the former as low context and the latter as high context. Hall asserts that

> a high-context (HC) communication or message is one in which most of the information is either in the physical context or is internalized in the person, while very little is in the coded, explicit, transmitted part of the message. A low-context (LC) communication is just the opposite; i.e., the mass of information is vested in the explicit code.[29]

Like individualism and collectivism, high-low context is best conceptualized along a cultural continuum (see Figure 2.3). No culture exists exclusively on one end of the continuum.

Characteristics of High- and Low-Context Cultures. Hall argues that the environmental, socio-relational, and perceptual contexts have an immense impact on communication. High-context cultures generally have restricted code systems. Users of a restricted code system rely more on the contextual elements of the communication setting for information than on the actual language code. In restricted code cultures, communication is not

Low Context ⟵⟶ High Context

Figure 2.3

general across individuals in content, but is specific to particular people, places, and times. Within a high-context transaction, the interactant will look to the physical, socio-relational, and perceptual environment for information. Of particular importance is the social relationship between the interactants, especially their status. As Hall notes,

> Twins who have grown up together can and do communicate more economically (HC) than two lawyers in a courtroom during a trial (LC), a mathematician programming a computer, two politicians drafting legislation, two administrators writing a regulation, or a child trying to explain to his mother why he got into a fight.[30]

Because interactants in a high-context culture know and understand each other and their appropriate role, words are not necessary to convey meaning. One acts according to one's role. Words and sentences may be collapsed and shortened. In this sense, restricted codes are not unlike local dialects, vernacular, or even jargon used by a well-defined group. Users of restricted codes interpret messages based on their accumulation of shared experiences and expectations.

Hall contends that persons communicating in high-context cultures understand that information from the physical, socio-relational, and perceptual environment already exists and need not be codified verbally. Therefore, high-context communication is fast, proficient, and gratifying. Unlike low-context communication, the burden of understanding in high-context communication rests with each interactant. The rules for communication are implicit, and communicators are expected to know and understand unspoken communication. High-context communication involves using and interpreting messages that are not explicit, minimizing the content of verbal messages, and being sensitive to the social roles of others. Although there are exceptions, many high-context cultures are collectivistic, including China, Japan, North and South Korea, Vietnam, and many Arab and African cultures.[31]

According to Hall, in a low-context transaction, the verbal code is the primary source of information. Low-context cultures generally rely on elaborated codes. Unlike users of restricted codes, users of elaborated codes rely extensively on the verbal code system for creating and interpreting meaning. Information to be shared with others is coded in the verbal message.

Although persons in low-context transactions recognize the nonverbal environment, they tend to focus more on the verbal context. Moreover, the rules and expectations are explicitly explained. Users of elaborated codes are dependent upon words to convey meaning and may become uncomfortable with silence. In low-context transactions, the communicants feel a need to speak. People using low-context communication are expected to communicate in ways that are consistent with their feelings. Hence, low-context communication typically involves transmitting direct, explicit messages. Although there are exceptions, many low-context cultures are individualistic, including Switzerland, Germany, Scandinavia, the United States, France, and the United Kingdom.[32]

Communication Consequences of Low- and High-Context Cultural Orientations. Members of high- and low-context cultures communicate differently, especially with the use of silence. Charles Braithwaite argues that one of the fundamental components of cultural and linguistic competence is knowing how and when to use silence as a communicative tactic.[33] During a high-context communicative exchange, the interactants generally are content with silence because they do not rely on verbal communication as their main source of information. Silence, in fact, communicates mutual understanding. Much of the meaning in communication is expected to be interpreted by the receiver. In communicative exchanges between persons of differing status, the person with lower status may recognize the higher status of the other through silence. Steven Pratt and Lawrence Weider contend that many Native American tribes use silence as a way of recognizing "Indianness." A "real" Indian recognizes another real Indian with silence rather than speech. A recognizable Indian knows that neither he nor the others has an obligation to speak and that silence on the part of all conversants is permissible.[34] In her book on the contemporary Japanese woman, Sumiko Iwao writes that most Japanese feel that expressing especially personal or intimate details is best done nonverbally and/or intuitively; that is, without words. Iwao writes,

> There is an unspoken belief among the Japanese in general that putting deep feelings into words somehow lowers or spoils their value and that understanding attained without words is more precious than that attained through precise articulation.[35]

Japan is considered a high-context culture. Unlike a high-context communication, during most low-context transactions silence is uncomfortable. Persons who do not talk are often perceived negatively. When someone is quiet in a low-context transaction, others may suspect that something is amiss. Silence somehow communicates a problem. Low-context communicators are expected to be direct and to say what they think.

Persons in low-context cultures typically separate the issue of communication from the person with whom they are interacting. A manager might say to an employee, "Don't take it personally" as he or she reprimands the person. High-context cultures, on the other hand, tend to see the topic of communication as intrinsic to the person. A person is seen as a role. If the issue is attacked, so is the person. This results in low-context cultures that deliver a direct style of communication whereas a high-context person prefers indirectness typified by extreme politeness and discretion.

AN INTERCULTURAL CONVERSATION: HIGH- AND LOW-CONTEXT CULTURES

In the following exchange, Mr. Hutchinson is the head of Information Technology (IT) within his organization. Mr. Wong is lead computer programmer. Mr. Wong was born and raised in Malaysia, a high-context culture. The two are discussing when Mr. Wong will put a computer program into production. Note that Mr. Hutchinson's speech is direct and to the point while Mr. Wong is indirect and subtle. In simple frequencies, Mr. Hutchinson uses four times as many words as Mr. Wong.[36]

Mr. Hutchinson:	*The program looks good and passed the test run with only minor errors. When do you think you can put it into production? I don't see any production schedule here. The changes need to go into the system by the end of the month. Is that possible? When do you want to go with this?*
Mr. Wong:	*Maybe I should review the requirements.*
Mr. Hutchinson:	*The errors were minor. Quality Control needs to know when it will go into production. Let's set the production date now. Just tell me when you'll fix the errors. I'll tell QC.*
Mr. Wong:	*Perhaps I can email you an estimate. I'll talk to the team.*
Mr. Hutchinson:	*Couldn't you just tell me when you'll have them fixed? Here, it's no big deal.* (Hands Mr. Wong the program) *Don't they seem like easy fixes?*

Mr. Wong:	(Looks at the program but says nothing—as if not hearing Mr. Hutchinson's suggestion)
Mr. Hutchinson:	*Mr. Wong? Just give me a date.*
Mr. Wong:	*Yes. Whenever you prefer is fine.* (Hands the program back to Mr. Hutchinson)
Mr. Hutchinson:	*I don't need this.* (Hands it back to Mr. Wong) *Well, it's got to go in by the first of next month. OK?*
Mr. Wong:	*Yes, that is fine.*

In the above dialogue, Mr. Hutchinson misses the hint that Mr. Wong is unable to set a production date. When Mr. Wong indicates that setting a date is difficult and will require some expertise, he is indirectly telling Mr. Hutchinson that he is not in a position to make the decision on his own and would prefer to discuss it with the team. Mr. Wong further signals his discomfort by telling Mr. Hutchinson that he could email him the date. Mr. Hutchinson ignores Mr. Wong's status in the organization and further complicates the issue by handing Mr. Wong the program. Trying to avoid any disagreement, Mr. Wong simply asks Mr. Hutchinson to set the date for production and agrees to whatever he says.

Assessing High- and Low-Context Communication. Communication researcher William Gudykunst and his colleagues have developed a survey designed to measure low and high communication styles. The instrument below is an adaptation of Gudykunst's scale.[37]

SELF-ASSESSMENT 2.2

Below are 32 statements regarding how you feel about communicating in different ways. In the blank to the left of each item, indicate the degree to which you agree or disagree with each statement. If you are unsure or think that an item does not apply to you, enter a 5 in the blank.

Strongly Disagree   1   2   3   4   5   6   7   8   9   Strongly Agree

1. ____ I catch on to what others mean, even when they do not say it directly.

2. ____ I show respect to superiors, even if I dislike them.

3. ____ I use my feelings to determine whether to trust another person.

4. ____ I find silence awkward in conversation.

5. ____ I communicate in an indirect fashion.

6. ____ I use many colorful words when I talk.

7. ____ In argument, I insist on very precise definitions.

8. ____ I avoid clear-cut expressions of feelings when I communicate with others.

9. ____ I am good at figuring out what others think of me.

10. ____ My verbal and nonverbal speech tends to be very dramatic.

11. ____ I listen attentively, even when others are talking in an uninteresting manner.

12. ____ I maintain harmony in my communication with others.

13. ____ Feelings are a valuable source of information.

14. ____ When pressed for an opinion, I respond with an ambiguous statement/position.

15. ____ I try to adjust myself to the feelings of the person with whom I am communicating.

16. ____ I actively use a lot of facial expressions when I talk.

17. ____ My feelings tell me how to act in a given situation.

18. ____ I am able to distinguish between a sincere invitation and one intended as a gesture of politeness.

19. ____ I believe that exaggerating stories makes conversation fun.

20. ____ I orient people through my emotions.

21. ____ I find myself initiating conversations with strangers while waiting in line.

22. ____ As a rule, I openly express my feelings and emotions.

23. ____ I feel uncomfortable and awkward in social situations where everybody else is talking except me.

24. ____ I readily reveal personal things about myself.

25. ____ I like to be accurate when I communicate.

26. ____ I can read another person "like a book."

27. ____ I use silence to avoid upsetting others when I communicate.

28. ____ I openly show my disagreement with others.

29. ____ I am a very precise communicator.

30. ____ I can sit with another person, not say anything, and still be comfortable.

31. ____ I think that untalkative people are boring.

32. ____ I am an extremely open communicator.

Scoring: Reverse your score for items 4, 6, 7, 10, 16, 19, 21, 22, 23, 24, 25, 28, 29, 31, 32. If your original score was 1, reverse it to a 9; if your original score was a 2, reverse it to an 8, etc. After reversing the score for those 15 items, simply sum the 32 items. Lower scores indicate low-context communication. Higher scores indicate high-context communication.

Source: Reprinted from Gudykunst, Matsumoto, Ting-Toomey, Nishida, Kim, & Heyman, "The Influence of Cultural Individualism-Collectivism, Self Construals, and Individual Values on Communication Styles Across Cultures," in *Human Communication Research, 22,* 1996, pp. 510-543. Reproduced with permission of Oxford University Press, Inc. via Copyright Clearance Center.

At this point in the chapter you have been given the opportunity to assess your own level of individualism-collectivism and the degree to which your communication style is high or low context. Whatever the outcome on these surveys, one style is not better than the other; they are simply different. The goal is for you to have a better understanding of yourself and those persons with different cultural backgrounds. Individualism-collectivism and high/low context are two dominant ways in which cultures differ. But perhaps what guides cultural behavior more than anything else are the values held by large collectives.

VALUE ORIENTATIONS

In his seminal book on values, Milton Rokeach argues that

the value concept, more than any other, should occupy a central position across all social sciences. . . . It is an intervening variable that shows promise of being able to unify the apparently diverse interests of all sciences concerned with human behavior.[38]

Values affect intercultural communication. When people from different cultures come together to interact, their messages are guided by and reflect their fundamental value orientations. People who strongly value individuality will likely interact differently from people who strongly value collectivism. An understanding of cultural value systems can help to identify similarities and differences between people from different cultures from which intercultural communication can proceed.

Like culture, values are learned; they are not innate or universal. Rokeach argues that values guide us in the selection and justification of social behavior.

Values prescribe what is preferred or prohibited. Values are the evaluative component of an individual's attitudes and beliefs. Values guide how we think about things in terms of what is right/wrong and correct/incorrect. Values trigger positive or negative emotions. Values also guide our actions.[39] Israeli psychologist Shalom Schwartz asserts that values are concepts or beliefs that pertain to outcomes and behaviors, guide the selection and evaluation of behaviors, and are rank ordered according to their relative importance to the individual.[40]

Hsu's Postulates of Basic American Values. Although any individual probably has a unique set of values, there are also sets of values that are representative of a particular culture. Francis Hsu, an anthropologist who has lived much of his life in China and the United States, has outlined what he thinks are the nine basic values of Americans. His list was generated from his personal experiences, American literature and prose, social science research, and studies of criminal behavior in the United States.[41]

Hsu's Postulates of Basic American Values

1. An individual's most important concern is self-interest; self-expression, self-improvement, self-gratification, and independence. This takes precedence over all group interests.

2. The privacy of the individual is the individual's inalienable right. Intrusion into it by others is permitted only by invitation.

3. Because the government exists for the benefit of the individual and not vice versa, all forms of authority, including government, are suspect. Patriotism is good.

4. An individual's success in life depends upon acceptance among his or her peers.

5. An individual should believe in or acknowledge God and should belong to an organized church or other religious institution. Religion is good. Any religion is better than no religion.

6. Men and women are equal.

7. All human beings are equal.

8. Progress is good and inevitable. An individual must improve himself/herself (minimize efforts and maximize returns); the government must be more efficient to tackle new problems; institutions such as churches must modernize to make themselves more attractive.

9. Being American is synonymous with being progressive, and America is the utmost symbol of progress.

Most of the values listed above reflect America's individualistic tendencies. In addition, they echo our emphasis on equality (which is discussed later under power distance), and our determination to push toward the future.

An interesting contrast with the values of America, an individualistic, low-context culture, are those of China, a collectivistic, high-context culture. A group of cross-cultural researchers calling themselves The Chinese Culture Connection (CCC) constructed a listing of 40 dominant Chinese values. The CCC is an international network of social scientists under the direction of Michael Bond, a professor in the Department of Psychology at Chinese University of Hong Kong. The members of the CCC approached a number of Chinese social scientists and asked each of them to prepare a list of 10 fundamental and basic Chinese values. Although their procedure resulted in considerable overlap, they were able to eliminate redundancy by creating a master list of 40 values.[42]

The Chinese Value Survey

1. Filial piety (obedience to parents, respect for parents, honoring of ancestors).
2. Industry (working hard).
3. Tolerance of others.
4. Harmony with others.
5. Humbleness.
6. Loyalty to superiors.
7. Observation of rites and social rituals.
8. Reciprocation of greetings, favors, and gifts.
9. Kindness.
10. Knowledge (education).
11. Solidarity with others.
12. Moderation, following the middle way.
13. Self-culturation.
14. Ordering relationships by status and observing this order.
15. Sense of righteousness.
16. Benevolent authority.

17. Non-competitiveness.

18. Personal steadiness and stability.

19. Resistance to corruption.

20. Patriotism.

21. Sincerity.

22. Keeping oneself disinterested and pure.

23. Thrift.

24. Persistence.

25. Patience.

26. Repayment of both the good and evil that another person has caused you.

27. A sense of cultural superiority.

28. Adaptability.

29. Prudence (carefulness).

30. Trustworthiness.

31. Having a sense of shame.

32. Courtesy.

33. Contentedness with one's position in life.

34. Being conservative.

35. Protecting your "face."

36. A close, intimate friend.

37. Chastity in women.

38. Having few desires.

39. Respect for tradition.

40. Wealth.

The CCC analyzed the list, noting the interrelations and underlying dimensions among many of the 40 values. They then reduced the list to four basic factors, labeled Integration, Confucian Work Dynamic, Human-Heartedness, and Moral Discipline.

Integration	Confucian Work Dynamic	Human-Heartedness	Moral Discipline
Tolerance	Ordering relationships	Kindness	Moderation
Harmony	Thrift	Patience	Keeping disinterested
Solidarity	Persistence	Courtesy	Having few desires
Filial piety	Sense of shame	Righteousness	Adaptability
Trustworthiness	Reciprocation	Patriotism	Prudence
Contentedness	Personal steadiness		
Conservative	Protecting your "face"		
Intimate friend	Respect for tradition		
Chastity in women			
Noncompetitiveness			

The CCC then asked people in 22 different cultures to rate the importance of the values.[43]

Cultures That Value Integration	Cultures That Value Confucian Work Dynamic
W. Germany	Hong Kong
Netherlands	Taiwan
Japan	Japan
New Zealand	S. Korea
Australia	Brazil
England	India
Brazil	Thailand
Sweden	Singapore
Canada	Netherlands
USA	Bangladesh

Cultures That Value Human-Heartedness	Cultures That Value Moral Discipline
Japan	Philippines
Philippines	S. Korea
Canada	Poland
Hong Kong	Pakistan
England	Japan
USA	W. Germany
Zimbabwe	India
New Zealand	Taiwan
Australia	Thailand
Singapore	Hong Kong

Schwartz's Universal Values. Shalom Schwartz and his colleagues have studied values across cultures. Schwartz's goal is to create a comprehensive classification scheme of the substantive content of human values that are shared across cultures. Although some disagree with his position, Schwartz argues that there is a universal structure to values recognized by all cultures. Schwartz's work focuses on the structure of values, not on the universality of their relative importance. Schwartz argues that values represent goals and/or motivations. He contends that values represent, in the form of goals, three universal requirements for human existence to which all cultures must be responsive: (a) the biological needs of individuals, (b) the need for social coordination, and (c) the survival and welfare needs of groups. Based on these three universal human requirements, Schwartz derived eleven distinct motivational types of values. These motivational types lead to the formation of specific values and their priorities. To make the meaning of each motivational type more concrete and explicit, the specific values used to measure the motivational type are in parentheses.[44]

Schwartz's Motivational Types of Values

1. *Self-Direction:* The defining goal of this value type is independent thought and action. (Freedom, Creativity, Independent, Choosing own goals, Curious, Self-respect)

2. *Stimulation:* The goal is derived from the need for variety and stimulation in order to maintain an optimal level of activation. Some of these needs are biological while others are learned/cultural. (An exciting life, A varied life, Daring)

3. *Hedonism:* The need and motivation for pleasure. (Pleasure, Enjoying life)

4. *Achievement:* The need and value of personal success and prestige. (Ambitious, Influential, Capable, Successful, Intelligent, Self-respect)

5. *Power:* Attainment of social status. (Social power, Wealth, Authority, Preserving my public image, Social recognition)

6. *Security:* Need for safety, harmony, and the stability of society and relationships. (National security, Reciprocation of favors, Family security, Sense of belonging, Social order, Healthy, Clean)

7. *Conformity:* Restraint of actions, inclinations, and impulses. (Obedient, Self-discipline, Politeness, Honoring of parents and elders)

8. *Tradition:* The value of religious rites, beliefs, and norms of behavior that, over time, are valued and passed on by a collective. (Respect for children, Devout, Accepting of my portion in life, Humble, Moderate)

9. *Spirituality:* The goal of inner harmony through the transcendence of everyday life. (A spiritual life, Meaning in life, Inner harmony, Detachment)

10. *Benevolence:* The need and motivation for positive interaction and affiliation. (Helpful, Responsible, Forgiving, Honest, Loyal, Mature love, True friendship)

11. *Universalism:* The value of understanding, appreciation, tolerance, and protection for the welfare of all people and for nature. (Equality, Unity with nature, Wisdom, A world of beauty, Social justice, Broad-minded, Protecting the environment, A world at peace)

Kluckhohn and Strodbeck's Value Orientations. In the early 1960s, Florence Kluckhohn and Fred Strodbeck developed the concept of value orientations. They argued that in every culture there are universal problems and conditions that must be addressed. For example, every culture must deal with the natural environment. All cultures must feed themselves. All cultures must face the issues of child-rearing, and so on. For a given culture, however, there are a limited number of solutions to these problems. These possible solutions are motivated by the values of the culture. Initially, Kluckhohn and Strodbeck created five sets of value orientations.[45] Several years later, communication researchers John Condon and Fathi Yousef extended the set to a total of 25 value orientations. Condon and Yousef organized the value orientations around six dominant themes: self, family, society, human nature, nature, and the supernatural.[46]

The Condon and Yousef set of value orientations provides a structure and vocabulary that can be used to compare cultures. Although there are exceptions, many of the values on the left of the continuum are representative of individualistic, low-context cultures, while those on the right are representative of collectivistic, high-context cultures (see Table 2.4).

The Self. In all cultures, people develop their self-identity. How that identity is fostered is influenced by the culture's values. For example, people in individualistic societies, such as the United States, tend to view their accomplishments and failures very personally. Conformity is viewed negatively. Hsu notes that in China, however, conformity and cooperation are highly valued. In the United States, a person is seen as a unique individual and strives for independence from others. When individuals succeed or win, they receive a great deal of attention and adulation, as in the case of winning an Olympic gold medal or an Academy Award. The individual is "put on a pedestal." Likewise, when individuals lose, they are often left to suffer alone. No one wants to be seen with a loser. Whether on top or on the bottom, the individual experiences intense emotions. Hsu contends

Table 2.4

	Individualistic Low Context		Collectivistic High Context
SELF			
1. Individualism	Individualism	Individuality	Interdependence
2. Age	Youth	Middle years	Old age
3. Sex	Equality of sexes	Female superiority	Male superiority
4. Activity	Doing	Being-in-becoming	Being
THE FAMILY			
1. Relational Orientations	Individualistic	Collateral	Lineal
2. Authority	Democratic	Authority centered	Authoritarian
3. Positional Role Behavior	Open	General	Specific-prescribed
4. Mobility	High mobility	Phasic mobility	Low mobility-stasis
SOCIETY			
1. Social Reciprocity	Independence	Symmetrical-obligatory	Complementary-obligatory
2. Group Membership	Many-brief membership	Balanced	Few-prolonged membership
3. Intermediaries	Few	Specialist only	Essential
4. Formality	Informal	Selective formality	Pervasive formality
5. Property	Private	Utilitarian	Communal
HUMAN NATURE			
1. Rationality	Rational	Intuitive	Irrational
2. Good/Evil	Good	Mixture	Evil

(Continued)

Table 2.4 (Continued)

	Individualistic Low Context		Collectivistic High Context
3. Happiness/ Pleasure	Happiness as goal	Inextricable bond of happiness and sadness	Life is mostly sad
4. Mutability	Change, growth, learning	Some change	Unchanging

NATURE

1. Relationship between Humans and Nature	Humans dominate nature	Harmonious	Nature dominates humans
2. Ways of knowing Nature	Abstract	Circle of induction and deduction	Specific-direct
3. Structure of Nature	Mechanistic	Spiritual	Organic
4. Concept of Time	Future	Present	Past

SUPERNATURAL

1. Relationship between Human and the Supernatural	Humans as God	Pantheism	Humans controlled by supernatural
2. Meaning of Life	Physical/ material goals	Intellectual goals	Spiritual goals
3. Providence	Good is unlimited	Balance of good and misfortune	Good in life is limited
4. Knowledge of Cosmic Order	Order is comprehensible	Faith and reason	Mysterious and unknowable

that strong emotions are unavoidable because they are concentrated in one individual. The Chinese, however, are interdependent with others, where responsibility and accountability are shared and divided among the group members. If the group wins, everyone in the group wins; there is no "most valuable player," so to speak. Therefore, the intense emotions experienced by winning or failing are tempered and moderated because they are shared.[47]

The second variation on the self continuum is age. Western, individual-istic, low-context cultures tend to value youth. Conversely, old age is valued in many cultures, such as Nigeria, where it is associated with wisdom. Accord-ing to Harris and Moran, in Nigeria the elderly are respected because they have much experience and can pass on family history and tradition. Harris and Moran suggest that when conducting business with Nigerians, a busi-ness would be wise to send an older person to meet with prospective busi-nesspersons, as this will show a certain amount of respect for Nigeria's emphasis on age.[48]

The third variation on the self is activity. Americans identify themselves in terms of their activities, usually professions and occupations. Condon and Yousef hold that many English names indicate "doers," such as Baker, Smith, and Carpenter, for example. In the United States, people are often asked about what they "do" for a living. Non-Western cultures emphasize being, a form of self-actualization. Life is an organic whole; it is human to embrace life and to become one with the universe and oneself.[49]

Family. Familial relationships differ across cultures. Harris and Moran write that in Nigeria, for example, the family is the core group of society. Nigerians value one's family lineage through the male head of the house-hold. A Nigerian is known by his or her family lineage and may have privi-leges and responsibility based on family name. Furthermore, marriage is seen as a way of producing more children to contribute to this lineage. If one's spouse is sterile, it is grounds for divorce. Nigerians also practiced polygamy. Wives are often acquired through the payment of a bride price to the bride's parents.[50]

Positional role behavior within families refers to how strictly roles are prescribed among family members. The Guatemalan Ladinos (a term used to refer to people born through interracial relationships or those who have Spanish and Indian blood) define a man's and woman's role within the family quite differently. Mike Keberlein argues that Machismo is a Spanish concept that deals mainly with how male and female roles are performed in the home. Ladinos view the men as protectors and providers and women as child-rearers and homemakers. Children are taught early by the mother to recognize their responsibilities as men and women. A boy may be sent to work in the fields as early as five years old. A young girl might start house-hold chores at the same age, where she is taught to care for younger children of the house and to cook. Young boys are expected never to cry or show signs of pain, whereas young girls are taught to show emotion when-ever appropriate.[51]

Society. According to Condon and Yousef, social reciprocity refers to the mutual exchanges people make in their dealings with others. What is perceived as a relatively innocuous request in one country may be inter-preted quite seriously in others. In the United States a request to do a favor (e.g., "Can I borrow your car") may imply no necessary reciprocity. In other cultures, one is required to return favors and obligations in kind. Equal exchanges are expected and obligated.[52]

The second value orientation, group membership, differs greatly among individualistic and collectivistic cultures. According to Condon and Yousef, members of individualistic cultures tend to join many groups throughout their lifetime, yet their affiliation with any particular group may be quite brief. The group is subordinate to the individual needs. In the United States, for example, people join political groups, social groups, hobby groups, occu-pational groups, self-help groups, fraternal groups, and so on. In collectivis-tic cultures, people tend to belong to fewer groups (e.g., family and occupational) but belong for a lifetime.[53]

An intermediary is a go-between; intermediaries are more common in collectivistic than individualistic cultures. Many Chinese prefer to work through an intermediary. According to De Menthe, the concept of *mian-zi,* or "face," is a critical ingredient for Chinese. The Chinese believe that respect for others binds society together. *Mian-zi* is a sort of social status, or how a person is ranked in relation to others. This is sometimes referred to as one's "face." A person's face is determined by such things as wealth and power. The more face a person has, the more he/she can "buy" with it. De Menthe writes that, like a checking account, *mian-zi* can be overdrawn, and people are expected to balance their accounts. Chinese are very conscious of their face as well as the face of others. The higher in rank a person is, the more critical the concern with face. In business dealings and in personal relationships, it is critical to the Chinese that they maintain face and avoid offending the face of others. Hence, it is difficult for the Chinese to be straightforward and open in their daily interaction with others. Intermediaries are therefore essential in both personal and business relationships.[54]

Human Nature. The human nature orientation deals with how cul-tures perceive human character and temperament. In Western cultures such as the United States, people are viewed as essentially rational. American children are taught to "use their heads" when making decisions.

Americans frequently tell their friends to "stop being so emotional," as if being emotional implied some character flaw. Japanese children, on the other hand, are often taught to follow their intuition or to lead with their hearts.

Condon and Yousef note that in the United States, happiness is viewed as a practical goal, even the primary goal; hence the popular song titled "Don't Worry, Be Happy." Moreover, the Declaration of Independence states that people "are endowed by their creator with certain unalienable rights, that among these are life, liberty, and the pursuit of happiness." Other societies and cultures view happiness and sadness as inseparable, as in the yin-yang philosophy of many Asian cultures. A Chinese proverb reads, "If a man's face does not show a little sadness, his thoughts are not too deep." Another one reads, "One should not miss the flavor of being sick, nor miss the experience of being destitute."[55]

Nature. In the United States, high school students learn about the structure of nature in their biology, geography, and physics classes, among others. Students learn about things they may never actually see, such as the structure of DNA. The models they see are not literal reproductions, but dramatic abstractions. Much of the education taught in the United States is based on abstract concepts and constructs. Condon and Yousef maintain that in other cultures, perhaps those with little formal education, what a person knows about nature is learned through direct experience. Many Western cultures view nature as mechanistic, meaning that nature is structured like that of a machine or clock. The brain, for example, is explained in computer analogics. Models of DNA look like double helixes. The organic orientation likens nature to that of a plant, where nature is seen as an organic whole that is interdependent with all other natural forces.[56]

Supernatural. Condon and Yousef assert that a culture's perspective on the cosmos reflects its philosophy about its people's relationship with the supernatural and spiritual world. In many Western cultures, the supernatural is studied almost scientifically. Scientists study the structure of space and seek, through scientific means, to find the origins of the universe. We send out satellites equipped with printed messages and recordings in a (perhaps vain) attempt to communicate with extraterrestrials. Most Western cultures believe that the order of the cosmos is knowable. Conversely, other cultures see the cosmos with a great deal of fear and uncertainty. Condon and Yousef point to a farmer in Peru who relies on the phases of the moon and the cycles of the seasons to tell him when to plant or harvest his fields. The farmer thinks of the cosmos with a great deal of superstition and fear. To him, these mysteries are unexplainable.[57]

The organization of the value orientations presented above are neither mutually exclusive nor exhaustive. They are representative of the kinds of values held by cultures and the difference in those values. They also serve as a starting point for researchers to compare and contrast the myriad cultures that cohabit the planet.

POWER DISTANCE

According to Hofstede, while many cultures declare and even legislate equality for their members, all cultures must deal with the issue of human inequality. A fundamental tenet expressed in the beginning of the Declaration of Independence, the document upon which the United States was founded, states that "we hold these truths to be self-evident, that all men are created equal." In the United States, we generally try to treat others as equal, in both our personal and professional lives. Although some cultures, like the United States, affirm equality for its members, some form of inequality exists in virtually every culture. Inequality can occur in areas such as prestige, wealth, power, human rights, and technology, among others. Issues of inequality fall within the rubric of what Hofstede calls "power distance." In his landmark survey research, Geert Hofstede defined power distance as "the extent to which the less powerful members of institutions and organizations within a country expect and accept that power is distributed unequally."[58] Power distance can be seen in families, bureaucracies, and even in friendships. For example, inequality of power within organizations is inevitable and desirable in many cases for organizations to function effectively. Military organizations are defined by power distance.

Hofstede categorizes cultures as possessing either large or small power distance. Cultures with a smaller power distance emphasize that inequalities among people should be minimized and that there should be interdependence between less and more powerful people. In cultures with small power distance (e.g., United States, Canada, Austria), family members are generally treated as equal and familial decisions are reached democratically. According to Hofstede, in low power distance schools, teachers expect a certain amount of initiative and interaction with students. The overall educational process is student-oriented. In class, students are expected to ask questions and perhaps even challenge their teachers. In organizations, decentralization is popular, where subordinates engage in participative decision making. The organizational power hierarchy is mostly for convenience, where the persons who occupy powerful roles may change regularly. In fact, workers are expected to try and "climb the ladder of success" to more power and prestige. In this sense persons in small power distance cultures may recognize "earned" power; that is, power that people deserve by virtue of their drive, hard work, and motivation. Moreover, small power distance cultures

Figure 2.4   In many cultures, there is a strict hierarchy among family members

tend to resent those whose power is decreed by birth or wealth (i.e., positional power).[59]

Hofstede maintains that in cultures with a larger power distance, inequalities among people are both expected and desired. Less powerful people should be dependent on more powerful people (see Figure 2.4). In larger power distance cultures (e.g., Philippines, Mexico, India), children are expected to be obedient. In many larger power distance cultures there is a strict hierarchy among family members where typically the father rules authoritatively, followed by the eldest son and moving down the ladder by age and sex. In educational settings, teachers are treated as parents, with respect and honor, especially older teachers. Students who disobey may by punished severely. In the workplace, power is usually centralized where workers and bosses are treated unequally. In many large power distance cultures, Hofstede observed that workers are generally uneducated and superiors are entitled to special privileges and status—in some cultures, by law.[60]

Table 2.5

Small Power Distance Cultures	Large Power Distance Cultures
Austria	Malaysia
Denmark	Guatemala
New Zealand	Panama
Ireland	Phillippines
Sweden	Mexico
Norway	Venezuela
Finland	Ecuador
Switzerland	Indonesia
Great Britain	India
Germany	Brazil

There appears to be a direct link between power distance and the latitude of the country. In a study conducted at 40 universities in the United States, Peter Andersen and his colleagues found a strong correlation between latitude and authoritarianism. Residents in the northern U.S. states were less authoritarian than those in the southern United States. The population of a country may be another predictor of power distance. Generally, larger cultures tend to be higher power distance (see Table 2.5). As the size of any group increases, it becomes unwieldy and difficult to manage informally.[61]

Large and small power distance cultures may value different types of power. Large power distance cultures tend to emphasize positional power. Positional power is based on formal authority (e.g., family rank). Persons with positional power have control over rewards, punishments, and information. Small power distance cultures recognize and respect earned power. Earned power is based on an individual's accomplishments, hard work, and effort.

Measuring Power Distance

SELF-ASSESSMENT 2.3

Below are 10 statements regarding issues we face at work, in the classroom, and at home. Indicate in the blank to the left of each statement the degree to which you (1) strongly agree, (2) agree, (3) are unsure, (4) disagree, and (5) strongly disagree with the statement. For example, if you strongly agree with the first statement, place a 1 in the blank. Work quickly and record your initial response.

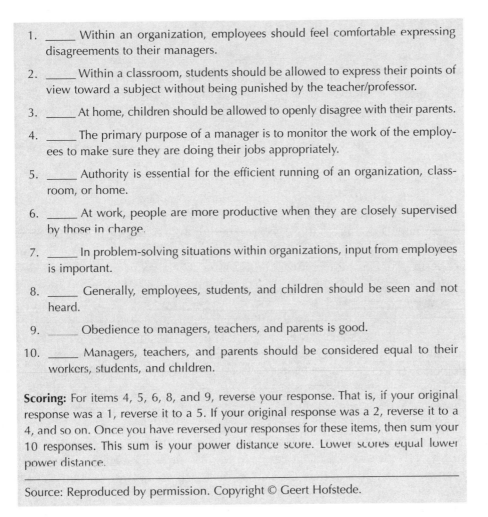

1. _____ Within an organization, employees should feel comfortable expressing disagreements to their managers.

2. _____ Within a classroom, students should be allowed to express their points of view toward a subject without being punished by the teacher/professor.

3. _____ At home, children should be allowed to openly disagree with their parents.

4. _____ The primary purpose of a manager is to monitor the work of the employees to make sure they are doing their jobs appropriately.

5. _____ Authority is essential for the efficient running of an organization, classroom, or home.

6. _____ At work, people are more productive when they are closely supervised by those in charge.

7. _____ In problem-solving situations within organizations, input from employees is important.

8. _____ Generally, employees, students, and children should be seen and not heard.

9. _____ Obedience to managers, teachers, and parents is good.

10. _____ Managers, teachers, and parents should be considered equal to their workers, students, and children.

Scoring: For items 4, 5, 6, 8, and 9, reverse your response. That is, if your original response was a 1, reverse it to a 5. If your original response was a 2, reverse it to a 4, and so on. Once you have reversed your responses for these items, then sum your 10 responses. This sum is your power distance score. Lower scores equal lower power distance.

Source: Reproduced by permission. Copyright © Geert Hofstede.

If we know the position of a culture on the power distance scale relative to our own culture, then we have a starting point from which to proceed in our understanding of that culture. In large power distance cultures subordinates are extremely submissive whereas in low power distance cultures subordinates are confrontational. Power distance tells us about dependence relationships in a given culture. In those countries where a small power distance is observed (e.g., Austria, Norway), there is limited dependence. Workers in these cultures prefer managers who consult with them in decision making. Here, subordinates are generally comfortable approaching and interacting with their superiors. In cultures with large power distance (e.g., Malaysia, Mexico, India), there is considerable dependence of subordinates on superiors.

COMMUNICATION AND POWER DISTANCE

Power distance affects the verbal and nonverbal behavior of a culture. Several studies have investigated power distance and communication during conflict. In their research Tyler, Lind, and Huo found that power distance influences the way that people react to third-party authorities in conflict situations. Specifically, they found that when making evaluations of authorities, persons in small power distance cultures placed more value on the quality of their treatment by authorities. In contrast, those with higher power distance values focused more strongly on the favorability of their outcomes. Tyler, Lind, and Huo suggest that the degree to which authorities can gain acceptance for themselves and their decisions through providing dignified, respectful treatment is influenced by the cultural values of the disputants. Specifically, they found that dispute resolution methods, such as mediation, are more likely to be effective among those who have low power distance values. In another study, Smith, Dugan, Peterson, and Leung examined how managers handled disagreement with their subordinates. Their results showed that the larger the power distance, the more frequent are reports of outgroup disagreements; the smaller the power distance, the more likely managers are to ask peers to handle disagreements; and the smaller the power distance, the more likely the manager is to use subordinates to handle disagreements. The authors conclude that in small power distance cultures managers minimize status differences during conflict and rely on peers and subordinates to assist in mediating conflict.

Ting-Toomey has examined power distance and the concepts of *face* and *facework* in conflict situations. Ting-Toomey and others argue that persons in all cultures have face concerns. Face represents an individual's sense of positive self-image in the context of communication. According to Ting-Toomey, everyone, in all cultures, has face concerns during conflict. *Self-face* is the concern for one's own image, *other-face* is concern for another's image, and *mutual-face* is concern for both parties. *Facework* is used to manage these face concerns during conflict. Ting-Toomey's research has shown that small power distance cultures have a greater self-face concern, have lesser other- and mutual-face concerns, use more dominating facework, and use less avoiding facework.[62]

Other research has investigated how power distance affects reactions to messages about alcohol warnings. Perea and Slater examined the responses of Mexican American and Anglo young adults to four televised drinking and driving warnings. The messages were manipulated into large and small power distance appeals by attributing or not attributing them to the Surgeon General; that is, an authority with power. Anglos (small power distance) rated the warnings without the Surgeon General as more believable than warnings with the Surgeon General; the opposite was true for Latinos (high power distance).[63]

Power distance also affects the nonverbal behavior of a culture. In many large power distance cultures, persons of lower status are taught not to give direct eye contact to a person of higher status. Indirect eye contact from a subordinate signals to the superior that the subordinate recognizes his or her lower status. In large power distance cultures, when a person of high status hands something to a person of lower status (e.g., a book), the lower-status person will often use both hands to receive the item; again, recognizing his or her lower status. Andersen, Hecht, Hoobler, and Smallwood have observed that many large power distance cultures prohibit interclass dating, marriage, and contact. They also suggest that persons of lower power must become skilled at decoding nonverbal behavior, and that persons of lower status must show only positive emotions to those of higher status. Moreover, in large power distance cultures, persons of lower status smile more in an effort to appease those of higher status.[64]

AN INTERCULTURAL CONVERSATION: LARGE AND SMALL POWER DISTANCE CULTURES

Different power distance orientations manifest themselves in interaction. In the dialogue below, Jim Neuman is a U.S. high school exchange student in Guatemala. Coming from a smaller power distance culture, Jim is accustomed to interacting with his teachers. Raising one's hand in a U.S. classroom is not only acceptable, but encouraged. In Guatemala, a larger power distance culture, the classroom is teacher-centered. In Mr. Gutierrez's classroom, there is to be strict order, with Mr. Gutierrez initiating all of the communication. Teachers are to be treated with deference.

Mr. Gutierrez: *This morning I will be discussing some points about Guatemala's geography. Guatemala is the northernmost country of Central America* (Jim Neuman raises his hand). *To the north it borders the countries of El Salvador and Honduras. To the west, its natural border is the Pacific Ocean. In the east is another natural border, the Atlantic Ocean, as well as the country of Belize.*

Jim Neuman: (raising his hand and waving it slightly). *Mr. Gutierrez?*

> **Mr. Gutierrez**: *Guatemala is called the "Land of the Eternal Spring." There are all of the same kinds of natural land forms as in Mexico, but are* (Jim Neuman interrupts)
>
> **Jim Neuman**: *Mr. Gutierrez, I have a question.*
>
> **Mr. Gutierrez**: *Jim, stop interrupting, please.*
>
> **Jim Neuman**: *May I ask a question?*
>
> **Mr. Gutierrez**: *No! If you continue to disobey, I will punish you! Be quiet!*

In the above dialogue Jim does not understand Mr. Gutierrez's harsh reprimand. Coming from a low power distance culture, Jim recognizes that teachers have more power than students, but does not see their power as absolute. Jim sees himself as an active participant of the class. After all, for most of his life Jim's teachers have encouraged him to speak up in class. Mr. Gutierrez, on the other hand, sees the classroom as his domain, one that he rules absolutely. By raising his hand, Jim demonstrates his insolence toward Mr. Gutierrez.

To some extent, a certain degree of power distance is essential if cultures are to survive. Legitimate power is a necessity of civil life. Yet independence from power, liberation, and freedom of choice are politically attractive alternatives. Perhaps the ideal situation is one where individual families operate with internally driven large power distances while the larger cultural milieu restricts overbearing, omnipotent, and intimidating governments.

UNCERTAINTY AVOIDANCE

Gudykunst and Kim state that communicating with someone from an unknown culture can be uncomfortable because such situations are replete with uncertainty and unpredictability. When uncertainty is high, anxiety is usually high and communication can be difficult and awkward. This may account for why some people avoid interacting with people from other cultures. By reducing uncertainty, however, anxiety can be reduced, which, in turn, facilitates effective and successful communication. Although uncertainty is probably a universal feature of initial intercultural communication, one's level of tolerance for uncertainty and ambiguity varies across cultures.

In addition, argue Gudykunst and Kim, the communicative strategies for reducing uncertainty also vary across cultures. Persons in high-context cultures, for example, look to the environmental, socio-relational, and perceptual contexts for information to reduce uncertainty. People in low-context cultures tend to rely on verbal information-seeking strategies, usually by asking lots of questions.[65]

Hofstede asserts that although the extent to which an individual experiences uncertainty and the subsequent strategies for reducing it may be unique to that person, a general orientation toward uncertainty can be shared culturally. According to Hofstede, tolerance for uncertainty is learned through cultural socialization. Hofstede notes that a culture's technology, system of laws, and religion are markers for how that culture addresses and attempts to avoid or reduce uncertainty. For example, some kinds of technology help a culture manage natural uncertainty (e.g., weather), systems of law are designed to prevent and account for behavioral uncertainties (e.g., crime), and religion can help a culture cope with supernatural uncertainty (e.g., death). A culture's technology, law, and religion are ingrained in the individual through socialization, education, and occupation. Hence, they lead to collective patterns of tolerance for ambiguity and uncertainty.[66]

Uncertainty avoidance is the degree to which the members of a particular culture feel threatened by uncertain or unknown situations. Hofstede contends that this feeling is expressed through nervous stress and in a felt need for predictability and a need for written and unwritten rules. Cultures possess either a weak or a strong uncertainty avoidance orientation. In cultures with a weak uncertainty avoidance orientation, uncertainty is seen as a normal part of life, where each day is accepted as it comes. The people are comfortable with ambiguity and are guided by a belief that what is different is curious. In school settings, students are comfortable with open-ended learning situations and enjoy classroom discussion. In the workplace, time is needed only as a guide, not as a master. Precision and punctuality are learned because they do not come naturally. Workers are motivated by their achievements and personal esteem or belongingness. There is also a high tolerance for innovative ideas that may conflict with the norm.[67]

Conversely, cultures with a strong uncertainty avoidance orientation sense that uncertainty in life is a continuous threat that must be fought. Life can be stressful where a sense of urgency and high anxiety are typical. Hofstede maintains that strong uncertainty avoidant cultures are guided by the belief that what is different is dangerous. Uncertainty avoiding cultures evade ambiguity in most situations and look for structure in their business organizations, home life, and relationships. At school, students are most comfortable in structured environments. The teachers are supposed to have

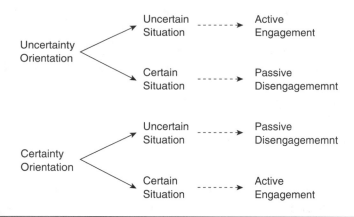

Figure 2.5

all the right answers. On the job, time is money, where punctuality and precision are expected. There is generally a resistance to innovative ideas, and workers are motivated by job security.[68]

A THEORY OF UNCERTAINTY ORIENTATION

Related to Hofstede's concept of uncertainty avoidance is the theory of uncertainty orientation. According to this variation of Hofstede's ideas, some individuals are considered uncertainty oriented and others are considered certainty oriented. Uncertainty-oriented individuals have a weak uncertainty avoidance while certainty-oriented individuals have a strong uncertainty avoidance tendency. Uncertainty-oriented persons' preferred method of handling uncertainty is to seek out information and to engage in activity that will directly resolve the uncertainty. These people try to understand and discover aspects of the self and the environment about which they are uncertain. Certainty-oriented people, on the other hand, develop a self-regulatory style that circumvents uncertainty. Given the choice, persons who are certainty oriented will undertake activity that maintains clarity; when confronted with uncertainty, they will rely on others and/or on heuristic devices more than more direct methods of resolving uncertainty (see Figure 2.5).

Generally, Eastern cultures have a preference for certainty, whereas Western cultures are uncertainty oriented (see Table 2.6). The tendency to be individualistic or self-oriented in Western populations exists because uncertainty-oriented people like to find out new information about the self. The more personally relevant or uncertain the situation, the more uncertainty-oriented persons will be actively engaged in the situation. Certainty-oriented

Table 2.6

Certainty-Oriented Cultures	*Uncertainty-Oriented Cultures*
Japan	United States
Guatemala	Canada
Portugal	New Zealand
Peru	Sweden
El Salvador	Ireland
Panama	Great Britain
Chile	Denmark
Spain	South Africa
Uruguay	Norway

people, however, are more group oriented, as the group provides a clear standard for norms and behavior, a standard that can be embraced by the certainty oriented. Western societies tend to be more uncertainty oriented because of their self-oriented and individualistic approaches to life than do people in Eastern societies, who, in turn, should be more certainty oriented as a function of their heavy reliance on groups.[69]

AN INTERCULTURAL CONVERSATION: WEAK AND STRONG UNCERTAINTY AVOIDANCE

There are any number of ways one's uncertainty avoidance orientation may manifest itself in interaction. In the dialogue presented below, Kelly and Keiko are interacting about a dinner invitation. Kelly, from the United States, possesses a relatively weak uncertainty avoidance index, while Keiko, from Japan, comes from a culture with a relatively strong uncertainty avoidance index.

Keiko: *Hey, Kelly, let's do something tonight.*

Kelly: *All right.*

Keiko: *Please come over to my house and I'll cook dinner for you.*

Kelly: *I have invited some friends over to my house for dinner tonight, but I don't know if they're coming.*

Keiko: *Well . . . as soon as you know if they're coming, let me know.*

Kelly: *I won't know until tonight.*

Keiko: *What time?*

Kelly: *I won't know until they call me. They'll probably call later this afternoon.*

Keiko: *How will you know whether or not to cook enough for everyone?*

Kelly: *Oh, I'll make up something on the spot. I like to cook. I'll whip up something fast.*

Keiko: *But . . . what if they don't come? Won't they call and let you know?*

Kelly: *No . . . if they don't come, I'll know that something else came up. I'll let you know as soon as I can.*

Keiko: *Maybe we should plan my dinner for some other night.*

In the above dialogue, Keiko is confused by Kelly's easygoing attitude toward the evening's plans. Coming from a strong uncertainty-avoidant culture, Keiko would prefer to plan ahead to avoid uncertainty and prepare her script for the evening. Kelly, on the other hand, is perfectly comfortable making plans based on how the evening progresses. Without a plan, how will Keiko know how to act?

Although the feelings associated with uncertainty are personal and subjective, they can be shared by whole cultures. Although anxiety creates the same physiological responses in humans, what triggers anxiety and one's level of tolerance for it are learned. A culture's orientation toward uncertainty can be found in its families, schools, and institutions. But uncertainty avoidance ultimately manifests itself in human interaction.

CHAPTER SUMMARY

In the contextual model of intercultural communication, culture is the largest context, surrounding all of the other contexts. This chapter has presented the paradox of culture. On one hand, culture is amorphous; it is shapeless, vague, and nebulous. Most of us are not aware of its influence on our daily behaviors. On the other hand, culture is arguably the strongest influence on an individual's cognitive, affective, and behavioral choices. Over the past few decades, anthropologists, psychologists, and sociologists have isolated several dimensions of cultural variability by which cultures can be compared. This chapter has focused on five of these dimensions, including the extent to which we place individual goals over those of the group (i.e., individualism) or the degree to which we see ourselves as members of a group first, then as an individual (i.e., collectivism). Another dimension is high-low context, which refers to the extent to which we gather information from the physical, social, and psychological context (i.e., high context), or the extent to which we gather information from the verbal code (i.e., low context). One of the most influential features of our lives is our value orientations. A culture's values guide its decisions as to what is right or wrong, decent or indecent, moral or immoral. Cultures also differ regarding the extent to which people accept and expect that power is distributed unequally (high power distance) or whether they believe that people are inherently equal (low power distance). And finally, cultures differ in the extent to which people accept and tolerate uncertainty and unpredictability in their lives (i.e., strong uncertainty avoidance), or the extent to which uncertainty should be fought and conquered (i.e., weak uncertainty avoidance). These dimensions provide a starting point for our future examination of intercultural communication.

GLOSSARY OF TERMS

Collectivism: Cultural orientation that the group is the primary unit of culture. Group goals take precedence over individual goals.

High Context: Cultural orientation where meanings are gleaned from the physical, social, and psychological contexts.

Horizontal Collectivism: Cultural orientation where the self is seen as a member of an ingroup whose members are similar to each other.

Horizontal Individualism: Cultural orientation where an autonomous self is valued, but the self is more or less equal with others.

Individualism: Cultural orientation that the individual is unique and that emphasizes individual goals over group goals.

Low Context: Cultural orientation where meanings are encoded in the verbal code.

Power Distance: The extent to which members of a culture expect and accept that power is unequally distributed.

Uncertainty Avoidance: The degree to which members of a particular culture feel threatened by unpredictable, uncertain, or unknown situations.

Values: Criteria for selecting and justifying behavior. Values have a cognitive, affective, and behavioral component.

Vertical Collectivism: Cultural orientation where the individual sees the self as an integral part of the ingroup but whose members are different from each other (e.g., status).

Vertical Individualism: Cultural orientation where an autonomous self is valued and the self is seen as different from and perhaps unequal with others.

REFERENCES

1. Hall, E. T. (1959). *The Silent Language,* Greenwich, CT: Fawcett, (p. 39).
2. Keesing, R. M. (1974). "Theories of Culture," in B. J. Siegel (Ed.), *Annual Review of Anthropology,* (pp. 73–97), Palo Alto, CA: Annual Reviews, Inc.
3. Yurkovich, D., Pliscott, K., & Halverson, R. (1996). "The Norwegian Culture." Unpublished student manuscript, St. Norbert College, DePere, WI; Gayle, A. R., & Knutson, K. P. (1993). "Understanding Cultural Differences: Janteloven and Social Conformity in Norway." *Et Cetera, 49,* 449.
4. Triandis, H. C. (2001). "Individualism-Collectivism and Personality." *Journal of Personality, 69,* 907–924; Triandis, H. C. (1990). "Cross-cultural studies of individualism and collectivism." In J. J. Berman (Ed.), *Nebraska Symposium on Motivation: 1989,* (pp. 41–133). Lincoln: University of Nebraska Press; Triandis, H. C. (1993). "Collectivism and Individualism as Cultural Syndromes," *Cross Cultural Research, 27,* 155–180; Triandis, H. C. (1995). *Individualism & Collectivism,* Boulder, CO: Westview.
5. Triandis, "Individualism-Collectivism and Personality"; Triandis, *Individualism & Collectivism.*
6. Ibid.
7. Ibid.
8. Triandis, *Individualism & Collectivism;* Hsu, F. L. K. (1981). *American and Chinese: Passage to Differences,* (3rd ed.), Honolulu: University of Hawaii Press; Schwartz, S. H. (1990). "Individualism-Collectivism: Critique and Proposed Refinement," *Journal of Cross-Cultural Psychology, 21,* 139–157; Lustig, M., & Koester, J. (1996). *Intercultural Competence: Interpersonal Communication Across Cultures,* New York: HarperCollins.
9. Triandis, *Individualism & Collectivism;* Hsu, *American and Chinese: Passage to Differences.*
10. Triandis, "Cross-Cultural Studies of Individualism and Collectivism."
11. Triandis, "Cross-Cultural Studies of Individualism and Collectivism";Triandis, *Individualism & Collectivism;* Schwartz, "Individualism-Collectivism: Critique and Proposed Refinement."
12. This dialogue is adapted from a scene in Copeland, L. (Producer). *Managing the Overseas Assignment* [videorecording], San Francisco, CA: Copeland Griggs Productions, 1983.

13. Feldhausen, J. (1998). "Collectivism and Individualism in Denmark." Unpublished student manuscript, St. Norbert College, De Pere, WI; Triandis, "Individualism-Collectivism and Personality."

14. Vandello, J. A., & Cohen, D. (1999). "Patterns of Individualism and Collectivism Across the United States." *Journal of Personality and Social Psychology, 77*(2), 279–292.

15. Ibid.

16. Triandis, "Individualism-Collectivism and Personality"; Triandis, *Individualism & Collectivism.*

17. Gudykunst, W. B., Matsumoto, Y., Ting-Toomey, S., Nishida, T., Kim, K. S., & Heyman, S. (1994). *Measuring Self Construals Across Cultures,* Paper presented at the International Communication Association, Sydney, Australia.

18. Triandis, *Individualism & Collectivism;* Hsu, *American and Chinese: Passage to Differences.*

19. Markus, H., & Kitayama, S. (1991). "Culture and Self: Implications for Cognition, Emotion, and Motivation," *Psychological Review, 98,* 224–253.

20. Triandis, "Individualism-Collectivism and Personality"; Triandis, *Individualism & Collectivism.*

21. Gudykunst, W. B., Matsumoto, Y., Ting-Toomey, S., Nishida, T., Kim, K. S., & Heyman, S. (1996). "The Influence of Cultural Individualism-Collectivism, Self Construals, and Individual Values on Communication Styles Across Cultures," *Human Communication Research, 22,* 510–543; Gudykunst, Matsumoto, Ting-Toomey, Nishida, Kim, & Heyman, "Measuring Self Construals Across Cultures."

22. Schwartz, "Individualism-Collectivism: Critique and Proposed Refinement," 139–157.

23. Singelis, T. M., Triandis, H. C., Bhawuk, D. P. S., & Gelfand, M. J. (1995). "Horizontal and Vertical Dimensions of Individualism and Collectivism: A Theoretical and Measurement Refinement," *Cross Cultural Research, 29,* 240–275.

24. Triandis, H. C. (1990). "Cross Cultural Studies of Individualism and Collectivism," in J. J. Berman (Ed.), *Nebraska Symposium on Motivation, 1989* (pp. 41–133), Lincoln: University of Nebraska Press; Singelis, Triandis, Bhawuk, & Gelfand, "Horizontal and Vertical Dimensions of Individualism and Collectivism: A Theoretical and Measurement Refinement."

25. Singelis, Triandis, Bhawuk, & Gelfand, "Horizontal and Vertical Dimensions of Individualism and Collectivism: A Theoretical and Measurement Refinement."

26. Hui-Ching, C. (1996). *"Collectivism" or "Competitive Bidding": An Alternative Picture of Chinese Communication.* Paper presented at the annual convention of the Speech Communication Association, San Diego, CA (p. 10).

27. Chang, H., & Holt, R. (1991). "More Than a Relationship: Chinese Interaction and the Principle of Kuan-his," *Communicatin Quarterly, 39,* 251–271; Gaertner, L., Sedikides, C., Vevea, J. L., & Iuzzini, J. (2002). "The 'I,' the 'We,' and the 'When': A Meta-Analysis of Motivational Primacy in Self-Definition," *Journal of Personality and Social Psychology, 83,* 574–591; Mortenson, S. T. (2005). "Clarifying the Link Between Culture and Self-Construal Through Structural

Equation Models." *Journal of Intercultural Communication Research, 34,* 1–22; Sedikides, C., Gaertner, L., & Toguchi, Y. (2003). "Pancultural Self-Enhancement," *Journal of Personality and Social Psychology, 84,* 60–79; Yamaguchi, S. (1994). "Collectivism Among the Japanese: A Perspective From the Self." In U. Kim, H. C. Triandis, C. Kagitcibasi, S. H. Choi, & G. Yoon (Eds.), *Individualism and Collectivism: Theory, Method, and Applications* (pp. 175–188). Thousand Oaks, CA: Sage; Voronov, M., & Singer, J.A. (2002). "The Myth of Individualism-Collectivism: A Critical Review." *Journal of Social Psychology, 142*(4), 461–480.

28. Gaertner, L., Sedikides, C., & Graetz, K. (1999). "In Search of Self-Definition: Motivational Primacy of the Individual Self, Motivational Primacy of the Collective Self, or Contextual Primacy?" *Journal of Personality and Social Psychology, 76,* 5–18.

29. Hall, E. T. (1976). *Beyond Culture,* Garden City, NY: Anchor Press/Doubleday, (p. 79).

30. Ibid. (Quote on page 79).

31. Ibid.

32. Ibid.

33. Braithwaite, C. A. (1990). "Communicative Silence: A Cross-Cultural Study of Basso's Hypothesis," in D. Carbaugh (Ed.), *Cultural Communication and Intercultural Contact,* (pp. 321–328), Hillsdale, NJ: Erlbaum.

34. Weider, D. L., & Pratt, S. (1990). "On Being a Recognizable Indian Among Indians," in D. Carbaugh (Ed.), *Cultural Communication and Intercultural Contact,* (pp. 45–64), Hillsdale, NJ: Erlbaum.

35. Iwao, S. (1993). *The Japanese Woman: Traditional Image & Changing Reality,* Cambridge, MA: Harvard University Press (p. 98).

36. Although different, the model for this dialogue is adapted from Storti, C. (1994). *Cross-Cultural Dialogues: 74 Brief Encounters With Cultural Differences.* Yarmouth, ME: Intercultural Press.

37. Gudykunst, Matsumoto, Ting-Toomey, Nishida, Kim, & Heyman, "The Influence of Cultural Individualism-Collectivism, Self Construals, and Individual Values on Communication Styles Across Cultures."

38. Rokeach, M. (1973). *The Nature of Human Values,* New York: The Free Press, (p. 3).

39. Rokeach, *The Nature of Human Values.*

40. Schwartz, S. H. (1992). "Universals in the Content and Structure of Values: Theoretical Advances and Empirical Tests in 20 Countries," in M. P. Zanna (Ed.), *Advances in Experimental Social Psychology, Vol. 25,* (pp. 1–66), San Diego, CA: Academic Press.

41. Hsu, F. L. K. (1969). *The Study of Literate Civilizations,* New York: Holt, Rinehart and Winston; Hsu, F. L. K. (1970). *Americans and Chinese: Reflections on Two Cultures and Their People,* Garden City, NY: Doubleday; Hsu, *American and Chinese: Passage to Differences;* Seelye, H. N. (1993). *Teaching Culture Strategies for Intercultural Communication.* Lincolnwood, IL: National Textbook Company.

42. The Chinese Culture Connection. (1987). "Chinese Values and the Search for Culture-Free Dimensions of Culture," *Journal of Cross-Cultural Psychology, 18,* 143–164.

43. Ibid.

44. Schwartz, S. H. "Universals in the Content and Structure of Values: Theoretical Advances and Empirical Tests in 20 Countries."

45. Kluckhohn, F., & Strodtbeck, F. (1961). *Variations in Value Orientations,* Evanston, IL: Row, Peterson; Condon, J. C., & Yousef, F. (1975). *An Introduction to Intercultural Communication,* Indianapolis, IN: Bobbs-Merrill.

46. Condon & Yousef, *An Introduction to Intercultural Communication;* Hsu, *Americans & Chinese: Passage to Difference.*

47. Hsu, *Americans and Chinese: Passage to Difference;* Hsu, *Americans and Chinese: Reflections on Two Cultures and Their People.*

48. Harris, P. R., & Moran, R. T. (1996). *Managing Cultural Differences,* (4th ed.), Houston, TX: Gulf.

49. Condon & Yousef, *An Introduction to Intercultural Communication.*

50. Harris & Moran, *Managing Cultural Differences.*

51. Keberlein, M. (1993). *A Cultural Profile of the Guatemalan Ladinos,* Unpublished student manuscript, St. Norbert College, DePere, WI.

52. Condon & Yousef, *An Introduction to Intercultural Communication.*

53. Ibid.

54. Amraen, B. (1994). *China: A Populous Nation,* Unpublished student manuscript, St. Norbert College, DePere, WI; De Menthe, B. (1992). *Chinese Etiquette & Ethics in Business,* Lincolnwood: NTC Publishing Group.

55. Condon & Yousef, *An Introduction to Intercultural Communication.*

56. Ibid.

57. Ibid.

58. Hofstede, *Cultures and Organizations: Software of the Mind;* Hofstede, G. (1980). *Culture's Consequences: International Differences in Work-Related Values,* Beverly Hills, CA: Sage.

59. Ibid.

60. Ibid.

61. Andersen, P. A., Hecht, M. L., Hoobler, G. D., & Smallwood, M. (2003). "Nonverbal Communication Across Cultures." In W. B. Gudykunst (Ed.), *Cross-Cultural and Intercultural Communication,* (pp. 73–90), Thousand Oaks, CA: Sage; Andersen, P. A., Lustig, M. W., & Andersen, J. F. (1990). "Changes in Latitude, Changes in Attitude: The Relationship Between Climate and Interpersonal Communication Predispositions." *Communication Quarterly, 38,* 291–311; Lustig, M. W., & Koester, J. (2003). *Intercultural Competence.* Boston: Allyn and Bacon.

62. Tyler, T. R., Lind, E. A., & Huo, Y. J. (2000). "Cultural Values and Authority Relations: The Psychology of Conflict Resolution Across Cultures," *Psychology, Public Policy, and Law,* 6(4), 1138–1163; Smith, P. B., Dugan, S., Peterson, M. F., & Leung, K. (1998). "Individualism-Collectivism and the Handling of

Disagreement: A 23 Country Study," *International Journal of Intercultural Relations, 22*, 351–367; Ting-Toomey, S., & Oetzel, J. G. (2003). "Cross-Cultural Face Concerns and Conflict Styles." In W. B. Gudykunst (Ed.), *Cross-Cultural and Intercultural Communication* (pp. 127–147), Thousand Oaks: Sage; Oetzel, J., Ting-Toomey, S., Chew-Sanchez, M. I., Harris, R., Wilcox, R., & Stumpf, S. (2003). "Face and Facework in Conflicts With Parents and Siblings: A Cross-Cultural Comparison of Germans, Japanese, Mexicans, and US Americans." *Journal of Family Communication, 3*, 67–93.

63. Perea, A., & Slater, M. D. (1999). "Power Distance and Collectivistic/Individualistic Strategies in Alcohol Warnings: Effects by Gender and Ethnicity," *Journal of Health Communication, 4*, 295–310.

64. Andersen, P. A., Hecht, M. L., Hoobler, G. D., & Smallwood, M. (2003). "Nonverbal Communication Across Cultures." In W. B. Gudykunst (Ed.), *Cross-Cultural and Intercultural Communication,* (pp. 73–90). Thousand Oaks: Sage.

65. Gudykunst, W. B., & Kim, Y. Y. (1997). *Communicating With Strangers: An Approach to Intercultural Communication,* New York: McGraw-Hill.

66. Hofstede, *Cultures and Organizations: Software of the Mind.*

67. Ibid.

68. Ibid.

69. Shuper, P. A., Sorrentino, R. A., Otsubo, Y., Hodson, G., & Walker, A. M. (2004). "A Theory of Uncertainty Orientation: Implications for the Study of Individual Differences Within and Across Cultures." *Journal of Cross-Cultural Psychology, 35*, 460–480.

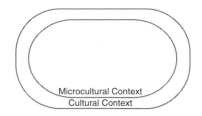

CHAPTER 3

The Microcultural Context

"For those of us who live in/between, being required, on the one hand, to cast off our cultural selves in order to don the worldview and ethos of an alien culture, on the other hand to cast off the influences of the alien culture as a means of purification and identification is more than a personal dilemma; it is always and most of all a condition of living in/between."[1]

— Richard Morris

Chapter Objectives

After reading this chapter, you should be able to

1. Define and explain the concept of a microculture.
2. List and illustrate the five criteria for membership in a microculture.
3. Recount the fundamental assumptions of the Muted Group Theory.
4. Provide examples of the various microcultures in the United States.
5. Identify and discuss two cultural values of the Hispanic microculture.
6. Identify and discuss at least three aspects of African-American communication.
7. Identify and discuss at least three aspects of Amish communication.
8. Identify and discuss at least three aspects of Hmong communication.

Within most cultures there are groups of people who differ in some custom, habit, or practice from the general societal culture. These groups are sometimes called minorities, subcultures, or co-cultures. In this book the term *microculture* is used to refer to those identifiable groups of people who share the set of values, beliefs, and behaviors of the macro-culture, possess a common history, and use a verbal and nonverbal symbol system. In some way, however, the *micro*culture varies from the larger, often dominant cultural milieu. Most *micro*cultural groups are groups of individuals who have much in common with the larger macro-culture yet are bonded together by similar experiences, traits, values, or in some cases, histories. Hence the term *microculture* includes different types of groups that could be classified by age, class, geographic region, sexual preference, disability (e.g., deaf), ethnicity, race, size, or even occupation. These are groups often studied by sociologists, and are called sociocultural groups as well. Perhaps most Americans are members of some kind of microcultural group.

Microcultures can be different from the larger culture in a variety of ways, often because of race or ethnicity. In the United States, for example, approximately 75 percent of the population is classified as White or Caucasian.[2] In this context, African-Americans, Hispanics, and Hmong might be considered microcultural groups. Microcultures can also differ from the larger culture on account of language or religion. For example, Protestants, Catholics, Jews, or Muslims (persons of Islamic faith) might be considered microcultural groups.

Finally, persons might be classified as members of microcultures because of their behavioral practices. Persons who use drugs are often said to belong to a "counter" or "drug" culture, not because of their race, ethnicity, or religion, but because they use drugs. Gays or lesbians could be considered a microculture because of their sexual orientation. Such microcultures often develop their own language for communicating outside of the dominant or majority culture's context or value system. Indeed, deaf persons, who communicate using sign language, can be considered a microculture.

Though not always, microcultural groups generally have less power than the majority or "macro" culture. The majority group's power may be legal, political, economic, or even religious. The group with the most power is the dominant or majority group, while the less powerful groups have been known as minority groups. Sociologist Richard Schaefer argues that the term *minority group* is a misnomer, however, in that it does not refer to the relative size of a group. According to Schaefer, a minority group is defined as "a subordinate group whose members have significantly less power and control over their own lives than members of the dominant or majority group."[3] Although defined as a minority, such groups may actually be larger (in population) than the majority group. For example, until recently, Whites, who were greatly outnumbered by Blacks, ruled in South Africa under the political system of apartheid. In many countries colonized by Europeans, the indigenous people outnumbered the dominant Europeans. And, in parts of the United States, certain ethnic/cultural groups outnumber the "dominant" group.

The term *subculture* is often used to refer to microcultural groups. Like *minority group,* the term *subculture* carries negative connotations. By definition, *sub-* means beneath, below, and inferior. The perspective of this book is that no cultural group is beneath or below any other cultural group. To be sure, some cultures are subordinate (i.e., meaning they have less power) to other groups, but such groups should not be considered inferior. Hence for the reasons cited above, the term *microcultural group* has been chosen as a more appropriate label for these groups.

MICROCULTURAL GROUP STATUS

In many cultures, including the United States, microcultural group status is determined by one's membership in sex, racial, ethnic, or religious groups. Schaefer notes that social scientists generally recognize five characteristics that distinguish microcultural groups from the dominant culture. The first characteristic is that members of the group possess some physical or cultural trait that distinguishes them from others. Two obvious physical properties that distinguish one group from another are skin color and sex. In the United States, for example, Blacks and women are considered minorities (even though women constitute about 51% of the population). White males are considered the most powerful political and economic group in the United States. Blacks are also considered a minority in Brazil, which depended on slave trading much more than the United States. In fact, Brazil imported eight times the number of slaves brought to the United States.[4]

Other traits that can distinguish a microcultural group include language or distinctive dress habits. A microcultural group in Jamaica is the Rastafarians. According to Penasa, Peters, and Smits, the "Rastas" are a relatively small group of about 14,000 persons. Rastas are recognizable by their dreadlock hair and unique dress habits. Rastafarians also speak Patios, an unofficial language that has a sort of lyrical annunciation scheme. Patios has been traced back to slavery, when slaves were forced to learn the language of their masters (i.e., English). Although it is mostly English, Patios took from African languages while borrowing words and phrases from other languages, including Spanish, French, and Portuguese. For example, the word "that" becomes "dat" and "the" becomes "de." Another difference is the use of "me" for "I, me, and my." Thus, the phrase "I am Jamaican" becomes "Me Jamaican."[5] Regardless of culture, the dominant group decides, perhaps arbitrarily, on what characteristics render a group its minority status. Such traits vary considerably across cultures.

The second distinguishing characteristic is that minority group/micro-cultural membership is not voluntary. People are generally born into their microculture. For example, people cannot choose to be of a certain race, ethnicity, or gender. Although people can choose their religion, most people are born into a religion and find it very difficult to leave. In tracing its history, Richard Schaefer notes that the roots of the violence in Northern Ireland are based in religion. Northern Ireland is two thirds Protestant and one third Catholic. The Catholics in Northern Ireland, a minority in both numbers and power, complain of inadequate housing and education, low income, and high unemployment. They often blame the Protestant majority for their problems. Armed conflict has been the result.[6]

The third property that distinguishes a microcultural group from the macro-culture is that microcultural group members generally practice endogamy (i.e., marrying within the ingroup). In many cultures, the dominant group staunchly discourages or even prohibits exogamy (marrying out of one's own group). Ethnologist Suzan Ilcan of the University of Windsor writes that majority groups believe that endogamy strengthens familial ties, preserves family property through inheritance, and upholds cultural and group traditions. Ilcan's work has focused on marital practices in Turkey, where endogamous marriages are viewed as a family or community affair. According to Ilcan, in the village of Sakli, in the northwestern region of Turkey, spousal selection and all aspects of marriage are controlled by certain members of the family. Couples have little to do with the arrangements. Moreover, any meaningful romance between unmarried persons is not valued. Love and mutual attraction are expected to come after marriage and even then are not considered necessities. In Sakli, people are considered suitable marriage partners based on the compatibility of their families. Familial reputation and comparable economic and social classes are the crucial elements for a marriage.[7] In cultures such as Japan, Pakistan, China, India, and Laos, among others, endogamous marriages are often arranged.

The fourth characteristic that distinguishes a microcultural group from the dominant group is that the group members are aware of their subordinate status. Because they know that they are less powerful within a particular culture, some microcultural groups are very cohesive. In the United States, for example, Blacks have gained significant political and economic strength and are arguably the most powerful microcultural group in the country.

Finally, perhaps the most disturbing aspect of microcultural group membership is that such groups often experience unequal treatment from the dominant group in the form of segregation and discrimination. Catholics in Northern Ireland, Blacks in the United States, and Muslims in Bosnia are all vivid examples of how membership in a minority group or microculture can affect one's life negatively.[8]

MUTED MICROCULTURAL GROUPS

The experiences and perceptions of subordinate microcultural groups are often different from those of the dominant cultural group. For example, microcultural groups often are not able to communicate as freely as the dominant group does. Historically in the United States, for example, women and Blacks could not vote or join the armed services. Only recently have Black South Africans been granted the right to vote in their country. Hence, they had no legal voice or representation. In many cultures, the subordinate microcultural groups do not contribute to the construction of the language of the dominant group. In this sense, the language of a particular culture does not benefit its members equally. Yet the language of the dominant group may not provide the words and symbols representative of the microcultural group's perceptions and experiences. Thus, because such groups are forced to communicate within the dominant mode of expression, they become "muted." In essence, the language of the dominant cultural group contributes to the microcultural group's subordination. This idea is known as "the Muted Group Theory."[9]

The manifestations of the Muted Group Theory are that microcultural groups' speech and writing are not valued by the dominant cultural group. Moreover, microcultural groups experience difficulty expressing themselves fluently within the dominant mode of expression, and "micro-macro" interaction is difficult. Because the microcultural groups must communicate within the dominant mode, they must achieve some level of competence to survive. The same is not true of the dominant group, however. In fact, the dominant cultural group experiences more difficulty than the microcultural groups in understanding the communication of the microcultural groups because the dominant group is not required to learn the microcultural groups' codes. Indeed, the communication style of the microcultural group is often considered substandard and/or inferior by the dominant group and is rejected as a legitimate form of communication.

Shirley Weber contends that microcultural groups may respond to the dominant mode of expression in two ways. Some will refuse to live by the standards set forth by the dominant group and will try to change the dominant mode of expression. In the United States, for example, the replacement of words such as *chairman* with simply *chair* or *mailman* with *mail carrier* is demonstrative of this phenomenon. Another way subordinate groups respond is by using their own "private" language. They create symbols that are not understood or used by the dominant group. They use their own language in order to express their unique experiences. Weber argues that sometimes the language of the subordinate group serves as a political statement that the microcultural group has not relinquished or abandoned its political or social identity. The group's ability to sustain a living language indicates that the members have control over a certain aspect of their lives and their determination to preserve their culture. As Weber notes, one's language is a model of his or her culture's adjustment to the world.[10]

Many social scientists consider the hip hop/rap music generation a microcultural group that has been muted by mainstream culture. Christopher Tyson argues that hip hop/rap has been the defining African-American cultural movement in the United States over the past 30 years. As most college students know, rap is a very fast, rhythmical, and accentuated singing and speaking style. Historically, the roots of rap are in African-American popular music. Tyson contends that hip hop culture and rap music are a by-product of the African-American cultural heritage of jazz and blues. Unlike jazz or blues, however, rap music reflects the growing flux of non-conformity among young African-Americans (and, now, other microcultural groups) in mainstream culture and the backlash against middle-class values.[11] Aino Konkka asserts that one of the most recognized styles of rap music is called *gangsta rap*. This style was invented on the West Coast, where inner-city gangs are prominent. Gangsta rap lyrics often tell the story of the desperate situation faced by many inner-city youths, who feel rejected and alienated by the dominant culture. Because the lyrics of gangsta rap are often profane, dealing with drugs and violence, especially violence against women and law enforcement, gangsta rap music has received a great deal of criticism from mainstream cultural critics. But, as Konkka argues, it is the language that young African-Americans understand. According to Konkka, "Using language that children can relate to, added with humor and catchy rhythms, helps getting the message through."[12]

Consistent with the tenets of the Muted Group Theory, rappers have created and developed a unique vocabulary that they use in their music and to communicate with each other. Although rappers speak English, the vocabulary, and its meaning, differs considerably from mainstream culture. Table 3.1 has some examples of rap vocabulary.

Another example of a microcultural group is the Amish. Many Amish groups in the United States are trilingual. They speak low German at home, high German at church, and English at school or with outsiders. High German is more formal, whereas low German is a more relaxed oral dialect spoken at home. Koslow notes that in Canada, the people of Quebec define themselves as culturally unique from the rest of Canada because they speak

Table 3.1

Rap Vocabulary	Meaning
"All that"	In possession of all good qualities
"Ay yo trip"	Phrase to seek attention, similar to "check this out."
"Bang"	To fight or kill.
"Be geese"	To leave, "Yo, we be geese."
"Bitch"	Label generally for females, but not necessarily derogatory, and not necessarily limited to women, as in "all yo niggas be bitches."
"Bone"	To have sexual intercourse. "Your aim is to bone."
"Cave boy"	A white person.
"Chill"	To relax.
"Homeboy"	Close friend
"Hood"	The neighborhood, usually a poor community.
"Nigga"	Originally considered racist and profane, now used by rappers to express pride; my friend, as in "my nigga."
"Peckerwood"	Derogatory term for a white person.
"Roll up"	To arrive on the scene.
"Shank"	A custom-made knife used in prisons.
"Tag"	The act of writing graffiti, as in "tagging up."
"Tight"	Feeling really good at the moment.

Source: P. Atoon, *The Rap Dictionary*, (2005), (www.rapdict.org).

French. In Quebec, the language debate is so great and emotional that many Quebecers are pushing for sovereignty. Quebecois (those who speak French) use French as a model and insist on keeping French in the home and on the street signs throughout the province.[13]

MICROCULTURES IN THE UNITED STATES

Many microcultures exist in the United States. The formation of micro-cultural groups is often the result of immigration, annexation, or colonization.[14] In this chapter, four U.S. microcultures will be explored, with particular attention paid to their communication and how it differs from the dominant macro-culture. The first microcultural group to be examined is the Hispanic/Latino group. Hispanics/Latinos represent the largest micro-cultural group in the United States. The second group is African-Americans, whose many ancestors were brought to the United States as slaves. The group was selected because it represents perhaps the most powerful microcultural group in the United States. And, although African-Americans have made strides in social, legal, economic, and political power in the United States in the past century, they remain socially disenfranchised by many of the dominant culture.

The third group is the Amish. The Amish immigrated to the United States from Europe, escaping religious persecution. The Amish were chosen because, perhaps more than any other microcultural group, they have managed to maintain their cultural traditions in the face of immense pressure from the dominant culture to conform and yet have managed successfully to co-exist within the dominant cultural milieu. The final group to be explored is the Laotian Hmong (pronounced "mung"), who began their immigration to the United States after the end of the Vietnam War in 1975. This group was chosen because its members represent perhaps the newest microculture. They are also a relatively powerless group who lack social, political, and economic power.

HISPANICS/LATINOS

For the first time in the history of the United States, Hispanics/Latinos comprise the largest microcultural group in the country, surpassing African-Americans. According to the U.S. Department of Commerce, in 2003 there were 38 million Hispanics in the United States. That is just over 13 percent of the population. Recall from Chapter 1 that the U.S. government distinguishes between race and Hispanic origin. The government considers the two to be separate and distinct. Hence, Hispanics are not considered a racial group. Specifically, the government defines Hispanic or Latino as "a person of Cuban, Mexican, Puerto Rican, South or Central American, or other Spanish culture or origin regardless of race." According to census data, nearly half of all Hispanics report their race as White. Six percent reported they were of two or more races, two percent reported their race as Black or African-American, while just over one percent indicated they were American Indian or Alaskan native. Forty-two percent of Hispanics indicated "Some other race."[15]

So, What Color Is Hispanic?

Given the above discussion, the term *Hispanic* is confusing to many. Crouch argues that the term *Hispanic* is a cultural reference, a way of identifying people that is neither racial nor geographic. According to Crouch, persons who consider themselves Hispanic may be Black, as in the Dominican

Table 3.2   Facts About U.S. Hispanics/Latinos[18]

More than 1 in 8 people in the United States are of Hispanic origin.

Hispanics are more geographically concentrated than non-Hispanic Whites.

Hispanics tend to live inside the central cites of metropolitan areas.

Hispanics are more likely than Whites to be under the age of 18.

Three out of 5 Hispanics are born in the United States.

Hispanics tend to live in households that are larger than those of non-Hispanic Whites.

Nearly 60 percent of Hispanics over the age of 25 have not graduated from high school.

Hispanics are more likely than Whites to work in service occupations.

Hispanics are more likely than Whites to live in poverty.

Republic, or White, as in Argentina, or of mixed racial heritage, as in Mexico. Racially, most Mexicans are correctly referred to as *mestizos,* meaning mixed blood, usually native and Spanish. Crouch argues that *Hispanic* is a cultural reference to people from any Spanish-speaking country except Spain (where the native peoples insist that they are Spanish, not Hispanic). In addition, Crouch also argues that the term *Latino* is a cultural reference that is more or less interchangeable with *Hispanic.*[16]

Due mostly to immigration and high fertility rates, the Hispanic population in the United States increased by nearly 60 percent from 1990 to 2000 compared with an increase of approximately 13 percent for the rest of the population. Of the various groups represented under the Hispanic label, the Mexican population represents nearly 67 percent, Puerto Ricans comprise just under 9 percent, and Cubans represent 3.7 percent. The remaining Hispanics of "some other origin" include Central and South Americans (14 percent), and Dominicans (2 percent). The remaining approximately 16 percent are labeled "all other Hispanics."[17] See Table 3.2 for some facts about U.S. Hispanics/Latinos.

Like other micocultural groups, Hispanics are concentrated in certain geographical areas in the United States. In fact, half of all Hispanics live in California and Texas. Other states with concentrated Hispanic populations include Arizona, Florida, Illinois, New Jersey, and New York. On the other hand, many states have very small Hispanic populations, such as Alabama, Kentucky, Maine, Mississippi, New Hampshire, North Dakota, South Dakota, Vermont, and West Virginia.[19]

In addition to its overall population trends, the Hispanic population has unique demographics compared to the rest of the United States. Generally, the Hispanic population is younger than the U.S. population. Approximately 23 percent of the U.S. population is under the age of 18, compared with 35 percent of the Hispanic population. Nearly 27 percent of Hispanic households, in which a Hispanic was considered the "householder," consisted of five or more people, while only 11 percent of households were this large in the U.S. population. In terms of education, 27 percent of the Hispanic population has less than a ninth-grade education. Only 46 percent have a high school diploma and only 10 percent have a college degree. Economically, Hispanics are more likely than the general U.S. population to be unemployed. In 2000, almost 7 percent of Hispanics were unemployed compared to 3.4 percent of non-Hispanic Whites. In addition, when working, Hispanics tend to work in different jobs and earn less than non-Hispanic Whites. Specifically, Hispanics are more likely to work in service occupations and much less likely to work in management or professional occupations. Among workers, just over 23 percent of Hispanics made $35,000 or more, compared with nearly half of non-Hispanic Whites earning that much. Furthermore, the percentange of Hispanic earning more than $50,000 was about 10 percent for Hispanics compared to 27 percent of non-Hispanic whites. Thus, in the year 2000, almost 23 percent of Hispanics lived in poverty compared to about 8 percent of non-Hispanic Whites. Hispanic children represent about 16 percent of all children in the United States, but constituted nearly 30 percent of all persons living in poverty.[20]

Cultural Values of Hispanics

Although very diverse, the Hispanic microculture is united by values, language, and religion. Consultants Anne Marie Pajewski and Luis Enriquez argue that, in Hispanic society, the family or group needs take precedence over individual needs. This collectivistic tendency conflicts with the dominant U.S. culture's emphasis on individualism. Hispanics seem collectivistic across a variety of contexts, including academics. According to Pajewski and Enriquez, in school settings Hispanic students tend to be cooperative, whereas White students tend to be competitive and individualistic. When Hispanic students work in groups, not everyone is expected to do his or her equal share. A group member who does not work is not sanctioned, while in an Anglo group, each is expected to do his or her share. Moreover, Pajewski and Enriquez report that some Hispanic students are baffled by the idea of "cheating" in U.S. schools. During examinations, Hispanic students sometimes allow other students to copy their work. This is not considered cheating by Hispanic students. Instead, such behavior is viewed as cooperative.[21]

Perhaps nowhere is the Hispanic group orientation more prevalent than in the family, or *familia*. Vasquez argues that commitment to the family is a dominant cultural value among virtually all Hispanics. According to Vasquez and others, family loyalty, the belief that a child's behavior reflects on the family honor, that sibling relationships are hierarchically ordered, and that family needs are met before individual needs are dominant values in most Hispanic communities. Indeed, Schaefer argues that, among Hispanics, the family is the primary source of both social interaction and caregiving. Griggs and Dunn maintain that the influence of the Hispanic family can be observed in the behavior of Hispanic adolescents, who are more likely than Anglo adolescents to model and adopt their parents' religious and political beliefs, occupations, and overall lifestyle.[22] Indeed, Crouch argues that

> the group bonding process begins the minute Mexican children are brought home from the hospital and put into the children's room— not their own, separate little pink or blue nursery. Their families tend to congregate in one large room. They are taught to play nicely with each other. Toys are toys and are played with by all the children. They are not owned by boy number one or girl number three. In Anglo culture, the more we misbehave with our siblings, the more attention we get . . . but beyond the conflicting pressures of adolescence, we seem to emerge as individualists . . . unlike the Mexicans, who believe that the more they conform, the more they will all prosper.[23]

In general, Hispanics are a very religious people, with as many as 90% of all Hispanics belonging to the Roman Catholic faith. Clutter and Nieto point out that the church is a strong influence on Hispanic family life. In addition, many Hispanic communities celebrate their patron saint's day with more importance and ceremony than individuals do for their own personal birthdays. Pajewski and Enriquez have observed that, although Hispanics are generally very religious, they tend to believe in supernatural powers beyond their religious teachings. Many Hispanics believe in witchcraft and the *curadora,* as well as the healing powers of women and certain herbs.[24]

Spanglish: The Language of Hispanic Americans

The communication style of most Hispanics is more formal than that of the dominant U.S. American culture. Pajewski and Enriquez maintain that Hispanics are sensitve to rank and customarily make use of formal titles. They also report that Hispanics tend to demonstrate affection nonverbally through touching, hugging, pats of the back, and cheek kissing.[25] Verbally, many Hispanics speak Spanglish, a combination of Spanish and English. Linguists (people who study language) have noted that when groups of people from different cultures who speak different languages come together and live in the same society, a hybrid language sometimes evolves. This new language will take some of the phonological features (i.e., sounds) and syntactic structures (i.e., grammar) from each group's language and blend them, creating a hybrid language that serves as a vehicle for communication between the groups. This very phenomenon is happening in the United States. According to Ilan Stavans, Spanglish is the intersection, perhaps the marriage (or divorce), of English and Spanish. Hispanics have taken English words and "Spanish-ized" them and have taken Spanish words and "English-ized" them. The result is what linguists call "Spanglish"—part Spanish and part English. Although Spanglish appears to be a fairly recent phenomenon, Stavans argues that it has been around for more than 150 years, tracing its origins to the U.S. annexation of Mexican territories in the early to mid-19th century. Moreover, Stavans explains that there are many varieties of Spanglish, including that which is spoken by Cuban Americans, called *Cubonics*.[26]

Scholars and laypeople alike agree that Spanglish unites the Hispanic community. Jane Rifkin of the *Hispanic Times Magazine* points out that Spanglish is a widely accepted communication tool used by Spanish-speaking immigrants and native-born Americans. Although some reject Spanglish as intellectually unsophisticated, Rifkin believes that the hybrid language is an expression of friendship, acceptance, and approval. Rifkin refers to Spanglish as the new national slang and contends that Spanglish is "truly a form of communicating among people that has a warmth about it and an inviting expression meant to be non-threatening to people who come together in spite of language barriers."[27]

Stavans argues that there are many variations of Spanglish depending on the nationality, age, and class of its users. He contends that the Spanglish spoken by Cuban-Americans (i.e., Cubonics) is different from that spoken by Dominicans, which is different still from Ganga Spanglish used by urban Hispanic gangs.[28] Although there may be many variations of Spanglish in the United States, Bill Cruz and Bill Teck, editors of *Generation ñ*, a magazine targeted primarily at Cuban American youths, argue that authentic Spanglish is heard when a speaker switches from English to Spanish, or from Spanish to English, within the same sentence. They argue that Spanglish is commonplace in the homes of Hispanics who, as children, were educated in American schools but spoke Spanish at home. In their defense of Spanglish

Table 3.3

Spanglish	*English Example*
No creo que voy on the trip with you	"I don't think I'm going on the trip with you."
lonchando: (Having lunch)	"I'm lonchando, I don't wanna talk to him now."
bacunclíner: (Vacuum cleaner)	"Aye! I think the bacunclíner just swallowed my earring!"
tiempo is money	"Time is money."
frizando: (To make frozen, or freezing)	"Turn up the heat, estoy frizando!"
el autopar	local auto parts store
guarejaus	a warehouse
Pisa Ho	Pizza Hut restaurant
Macdonal	McDonald's fast food restaurant
Sebenileben	7-11 convenience store
Guendis	Wendy's fast food restaurant

as a legitimate language, Cruz and Teck maintain that often there are no words in English (or Spanish) that accurately express the speaker's intent. In such cases, the blending of the two languages allows the speaker to capture the essence of one culture in the language of the other. Cruz and Teck have compiled what they call *The Official Spanglish Dictionary*. Table 3.3 shows some examples of Spanglish, taken from their work.[29]

Chicano English

As immigrants from Mexico settled in California and other parts of the Southwest, they soon formed communities of people who spoke only Spanish. As usual, many of these people began learning English. And, as is typical of immigrants, they took phonological and grammatical complexes from each language and combined them. But the children of these immigrants grew up using both Spanish and English, and as the communities began to grow, a new dialect of English, called Chicano English, evolved. Carmen Fought, a professor of linguistics, studies Chicano English. Fought maintains that Chicano English is neither Spanglish nor a version of nonstandard Spanish, but is a unique dialect used by speakers who are typically not bilingual. In fact, Fought argues that most speakers of Chicano English do not know any Spanish at all.[30]

Fought notes that because of its origins, Chicano English shares many of the phonological features of Spanish. For example, in endings like *going* or *talking,* Chicano English speakers tend to have a higher vowel, more like the "i" of Spanish (as in *si*), so that the words sound like "goween" and "talkeen." According to Fought, people who hear Chicano English typically assume that they are hearing the "accent" of a native Spanish speaker. But Fought maintains that many speakers of Chicano English are not bilingual and may not know any Spanish at all. To be sure, notes Fought, these Mexican-American speakers have learned English natively and fluently, like most children growing up in the United States. They just happened to have learned a nonstandard variety that retains indicators of contact with Spanish.[31]

Stereotypes of Hispanics

In most cultures, microcultural groups are often stereotyped by the dominant cultural group. In the United States, the Hispanic microculture has been the target of several unfortunate stereotypes. Perhaps the most common, and the most hotly debated, stereotype about Hispanics revolves around the construct of male gender identity called *machismo.* Machismo centers on the notion of Hispanic masculinity and male superiority and dominance in the traditional patriarchical Hispanic society. Stereotypical characteristics associated with machismo males include aggressiveness, violence, dominance and supremacy over women, infidelity, and emotional insensitivity.[32] Manuel Roman, a Puerto Rican psychiatrist, argues that the concept of machismo is power based. He says,

> Men are physically more powerful than women. And machismo is derived from the natural state of being bigger, more muscular. It has to do with dominance, autocracy, having power over others. A macho man is somebody who is expected to be sexually knowledgeable and aggressive with women, and to be fearlesss in his interactions with other males.[33]

To be sure, scholars disagree about the uniqueness of machismo in Hispanic culture. Counseling psychologist J. Manuel Casas and his associates argue that machismo has never been a uniquely Hispanic phenomenon. Instead, they argue that many of the traits associated with machismo can be found in virtually every culture. They note, however, that differences may exist in how the equivalent of the machismo construct is defined across cultures.[34] In other words, there may be many cultures in which the male gender identity is associated with aggressiveness, male supremacy, infidelity, and so on. Although there has not been a substantial amount of research conducted on the machismo identity, some data indicate that at least one characteristic associated with machismo, infidelity, is not unique to Hispanic males. University of Chicago sociologists Michael, Gagnon, Laumann, and Kolata, authors of the widely publicized "Sex in America" study, found that the infidelity rate among Hispanics in the United States is about the same as for the general U.S. population.[35]

U.S. media, especially advertisers, have been particularly culpable in the dissemination of Hispanic stereotypes. Octavio Nuiry points out that one of the earliest images of Hispanics, and particularly Mexicans, is that of the ruthless bandito. This image has been depicted in all sorts of media from movie westerns to the famous advertising campaign for Frito corn chips. In 1967, Frito-Lay Corporation launched an advertising campaign for its brand of corn chips. The ads featured a cartoon character called the "Frito Bandito," whose persona was replete with a thick Spanish accent, a long handlebar mustache, a sombero, and a pair of six-shooters. In the ads, the bandito was described as "cunning, clever, and sly." Contemporary ads, such as those of Taco Bell, encourage taco lovers to "Run for the Border!" in an apparent reference to the immigration issue. Interestingly, in what advertisers call crossover commercials, a Miller Lite beer advertisement features boxing champion Carlos Palomino encouraging viewers to "Drink Miller Lite, but don't drink the water."[36]

The influences of the Hispanic microculture in the United States are growing. Now more than ever, Hispanics are noticed by the dominant culture. We see images of Hispanics in television and movies. Hispanic cuisine is more popular than ever. Although their unemployment rates are high and their incomes are low, as a microcultural group, Hispanics are increasing their political and economic power. Soon, their voices will not be muted.

AFRICAN-AMERICANS

According to Richard Schaefer, the history of African-Americans in the United States dates as far back as the history of Euro-Americans (persons of European descent). Blacks arrived in the new world with the first White explorers. Schaefer reports that in 1619, twenty Africans arrived in Jamestown as indentured servants. At that time, their children were born free people. By the 1660s, however, the British colonies passed laws making Africans slaves for life.[37]

According to Schaefer, the proportion of Blacks in the United States has varied over the centuries and actually declined until the 1940s, primarily because White immigration (mostly from Europe) far outdistanced population growth by Blacks. In 1790 Africans represented a little over 19% of the total population of the United States. That percentage continued to decline to 9.7% in 1910. Today, Blacks, or African-Americans, represent nearly 13 percent of the population[38] and are the second largest microcultural group in the United States. In 2005, Blacks and Hispanics comprise nearly 27 percent of the U.S. population. Unlike the rapid and disproportionate growth of the Hispanic population since 1990, the rate of Black population growth remains relatively stable.

African-Americans have made significant progress in the 20th century due mostly to the civil rights movement. Although there remain significant gaps between Blacks and Whites in such areas as income, education, employment, and housing, Blacks have made significant progress in the past 50 years. For example, in 2005 nearly 30 percent of all Black families had incomes of $50,000 or more. Politically, the number of Black elected officials has increased 271 percent since 1972. Schaefer notes also that an interesting phenomenon is developing: An ever-growing proportion of the Black population consists of Blacks that are foreign born. Since 1984 the percent of Blacks in the United States born outside the United States (mostly in the Caribbean) has almost doubled.[39]

Black English, Dialect, and Ebonics

One of the primary ways in which members of cultural groups define themselves and establish ingroup and outgroup identities is through verbal and nonverbal language; that is, through conversation. As groups residing in the same geographical country, African-Americans and Euro-Americans differ significantly in their use of language codes. Some linguists maintain that 80 to 90 percent of African-Americans engage in what is frequently labeled "Black Language," "Black Dialect," "Black English," or African American English (AAE). Geneva Smitherman argues that Black language is "an Africanized form of English reflecting Black America's linguistic-cultural African heritage."[40]

Recently there has been a veritable fervor over the use of Ebonics in California school districts. The term *Ebonics* (from *ebony* and *phonics*) was first coined in 1973 and refers to a grammatically complex African-American speech pattern. Ebonics, or Black language, is the language of the descendants of slaves that combines English vocabulary with a Niger-Congo grammatical structure. Many linguists recognize Black language as a Creole that developed as a result of contact between Africans and Europeans; a new language was formed that was influenced by both languages and took on a variety of forms depending on whether there was French, Portuguese, or English influence. According to Weber, there is evidence that these languages were spoken on the western coast of Africa as early as the 1500s.

Some linguists believe that Africans responded to the English language as do all other non-native speakers; that is, from the phonological and grammatical constructs of their native language.

Historically, Blacks have been a muted group in the United States. Slaves and their descendants were denied access to educational institutions for 200 years. Hence, there was no bilingual educational system available to them to teach them English. In fact, slaves who risked learning English and were caught speaking it were often put to death. Moreover, they were not allowed to speak their own native language and were often separated from their ethnic groups when sold as slaves. Over time, Africans were forced to use English without the benefit of formal education and the result was what some now call Black language or Ebonics. In Ebonics, the verb "to be" is not conjugated ("I be laughing at you"). The language is spoken very rhythmically and flows like other African languages in a consonant-vowel-consonant pattern, where some syllables are held longer and accented more strongly than in standard English, as in "DEE-troit."[41]

According to Ebonics scholar John Rickford, typical Ebonic pronunciations include the omission of the final consonant in words like "pas" (i.e., past) or "han" (i.e., hand), and the pronunciation of the th in "bath" as t (i.e., bat), and the pronunciation of the vowel in words like "my" and "ride" as long ah, as in "mah rahd." According to Rickford, Ebonics pronunciations are systematic and the result of regular rules and restrictions found in any and all languages. Ebonics rules are not random mistakes made by lazy speakers of the language. For instance, speakers regularly produce sentences without present tense *is* and *are*, as in "Joe trippin'" or "They allright." But they don't omit present tense *am*. Instead of the ungrammatical "Ah walkin'," Ebonics speakers would say "Ahm walkin'." Ebonics speakers use an invariant *be* in their speech (e.g., "They be goin' to school every day"); however, this *be* is not simply equivalent to *is* or *are*. Invariant *be* refers to actions that occur regularly or habitually rather than on just one occasion.[42]

In addition to its phonological and syntactic elements, Black language includes other communication dimensions that distinguish it from other languages and mark its speakers as members of a unique group. Thomas Kochman argues that African-American expression is characteristically "emotionally intense, dynamic, and demonstrative," whereas Euro-American expression is "more modest and emotionally restrained."[43]

In comparing African-American and Euro-American modes of expression, Kochman asserts that when engaging an issue, Euro-Americans use a detached and unemotional form of "discussion" whereas African-Americans use an intense and involving form of "argument." Kochman maintains that Euro-Americans tend to understate their talents whereas African-Americans tend to boast about theirs. In essence, African-American speech acts and events are more animated, lively, and forceful than Euro-American speech acts. According to Kochman, the animation and vitality of Black communication is due to the emotional force and spiritual energy that Blacks invest in their public presentations and the functional role that emotions play in realizing the goals of Black interactions, activities, and events. For example, a common goal of many African-American speech events is to energize the audience into an emotional and spiritual release. Such speech events require a strong speaker, a medium that facilitates the emotional and spiritual release, and active participation from the audience. One type of communication that captures the essence of such revitalization is the "call-and-response" pattern involving reciprocal speech acts between speaker and audience. In the typical call-and-response mode, a speaker begins by calling; that is, making some point or assertion to which the audience responds. African Studies professor Shirley Weber describes an instance of call and response while teaching:

> During the lecture, one of my more vocal black students began to respond to the message with some encouraging remarks like "all right," "make it plain," "that all right," and "teach." She was soon joined by a few more black students who gave similar comments. I noticed that this surprised and confused some of the white students. When questioned later about this, their response was that they were not used to having more than one person talk at a time, and they really could not talk and listen at the same time. They found the comments annoying and disruptive. As the lecturer, I found the comments refreshing and inspiring.[44]

African-Americans often engage in call-and-response modes in a variety of formalized settings, such as church meetings, and during informal, everyday gatherings.

The Dozens

Weber outlines other modes of African-American communication, including rappin', runnin' it down, and doin'/playin' the dozens. The original meaning of the term *rappin'* refers to a dialogue between a man and woman wherein the man generates creative and imaginative statements designed to win the affection of the woman. Runnin' it down is a speech event where the speaker's goal is to describe some event or situation in such detail that there is complete agreement and comprehension between speaker and audience. Doin'/playin' the dozens is a verbal battle of insults between speakers who are judged for their originality and creativity by a small group of listeners. This is the highest form of verbal warfare and impromptu speaking. The term *dozens* was used during slavery to refer to a selling technique used by slave owners. If an individual slave had a disability, he or she was considered damaged goods and was sold with eleven other damaged slaves at a discount rate. The term *dozens,* then, refers to negative physical attributes.[45]

In the early 1970s, University of Pennsylvania linguist William Labov conducted extensive field research in the inner cities of some of the major cities in the United States. Labov was interested in the language of the inner city used primarily by African-Americans, and he called the language Black English vernacular (BEV). One form of BEV studied by Labov is called Playin' the Dozens. The Dozens is game-like interaction according to a set of rules in which two players compete, in the form of insulting each other, for the admiration of the audience. There is a minimum of two players, and anyone within speaking distance can be forced by social pressure to play (see Figure 3.2). Playin' the dozens is also known as soundin', signifyin', woofin', cuttin', and so on depending on the particular location. The Dozens is a highly rule-oriented speech event in which players insult (called sounding) each other, and an audience of listeners evaluates and selects a winner. Sounding is almost always about someone's mother—her age, weight, ugliness, Blackness, smell, the food she eats, the clothes she wears, her poverty, and her sexual activity. An important point here is that ritual insults are not intended as factual statements; they are not to be denied. The players and the audience know that these propositions are not true. For example, to say *I fucked your mother* is not obviously untrue and could be interpreted as a personal insult. But to say *I fucked your mother from tree to tree* is obviously untrue and is interpreted as a ritual insult. Playin' the dozens is a language game of ritual insults.[46]

Outgroups or strangers are generally not welcome to join in sounding. Extended ritual sounding is an ingroup process representing ingroup rules. Moreover, obscenity does not play as large a role as one might think. To be sure, many of the sounds are obscene, but only within the rule structure of the dominant White adult middle-class society. The significance of the sound would be meaningless without reference to middle-class norms. In this sense, they violate the rules of the middle-class speech community.

Whether a sound is good or bad is determined by the amount of laughter it receives. But, as Labov notes, an even more forceful mode of approving sounds is for the audience members to repeat them. Negative reactions include the absence of laughter. Black English vernacular is the vehicle of communication used by some of the most talented and effective speakers of the English language.[47]

Figure 3.2   Black language includes many different communication dimensions that distinguishes it from other languages

Source: Copyright © Kristin Finnegan/Getty Images.

Origins of Black Language

The origins of many of these African-American communicative modes can be traced to ancient African philosophies about the relationship between humans, the spoken word, and the fostering of community. According to African scholar Janheinz Jahn, the traditional African view of the world is one of extraordinary harmony. All being, all essence, in whatever form it is conceived, is subsumed under one of four categories: (a) *muntu,* or human being; (b) *kintu,* or thing; (c) *hantu,* or place and time; and (d) *kuntu,* or modality. Everything that exists must necessarily belong to one of these four categories and is conceived of not as some tangible substance but as a force that affects and is affected by the other forces. All of the forces are interrelated and work together to accomplish a common goal. For example, "scholar" belongs in the *muntu* category, "pen" in the *kintu* category, "university" in *hantu,* and "knowledge" in *kuntu.* Anything that exists has distinct characteristics that combine and relate with characteristics in the other categories. For example, the most distinguishing characteristic of *muntu* is the possession of *nommo;* that is, the magic power of the word. Through *nommo,* humans establish their mastery over the other things. According to Jahn, *nommo* is

> the life force, is the fluid as such, a unity of spiritual-physical fluidity, giving life to everything, penetrating everything, causing everything. . . . And since man has the power over the word, it is he who directs the life force. Through the word he receives it, shares it with other beings, and so fulfills the meaning of life.[48]

Nothing exists without *nommo,* it is the force that fosters the sense of community between speaker and audience wherein they become one as senders and receivers.

Shirley Weber argues that the philosophy of *nommo* has been carried into contemporary African-American society, where the audience listening and responding to a message is equally as important as the speaker. One of the foremost goals within any African-American communicative context is to bring speaker and audience together as one; hence the call-and-response mode. In contemporary and traditional African-American speech contexts, the speaker and audience share the platform.[49]

The above discussion suggests that there are distinct differences in the language use of African-Americans and Euro-Americans, and that the reason for such differences may lie in its purpose. African-Americans, more so than Euro-Americans, tend to use language to establish and maintain a sense of community. The use of a language that expresses their unique history, bridges social and economic gaps, and helps build their future is a critical ingredient in African-American communication and membership in their microcultural group.

THE AMISH

One microcultural group that continues to fascinate much of America is the Amish. John Andrew Hostetler is a former Amish member who left his community and is considered the country's leading expert on Amish custom.

Hostetler describes them as "a church, a community, a spiritual union, a conservative branch of Christianity, a religion, a community whose members practice simple and austere living, a familistic entrepreneuring system, and an adaptive human community."[50]

The Amish, sometimes called "The Plain People" or "Old Order Amish," are an Anabaptist religious group that emigrated from Europe to the United States in the early 1700s. Today, Amish groups have settled in about 22 states and Ontario, Canada. Historically, the Amish immigrated to the United States to escape religious persecution. Their name is derived from one of their earliest leaders, Jacob Amman, a young Alsatian bishop and farmer who held a strong Bible-centered faith and was staunchly conservative. To his followers, Amman advocated nonresistance, adult baptism, disciplinary dress standards, and separatism from worldly fashion and influence. From 1730 through 1770, between 50 and 100 Amish families arrived in the United States and initially settled in Pennsylvania. Since then, several groups of Amish have moved farther west to settle in Ohio, Indiana, Illinois, Iowa, and Wisconsin, among other areas. Today, some 90,000 Amish inhabit the United States, and more than 80% of them live in Pennsylvania, Ohio, and Indiana.[51]

An Isolated Microculture

Perhaps more than any other microcultural group, the Amish have been relatively successful at isolating themselves from the influences of the dominant culture. Living what they call nonresistant lives, they do not serve in the military. According to Rich Huber, who was raised a Mennonite in Lancaster County, Pennsylvania, the Amish follow the Bible as literally as possible, citing "Be ye not conformed to the world" (Romans 12:2) as their fundamental principle. Based on their interpretation of this Biblical passage, the Amish believe that true followers of Christ are to be separate from the world. Hence, to evade worldliness and the corruption and sin associated with it, the Amish have drawn strict boundaries between themselves and the dominant cultural milieu.[52]

Although they are successful at avoiding contemporary American society, the Amish are considered American citizens and observe most U.S. laws. Hostetler notes that the Amish pay income, property, and sales taxes like everyone else. They do not pay Social Security taxes, nor do they receive Social Security benefits or any other type of government aid (e.g., food stamps, welfare, and so on). In addition, they avoid the courts in settlings of disputes, are forbidden to take oaths, do not serve on juries, and do not collect settlements by the courts.[53] Moreover, they take full responsibility for the education of their children and generally do not send their children to public schools. In fact, in 1972, the Supreme Court heard the case of *Wisconsin v. Yoder* wherein the court exempted the various Amish sects from compulsory school attendance laws beyond eighth grade. *Wisconsin v. Yoder* represented the first time conflicts over education between the Amish and the government had been argued before the Supreme Court. This is significant because most Amish follow a "turn the other cheek" mentality and do not defend themselves. MacKaye notes that, when confronted, many Amish simply pack up their belongings and move somewhere else in order to be left alone.[54]

Today, most Amish children are taught in one-room schoolhouses by teachers with no more than an eighth-grade education. Amish children attend school until the eighth grade, after which they are educated at home and go to work on the family farms. The Amish consider their society as a form of schooling. The Amish train their children vocationally. Almost exclusively, Amish boys become farmers, carpenters, or tradesmen and girls become homemakers. The Amish have virtually no unemployment.[55]

Like other religiously oriented microcultural groups, the Amish believe that God is the absolute power in the universe. They believe that their life on earth is preparation for their afterlife in heaven. As a result, many of the values and behaviors of the Amish may be similar to mainstream America, but for very different reasons. By the time they die, the Amish want their earthly sins settled. Hence, every day is to be lived well so to please God. The Amish do not believe that entrance to heaven is guaranteed, however.[56] As Hostetler notes, complete assurance of heaven is seen as obnoxious because it smacks of pride and boasting. Hence, humility, self-denial, and submissiveness are at the core of Amish values.[57]

Because the Amish very much want their group to remain much as it was in the seventeenth century, they are very slow to change. They choose to examine change very carefully before they accept it. If a new idea or change does not help them keep their lives simple and their families together, they will probably reject it. Hence, the Amish eschew most modern technologies such as electricity, automobiles, and other conveniences (see Figure 3.3).[58] Also, based on the Biblical passage "Thou shalt not make unto thee any graven image, or any likeness of anything that . . . is in the earth . . ." (Exodus 20:4), the Amish do not take photographs.[59]

Unlike mainstream American society, the Amish are a collectivistic community, what they call *Gemeinde,* which translates to "redemptive community." From this perspective, individuals depend on their community for their identity. The Amish believe that a person's self-worth is defined by his or her role in the community. Individual achievement, self-ambition, power, and worldly acquisitions are not valued. Sharing, community effort, and

Figure 3.3   The Amish eschew most modern technologies

Source: Copyright © Sylvain Grandadam/Getty Images.

trading are the core values of most Amish communities. The Amish believe that community service gains access to God and eternal life.[60] Because of their collectivistic orientation, each member of the group has a well-defined role. For example, sex roles among Amish men and women are very clearly prescribed. Patterns of dress and a strict division of labor separate men and women in Amish society. Exclusively, Amish women are homemakers and Amish men are farmers, with the exception of those men who join the ministry.[61]

Verbal Communication of the Amish

Most Amish are trilingual; that is, they speak three languages. They speak a dialect of German, called high German, during church services. At home or during informal gatherings, they speak low German, sometimes called Pennsylvania Dutch (the term derived from non-Amish mispronunciation of *Deutsche*). They learn and speak English at school and when interacting with non-Amish persons. Like all other microcultures, the Amish frequently use phrases and sayings that carry meaning to them. In their study of Amish verbal phrases and colloquialisms, Moellendorf, Warsh, and Yoshimaru report that one traditional Amish saying in German is "Das alt Gebrauch ist besser" which translates to "The old way is the better way." According to Moellendorf and her colleagues, the Amish believe that past traditions and the old way of living are superior to the conveniences of modern life and its new technologies. Occasionally, outsiders look to the Amish as an idyllic community. They see the Amish lifestyle as free from the pressures of the modern world. To this, the Amish say, "It's not all pies and cakes," meaning that the life of the Amish may appear simple and serene, but in reality, the life of an Amish person is hard, disciplined, and strenuous. Although it happens only infrequently, sometimes an individual will leave the Amish community and join a less demanding church, such as the Mennonites, or another community. To this, the Amish say, "He got his hair cut" as a polite way of communicating that the individual was unable to meet the rigorous standards of the Amish. The saying also suggests that the person has lost his masculine tie (i.e., his long hair) to the community. Another way of communicating a similar phenomenon is "He went English," which is said when an Amish member has left the community to become a part of mainstream American culture.[62]

To enforce church order and discipline, the Amish engage in a form of excommunication called "the ban" or "shunning." Shunning includes prohibiting attendance at church and, in its most extreme form, most types of involvement with members of the community. The ban is particularly difficult for other members of a family who may have a member shunned. In such cases they are expected to cut off all communication with that person.[63]

Nonverbal Communication of the Amish

Moellendorf and her colleagues also studied the nonverbal communication of the Amish and found that the Amish have a very distinct nonverbal communication system. According to Moellendorf, one's role in an Amish community is nonverbally communicated by his or her physical appearance and dress. For example, the style of hats worn by Amish men communicate their age and marital status. A black hat with three or more inches of brim is given to Amish boys at about the age of two. The larger brim is to communicate the young boy's innocence. A bridegroom's hat has a crease around the top and a wide seam along the brim signaling his marriage. Amish fathers wear hats with flat crowns. An Amish woman's bonnet is her way to communicate her marital status. All Amish women wear bonnets over the back part of their hair. Young girls wear colored bonnets and begin to wear black bonnets at about the age of nine. Married Amish women wear white bonnets.[64]

In addition to their hats and bonnets, Amish hairstyles communicate status. Young girls wear braids that are fastened around their forehead. At about the age of ten, their hair is arranged into a bun. Adult Amish women never cut their hair; they part it in the middle and wear a bun. Most Amish women do not shave their legs or trim their eyebrows, as such behavior is seen as interfering with God's work. Amish men shave until marriage, at which time they grow beards, which are analogous to wedding rings. If a single man reaches the age of forty, he may grow a beard. In all cases, married or not, the beard is left untrimmed, and moustaches are not allowed because of their long association with the military.[65]

To communicate submissiveness and pride, enhance group unity, and indicate the desire to be separate from the rest of the contemporary world, only very plain clothing is worn by the Amish. To the Amish, dress is a statement of conformity to group values. A man's shirt is pocketless, and his trousers do not have hip pockets and are worn with suspenders so that they are not tight. For women, ribbons, bows, makeup, and jewelry are forbidden as they are seen as haughty and vain. The dresses of older Amish women close in front with skirts that touch the tops of their shoes. Women are never allowed to wear pants and typically wear an apron over the dress. Generally the colors of both men and women's clothing are restricted to white, green, blue, or purple.[66]

Another nonverbal dimension to the Amish is the horse and buggy. Kraybill argues that the horse and buggy serve as the prime symbol of Amish life. To the Amish, the horse communicates tradition, time, and proof that the Amish have not succumbed to the conveniences of modern life. The buggy, which is typically gray, communicates *Gelassenheit,* which means a surrender to communal values and modesty. Moreover, because the buggies all look alike, they serve as a kind of equalizer among the Amish.[67]

Amidst incredible societal and technological change, the Amish have maintained their lifestyle for more than 200 years. Although they are generally a quiet and reserved microculture that prefers to be isolated from the dominant culture, some Amish have recently become the target for hate crimes. Ironically, their nonflamboyant appearance and subdued behavior, along with their horses and buggies and their refusal to adapt the modern technologies, have rendered the Amish an easy target. In a recent example where a young man shot at an Amish buggy full of children and then raped a young Amish woman, the assailant was quoted as saying that he wanted the Amish to know that they do not own this world and that there are other people in the world.[68] Father J. Mahoney, a priest who has studied various religious groups, argues that the Amish have tried to freeze their culture in the late seventeenth century. Throughout the centuries, as the mainstream culture of the United States progressed technologically, the Amish have tried to preserve their lifestyle, creating a disparity between them and the dominant culture. That disparity, and disagreements as to how far they should go in accommodating to it, will remain the major challenge in the coming decades for the Amish.[69] As Hostetler notes,

> Over the past three centuries the Amish and other Anabaptist groups have been suspended between two opposing forces: the political forces that would eliminate ethnicity from the face of the earth and the human communities who regard ethnicity as a natural and necessary extension of the familial bonds that integrate human activities. Caught between these forces the "plain" people have sometimes prospered and sometimes suffered for their faith.[70]

THE HMONG

While most students in the United States learn about America's involvement in the Vietnam War, probably few ever learn of the "Secret War" fought on behalf of the United States during this time. The "Secret War" refers to the thousands of Hmong who were recruited by the U.S. military through the Central Intelligence Agency (CIA) to help fight the war against Communism in Southeast Asia. According to Daphne Winland, the Hmong belong to the Sino-Tibetan language family. Being culturally similar to the Chinese, Hmong origins can be traced back to China, where they lived peacefully for hundreds of years. Approximately 150 years ago, Chinese rulers began a campaign of persecution to extinguish the Hmong language. The Hmong moved southward and westward out of China and organized communities in Burma, Thailand, North Vietnam, and the mountains of Laos. Winland points out that the Hmong, which means "free people" or "mountain people," were singled out by the CIA during the Vietnam War because of their geographically strategic location in the mountains of Laos.[71]

In the 1960s, the CIA began secretly enlisting Hmong to prevent North Vietnamese troops from entering and moving supplies to South Vietnam through Laos. They also set up navigational aids for American bombers and fought to protect them when they were attacked by the North Vietnamese.

In addition, Hmong soldiers were highly skilled in the operations required to rescue American pilots shot down over Laos (the United States flew more tactical missions over Laos than it did over Vietnam).[72] The Hmong were fierce fighters yet suffered devastating losses estimated at more than 100 times greater (proportionately) than the United States. Although estimates vary, most experts agree that more than 25,000 Hmong lost their lives fighting for the United States during the Vietnam War.[73] Due to intense political pressures at home, the United States had vowed not to escalate the war into Laos. Hence, the Hmong became known as "The Secret Army," and their participation in the war was called "The Secret War."[74]

In 1975, the United States withdrew its forces from Vietnam. Concurrently, a Communist-backed government, supported by the Vietnamese and Soviets, assumed power in Laos. One of the foremost goals of the new Laotian government was to annihilate the Hmong people because of their alliance with the United States. The Communists tortured, raped, and murdered thousands of Hmong. They napalmed their villages and slaughtered their cattle. There is evidence that the Communists used chemical and biological weapons in their attempt to wipe out the Hmong. With the United States having withdrawn from Vietnam, the Hmong were left without any allies in the midst of their enemies and a new war.[75] More than 200,000 Hmong fled to Thailand, where they were housed in prison-like conditions in refugee camps. Many Hmong immigrated to the United States, Australia, and France. Approximately 100,000 or so made it to the United States. Today, approximately 150,000 Hmong reside in the United States with large concentrations in California, Wisconsin, and Minnesota. Although they were hired and paid by the United States, Hmong soldiers have received little or no recognition for their efforts and do not receive veteran benefits. In May 1997, the United States finally acknowledged Hmong veterans with a granite marker in Arlington National Cemetery that reads "The U.S. Secret Army in the Kingdom of Laos 1961–1973." In both Laos and Hmong languages, the marker also reads "You will never be forgotten." In 1995 there were still as many as 40,000 Hmong residing in refugee camps in Thailand.[76]

Duffy alleges that life in the United States has been very difficult for many Hmong. For the most part, Hmong immigrants have not been welcome. Unfortunately, many people inaccurately associate the Hmong with the "enemy" in the Vietnam War. To add to their arduous situation, many stereotypes preceded their immigration to the United States. News coverage of the Hmong often referred to them as a "pre-literate," "primitive," and "hilltribe" group.[77] Moreover, writes Winland, during this time period just about anything associated with the Vietnam War was anathema. Hence, the Hmong entered the United States being doubted and distrusted by many, and facing the straightforward bigotry of others. The Hmong find themselves in a situation of relative dependency on U.S. culture while simultaneously facing a real sense of cultural isolation.[78]

Unlike the African-Americans or the Amish, who have been in the United States for centuries, the Hmong are unique in that they are first-generation immigrants. Their values, customs, and modes of communication have collided head-on with mainstream American culture. For example, like many of their Asian cousins, the Hmong are a collectivistic culture. According to Katie Thao, a native Hmong who immigrated to the United States when she was a teenager, the most important group is the family clan. Hmong family clans are patrilineal. Hmong males are given two names—one in childhood and the other when they reach adulthood. When children are born they are given their father's clan name. When women marry, they keep their father's clan name and do not adopt their husband's even though they become formal members of his clan. Conversely, Hmong women do not receive an adult name, but become known by their husband's clan name. There are between twenty and thirty clan names. The most common clan names in the United States include Cha, Hang, Her, Kong, Kue, Moua, Lee, Lo or Lor, Thao or Thor, Vang, Vue, Xiong, and Yang.[79]

Role Relationships and Marriage

According to Ray Hutchison and Miles McNall, many of the Hmong customs associated with clan membership that have been imported to the United States include sex role relationships and marriage practices (see Figure 3.4). For the most part, these practices clash with American customs. For example, in traditional Hmong culture, women maintain clearly subordinate roles. Their role is to bear children, maintain the household, and be subservient to their husbands. One way Hmong women demonstrate their subordinate status is by walking directly behind their husbands when in public. Moreover, they have little or nothing to say in the decision making or political affairs of their clans. Some husbands refuse to allow their wives to learn English, hence keeping them muted and powerless in American culture. For the most part, first-generation Hmong women are not allowed an education and are expected to marry early, between the ages of 13 to 18 (whereas men marry between the ages of 18 and 30). Although the practices are gradually changing in the United States, many Hmong marriages in the United States are still arranged. Many communities report that a high percentage of Hmong girls drop out of high school to get married. Indeed, Hmong women have the youngest average age of marriage of all Southeast Asian refugee groups. Moreover, Hmong fertility

Figure 3.4   Many customs are imported to the United States, such as sex role relationships and marriage practices

Source: Copyright © Keren Su/Getty Images.

rates in the United States are much higher than those of any other refugee or immigrant group.[80]

Katie Thao participated in an arranged marriage. She did not meet her husband-to-be until the day of her wedding. To many Americans an arranged marriage seems ridiculous and absurd. But Thao asserts that she was completely comfortable with the idea because she had confidence in her parents, especially her father, to negotiate a good husband for her. Thao contends that an arranged Hmong marriage is a matter of considerable maneuvering and bargaining. Typically each family selects an elderly male spokesman. These spokesmen, usually the fathers, then negotiate and bargain a bride price that is to be paid to the bride's parents. The philosophy behind "buying a wife" is to ensure that she will be highly valued by her new family. In many cases, the parents of the bride hold a feast of roasted pig in their home in celebration of the wedding. After the wedding ceremony, the souls and good fortune of the bride and groom are symbolically wrapped in an umbrella that is carried in procession to the groom's home, where another feast is held. If the bride is entering the groom's home for the first time (which is usually the case because the bride and groom are strangers), a rooster is waved over the bride to symbolize her membership in the groom's clan. In most cases a Hmong marriage is seen not as a bonding of two people but a union of two family clans. In some cases, if a married Hmong woman's husband dies, she automatically becomes the wife of his younger brother.[81]

Communication Patterns of the Hmong

Like most microcultural groups, the Hmong share some unique verbal and nonverbal communication patterns. The overwhelming majority of the first Hmong immigrants entering the United States did not speak English. Historically, because the Hmong emigrated so often, their written language was eventually lost. Not until the 1950s were orthographies of the written language developed. Well over half of the Hmong who immigrated to the United States could not read or write. For the Hmong who immigrated to Laos, they were taught in Buddhist temples in Lao language and Lao alphabet. In Laos today, there are two major dialects of Hmong language. One is "Hmoob Dawb," meaning White Hmong, and the other is "Hmoob Ntsuab," meaning Blue Hmong. Because the White Hmong are in the majority, Hmoob Dawb is spoken more frequently.[82]

According to Thao, the phrase "Playing a flute into a water buffalo's ear" is used by the Hmong when someone is trying, without success, to explain something to another who simply does not understand. Often, Hmong will refer to someone who does not understand a message as some kind of animal, often a water buffalo. The idea of a flute is significant because in traditional Hmong culture, the flute communicates emotions, such as sorrow, love, and even anger or depression. Another phrase "The grinder doesn't taste salty" is used to refer to a person who is bankrupt. Salt is a very valuable ingredient to the Hmong, and when there is no salt, it is an indication that the family is out of money.

The Hmong are animistic, meaning that they believe that everything has a spirit. According to Thao, the supernatural is a very real part of Hmong life. Evil spirits are thought to exist in unpopulated areas, therefore many Hmong are afraid to travel alone in uninhabited places. The phrase "The devil will not eat or chew anyone for it" is said when an act or crime is committed wherein no one will be caught or found guilty. The Hmong believe that evil spirits such as the devil are omnipresent and can hear and see everything. If the devil will not eat anyone, then the act will go unpunished. "Go check the mousetrap" is made in reference to a meal that is shared by an entire clan or village. The phrase is used when someone goes to the meal, similar to when a mouse goes to the trap in search of food and gets trapped. When a person goes to a meal, he or she gets trapped in the company of the clan or family. Many of the Hmong sayings and colloquialisms are indirect expressions. The Hmong believe that if the truth is spoken directly, evil spirits or unwanted guests can overhear it. Thao says that a Hmong farmer might call out to his family "Come sharpen your knives" rather than calling out "It's time to eat" because the latter might attract the evil spirits or animals, who will eat up the meal.[83]

One of the most significant forms of nonverbal communication for the Hmong are their *paj ntaub,* pronounced "pandoa." Paj ntaub, meaning "flower cloth," are sophisticated stitched quilts embroidered with bright threads. They often feature picturesque geometric designs that occasionally feature animals or other creatures. Since their immigration to the United States, paj ntaub have evolved into "storycloths" often depicting the history and life experiences of the Hmong culture. Evolving from the Thai refugee camps, story cloths were a means to teach written language to Hmong children and others. Now they are treated as works of art and a vehicle for the Hmong to document their history and retain their cultural identity. Created exclusively by Hmong women, the cloths carry much significance. The quality of the needlework communicates the skill and creativity of the women who make them and may bring them a higher bride-price at the time of marriage bargaining.[84]

Other nonverbal gestures used in Hmong culture include twitching the eyes to communicate contempt to another. Twitching the eyes during a long stare is very offensive and may lead to a physical confrontation. Slapping oneself on the buttocks is a nonverbal way of saying "kiss my ass" or "lick my ass." Kneeling is done only by men when they want to express their thanks or to ask another for mercy and forgiveness. A woman's kneeling has little or no value because of her low rank and position in Hmong clans.[85]

Elliot Barkan writes that acculturation in the United States has been difficult for the Hmong. The first-generation Hmong, arriving in the United States in the mid-1970s, have tried hard to preserve their culture, whereas their children, exposed to the values and communication system of the dominant culture, are caught in between two cultures. The older Hmong try to preserve the traditional ways while contemporary culture, including the educational system, encourages their assimilation. Acculturation for the elderly Hmong has been particularly difficult. The age and sex hierarchies that prescribed their superior status are gone. In Laos, women have few, if any, rights. In the United States, of course, wives have equal rights. Language has played a key role as well. A Hmong child's quick acquisition of English almost reverses traditional family roles. Unlike the traditional ways, the parents are now dependent on the child's communication skills to get along. Many parents feel that the learning of such skills undermines their authority. Hence some parents develop a sense of loss and worthlessness and fall into deep depressions.[86]

ARAB-AMERICANS

Since the attacks on the World Trade Center towers in New York and the Pentagon in Washington, DC, in September 2001, increased racial, ethnic, and religious hostility has left Arab-Americans, Middle Easterners, and those who bear physical likeness to members of these groups in a precarious state. Arab-American groups (such as the American-Arab Anti-Discrimination Committee) report numerous attacks on people from these various cultural and ethnic groups since September 11, 2001. Hundreds of people have been beaten, killed, threatened, ridiculed, and harrassed because they were thought to be Arabian and somehow associated with those who attacked the United States. But of all the microcultural groups discussed in this chapter thus far, these groups (i.e., Arab-Americans, Middle Easterners) are perhaps the most ethnically, racially, and religiously diverse group in the country. In fact, to classify these people into one group is impossible.

For the first time in its history, in 2000, the U.S. Census Bureau classified persons in the United States who had Arab ancestry. According to the Census Bureau, people with ancestries originating from Arabic-speaking countries or areas of the world were classified as Arab. The census results indicate that in 2003, 1.2 million people living in the United States consider themselves as having Arab ancestry, an increase of nearly 40 percent since 1990.

The problem with this classification is that a person is included in the Arab ancestry category if he or she reported being Arab, Egyptian, Iraqi, Jordanian, Lebanese, Middle Eastern, Moroccan, North African, Palestinian, Syrian, and so on. Yet many people from these countries do not consider themselves to be Arab, and conversely, some people who consider themselves Arab may not be included in this classification. For example, groups such as Kurds and Berbers who are typically not considered Arab were included in this definition for consistency with the 1990 and 2000 census. Moreover, some groups such as Mauritanian, Somalian, Djiboutian, Sudanese, and Comoros Islander who may consider themselves Arab were not included.[87]

Often, people of Arab ancestry are thought to be Muslim. The followers of Islam are called Muslims. Muslims are not to be confused with Arabs. Muslims may be Arabs, Filipino, Turks, Persians, Indians, Pakistanis, Malaysians, Indonesians, Europeans, Africans, Americans, Chinese, or other nationalities. An Arab could be Muslim, Christian, Jewish, or an atheist. The language of the Qur'an (the Holy Book of Islam) is Arabic. Muslims all over the world try to learn Arabic so that they may be able to read the Qur'an and understand its meaning. Most Muslims pray in the language of the Qur'an, namely Arabic. Supplications to God could be in any language, however. Whereas there are one billion Muslims in the world, there are about 200 million Arabs. Among them, approximately ten percent are not Muslims. Thus, Arab Muslims constitute only about twenty percent of the Muslim population of the world.[88]

CHAPTER SUMMARY

Within most cultures, there are groups of people who differ in some significant way from the general societal culture. In this book, the term *microculture* is used to refer to those identifiable groups of people who share a set of values, beliefs, and behaviors and who possess a common history and a verbal and nonverbal symbol system that is similar to the dominant culture but varies in some way, perhaps subtly. Microcultures can be different from the larger culture in a variety of ways, most often because of race, ethnicity, language, or behavior. But one's age group or occupation might also render one a member of a microcultural group. Perhaps every member of a culture is also a member of a microcultural group.

In this chapter Hispanics, African-Americans, Amish, and Hmong were profiled as microcultural groups in the United States. Mostly because of immigration and high fertility rates, Hispanics are now the largest microcultural group in the United States. Like many microcultural groups, Hispanics experience lower incomes, higher poverty, and higher unemployment rates than the non-Hispanic White groups. The U.S. government estimates that the Hispanic population will continue to grow through the first half of the 21st century. By then, Hispanic economic influence will be significant.

As an economic, political, and socially powerful group, African-Americans have maintained an important part of their history; that is, their language. African-American history is expressed in the language games that African-Americans play and in their daily communication with others in the form of Ebonics. The Amish were also profiled in this chapter. More than any other microcultural group, the Amish have preserved their traditional culture while peacefully co-existing within the rule structure of the dominant cultural milieu. Unlike any other microcultural group, the Amish have successfully isolated themselves from most of mainstream American culture. Finally, possibly the newest microcultural group in the United States is the Hmong. The Hmong are a group of people who fought alongside American troops in the Vietnam War, only to be abandoned when the war was lost. Having immigrated to the United States, the Hmong try desperately to adapt to U.S. culture while simultaneously maintaining some aspects of their traditional culture. Like African-Americans, the Hmong face a great deal of racism and resentment.

Although each of the microcultural groups portrayed in this chapter is obviously different from the others, they share at least one major feature; that is, language. Each group, while adapting and accommodating to the dominant cultural surroundings, has successfully preserved a part of the original culture through communication. The verbal and nonverbal language of any cultural group maintains its heritage and allows its people to pass along its ancestry for future generations.

GLOSSARY OF TERMS

African-Americans: Microcultural group in the United States whose ancestors were brought to the United States as slaves.

Amish: A microcultural religiously oriented group whose members practice simple and austere living.

Arab: A person with ancestries originating from Arabic-speaking countries or areas of the world.

Dozens: A verbal battle of insults between speakers who are judged for their originality and creativity by a small group of listeners. This is the highest form of verbal warfare and impromptu speaking in many African-American communities.

Ebonics: From the terms *ebony* and *phonics,* a grammatically robust and rich African-American speech pattern whose roots are in West Africa.

Hispanic: Defined by the U.S. government as a person of Cuban, Mexican, Puerto Rican, South or Central American, or other Spanish culture or origin regardless of race.

Hmong: Microculture belonging to the Sino-Tibetan language family and culturally similar to the Chinese. The Hmong, which means "free people" or "mountain people," fought for the United States during the Vietnam War, and many have immigrated to the United States since the end of the war.

Microculture: An identifiable group of people who share a set of values, beliefs, and behaviors and who possess a common history and a verbal and nonverbal symbol system that is similar to but systematically varies from the larger, often dominant cultural milieu.

Minority Group: A subordinate group whose members have significantly less power and control over their own lives than members of the dominant or majority group.

Muslim: A person who practices Islam.

Muted Groups: Microcultures whose members are forced to express themselves (e.g., speak, write) within the dominant mode of expression.

Spanglish: Hybrid language combining the phonological features (i.e., sounds) and syntactic structures (grammar) of English and Spanish.

REFERENCES

1. Morris, R. (1997). "Living in/between." In A. Gonzales, M. Houston, & V. Chen (Eds.), *Our Voices: Essays in Culture, Ethnicity and Communication*, (pp. 163–176). Los Angeles: Roxbury.
2. "Profiles of General Demographic Characteristics: 2000 Census of Population and Housing." U.S. Department of Commerce, U.S. Census Bureau, Washington, DC. U.S. Government Printing Office, 2001.
3. Schaefer, R. T. (2003). *Racial and Ethnic Groups.* (9th Ed.), New York: Prentice Hall.
4. This discussion of the defining characteristics of minority groups is based on the following sources: Wagley, C., & Harris, M. (1958). *Minorities in the New World: Six Cases.* New York: Columbia University Press; Meyers, B. (1984). "Minority Group: An Ideological Formulation." *Social Problems, 32,* 1–15.; Schaefer, *Racial and Ethnic Groups.*
5. Penasa, A., Peters, M., & Smits, S. (1996). *Jamaica: Out of Many, One People.* Unpublished Student Manuscript, St. Norbert College, DePere, WI.; Lunatta, K. (1993). *Jamaica Handbook.* Chico, CA: Moon Publications.
6. Schaefer, *Racial and Ethnic Groups.*
7. Ilcan, S. M. (1994). "Marriage regulation and the rhetoric of alliance in Northwestern Turkey." *Ethnology, 33,* 273–297.
8. Schaefer, *Racial and Ethnic Groups.*
9. The Muted Group Theory was first articulated by Shirley and Edwin Ardener. The sources used for this discussion are Kramarae, C. (1981). *Women and men speaking.* Rowley, MA: Newbury House; Ardener, S. (Ed.), (1975). *Perceiving Women.* London: Malaby Press.
10. Weber, S. N. (1991). "The Need to Be: The Socio-cultural Significance of Black Language," in L. A. Samovar & R. E. Porter, (Eds.). *Intercultural Communication: A Reader.* (6th Ed.), (pp. 277–283), Belmont, CA: Wadsworth.
11. Tyson, C. "Exploring the Generation Gap and Its Implications on African American Consciousness," *Doula, The Journal of Rap Music and Hip Hop Culture* (2001), (www.urbanthinktank.org).
12. Konkka, A. "Power, Pride, and Politics in Rap Music," Department of Translation Studies, University of Tampere, (www.uta.fi/FAST/US8/PAPS/ak-rap.html).

13. Koslow, J. (1995). *A World of Difference: An Introduction to the Culture of Quebec.* Unpublished Student Manuscript, St. Norbert College, DePere, WI.

14. Schaefer, *Racial and Ethnic Groups.*

15. Grieco, E. M., & Cassidy, R. C. "Overview of Race and Hispanic Origin: Census 2000 Brief." U.S. Department of Commerce, U.S. Census Bureau, Washington, DC. U.S. Government Printing Office, 2001.

16. Crouch, N. (2004). *Mexicans & Americans: Cracking the Cultural Code.* Yarmouth, ME: Intercultural Press.

17. Ramirez, R. R., & de la Cruz, G. P. (2003). "The Hispanic Population in the United States," March, 2002. U.S. Department of Commerce: Economics and Statistics Administration. U.S. Cenus Bureau; B. Guzman, "The Hispanic Population: Census 2000 Brief." U.S. Department of Commerce, U.S. Census Bureau, Washington, DC. U.S. Government Printing Office, 2001.

18. Ibid.

19. Ibid.

20. Therrien, M., and Ramirez, R. R. "The Hispanic Population in the United States: Population Characteristics." U.S. Department of Commerce, U.S. Census Bureau, Washington, DC. U.S. Government Printing Office, 2001; Ramirez and de la Cruz, "The Hispanic Population in the United States."

21. Pajewski, A., & Enriquez, L. *Teaching From a Hispanic Perspective: A Handbook for Non-Hispanic Adult Educators.* (Phoenix, The Arizona Adult Literacy and Technology Resource Center, Inc., 1996).

22. Vasquez, J. "Teaching to the Distinctive Traits of Minority Students," *The Clearing House, 63* (1990), 299–304. Schaefer, *Racial and Ethnic Groups;* Griggs, S., & Dunn, R. "Hispanic-American Students and Learning Style," ERIC Clearinghouse on Elementary and Early Childhood Education, (Urbana, IL: 1996). ERIC Identifier 393607.

23. Crouch, *Mexicans and Americans.*

24. Clutter, A. W., & Nieto, R. D. "Understanding Hispanic Culture," Ohio State University Fact Sheet, (Columbus, Ohio State University Extension, 2000). Pajewski and Enriquez, *Teaching From a Hispanic Perspective.*

25. Pajewski and Enriquez, *Teaching From a Hispanic Perspective.*

26. Stavans, I. (2003). *Spanglish: The Making of a New American Language.* New York: Rayo (HarperCollins). I. Stavans, "The Gravitas of Spanglish," *Chronicle of Higher Education, 47,* (October 13, 2000), B7–B10.

27. Rifkin, J. M. "No Problema-Spanglish Language Abounds," *Hispanic Times Magazine, 11* (1990), 30–31.

28. Stavans, "The Gravitas of Spanglish."

29. Cruz, B., & Teck, B. "The Official Spanglish Dictionary," *Hispanic, 11* (1998), 34–36; These examples of Spanglish can be found in B. Cruz , B. Teck, and the Editors of *Generation ñ,* "The Official Spanglish Dictionary: Un User's Guia to More Than 300 Words and Phrases That Aren't Exactly Espanol or Ingles." (New York: Fireside, 1998).

30. Fought, C. (2001). Facts and Myths About Chicano Language. *Language Magazine,* 1, 3.

31. Ibid.
32. Mayo, Y. Q., & Resnick, R. P. "The Impact of Machismo on Hispanic Women," *Journal of Women & Social Work, 11* (1996), 257–278; Casas, J. M., Wagenheim, B. R., Banchero, R., & Mendoza-Romero, J. "Hispanic Masculinity: Myth or Psychological Schema Meriting Clinical Consideration," *Hispanic Journal of Behavioral Sciences, 16* (1994), 315–332.
33. Anders, G. "Machismo: Dead or Alive?" *Hispanic, 6* (1993), 14–18.
34. Casas et al., "Hispanic Masculinity: Myth or Psychological Schema Meriting Clinical Consideration."
35. Michael, E. T., Gagnon, J. H., Laumann, E. O., & Kolata, G. *Sex in America: A Definitive Survey,* (New York, Warner Books, 1995).
36. Nuiry, O. E. "Ban the Bandito!" *Hispanic, 9* (1996), 26–31.
37. Schaefer, *Racial and Ethnic Groups.*
38. Ibid.
39. Ibid.
40. Smitherman, G. (1972). *Talkin' and Testifyin'.* Boston: Houghton-Mifflin, (p. 2).
41. This discussion of Black language and Ebonics is based on the following sources: Weber, S. N. (1994). "The Need to Be: The Sociocultural Significance of Black Language." In L. A. Samovar & R. E. Porter (Eds.), *Intercultural Communication: A Reader,* (7th ed.), Belmont, CA: Wadsworth; Leland, J., Joseph, N., & Rhodes, S. (1997). "Hooked on Ebonics." *Newsweek, 129,* 78–79; "A Case for Ebonics: An Interview With Noma Le Moine." (1979). *Curriculum Review, 36,* 5–6; Blackshire-Belay, C. A. (1996). "The Location of Ebonics Within the Framework of the Africological Paradigm." *Journal of Black Studies, 27,* 5–24.
42. Rickford, J. C. (2004). *What Is Ebonics (African-American Vernacular English)?* Washington, DC: Linguistics Society of America.
43. Kochman, T. (1990). "Cultural Pluralism: Black and White styles." In D. Carbaugh, (Ed.), *Cultural Communication and Intercultural Context,* (pp. 219–224). Hillsdale, NJ: Erlbaum.
44. Weber, "The Need to Be: The Sociocultural Significance of Black Language" (p. 279).
45. Weber, "The Need to Be: The Sociocultural Significance of Black Language."
46. This discussion of "The Dozens" is based entirely on Labov, W. (1976). *Language of the Inner City: Studies of the Black English Vernacular.* Philadelphia: University of Pennsylvania Press.
47. All of the examples presented here are from Labov, *Language of the Inner City: Studies of the Black English Vernacular.*
48. Jahn, J. (1961). *Muntu.* New York: Grove Press.
49. Weber, "The Need to Be: The Sociocultural Significance of Black Language."
50. Hostetler, J. A. (1993). *Amish Society.* Baltimore, MD: Johns Hopkins University Press. (Quote on page 4)
51. Pennsylvania Dutch Country Welcome Center. (1998). *The Amish, the Mennonites, and "the Plain People"* [On-line]. Available: www.800padutch.com/amish.html; Schlabach, D. (1998). *An Amishman's Personal Expression.* [On-line]. Available: www.amish-heartland.com/amish/stories/anamishman.htm

52. Huber, R. (1997). *Be Ye Not Conformed to This World.* [On-line]. Available: www.columbia.edu/cu/sipa/PUBS/SLANT/SPRING97/huber.html

53. Hostetler, *Amish Society;* Pearce, S., Suminski, S., & Tschudy, K. (1996). *The Amish: Simple Values in a Complex World.* Unpublished Manuscript, St. Norbert College, De Pere, WI.

54. MacKaye, W. R. (1971, December 9). High court hears Amish school case. *The Washington Post.*

55. *Origins of the Old Order Amish.* [On-line]. Available: holycrosslivonia.org/amish/origin.htm.

56. S.A. (1998). *Influences of World View on Individual Life and Culture.* [On-line]. Available: www.missouri.edu/~rsocjoel/rs150/papers/sall.html.

57. Hostetler, *Amish Society.*

58. Pennsylvania Dutch Country Welcome Center, *The Amish, the Mennonites, and "the Plain People."*

59. Huber, *Be Ye Not Conformed to This World.*

60. *Influences of World View on Individual Life and Culture.*

61. P. D. (1998). *Gender, Work, and Worldview: Reflections on Amish and American Society.* [On-line]. Available: www.missouri.edu/~rsocjoel/rs150/papers/pdun.html

62. Moellendorf, Warsh, and Yoshimaru, *The Amish Culture: A Closer Look at the People of Lancaster County.* Unpublished student manuscript, St. Norbert College, DePere, WI, 1997; Hostetler, *Amish society;* Kraybill, D. B. (1989). *The Riddle of Amish Culture.* Baltimore, MD: Johns Hopkins University Press.

63. Ontario Consultants on Religious Tolerance. (1998). *The Amish* [On-line]. Available: religioustolerance.org/amish.htm; Mahoney, J. (1998). *European free-church family* [On-line]. Available: www.jmahoney.com/european.htm.

64. Moellendorf, Warsh, and Yoshimaru, *The Amish Culture;* Buch, B. B. (1997). *The Nonverbal Cues of Amish Dress.* Unpublished Manuscript, St. Norbert College, DePere, WI; Hostetler, *Amish Society;* Kraybill, *The Riddle of Amish Culture.*

65. Ibid.

66. Ibid.

67. Ibid.

68. P. D. (1998). *Amish and Mainstream Culture Clash.* [On-line]. Available: www.missouri.edu/~rsocjoel/rs150/papers/pd4.html.

69. Mahoney, *European Free-Church Family.*

70. Hostetler, J. A. (1992). "An Amish Beginning." *American Scholar, 61,* 552–563. (Quote on page 562).

71. Winland, D. N. (1992). "The Role of Religious Affiliation in Refugee Resettlement: The Case of the Hmong." *Canadian Ethnic Studies, 24,* 96–120.

72. Tyson, J. L. (1994). "Congress and State Department Ignore Persecution of Hmong." *Human Events, 50,* 12–14.

73. "Honoring the Secret Warriors." (1997, May 26). *US News & World Report, 122,* 13.

74. Duffy, J. (1996). *Who Are the Hmong? Legends of Literacy, History of Struggle* [On-line]. Available: www.adone.com/ttj/news/050296/ent3.htm

75. Thao, K. (1995). *The Hmong Culture.* Unpublished Student Manuscript, St. Norbert College, De Pere, WI.

76. "Honoring the Secret Warriors."

77. Duffy, *Who Are the Hmong?*

78. Winland, "The Role of Religious Affiliation in Refugee Resettlement."

79. Thao, *The Hmong Culture.*

80. Hutchison, R., & McNall, M. (1994). "Early Marriage in a Hmong Cohort." *Journal of Marriage & the Family, 56,* 579–591.

81. Thao, *The Hmong culture.*

82. Ibid.

83. Ibid.

84. Guensburg, C. (1996, June 16). "The Fabric of Their Lives." *Milwaukee Journal Sentinel;* Lee, J. H. (1998). *Hmong Quilts—Pa Ndau—Reflect Hmong History* [On-line]. Available: www.stolaf.edu/people/cdr/hmong/culture/pandau2.html

85. Thao, *The Hmong culture.*

86. Barkan, E. R. (1995). "Out of Carnage and Into the Crucible: Southeast Asian Refugees' Journey From Old Worlds to a New One." *Journal of American Ethnic History, 14,* 53–58.

87. de la Cruz, G. P., & Brittingham, A. (2003). *The Arab Population: 2000.* U.S. Census Bureau. Washington, DC: U.S. Department of Commerce.

88. Sakr, A. H. (2005). *Introduction to Islam.* Chicago: The Institute of Islamic Information and Education.

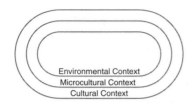

CHAPTER **4**

The Environmental Context

"Environment is heir to psyche."

—Howard F. Stein[1]

Chapter Objectives

After reading this chapter, you should be able to

1. Compare and contrast high- and low-load environments.

2. Discuss the relationship between culture and the natural environment.

3. Identify and describe fixed, semi-fixed, and informal built environments.

4. Compare and contrast housing patterns of Japanese, Navaho, and Marakwet cultures.

5. Assess your orientation toward privacy.

6. Assess your monochronic/polychronic orientation.

All human communication occurs within a physical and perceptual environment. These environments have a pervasive influence on the nature of communication. Consider the following two scenarios[2]:

Scenario #1: It is early evening, and you are alone in your dorm room. You're sitting on your bed reading a chapter in your intercultural communication textbook. You have some quiet music in the background that helps you concentrate. The room is quiet, as is the rest of the dormitory. Most of your friends are studying in their rooms as well.

Scenario #2: You are walking through the international terminal of a major airport. The terminal is very crowded with people rushing to and from the various ticket counters. Announcements are coming in over the airport intercom system. The airport is very noisy with people conversing, yelling, and laughing. You can hear the various jets landing and taking off as you rush to your gate. The lights are bright.

How would you compare these two environments? How might your verbal and nonverbal communication differ in each scenario? Do you feel and react the same in Scenario #1 as in Scenario #2?

The purpose of this chapter is to explore the environmental context of intercultural communication. In the contextual model of intercultural communication presented in Chapter 1, the environmental context is the third largest circle surrounding the interactants. Recall that, in the model, the cultural and microcultural contexts encircle the environmental context. How humans perceive the physical environment is very much affected by their culture and microculture. Furthermore, like the cultural and microcultural contexts, the influence of the physical environment is generally outside of our conscious awareness.

How we see the physical world around us is very much influenced by our individual psychological perceptions, which, in turn, are shaped by culture. People from all cultures project their mental perceptions onto the physical environment and act as though what is projected is, in fact, the true quality of the physical world. In other words, even the physical environment is subject to cultural interpretation. As Stein notes, far from being a passive component of culture, the environment is an active ingredient of the human experience.[3] In addition, the physical environment has a considerable impact on our communication. As we move from one physical location to another, our verbal and nonverbal messages adapt accordingly. The types of messages we send and receive in the classroom differ significantly from those we exchange in our dorm room or when we are out shopping in the mall. As the environment changes, our messages change.

In this chapter several aspects of the environment will be discussed, including the information load of an environment, the relationship between cultures and their natural environment, the *built* dimension of the physical environment, cross-cultural comparisons of housing, dimensions of privacy, and monochronic and polychronic time orientations. Each of these environmental dimensions affects how we communicate with others, and each varies considerably across cultures.

ENVIRONMENTS AND INFORMATION LOAD

Albert Mehrabian is well known for his work in environmental psychology. According to Mehrabian, there are a number of ways to compare one environment to another (e.g., Scenario #1 with Scenario #2 above). One way is to calculate the *information rate;* that is, the amount of information contained or perceived in the environment per some unit of time. According to Mehrabian, the more information available to process, the greater the information rate. An environment having a high information rate has a *high load,* whereas one with a low information rate has a *low load.* Mehrabian and his colleagues developed a list of descriptive adjectives to describe the load of any given environment (see Table 4.1).[4]

An environment containing several of the left-hand adjectives has a high load, whereas one that can be described with right-hand terms has a low load. Some environments might contain a blend of both left- and right-hand terms. In comparing Scenario #1 to Scenario #2 many of the right-hand terms apply to Scenario #1, including *simple, small scale, sparse, uncrowded, homogeneous, symmetrical, still, patterned,* and *probable.* On the other hand Scenario #2 could be described using several of the left-hand terms, such as *varied, complex, large scale, contrasting, dense, surprising, heterogeneous, crowded, asymmetrical, moving, random,* and *improbable.* Based on this comparison Scenario #1 has a low information load and Scenario #2 has a high information load.[5]

Mehrabian argues that, to some extent, information load is equivalent to the level of uncertainty in a particular environment. The higher the information load the higher the uncertainty, especially in novel and complex environments. The more familiar we are with a situation the less uncertainty we experience. Of all the environmental factors, people are perhaps the greatest source of uncertainty. This is especially true of strangers, including people from different cultures. Hence, a crowded room of strangers contains high levels of uncertainty and a heavy information load. Hence, the probability is high that when we are interacting with people from a different culture (especially in their environment) the information load will be high.[6]

Table 4.1   High Versus Low Load Descriptors

Environment Type	
High Load	Low Load
Uncertain	Certain
Varied	Redundant
Complex	Simple
Novel	Familiar
Large-Scale	Small-Scale
Contrasting	Similar
Dense	Sparse
Intermittent	Continuous
Surprising	Usual
Heterogeneous	Homogeneous
Crowded	Uncrowded
Asymmetrical	Symmetrical
Immediate	Distant
Moving	Still
Rare	Common
Random	Patterned
Improbable	Probable

Mehrabian contends that the information load of a particular environment can affect people's feelings in three ways: arousal-nonarousal, pleasure-displeasure, and dominance-submissiveness.[7] The arousal dimensions refers to your level of stimulation and excitability. Pleasure refers to your degree of happiness and satisfaction. Dominance refers to your feelings of control or command of the situation. These emotional responses cause people to approach or avoid the environment. Generally, lower load environments produce less negative arousal, are more pleasant, and are controllable. Hence, we're likely to approach these kinds of environments. Conversely, the heavily loaded environments produce anxiety (e.g., negative arousal), are unpleasant, and are less controllable. We may be more likely to avoid these situations.[8] Consider Scenario #1 and Scenario #2 from the beginning of this chapter. If you had the chance to choose one of the two scenarios, which would you choose? Of the two, which produces the most positive arousal, is more pleasant, and more controllable? Likewise, how do you feel about approaching or avoiding communication situations with people from different cultures? Because such situations may be highly loaded, you may prefer to avoid them.

CULTURE AND THE NATURAL ENVIRONMENT

Jon T. Lang, a professor in the Urban Design Program at the University of Pennsylvania, has written extensively about the relationship between people, culture, and their environment. Lang explains that the natural, or *terrestrial,* environment includes the physical geography of the earth, its climate, and its natural processes. The terrestrial environment for every person is the planet Earth.[9] Environmental psychologist Richard Knopf maintains that the natural environment is valued differently for different people. A culture's relationship with nature is culture-bound. According to Knopf, culture influences how much people value nature and the symbols they use to communicate about it. Aivilik Eskimos, notes Knopf, have more than a dozen different terms to describe the winds and different snow conditions. People perceive and create symbols of their environment based on their cultural experiences with it. Knopf argues that it is not the natural environment per se that generates affect, but rather the verbal and nonverbal symbols that we use to communicate about nature. Moreover, how a culture values and treats the natural environment can change quickly, especially if that culture experiences shifts in religion or dramatic advances in science and technology.[10] The 20th century in the United States, for example, witnessed immense changes in how we treat the natural environment. Because of scientific and technological progress, we now see the environment as something we control and dominate.

Although all cultures exist within specific terrestrial contexts, some aspects of the terrestrial environment exist in every culture while others do not. Gravity, for example, exists everywhere on earth. Oceans, lakes, streams, mountain ranges, deserts, valleys, trees, and forms of vegetation vary considerably across cultures, however. Indonesia, for example, is composed of more than 13,000 islands covering more than 700,000 square miles. The vegetation in Indonesia is very diverse, with more than 40,000 species of flowering plants, including 5,000 species of orchids.[11] The country of Laos in Southeast Asia has a monsoonal climate wherein heavy rainfall sometimes averages 90 inches a year.[12] Conversely, in some areas of South Yemen, which lies in the southwest corner of the Arabian peninsula, only four inches of rain fall in a given year. Some northern and eastern sections of the country can go without rain for years.[13] Russia is the largest country in the world (i.e., geographically) with a land mass of more than six and a half million square miles and dramatic climate extremes. Northern Siberia, for example, is covered with permafrost, where snow drifts can reach as high as sixty feet and little vegetation is found.[14] Norway's land mass is just over 100,000 square miles—slightly larger than Arizona—and only three percent of the land is usable as farmland.[15] As the physical environment of a culture varies, so will the vocabulary of the culture. Cultures with different environments create verbal and nonverbal symbols that enable them to adapt to and communicate about their environment.

Lang asserts that the natural environment of any culture influences life in that culture. Physical and climatic aspects of the environment can restrict the kinds of activities that occur.[16] In many cultures the pace of daily activities reflects the natural climate of the area. A quick example may help illuminate this point. In some southern European countries (e.g., Spain, southern Italy), during the warm weather season many shop owners close their stores from about midday until late afternoon. They do this to avoid working through the hottest part of the day, when the temperatures can rise above 100 degrees Fahrenheit. Most of the stores in these countries are not air conditioned. Visitors from other countries, particularly the United States, may interpret this custom as laziness on the part of the shop owners, but in reality, the store owners are simply adjusting to the conditions of their natural climate.

World Views of the Natural Environment. Harvard University sociologist Florence Kluckhohn says that cultures can be described as having one of three orientations toward nature, depending on what their members believe: that people are subjugated to nature, that they are an inherent part of nature, or that they are dominant over nature.[17] A culture's orientation toward nature affects how people within that culture communicate about nature and organize their daily activities. Knowing and understanding a particular culture's orientation toward nature is a helpful step in becoming a competent intercultural communicator.

Irwin Altman and Martin Chemers argue that in cultures where nature is viewed as supreme, people believe they are at the mercy of an omnipotent nature. According to Altman and Chemers, in such cultures, nature is perceived as a dominant and unmanageable power. In Biblical times, and even more recently, the natural environment and nature were viewed as threatening and dangerous. Altman and Chemers note that Western fairly tales are replete with references to such environmental features as "dark forests," where danger is lurking at every corner.[18] In her research on East India, Rebecca Jo Bishop found that many East Indians believe that the elements of the natural environment dictate the health and well-being of the people. Indeed, astrologers play an important role in India as the people believe that nothing in nature is accidental, and the universe and all living components have a fundamental order over which they have no control.[19]

Kluckhohn claims that many cultures attempt a balancing act with nature and try to live in harmony with it. Indeed, argue Altman and Chemers, in these types of cultures the natural environment is seen as orderly and cyclical. The days and seasons recur regularly and natural events repeat themselves in consistent patterns. People and environment are viewed as one, changing together, in what Altman and Chemers describe as a timeless mutual relationship.[20] Reick and Ogura hold that in many Eastern societies nature is perceived as an ally that people draw on for spiritual support. The people of the island nation of Sri Lanka, which sits 20 miles off the southern coast of India, attempt a balancing act with nature. According to Reick and Ogura, the source of their belief has its roots in Buddhism, which professes equality among all living things.[21] The Japanese are well known for their attempt to harmonize their relationship with nature, which can be seen in Japanese art forms such as gardening and flower arrangements and Haiku poetry (which makes reference to the seasons). Altman and Chemers assert that the Pygmies of Zaire, Africa, view themselves as an intrinsic part of the rainforest where they dwell. To them, the forest is their mother and father with whom they communicate on a personal basis.[22]

Kluckhohn's third orientation is seen in many Western societies, where people believe that nature is something to be controlled, domesticated, and subjugated.[23] According to Altman and Chemers, some scholars attribute this view to Judeo-Christian doctrine, where God is seen as the creator of the universe and put humans on the Earth to do His will. People are not just part of the environment, like trees, plants, or animals, but are of divine origin. Such philosophies have led to a separation between humans and the environment. When the scientific revolution developed, nature was seen as mechanistic, further separating people from nature. Through technology, buildings, and modern agricultural methods, humans were able to dominate their natural setting to their liking. In the United States, people separate themselves from nature and believe they have the power, even the right, to dominate nature in just about any way they can. Many of our proudest achievements (e.g., moon landings, dams, indoor sports facilities) are based on conquering or exploiting nature. Like other countries where European settlement has occurred, the environment is seen as an entity to be conquered. Much of Australia's economic activity is based on the extraction of natural resources such as timber, minerals, natural gas, and oil.[24]

Culture and Natural Disasters. A culture's relationship with nature can be seen in how it deals with natural disasters. Whether it be drought, tornadoes, hurricanes, floods, or earthquakes, natural disasters occur in all cultures. How people manage such disaster is shaped by the culture and its view of nature. Moreover, many times when natural disasters strike, people from all over the world come together to help. Understanding the stricken culture's relationship with nature can facilitate communication among those directly affected and those offering aid and comfort. The Red Cross, for example, has people stationed all over the world to help in times of need. Ironically, natural disasters provide an opportunity for intercultural communication.

One model of human responses to natural disasters, reviewed by Sorenson and White, segregates cultures into three types: folk or preindustrial, transitional, and industrial. Preindustrialized cultures such as Nigeria, Malawi, and rural China are characterized by primarily rural agrarian land use and have low income and literacy levels, underdeveloped communication systems, and simple technology. In these cultures, land use is primarily farming in small plots of land. Housing is typically adobe or mud. Many preindustrialized cultures believe in a harmonious relationship with nature. According to Sorenson and White, these societies have a low level of resource use, low material wealth, and less exposure to hazard risk; hence, they are the least vulnerable to catastrophic natural events. They display resonance with the environment and have great resilience to most natural hazards. Although most people in most cultures believe that natural disasters are random occurrences, individuals in preindustrial cultures are more likely to perceive environmental hazards as cyclical or clustered than those in industrialized societies.[25]

According to Sorenson and White, transitional societies such as Sri Lanka, rural Turkey, and Brazil are characterized by rural to urban migration. These cultures may be investing in industry; see shifts from labor to capital-intensive land use; and have low to moderate income, basic level literacy rates, developing communication systems, and some trade. Land use may be semimechanized, and housing is unreinforced concrete and frame. Many transitional societies view nature as dominating. They have more wealth and more people living in high-risk areas than preindustrialized societies. Sorenson and White claim that because of their marginal economic status, which restricts their ability to prevent and recover from loss, these cultures are quite vulnerable to hazards and their adaptability to disaster is low. Like preindustrialized cultures, people in transitional societies are more likely to perceive natural disasters as cyclical than people in industrialized cultures.[26]

Industrial societies such as Great Britain, urban Japan, and Australia can be classified as primarily urban land use. According to Sorenson and White, these cultures are capital intensive and heavily mechanized, and they have high income and literacy levels, highly developed communication systems, and high trade. Land use is urban, suburban, residential, and industrial. Agriculture is highly mechanized with large corporate farming operations. Contemporary architecture and housing in many industrialized societies is earthquake resistant. These types of cultures believe that they are dominant over nature in a master/slave-like relationship. Although these societies have increased their exposure to natural disasters through intensive land use, their advanced technologies and greater wealth reduce the overall risk. Resilience is low, but different from that of transitional societies because the vulnerability to disaster is decreased.[27]

Figure 4.2   The architecture of different cultures affects the interaction between people and the natural environment

Source: Copyright © James Neuliep.

THE BUILT ENVIRONMENT

Jon Lang explains that the built environment of any culture consists mainly of adaptations to the terrestrial environment, including architecture, housing, lighting, and landscaping (see Figure 4.2). The built environment artificially changes natural patterns of behavior, heat, light, sound, odors, and human communication. Hence, the built environment affects the interaction between people and the natural environment. Moreover, many of these changes are specifically designed to facilitate or restrict human interaction. The built environment is not random; it is an intentionally designed pattern of spatial relationships between objects and objects, objects and people, and people and people. The built environment organizes and manages human communication between people and it varies considerably across cultures.[28]

Lang notes that while sometimes designed for purely aesthetic reasons, the built environment is typically structured for specific activities. Classrooms, for example, are designed for a specific kind of communication. The size of the room, the positioning of the blackboards, and so on are all fashioned to facilitate interaction between teacher and student. Culture affects how the built environment is designed. Amos Rapoport argues that the interior of any given built environment influences and directs the way activities are carried out, how the family is structured, how gender roles are played, attitudes toward privacy, and the overall process of social interaction. Moreover, says Rapoport, how the built environment is planned and constructed reflects the values, motivations, and resources of the culture wherein it exists. The overall economic, political, and legal system of a particular culture affects how that culture designs its built environment, including homes, schools, government, and private business buildings. As the built environments of cultures differ, so do communication patterns.[29]

Lang argues that the degree of ease or difficulty afforded by the built environment when moving from one place to another is a major predictor of human communication patterns. People are more likely to communicate with each other in those environments where access to others is facilitated by the built environment than in environments where access is restricted.[30] Anthropologist Edward Hall has identified three fundamental types of layout patterns in built environments: fixed-feature space, semifixed-feature space, and informal space. Fixed-feature space is defined by immoveable or permanent fixtures such as walls, floors, windows, and so on. Semifixed space includes that which is moveable (usually within fixed-feature space), such as furniture. Informal space is perceptual and varies according to the movement of the interactants. Informal space lasts only as long as the interactants communicate; it is not stated space and is usually outside the awareness of the people interacting.[31]

The variability of fixed, semifixed, or informal space influences human communication. Some environments must be restructured for certain kinds of activities, whereas others need not be adjusted at all. According to Lang, these kinds of environments are called adaptable or flexible. For example, in an adaptable fixed-feature space such as a gymnasium, many kinds of activities can occur without any changes to the fixed features, such as sporting events, gym classes, commencement ceremonies, dances, plays, speeches, and so on. In a flexible semifixed-feature space, changes are made to accommodate certain kinds of activities. Some schools and office buildings, for example, have portable walls. Informal (or dynamic) space between people is controlled, regulated, and managed by the nature of the relationship between the interactants.[32]

In addition to classifying fixed, semifixed, and informal space, Hall also developed a four-level classification of social distances. Hall argues that the physical environment guides behavior and the way that people define the space between themselves and others. Hall's classification scheme was modeled after the findings of ethologists (i.e., people who study animal behavior), who observed the various distances that animals maintain in their environments. Hall maintains that spatial distance between people is a vehicle for communication, much like that of sight, sound, smell, and touch. As distance decreases, people can see, hear, touch, and smell others differently from when distance increases. As the distance between interactants increases, the available visual, auditory, olfactic, thermal, and kinesthetic information decreases. As distance increases, the privacy of the person increases but the privacy of the interaction decreases.[33]

Hall's four-level classification specifies intimate, personal, social-consultative, and public distances. Intimate distance is reserved for close intimate contact, including touching. In this distance there is much visual, auditory, and olfactic sensation. In the United States, intimate distance is 9 to 18 inches and is usually reserved for highly personal relationships. The second type, personal distance, is 1.5 to 4 feet. This is sometimes called "arm's length" distance because a comfortable distance between interactants is literally about one human arm length. Social-consultative distance is the spacing people practice at casual gatherings and in working situations. In the United States this distance is 4 to 12 feet. In social distance there is a more formal atmosphere. Public distance is used for talking across a room and for public speaking situations. In the United States this distance extends from 12 feet and beyond. There is little olfactic sensation in this distance.[34]

To be sure, intimate, personal, social, and public distances vary by culture and Hall's classification may not be universal. Hall argues that other factors, such as the relationship between interactants or external environmental factors, may influence distances between people. In addition, the built environment plays a key role in how space is used. Smaller, more confined spaces, insists Hall, increase interaction distances whereas larger environments motivate people to adopt smaller distances. Lustig and Koester note, for example, that people in so-called high-contact cultures (Arabs, Latin Americans, Southern Europeans) tend to use closer interaction distances than people from low-contact cultures. People in the United States, for example, prefer greater distances between themselves and others than do persons living in many Latin American cultures. People from colder climates have a tendency to use large physical distances when they communicate. Conversely, people from warm weather climates tend to use small physical distances. Northern Europeans (e.g., England, Germany, Scandinavia) are said to have larger personal space "bubbles" than Southern Europeans (e.g., Greece, Italy, Spain).[35] In some Middle Eastern cultures, people stand close enough to smell each other's breath. Aiello has reviewed several studies and found that Indonesians used less space than Australians and were more likely to initiate a conversation with a stranger. Other studies comparing Americans with other cultures have found no differences; that is, they have found common spatial behavior patterns. American, Australian, British, and South African young adults placed figures representing mental patients at approximately the same distances. In a similar study, American, British, Scottish, Swedish, and Pakistani subjects all rated different seating distances similarly for intimacy level. In an interesting study, it was found that when the bilingual Japanese subjects spoke in their native tongue, they sat farther from a same-sex, same nationality confederate than either Americans or bilingual Venezuelans. But when all subjects spoke English, the three groups approximated the American seating pattern.[36]

CROSS-CULTURAL COMPARISONS OF HOUSING

The use of space is an integral part of every human being's communication. Decisions about where and when to perform our daily activities are based on spatial patterns that are learned culturally. We become so accustomed to our spatial definitions and boundaries that many of us experience anxiety when forced to interact in novel or unusual environments. Many people complain that they do not sleep well when outside of their regular home environments. How we organize space within the built environment says much about our culture—its values and way of life. Perhaps more than any other aspect of the built environment, the home presents a particularly rich source of information about a culture's perception and use of space.

Japanese Housing

In the past 150 years much has been written in the West about Japanese architecture, especially the Japanese home. Since World War II, great changes have occurred in Japanese housing. Many of the traditional Japanese homes, where most of the daily activities occurred in one room, have been replaced by Western-style homes and high-rises where space is defined by walls.[37]

Houses of various types and styles can be found side by side in contemporary Japan. According to Kiyosi Sieke and Charles Terry, a fair number of homes still exist that reflect traditional Japanese architecture dating back to the eighteenth century. Other homes reveal clear European influences. Many others, perhaps the majority, have almost completely adopted a Western look. Sieke and Terry believe that the design of contemporary Japanese homes has been influenced by the breakdown of the traditional family system in Japan. Many young people are leaving the traditional multigeneration family home situation and moving to apartments or small houses of their own. In homes where two or three generations still live together, the main part of the house is intended for the second-generation husband and wife. A special section of the house might be designated for the family elders, and another section especially for the children. In many homes like this, the elders' section is organized and decorated in traditional Japanese style, the children's section will be completely Western, and the husband's and wife's part a combination of the two styles. This type of home was unheard of before the war.[38]

Although many contemporary Japanese houses reflect a Westernized design, the Japanese attitude about life has not changed. Charles Terry, past editor of *The Japan Architect,* asserts that an essential point about Japanese houses and Japanese culture is the gap between the public and private Japanese person. According to Terry, the impression that a Japanese presents to society may be very different from how a Japanese actually thinks or feels. In public settings, Japanese act according to clearly prescribed social rules. In private, Japanese think and act as they please. This philosophy is reflected in the contemporary Japanese home and its Western influence. According to Terry, most Japanese who build Western-style homes do so because it is fashionable and expected of them. Terry alleges that most Japanese probably prefer the traditional, however.[39] Atsushi Ueda, a Japanese author and scholar of traditional Japanese urban architecture, argues that the contemporary Japanese house is caught between tradition and modernism.[40]

Tetsuro Yoshida, one of Japan's leading contemporary architects, writes that because of their belief in harmony with nature, the traditional Japanese home fits unobtrusively into the landscape, not appearing human-made. The traditional Japanese house is a detached house with a garden. Yoshida states that among traditional Japanese, there is an intimate relationship between the house and garden.[41]

Since ancient times the Japanese garden has been considered more like a work of art than a simple plot of land where flowers and vegetables are cultivated. Instead, the Japanese garden is treated as a painting or sculpture to be appreciated from some distance. Yoshida describes the Japanese garden as a quiet monochrome compared to the colorful European or American garden.[42] In contrast, writes Ueda, one seldom encounters anything resembling a proper Japanese garden in contemporary Japanese homes. Instead, one of the most visible features of the modern Japanese home is a car or a garage.[43]

In traditional Japanese homes, writes Ueda, rooms are separated by *shoji* or *fusuma;* meaning opaque sliding screens. A *shoji* panel is usually made of cedar lattice with translucent paper stretched over it. *Shoji* panels are very lightweight and easily slide open or closed with one finger. The purpose, and major advantage, to *shoji* is that they can be removed easily to convert an entire floor of a house into a single open room. The traditional Japanese house is fundamentally a one-room home that is partitioned by *shoji.* Because of the versatility of *shoji,* the plan of a house is flexible where the divisions of the rooms are easily changed. According to Ueda, this is the major characteristic of space allocation in the Japanese home.[44]

Ueda alleges that regardless of how Westernized they may have become, the Japanese have not abandoned the custom of taking off their shoes when entering a house and sitting on the floor. The Japanese *yuka* (i.e., floor) developed as a result of this custom. The Japanese *yuka* is actually a raised floor and was developed out of a need to maintain sanitary conditions. Even contemporary homes have a raised floor. According to Ueda, the size of a room in a Japanese home is measured by its number of *tatami mats.* The *tatami mat* is a modular floor mat made from straw that is used to cover the floor and upon which one sits or sleeps. The principal room in a traditional Japanese home is the reception room, also called the sitting room. The average size of the room is eight to ten mats. The room usually faces the garden and incorporates an alcove, called the *tokonoma.* According to Ueda, the tokonoma is a recess arranged with staggered shelves, artistic ornaments, hanging scrolls, and perhaps a flower arrangement. The tokonoma is the most sacred place in the home, holding a sort of spiritual or moral place. The space immediately in front of the tokonoma is the most honored place in a traditional Japanese home.[45]

Two rooms not much discussed, but of primary importance in the Japanese home, are the kitchen and bathroom. The kitchen, even in modern Japanese homes, is the domicile of the wife. The kitchen is her place, not to be disturbed by other household members, and not to be entered or even observed by guests. The kitchen is a private place. In both traditional and contemporary Japanese homes, the bath is of utmost importance, and is thought of as a time of recuperation and solitude. The bathroom, which is in a separate room from the toilet, consists of two separate places, one for bathing and the other for soaking. Initially, the Japanese will wash themselves with soap under a shower that is next to the bathtub. Following the shower, the Japanese will crouch into the tub, which is designed for sitting, not lying. The water is warmed and sometimes scented with flowers or lemons. The purpose is to relax and soothe the body. The water is kept for several days and used by all family members.

Japanese architect and author Atsushi Ueda maintains that the traditional Japanese house is a thing of the past. However, the contemporary Japanese house, he writes, is "nervously confessing its own insecurity."[46] Though dramatic changes have occurred in Japan in the past 50 years, much of the psychology driving the design of the traditional Japanese house lives in the contemporary people.

American Navajo Housing

Susan Kent, an ethnoarchaeologist, has studied extensively the use of space in Native American Navajo housing. In her pioneering work, Kent compared the use of space across three American co-cultural groups: Native American Navajo, Spanish-Americans, and Euro-Americans. Of particular interest is her work with Navajos. According to Kent's studies, many of the Navajos live in remote parts of reservations and have very limited contact with White Americans. Traditional Navajo families speak mostly Navajo and live in aboriginal dwellings called hogans. Hogans typically consist of three large converging support posts that interlock at the top with smaller support posts. The hogan is covered with earth. In addition to the hogan, the Navajo camp may consist of a wooden ramada, a wood-chip storage area, a horse corral, and small fields of corn. The hogan is occupied in the winter and the ramada is used in the summer (see Figure 4.3). The hogan is used for storage during the summer months. Water is hauled in from tribal wells. There is no outhouse. Some camps will have a sweat house.[47]

Navajo Hogan and Ramada

In her research Kent[48] discovered that the space inside the hogan was used differently by the occupants according to their sex. The men stayed almost exclusively in one half of the hogan while the women and children used the other half. Food preparation always took place in the half occupied by the women and children, but was consumed in the half occupied by men.[49]

Kent writes that in contrast to the sex-defined spaces inside the hogan, both sexes of all ages performed activities at the same locale both out-of-doors and in the ramada. Not only did both sexes use the same activity area outside the hogan, but different types of activities were performed at the same place, including stripping hides, weaving, butchering, and washing. An individual's mood and season seemed to be the only factors affecting the activity areas of the Navajo camp.[50]

Kent observed that the use of space within the ramada differed significantly from the hogan. The men were active in all parts of the ramada. The

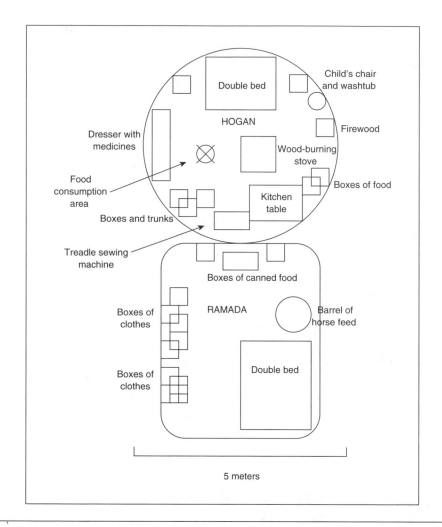

Figure 4.3

women and children also used most of the ramada without restriction. Chairs and beds were used by each family member regardless of sex or age. Kent also observed that the Navajos seemed to place little emphasis on the differences between the sexes and did not prescribe a traditional division of labor seen in many Euro-American homes. Moreover, asserts Kent, the Navajo had only a few sex-specific activities or sex-specific artifacts, and very few single-function activity areas or artifacts. In fact, the only sex-specific activity areas used by the Navajos, observed Kent, were in the hogan, where traditional Navajos segregate space into sex-specific areas. In the ramada there were no sex-specific areas, although identical activities of daily living occur in both. Kent speculates that the reason for this is that the hogan is perceived as a sacred dwelling, whereas the ramada is not. According to Kent, the hogan is mentioned in important myths and prayers, and specific ceremonies must be conducted only in a hogan. Kent suggests that the circular hogan symbolizes the circular cosmos, whereas the rectangular ramada and out-of-doors do not. The round sacred hogan is divided into the same male and female areas as is the round, sacred cosmos.[51]

Housing of the Marakwet of Kenya

The Marakwet people are a part of the Kalenjin tribe, which lives in western Kenya. Prior to 1900 very little had been written about this group. In 1986 Henrietta Moore published an extensive anthropological study of the Marakwet people focusing specifically on their use of space. The following discussion of the Marakwet is based on Moore's analysis.[52]

According to Moore, Marakwet country is one of the most secluded parts of Kenya. The Marakwet are divided into a number of villages called *kor*. The village is composed of family compounds consisting of a family house, store, and goat house. According to Moore, the Marakwet people are emotionally attached to the land and see themselves and the land they occupy as inseparable.[53]

Marakwet houses and their associated structures (i.e., stores and goat houses) are the only forms of built environment in the Marakwet village. There is no physically constructed space outside of the family compound. According to Moore,

> The nature of village organisation is an interlocking set of social units which are also territorial units. At every moment, the life of the villages focuses down on the household, and that of the household expands out to meet the world of the village: a world where social relations are also spatial relations.[54]

The Marakwet insist that a house must never face out over the valley. In addition, the houses within a particular compound must always face each other. The majority of Marakwet houses are sub-circular with a single entrance and a window and are made of wattle and daub. Wattle is a fabrication of poles interwoven with branches or reeds. Daub is a covering of some type, usually earth. The houses have thatched roofs. In the dry season the houses are virtually indistinguishable from the natural terrain of the escarpment.

In her study, Moore observed that each house is divided into three areas, including the sleeping area, the cooking area, and the area beneath the roof store. The bed is typically placed behind the door and is considered

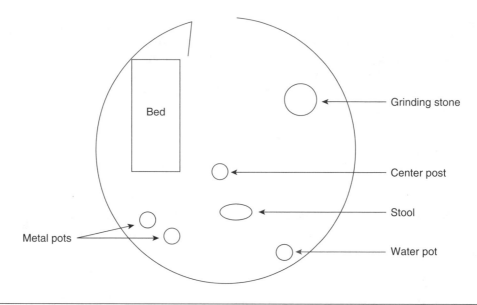

Figure 4.4   The Interior of a Traditional Marakwet House in the Sibou Village[56]

the most private place in the house. The fireplace/cooking place is just behind and to the side of the center post. The area beneath the roof store, then, is on the opposite side from the bed. Most family compounds within villages contain at least one house and a store or goat house. Like the houses, the stores are made of wattle and daub and are always elevated on stone stilts with a thatched roof. Stores must always be placed to the back of the family compound. Every Marakwet man starts with one house. After he marries he may build a second house. Ideally, the second house would be for his wife.[55]

Based on her observations, Moore concluded that the internal organization of the Marakwet houses is based on the social relationships between family members. In terms of the space, men and women are segregated. In Marakwet society women are subordinate to men. Men spend the majority of their time away from the house while women spend the majority of their time within the family house and compound. Men use the house primarily for sleeping and storage while women use the house for cooking, child bearing and rearing, entertaining, and family maintenance. Men spend most of their time tending to the herds or attending meetings with the other men in the village. Moore notes that because the women spend most of their time in the house, they exert considerable control over its possessions. For example, fellow villagers must ask for and receive permission to enter a house or to remove something from it. Although Marakwet women are subordinate to Marakwet men, they wield a great deal of power within the boundaries of the household.[57]

Moore explains that of particular importance to the Marakwet is the organization and disposal of refuse, which she argues also reflects a clear male-female dichotomy. The majority of refuse for the Marakwet is made up of ash, animal dung, and chaff (i.e., seed coverings). The three types of refuse hold symbolic meaning and have distinct disposal locations. Ash is the result of cooking and burning; that is, a woman's job. Hence ash is associated with womanness and female fertility. Ash, then, is always thrown behind the house. Chaff is placed in front of the compound, and dung is placed near the animal compound. Women are buried near the chaff because their work is to dig and remove chaff. Men are buried near the animal dung because their work is to herd the cattle. Goat dung is symbolic of male fertility. The Marakwet are adamant about not mixing the three types of refuse because of their relationship to burial locations and their symbolic meaning.[58]

PRIVACY

Most social scientists agree that human beings, regardless of culture, are a social species with an innate propensity to affiliate and communicate with other human beings. At the same time, however, humans beings cannot tolerate extended physical contact with other humans and need privacy.[59] According to Alan Westin these same competing needs are found in the animal kingdom. Westin maintains that virtually all animals seek periods of time when they desire the company of other animals and other times when they seek individual seclusion.[60]

Although the need for privacy is innate and universal, the degree to which an individual human feels the need for seclusion varies considerably across cultures. For example, Americans value privacy so much that they have made it law. Junior high school students learn that Article Four of the Bill of Rights of the Constitution of the United States guarantees every citizen the right to be secure in their persons, houses, papers, and effects against unreasonable searches and seizures. Americans literally believe that they have a *right to privacy*. Anthropologists contend that individuals in virtually all cultures engage in a continuous process of seeking privacy at some times and companionship at others (see Figure 4.5). In this sense privacy is culture bound and is considered a learned response to particular social situations. Irwin Altman argues that privacy is a "boundary control" process whereby people sometimes make themselves accessible to others and sometimes close themselves off from others. The behavioral and environmental

Figure 4.5   People of all cultures seek privacy at some times and companionship at others

strategies that people use to accomplish this process are defined by culture.[61]

Westin maintains that privacy is a necessary condition for acceptable social behavior. In some circumstances, privacy is literally required in order to not violate cultural norms. Most cultures specify (sometimes legally) that certain behaviors must be enacted in private. Such rules and norms vary from culture to culture.[62] Even within cultures, microcultural groups have different perceptions of privacy. In the United States, for example, African-American opinions and policy preferences toward privacy differ from those of the White majority. In comparison with Whites, African-Americans are more concerned, and believe others are more concerned, with invasions of privacy.[63]

Jon Lang states that privacy is closely linked to the built environment because it can be designed and/or maneuvered in a number of ways to promote, encourage, or restrict communication with others.[64] In his seminal work on privacy, Alan Westin identified four types of privacy: (a) solitude, or the state of being free from observation of others; (b) intimacy, or the state of being with another person but free from the outside world; (c) anonymity, or the state of being unknown even in a crowd; and (d) reserve, or the state in which a person employs psychological barriers to control unwanted intrusion.[65] These different forms of privacy serve different purposes, including personal autonomy, release of emotions, self-evaluation, and communication. Westin argues that the type and degree of privacy desired depends on the type of behavior in which one engages, the culture, and the individual personality traits of the individual. The location of sexual intercourse, for example, may vary from culture to culture. In cultures such as the United States, where the nuclear family resides in a walled house that provides for privacy, sexual intercourse is likely to occur within the household. In cultures where the extended family lives together in a communal dwelling without clear spatial divisions, sexual intercourse probably occurs outside the built environment.[66]

Extending on Westin's four categories of privacy, Darhl Pedersen identified six types of privacy: (a) reserve, (b) isolation, (c) solitude, (d), intimacy with family, (e) intimacy with friends, and (f) anonymity. Reserve indicates an *unwillingness* to be with others, especially strangers. Isolation is defined as total separation and detachment from others. Solitude implies the absence from others. Intimacy with family is being alone with members of one's own family. Intimacy with friends is being alone with friends. Anonymity is a desire to go unnoticed in a crowd. With the exception of isolation and solitude, these types of privacy are independent; that is, one type of privacy does not necessarily go with another. A privacy profile may be expected to be unique for a particular person or culture.[67]

Assessing Dimensions of Privacy. In his work on privacy, Darhl Pedersen developed a privacy questionnaire for measuring the types of privacy preferred by individuals. This questionnaire has been used in cross-cultural comparisons. The questionnaire contains 30 statements regarding the "privacy sphere" and is presented below.

SELF-ASSESSMENT 4.1

Dimensions of Privacy Questionnaire[68]

To complete the questionnaire, indicate how often you engage in the activity or state represented in each statement by marking whether it (1) never, (2) rarely, (3) occasionally, (4) sometimes, (5) often, or (6) usually applies. Scoring procedures are outlined following the scale.

1. _____ I sometimes need to be alone and away from anyone.

2. _____ I would be reluctant to engage in a prolonged conversation with someone I had just met.

3. _____ I like to go on vacation with just my family.

4. _____ I like my friends to sympathize with me and to cheer me up when I am depressed.

5. _____ I have to be encouraged to put on a stunt at a party even when others are doing the same sort of things.

6. _____ I want my thoughts and ideas to be known by others.

7. _____ I'd like to work on a farm all by myself for a summer.

8. _____ I like to be the center of attention in my group.

9. _____ I like living in an apartment house because it prevents you from being alone.

10. _____ I do not like to be disturbed when I am at home engaged in a family activity.

11. _____ It would be fun to be alone on a high mountain peak surveying the scene below.

12. _____ I like to be alone at home where it is peaceful and quiet.

13. _____ I like to be at home with nobody else around.

14. _____ I have a special person that I can confide in.

15. _____ I like to attend meetings if I do not know others.

16. _____ At parties I am more likely to sit by myself than to join the crowd.

17. _____ I would like to have a mountain cabin where my family and I could be alone together.

18. _____ I like my friends to fuss over me when I am sick.

19. _____ I like other people to notice me when I am in public.

20. _____ It pleases me when my accomplishments obtain recognition from my friends.

21. _____ I reserve displays of physical affection for a select few friends and family.

22. _____ I'd be happy living all alone in a cabin in the woods.

23. _____ Sometimes I like to be alone where I cannot be observed by anyone.

24. _____ I tell my problems only to my family.

25. _____ My personal relations with people are cool and distant.

26. _____ I think I'd like the kind of work a forest ranger does.

27. _____ I prefer doing things with only my family.

28. _____ I like to meet new people.

29. _____ Whenever possible, I avoid being in a crowd.

30. _____ I like being in a room by myself.

Scoring:

Reverse your score for items 6, 8, 9, 15, 19, and 28, then follow the directions below.

Add your responses to items 1, 12, 13, 23, and 30. This represents your Solitude score.

Add your responses to items 4, 14, 18, 19, and 20. This represents your Intimacy with Friends score.

Add your responses to items 2, 16, 25, 28, and 29. This represents your Reserve score.

Add your responses to items 7, 9, 11, 22, and 26. This represents your Isolation score.

Add your responses to items 3, 10, 17, 24, and 27. This represents your Intimacy with Family score.

Add your responses to items 5, 6, 8, 15, and 21. This represents your Anonymity score.

Scores of 20 or higher on these subscales indicate a greater preference for the specific type of privacy.

PERCEPTIONS OF PRIVACY IN THE UNITED STATES

Although the United States literally legislates privacy, perceptions of privacy differ throughout the country and among microcultural groups. Moreover, attitudes about privacy have changed dramatically in the past decade or so. Clay Calvert, a professor who holds degrees in communication and law, argues that Americans live in a "voyeur nation." A voyeur is one who seeks sexual stimulation by visual means and/or is a prying observer of sordid or scandalous material. Calvert maintains that voyeurism has become a central theme of American entertainment and culture. Calvert argues that the American public has access to information not originally intended for public consumption, made available over television and the Internet, in what he calls "mediated voyeurism." Calvert categorizes four types of mediated voyeurism. The first type is video verite voyeurism; that is, unrehearsed and unscripted moments of actual events filmed by a video camera. The Rodney King beating and the television program "Cops" are included as examples of video verite voyeurism. The second type is reconstruction voyeurism, where some actual event is dramatized for the benefit of the viewer. The television show "America's Most Wanted" is an example of reconstructed voyeurism. The third type is called tell-all/show-all voyeurism typical of television shows such as "Jerry Springer." Finally, the fourth type is sexual voyeurism, characterized by explicit Internet sites where hidden cameras are put into bathrooms, bedrooms, up women's skirts, and so on. Calvert maintains that the American voyeur mentality has serious implications for an individual's constitutional right to privacy. Frankly, Calvert is not particularly sanguine (optimistic) about the future of privacy rights in the United States.[69] Sociologist Sherry Turkle argues there is a tension in American culture between the individual's desire for, and right to, privacy and the invasion of personal privacy brought on by the computer age.[70] Because so much personal information about people is stored electronically, it is relatively easy to gain access to it, including virtually all of one's financial and medical data. According to Carole Lan, a paid Internet searcher,

> In a few hours, sitting at my computer, beginning with no more than your name and address, I can find out what you do for a living, the names and ages of your spouses and children, what kind of car you drive, the value of your house and how much taxes you pay on it.[71]

Different groups of people throughout the United States have different concerns about privacy. Many college students, for example, are concerned about what type of information, and how much, their college or university can disclose about them. The 1974 Family Educational Rights and Privacy Act, also known as the Buckley Amendment, forbids colleges from disclosing academic records without student approval. In October 1998, the U.S. Congress passed an amendment to the Family Educational Rights and Privacy Act that allows colleges and universities to inform parents any time a student under the age of 21 violates drug or alcohol laws. The privacy act still prohibits colleges and universities from releasing students' grades, but many colleges and universities are routinely calling parents and informing them of drug and alcohol policy violations. Moreover, colleges are not required to alert students when they have notified their parents. The new laws also allow colleges to disclose information regarding any violent crimes committed by students, and the new amendment now permits a college to release a student's grades to a court.[72]

African-Americans seem to have different views on privacy compared with Whites. For example, Gandy reports that educated African-Americans extend broad privacy rights to individuals and, unlike Whites, do not view information-gathering techniques used by businesses as invasions of privacy. In addition, when African-Americans are concerned about privacy it is because they sense that a loss of control over personal information renders them more susceptible to discrimination, especially in terms of employment, insurance, and credit. According to Gandy, African-Americans are most concerned about privacy issues as they relate to relationships between individuals and the government, but not more so than other groups (e.g., Whites).[73]

Cross-Cultural Variations on Privacy. Pedersen's privacy questionnaire can be useful in determining the privacy preferences of a variety of cultural groups. Knowing a culture's preferences about privacy can help you determine when and where communication can and should take place. For example, if you know when and how a culture desires privacy, you would know when to restrict communication with persons from that culture. Invasions of privacy are negatively perceived across cultures and will be interpreted as a sign of incompetent communication.

Pedersen and Frances found that within the United States, men tend to score higher on isolation while women are higher on intimacy with family and intimacy with friends. People from the mountain states region preferred isolation, anonymity, and solitude more than people from the western states, where a preference for solitude ranked significantly higher. Persons from the southeast region showed a preference for isolation and a high preference for anonymity.[74]

Rustemli and Kokdemir administered Petersen's privacy questionnaire to Turkish students, and the results of their study are comparable to Americans. The overall preferences for solitude, isolation, anonymity, and intimacy are virtually the same for Americans and Turks. Preferences for reserve and intimacy with family differed across cultures, however. Unlike American subjects, the Turkish subjects demonstrated a lower preference for reserve and intimacy with family members. The Turkish subjects preferred intimacy with friends over intimacy with family. This may be due to the family structure in Turkish culture, where the family is an intact group with intense care for children. In the typical Turkish family, the children develop a very intimate and dependent, but restricted, relationship with their parents. The children become very dependent on their parents but have limited intimate communication with them. Thus, issues of personal identity and intimacy are directed toward peers rather than parents.[75]

In referring to a paper delivered by Clifford Geertz, Westin describes the living arrangements of the people living in Java. According to Westin, the Javanese live in small, bamboo-walled houses that have no interior walls or doors. Except for the bathroom, there are no really private areas. Westin claims that because the Javanese have no physical privacy, they have developed a kind of psychological privacy in their everyday behaviors and communication. They speak softly, conceal their feelings, are emotionally restrained, and are very indirect in their verbal and nonverbal communication.[76]

Irwin Altman has reviewed the privacy behaviors of several groups, including the Mehinacu Indians, a tribal culture in central Brazil. According to Altman, the Mehinacu live in communal villages where there is virtually no privacy in their houses. Instead of achieving privacy within their homes, the Mehinacu create privacy by actually leaving the village for extended periods of time, even years. Newly born children and their parents are isolated from the village in their homes for several weeks or months. Young boys are required to stay within the home behind a wooden partition where they have virtually no communication with anyone. Food and bathing materials are brought to them. Altman states that during their seclusion, the boys are taught to speak quietly, are not allowed to play, and must abstain from emotional displays. Young women also go through a similar seclusion after their initial menstruation. Other forms of seclusion occur after the death of a spouse. Altman notes that the typical Mehinacu Indian may spend as much as 7 to 8 years of his or her life in isolation from others.[77]

While the Javanese and Mehinacu cultures may be characterized by having minimal privacy, the Balinese and Tuareg cultures desire maximum privacy. According to Altman, the Balinese live in houses surrounded by high walls and narrow doorways. The Tuareg, a Moslem culture in North Africa, wear clothes that cover the entire body except for the eyes. In addition, they wear a sleeveless undergarment and a flowing outer garment that reaches from the shoulder to the ankle. A veil and headdress covers the forehead and bridge over the nose that are worn continuously throughout one's life. Altman suggests that the veil is not unlike a door that allows some to enter and keeps others out.[78]

Hesselink, Mullen, and Rouse have studied privacy in Moroccan culture. They claim that Moroccans value privacy as a way of protecting themselves from the external environment. Moroccans keep private the things they value most. The outside surface of Moroccan homes, for example, is very plain so as to expose little information about the people who live there. Hesselink notes that the walls of the homes are so tall that the only way to see into a home is to walk from the rooftop of one house to another. Moroccan women are also considered private and are hidden when males who are not a part of the immediate family enter a Moroccan home.[79]

The built environment is only one way a culture defines its communication with others. The way in which a particular culture achieves privacy involves a complex formula of environmental, verbal, nonverbal, and cultural factors. Focusing on only one of these dimensions provides a distorted view of the privacy regulation system of any culture.

MONOCHRONIC VERSUS POLYCHRONIC TIME ORIENTATION

In addition to its physical and spatial components, the built environment also contains a perceptual-temporal feature. Human communication occurs in a physical space and *perceptual time*. Edward Hall is well known for his discussion of time across cultures. As Hall asserts,

> Time talks. It speaks more plainly than words. The message it conveys comes through loud and clear. Because it is manipulated less consciously, it is subject to less distortion than the spoken language. It can shout truth where words lie.[80]

Like other components of the environment, the perception and use of time is cultural. Unlike other elements of the built environment, time is not physical or tangible; it is a *psychological* component of the environment. Regarding time, Hall categorizes cultures as either monochronic or polychronic. Monochronic- and polychronic-oriented cultures organize time and space differently. According to Hall, monochronic (M-time) orientations emphasize schedules—the compartmentalization and segmentation of measurable units of time. Conversely, polychronic (P-time) orientations see time as much less tangible and stress multiple activities with little emphasis on scheduling. P-time cultures stress involvement of people and the completion of tasks as opposed to a strict adherence to schedules. Hall maintains that the two orientations are incompatible.[81]

In M-time cultures, such as the United States, time is thought of as almost physical, like something you can touch and hold in your hand. Time is treated like money. We talk of saving, spending, wasting, and losing time. Hall argues that for M-time people, time is linear and compartmentalized into discrete units (e.g., minutes, hours, days, and so on). The schedule is paramount in monochronic cultures. In M-time cultures, scheduling dictates just about every activity of every day. But in some ways scheduling is like a computer program, specifying what actions will be performed while prohibiting others. Moreover, asserts Hall, scheduling allows only a limited number of activities to be performed in one place at one time. In M-time cultures, people are concerned with doing only one activity at a time. We have often said aloud that "I can only do one thing at a time!"[82]

Hall explains that by its very nature, scheduling segments people from one another and dictates how people conduct their relationships. Because time is viewed as so valuable, people with the most power and prestige are given the most time (and space) and are allowed more flexibility and less accountability with their time. Physicians, for example, are routinely late for appointments without sanction. Late or "no show" patients, on the other hand, may pay heavily for their inconsideration of the physician's time.

Hall maintains that although an M-time orientation is learned and completely arbitrary, it becomes so ingrained in people that they have no other way of thinking about their world. At an early age, children are taught the importance of time, scheduling, and promptness. Moreover, they are often punished if they fail to adhere. A child learns when to eat, nap, and play. In schools, subjects are taught at certain times of the day for a specific duration. Through compartmentalizing and segmenting time, a person's day is completely planned and scheduled, including sleep, work, leisure, and even sex. Hall notes that tardiness and missed appointments are a source of extreme anxiety for many M-timers. Hall points out that perhaps the most important consequence of M-time is that it *denies the natural context and progression of human communication*. Rather than completing an assignment or finishing a conversation, scheduling forces people into an artificial pattern and sequence of behavior. Many M-time cultures are low context, including the United States, Germany, Scandinavia, Canada, France, and most of northern Europe.[83]

On the other hand, Hall argues that in P-time cultures, schedules are not important and are frequently broken. Polychronic people can do many things at once, and relationships take priority over schedules. P-timers are often distractible and tolerant of interruptions. In P-time cultures, time is not thought of as tangible and a person may be engaged in several activities, in the same space with several people, simultaneously. P-time people are more interested in completing the task at hand than leaving it because of some predetermined schedule. Hall contends that P-time cultures are not slaves to schedules and are frequently late for appointments or may not show up at all. The guiding principle behind polychronic cultures is that the natural context, *in the present,* guides behavior. Many P-time cultures are high context, including southern Europe, Latin America, and many African and Middle Eastern countries.[84]

Consequences of Monochronic and Polychronic Orientations. Monochronic people have a particularly difficult time adjusting to poly-chronic-oriented cultures. To an M-timer, people in P-time cultures may appear disorganized or even lazy. Harris and Moran warn American busi-nesspersons traveling to Arab countries that they may find themselves wait-ing for days or even weeks to meet with their Middle Eastern affiliates. "Bukra insha Allah," meaning "tomorrow if God wills," is a favorite expres-sion of the traditional Arab. Unlike M-timers, Arabs believe that time is con-trolled by Allah. Hence, when trying to schedule an appointment, the Arab may respond "insha Allah," or "if Allah wills," and he means this quite liter-ally. To the Arab, a person who tries to influence the future via scheduling is either insane or irreligious.[85]

M-time and P-time cultures organize their space in much the same way as their time. Hence, the M-timer has a specific space set aside for specific activities, and, generally, these are the only activities allowed in that space. In M-time office buildings, for example, people have their own private offices to conduct their business. Likewise, in P-time cultures, where multi-ple activities occur simultaneously, multiple activities are conducted in the same place. Keberlein describes the inside of the municipal building in a small Guatemala town that has no interior walls to cordon off people from each other. Instead the building is one large room where all of the town's municipal needs are handled. There may be one desk surrounded by many people vying for the attention of the local mayor, who seems to be interact-ing with two or three people simultaneously. No lines are formed, and people compete for the mayor's attention. The mayor probably is a very important and informed person in this town.[86] Hall has observed that in many P-time cultures there is a defined centralization of bureaucratic con-trol. This is because the leaders interact with many people, and the people are informed because they interact with each other. Polychronic people tend to be well informed of each other's business. Hall argues that their involvement with each other is the essence of their existence. Consequently P-time bureaucracies can be slow and difficult to penetrate unless one knows an "insider."[87]

A similar contrast can be seen in the homes of M-time and P-time cul-tures. In most M-time cultures, the home is carefully planned and organized. The home is compartmentalized with individual rooms, each with its specific purpose (e.g., kitchen, dining room, bedroom, laundry room, bathroom). Many P-time homes, on the other hand, may be defined by one large living area. In traditional Japanese homes, for example, the main living area is a single room where the entire family eats, sleeps, and interacts as a group.

Some cultures possess elements of both M-time and P-time. Vandehey, Buerger, and Krueger explain that the Masai, a nomadic culture of Kenya, do not compartmentalize time into seconds, minutes, and hours, but instead have specific periods of the day that are scheduled around the rising and setting sun and the feeding of their cattle. The typical Masai day begins just prior to sunrise when the cattle go to the river to drink. This period is called "The Red Blood Period" because of the color of the sunrise. The afternoon consists of a period of time when the "shadows lower themselves." The evening begins when the cattle return from the river.[88]

According to Vandehey and her colleagues, the Masai have a unique way of classifying people by age. Rather than using a calendar of years, as most cultures do, the Masai belong to age sets. One's age set determines his or her privileges and responsibilities. Instead of a calendar, the Masai measure time periods by seasons and months whose duration is determined by rainfall. Although the Masai compartmentalize time into months, they are not restricted to any set time. For example, a particular month lasts as long as the rains continue. A new month does not begin until the rains have ceased.[89]

AN INTERCULTURAL CONVERSATION: MONOCHRONIC AND POLYCHRONIC CULTURES

Mr. Paul Bersik is the international sales representative for his computer equipment company. His most recent trip takes him to Saudi Arabia, where he is scheduled to meet with his Saudi counterpart, Abdul Arami. In the following scenario, Mr. Bersik comes face to face with P-time. Mr. Bersik and his training team arrived in Saudi Arabia three days ago for a scheduled appointment with Mr. Arami. Mr. Arami had not yet met with Mr. Bersik or his team. Finally, a call to Mr. Bersik's hotel room indicates that Mr. Arami is prepared to meet with him. When he arrives at the location, Mr. Bersik is asked to wait outside Mr. Arami's office. As he waits he notices many people entering and leaving Mr. Arami's office at a very quick pace. The hallways of this building are a hustle and bustle of activity with people shuffling in and out of many rooms. Finally, after several hours, Mr. Bersik is called in to meet Mr. Arami.[90]

Mr. Bersik: *Ah, Mr. Arami, it's so good to finally see you. Gosh, I've been waiting for days. Did you forget our appointment?*

Mr. Arami: *Hello Mr. Bersik, please sit down. Everything is fine?*

Mr. Bersik: *Actually no . . . (phone rings) . . . the problem is . . .*

Mr. Arami: *Excuse me . . .* (takes the phone call and speaks in Arabic. After several minutes he concludes the phone conversation) *Yes, now . . . everything is fine?*

Mr. Bersik: *Well, actually, I've got a small problem. You see the computer equipment you ordered . . .* (a staff person enters the room and hands Mr. Arami something to sign).

Mr. Arami: *Oh, excuse me* (signs the document). *Yes, now, everything is fine?*

Mr. Bersik: *As I was saying . . . all of the computer equipment you ordered is just sitting on a ship in the dock. I need your help in getting it unloaded. I mean it's been there for two weeks!*

Mr. Arami: *Hmmm. I see . . . This is no problem.*

Mr. Bersik: *Well, if it sits in the heat much longer it could be damaged. Could I get you to sign a work order to have it unloaded by Friday?*

Mr. Arami: *There is no need for that. The job will get done, insha Allah.*

Mr. Bersik: *Well, could we set up some kind of deadline? You see, I have a staff of people here waiting to train your people on the equipment. I need to let them know when it will be ready. How about this Friday? Could we do it then? My people are here now and they're waiting to begin training.*

Mr. Arami: *There is no great rush. We have lived for many generations without this equipment. We can wait a few more weeks, if necessary. This is not a problem.* (Two men enter the room and begin a conversation with Mr. Arami.)

There is little chance that Mr. Arami will sign any kind of work order for Mr. Bersik. Within the context of the Saudi culture, Mr. Bersik's behavior is inappropriate. His emphasis on deadlines is perceived by Mr. Arami as either insane or irreligious. Mr. Bersik is also distressed by the constant interruptions. To Mr. Arami, Mr. Bersik is in too much of a hurry. When Mr. Arami says to Mr. Bersik that the job will get done "insha Allah," he means it quite literally. Unless God decrees it, a plan or schedule is useless. In the future, Mr. Bersik must learn that the Saudi's perception of time is very different from his own. Mr. Bersik is monochronic, whereas Mr. Arami is polychronic. When he does business in Saudi Arabia, Mr. Bersik must understand the temporal feature of the culture.

SELF-ASSESSMENT 4.2

Assessing Time Orientation

Below is a scale designed by Charles Phipps. The scale is designed to measure one's monochronic and/or polychronic time orientation. In the blank before each item, indicate the degree to which you (1) strongly agree, (2) agree, (3) are neutral, (4) disagree, or (5) disagree with the statement. There are no right or wrong answers, and many of the statements are similar; this is by design. Work quickly and record your first impression.[91]

1. _____ I usually feel frustrated after I choose to do a number of tasks when I could have chosen to do one at a time.

2. _____ When I talk with my friends in a group setting, I feel comfortable trying to hold two or three conversations at a time.

3. _____ When I work on a project around the house, it doesn't bother me to stop in the middle of one job to pick up another job that needs to be done.

4. _____ I like to finish one task before going on to another task.

5. _____ At church it wouldn't bother me to meet at the same time with several different people who all had different church matters to discuss.

6. _____ I tend to concentrate on one job before moving on to another task.

7. _____ The easiest way for me to function is to organize my day with activities with a schedule.

8. _____ If I were a teacher and had several students wishing to talk with me about assigned homework, I would meet with the whole group rather than one student at a time.

9. _____ I like doing several tasks at one time.

10. _____ I am frustrated when I have to start on a task without first finishing a previous one.

11. _____ In trying to solve problems, I find it stimulating to think about several different problems at the same time.

12. _____ I am mildly irritated when someone in a meeting wants to bring up a personal topic that is unrelated to the purpose of the meeting.

13. _____ In school, I prefer studying one subject to completion before going on to the next subject.

14. _____ I'm hesitant to focus my attention on only one thing because I may miss something equally important.

15. _____ I usually need to pay attention to only one task at a time to finish it.

Scoring: For items 2, 3, 5, 8, 9, and 11, reverse your response: (5 = 1), (4 = 2), (3 = 3), (2 = 4), or (5 = 1). For example, if your response to Item #2 was 5, reverse it to 1. If your response to Item #3 was 4, reverse it to a 2. Once you have reversed your responses to those six items, sum the scores of all 15 items. Scores of approximately 30 and below indicate a monochronic orientation. Scores of approximately 42 and above indicate a polychronic orientation.

CHAPTER SUMMARY

The relationship between humans and their environment is complex. By its very nature the environment, natural or built, is loaded with information. How that information is perceived and processed is strongly influenced by culture and can dramatically affect communication. In this chapter we saw that cultures vary considerably with how they view the natural environment. Some see the environment as a dominating force, one that cannot be harnessed. Other cultures prefer a balancing act between the environment and their needs. These cultures try to co-exist with nature peacefully. Still others see nature as a slave and try to control and rule it. Whether dominated by it, living in harmony with it, or treating it as a slave, humans are in constant interaction with their environment. As the contextual model of intercultural communication shows, all human communication exists within some kind of environment. Most human communication occurs within a built environment. The built environment is specifically designed to either restrict or facilitate human interaction. How a culture designs its built environment says much about how it approaches communication, especially through its housing. Understanding how cultures manage the built and home environments leads one to a better understanding of cultures and to be a more competent intercultural communicator.

This chapter also discussed issues of privacy. People of all cultures have an innate inclination to affiliate and communicate with other human beings. At the same time, however, people cannot tolerate extended physical contact with others and develop a need for privacy. The degree to which one senses privacy is learned and varies from culture to culture. Finally, this chapter described two orientations toward the perceptual environmental variable of time: monochronic and polychronic. Monochronic orientations emphasize schedules, the compartmentalization and segmentation of measurable units of time, and promptness. Conversely, polychronic orientations see time as much less tangible and stress multiple activities at once with little emphasis on scheduling. P-time cultures stress involvement of people and the completion of tasks as opposed to a strict adherence to artificial schedules. The natural, built, and perceptual aspects of the environment are pervasive influences on how people communicate with each other. Moreover, our perceptions of the environment are largely molded by our culture.

GLOSSARY OF TERMS

Built Environment: Adaptations to the terrestrial environment, including architecture, housing, lighting, and landscaping.

Fixed-Feature Space: Space bounded by immovable or permanent fixtures, such as walls.

High Load: Situation with a high information rate.

Informal Space: Space defined by the movement of the interactants.

Information Rate: The amount of information contained or perceived in the physical environment per some unit of time.

Low Load: Situation with a low information rate.

Monochronic Time Orientation: Cultural temporal orientation that stresses the compartmentalization and segmenting of measurable units of time.

Polychronic Time Orientation: Cultural temporal orientation that stresses the involvement of people and the completion of tasks as opposed to strict adherence to schedules. Time is not seen as measurable.

Privacy: The degree to which an individual can control the visual, auditory, and olfactic interaction with others.

Semifixed-Feature Space: Space bounded by movable objects such as furniture.

Terrestrial Environment: The physical geography of the Earth.

REFERENCES

1. Stein, H. F. (1987). *Developmental Time, Cultural Space*. Norman: University of Oklahoma Press.
2. Although different, the idea to compare two scenarios is adapted from Mehrabian, A. (1976). *Public Places and Private Spaces: The Psychology of Work, Play, and Living Arrangements*. New York: Basic Books.

3. Stein, *Developmental Time, Cultural Space.*
4. Mehrabian, *Public Places and Private Spaces.*
5. Ibid.
6. Ibid.
7. Ibid.
8. Ibid.
9. Lang, J. (1987). *Creating Architectural Theory: The Role of the Behavioral Sciences in Environmental Design.* New York: Van Nostrand Reinhold.
10. Knopf, R. C. (1987). "Human Behavior, Cognitions, and Affect in the Natural Environment." In D. Stokols & I. Altman (Eds.), *Handbook of Environmental Psychology* (Vol. 1, pp. 783–826). New York: Wiley.
11. Wibisono, A. K., & Schultz, W. (1996). *Cultural Examination of Indonesia.* Unpublished student manuscript, St. Norbert College, DePere, WI; Safra, J. E. (1997). "Indonesia." *The New Encyclopedia Britannica,* (Vol. 6, pp. 298–299). Chicago: Encyclopedia Britannica.
12. Thao, K. (1995). *The Hmong Culture.* Unpublished student manuscript, St. Norbert College, DePere, WI; Yang, D. (1993). *Hmong at the Turning Point.* Minneapolis, MN: Worldbridge Associates.
13. Bichler, S., Jaeger, R., & Schiefelbein, B. (1996). *Life and Culture in South Yemen.* Unpublished student manuscript, St. Norbert College, DePere, WI; Nyrop, R. F. (Ed.). (1986). *The Yemens: Country Studies.* Washington, DC: U.S. Government Printing Office.
14. Westfahl, G., Koltz, R., & Manders, A. (1996). *Ethnic Russian Culture and Society.* Unpublished student manuscript, St. Norbert College, DePere, WI; Shoemaker, M. W. (1996). *Russia, Eurasian States, and Eastern Europe: 1996.* Harpers Ferry, WV: Stryler-Post.
15. Yurkovich, D., Pliscott, K., & Halverson, R. (1996). *The Norwegian Culture.* Unpublished student manuscript, St. Norbert College, DePere, WI; Central Intelligence Agency. (1995). *The World Fact Book.* Washington, DC: U.S. Government Printing Office.
16. Lang, *Creating Architectural Theory.*
17. Kluckhohn, F. R. (1953). "Dominant and Variant Value Orientations." In Kluckhohn, C., Murray, H. A., & Schneider, D. M. (Eds.), *Personality in Nature, Culture and Society* (pp. 342–357). New York: Knopf.
18. Altman, I., & Chemers, N. M. (1980). "Cultural Aspects of the Environment-Behavior Relationship." In Triandis, H. C., & Brislin, R. W. (Eds.), *Handbook of Cross-Cultural Psychology* (Vol. 5, pp. 335–394). Boston: Allyn & Bacon.
19. Bishop, R. J. (1995). *Cultural Profile, Examination of Value Orientations and Sociocultural Influences, and Verbal And Nonverbal Language Aspects of the East Indian Culture.* Unpublished manuscript, St. Norbert College, DePere, WI; Srinivasan, R. (1951). *India.* New York: Marshall Cavendish; Harris, P. R., & Moran, R. T. (1996). *Managing Cultural Differences* (4th ed.). Houston, TX: Gulf.
20. Kluckhohn, "Dominant and Variant Value Orientations."

21. Rieck, S., & Ogura, M. (1996). *Sri Lanka: The Pearl of the Indian Ocean.* Unpublished student manuscript, St. Norbert College, DePere, WI; Borden, G. A., Conaway, W. A., & Morrison, T. (1993). *Kiss, Bow, or Shake Hands.* Holbrook, MA: Bob Adams, Inc.

22. Altman and Chemers, "Cultural Aspects of the Environment-Behavior Relationship."

23. Kluckhohn, "Dominant and Variant Value Orientations."

24. Altman and Chemers, "Cultural Aspects of the Environment-Behavior Relationship"; Thorne, R., & Hall, R. (1987). "Environmental Psychology in Australia." In D. Stokols & I Altman (Eds.), *Handbook of Environmental Psychology* (Vol. 2, pp. 1137–1154). New York: Wiley.

25. Sorenson, J. H., & White, G. F. (1980). "Natural Disasters: A Cross-Cultural Perspective." In I. Altman, A. Rapoport, & J. F. Wohlwill (Eds.), *Human Behavior and Environment: Advances in Theory and Research* (Vol. 4: Environment and culture, pp. 279–318). New York: Plenum.

26. Ibid.

27. Ibid.

28. Lang, *Creating Architectural Theory;* Rapoport, A. (1980). "Cross-Cultural Aspects of Environmental Design." In I. Altman, A. Rapoport, & J. F. Wohlwill (Eds.), *Human Behavior and Environment: Advances in Theory and Research* (pp. 7–46). New York: Plenum.

29. Rapoport, A. (1969). *House Form and Culture.* Englewood Cliffs, NJ: Prentice-Hall.

30. Lang, *Creating Architectural Theory.*

31. Hall, E. T. (1966). *The Hidden Dimension.* New York: Doubleday.

32. Lang, *Creating Architectural Theory.*

33. Hall, *The Hidden Dimension;* Altman, I., & Vinsel, A. M. (1977). "Personal Space: An Analysis of E. T. Hall's Proxemics Framework." In I. Altman & J. F. Wohlwill (Eds.), *Human Behavior and Environment: Advances in Theory and Research* (Vol. 2, pp. 181–260). New York: Plenum.

34. Hall, *The Hidden Dimension.*

35. Lustig, M. W., & Koester, J. (1996). *Intercultural Competence: Interpersonal Communication Across Cultures* (2nd ed.). New York: HarperCollins.

36. For an excellent summary of research related to personal space across cultures, see Aiello, J. (1987). "Human Spatial Behavior." In D. Stokols & I. Altman (Eds.), *Handbook of Environmental Psychology* (Vol. 1. pp. 389–504). New York: Wiley.

37. Hagino, G., Mochizuki, M., & Yamamoto, T. (1987). "Environmental Psychology in Japan." In D. Stokols & I. Altman (Eds.), *Handbook of Environmental Psychology* (Vol. 2, pp. 1155–1170). New York: Wiley.

38. Sieke, K., & Terry, C. S. (1970). *Contemporary Japanese Houses.* Tokyo: Kodansha.

39. Ibid, (pp. 11–12).

40. Ueda, A. (1990). *The Inner Harmony of the Japanese House.* Tokyo: Kodansha.

41. Yoshida, T. (1969). *The Japanese House and Garden.* London: Pall Mall Press.

42. Ibid.

43. Ueda, *The Inner Harmony of the Japanese House.*

44. Ibid.

45. Ueda, *The Inner Harmony of the Japanese House;* Yoshida, *The Japanese House and Garden.*

46. Ueda, *The Inner Harmony of the Japanese House,* (p. 9).

47. Kent, S. (1984). *Analyzing Activity Areas: An Ethnoarchaeological Study of the Use of Space.* Albuquerque, NM: University of New Mexico Press.

48. Though not an exact duplication, this graphic is based on those present in Kent's *Analyzing Activity Areas.*

49. Kent, *Analyzing Activity Areas.*

50. Ibid.

51. Ibid.

52. Moore, H. L. (1986). *Space, Text and Gender: An Anthropological Study of the Marakwet of Kenya.* Cambridge, UK: Cambridge University Press.

53. Ibid.

54. Ibid., (p. 45).

55. Ibid.

56. Though not an exact duplication, Figure 4.4 is based on Moore's.

57. Ibid.

58. Ibid.

59. Burgoon, J. K. (1978). "A Communication Model of Personal Space Violations: Explication and an Initial Test." *Human Communication Research, 4*(2), 129–142.

60. Westin, A. F. (1967). *Privacy and Freedom.* New York: Atheneum.

61. Altman, I. (1977). "Privacy Regulation: Culturally Universal or Culturally Specific?" *Journal of Social Issues, 83*(3), 66–84.

62. Westin, *Privacy and Freedom.*

63. Gandy, O. H. (1993). "African-Americans and Privacy: Understanding the Black Perspective in the Emerging Policy Debate." *Journal of Black Studies, 42*(2), 178–195.

64. Lang, *Creating Architectural Theory.*

65. Westin, *Privacy and Freedom.*

66. Ibid.

67. Pedersen, D. M. (1979). "Dimensions of Privacy." *Perceptual and Motor Skills, 48,* 1291–1297.

68. Ibid. Reprinted by permission.

69. Calvert, C. *Voyeur Nation: Media, Privacy, and Peering in Modern Culture* (Boulder, CO: Westview Press, 2000). Stepp, C. S. "Playing at Peeping Tom," *American Journalism Review,* 23, (2001), 58.

70. Quittner, J., & Dowell, W. "Invasion of Privacy" *Time,* 150, (1997), 28–36.

71. Ibid.

72. Burd, S. "Colleges Allowed to Tell Parents About Alcohol Use." *Chronicle of Higher Education,* 46, (2000) A31; Reisberg, L. "2 Years After Colleges Started Calling Home, Administrators Say Alcohol Policy Works." *Chronicle of Higher Education,* 47 (2001), A34.

73. Gandy, "African-Americans and Privacy."

74. Pedersen, D. M., & Frances, S. (1990). "Regional Differences in Privacy Preferences." *Psychological Reports, 66,* 731–736.

75. Rustemli, A., & Kokdemir, D. (1993). "Privacy Dimensions and Preferences Among Turkish Students." *Journal of Social Psychology, 133*(6), 807–814.

76. Westin, *Privacy and Freedom.*

77. Altman, Privacy regulation: Culturally universal or culturally specific? (pp. 66–84).; Roberts, J. M. & Gregor, T. A. (1971). Privacy: A cultural view. In J. R. Pennock & J. W. Chapman (Eds.), *Privacy.* New York: Atherton Press.

78. Altman, "Privacy Regulation."

79. Hesselink, R. C., Mullen, R. T., & Rouse, J. M. (1996). *Moroccan Culture: An In-Depth Study.* Unpublished manuscript, St. Norbert College, DePere, WI; Bowles, P. (1993). *Morocco.* New York: Harry N. Abrams, Inc.; Seward, P. (1995). *Cultures of the World: Morocco.* New York: Marshall Cavendish; Overview of Islamic Architecture [online]. Available: http://venture.cob.ohio-state.edu:1111/khalid/pages/archtcre/ overview.htm

80. Hall, *The Silent Language* (quote on p. 15).

81. Hall, E. T. (1983). *The Dance of Life.* New York: Doubleday; Hall, *The Silent Language.*

82. Ibid.

83. Ibid.

84. Ibid.

85. Harris and Moran, *Managing Cultural Differences.*

86. Keberlein, M. C. G. (1993). *A Cultural Profile of the Guatemalan Ladinos.* Unpublished manuscript, St. Norbert College, DePere, WI.

87. Hall, *The Silent Language.*

88. Vandehey, K., Buerger, C., & Krueger, K. (1996). *Traditional Aspects and Struggles of the Masai Culture.* Unpublished manuscript, St. Norbert College, DePere, WI; Hollis, A. C. (1995). *The Masai: Their Language and Folklore.* (Rev. Ed.), New York: Clarendon Press.

89. Ibid.

90. Although different, the model for the dialogue is adapted from Copeland, L. (Producer). *Managaing the Overseas Assignment* [videorecording]. San Francisco: Copeland Griggs, 1982.

91. This scale was developed by Charles A. Phipps as a part of his Senior Honors Thesis titled "The Measurement of Monochronic and Polychronic Cognitions Among Hispanics and Anglos," Abilene Christian University, 1987.

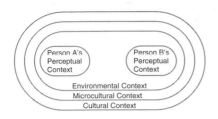

CHAPTER 5

The Perceptual Context

*"It seems to me that we have sound reasons for thus considering
theoretical knowledge as more objective than immediate experience."*

—Michael Polyani[1]

Chapter Objectives

After reading this chapter, you should be able to

1. List and discuss the three stages of human information processing.
2. Discuss cross-cultural differences in perception.
3. Define and discuss short- and long-term memory.
4. Discuss cross-cultural differences in memory and recall.
5. Define and discuss at least four types of mental categories.
6. Define and discuss racial and ethnic stereotypes.
7. Identify and discuss at least two reasons why people stereotype.
8. Define and discuss the nature of ethnocentrism.
9. Define and discuss the nature of racism.

Consider the following interaction between Jim, an American college student, and Olga, a Ukrainian exchange student studying at the same college as Jim in the United States.

Jim: *Ya know, Olga, I've been thinking about America's involvement in the war in Afghanistan. I see reports of people starving and dying and it's just so depressing. I hope this is over soon.*

Olga: *Yes, I know, it's a terrible thing. My country has experienced a lot of starvation and war.*

Jim: *Really?*

Olga: *Oh yes. My country has been fought over and suppressed for centuries. We gained our independence from Russia for a short time between 1917–1920, but that was followed by ruthless Soviet rule that was responsible for two famines in which over 8 million people died. Can you relate to that, Jim? And then World War II, where the German and Soviet armies killed some 7 million of my people. So in the 20th century alone, over 15 million people died, some say for no good reason.*

Jim: *I had no idea. I can't imagine how that makes you feel.*

Olga: *Right, I understand. Our history gives my people a whole different perspective on life and how we see and live our lives. It's almost impossible to not carry a little sadness in our hearts.*

Jim: *My generation has never experienced anything like that. This is brand new to us. It's very confusing.*

Whenever two people come together and interact, like Jim and Olga, they process great quantities of information. In addition to the cultural, microcultural, and environmental contexts influencing their interaction, Jim and Olga both bring with them their unique perceptual experiences. The perceptual context refers to how people take in, store, and recall information. In this brief conversation, Jim and Olga encode, decode, and interpret a vast amount of information about themselves, their culture's histories, current events, their surroundings, and each other. Because they come from different cultures, they see the world differently. Their interpretation of world events differs dramatically. Intercultural communication is a process of connecting perceptual contexts.

The higher mental processes required for human communication include the gathering, storing, and retrieval of information. Although human information processing is a universal phenomenon, it is influenced by culture. This chapter is about the higher mental activities of the individual that constitute the perceptual context of intercultural communication. In addition to the cultural, microcultural, and environmental contexts, the perceptual context affects how people interact. Every time we enter into a communicative exchange with someone, we bring with us a perceptual frame of reference through which all of our messages are filtered. The cultural, microcultural, environmental, and perceptual contexts are interdependent influences that combined in a complex formula and that ultimately define our interaction with others.

From an information-processing perspective, the human mind is seen as a complex information-processing system that takes in, stores, and retrieves information. The first part of this chapter introduces the idea of culture and cognition and outlines a model of human information processing. The second part of the chapter explains a common form of information processing called categorization. The third part of the chapter focuses on two attitudinal dimensions of information-processing: stereotyping and ethnocentrism. The overall purpose of the chapter is to explain how the human mind processes information during communication, especially intercultural communication.

CULTURE AND COGNITION

People from different cultures think about different things. The Aleutian Eskimos of western Alaska and the Marakwet tribe in western Kenya think about different things because of the extreme differences in their natural environments. Moreover, people from different cultures think differently about their life experiences. The life experiences of a Guatemalan Ladino are markedly different from those of a Ukrainian. Few people question that the content of thought for people in different cultures varies. What is open to speculation, however, is whether higher mental processes, such as perception and remembering, differ across cultures. How much do the cultural, microcultural, and environmental contexts affect how the human brain processes information?

A Model of Human Information Processing

Roy Lachman and his colleagues maintain that when it comes to processing information, the human mind is analogous to a computer. Information is entered, stored, and retrieved in a sequence of stages where each stage performs a specific operation on the information.[2] According to Lachman, Lachman, and Butterfield, during Stage 1, the input stage, information is taken in via the senses, attended to, and then interpreted. In the storage stage, information is held in short-term and long-term memory. During the retrieval stage, information is recalled. In order for people to communicate with each other, in any culture, they are required to take in, store, and recall information. Although these stages are probably universal, culture influences the specific strategies and styles of processing information in each stage.

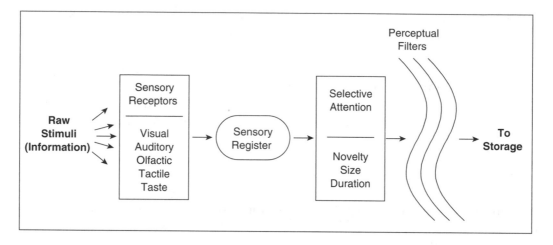

Figure 5.2

Stage #1: Input. The first stage of information processing is the input stage where information is taken in and interpreted, and Figure 5.2 represents this process. This is the stage where raw information is taken in through the senses and interpreted by the brain. The essential cognitive process during this stage is *perception.* Margaret Matlin defines perception as the mental interpretation of external stimuli via sensation.[3]

According to Matlin, at any given point in time, especially during human communication, human beings are bombarded with external stimuli. Humans take in visual stimuli with their eyes, auditory stimuli with their ears, olfactic stimuli with their nose, taste stimuli with their mouth, and tactile stimuli through the skin (see Figure 5.3).

Although humans tend to favor visual and auditory sensations, olfactic, tactile, and taste sensations are very informative as well. Although most stimuli come from external sources, information can come from within the human processor as well. During intercultural communication many of the stimuli come from the cultural, microcultural, and environmental context. Matlin maintains that at the point of sensation, the external stimuli are raw and unprocessed. At the very moment the stimuli are sensed, they are transferred to a sensory register, which holds the unprocessed stimuli for a very short period of time until they can be further processed and interpreted. Matlin points out that information in the sensory register is a nearly literal record of its sensory image. The entry of information into the sensory register is passive and is lost very quickly.[4] Visual sensory memory (called iconic memory) can be demonstrated by taking a flashlight into a dark room.

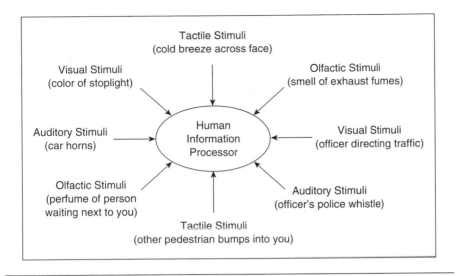

Figure 5.3

Holding the flashlight firm and pointing it at a wall, make a circular motion with the flashlight in such a way as to produce a "circle" of light on the wall. You can actually see the complete circle even though the light is only at one physical location on the wall at any time. Tactile sensory memory can be easily demonstrated by loudly clapping the hands. The clap can be felt after the completion of the act.[5]

The sensory register holds stimuli long enough for an individual to decide which stimuli to process further and which to ignore. This is the attention phase of perception, where the human processor becomes conscious of the incoming stimuli. During the attention phase, the individual selects which information to process further. Because the person is bombarded with so many stimuli, only certain kinds will be attended to while others will be ignored. According to Jim McCroskey and Virginia Richmond, for example, novel or unusual stimuli generally attract attention. Hence, interacting with someone from a different culture may heighten one's attention span. If you have ever walked through the international terminal of a major airport, you may have found yourself staring at people you considered "different" or "unusual." If the cultural or environmental context is unusual or new, an individual may sense information overload. Although there may not be any more stimuli in one context than another, the novelty of one context may lead one to think there are more stimuli. This may account for why entering a new culture may be overwhelming to some. McCroskey and Richmond point out that the size of the stimuli also affects attention; generally, the larger the stimulus, the more likely one is to attend to it. Finally, the duration of the stimuli will also affect one's attention. Stimuli that fade quickly may not be attended to while stimuli that last for excessively long periods of time may eventually be ignored.[6]

Immediately after information passes through the sensory register and is attended to, it passes through perceptual filters. Perceptual filters alter and change how humans interpret incoming information. According to Blaine Goss, people filter information physiologically, sociologically, and psychologically.[7] Physiological filters include the natural or genetic differences in how one sees, hears, smells, tastes, or feels. For example, eyesight varies considerably from person to person. Many people are required to wear eyeglasses to accommodate for poor visual sensation. When light waves are sensed by the eye, they are transmitted via the optical nerve to the brain. The brain then interprets the stimuli. The eyes of a nearsighted person sense visual stimuli (i.e., lightwaves) differently from the eyes of a farsighted person. Hence, the brain of the nearsighted person interprets the stimuli differently from the brain of a farsighted person. People everywhere have natural physiological differences in their ability to see, hear, taste, touch, and smell incoming stimuli.

Sociological filters represent demographic data and one's membership in groups, including one's culture, microculture, and hometown, for example. The groups to which people belong influence how they perceive incoming stimuli. For example, in the National Football League, a fierce rivalry exists between the Chicago Bears and the Green Bay Packers. People from Chicago and Green Bay view their respective football teams differently. In the last seconds of a game played several years ago, the quarterback for the Green Bay Packers threw a touchdown pass that would have won the game for the Packers. A penalty was called on the play indicating that the quarterback had stepped over the line of scrimmage—a violation of the rules that nullifies the winning touchdown. Upon further review, the penalty was reversed, the touchdown was counted, and Green Bay won the game. Chicago fans were outraged because they were convinced the quarterback had crossed the scrimmage line. Packer fans were joyous because they could see that he had not crossed the line. Even to this day, Chicago fans watching replays of that play are certain the quarterback crossed the line while Green Bay fans, watching the very same replay, are equally convinced he did not. Both sets of fans perceiving the very same play have very different perceptions.

The third set of filters outlined by Goss is psychological filters, which include the attitudes, beliefs, and dispositions of the individual. A person's likes, dislikes, and beliefs about what is right or wrong filter the perception of incoming stimuli. If someone has a negative attitude about a professor, he or she may perceive that class as especially boring or uninformative. If people believe that abortion is immoral, then they may perceive an abortion rights speaker as unattractive. At the point of passing through the perceptual filters, the information is no longer considered raw and unprocessed. Although all of us are bombarded with the same visual, auditory, tactile, olfactic, and taste stimuli, our sensations and perceptions of those stimuli will differ considerably, especially if we come from different cultures.

Cross-Cultural Differences in Sensation and Perception

Data from some studies suggest that people differ across cultures in their ability to gather incoming information. John Berry and his associates outline four explanations for cross-cultural differences in the perception of sensory stimuli: (a) conditions of the physical environment, (b) indirect environmental conditions, (c) genetic differences, and (d) cultural differences in how people interact with their environment.[8] Regarding conditions in the physical environment, in the early 1970s Reuning and Wortley conducted a cross-cultural study on auditory acuity (i.e., sharpness). In their comparison of Kalahari Bushmen, Danish, and American subjects, they found less hearing loss in the Kalahari sample than in the Danish or American samples, particularly among older subjects. Reuning and Wortley attributed their findings to low levels of ambient noise in the Kalahari desert region. They also cited other studies that found a slower loss of hearing in nonindustrialized societies. This may suggest that environmental noise, such as that heard in industrialized societies, may have a negative effect on hearing.[9]

In his study, Wyndham attributed an indirect environmental factor, specifically poor nutrition, as the reason for slower dark adaptation among Black South African miners than among Whites. Wyndham found that it took longer for the eyes of Black miners to adapt to the dark conditions than for white miners. Wyndham suggests that many of the Black mine workers might suffer from forms of liver ailments, which in turn were associated with nutritional deficiencies in early childhood.[10]

Berry and his associates argue that genetic factors seem to account for red-green color-blindness, taste-blindness, and the "alcoholic flush" phenomenon. Many studies have demonstrated that the frequency of red-green color blindness is much lower in non-Caucasian groups than among Caucasians. Approximately 30 percent of all Caucasians are taste blind to certain substances that taste bitter to Africans and Native American Indians. The alcoholic flush, a reddening of the face after consuming only a few alcoholic drinks, is much more common in Asian populations than in Caucasians.[11]

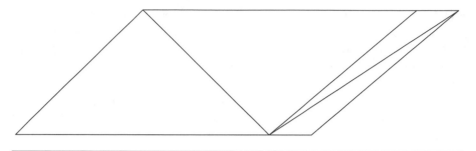

Figure 5.4   The Sander parallelogram

According to Berry, one's experience and enculturation with the environment play a role in sensory stimulation. People can be conditioned to prefer and select some stimuli over others. Children are taught to pay attention to certain kinds of stimuli. Africans, for example, tend to excel in auditory tasks, whereas Europeans tend to excel at visual tasks. Cultural groups are taught to favor some sensory receptors over others. These people are called sensotypes; that is, the relative importance of one sensory modality over the others.[12]

An extensive body of cross-cultural research on perception has been conducted by Marshall Segall and his colleagues.[13] Segall believes that repeated experience with perceptual objects affects how those objects are perceived. His study involved the perception of *optical illusions.* Almost 2000 subjects, from fourteen non-Western cultures (mostly in Africa) and three Western cultures, participated in the study. Each participant was shown a series of optical illusions. Segall argued that optical illusions occur because previously learned interpretations of visual cues are misapplied due to unusual or misleading characteristics of stimuli. One hypothesis that explains vulnerability to illusions is called the carpentered world hypothesis.[14]

According to Segall and the carpentered world hypothesis, there is a learned tendency among those raised in an environment shaped by carpenters (e.g., rectangular furniture, houses, right angles) to interpret nonrectangular figures as representations of rectangular figures seen *in perspective.* Segall described this hypothesis by applying it to the Sander parallelogram (see Figure 5.4).

For this drawing, people living in carpentered societies tend to judge the left-most diagonal line within the parallelogram as longer than the two lines on the right side. This is a result of a tendency to perceive a parallelogram drawn on a flat surface as a representation of a rectangular surface extended in space. Here the viewer is actually judging distance covered by

Figure 5.5   The Muller-Lyer Illusion

the left diagonal as greater than the distance covered by the right diagonal. Subjects in Segall's study were also shown the Muller-Lyer illusion (see Figure 5.5).

Again, Segall assumed that people from carpentered societies would perceive the figures as representations of three-dimensional objects, extended in space. For example, these illusions can be found in the corners of rooms extending away from the observer. The figure on the right tends to be interpreted as further away and therefore is seen as longer. The figure on the left is found in corners of objects extending toward the observer, and therefore the line is seen as shorter.

In related research, Dawson, Young, and Choi compared optical illusion susceptibility of Hong Kong Chinese, Americans, and Australian Aboriginal Arunta desert dwellers. In the case of the Muller-Lyer and the Sander parallelogram illusions, the American subjects were the most susceptible, followed by the Chinese, and then the Arunta. With the horizontal/vertical illusion, the Arunta showed the greatest susceptibility, followed by the Americans, and then the Chinese. These results lend support to Segall's carpentered world hypothesis.[15]

Segall spent many years gathering data and found that strong tendency for illusion susceptibility across cultural groups. Although Segall's findings have not gone unchallenged, the general consensus among most cognitive psychologists is that learned experiences do, in fact, affect how people perceive their surroundings. Culturally learned experiences filter how we see, hear, smell, feel, and taste the world around us.[16]

Stage #2: Storage. Lachman, Lachman, and Butterfield argue that once information has passed through the perceptual filters, it is processed into memory. Memory involves maintaining information over time.[17] Memory is required for virtually all human communication. Without the ability to store information over time, we could not communicate with others. Imagine not being able to remember your own name, or recognize your family members. Without memory, you could not read this book, nor would you be able to construct a single spoken sentence! The importance of mem-

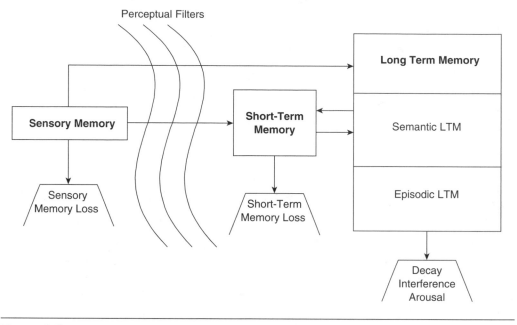

Figure 5.6

ory is why many cultures regard memory as the most important component of human intelligence.

According to Lachman and his colleagues, cognitive psychologists recognize three kinds of memory: sensory register (discussed above), short-term memory, and long-term memory. These three memory stores preserve information in different formats, for different time intervals, and in different ways.[18]

As mentioned above, sensory memory may last only a second or two, and the information is generally stored in its original form. Once the information has passed through the perceptual filters, it travels either directly to long-term memory or through short-term memory (see Figure 5.6). According to Robert Logie, short-term memory, sometimes called working memory or active memory, refers to the cognitive storage area where small amounts of information are held for relatively brief periods of time.[19] In some cases the information is committed to long-term memory, and in many other cases the information is simply lost. The amount of information stored in short-term memory is quite limited. Although psychologists disagree, many concur with George Miller's conclusion that short-term memory is limited to seven items, plus or minus two. In what is now considered a classic article, Miller coined the phrase "The Magical Number Seven Plus or Minus Two" in referring to the storage capacity of short-term memory.[20]

Lachman, Lachman, and Butterfield suggest that short-term memory is relatively fragile. Information held in short-term memory is easily lost due to interference from other information entering the cognitive system or from other external distractions, such as noise. Although short-term memory is temporary, limited, and fragile, it is essential for human communication. Most communicative tasks are entirely dependent on the ability to maintain information for short periods of time, such as reading, writing, listening, and speaking. The ability to finish a spoken sentence is contingent on remembering its first words.[21]

On the other hand, according to Robert Howard, long-term memory is a virtual warehouse of stored information. A major difference between short-term and long-term memory is the duration of storage. Unlike short-term memory, information in long-term memory may be held for a lifetime. People may be able to recall events that took place 30 or 40 years ago. A second major difference between the two stores is their capacity. Whereas the short-term store may be limited to seven items, plus or minus two, the storage capacity in long-term memory is virtually unlimited. Another difference between the two memories is their method of forgetting. Information in short-term memory seems to be lost due to decay; that is, if the information is not used, it simply fades away. Although long-term memories also decay, long-term store seems most disrupted by interference; that is, other information gets in the way of stored information.[22]

Many cognitive psychologists distinguish between two types of long-term memory: episodic long-term memory and semantic long-term memory.[23] According to Endel Tulving, episodic long-term memory refers to that type of stored information pertaining to the unique experiences of the individual. Episodic memory is autobiographical. One's birthday, first-grade teacher, first date, and so on are different for each person and are representative of the type of information stored in episodic long-term memory. On the other hand, according to Tulving, semantic long-term memory preserves a person's general conceptual information, world knowledge, and language abilities. How to spell, ride a bike, and construct sentences would be information preserved in semantic long-term memory. Semantic long-term memory is not autobiographical. Although these two types of long-term memory appear to be different, they are also highly interconnected and probably operate in tandem.[24]

Stage #3: Retrieval. Once information has been stored, it is relatively useless unless it can be retrieved. The human information processor excels at retrieval. Information that has been stored for a lifetime yet rarely used can be recalled in an instant. Other times, however, recently stored information seems very difficult to recall. Most adults can easily recall the name of their first-grade teacher but cannot remember what they had for dinner three nights ago. Moreover, the quality of human information retrieval is typically approximate rather than literate. People have global memories of conversations or events rather than verbatim transcriptions.

According to Lachman and his colleagues, forgetting is memory failure; the inability to recall or recognize stored information. Forgetting in sensory or short-term store is necessary in order to process new incoming information. Forgetting information in long-term storage may have serious consequences, especially on a multiple-choice or essay exam. Cognitive psychologists now treat long-term memory forgetting as an asset rather than a liability because it is a useful way to prevent long-term memory from being cluttered up with information that is not being used. Forgetting often follows what is called a "negatively accelerated curve." Most forgetting occurs rapidly then levels off over time. Other researchers contend that information is never really forgotten; people just lose access to it.[25]

Matlin points out that there are many reasons why we might forget something, including decay, interference, arousal, trauma, and depth of processing. Forgetting that is due to decay occurs when a memory is not rehearsed or used over time. Eventually the information diminishes or fades from memory. Interference occurs when other information intrudes on stored information. Sometimes forgetting occurs when old memories interfere with the storage of new information. Other times forgetting occurs when new information disrupts previously stored "old" memories. Matlin devised a mini-experiment that demonstrates the effect of interference.

Interference Forgetting Mini-Experiment[26]

Present the following word list to a friend or roommate:

River	Card
Door	Test
Cat	Tree
Plate	Ball
Book	Road

Allow a few moments for your friend to read the list. After he/she finishes, ask him/her to either write down or recite orally a list of 10 vegetables. When he/she has finished the list ask him/her to recall the words on the list. See how many he/she recalls and with what degree of accuracy. Repeat the experiment with another friend, but this time delete the vegetable list exercise. Compare their results. Theoretically, the vegetable word list exercise should interfere with your friend's ability to store the word list in memory.

Negative arousal, or anxiety, may be another source of forgetting. One study that supports this view was conducted by Goss, Neuliep, and O'Hair. In their study two groups of students were shown the same videotaped conversation between a student and teacher interacting about an alleged cheating incident. The student in the video was being accused of cheating by the teacher. One week later students from one of the two groups were individually taken to a room where they were told they were about to testify before a university tribunal where the student who was in the videotape was on trial for cheating (there was no actual trial). Prior to entering the trial each student was given a multiple-choice recall test and was asked to recall as much as he or she could about the videotape seen one week earlier. The other group of students was given the same recall test but was not informed of any trial. In a comparison of the recall tests, the students in the group being told to testify scored significantly lower than the other group. Goss, Neuliep, and O'Hair attributed the lower recall scores to increased negative arousal.[27]

According to Matlin, another form of forgetting may be due to repression. This occurs when people actively, but unconsciously, forget unpleasant material. Similarly, pleasant material may be processed more easily than unpleasant. Refer back to the interference forgetting mini-experiment above. After your friend completes the experiment, make note of the first few and the last few vegetables on the list. Chances are that those vegetables listed first are the ones your friend enjoys while those listed toward the end are those that he or she dislikes.[28]

Matlin suggests that the effort required to gather and store information may also affect its retrieval. Meaningful information that requires deeper cognitive processing may be easier to recall than information that requires minimal effort to encode. Likewise, the context in which the information is encoded may facilitate recall. Called *encoding specificity,* the contextual cues present during the gathering and storing of information may serve as cues for the memory of stored information.[29]

Cross-Cultural Differences in Memory and Retrieval

Several studies indicate that culture affects information retrieval. In addition to culture, age and education are two other variables strongly linked to recall. Age and recall are curvilinearly related (see Figure 5.7). Up to a point, one's age facilitates recall.

When many people reach a certain age, however, their memory skills deteriorate. Likewise, educated persons seem to employ different kinds of memory strategies. Barbara Rogoff claims that to the extent that cultures have different educational systems and methods, their peoples may have different memory skills. Persons educated in industrialized cultures have been

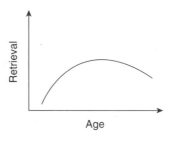

Figure 5.7

taught to remember disconnected bits of information, such as names and dates. These persons may be more likely than nonschooled individuals to use memory strategies that facilitate the organization of unrelated items. Moreover, Rogoff asserts that schooled individuals are more likely to classify similar objects together, whereas nonschooled persons classify objects based on their functional similarity. For example, in many memory tests, persons are presented with lists of unrelated pieces of information, not unlike the word list presented above in the interference forgetting mini-experiment. This type of information may be remembered better if the person employs some sort of mnemonic (pronounced "neh-monic," meaning a technique for improving memory) device such as rehearsing or classifying. Nonschooled persons, including preschool children, generally do not employ such mnemonic strategies and have difficulty with such tasks.[30]

With contextually organized information, however, fewer memory differences are observed between schooled and nonschooled persons. In one study reported by Rogoff, for example, Guatemalan Mayan and American 9-year-olds watched an experimenter place 20 miniature objects such as cars, animals, furniture, people, and household items into a panorama model of a town. The 20 items were then removed from the panorama and put into a pool of 80 other objects. The children were then asked to reconstruct the panorama using as many of the original 20 items as they could remember. The Mayan children performed slightly better than the American children. The performance of the Mayan children may have been due to the fact that about one third of the American children used rehearsal strategies typical for remembering unrelated bits of information, such as rehearsing the names of the objects. This type of strategy may be inappropriate for remembering spatially oriented, contextual information.[31] In related research Yoshida, Fernandez, and Stigler explored Japanese and American students' recognition memory for statements made during a videotaped mathematics lesson. Japanese and American fourth and sixth graders watched either a Japanese or English version of the same lesson and then were tested for recognition of teacher statements that were relevant or irrelevant to the content of the lesson. The Japanese and American students were equally successful at recognizing relevant statements but American students remembered more irrelevant statements than the Japanese.[32]

Cole and Gay assert that a culture's language and literacy rate may affect recall. Some evidence indicates that nonliterate societies develop mnemonic skills different from those of literate societies. In nonliterate societies, there may be no written language to facilitate memory. Imagine studying for an examination for which you have no notes! Cole and Gay note that in nonliterate societies people must store information in memory rather than on a piece of paper. Likewise, the histories of nonliterate societies must be stored in the memories of their peoples rather than on paper or in books.[33] In a study conducted by Ross and Millson, two groups of university students, one from Ghana and the other from New York, were read several stories aloud and then asked to recall them. Generally, the Ghana students had better recall of the stories than the American students. Researchers in a related study examined the effects of culturally based knowledge on memory for stories about people performing common activities.[34] In a study by Harris, Schoen, and Hensley, college students from America and Mexico read three brief stories of everyday activities. There were two versions of the same story, consistent with either an American or a Mexican cultural script. The students read each version. Researchers then administered memory tests immediately after reading the story, 30 minutes after reading the story, and 1 week after reading the story. After 1 week both groups of students mistakenly recalled the stories from the other cultures as being more like their own culture than they in fact were.[35] Other memory research reviewed by Liu indicates that Chinese persons may have superior memory. For example, in word pair association memory tasks, Chinese college students usually attain perfect recall within two or three trials compared to other cultures, whose accuracy is typically below 70%.[36]

Until more is known, final conclusions about the relationship between culture and memory should be made with some degree of caution. Although several studies indicate a connection between culture and memory, these studies may actually be revealing differences in other factors that affect recall, such as socialization or education. Because cultures differ in so many ways, it is difficult to pinpoint culture as the sole mechanism for memory ability.

Categorization and Mental Economy

Humans are besieged by so many stimuli simultaneously that they cannot possibly process all of it. In order to manage the enormous quantities of information, humans tend to engage in mental economy strategies. One such strategy is called categorization. Categorization is classifying, sorting, or arranging information into identifiable compartments that share certain features or characteristics. Most cognitive psychologists argue that all people, regardless of culture, engage in categorization. Gordon Allport argues that humans cannot avoid categorization and that orderly living depends on it.[37] Gudykunst and Kim suggest that categories are useful because they help the information processor reduce uncertainty and increase the accuracy of predictions about others. Moreover, categories help us to make attributions about the behavior of others and help us recall and recognize information. Understanding categorization is particularly important for intercultural communication because whenever we interact with someone from a different culture, we are faced with high levels of uncertainty and unfamiliar stimuli to process.[38]

Richard Brislin argues that people categorize for a number of reasons, including the reduction of uncertainty and the maintenance of self-esteem. According to Brislin, the kinds of information upon which people form categories includes, but is not limited to, conspicuous differences, familiarity, functional importance, maximizing the relative advantage of the ingroup, projection and externalization, belief similarity, desirable and undesirable qualities, and salient information. The examples provided here are particularly relevant to intercultural communication. Keep in mind that these examples are not the actual categories themselves; rather, they illustrate the kinds of information used to formulate categories.[39]

Conspicuous differences categories are based on easily seen similarities or differences. According to Brislin, these types of categories are formed quickly during initial interaction with someone from a different culture. Conspicuous similarities or differences help us classify others as members of ingroups and outgroups. Conspicuous differences may stem from skin color, dress, language, or occupation.[40]

Sometimes we form categories based on information that is familiar to us. Brislin points out that although people from different cultures may be conspicuously different from us, we may be quite familiar with them and their culture. Familiar stimuli are processed more efficiently than unfamiliar stimuli. The use of familiar categories facilitates accurate predictions about the behavior of others.[41]

Sometimes categories are formed that help us adjust and function. These functionally important categories may help us to meet needs and achieve goals. For example, when needed, a person may categorize him- or herself as a member of a particular kind of group that receives special benefits or entitlements. At other times, the same person may not categorize him- or herself that way because it is not "functionally important." For example, a student wishing to obtain a scholarship or loan may highlight his or her membership in an ethnic or racial group in order to obtain the assistance. Group membership, in this circumstance, becomes functionally important.[42]

Most persons have a tendency to think of others in terms of ingroup and outgroup membership. In doing so, people also have a tendency to create categories that maximize the advantage of the ingroup. An example provided by Brislin suggests that when members of the ingroup constantly lose at sporting competitions, they may be categorized as "sportsmanlike." If ingroup members share their resources, they may be categorized as "generous." Conversely, if the outgroup members lose at sporting events, they are categorized as "losers," and when they share their resources, they are categorized as "irresponsible."[43]

Projection refers to a shift of one's negative feelings onto someone or something else. In the case of categories, people may project ingroup troubles to an outgroup. For example, if a high percentage of the members of an ingroup are unemployed, they might blame members of the outgroup for taking all of "their" jobs. Brislin claims that externalization is related to projection in that people categorize members of the ingroup as more like themselves than may actually be the case. For example, a student may complain to his or her advisor that "all students" hate to take the required math class when, in fact, not "all" students claim so.[44]

Perceived similarity may be the best predictor of positive affect toward others. People who perceive an outgroup as similar to their ingroup are likely to think positively about that outgroup and to engage the members in interaction. People can perceive themselves as similar to others in a variety of ways—physically, socially, morally, experientially, economically, and so on. When people categorize others as similar they reduce uncertainty about them, which, in turn, facilitates interaction (see Figure 5.8).[45]

People have a tendency to label outgroups with undesirable qualities while classifying ingroups with desirable qualities. For example, outgroup members may be categorized as bitter, arrogant, or strange, whereas ingroup members are categorized as loyal, honest, and trustworthy. Brislin argues that people are socialized to believe in the superiority of the groups of which they are members.[46]

Salient information is that which is most noticeable, pronounced, or striking. When interacting with someone from another culture for the first time, there may be many salient features about that person that could lead to categorizing the entire culture. For example, when entering into another culture, if the first person with whom you interact treats you disrespectfully, you may categorize the entire population as such.[47]

Figure 5.8 People can perceive themselves as similar to others in a variety of ways—physically, socially, morally, etc.

Brislin asserts that there are several consequences of categorization, some positive and others potentially negative. On the positive side, categorization helps to confirm thinking. Categorization reduces the amount of incoming information to a manageable size and increases the availability of incoming information. Categorization also reduces uncertainty and stress, especially in situations where we are interacting with someone for the first time who belongs to a culture with which we are unfamiliar. Categorization also helps integrate incoming information and may help to link our own culture with others. On the potentially negative side, when we categorize others we ignore individual elements of the person. We must be careful not to categorize too quickly or carelessly. We must be conscious that categorizing minimizes ingroup differences while maximizing outgroup differences.[48]

STEREOTYPING

By constructing categories, the human mind processes information more efficiently. Once created, categories are the basis of prejudgment, such as stereotyping. Considered a subset of categorization, stereotyping involves members of one group attributing characteristics to members of another group. These attributions typically carry a positive or negative evaluation. In this sense, stereotypes are categories with an attitude. Stereotypes typically refer to membership in social categories, such as sex, race, age, or profession, that are believed to be associated with certain traits and behaviors. In the United States, race and gender groups are often stereotyped. The meaning of the term *stereotype* has changed considerably since its introduction in 1824 by James Morier. Morier coined the term to describe a printing duplication process "in which the original is preserved and in which there is no opportunity for change or deviation in the reduplications."[49] A century later Walter Lippman defined stereotypes as "pictures in our heads" and argued that stereotypes are not merely descriptions of others, but include an affective component that is driven by one's self-respect and value orientations.[50] In more recent times, the word *stereotype* has taken on negative connotations. In 1998, Richard Schaefer defined stereotypes as exaggerated images of the characteristics of a particular group held by prejudiced people who hold ill feelings toward that group.[51] Gudykunst and Kim define stereotypes as cognitive representations of another group that influence one's feelings about the group. They argue that stereotypes provide the content of social categories.[52]

Although it is hard to admit it, we all stereotype. Stereotyping is a natural and universal information-processing strategy. Taylor and Porter maintain that stereotyping should be seen as a normal process that is a useful information-processing tool in diverse societies. The difficulty arises when stereotypes carry a negative valence and are used to overgeneralize negative traits to an entire group of people when, in reality, few members of the group actually possess such traits.[53] Victoria Esses and Mark Zanna found that simply being in a "bad mood" may incline people to stereotype negatively. Several studies have demonstrated that when individuals are in a negative mood, they are especially likely to attribute stereotypes that they consider to be very unfavorable to certain ethnic groups.[54] In this way, stereotyping can lead to ethnocentrism, prejudice, and discrimination.

Racial and Ethnic Stereotypes

Social scientists have long been interested in stereotypes and prejudice, two concepts that are often related. The systematic study of racial and ethnic stereotypes in the United States began in the 1930s with a study conducted by David Katz and Kenneth Braly. In their study, college students were presented with a list of 84 adjectives (e.g., lazy, ignorant, arrogant, intelligent, and so on) and were asked to indicate which traits were characteristic of ten ethnic groups: Americans, Blacks, Chinese, English, Germans, Italians, Irish, Japanese, Jews, and Turks. The results of their study showed that the college students consistently agreed on which traits described which group. The results were particularly consistent for Blacks and Jews.[55]

Traits Associated with Blacks (Katz and Braly 1933)
Superstitious
Lazy
Happy-go-lucky
Ignorant
Stupid
Dirty (physically)
Musical
Religious

Traits Associated with Jews (Katz and Braly 1933)
Shrewd
Mercenary (selfish)
Sly
Aggressive
Industrious
Intelligent
Ambitious

In their original study, Katz and Braly found a high level of consistency in the adjectives respondents associated with the Black stereotype. Moreover, the adjectives selected were generally negative. Since their original work, several other researchers have replicated Katz and Braly's stereotype checklist method using the same 84 adjectives as in the original study—Gilbert in 1950 and Gordon in 1969 and 1982. Patricia Devine and Andrew Elliot replicated the research in 1995. In their work, however, Devine and Elliot added nine new characteristics to the original 84-item adjective checklist.[56]

Traits Associated with Blacks (Devine and Elliot 1995)
Lazy
Ignorant
Dirty (physically)
Loud
Athletic
Rhythmic
Unintelligent
Poor
Criminal
Hostile

Devine and Elliot argue that despite a shift in social norms discouraging the overt expression of prejudice and discrimination, stereotypical images of Blacks remain salient in U.S. culture. Devine and Elliot conclude,

> Although efforts such as affirmative action and increased sensitivity to media portrayals of Blacks may ultimately have positive effects and facilitate the fading of cultural racial stereotypes, it is likely that such changes will take place over a protracted period of time.[57]

American Stereotypes

Canadian psychologists Donald Taylor and Lana Porter examined some of the socially desirable aspects of stereotyping and allege that the negative connotation associated with stereotyping may be uniquely American. They argue that, historically, the study of stereotypes in the United States has mainly focused on White stereotypes of African-Americans, which have been particularly brutal and negative (see Figure 5.9). Second, Taylor and Porter suggest that the essence of the political doctrine in the United States is modeled after the "melting pot" metaphor wherein the peoples of all the different cultures immigrating to the United States get "stirred up in the great pot until cultural differences are boiled away and a single culture remains—American." Because stereotyping, by definition, recognizes and highlights differences among groups, it directly conflicts with the melting pot image. Third, Taylor and Porter suggest that psychologists studying interpersonal attraction have long understood that perceived similarity is a major determinant in how much

Figure 5.9   Often White stereotypes of African Americans have been brutal and negative

people are attracted to and like others. The more we perceive people to be similar to us, the more likely we are to be attracted to and like them. Hence, stereotypes that emphasize group differences essentially block the potential for intergroup friendships. Given these trends, Taylor and Porter assert that there are compelling reasons why Americans view stereotyping as a destructive social force. This, they argue, has led to an enormous investment in human and financial resources to rid people of their stereotypes.[58]

Taylor and Porter recognize that people in countries different from the United States are brought up in entirely different cultural contexts where it is perfectly acceptable to categorize people into groups. In Europe and Canada, for example, people presume that society is culturally diverse and are proud of their various group memberships. Taylor and Porter suggest that this philosophy contrasts sharply with the American melting pot metaphor, which emphasizes cultural homogeneity. In other countries the significance of cultural diversity is symbolized through metaphors very different from the melting pot, such as a mosaic or montage; that is, an assortment of people in the same place, but not necessarily blending together.

Taylor and Porter claim that a fundamental feature of any pluralistic society is that ethnic attitudes exist between different groups, particularly ingroups and outgroups. Ethnic attitudes and stereotypes are a part of all cultures, and no one can avoid learning them.[59] In fact, research conducted by Trice and Rush indicates that stereotypes are well established in children's memories well before they acquire the intellectual ability to question or evaluate them. In their study of American four-year-olds, Trice and Rush found that boys were significantly more likely to accept male-stereotyped occupations (e.g., police officer, truck driver, housebuilder) than female-stereotyped occupations (e.g., teacher, nurse, secretary). Likewise, girls were significantly more likely to accept female-stereotyped occupations than male-stereotyped occupations.[60]

Attitudes about ethnic groups may be relatively independent of ethnic group stereotypes, however. That is, although people may have knowledge of a stereotype, their personal beliefs may or may not be congruent with the stereotype. Some studies indicate that the degree of stereotyping of an ethnic group is unrelated to the evaluation of that group. Indeed, other studies demonstrate that stereotypes and personal beliefs are conceptually distinct cognitive structures. Patricia Devine, a psychologist at the University of Wisconsin, has shown that stereotyping is an *automatic* information-processing strategy whereas prejudice is a *controlled* process.[61] According to Devine, automatic information processing is the unintentional and/or instinctive activation of thoughts that have been learned through repeated stimulation in memory. Automatic processes are largely unconscious and appear to be triggered by environmental stimuli (e.g., a person from a different ethnic or cultural group). Devine notes that an important point about automatic processes is that they seem to be inescapable despite our conscious attempts to ignore them. Controlled processes, on the other hand, are intentional and require the conscious attention of the processor. Because they are intentional, controlled processes are useful in decision-making and problem-solving tasks.

Devine's model assumes that high- and low-prejudiced persons are equally knowledgeable of cultural stereotypes. Moreover, because stereotypes are learned at such an early age, they become automatically activated in the presence of a member of the stereotyped group. Devine contends that although just about everyone possesses knowledge of cultural stereotypes, not everybody believes or endorses them. Devine argues that the unintentional activation of the stereotype is equally strong and inescapable for the high- and low-prejudiced person. Devine's major thesis is that high- and low-prejudiced persons differ with respect to their personal beliefs about the stereotype. High-prejudiced persons have personal beliefs consistent with the stereotype, whereas low-prejudiced persons understand that the stereotype is inappropriate or inaccurate. Instead of believing in the stereotype, low-prejudiced persons create new thoughts or images (of the person or group) that require intentional activation. In her research, Devine found that high- and low-prejudiced individuals do not differ in their knowledge of stereotypes but diverge sharply in their sanction of the stereotype. For example, whereas most White Americans possess knowledge of the Black stereotype, only a subset of these individuals actually endorses the stereotype and believes its validity. Such findings lend support to the idea that ethnic stereotyping simply may be a useful information-processing approach that is relatively innocuous.[62]

When stereotyping is viewed as a natural information-processing strategy, there are several explanations as to why it is so common and universal, none of which relate to prejudice. One explanation is called the outgroup homogeneity effect. According to Judd and Park, the outgroup homogeneity effect is the tendency for people to see members of an outgroup as less diverse and more stereotypic than the members of that group see themselves. We have a tendency to see outgroup members as highly similar (i.e., homogeneous) yet view ourselves and our ingroup members as unique and individual. For example, students may think that all professors are the same. Likewise, professors may think that all students are alike. Yet neither professors nor students see themselves as "just like" all the others. The outgroup homogeneity effect is not necessarily the consequence of prejudice. Taylor and Porter contend that because ingroups and outgroups do not interact much, they may be unable to develop accurate representations of each other.[63]

A second plausible explanation for stereotyping is called the illusory correlation principle. According to Taylor and Porter, when two objects that are unfamiliar or unusual in some way are observed to be connected on some occasion, we have the tendency to believe that they are always connected. For example, if we observe an outgroup member participating in some atypical incident or behavior, such as a felony, then outgroup members and felonies become associated in our minds. Then, the next time we see a member of the same outgroup we will stereotype him or her as a felon. The correlation between the outgroup members and felonies is illusory and/or unreal because the outgroup is now linked to felonies on account of only one, or relatively few, observed occurrences.[64]

Neither the outgroup homogeneity effect nor the illusory correlation principle is necessarily wrong or socially "bad." Both are naturally occurring information-processing strategies that are a part of everyone's normal cognitive repertoire. The problem is that they may lead to negative attitudes and subsequent prejudice. If people understand their information-processing functions and are informed of these kinds of strategies, then they can become mindful of the process and ward off any potentially harmful negative consequences that may result.

Richard Schaefer offers two other reasons why stereotypes are so widely held by groups of people. First, he argues that stereotypes may arise out of real conditions. For example, a disproportionate number of people from a particular racial or ethnic group may live in poverty, and so members of other groups stereotype all of them as poor or even lazy. A second explanation of stereotypes is their role in self-fulfilling prophecies. The dominant group in a particular culture may construct social or legal obstacles, making it hard for members of the stereotyped group to act differently from the stereotype. Hence, conformity to the stereotype, although forced, validates the stereotype in the minds of the dominant group. For example, members of a subordinate stereotyped group may have difficulty obtaining high-paying, prestigious employment because members of the dominant group refuse to hire them. Hence, they accept low-paying, less prestigious jobs and become stereotyped.[65]

Henri Tajfel contends that another reason why people retain stereotypes is that they help us develop and maintain a positive self-esteem. Our memberships in various groups constitute a major aspect of our self-concept. Our social identities essentially are made up of our group memberships (e.g., husband, professor, colleague, friend, counsel). Tajfel asserts that our sense of esteem is nourished when we differentiate our ingroups from outgroups, usually by assigning traits (i.e., stereotypes) that are favorable to the ingroup and negative to the outgroup. Typically, we differentiate our ingroups on the basis of power, ancestry, religion, language, culture, race, or a whole host of other variables.[66]

According to Steele and Aronson, some members of stereotyped groups actually start to believe the stereotype. They call this phenomenon *stereotype threat.* Stereotype threat occurs when we sense that some aspect of our self (e.g., our behavior, physical characteristics, or social condition) seems to match the stereotype, making it appear valid. Steele and Aronson believe that stereotype threat is experienced essentially as a self-evaluative threat. Culturally held stereotypes pose the most danger for stereotyped groups because large numbers of people may hold them, leading members of the group to sense that the stereotype is valid. When the stereotype is negative,

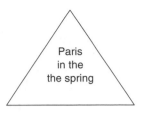

Figure 5.10

the effects can be disastrous to the stereotyped group. In their research on stereotype threat, Steele and Aronson varied the stereotype vulnerability of African-Americans taking a difficult verbal test. In one condition the African-Americans were told that the test was a valid measure of intellectual ability. In a second condition, they were told that the test was simply a problem-solving activity that was not designed to measure ability. Their results showed that African-Americans performed worse than Whites when the test was presented as a measure of their intellectual ability but improved dramatically, matching the performance of Whites, when the test was presented as less reflective of ability. Steele and Aronson theorize that stereotype threat inhibits efficient information processing like that caused by other evaluative pressures. Stereotype-threatened persons alternate their attention between trying to accomplish the task at hand and trying to assess their self-significance. This leads to reduced speed and accuracy.[67]

Although evidence suggests that stereotyping may be independent of one's attitudes about others, some studies have demonstrated that stereotypes distort social perception of others. Human perception is not necessarily accurate and honest. Perception is influenced by one's needs, wishes, and expectations. In many cases people perceive what they expect to perceive regardless of reality. Figure 5.10 is a popular illustration of how expectations affect perception.

Most read the words in the triangle as "Paris in the spring" failing to notice the duplication of the word "the." By definition, stereotyping is categorizing people according to some easily identifiable characteristic and then attributing to them qualities or behaviors believed to be typical of members of that classification. In this sense, stereotyping leads to expectations that, in turn, affect our social perception of others. In what is now considered a classic experiment, Bruner and Goodman found that persons of lower socioeconomic status tended to accentuate the size of coins.[68] In related research Duncan found that perceptions of an ambiguously aggressive act are strongly influenced by racial stereotypes. In his study, White male college students coded the behaviors observed in what they thought was a live conversation on a television monitor. The conversation ended with an ambiguous shove. Approximately half of the students witnessed a Black actor shove another person, whereas the other half observed the identical act by a White actor. Thirty-five of the 48 observers coded the shove as violent behavior when it was performed by a Black actor, yet only 6 of 48 observers coded the identical act as violent behavior when it was performed by a White actor. Duncan argued that because of stereotypes associating Blacks with violence, the violent behavior category is cognitively more accessible to observers viewing a Black perpetrator than to those viewing a White one.[69] The results of Duncan's study were replicated by Sagar and Schofield, who studied Black and White sixth graders. The students were shown a variety of ambiguously aggressive acts performed by Black and White actors. Both Black and White students rated the behaviors of Black actors as more mean and threatening than when the identical acts were performed by White actors. Sagar and Schofield argue that stereotypes create expectations and conclude that "in the existing social order, the stereotype is all too real. To activate it, the person engaging in an ambiguous behavior need only be black."[70]

AN INTERCULTURAL CONVERSATION: STEREOTYPING

Akira is an exchange student from Japan who is spending a semester at an American University. Jim is a student at the same university. Jim was born and raised in Milwaukee. Jim and Akira meet for the first time. Below is an excerpt from their initial interaction.

Jim:	*Hi.* (Thinks to himself—"Man, he's so short, he's just like all the other Asians I've seen.")
Akira:	*Hi. I'm Akira.* (Thinks to himself—"Wow, he's pretty tall.")
Jim:	*I'm Jim, are you a student here?* (Thinks to himself—"He's probably a math major.")
Akira:	*Yes.* (Thinks to himself—"He probably thinks I'm Chinese.")
Jim:	*Are you from Japan?* (Thinks to himself—"He probably wonders if I drive a Honda. I wonder if he realizes how many Americans are unemployed because of all the imported Japanese cars.")
Akira:	*Yes, I am.* (Thinks to himself—"What will he ask me now. These Americans are so impolite.")

> **Jim**: *Yeah? That's cool. How do you like it in the United States? Have you been here before?* (Thinks to himself—"He must love it here . . . it's got to be better than his country.")
>
> **Akira**: *I like it here a lot.* (Thinks to himself—"I'd better not tell him that the food here is horrible. It might upset him.")

In this brief exchange, both Jim and Akira engage in categorization and stereotyping. Initially Jim categorizes Akira based on conspicuous differences ("Man, he's short"), familiarity ("He's probably a math major"), and projection ("I wonder if he realizes how many Americans are unemployed because of all the imported Japanese cars"). Jim also stereotypes Akira as good in math. Akira categorizes and stereotypes Jim in much the same way.

ETHNOCENTRISM

One of the central concepts in understanding outgroup attitudes and intergroup relations is ethnocentrism. Sumner originally defined it as "the technical name for this view of things in which one's own group is the center of everything, and all others are scaled and rated with reference to it."[71] Many researchers recognize it as a universal phenomenon experienced in all cultures.[72] Many scholars maintain that ethnocentricity is a natural condition and that most peoples of the world do not like foreigners and openly display feelings of hostility and fear toward them.[73] Lustig and Koester contend that all cultures have an ethnocentric tendency.[74] At the core of ethnocentrism, asserts Segall, is the tendency for any people to put their own group in a position of centrality and worth while creating and reinforcing negative attitudes and behaviors toward outgroups.[75] As Dutch sociologist Geert Hofstede argues, ethnocentrism is to a people what egocentrism is to an individual.[76] The term comes from the Greek words *ethnos,* which refers to nation, and *kentron,* which refers to center.[77] Neuliep and McCroskey assert, however, that the term can also be applied to an ethnic or microcultural group within a country. Similar views can be held based on religion (e.g., Judaism is the only true religion) or a region of origin (e.g., Texans are the only real Americans).[78]

Ethnocentric persons hold attitudes and behaviors toward ingroups that are different from attitudes and behaviors toward outgroups. Specifically, the attitudes and behaviors of ethnocentric persons are biased in favor of the ingroup, often at the expense of the outgroup. Although ethnocentrism is generally thought to be a negative trait, ethnocentrism fosters ingroup survival, solidarity, conformity, cooperation, loyalty, and effectiveness. In his seminal work, Levinson argued that ethnocentrism is

> based on a pervasive and rigid ingroup-outgroup distinction; it involves stereotyped, negative imagery and hostile attitudes regarding outgroups, stereotyped positive imagery and submissive attitudes regarding ingroups, and a hierarchical, authoritarian view of group interaction in which ingroups are rightly dominant, outgroups subordinate.[79]

In related research, Taylor and Jaggi introduced a phenomenon called *ethnocentric attributional bias*. According to this theory, ethnocentrics construct internal attributions for the positive behavior of ingroup members while making external attributions for their negative behavior. For example, if ingroup members perform well on some task, the attribution is that they possess the essential ingredients to accomplish such a task (e.g., "they're smart," "they're hard workers," and so on.). Yet if ingroup members perform marginally on some task, the fault lies elsewhere (e.g., "trick questions," "bad calls by the umpire," and so on.). On the contrary, external attributions are made for the positive behavior of outgroup members (e.g., "they got lucky"), and internal attributions are made for their negative behavior (e.g., "they're born liars").[80]

A CONTEMPORARY CONCEPTUALIZATION OF ETHNOCENTRISM

Neuliep and McCroskey have offered a contemporary conceptualization of ethnocentrism. We argue that ethnocentrism should be viewed along a continuum; that everyone is, to some extent, ethnocentric. As newborns, humans are entirely, and naturally, egocentric. Eventually, we develop an awareness of others around us. By age two or three we engage in social perspective taking of those most central to us. These people, our biological or adopted families, are the center of our universe. As we become socialized, we observe that our families coexist with other families, and that this culmination of people constitutes some form of neighborhood, clan, tribe, community, city, society, and finally culture. By the time we realize that we are a part of some much larger whole, we are officially enculturated and ethnocentric.[81]

Ethnocentrism is essentially descriptive, not necessarily pejorative. On one end of the ethnocentrism continuum, ethnocentrism may serve a very valuable function when one's central group is under actual or threat of

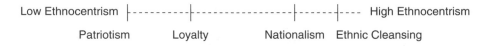

Figure 5.11 Ethnocentrism Continuum

attack. Ethnocentrism forms the basis for patriotism and the willingness to sacrifice for one's central group. On the other end of the continuum, the tendency for people to see their own way as the only right way can be dangerous and lead to pathological forms of ethnocentrism that result in prejudice, discrimination, and even ethnic cleansing (see Figure 5.11).[82]

To the extent that humans are ethnocentric, we tend to view other cultures (and microcultures) from our own cultural vantage point. That is, our culture is the standard by which we evaluate other cultures and the people from those cultures. Most deviations from that standard are viewed negatively and will be used as evidence of the inferiority of people from the other culture.

ETHNOCENTRISM, INTERCULTURAL COMMUNICATION, AND INTERPERSONAL PERCEPTION

Ehnocentrism negatively influences intercultural communication. Gudykunst points out that one's cultural orientation acts as a filter for processing incoming and outgoing verbal and nonverbal messages. To this extent, all intercultural exchanges are necessarily, to a greater or lesser degree, charged with ethnocentrism.[83] Indeed, most cross-cultural researchers recognize that human communication is replete with cultural noise that interferes with the transmission of information. Guan points out that ethnocentrism leads to "self-centered dialogue" where interactants use their own cultural standards to evaluate and communicate with others.[84] Gudykunst and Kim assert that high levels of ethnocentrism are dysfunctional with respect to intercultural communication and expand upon Peng's concept of communicative distance and Lukens's concept of ethnocentric speech.[85] Peng alleges that ethnocentric attitudes are reflected in linguistic diversity and create communicative distance between interactants that manifests itself in the expressions, idioms, and words of the speakers.[86] Lukens claims that ethnocentric speech results in three types of communicative distance: indifference, avoidance, and disparagement.[87] The distance of indifference is communicated in speech patterns such as talking loudly and slowly to a nonnative speaker of the language, including exaggerated pronunciation and simplification. The communicative distance of indifference is also communicated in such expressions as "Jew them down," "top of the totem pole," and "the blind leading the blind." The distance of avoidance communicates that the speaker prefers to minimize or avoid contact with persons from other cultures through the use of ingroup jargon or slang that members of other cultures or outgroups do not understand. The distance of disparagement is communicated to openly express contempt for persons of different cultures and is communicated through ethnophaulisms such as "nigger," "nip," "chink," and so on.[88]

Neuliep and McCroskey contend that ethnocentrism acts as a perceptual filter that affects not only the perceptions of verbal and nonverbal messages, but also perceptions of their source. For the most part, we tend to initiate and maintain communication with those to whom we are attracted. When we interact with someone from another culture, however, our perception of the other's attractiveness is affected by our degree of ethnocentrism. Moreover, many studies indicate that perceived similarity is related to attraction. Thus, if we perceive someone as similar to ourselves, we are more likely to be attracted to that person. But, by definition, ethnocentrics perceive themselves as dissimilar to outgroups. Specifically, ethnocentrics perceive themselves as superior to outgroups (e.g., ethnic/racial groups). Hence, when interacting with people from a different culture or ethnicity, high ethnocentrics are likely to perceive outgroup members as less attractive than ingroup members. Judgment of another's credibility is also affected by ethnocentrism. Persons are thought to be credible to the degree that they are perceived to be informed, qualified, trained, intelligent, trustworthy, and so on. However, because they see themselves as superior, ethnocentrics tend to judge outgroup members as less competent, less honest, less trustworthy, and so on.[89]

ETHNOCENTRISM AND COMMUNICATION IN THE WORKPLACE

The effects of ethnocentrism are manifest in any social context, including organizational environments where persons of different cultural backgrounds interact in the workplace. In their research Neuliep, Hintz, and McCroskey investigated the effects of ethnocentrism in an employment interview. In their study, U.S. students watched a videotaped interview of a Korean national student being interviewed for a job in the financial aid office of her U.S. college. The students then completed measures of ethnocentrism, interpersonal attraction, and credibility, and they were asked to give a hiring recommendation. Their results showed that ethnocentrism was negatively and significantly correlated with perceptions of social attraction, competence, character, and hiring recommendations.[90] Their results are consistent with House, who reports that cultural and/or ethnic similarity between interviewee and interviewer may play a role in hiring decisions. House maintains that interviewers are more likely to hire people with whom they feel they have the most in common (e.g., culture and/or ethnicity). This effect may be enhanced by ethnocentrism.[91]

In additional research, Neuliep, Hintz, and McCroskey investigated the effects of ethnocentrism on manager-subordinate communication. In this study, participants watched a video of an Asian student manager reprimanding a White student worker. A different group of participants watched a nearly identical video of a White student manager reprimanding the same White student worker (the same scripts were used for both videos). After watching the video, each group of participants completed measures of ethnocentrism, interpersonal attraction, credibility, attitudes about the manager, and managerial effectiveness. For the group of participants that watched the Asian student manager reprimanding the White student worker, ethnocentrism was negatively and significantly correlated with perceptions of the manager's physical, social, and task attraction; competence; and general attitudes about the manager. For the group of participants that watched the White student manager, there were no significant correlations between ethnocentrism and any of the other variables.[92]

The implications of these results are significant. In an increasingly diverse workplace, managers and subordinates of different cultures and ethnicities are likely to find themselves interacting together. To the extent that such interactants are ethnocentric, interpersonal perceptions and communication will be influenced negatively. In addition to providing leadership functions, one of the primary functions of management, in any organization, is performance appraisal of subordinates. The results of this study suggest that in cases where managers and subordinates are of different cultures or ethnicities, subordinate ethnocentrism may interfere with the interpretation of managerial appraisals. If ethnocentric subordinates perceive managers of different cultures/ethnicities to be less attractive, less competent, and less credible, they may be less likely to accept their appraisal and any of the recommendations contained therein. Moreover, the position of an effective manager is one that fosters a certain level of obedience and compliance by subordinates. To the extent that managers are perceived as credible, subordinates are more likely to comply with them. As Neuliep, Hintz, and McCroskey found, in manager-subordinate transactions, ethnocentrism interferes with perceptions; that is, ethnocentric managers perceive out-group subordinates as less attractive and/or credible. Similarly, ethnocentric subordinates may perceive outgroup managers as less credible and/or attractive. Other research has found that the consequences of racial and/or ethnic differences between managers and subordinates are most clearly evident in performance appraisals. For example, Landay and Farr, and Kraiger and Ford found that African-American and White managers consistently gave more positive appraisals to members of their own race. Manager or subordinate ethnocentrism may amplify this effect.[93]

Ethnocentrism and Racism

Although the terms *racism* and *ethnocentrism* are not synonymous, they are related. Ethnocentrism refers to the degree to which one sees his or her culture as superior and the standard by which other cultures should be judged. Racism refers to a belief that one racial group is superior to others, and that other racial groups are necessarily inferior. To be ethnocentric, but not racist, is possible. To be racist, and not ethnocentric, is probably unlikely. In other words, you may believe your culture is superior to other cultures, but do not necessarily believe that your race is superior. However, if you believe that your race is superior, chances are very good that you also believe your culture is superior. There is a biological component at the core of racist ideology that does not exist in the concept of ethnocentrism. Racist ideology is a belief in the moral or intellectual superiority of one race over the others. This superiority is biologically based. Because such superiority is biological, rather than social, it cannot be conditioned by culture or education. However, racist ideology asserts that racial-biological superiority does, in fact, translate into cultural and/or social superiority. Hence superior race produces superior culture. Whereas racism refers to the hierarchical ranking of one race above the others, ethnocentrism refers to the strong preference for one's own culture over other cultures. Just as racism is rooted in biology, ethnocentrism is rooted in ethnicity and culture. Racial groups are biological. Ethnic groups can be based on blood, common history, nationality, religion, or even geographic region.[94]

In addition to their conceptual differences, racism and ethnocentrism have different origins. As mentioned previously, many scholars believe that ethnocentrism is a universal phenomenon that reflects a biologically rooted survival instinct experienced, to some degree, by all people in all cultures. Hence, it is thought that ethnocentrism is innately human; that is, we are born ethnocentric. Racism, on the other hand, is not universal and is thought to be learned. This begs the question, Why would anyone teach others to be racist? One argument, espoused by scholars from across a wide variety of disciplines, is that racism is the by-product of ignorance, fear, and hate. Although this argument is attractive, it fails to take into account the fact that many of the leading philosophers of Western civilization espoused undeniably racist views. David Hume wrote that "I am apt to suspect that Negroes, and in general all the other species of men, to be naturally inferior to the whites." Immanuel Kant wrote that "The Negroes have received from nature no intelligence that rises above the foolish." Georg Hegel wrote, "The Negro race has perfect contempt for humanity."[95]

Although slavery is not unique to the United States, in American history, racism is often associated with the forced immigration and enslavement of Africans. Because the U.S. Constitution was predicated on the tenet that all men are created equal, slavery presented a moral dilemma for the country. The enslavement and brutal treatment of Africans was a blatant violation of any sort of equality creed. But if Whites could define Blacks as biologically inferior, then they could justify slavery and do so with a clear conscience. Hence, the institutionalization of a flagrantly racist system of unequal treatment was established.[96]

Many political scientists offer a socioeconomic-political explanation of the causes of racism, frequently called the frustration-aggression hypothesis. During times of social, economic, or political stress (e.g., depressed economy, mass immigration), the dominant cultural group often will place blame on subordinate racial groups. Racism becomes a way of releasing the stress and frustration associated with difficult social, economic, or political times. In these situations, the dominant group often will act out its frustration against the subordinate racial group via prejudice and discrimination.[97] Racism, stereotyping, prejudice, and discrimination are often linked. When a racial group is labeled inferior, stereotypes emerge, such as those presented earlier in this chapter. Because racial stereotypes are often negative, people become prejudiced toward the racial group and discriminate against it. Prejudice is how people feel or think about a particular group, and discrimination is the behavioral outcome; that is, action against the prejudiced group.

CHAPTER SUMMARY

The purpose of this chapter was to describe and explain the psychological context of intercultural communication. Whenever two people come together and interact, they process immense amounts of information. Some communicative situations, especially intercultural communication contexts, have higher information rates than others and require the interactants to reduce more uncertainty than usual. Another important point of this chapter is that regardless of culture, human beings, for the most part, process information similarly. Although culture affects the types of information we process, all humans take in, store, and recall information in much the same way. Culture's role in this process leads us to make different kinds of interpretations about the information we process. All persons categorize, stereotype, and to some extent are ethnocentric with the information they process.

GLOSSARY OF TERMS

Carpentered-World Hypothesis: Learned tendency by those living in industrialized cultures to interpret nonrectangular figures as rectangles in perspective.

Categorization: Classifying or sorting of perceived information into distinct groups.

Cognition: Higher mental processes, such as perception and memory.

Decay: Memory loss due to lack of use.

Episodic Memory: A component of long-term memory where private individual memories are stored.

Ethnocentric Attributional Bias: The tendency to make internal attributions for the positive behavior of the ingroup while making external attributions for its negative behavior.

Ethnocentrism: Tendency to place one's own group or ethnicity in a position of centrality and worth while creating negative attitudes and behaviors towards other groups.

Illusory Correlation Principle: When two objects or persons are observed to be linked in some way, people have a tendency to believe they are always linked (or correlated).

Interference: During recall, when new or old information blocks or obstructs the recall of other information.

Long-Term Memory: Cognitive storage area where large amounts of information are held relatively permanently.

Memory: The storage of information in the human brain over time.

Outgroup Homogeneity Effect: The tendency to see members of an outgroup as highly similar while seeing the members of the ingroup as unique and individual.

Perception: The mental interpretation of external stimuli via sensation.

Perceptual Filters: Physical, social, and psychological processes that screen and bias incoming stimuli.

Recall/Retrieval: To call to the mind or recollection of stored information.

Semantic Memory: A part of long-term memory where general information such as how to read and write and the meanings of words are stored.

Sensation: Gathering of visual, auditory, olfactic, haptic, and taste stimuli/information.

Sensory Receptors: Eyes, ears, nose, mouth, and skin.

Sensory Register: Storage center for raw sense data.

Short-Term Memory: Cognitive storage area where small amounts of information are held for short periods of time, usually less than 20 seconds.

Stereotypes: A subset of categorizing and involving the attribution of characteristics of a group to an individual based on the individual's membership in that group. Stereotypes are categories with an attitude.

REFERENCES

1. Polyani, M. (1958). *Personal knowledge: Towards a post-critical philosophy.* Chicago: University of Chicago Press.
2. Lachman, R., Lachman, J. L., & Butterfield, E. C. (1979). *Cognitive psychology and information processing: An introduction.* Hillsdale, NJ: Erlbaum; see also Stillings, N. A., Weisler, S. E., Chase, C. H., Feinstein, M. H., Garfield, J. L., & Rissland, E. L. (1995). *Cognitive science: An introduction.* Cambridge: Massachusetts Institute of Technology Press
3. Matlin, M. (1983). *Cognition.* New York: Holt, Rinehart and Winston.
4. Ibid.
5. These demonstrations are from Matlin, *Cognition.*
6. McCroskey, J. C., & Richmond, V. P. (1996). *Fundamentals of human communication: An interpersonal perspective.* Prospect Heights, IL: Waveland.
7. Goss, B. (1989). *The psychology of human communication.* Prospect Heights, IL: Waveland.
8. Berry, J. W., Poortinga, Y. H., Segall, M. H., & Dasen, P. R. (1992). *Cross-cultural psychology: Research and applications.* Cambridge, UK: Cambridge University Press.

9. Reuning, H., & Wortley, W. (1973). Psychological studies of the Bushmen. *Psychologia Africana* (Monograph Supplement #7); cited in Berry et al., *Cross-cultural psychology*.

10. Wyndham, C. H. (1975). Ergonomic problems in the transition from peasant to industrial life in South Africa. In A. Chapanis (Ed.), *Ethnic variables in human factor engineering* (pp. 115–134). Baltimore: Johns Hopkins University Press; see also Berry et al., *Cross-cultural psychology*.

11. Berry et al., *Cross-cultural psychology*.

12. Ibid.

13. Segall, M. H. (1994). A cross-cultural research contribution to unraveling the nativist-empiricist controversy. In W. J. Lonner & R. Malpass (Eds.), *Psychology and culture* (pp. 135–138). Boston: Allyn & Bacon.

14. Ibid.; Segall, M. H. (1979). *Cross-cultural psychology: Human behavior in global perspective*. Monterey, CA: Brooks/Cole.

15. Dawson, S. L. M., Young, B. M., & Choi, P. P. C. (1973). Developmental influences on geometric illusion susceptibility among Hong Kong Chinese children. *Journal of Cross-Cultural Psychology, 4,* 49–74.

16. Segall, *Cross-cultural psychology*.

17. Lachman, Lachman, & Butterfield, *Cognitive psychology and information processing*.

18. Ibid.

19. Logie, R. H. (1995) *Visual-spatial working memory*. Hillsdale, NJ: Erlbaum.

20. Miller, G. A. (1956). The magical number seven, plus or minus two: Some limits on our capacity for processing information. *Psychological Review, 63,* 81–97.

21. Lachman, Lachman, and Butterfield, *Cognitive psychology and information processing*.

22. Howard, R. W. (1995). *Learning and memory: Major ideas, principles, issues and applications*. Westport, CT: Praeger.

23. Howard, *Learning and memory;* Stillings et al., *Cognitive science*.

24. Tulving, E. (1972). Episodic and semantic memory. In E. Tulving & W. Donaldson (Eds.), *Organization of memory*. New York: Academic Press.

25. Lachman, Lachman, & Butterfield, *Cognitive psychology and information processing;* Howard, *Learning and memory*.

26. Matlin, *Cognition*.

27. Goss, B., Neuliep, J. W., & O'Hair, D. (1985). Reduced conversational recall as a function of negative arousal: A preliminary analysis. *Communication Research Reports, 2,* 202–205.

28. Matlin, *Cognition*.

29. Ibid.

30. Rogoff, *Apprenticeship in thinking*.

31. Ibid.

32. Yoshida, M., Fernandez, C., & Stigler, J. W. (1993). Japanese and American students' differential recognition memory for teachers' statements during a mathematics lesson. *Journal of Educational Psychology, 85,* 610–617.

33. Cole, M., & Gay, J. (1972). Culture and memory. *American Anthropologist, 74,* 1066–1084.

34. Ross, B. M., & Millson, C. (1970). Repeated memory of oral prose in Ghana and New York. *International Journal of Psychology, 5,* 173–181.

35. Harris, R. J., Schoen, L. M., & Hensley, D. I. (1992). A cross-cultural study of story memory. *Journal of Cross-Cultural Psychology, 23,* 133–147.

36. Liu, I. (1986). Chinese cognition. In M. H. Bond (Ed.), *The psychology of the Chinese people* (pp. 73–105). Hong Kong: Oxford University Press.

37. Allport, G. (1958). *The nature of prejudice.* New York: Doubleday.

38. Gudykunst, W. B., & Kim, Y. Y. (1997). *Communicating with strangers: An approach to intercultural communication.* New York: McGraw-Hill.

39. Brislin, R. (1981). *Cross-cultural encounters.* Elmsford, NY: Pergamon.

40. Ibid.

41. Ibid.

42. Ibid.

43. Ibid.

44. Ibid.

45. Ibid.

46. Ibid.

47. Ibid.

48. Ibid.

49. Rudmin, F. (1989). The pleasure of serendipity in historical research: On finding "stereotype" in Morier's (1824) Haiji Baba. *Cross-Cultural Psychology Bulletin, 23,* 8–11; Taylor, D. M., & Porter, L. E. (1994). A multicultural view of stereotyping. In W. J. Lonner & R. Malpass (Eds.), *Psychology and culture* (pp. 85–90). Boston: Allyn & Bacon.

50. Lippman, W. (1922). *Public opinion.* New York: Macmillan.

51. Schaefer, R. T. (2003). *Racial and ethnic groups* (9th ed.). New York: Prentice Hall.

52. Gudykunst & Kim, *Communicating with strangers.*

53. Taylor & Porter, "A multicultural view of stereotyping"; Berry et al., *Cross-cultural psychology.*

54. Esses, V. M., & Zanna, M. P. (1995). Mood and the expression of ethnic stereotypes. *Journal of Personality and Social Psychology, 69,* 1052–1068.

55. Katz, D., & Braly, K. W. (1933). Racial stereotypes of one hundred college students. *Journal of Abnormal Sociology and Psychology, 28,* 280–290.

56. Katz & Braly, "Racial stereotypes of one hundred college students"; Gilbert, G. (1951). Stereotype persistence and change among college students. *Journal of Abnormal and Social Psychology, 46,* 245–254; Gordon, L. (1973). The fragmentation of literary stereotypes of Jews and Negroes among college students. *Pacific Sociological Review, 16,* 411–425; Gordon, L. (1986). College student stereotypes of Blacks and Jews on two campuses: Four studies spanning 50 years. *Sociology and Social Research, 70,* 200–201; Devine, P G., & Elliot, A. J. (1995). Are racial stereotypes really fading? The Princeton trilogy revisited. *Personality and Social Psychology Bulletin, 21,* 1139–1150.

57. Devine & Elliot, "Are racial stereotypes really fading?"

58. Taylor & Porter, "A multicultural view of stereotyping."

59. Ibid.

60. Trice, A. D., & Rush, K. (1995). Sex-stereotyping in four-year-olds' occupational aspirations. *Perceptual and Motor Skills, 81,* 701–702.

61. Devine, P. G. (1989). Stereotypes and prejudice: Their automatic and controlled components. *Journal of Personality and Social Psychology, 56,* 5–18.

62. Ibid.

63. Judd, C. M., & Park, B. (1988). Outgroup homogeneity: Judgments of variability at the individual and group levels. *Journal of Personality and Social Psychology, 54,* 778–788; Park, B., & Judd, C. M. (1990). Measures and models of perceived outgroup variability. *Journal of Personality and Social Psychology, 59,* 173–191; Taylor & Porter, "A multicultural view of stereotyping."

64. Taylor & Porter, "A multicultural view of stereotyping."

65. Schaefer, *Racial and ethnic groups.*

66. Tajfel, H. (1978). *Differentiating between social groups: Studies in intergroup behavior.* London: Academic Press.

67. Steele, C. M., & Aronson, J. (1995). Stereotype threat and the intellectual performance of African Americans. *Journal of Personality and Social Psychology, 69,* 797–811.

68. Bruner, J. S., & Goodman, C. C. (1947). Value and need as organizing factors in perception. *Journal of Abnormal Social Psychology, 42,* 33–44.

69. Duncan, B. L. (1976). Differential social perception and attribution of intergroup violence: Testing the lower limits of stereotyping of Blacks. *Journal of Personality and Social Psychology, 34,* 590–598.

70. Sagar, A. H., & Schofield, J. W. (1980). Racial and behavioral cues in Black and White children's perceptions of ambiguously aggressive acts. *Journal of Personality and Social Psychology, 39,* 590–598.

71. Sumner, W. G. (1906). *Folkways.* Boston: Ginn.

72. Segall, *Cross-cultural psychology.*

73. Lewis, I. M. (1985). *Social anthropology in perspective.* Cambridge, UK: Cambridge University Press; Lynn, R. (1976, July). The sociobiology of nationalism. *New Society,* pp. 11–14; Rushton, J. P. (1984). Genetic similarity, human altruism, and group selection. *Behavioral and Brain Sciences, 12,* 503–559.

74. Lustig, M. W., & Koester, J. (2003). *Intercultural competence: Interpersonal communication across cultures.* Boston: Allyn & Bacon.

75. Segall, *Cross-cultural psychology.*

76. Hofstede, G. (1991). *Cultures and organizations: Software of the mind.* London: McGraw-Hill.

77. Klopf, D. W. (1995). *Intercultural encounters: The fundamentals of intercultural communication.* Englewood, CO: Morton.

78. Neuliep, J. W., & McCroskey, J. C. (1997). The development of a U.S. and generalized ethnocentrism scale. *Communication Research Reports, 14,* 385–398.

79. Levinson, D. J. (1950). Politico-economic ideology and group memberships in relation to ethnocentrism. In T. W. Adorno, E. Frenkel-Brunswik, D. J. Levinson, & R. N. Sanford (Eds.), *The authoritarian personality* (pp. 151–221). New York: Harper & Brothers. Quote on page 151.

80. Taylor, D. M., & Jaggi, V. (1974). Ethnocentrism and causal attribution in a South Indian context. *Journal of Cross-Cultural Psychology, 5,* 162–171.

81. Neuliep & McCroskey, "The development of a U.S. and generalized ethnocentrism scale."

82. Ibid.

83. Gudykunst & Kim, *Communicating with strangers.*

84. Guan, S. J. (1995). *Intercultural communication.* Beijing: Peking University Press.

85. Gudykunst & Kim, *Communicating with strangers.*

86. Peng, F. (1974). Communicative distance. *Language Science, 31,* 32–38.

87. Lukens, J. (1978). Ethnocentric speech. *Ethnic Groups, 2,* 35–53.

88. Gudykunst & Kim, *Communicating with strangers;* Peng, "Communicative distance"; Lukens, "Ethnocentric speech."

89. Neuliep & McCroskey, "The development of a U.S. and generalized ethnocentrism scale."

90. Neuliep, J. W., Hintz, S. M., & McCroskey, J. C. (2005). The influence of ethnocentrism in organizational contexts: Perceptions of interviewee and managerial attractiveness, credibility, and effectiveness. *Communication Quarterly, 53*(1), 41–56.

91. House, T. (2001). Equal hiring a must. *Computerworld, 35,* 32–34.

92. Neuliep et al., "The influence of ethnocentrism in organizational contexts."

93. Kraiger, K., & Ford, J. K. (1985). A meta-analysis of ratee race effects in performance ratings. *Journal of Applied Psychology, 70,* 56–65; Landy, F., & Farr, J. (1980). Performance rating. *Psychological Bulletin, 87,* 72–107.

94. This discussion of racism is based on de Benoist, A. (1999). What is racism? *Telos, 114,* 11–49; D'Souza, D. (1995). *The end of racism: Principles for a multiracial society.* New York: Free Press.

95. These quotes were taken from D'Souza, *The End of Racism,* pp. 28–29.

96. This slavery argument is found in a variety of sources. The sources used here are "A Learned Behaviour," *Canada & the World Backgrounder, 61* (1996), 4–10; M. T. Briggs, director and producer. (1987). *Ethnic notions* [Film]. Available from California Newsreel, Berkeley, CA.

97. Wolfe, C. T., & Spencer, S. J. (1996). Stereotypes and prejudice. *American Behavioral Scientist, 40,* 177–187; Castle, S. (1993). Explaining racism in the new Germany. *Social Alternatives, 12,* 9–13.

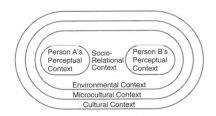

CHAPTER 6

The Socio-Relational Context

"Americans of all ages, all conditions, and all dispositions form associations . . . associations of a thousand different kinds—religious, moral, serious, futile, extensive, or restricted, enormous or diminutive."

—Alexis de Tocqueville[1]

Chapter Objectives

After reading this chapter, you should be able to

1. Compare and contrast membership and nonmembership groups.
2. Compare and contrast voluntary and involuntary groups.
3. Define and discuss the significance of reference groups.
4. Define and discuss the concept of group roles.
5. Compare and contrast formal and informal roles across cultures.
6. Compare and contrast sex roles across cultures.
7. Compare and contrast family roles across cultures.

All human beings, regardless of culture, belong to groups. Although some cultures (like the United States) promote individuality and independence, our survival depends on our interdependency and cooperation with other humans. This, of course, requires human communication. Historians believe that it was through social cooperation, social organization, the initiation of group hunting methods, a system of distributing work, and our ability to share knowledge that empowered our human ancestors to survive when other related species, such as Neanderthals, became extinct.[2]

In many ways, intercultural communication is a group phenomenon experienced by individuals. In other words, when people from different cultures come together to interact, they typically view each other not as unique individuals, but as members of a different cultural *group*. Think about your own communication experiences with strangers from different cultures. When you meet a stranger from a different culture, do you see that person as an individual or as a member of a cultural group that is different from your own? Even intraculturally, that is, within our own culture, when we meet strangers, we typically see them in terms of the groups to which they belong (e.g., sex, race, age, and so on.). In fact, there is no other way to describe a stranger than by the groups to which he or she belongs. The *socio-relational context,* then, refers to how group memberships affect communication. Whenever people from different cultures come together to interact, their verbal and nonverbal messages are defined by, and filtered through, their group memberships. The social relationship they develop is significantly influenced by the groups to which they belong, hence the term *socio-relational context.*

Although all people belong to groups, the nature of group membership and group behavior, especially group communication, differs considerably across cultures. The number of social groups to which a person belongs, the length of association with those groups, whether group membership is determined by birth or eligibility, and the purpose of the groups varies from one culture to the next. Our membership in groups represents the socio-relational context of intercultural communication.

The purpose of this chapter is to explore the idea of groupness and how social groups vary across cultures. The first part of this chapter focuses on definitional aspects of group memberships and categories of groups. The second part of the chapter discusses role relationships, social hierarchies, and stratification across cultures. The third part of the chapter looks at family groups, and the final part of the chapter examines gender groups.

DIMENSIONS OF GROUP VARIABILITY

Membership and Nonmembership Groups

Much of what makes each of us human is our membership in social groups. Regardless of our culture, we all belong to groups. For individuals in any culture there are those groups to which they belong, called membership groups, and those groups to which they do not belong, called nonmembership groups. There are two classes of membership groups, voluntary and involuntary. Involuntary membership groups are those groups to which people have no choice but to belong. Examples of involuntary membership groups include one's age, race, sex, and biological family group. Obviously, we cannot choose our age, race, or sex. Although we may choose to interact or not with our biological family group, we cannot choose our biological father, mother, brother, or sister. Voluntary membership groups are those groups to which people consciously choose to belong. Examples of voluntary groups include one's political affiliation, religion, occupation, and to some extent, economic status, among others.[3] Whether group membership is voluntary or involuntary varies according to culture. In some cultures, such as China, people may have no choice but to belong to a particular religion or political party. In fact, there may be strong sanctions for not belonging to a group. For example, Islam is the official religion of the Kingdom of Saudi Arabia. According to Saudi law, the public practice of any religion other than Islam is illegal. Hence, essentially 100% of the native population practices some form of Islam. According to Anne Wolter, who lived in Saudi Arabia, the Saudi government is a monarchy where the citizens have virtually no participation in governmental matters.[4] In a stark comparison with Saudi Arabia, there are more than 130 organized religions in the United States and a person can choose to belong to any one of them. As we all know, the U.S. Constitution guarantees freedom of religion.

Nonmembership groups are those groups to which people do not belong. Like membership groups, nonmembership groups can be voluntary or involuntary. Some people may want to belong to a group but are ineligible to join because they do not possess the needed qualifications (e.g., age, education, and so on.). In other cases people might be eligible for membership in a group but choose not to join. The distinction is important because people who are eligible to join a group but choose not to belong may be more likely than ineligible nonmembers to accept and embrace the norms and behaviors of the group. Nonmembers may also differ regarding their ability and motivation to become members. For example, some nonmembers may aspire to membership, some may be indifferent, and others may be motivated to remain unaffiliated. In India, people are divided into social classes called castes. According to Bishop, there are dramatic social disparities between the different levels of the caste system. Usually, members of the lower levels are exploited and treated very harshly. The four main castes, from highest to lowest, are Brahmans, Kshatriyas, Vaisyas, and Sudras. In India, a native person is born into a caste and cannot leave it until the beginning of the next lifetime. Hence one is born into a membership caste group (i.e., involuntary membership group) and is ineligible for membership in any other caste.[5]

Ingroups and Outgroups

In 1906 sociologist William Graham Sumner introduced the concepts of ingroup and outgroup when he wrote,

> A differentiation arises between ourselves, the we-group, or ingroup, and everybody else, or the others-group, out-group. The insiders in a we-group are in a relation of peace, order, law, government and industry, to each other. Their relation to all outsiders, or others-group, is one of war and plunder, except as agreements have modified it. . . . The relation of comradeship and peace in the we-group and that of hostility and war towards the others-group are correlative to each other.[6]

Based on Sumner's thesis, ingroups represent a special class of membership group characterized by a potent internal cohesiveness among its members and a sometimes intense hostility toward outgroups (see Figure 6.2). To be sure, however, earnest loyalty to one's membership group does not necessarily mean that you will feel hostility toward nonmembership groups or outgroups. Sumner's dichotomy of ingroup-outgroup animosity can be seen in cases of extreme nationalism. According to Merton, nationalists are members of a group, usually ethnic and/or religious, who believe that their group should dominate and rule a political entity such as a state or nation. A nationalist state, then, is dominated by an ethnic or religious group. The symbols and laws of a nationalist state are reflective of the particular ethnic or religious group. Nationalist groups believe that political organizations within the state or nation should be ethnic or religious in character and may take extreme measures to see that they are. Intense nationalism has been blamed for the atrocities in the war in the former Yugoslavia. In countries such as Bosnia, Serbia, Croatia, and Herzegovina, being a member of an outgroup (e.g., Muslim) has cost more than 200,000 people their lives. The term *ethnic cleansing,* used often to describe aspects of the conflict in Yugoslavia, refers to a process of systematically killing people on the basis of their ethnicity and/or religion. Although this is an extreme example of the ingroup-outgroup phenomenon, it vividly demonstrates how much group membership and nonmembership can affects our lives.[7]

Harry Triandis defines an ingroup as a group whose norms, aspirations, and values shape the behavior of its members. An outgroup, on the other hand, is a group whose attributes are dissimilar from those of the ingroup, or that opposes the accomplishment of the ingroup's goals. Triandis maintains that in order to be classified as an outgroup, the group must be perceived as threatening in some way to the ingroup, be relatively stable and impenetra-

Figure 6.2 Ingroups are characterized by a potent internal cohesiveness among its members and sometimes an intense hostility toward outgroups

ble, and dissimilar. An important point articulated by Triandis is that persons can be perceived as ingroup members in one context and outgroup members in another.[8] For example, a White American might view a Black American as a member of an outgroup within the boundaries of the United States, but sees the same person as an ingroup member while visiting a foreign country. Furthermore, definitions of ingroups and outgroups differ widely across cultures. In Greece, for example, family and close friends are considered ingroup members whereas other Greeks are outgroup members.

Brewer and Campbell assert that the tendency to distinguish between ingroups and outgroups is universal.[9] As mentioned in Chapter 5, when we meet someone from a different culture for the first time, we immediately categorize him or her as an ingroup or outgroup member. Attributions about ingroup and outgroup members are typically biased in favor of the ingroup at the expense of the outgroup. Some theorists argue that ingroup biases function to promote, enhance, protect, and maintain the ingroup's self-esteem. Others maintain that ingroup biases function to preserve ingroup solidarity and justify the exploitation of outgroups. Tajfel and Turner argue that the mere presence of an outgroup is sufficient to provoke intergroup competition or discriminatory responses from the ingroup. Moreover, the magnitude of ingroup and outgroup dissimilarity tends to intensify ingroup biases. That is, the more the groups appear different (e.g., sex, race, religion, status, and so on), the greater the extent of ingroup bias.[10]

Richard Schaefer points out that ingroup bias can manifest itself in what he calls ingroup virtues and outgroup vices. The behaviors and practices of the ingroup often are perceived by the ingroup as virtuous (i.e., ingroup virtues) yet when the very same behaviors are practiced by the outgroup, they are seen as unacceptable (outgroup vices).[11] For example, Christians may view the fervor with which they practice their religion as commendable, yet think of Islamic or Jewish fundamentalism as unprogressive and backward. White students on some college campuses complain that formation of Black student unions and Black fraternities and sororities constitutes a kind of "self-segregation" of Blacks. Blacks, however, may label their behavior as "self-affirmation."[12]

Reference Groups

Another type of group that affects our communication and our relationships with others is the reference group. A reference group is a group to which we may or may not belong, but we identify with it in some important way. A reference group possesses some quality to which we aspire and hence serves as a "reference" for our decisions or behavior. From time to time we are faced with decisions about matters of which we know very little or need direction. We may not know how to feel about a particular political issue or which way to vote in an upcoming referendum. In these kinds of situations we often look to others whose opinion we value and trust to help us make our decision. For example, students often look to teachers for guidance. In this way teachers are a reference group for students. Attorneys may be a reference group for law students. We use the group's position on an issue as a reference, standard, or barometer in developing our own attitudes. Reference groups can be membership or nonmembership and positive or negative. For example, in deciding for which political candidate to cast your vote, you may look to your political party (i.e., a membership group) for guidance. A law student, for example, might view lawyers or judges as a reference group but does not yet belong to the group. Usually, though not necessarily, voluntary membership ingroups serve as positive reference groups whereas voluntary nonmembership outgroups are seen as negative reference groups.

Napier and Gershenfeld point out that reference groups serve two functions—a comparative function and a normative function.[13] We often use reference groups to compare ourselves in making judgments and evaluations. For example, when professors return examinations, students try very hard to see the grades of their peers in an effort to determine their own relative standing. If a student fails an examination but learns that most of the class failed, then she or he does not feel so bad. A failing grade has less impact if several other students failed as well.

Individuals also use reference groups to establish the norms and standards to which they conform. For example, many students on college campuses dress according to how other students dress. Our reference groups influence our self-concept, self-esteem, and our relationships with others. For example, in most cultures children look to their elders as a positive reference group. The elders of the Masai culture of southern Kenya are an important reference group. Social power in Masai culture is based on age. This is called a gerontocracy. In the Masai gerontocracy, wisdom, insight, and sound judgment stem from age and are highly respected. The elders have moral and political authority, and the younger Masai age groups look to them for advice and direction. Through their age-based level in the hierarchy, the elders are the central reference group of their culture.[14]

ROLE RELATIONSHIPS, SOCIAL STRATIFICATION, AND HIERARCHY

Role Relationships

Whenever we join a group, voluntarily or involuntarily, we assume a role. A role is one's relative position in a group; that is, one's rank. Any group role exists in relation to some other role in that group. In fact, roles cannot exist in isolation; they are always related to some other role. You cannot be a son without a father. You cannot be a student without a teacher. Leaders cannot lead without followers.

With all roles, in all groups, certain behaviors are expected. A role, then, can be defined as one's relative position in a group with an expected set of verbal and nonverbal behaviors. By virtue of our membership in groups, even family groups, we are expected to behave in certain ways, usually according to some set of standards or norms established by the group. In your role as student, for example, you are expected to attend class, write papers, and complete examinations, among other behaviors. Within groups, roles are hierarchically organized, where some roles have more influence and prestige than others. In this sense, our role in a group represents our relative position or rank in the group.[15]

There are two types of roles in most cultures: formal and informal.[16] Formal roles have very well defined, and often contractual, behavioral expectations associated with them. The chief executive officer of a corporation, the president of your college or university, and the President of the United States have a clearly prescribed set of behaviors that they are expected to enact by virtue of their role. Most fraternities/sororities and academic organizations have constitutions or charters that very specifically spell out the roles of their officers and members. In many cases, the person assuming a formal role takes an oath declaring his or her allegiance to the group and faithful effort to follow the expectations prescribed. Violations of such prescriptions are often subject to negative evaluation and even removal from the role. An important point about formal roles is that regardless of who assumes the role, the behavioral expectations remain the same. Formal roles and their prescriptions vary across cultures.

Informal roles are learned informally and are much less explicit than formal roles. Unlike formal roles, the behavioral expectations associated with informal roles must be mastered by experience and vary considerably from person to person and group to group. Your role as son or daughter, brother or sister, or even boyfriend or girlfriend, for example, is learned through experience. What it means to be a son or daughter in your family may be quite different from what it means to be a son or daughter in the family of your next-door neighbor. Informal roles and their prescriptions vary across and within cultures.

Roles and communication are integrally linked. Roles prescribe (1) with whom, (2) about what, and (3) how to communicate with others.[17] Because you are assuming the role of student, most of the people with whom you communicate include teachers, students, resident hall assistants, librarians, and so on. If not for your role as college student, you probably would not have communicated with any of the people with whom you have already communicated today. In addition to prescribing with whom you communicate, your role prescribes the topic of your communication. With teachers, for example, much of your interaction is about class-related topics and assignments. Finally, your role defines how you communicate, or your style of communication. When you are interacting with your professors about class-related topics, you probably engage in a more formal communication pattern than when you interact with other students. You probably use less slang and perhaps speak more politely with professors than with other students.

Henri Tajfel contends that our social identity is created by our total combination of roles. He argues that one's social identity is that part of the individual's self-concept derived from his or her membership in social groups together with the value and significance attached to that membership.[18]

Because the nature and prevalence of formal and informal roles varies so much across cultures, the roles we assume in our native culture may not be practiced or valued similarly in another culture. This would include the roles we assume in our cultural, national, ethnic, demographic, and various other ingroups.

Because roles and communication are so closely related, they must be considered cross-cultural; that is, roles vary significantly across cultures. For example, although there are probably teachers and students in every culture, what it means to be a teacher or student in the United States might differ remarkably from what it means in China or Japan. Gudykunst and Kim argue that there are at least four dimensions upon which roles vary across cultures and involve the degree of personalness, formality, hierarchy, and deviation from the ideal role enactment.[19] According to Gudykunst and Kim, roles can vary from personal to impersonal. Some role relationships are quite close and perhaps intimate, whereas others are distant. The degree of formality between roles varies from formal to informal. In some cases our role relationships are prim and proper, whereas others are casual and relaxed. The degree of hierarchy refers to how strictly roles are ranked from one another. In some cultures there may be a very rigid hierarchical distinction between student and teacher, whereas in others the difference is quite loose and flexible. The degree of deviation allowed refers to how much a person is permitted to deviate from the prescribed role expectation without significant negative sanction.

Using the roles of teacher and student in the United States and Korea illustrates how Gudykunst and Kim's four dimensions can be applied. In Korea, there is an old adage "One should not step even on the shadow of one's teacher." This expression, emphasizing the degree of respect accorded teachers, has been a guiding tenet in Korean education for years. Social order in Korea is based on Confucianism, whose central axiom is obedience to superiors. At just about any type of social gathering, who greets whom first, who sits where, who sits first, who speaks first, and so on, is of utmost importance. In Korea, special attention must be taken not to upset the social order, for to do so is interpreted as uncouth and lacking in social decorum. In Korea, the recognition of one's place in the social hierarchy is communicated via special vocabularies. These vocabularies consist of special terms and phrases for addressing one who is superior, equal, or of lower status.[20]

In the United States most students respect their teachers but do not recognize the strict adherence to formality and hierarchy to the degree that is seen in Korea. In Korea, the student/teacher role relationship is quite proper and formal, and the communication is scripted. Similarly, the difference in rank between Korean student and teacher is very strict and recognized.

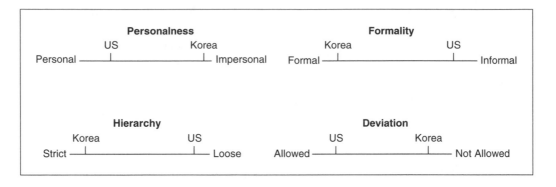

Figure 6.3

On the other hand, the student/teacher role relationship in the United States is more personal and probably allows for more deviation from the ideal role prescription. Students and teacher can interact informally and may even engage in activities outside the formal classroom. On the four role dimensions outlined by Gudykunst and Kim, we can see where the student/ teacher role relationship might fall in both cultures (see Figure 6.3). In most cases the student/teacher relationship in Korea is less personal, more formal, and more hierarchical, with less room for deviation from the ideal role enactment than in the United States.

AN INTERCULTURAL CONVERSATION: STUDENT/TEACHER ROLE POSITIONS

Because roles prescribe with whom, about what, and how people communicate, differences in the four role dimensions manifest themselves in communication. Below are two cross-cultural interactions between a student and a teacher. Scenario A is between a student and a teacher in the United States. Scenario B is between a student and a teacher in Korea. Note the differences in formality and personalness and the degree to which the students recognize the hierarchical difference between themselves and the teacher. In each case the student wishes to speak to the teacher about an assignment.

Scenario A	
Jeff:	(approaches Dr. Neuliep's office unannounced) *Hey, Dr. N., how's it goin'?*
Dr. Neuliep:	*Hey, Jeff, what's up?*

Jeff:	(Steps into the office) *I thought I would stop by an' see if I could talk to ya about my paper assignment.*
Dr. Neuliep:	*Sure, c'mon in, have a seat. What are you thinking about?*
Jeff:	*Well . . . I'm kinda havin' some trouble coming up with a topic. Do you have any ideas?*
Dr. Neuliep:	*I suggest doing something that's very interesting to you, otherwise the assignment might bore you to death. Stay away from topics that have very little research associated with them. Also . . . you might try doing a search on the Internet. Sometimes you'll find topics that you might not ever have thought of yourself.*
Jeff:	*Yeah . . . that's a good idea. If I find somethin', can I stop by and show it to you before I get started?*
Dr. Neuliep:	*Sure, just stop by or leave a message on my voice mail.*
Jeff:	*OK, yeah. OK, well . . . thanks a lot.*
Dr. Neuliep:	*Sure.*

Scenario B

Mino:	(approaches Dr. Choi's office and knocks on the door) *Good morning, Professor Choi.*
Dr. Choi:	*Hello, Mino.*
Mino:	*I am here for my appointment.*
Dr. Choi:	*Yes.*
Mino:	*May I come in?*
Dr. Choi:	*Yes.*
Mino:	*Thank you* (enters Dr. Choi's office). *I am here to approve my topic for the research paper assignment, as you requested.*
Dr. Choi:	*Yes, what have you decided?*
Mino:	*I would like to research the natural resources of northern India, if that is acceptable.*
Dr. Choi:	*Yes, that topic is fine.*
Mino:	*Thank you. Thank you for seeing me this morning.*
Dr. Choi:	*Yes, you are welcome. Good day.*

The conversation between Jeff and Dr. Neuliep was generally smooth and coordinated. The situation was informal enough that Jeff shows up unannounced, without an appointment. Jeff uses informal dialect (e.g., "havin'," "ya," and so on.) and refers to Dr. Neuliep as "Dr. N," demonstrating a degree of personalness. Dr. Neuliep invites Jeff to sit down, reducing the hierarchical distance between them. Generally, their conversation, though perfectly respectful, was informal. In Scenario B, Mino has set up an appointment with Dr. Choi prior to the meeting, shows up at the appointed time, and asks permission to enter the office. The conversation was rather formal and impersonal. Mino did not engage in any slang or informal vocabulary, did not sit down, and kept the conversation as short as possible. Unlike Jeff, Mino was prepared to state his choice of subject. To ask the professor for a suggestion, as Jeff did in Scenario A, would be impertinent in Korean culture, where responsibility rests entirely on the student.

Role Differentiation and Stratification

As mentioned earlier, whenever we assume a role in a group, that role represents our rank or relative position within the group. On a much larger scale, our roles are ranked by our culture as well. Some roles are at the top of the hierarchy, while others are at the bottom. In the United States, for example, physicians and attorneys are high-ranked roles, whereas used-car salespeople are low-ranked occupational roles. The rank ordering of roles within a culture is called social stratification. Social stratification varies across cultures, and not all roles are valued the same across cultures.

The complexity of the role hierarchy varies from culture to culture, too. Some cultures make relatively few distinctions, whereas others make many; this is called role differentiation. For example, a relatively undifferentiated culture might distinguish among only a few roles, such as family, social, and occupational roles. A highly differentiated culture may make numerous role distinctions, such as corporate roles (e.g., owner, vice president, manager, worker, retiree); religious roles (e.g., pope, cardinal, bishop, priest, parishioner); educational roles (e.g., superintendent, principal, teacher, senior, junior, sophomore, freshman); and military roles (e.g., general, colonel, major, captain, lieutenant), among others. According to cross-cultural researcher John Berry and his colleagues, social stratification exists in a culture with a highly differentiated role hierarchy that is organized in a vertical status structure. As mentioned above, most cultures have some form of role hierarchy that distinguishes among high- and low-ranking roles. Berry maintains that cultural role differentiation and stratification appear to be related to the ecological systems among cultures. For example, nomadic hunter-gatherer cultures tend to have less role differentiation and stratification, whereas industrialized urban cultures are typically quite differentiated and stratified. Sedentary agricultural societies fall somewhere in the middle.[21]

Although it is impossible to generalize across every culture, many collectivistic, high-context, and high power distance cultures possess a relatively strict hierarchical role stratification compared to low-context, individualistic, small power distance cultures. Recall from Chapter 2 that individualistic, small power distance cultures believe that all people are created equal and have inalienable rights. Collectivistic cultures, on the other hand, see people not as individuals, but as members of groups. In these cultures, one's level in the role stratification hierarchy often is based on one's membership in sex, age, family, and occupation groups. In such cultures, one person is almost always more powerful than another. Mike Keberlien points out that the Guatemalan Ladino stratification is vertically shaped, like a pyramid, with the wealthy on top and the poor on the bottom. Belonging to an upper class means owning a home and having land to work and rent. Members of the upper class have their own social ingroups, such as the International Rotary Club, to which only they are accepted for membership. Lower-class Ladinos are left to work the land. They are also the ones who attend church most often. The upper class, however, establishes the rules considered socially acceptable. Interestingly, according to Keberlien, the lower-class Ladinos practice the values of the culture more than any other social class.

Perhaps the most notorious system of social stratification is the caste system of India. According to Duley, castes (or jatis) are endogamous groups in which membership is by birth. A Hindu is born into a caste and cannot leave it until the beginning of the next lifetime. The caste system prescribes a very strict and practiced code of conduct. A person's social status depends on the caste to which he or she belongs. Although deemed illegal 50 years ago, the caste system still operates in many parts of India today, especially rural areas. Although the system contains literally thousands of subcastes, there are four or five generally recognized levels. At the top of the castes are the Brahmins. These are priests or seers who possess spiritual power. Next are the Kshatriyas; that is, warriors and rulers. The third level are the Vaishyas, or merchants. The fourth level are the Sudras, who may be farmers. Outside the caste system are the untouchables, or as Ghandi termed them, the Harijan, meaning "children of God." Untouchables are workers who take on the lowest of jobs, such as sweepers, butchers, potters, and so on. Also outside the system are trial groups (called adivasis) with unique ethnic, linguistic, and cultural histories.[22]

Because roles prescribe with whom, about what, and how to communicate with others, communication in cultures with a rigid social stratification system is very predictable. Verbal and nonverbal messages are prescribed according to one's role and rank in the social hierarchy. Accepted forms of address, vocabulary, nonverbal behavior such as eye contact, and social manners are defined for practically every social situation. When two strangers interact for the first time, much uncertainty is reduced simply by recognizing role differences. They only need to know each other's role in order to communicate appropriately. Although not exclusively, many of these cultures can be found in the East (e.g., China, Japan, India, Korea).

Many individualistic, low-context, low power distance cultures profess equality and minimize role stratification. In the United States, for example, children are taught that they are equal to everyone else. In fact, in many of these cultures, equality is legislated. Although role differences are recognized and respected, these cultures believe that a person occupying a role is a unique individual. In this sense, knowing someone's role provides only minimal information about the person. Hence, knowing one's role does not reduce as much uncertainty as it would in a high-context, high power distance culture. Many of these cultures can be found in the West, but there are certainly exceptions (e.g., Australia, New Zealand).

Understanding a culture's role differentiation and stratification is important for communication because special vocabularies exist for different roles. Donald Klopf notes, for example, that in Korea, the terms a husband will use to refer to his wife vary depending on with whom he is interacting. She is his *cho* when he is speaking to someone of higher rank, his *chip saram* when speaking to an equal, or his *ago omoni* when speaking to a person of lower rank or status.[23] Communication problems often result when persons from different cultures do not understand or recognize the role differences between cultures. Many international exchange students may find American teachers rather informal and personal compared to their teachers. Students from Eastern cultures, for example, find an American teacher's use of humor quite strange, because teachers in their cultures would never act in such a way.

AN INTERCULTURAL CONVERSATION: CROSS-CULTURAL ROLE POSITIONS

In cultures such as the United States, Canada, and Australia, among others, people are accustomed to treating everyone else as equal regardless of sex, age, occupation, and so on. This can lead to misunderstandings when interacting with people who, in their culture's role hierarchy, are accorded special privileges. In the following cross-cultural interaction, Mr. Mammen, an East Indian living in the United States, has taken his wife and family to a very nice restaurant. When he arrives at the restaurant he expects to be seated, even though he has not made dinner reservations. Because of his social standing, he assumes that he will be accommodated.[24]

Mr. Mammen:	(Approaches the host)
Host:	*Good evening, may I help you?*
Mr. Mammen:	*Yes, my wife and family are here for dinner.*
Host:	*Certainly, your name please?*
Mr. Mammen:	*I am Mr. Mammen.*
Host:	*I'm sorry, I don't see your name on our reservation listing.*
Mr. Mammen:	*I don't have reservations, but I can make them now.*
Host:	*I'm sorry, but this evening's dinner reservation list is completely full.*
Mr. Mammen:	*No . . . I disagree. This restaurant is not full. I see empty tables.*
Host:	*Yes, but these tables are reserved for those people who have reservations for this evening.*
Mr. Mammen:	*I will make reservation right now.*
Host:	*I'm sorry, but the evening is completely full.*
Mr. Mammen:	*I can see that it is not full. I want to see a manager right now! I am here to have dinner!*

Because of his cultural role position, in Mr. Mammen's native culture he probably would have been seated in the restaurant even though he did not have a reservation. In the United States, however, one's occupational role will not ensure any special favors outside of that occupation. The host of this restaurant is simply following his culture's way of treating everyone; that is, equally. In the illustration above, this has led to conflict and misunderstanding.

Family Groups

All human beings, regardless of culture, belong to a family. One's biological or adoptive family is the first and probably most significant socialization influence on a child. The structure of the family and the degree of influence a family has on its children differ notably across cultures. The nuclear family consists of the father, mother, and children. The extended family consists of the nuclear family plus other relatives, such as grandparents, uncles, aunts, cousins, and in-laws. As a unit, the nuclear family is prevalent in most low-context, individualistic, low power distance cultures such as the United States, Canada, and northern European cultures such as England, Ireland, Germany, and France. Extended families are common in Central and South America, Africa, the Middle East, and throughout Asia, although trends are changing even in these countries. There are clearly exceptions to the above list, such as African-American families in the United States, who have a cultural pattern of a very strong extended family interaction and kinship network. In collectivistic cultures, families are generally cohesive and well integrated. Familial relations are caring and warm, but also hierarchical. The decision-making process typically is not democratic. The interests of the family group take precedence over individual family members. Familial role prescriptions are clearly defined not only within the family, but also in the larger cultural context. In individualistic cultures, on the other hand, there is less emphasis on hierarchy and more emphasis on individual development. Family decisions may be more participative than in collectivistic cultures. Familial role prescriptions are open and may vary considerably across the cultural context.

In the Hmong culture of Laos, the most important sociocultural groups are the family and the clan, both of which are headed by men. According to Katie Thao, the Hmong clan system combines social, political, economic, and religious dimensions and is the primary guide for Hmong behavior. Within a clan, each person has certain obligations to others. When one shares with fellow clan members, the act is returned. Clan members of the same generation (but of different biological families) will call each other "brothers" and "sisters." Although the bond is not biological, it is so close that marriages between members of the same clan are seen as almost incestuous, leading to the Hmong practice of clan exogamy.[25]

In most cultures the family group is the most valued society structure. Familial role prescriptions, however, differ widely across cultures. For example, two important variables in understanding Korean family structure are family surname and Confucianism. According to Sungjong Paik, there are only about 250 family names in South and North Korea. In fact, more than half of the population uses one of five family names: Kim, Yi, Pak, Ch'oe, and Chong. One in five family names in Korea is Kim. Fifteen percent of Koreans use Yi, nine percent use Pak, five percent use Ch'oe, and four percent use Chong. In comparison, in many other countries, like the United States, literally hundreds of thousands of family names are used.[26]

Many Koreans believe that because of their common family names, they are descended from a common ancestor. Hence, many Koreans belong to formal family name organizations, called taejonghoe. According to Paik, taejonghoe are rather formal organizations with head offices in Seoul and hundreds of branch offices throughout the country. Taejonghoe publish newsletters, award scholarships, and sponsor sporting events. Paik argues that taejonghoe exercise great influence on Korean social life. For example, one's social status is often determined by membership in a specific family name lineage. Moreover, Paik asserts that many politicians try to use their family names to gain political influence.[27]

As in many cultures, the family is the foundation of Korean society. Historically and in traditional Korean society, family roles and social interaction were governed by patriarchal Confucianism. Kyung-Sup Chang asserts that patriarchal Confucianism prescribes a social structure of *authoritarian collectivism*. According to Chang, traditional Korean patriarchal Confucianism imposes a rigid hierarchy and inequality between different age groups and between men and women. Males dominate females, and elders dominate young. In traditional Confucian families, children are socialized to conform with traditional gender stereotypes and are segregated by sex. Following the father, the eldest son has the highest social status in the family.[28] Kim notes that in traditional Korean families, certain rooms in the home are reserved for communication. Men interacted only with men in the outer room (sarang-bang), and women interacted with only women in the anbang (inner room).[29] Communication in Confucian familial relationships would require the use of a restricted code. In the United States, when speaking to a brother or sister, aunt or uncle, English speakers use the generic terms *brother, sister, aunt,* or *uncle.* Linguistically, one's age or status is irrelevant. In Korean language (i.e., Hangul), the relationship term used to refer to a familial relative changes based on the sender's and receiver's familial rank, which is based on his or her age and sex.

As in many cultures, family life in Korea is changing. Levande, Herrick, and Sung maintain that while filial piety (i.e., loyalty and obedience to parents, elderly) remains a central value among Koreans, familial relationships between parents and children are changing from one of duty and obligation to intergenerational affection. Levande, Herrick, and Sung argue that Korean families are moving away from the authoritarian and patriarchal norms of the past to more egalitarian and reciprocal patterns of mutual support between generations. For example, younger Koreans, in pursuit of educational and occupational opportunities, are increasingly moving to urban areas. The effect has been a decrease in the number of multigenerational, co-residing nuclear families. For example, in 1975, more than 90 percent of elderly Koreans lived with their children. That number decreased to 53 percent in 1996. Such trends are observed mostly in rural areas, where elderly people constitute the majority of the population. In urban areas, such as Seoul, the capital of South Korea, 65 percent of persons 60 or older live with their children. The majority of these persons live with their married sons.[30] Kim argues that living apart does not necessarily translate into autonomy from parents. Korean sons are still responsible for the parents' well-being and are expected to provide emotional and material support for them. Kim maintains that, in contemporary Korean society, nuclear families are faced with the social dilemma of having to appear autonomous yet interdependent, and private yet communal, simultaneously. Chun and MacDermaid agree, and assert that contemporary Korean families still value connectedness over separateness. They maintain that in contemporary Korean families, children associate strict parental control with warmth rather than hostility.[31]

As in Korea, filial piety is the dominant force in Chinese families, in which the elders maintain complete control in the home. Michael Bond has written extensively about the Chinese, and he maintains that Chinese women are beginning to make inroads toward equality. For example, half of the physicians in China are women. In the past, Chinese families had many children, but today, family planning is required, and abortions are easy to obtain and sometimes forced. Although the Chinese government seems coercive, Chinese parents seem to be extremely lenient and even lax in their child-rearing attitudes toward obedience with infants and young children. This is in sharp contrast to the strict discipline they impose on older children (beginning at about 4 to 6 years of age). According to Bond, communication between parents and their children is based on obedience, morality, and the acceptance of social obligation. A child's adventurous or risky activities are discouraged. On the other hand, sex training and control of aggression are severe. The father is the harsher disciplinarian, and fathers seem more distant toward their children than do mothers. In terms of communication, some studies have demonstrated that Chinese babies are less vocal, less active, less likely to smile, and more apprehensive in social situations than Caucasian babies.[32]

According to Tehmina Basit, the family group represents the foundation of Islamic society. Basit argues that obedience and respect for parents are repeatedly stressed in Islamic teachings. Mohammed Haroun maintains that, in Islam, the individual is not allowed to be just an individual who is free to do whatever he or she desires. Haroun alleges that any political or social system that makes the individual the basic unit of society does not take into account the natural bonds and needs of family. He says that the most *natural* unit of society is the family, and that in Islam, three factors keep the family together: kinship or blood ties, marital commitments, and faith. The traditional Muslim household is multigenerational and typically includes grandparents; parents; married sons, their wives, and children; unmarried sons and daughters; and sometimes an unmarried, widowed, or divorced uncle or aunt. Although Islamic teachings stipulate that men and women are equal, within the context of marriage, the man is endowed with authority over the woman and the family setting. Pels maintains that the role of the eldest male is that of patriarch, and therefore his authority is undisputed and paramount.[33]

Sex and Gender Groups

One group to which every human being belongs, regardless of culture, is biological sex. Biological differences between males and females are universally recognized. But like any other group, to be a member of a sex group is to assume a role—in this case, a sex role. And like any other role, one's sex role, or gender, is a set of expectations about how one should behave.

The terms *sex* and *gender* often are used interchangeably, but as Sandra Bem notes, the terms are not synonymous. Sandra Bem has done considerable research on sex roles. Like others, Bem recognizes that sex refers to the biological and anatomical classifications of males and females. Gender, on the other hand, is a social and symbolic creation that we learn through enculturation and socialization. Whereas sex is innate, gender is learned. In most cultures, however, there is a close association between sex and gender. That is, most cultures establish norms and expectations that they assign people on the basis of their biological sex. According to Bem, our sex role orientation (i.e., gender) is based on the extent to which we internalize our culture's sex type expectations of desirable behavior of men and women. In most cases, there is a high correlation between biological sex and sex role orientation. In other words, most people assume the gender roles that their culture prescribes. We are taught by our parents, teachers, and peers how we should behave based on our culture's standards. Boys are taught to be masculine (however the culture defines it) and girls are expected to act feminine (however the culture defines it). Thus, when cultures recognize some behaviors as masculine and others as feminine, they are saying that the majority of people taking on this role should be male (for the former) and female (for the latter). Gender, then, can be defined as the behavioral, cultural, and psychological traits typically associated with one's sex. To be sure, as Bem notes, this is not to say that a certain sex cannot fulfill the other role, but rather that the characteristics of the person assuming the role are associated with that sex. Indeed, some people possess both feminine and masculine traits. These persons may be classified as androgynous, a term that combines *andro,* meaning male/masculine, and *gyne,* meaning woman.[34]

More than 30 years ago, Bem developed an instrument designed to measure an individual's sex role orientation. The instrument, called the Bem Sex Role Inventory (BSRI), consists of a list of 60 personality traits, 20 of which are considered masculine, 20 of which are considered feminine, and 20 of which are considered neither masculine nor feminine and are included as neutral traits.[35] Examples of masculine traits on the BSRI include the terms *assertive, dominant, forceful,* and *aggressive.* Examples of feminine traits on the BSRI include the terms *yielding, understanding, tender,* and *warm.* Neutral traits include the terms *helpful, moody, conscientious,* and *reliable.* In completing the BSRI, respondents are instructed to indicate, on a 7-point scale (1 = *never* to 7 = *always*), the extent to which each of the 60 traits describes them. Based on the respondents' self-ratings, they can be classified as androgynous (i.e., high masculine score and high feminine score), masculine (i.e., high masculine score and low feminine score), feminine (i.e., low masculine score and high feminine score), or undifferentiated (i.e., low masculine score and low feminine score).

The BSRI has been used in a number of cross-cultural studies. Typically, researchers will have people from one culture complete the BSRI, and then compare the results with people from a different culture. For example, Zhang, Norvilitis, and Jin compared BSRI scores between Americans and Chinese. Their results indicated that the majority of BSRI scores, for both the masculine and feminine traits, were lower among the Chinese sample compared to the American sample. Zhang, Norvilitis, and Jin reasoned that Chinese men are less male oriented than American men and that Chinese women are less female oriented than American women, according to American standards for gender roles. Another possible explanation is that according to Confucian philosophy, moderation is highly valued, where one is encouraged to take the "middle road." Such philosophy may have led the Chinese participants to respond differently from Americans when completing the BSRI; that is, they are less likely to use extreme scores (i.e., 1s and 7s) in their responses.[36]

The BSRI also has been used to examine masculinity and femininity in Japan. In traditional Japanese society, sex roles were clearly differentiated between men and women. According to Sugihara and Katsurada, Japanese males were taught to be strong and maintain control and dominance over children and women. Japanese women were taught to be subservient to their husbands and to their male children in their old age. Sugihara and Katsurada also point out that the Japanese adopted the traditional division of labor, where the man provides for his family through his occupation, and the woman stays at home and does housework and child-rearing.[37] In related work, Katsurada and Sugihara argue that contemporary Japanese society has changed over the years in terms of the number of Japanese women in higher education, increasing numbers of Japanese women in the workforce, women delaying marriage, high divorce rates, and low birth rates. In addition, the number of men involved in domestic activities and enrolling in women's studies courses is increasing.

Katsurada and Sugihara maintain that along with these changes in Japanese society, gender role expectations have changed accordingly. In two separate studies, Katsurada and Sugihara had Japanese college students complete the BSRI. In one study, their results showed that male students rated the feminine items significantly higher than female students in terms of their desirability for men. No gender difference was found in the desirability items of feminine characteristics for women, however. In another study, Sugihara and Katsurada found no significant differences between Japanese males and Japanese females on either the masculinity or femininity scales of the BSRI. However, a comparison of the masculinity and femininity scores within male and female samples indicated that both male and female students scored higher on the femininity scale than the masculinity scale of the BSRI.[38] In related work, Shimonaka, Nakazato, and Kawaai examined the BSRI scores among elderly Japanese men and women and found that, like the Japanese college students, both elderly men and women scored higher on the femininity scale than the masculinity scale.[39]

The value associated with masculinity seems to vary across cultures (see Table 6.1). Although he did not use the BSRI in his seminal cross-cultural survey of more than fifty countries, Dutch sociologist Geert Hofstede asked participants to rate the value of masculinity. According to Hofstede, masculinity stands for a society in which social gender roles are clearly distinct. In masculine cultures men are conditioned to be assertive, tough, and focused on material success. In these same cultures women are conditioned to be modest, tender, and concerned with the quality of life. Hofstede argues that feminine-oriented cultures see sex roles as overlapping in some cases.[40]

The expectations and behaviors associated with masculinity and femininity can vary remarkably across cultures. In his study of the Sambian society of Papua, New Guinea, anthropologist Gilbert Herdt found that adolescent boys are required to perform fellatio (oral sex) on older men as a part of the initiation into manhood. Their culture believes that a Sambian boy cannot mature physically or emotionally unless he ingests another man's semen over a period of several years. In Sambian culture, such behavior is considered masculine.[41]

When people deviate from their cultural sex role expectations, they are often negatively sanctioned. Some researchers have argued that collectivistic cultures are more traditional than individualistic cultures and are more

Table 6.1

Countries With High Masculinity Scores	Countries With Low Masculinity Scores
Japan	South Korea
Austria	Uruguay
Venezuela	Guatemala
Italy	Thailand
Switzerland	Portugal
Mexico	Chile
Ireland	Finland
Jamaica	Yugoslavia
Great Britain	Costa Rica
Germany (FR)	Denmark
Philippines	Netherlands
Colombia	Norway
South Africa	Sweden
Ecuador	
USA	

likely to punish persons who violate cultural sex role expectations. Recall from Chapter 2 that collectivistic cultures stress interdependence, prescribe very clear role expectations, and value conforming to the needs of the group. Violating one's role prescription (including sex role) disrupts the harmony of the group. Individualistic cultures, on the other hand, value independence, self-expression, and the pursuit of individual goals over group goals. Promotion of an individual's uniqueness is common in individualistic cultures. Therefore, when an individual violates a cultural sex role expectation, it is likely to be tolerated more in an individualistic culture than in a collectivistic culture.[42]

Gender Stereotypes

In most cultures, men and women carry out different sex roles, yet there is remarkable consistency in how cultures view the roles of men and women. Since 1990, John Williams and Deborah Best, professors of psychology at Wake Forest University, have conducted a series of cross-cultural studies investigating gender stereotypes. Williams and Best asked university students in more than 30 countries to consider a list of 300 adjectives and to indicate whether in their culture the adjectives are more frequently associated with men, women, or equally with both. The responses of the participants in each

Table 6.2

Male Associated		Female Associated	
Active	Loud	Affected	Modest
Adventurous	Obnoxious	Affectionate	Nervous
Aggressive	Opinionated	Appreciative	Patient
Arrogant	Opportunistic	Cautious	Pleasant
Autocratic	Pleasure-seeking	Changeable	Prudish
Bossy	Precise	Charming	Self-pitying
Capable	Progressive	Complaining	Sensitive
Coarse	Quick	Complicated	Sentimental
Conceited	Rational	Confused	Sexy
Confident	Realistic	Curious	Shy
Courageous	Reckless	Dependent	Softhearted
Cruel	Resourceful	Dreamy	Sophisticated
Cynical	Rigid	Emotional	Submissive
Determined	Robust	Excitable	Suggestible
Disorderly	Serious	Fault-finding	Talkative
Enterprising	Sharp-witted	Fearful	Timid
Greedy	Show-off	Fickle	Touchy
Hardheaded	Steady	Foolish	Unambitious
Humorous	Stern	Forgiving	Unintelligent
Indifferent	Stingy	Frivolous	Unstable
Individualistic	Stolid (detached)	Fussy	Warm
Initiative	Tough	Gentle	Weak
Interests Wide	Unfriendly	Imaginative	Worrying
Inventive	Unscrupulous	Kind	Understanding
Lazy	Witty	Mild	Superstitious

country were tallied to determine for each adjective the frequency with which it was associated with men and with women. A surprising degree of cross-cultural agreement was found among 100 of the 300 adjectives. The 100 adjectives are presented in Table 6.2. The countries surveyed included Canada, Finland, England, Italy, Pakistan, Malaysia, Nigeria, Singapore, India, Japan, Netherlands, Venezuela, Germany, United States, New Zealand, Peru, Australia, South Africa, and Brazil.

Williams and Best also scored each of the adjectives in terms of its affective meaning, (i.e., its favorability, strength, and activity). They found that the characteristics associated with men were generally stronger (e.g., "Tough") and more active (e.g., "Robust") than those associated with women, but that the adjectives were equally favorable for both men and women. Williams and Best also concluded that the male stereotypes were more favorable than the female stereotypes in certain countries such as Japan, South Africa, and Nigeria, whereas the female stereotypes were more favorable in countries such as Italy, Peru, and Australia. They also found that gender stereotypes were more differentiated in Protestant countries than in Catholic countries.[43]

In a related study, Williams and Best surveyed 5- and 8-year-old children in 25 countries. In this study the children were shown silhouettes of a man and a woman and were asked to select between the ones described in brief stories. Their story was written to reflect the more important features of the adult sex stereotype characteristics. For example, children were asked to select "the person who gets into the most fights" or to select "the person who cries a lot." Their results indicate that the children in each culture showed at least a beginning knowledge of the adult stereotypes. The stories most frequently associated with the male figures were those involving the strong, aggressive, and cruel characteristics, whereas the stories associated with women were emotional, weak, and soft-hearted. Pakistani children seemed to show the most developed gender stereotypes, and the Brazilian children showed the least. In each country there was a significant increase in stereotype knowledge when moving from the 5- to the 8-year-old children.[44]

SEX AND GENDER ROLES ACROSS CULTURES

The variability of sex roles across cultures is dramatic. But many anthropologists and some feminist writers contend that although the customs and practices with which women's subordination is expressed differ from culture to culture, the secondary status of women across the globe is one of the few universal cross-cultural truisms. No book or chapter could possibly describe all of the sex role differences between males and females across all cultures. Discussed below is a selection of cultures and their sex roles, with special attention to women's roles.

Morocco

Leila Hessini has written about women's roles in Moroccan culture and points out that Moroccan society defines physical space according to male and female roles. Private space within the home is for family and is considered female space. Public space, on the other hand, is male space. Women are to fulfill their roles inside the female space; that is, the interior of the home. Men fulfill their roles in public spaces; that is, almost anywhere outside the home. Men are free to sit in public spaces where women are not welcome. According to Hessini, Article 36 of the Moroccan Personal Status code, called the Mudwanna, was enacted in 1957 and stipulates a wife's duties to her husband, as follows: (a) fidelity; (b) obedience according to accepted custom; (c) breastfeeding of children; (d) management of the household; and (e) deference toward the husband's father, mother, and close relatives. Article 35 of the Mudwanna specifies the husband's duties to his wife, as follows: (a) financial support, (b) equal treatment of all spouses (i.e., in the case of polygamy), (c) authorization for his wife to visit her parents within the limits of socially accepted norms, and (d) protecting the wife's total freedom to administer her possessions independent of the husband's control. Hessini notes, however, that a gap has grown between what the Mudwanna legally stipulates and how people actually behave.[45]

Japan

Sumiko Iwao has written a fascinating book portraying the role of women in contemporary Japan. Sumiko notes that the "kimono clad, bamboo parasol-toting, bowing female walking three paces behind her husband" is still seen in some parts of Japan. But Iwao contends that the lives and attitudes of many younger contemporary Japanese women have undergone dramatic changes in the past 20 years. The postwar Japanese Constitution stipulates that all Japanese are equal under the law and outlaws discrimination on the basis of sex. To be sure, however, most private and political organizations that comprise the dominant Japanese culture are controlled by men. But Japanese women enjoy more freedom today than perhaps ever in their history (see Figure 6.4). Iwao remarks that although today's Japanese women are much more outspoken and direct than their mothers, even modern Japanese women recognize their secondary status and have not completely discarded their earmark passivity. Moreover, when asked, many Japanese women acknowledge their fate as a subordinate group. Even the modern Japanese woman's happiness remains tied to her family, so much so that she will repress her personal feelings to an extent that many American women would find unendurable. Following their collectivistic histories, most Japanese women continue to sacrifice personal goals for the sake of the harmony of the family. Because they have fewer opportunities than men, maintaining interpersonal harmony is of the utmost concern for Japanese women.[46]

Figure 6.4   Japanese women enjoy more freedom today than perhaps ever in their history

India

Margot Duley has written about women in India. According to Duley, the Preamble of the Indian Constitution guarantees all citizens "equality of status." Unfortunately, writes Duley, legal equality remains elusive for most Indian women. The subordination of women in India is primarily economically based. Most women work in agricultural jobs. But in the past few decades, India has developed a commercial market economy with capital-intensive production. Although laws favoring women's rights have been passed, they have not had much impact. For example, there are no uniform statutes governing marriage and inheritance laws. In most areas there is a very strong emphasis on purity and chastity of women. Most young women marry by the age of 17. The Dowry Prohibition Act of 1961 is largely ignored. The practice of giving a dowry has actually spread in recent years because of the overwhelming pressure on girls to marry. Women also have less access to education than men, and women's literacy rate (25%) is less than half the rate among men. Only 13% of women enroll in high school. Duley writes that because of the large dowries required at marriage, daughters receive poor nutrition and health care and less love and nurturance than their brothers. Essentially, women are seen as an economic liability.[47] In some areas female infanticide is still practiced.[48]

Saudi Arabia

Most Arab states (e.g., Saudi Arabia, Iraq) and Arab societies adhere to a patriarchal (i.e., male-ruled) social and political system in which a woman's position within and duties toward the family precede her rights as an individual. In September 2000, Amnesty International released a report that denounced Saudi Arabia for its treatment of women. According to the report, the situation for Saudi women is "untenable" by any legal or moral standard. The report contends that female domestic workers are often locked inside homes, beaten, and raped by their Saudi employers.[49] Saudi women are not allowed to vote, drive a car, sail a boat, or fly a plane. They cannot check into a hotel without a male family member. They cannot appear outdoors with hair, wrists, or ankles exposed. They cannot marry, work, study, travel, or obtain identification papers without the permission of a male guardian. If she does work, with the permission of her husband or a male guardian, she may not work alongside males. Although many women pursue university degrees, Saudi women make up just 5 percent of the private workforce (most women are teachers). Moreover, women and/or their guardians are not allowed to postpone marriages for the purpose of continuing education.[50]

In 2004, Saudi's reform-minded Crown Prince Abdullah initiated a series of forums on women's rights in Saudi Arabia. Saudis are now actively debating the pros and cons of women driving, how the court system and divorce laws favor men, the high unemployment rate among women, and whether desegregated workplaces violate Islamic law. To be sure, many outsiders assume that Islam is the source of discrimination of women, but this is not entirely accurate. Some scholars argue, for example, that religious texts are often distorted to fit existing traditions. The ban on women driving, for example, is unique to Saudi law; that is, other Islamic countries allow women to drive. The Saudi custom of *ikhtilat* (i.e., the mixing of men and women socially) also has no religious justification.[51]

Egypt

According to the 1971 constitution, all Egyptian citizens enjoy a constitutional right for public posts without discrimination between males and females. In addition, the constitution guarantees the protection of motherhood, childhood, and the existence of a harmony between the duties of a woman toward her family and her role in society. Even with such constitutional rights, gender segregation is an integral part of social etiquette and class structure in Egypt.

Nemat Guenena and Nadia Wassef have written extensively about the changing role of women in Egyptian society;[52] Egyptian women, together with children, represent about 70 percent of the population. According to Guenena and Wassef, Egyptian women have struggled for more than a century to establish their rights as equal partners with men. Their progress for equality has advanced as a result of numerous factors, including education, economic necessity, and significant political changes. Guenena and Wassef note, however, that the many advances women have made are contradicted by high rates of illiteracy, minimal political participation, declining representation in parliament, and the recurrence of modest dress.

Regarding education, a significantly greater proportion of women are illiterate. Nearly 62% of females as opposed to 38% of males are illiterate. This disparity is higher now, in 2005, than it has ever been before. In addition, Guenena and Wassef note that boys and girls receive different kinds of education. Girls are taught home economics, whereas boys are taught agricultural economics, topics that are considered gender appropriate.

Guenena and Wassef have observed that Egyptian media portray women and men in very different ways. Women are seen as mothers, wives, and daughters who are in need of protection from their fathers, husbands, and brothers. In exchange for such protection, women are required to submit to male authority. On the other hand, men are portrayed as wise, compassionate, generous, and knowledgeable about what is best for their women.

Finally, Guenena and Wassef note that women are not treated equally under Egyptian law. For example, the penalty for murdering one's spouse (upon discovery of adultery) is much harsher for the wife than the husband. Typically, men are given a prison sentence of not more than three years. Women are often sentenced to death or hard labor for life. Guenena and Wassef contend that this difference stems from the Egyptian attitude that a man's reputation is dependent upon his wife's high merit. Consequently, murdering one's adulterous wife is excusable, especially if committed in the heat of the moment.

Although rape in Egypt is penalized, forced or nonconsensual marital intercourse is not considered a criminal offense. One study found that 46 percent of Egyptian men believe they are entitled to force their wives into intercourse. Egyptian law also stipulates that husbands, but not wives, may physically punish their spouses in case of disobedience so long as no permanent damage is inflicted.[53]

CHAPTER SUMMARY

Our lives are inextricably tied to our group memberships and the roles that we play. How we see ourselves and how our culture treats us is based on the total accumulation of roles we assume. They represent our social standing in our culture. This chapter has focused on the socio-relational context of intercultural communication; that is, the group memberships we assume. All of us belong to any number of groups. Groups to which we belong are called membership groups. Some of these are voluntary, whereas others are involuntary. Voluntary ingroups often serve as reference groups, which help us make decisions about significant issues in our lives. The reference group serves as a standard by which we judge ourselves. As group members, we assume roles that define with whom, about, what, and how we communicate with others. Some of our roles are formal, whereas others are informal. Regardless, roles prescribe how we should communicate with others. Roles are a set of expectations that, if violated, are subject to negative sanctions. Roles vary considerably across cultures, especially family and sex roles. In order for us to be competent communicators across cultures, we must understand the expectations of the roles we assume. We must also understand and appreciate that the roles we assume in our native culture may be quite different in other cultures.

GLOSSARY OF TERMS

Gender: A socially constructed and learned creation usually associated with one's sex; masculinity and femininity. People are born into a sex group, but learn to become masculine or feminine. The meaning of gender stems from the particular culture's value system.

Ingroup: A membership group whose norms, goals, and values shape the behavior of the members. Extreme ingroups see the actions of an outgroup as threatening.

Involuntary Membership Group: A group to which a person belongs and has no choice but to belong, such as a person's sex, race, and age groups.

Involuntary Nonmembership Group: A group to which a person does not belong because of ineligibility.

Membership Group: A group to which a person belongs where there is regular interaction among members who perceive themselves as members.

Nonmembership Group: A group to which a person does not belong.

Outgroup: A group whose attributes are dissimilar from an ingroup and who opposes the realization of ingroup goals.

Reference Group: A group to which a person may or may not belong, but identifies in some way with the values and goals of the group.

Role: One's relative hierarchical position or rank in a group. A role is a prescribed set of behaviors that is expected in order to fulfill the role. Roles prescribe with whom, about what, and how to interact with others.

Sex: A designation of people based on biological genital differences.

Sex Role: A prescribed set of behaviors assigned to different sexes.

Social Identity: The total combination of one's group roles. A part of the individual's self-concept that is derived from the person's membership in groups.

Social Stratification: A culture's organization of roles into a hierarchical vertical status structure.

Voluntary Membership Group: A membership group to which a person belongs out of choice, like a political party or service organization.

REFERENCES

1. de Tocqueville, A. (1900). *Democracy in America.* (translated by Henry Reeve). (Volume II). New York: P. F. Collier & Sons. (Copyright 1900 by the Colonial Press). (p. 114).
2. Johnson, D. W., & Johnson, F. P. (1994). *Joining together: Group theory and group skills.* Boston: Allyn & Bacon.
3. This discussion of membership, nonmembership, voluntary, and involuntary groups can be found in a number of textbooks. The source used here is Merton, R. K. (1959). *Social theory and social structure.* Glencoe, IL: Free Press.
4. Wolter, A. (1994). *Saudi Arabia and its culture.* Unpublished manuscript, St. Norbert College, DePere, WI; *Saudi Arabia culture and religion.* (1997). [On-line]. Available: www.arab.net/saudi/culture
5. Merton, *Social theory and social structure;* Bishop, R. J. (1995). *Cultural profile, examination of value orientations and sociocultural influences, and verbal and nonverbal language aspects of the East Indian culture.* Unpublished manuscript, St. Norbert College, DePere, WI; Gudykunst, W. B., & Kim, Y. Y. (1997). *Communicating with strangers: An approach to intercultural communication.* New York: McGraw-Hill.
6. Sumner, W. G. (1906). *Folkways.* Boston: Ginn (pp. 12–13).

7. Merton, *Social theory and social structure.*

8. Triandis, H. (1990). Cross-cultural studies in individualism and collectivism. In J. J. Berman (Ed.), *Nebraska symposium on motivation, 1989* (pp. 41–133). Lincoln: University of Nebraska Press.

9. Brewer, M. B., & Campbell, D. T. (1976). *Ethnocentrism and intergroup attitudes.* New York: Wiley.

10. Weber, J. (1994). The nature of ethnocentric attribution bias: Ingroup projection or enhancement? *Journal of Experimental Social Psychology, 30,* 482–504; Brewer, M. B. (1979). Ingroup bias in the minimal intergroup situation: A cognitive motivational analysis. *Psychological Bulletin, 86,* 307–324. Tajfel, H., & Turner, J. (1979). An integrative theory of intergroup conflict. In W. Austin & S. Worchel (Eds.), *The social psychology of intergroup conflict.* Monterey, CA: Brooks/Cole.

11. Schaefer, R. T. (2004). *Racial and ethnic groups* (9th ed.). New York: Longman.

12. These examples of Christians and Jews are adapted from Schaefer, *Racial and ethnic groups.*

13. Napier, R. W., & Gershenfeld, M. K. (1993). *Groups: Theory and experience* (5th ed.). Boston: Houghton Mifflin.

14. Spear, T., & Waller, R. (Eds.). (1993). *Being Maasai.* London: James Currey. Vandehey, K., Buerger, C. M., & Krueger, K. (1996). *Traditional aspects and struggles of the Masai culture.* Unpublished manuscript, St. Norbert College, DePere, WI.

15. The discussion of roles can be found in any number of group textbooks. The particular one used here is Fisher, B. A., & Ellis, D. G. (1990). *Small group decision-making.* (3rd ed.). New York: McGraw-Hill.

16. This discussion of formal and informal roles was based on Brilhart, J. K., & Galanes, G. J. (1998). *Effective group discussion* (9th ed.). Boston: McGraw-Hill.

17. Adler, R. B., & Towne, N. (1996). *Looking out looking in* (8th ed.). Fort Worth, TX: Harcourt Brace.

18. Gudykunst & Kim, *Communicating with strangers;* Tajfel, H. (Ed.). (1978). *Differentiation between social groups.* London: Academic Press. (p. 63).

19. Gudykunst & Kim, *Communicating with strangers.*

20. This information about Korea was found on the following Web page: *Customs and traditions in Korea.* (1997). [On-line]. Available: www.emb.washington.dc.us/Korea/Scustoms.html

21. Berry, J. W., Poortinga, Y. H., Segall, M. H., & Dasen, P. R. (1992). *Cross-cultural psychology: Research and applications.* Cambridge, UK: Cambridge University Press.

22. Keberlein, M. (1993). *A cultural profile of the Guatemalan Ladinos.* Unpublished manuscript, St. Norbert College, DePere, WI; Duley, M. I. (1986). Women in India. In M. I. Duley & M. I. Edwards (Eds.), *The cross-cultural study of women* (pp. 127–236). New York: Feminist Press; Bishop, *Cultural profile, examination of value orientations and sociocultural influences, and verbal and nonverbal language aspects of the East Indian culture.*

23. Klopf, D. (1995). *Intercultural encounters: The fundamentals of intercultural communication* (3rd ed.). Englewood, CO: Morton.

24. Although different, this dialogue is adapted from a scene in Copeland, L. (Producer). (1982). *Managing the overseas assignment* [videorecording]. San Francisco, CA: Copeland Griggs.

25. Chan, S. (1984). *Hmong means free.* Philadelphia: Temple University Press; Thao, K. (1995). *The Hmong culture.* Unpublished manuscript, St. Norbert College, DePere, WI.

26. Paik, S. (2000). The formation of the united lineage in Korea. *History of the Family, 5,* 75–90.

27. Ibid.

28. Chang, K. S. "Modernity Through the Family: Familial Foundations of Korean Society." *International Review of Sociology* 7, (1997), 51–64.

29. Kim, M. "Transformation of Family Ideology in Upper-Middle-Class Families in Urban South Korea," *Ethnology* 32, (1993), 69–86.

30. Lavande, D. Herrick, J., & Sung, K., "Eldercare in the United States and South Korea," *Journal of Family Issues* 21, (2000), 632–652.

31. Kim, "Transformation of Family Ideology in Upper-Middle-Class Families in Urban South Korea"; Chun, Y,. & MacDermid, S. M. "Perceptions of Family Differentiation, Individuation, and Self-Esteem Among Korean Adolescents," *Journal of Marriage and the Family* 59, (1997), 451–463.

32. Bond, M. H. ed., *The Psychology of the Chinese People* (Hong Kong: Oxford University Press, 1986); Amraen, B. "China: A Populous Nation" (unpublished manuscript, St. Norbert College, DePere, WI, 1994).

33. Basit, T. "'I Want More Freedom, But Not Too Much': British Muslim Girls and the Dynamism of Family Values," *Gender & Education* 9, (1997), 425–440; Haroun, M. "Family Life in Islam," *The Lahore Ahmadiyya Movement for the Propagation of Islam* [online]. Available: www.aaiil.org/text/articles/others/familylifeinislam.shtml; Pels, T. "Muslim Families From Morocco in the Netherlands: Gender Dynamics and Fathers' Roles in a Context of Change," *Current Sociology* 48, (2000), 75–94.

34. Bem, S. L. "The Measurement of Psychological Androgyny," *Journal of Consulting and Clinical Psychology* 81, (1974), 506–520; Wood, J. "Gender, Communication, and Culture," In *Intercultural Communication: A Reader,* 9th ed., Samovar L. A., & Porter, R. E. eds. (Belmont, Calif.: Wadsworth, 2000), pp. 170–179.

35. Bem, "The Measurement of Psychological Androgyny."

36. Zhang, J. Norvilitis, J. M., & Jin, S. "Measuring Gender Orientation with the Bem Sex Role Inventory in Chinese Culture," *Sex Roles* 44, (2001), 237–251.

37. Katsurada, E., & Sugihara, Y. "Gender Differences in Gender-Role Perceptions Among Japanese College Students," *Sex Roles* 41, (1999), 775–786; Sugihara, Y., & Katsurada, E. "Masculinity and Femininity in Japanese Culture: A Pilot Study," *Sex Roles* 40, (1999), 635–646.

38. Ibid.

39. Shimonaka, J. Nakazato, K., & Kawaai, C. "Rounenki Ni Okeru Seiyakuwari To Shinnritekitekiou" [Sex Roles and Psychological Adjustment in Old Age], *Shakai Ronenngaku* 31, (1990), 3–11.

40. Hofstede, G. *Cultures and Organization: Software of the Mind* (New York: McGraw-Hill, 1991).

41. Herdt, G. H. ed., *Ritualized Homosexuality in Melanesia* (Berkeley and Los Angeles: University of California Press, 1984).

42. Lobel, T. E., Mashraki-Redhatzur, S., Mantzur, A., & Libby, S. "Gender Discrimination as a Function of Stereotypic and Counterstereotypic Behavior: A Cross-Cultural Study," *Sex Roles* 43, (2000), 395–406.

43. Williams, J. E., & Best, D. L. *Measuring Sex Stereotypes Across Cultures: A Multi-Nation Study* (Newbury Park, Calif: Sage, 1990).

44. Williams, J. E., & Best, D. L. "Cross-Cultural Views of Women and Men," in Lonner, W. J., & Malpass, R. eds., *Psychology and Culture* (Boston: Allyn & Bacon, 1994), pp. 191–196.

45. Hessini, L. "Wearing the Hijab in Contemporary Morocco: Choice and Identity," in Gogek, F. M., & Balaghi, S. eds., *Reconstructing Gender in the Middle East* (New York: Columbia University Press, 1994), pp. 40–56.

46. Iwao, S. *The Japanese Woman: Traditional Image and Changing Reality* (Cambridge, Mass: Harvard University Press, 1993); Sugihara and Katsurada, "Masculinity and Femininity in Japanese Culture."

47. Dulcy, M. I. "Women in India," in *The Cross-Cultural Study of Women,* ed. Duley, M. I., & Edwards, M. I. (New York: Feminist Press, 1986), pp. 127–236. "India: Dowry Deaths Still Increasing," *Women's International Network News* 22, (1996), 67; Mandelbaum, P. "Dowry Deaths in India," *Commonweal* 126, (1999), 18–21.

48. "India: Actions to Stop Feticide," *Women's International Network News* 26, (2000), 47.

49. Ahmad, K. (2000). Amnesty International denounces treatment of women. *The Lancet, 356,* 1252.

50. Ambah, F. S. (2004). In rare public dialogue, Saudi women talk rights. *Christian Science Monitor* 96, 1. "Out of the Shadows, into the World." *The Economist* 371, (2004), 8380.

51. Ibid.

52. Guenena, N., & Wassef, N. (1999). *Unfulfilled promises: Women's rights in Egypt.* Cairo: Population Council of West Asia and North Africa.

53. Ibid.

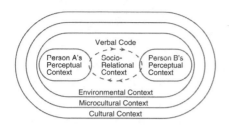

Verbal Code

Person A's Perceptual Context — Socio-Relational Context — Person B's Perceptual Context

Environmental Context
Microcultural Context
Cultural Context

CHAPTER 7

The Verbal Code

Human Language

The language faculty is a system, a subsystem of the brain . . . its major elements don't appear to exist in other similar organisms . . . to a large extent it appears to be determined by our biological endowment and is essentially invariant across the species.

—Noam Chomsky[1]

Chapter Objectives

After reading this chapter, you should be able to

1. Explain the relationship between language and culture.
2. Explain the principles of linguistic relativity and linguistic determinism.
3. Define the three levels of language.
4. Explain the principle of universal grammar.
5. List and define three universals of language.
6. Compare and contrast elaborated and restricted codes.
7. Compare and contrast cross-cultural communication and conflict styles.
8. Compare and contrast U.S. American dialects.

The capacity of the human brain to acquire language may be the distinguishing feature that separates humans from the rest of the living beings on the planet. Our ability to put thoughts into a code in order to communicate with someone else empowers us beyond imagination. Other living beings are larger, stronger, faster, and smaller, but no other living being has the capacity for language. Language has put humans on top of the evolutionary ladder. Because of their capacity for language, humans have become the most powerful living beings on earth. The purpose of this chapter is to explore the idea of language and how it varies across cultures. This chapter will outline the relationship between language and culture by first exploring the Sapir-Whorf hypothesis. The second part of this chapter will outline the fundamental structure of language, including a discussion of the concept of a universal grammar that applies to all languages. The third part of this chapter will look at universals of language that are shared across cultures. The fourth part of the chapter focuses on how the use of language differs across cultures, including a look at elaborate and restricted codes and cross-cultural comparisons of language style.

THE RELATIONSHIP BETWEEN LANGUAGE AND CULTURE

Linguist and cultural anthropologist Zdenek Salzmann points out that, historically, anthropologists and linguists often grouped language, culture, and race together as though any one of them automatically implied the other two. Contemporary linguistic anthropologists generally agree, however, that culture, race, and language are historically distinct. In other words, a person's race does not determine what language he or she will speak. As we saw in Chapter 5, however, the language of a particular culture and the thought processes of its people are closely related.[2]

Sapir-Whorf Hypothesis

In 1928, anthropologist and linguist Edward Sapir published a paper in the journal *Language* that changed the face of the study of language and culture. Sapir's thesis was that the language of a particular culture directly influences how people think. In the paper he wrote,

The network of cultural patterns of a civilization is indexed in the language which expresses that civilization. . . . Language is a guide to "social reality." . . . Human beings do not live in the objective world alone . . . but are very much at the mercy of the particular language which has become the medium of expression for their society.[3]

Sapir continued to argue that the ways in which people perceive the world around them, including their natural and social environments, are essentially dictated by their language. In fact, Sapir argued that the speakers of different languages see different worlds. Strongly influenced by Sapir was one of his students, Benjamin Whorf.[4] Whorf was persuaded by Sapir's writings and further developed this line of thought. In 1940, Whorf wrote,

> The background linguistic system (in other words the grammar) of each language is not merely a reproducing instrument for voicing ideas but rather is itself the shaper of ideas. . . . We dissect nature along lines laid down by our native languages.[5]

Like Sapir, Whorf believed the people who speak different languages are directed to different types of observations; therefore, they are not equivalent as observers and must arrive at somewhat different views of the world.[6] Sapir and Whorf's ideas received a great deal of attention and have become well-known as the Sapir-Whorf Hypothesis. Salzmann contends that the Sapir-Whorf hypothesis delineates two principles. One is the principle of linguistic determinism, which says that the way one thinks is determined by the language one speaks. The second is the principle of linguistic relativity, which says that the differences among languages must therefore be reflected in the differences in the worldviews of their speakers. These principles raise some important issues for cross-cultural communication. If how we think is a reflection of the language we speak, then the speakers of two very different languages must think very differently. This could render effective and successful intercultural communication extremely difficult, if not insurmountable.

Salzmann and other contemporary linguists and anthropologists maintain that the Sapir-Whorf hypothesis may be a bit exaggerated. Today, most linguists believe that the vocabulary and grammar of a particular language parallel the "nonverbal" culture. In other words, the geographic, climatic, kinesic, spatial, and proxemic aspects of a culture are emphasized and accented in a culture's language. Salzmann notes, for example, that in Pintupi (one of the aboriginal languages of Australia) there are at least ten words designating various kinds of holes. Mutara is a special hole in a spear, Pulpa refers to a rabbit burrow, Makarnpa is the burrow of a monitor lizard, and Katarta is the hole left by a monitor lizard after it has broken the surface after hibernation. Moreover, linguists believe that the syntactic features of a language influence how speakers of that language categorize and mentally organize their worlds. For example, speakers of English use the personal pronoun "you" whether they are addressing one or several children, adults, old persons, subordinates, or individuals much superior in rank than themselves. Other languages operate differently. When addressing someone, speakers of Dutch, French, German, Italian, Russian, and Spanish must choose between the "familiar" personal pronoun and the "polite" personal pronoun and/or the corresponding verb form. In English, the word *teacher* refers to a person who teaches, whether it is a man or a woman. In German, *lehrer* is the masculine form of teacher and *leherin* is the feminine form. In this way, speakers of Dutch, French, German, and Italian may be more conscious of the status differences between them and another person because their language requires them to use words designating the power differential.[7]

Therefore, most linguists now believe that the users of a particular language may overlook or ignore objects or events that speakers of another language may emphasize. John B. Carroll modifies the Sapir-Whorf hypothesis by arguing that to the extent that languages differ, language users organize their experiences differently based on the vocabularies and grammars provided by their respective languages. Carroll notes that these cognitions will affect behavior.[8]

THE STRUCTURE OF HUMAN LANGUAGE

All languages are a systematic set of sounds, combined with a set of rules, for the sole purpose of creating meaning and communicating.[9] Any human language is made up of a set of sounds. These sounds are represented symbolically in the language's alphabet. In English, for example, there are approximately 40 sounds represented in an alphabet of 26 letters. The Korean script, called Hangul, consists of 16 consonants, of which there are five basic forms, and 10 vowels. According to Kenneth Katzman, the Hebrew alphabet of twenty-two letters (five of which have a different form when they appear at the end of a word) consists entirely of consonants. The language is written from right to left without vowels. Thus, the word *kelev* (i.e., dog) appears as the Hebrew equivalents of, from right to left, k, 1, and v. If you are not familiar with Hebrew it is impossible to know how to pronounce a word from the way it is written. During the 8th century, a system was developed for indicating vowels through the use of small dots and dashes placed above and below the consonants. These signs are still in use today, but they are confined to schoolbooks, prayer books, and textbooks for foreigners, and are not to

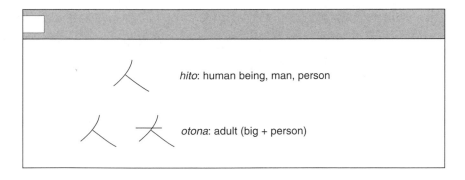

Figure 7.1   Kanji Examples

be seen in newspapers, magazines, or books for general use.[10] The written form of Japanese consists of three major alphabets. A fourth alphabet, called *romaji,* is a Romanization using English letters. All four alphabets are used simultaneously in any given piece of writing. The first alphabet, called *kanji,* consists of more than 5,000 borrowed characters from Chinese. The word *kanji* means "Chinese character." Kanji are the Chinese characters used in written Japanese. Each kanji character represents an idea or concept, rather than a simple sound. The meaning of the character changes when the combination of characters varies. For an example, see Figure 7.1.

To be able to read a Japanese newspaper, you would need to know and understand at least 2,000 basic characters. Moreover, you would have to learn the different readings or compounds of two or more kanji. There are more than 4000 kanji compounds. The Japanese also have two phonetic alphabets, called *hiragani* and *katakana.* Hiragani consists of 46 characters. These are phonetic sounds that make up the kanji and are used to change verb tenses. The katakana also consists of 46 sounds. The katakana sounds coincide with the hiragana but the characters are different. Katakana is used for all foreign words coming from outside of Japan.[11]

Sounds and Symbols

The letters of a language's alphabet are symbols representing sounds. These small units of sound are called phonemes. In English the letter *c* represents the sound "see" or "ka," the letter *a* represents the sound "ah," and the letter *t* represents the sound "tee." In combination, phonemes become words; that is, morphemes, the smallest meaning unit of sound. When coarticulated, the sounds "ka," "ah," and "tee" create the word/morpheme "cat."

There is no natural or inherent relationship between the sounds and their accompanying alphabet. That is, there is no intrinsic or immanent relationship between the symbol *c* and the "see" sound, the *a* and the "ah" sound, or the letter *t* and the "tee" sound. That *c* represents the "see" sound is completely random and arbitrary. Likewise, there is also no natural relationship between any word and its referent. In other words, there is no natural or necessary relationship between the word *cat* and that fuzzy little animal walking across the room. In Spanish, which uses a similar but different sound system, the fuzzy little animal walking across the floor is called *gato,* in Japan it is *neiko,* and in French it is *chat.* Each of the different languages uses a different set of sounds to refer to the same referent.

Although the letters and the sound systems of any two languages may be different, the function of an alphabet is the same across languages—to symbolize sound. A symbol is an arbitrarily selected and learned stimulus representing something else. The ability to represent sounds with symbols seems to be limited to humans. To be sure, animals can learn to associate sounds with behaviors, but they can do so only at a very rudimentary level. Jo Liska has developed a hierarchy of symbolic abstraction that allows us to see where humans and animals are distinct in terms of language and symbol use.[12] The hierarchy is, from bottom to top, symptoms, ritual semblances, iconic semblances, proper symbols, conceptual symbols, and syntactic symbols.

According to Liska, *symptoms* constitute the foundation for all animal communication. These are biologically "hard-wired" in the central nervous system. The employment of symptoms is unconscious and stimulated by events in the physiological conditions of the animal. Examples of symptoms are pupil dilation, blushing, piloerection, estrous, and vocalizations. A dog's growl at the sign of another dog is symptomatic. Liska maintains that these behaviors are fixed and immune to short-term environmental changes. Symptoms are automatic, involuntary, and primary. Liska labels *ritual semblances* as exaggerated symptoms that are relatively conscious. Examples include posed facial expressions, gestures of pantomime, begging, and signs of submission. Dogs and cats often exaggerate their begging routines in order to receive table scraps. *Iconic semblances* are related to ritual semblances in that these are signs that represent their referents. A map, blueprint, and photograph of a dog are iconic semblances that are isomorphic to their referents. Liska suggests that iconic semblances are probably restricted to humans. Early cave drawings by our ancestors might be considered iconic semblances. Moving up Liska's ladder of symbolic abstraction are *proper symbols.* These refer to a specific stimulus that labels some aspect of reality. Proper symbols provide the means for naming others, objects, or events. The word "cat" is a proper symbol for the fuzzy little animal. Proper symbols are acquired through stimulus-response learning. Over time, we learn to associate the fuzzy little animal with the word "cat." On the other hand, *conceptual symbols* create symbolic reality and refer to concepts that exist only in the minds of the users such as "liberty," "democracy," and "freedom." Unlike proper symbols, conceptual symbols have no physical referent. The stimulus-response pattern for acquiring proper symbols cannot account for the acquisition of conceptual symbols because there is no external stimulus (e.g., such as a cat) for which to associate the symbol. Finally, at the top of the symbolic hierarchy are *syntactic symbols.* These symbols express grammatical relationships between other symbols such as possession, function, and tense. Syntactic symbols are the means by which language is patterned, organized, and structured.[13]

According to Liska, many mammals and birds communicate using ritual semblances, and some species of primates seem to be able to acquire and use proper symbols. When well-trained and monitored, apes seem to acquire language presented to them visually. Yet their natural communication repertoire appears to be based on symptoms and ritual semblances. Apes seem to have the capacity for language, but as humans use it, language has not yet emerged among wild-living apes. Liska contends that all animals "communicate," but we humans have made it our single most distinguishing characteristic. To be sure, argues Liska, other animal species may possess "advanced" communication systems. Apes engage in a whole host of symptomatic and semblamatic signs. Whales sing intricate songs that vary over time. Killer whales (i.e., orcas) use calls that seem to vary from group to group. Wolves use a complicated set of postures for coordination of the pack. But unlike animals, we seem compelled to create and invent symbols. As Liska avows, humans seem to communicate because we *need* to (see Figure 7.2).[14]

Syntax and Universal Grammar

Along with a system of sounds, all languages have a set of rules for combining the sounds to create meaning. The set of rules, or grammar, is called syntax. Through syntax, sentences are generated. Through syntax, sound and meaning are connected. Noam Chomsky is perhaps the most recognized linguist in the world. For the past 50 years, Chomsky has developed a fascinating theory about syntax.[15] Chomsky contends that although the 5,000 or so languages that are spoken in the world today appear to be very different, they are, in fact, remarkably similar. Moreover, Chomsky asserts that the obvious differences among languages are actually quite trivial.

Figure 7.2   Humans, like other animals, have a *need* to communicate

Chomsky maintains that the languages spoken on the planet today are all dialects of one common language—human language.[16]

Chomsky argues that all human languages share a *universal grammar* that is innate in the human species and culturally invariant. Chomsky and other linguists claim that every normal child is genetically programmed for human language. Just as humans are programmed to walk upright, so are humans programmed with universal grammar. Chomsky says that language is as much a part of the human brain as the thumb is a part of the human hand. Lila Gleitman, a linguist at the University of Pennsylvania, maintains that human language is not innate in the same way as bee language or horse language may be innate, or in the sense that human visual sensation is innate. Humans do not "learn" how to see. Humans do, however, learn a specific language. The acquisition of a particular language (e.g., English, Japanese) is influenced by the specific cultural environment in which a child is born.[17] In other words, no individual language is universal to human beings. Children learn their specific language by being exposed to it in their cultural environment. Children born and raised in China learn to speak Chinese, whereas children born and raised in Norway learn to speak Norwegian, not because of their race or ethnicity, but because of their cultural environment. The commonalities between the different languages (e.g., Chinese and Norwegian) are so striking that Chomsky and other linguists are convinced that the fundamental syntax for all languages is universal and that the particular languages of a particular culture are simply dialects of the universal grammar. For example, there are two fundamental syntactical structures to all human languages. The first is that all languages, the world over, rely on either word order or inflections to convey meaning. Most languages rely on both to a greater or lesser extent. English, for example, relies heavily on word order. The phrase "The man is in the car" means something very different from "The car is in the man." English also uses inflection to carry meaning. Inflections are changes to words to indicate grammatical relationships such as number, case, gender, tense, and so on. For example, to indicate the plural of something in English, we add the letter "s" to the end of words. A single fuzzy little animal is called a "cat," and two fuzzy little animals are called "cats." The language of the Warlpiri people of Australia relies almost exclusively on inflection rather than word order. Latin also relies heavily on inflection. The point is that word order and inflections are a part of all languages. As linguist Dan Slobin asserts,

> In a way [language] it's like the human face. A human face is very simple, two eyes, a nose, and a mouth. You can draw a simple sketch of it. But look at the incredible diversity. Each one of us has a uniquely different face. Yet each face is obviously a human face. Languages are the same. Each one is obviously a different language but they're clearly examples of the same kind of system.[18]

Lila Gleitman forwards two additional arguments in favor of the universality of language.[19] The first is that language learning proceeds uniformly among children within and across cultures. Chinese children and Norwegian children learn language at the same time in their development. All normal children begin to use language at about the same time, across cultures. Linguist Steven Pinker of the Massachusetts Institute of Technology has observed that sometime around their first birthday, babies start to understand and use words. At about eighteen months, the children's vocabulary, across all cultures, increases at a rate of one word every two hours and continues to grow through adolescence. At this time, two-word strings appear. These two-word combinations are highly similar across cultures. Children announce when objects appear, disappear, and move about. According to Pinker, by the age of three years, a child's vocabulary grows dramatically and he or she can produce fluent grammatical conversation. Such sentences, though quite short, illustrate the child's knowledge and competence of the basic structure of language (e.g., appropriate word order, and so on.). For example, even though he or she has never had a lesson on English grammar, an English-speaking child might say "I want cookie," but would never say, "Want I cookie." By the age of five or so, children in normal learning settings begin to use complex sentences.[20]

Gleitman argues that even in cases where the learning environment changes, children learn language at essentially the same rate. For example, studies indicate that a child's language learning rate is basically unaffected by differences in mothers' speech. Furthermore, deaf and blind children learn language at the same time and rate as children with normal hearing and sight. Gleitman points out that the vocabulary and syntax of sign languages are essentially the same as in spoken languages. At about the age of two, deaf children start to put gestures together into elementary two- and three-gesture sentences. By five years of age they are constructing complex, multigesture sentences. In addition, blind children have little trouble acquiring terms that describe visual experiences. Gleitman suggests that because blind children are unable to see, phrases referring to sight (e.g., "Look at that!") might be absent from their speech. Yet such terms are some of the first to appear in the blind children's vocabulary. For example, in response to the command "look up," blind children raise their hands instead of their heads. When they are told that they can "look but not touch," blind children very slowly stretch out their hands and cautiously touch the object. When told "go ahead and look," they handle the object with enthusiasm (see Figure 7.3).[21]

The second point supporting the universality of language argument is that children across cultures acquire many linguistic generalizations that experience alone could not have taught them. Children of all cultures say things that no one could have taught them. Chomsky argues that in advance of experience, children of all cultures are already equipped with an understanding of the basic structure of any human language. Like walking, or growing hair, language is encoded into the genetic makeup of normal functioning human beings. By the age of three, for example, there are any number of things children cannot do, such as tie their own shoes, perform mathematical computations, or spell most words. By the age of three, however, children can construct meaningful sentences in ways that no one has ever taught them.[22] Moreover, as Pinker notes, the sentences they create are grammatically correct. Indeed, asserts Pinker, children never make some mistakes. For example, a child might ask "What did you eat your eggs with?" but the child would never say "What did you eat your eggs and?" which seems to be a straightforward extension of the statement "I ate ham and eggs." The interesting point here is that no one has ever taught the

Figure 7.3   Deaf and blind children learn language at the same time and rate as children with normal hearing and sight

Source: Copyright © James Neuliep.

child not to end sentences with the word *and*. Pinker and Chomsky argue that children never make such errors because to do so would violate some principle of universal grammar. Below is another example provided by Pinker. In this example, a language learner who hears the (a) and (b) sentences could quite sensibly extract a general rule that, when applied to the (c) sentence, would yield sentence (d). But the resulting sentence (d) is something no one would say.

(a) We expect the bird to fly.

(b) We expect the bird will fly.

(c) The bird is expected to fly.

(d) The bird is expected will fly.[23]

The proposition that all languages share a universal grammar that is innate to humans is widely accepted among contemporary linguists. But these linguists also recognize that all human languages are somewhat different. For example, although virtually all languages rely on some form of word order to construct sentences, the word order may vary across languages. For example, the word order for a sentence in most European languages is subject-verb-object, as in the sentence "I watch television." In Japanese, however, the order is subject-object-verb, as in the sentence "I television watch." In addition, Japanese, like other Asian languages, does not contain a grammatical equivalent to plurality, as can be found in English.[24] The Swahili alphabet lacks the letters *c, q,* and *x,* but contains a number of its own. The letter *dh* is pronounced like the *th* of "this," and *gh* like the German *ch.* Whereas English grammatical inflections occur at the end of a word, in Swahili everything is done at the beginning. *Kitabu* is the Swahili word for "book," but the word for "books" is *vitabu.* This word falls into the so-called Ki Mi class, one of eight in the Swahili language. Others are the M Mi class (e.g., *mkono* = hand, *mikono* = hands; *mji* = town, *miji* = towns); and the M Wa class, used mainly to refer to people (e.g., *mtu* = man, *watu* = men; *mjinga* = fool, *wajinga* = fools). Thus, "one big book" in Swahili is *kitabu kikubwa kimoja,* which translates as "book-big-one," but "two big books" is *vitabi vikubwa viwili.*

Many languages are read from left to right, as in English. Most languages of the Middle East, however, including Arabic, Hebrew, and Persian, are read from right to left. Korean writing differs considerably from most other languages, in that the letters of each syllable are grouped together into clusters, as if the English word "seldom" were written:

S D   S E L

E O   or   D O M

L M

The point here is that although human languages across the globe have much in common, each is unique in some way.[25]

All human languages have a set of rules that is used to combine the language's sounds into meaningful units. Complex languages exist even in remote parts of the world, where people have yet to be exposed to modern technology and media. Papua, New Guinea, for example, is where some of the most isolated people on earth live, and yet it is probably the most linguistically diverse country. Among the population of three million people, there are more than 750 languages spoken; about one-fifth of the total number of languages on Earth. Some of the languages are spoken by fewer than 1,000 people. In his longitudinal work with the Menya people of Papua, New Guinea, Carl Whitehead has found that the Menya use a language that is as complex as any other language. He argues that one of the most remarkable features of the Menya language is its verb system. Some Menya verbs, according to Whitehead, can have as many as 2,000 to 3,000 different forms as compared to English, where a verb can have up to five forms. Languages such as Menya are as highly rule governed as any other language. In this sense, there is no such thing as a primitive language.[26]

Universals of Language

Another reason why so many linguists believe that all languages evolved from a universal grammar is their numerous commonalities. All languages are remarkably similar. For example, all languages have some way of labeling objects, places, or things (like the English noun). All languages have a way of naming action (like the English verb). All human languages have some way of stating the negative (e.g., it is *not* raining out), a way to construct interrogatives, and a way of differentiating between singular and plural.[27]

According to Salzmann, the uniquely human way of communicating via speech, shares several other universal features, regardless of culture, race, and particular lexicon. First, Salzmann notes that all human speech is transmitted via a vocal-auditory channel. Conversely, some sounds produced by animals are not vocal or are not received auditorily (e.g., bees have no ears). An important advantage of the vocal-auditory channel for humans is that the rest of the body is left free to carry on other activities. Second, speech sounds are emitted from their source of origin in all directions, making it possible to determine the location of the source. Functionally this is important because the sender and the receiver do not have see each other to communicate. This is also important because it enables speakers to communicate without necessarily being face to face—for example, from around corners, or in the dark. Third, speech sounds are heard within a very limited range and only during production. Soon after, they are lost. In this sense speech is transitory. Fourth, speech is also interchangeable. We are capable of repeating what others say. This is not true of many animal species. Fifth, human speakers are equipped with complete intrapersonal feedback. As speakers, we can hear ourselves and are capable of monitoring our own messages. Sixth, speech is specialized. Human speech has only a single function; that is, to communicate. Seventh, speech can be displaced from time and space. We can talk about something that happened 1,000 years ago, or project what we think will happen 1,000 years from now. Eighth, what a person may say can be completely false. Ninth, speech is reflexive. We use language to talk about language. Finally, tenth, the speakers of any language can learn a second language or even several languages in addition to their native tongue.[28]

Generative Grammar

One of the most remarkable features of any language's rule structure is that it allows the speakers to generate sentences that have never before been spoken. Chomsky refers to this aspect of language as its *generative grammar.* From a finite set of sounds and a finite set of rules, speakers of any language can create an infinite number of sentences, many of which have never before been uttered yet are easily comprehended by other speakers of the same language.[29]

Most of the sentences you have produced today have never before been spoken by anyone on the planet, and yet everyone understood them. Linguist George A. Miller contends that any sentence more than 20 words in length has probably never before been spoken. Miller demonstrates this through example. According to Miller, suppose it is possible for someone to choose the next word that he or she is going to say from a list of 10 possible words. Continuing on, assume that the second word someone is going to speak is also one of 10 possible words. At this point the total number of possible combinations of two-word sentences is 10 times 10, or 100 possible two-word sentences. Now assume that the person is to select a third word out of a possible 10 words. The number of possible three-word sentences is 10 to the third power, or 1,000 possible sentences (see Figure 7.4).

Moving on to a fourth possible word, out of a list of 10 possible words, the number of potential four-word sentences is 10 to the fourth power, or 10,000 possible sentences. The number of possible messages is increasing very rapidly as the length of the message increases. Following this example, the number of possible 20-word sentences is 10 to the 20th power, or 100,000,000,000,000,000,000 possible sentences. Based on this example, Miller alleges that the number of possible sentences in any language is essentially infinite.[30]

ELABORATED AND RESTRICTED CODES

Although the world's 5,000 or so languages have much in common, the style or fashion in which they are used by the people who speak them differs from culture to culture. In fact, speakers of the same language often use it differently. Some of these differences may be explained by Hall's concept of high- and low-context cultures. Persons in high-context cultures generally rely more on their nonverbal code than on their verbal code to communicate, whereas members of low-context cultures rely extensively on the verbal code during communication.

Basil Bernstein argues that the use of linguistic codes is closely related to the social structure of a particular culture. First, Bernstein differentiates

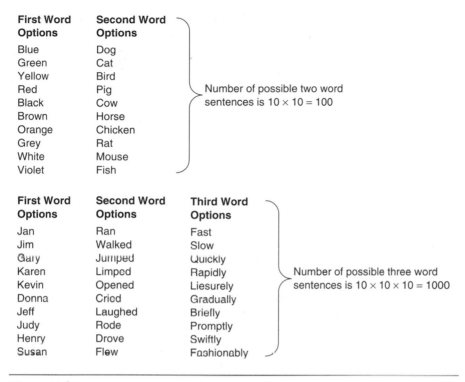

Figure 7.4

between language and speech. As it is described above, Bernstein agrees that language is a system of sounds and syntax that allows speakers to represent their reality and generate an infinite number of sentences. In fact, he argues that all languages are equal in terms of their ability to represent reality. Speech, on the other hand, is at the mercy of the social circumstances wherein it is employed. Bernstein maintains that whereas language symbolizes what is *possible* to do, speech symbolizes what is actually occurring. The social context of communication sets up the boundaries for the type of speech that is preferred, obligated, or prohibited. As the social context varies, the speakers of the language will generate different kinds of speech, even if they speak the same language. The social system delimits the speaker's options in terms of language use. The speech codes, then, are not defined in terms of lexicon or syntax, but by the social structure of the culture.[31]

Broadly speaking, Bernstein identifies two types of linguistic/speech codes: elaborated and restricted. A restricted code is one wherein the options (not necessarily the vocabulary) are limited as to what the speakers can say or do verbally. A restricted code is considered a status-oriented speech system. The code reinforces the social system by restricting or limiting its speakers to a limited number of linguistic options during communication. Restricted codes are most often seen in high-context cultures wherein the status of the interactants dictates who says what to whom and how it is said. When interactants of a high-context, collectivistic culture communicate, their words and phrases are strictly prescribed, leaving them little choice about what to say or how to say it. In this way, their code is "restricted" and is highly predictable. Bernstein points out that the Chinese, for example, operate with a restricted code, yet have one of the most complex languages on earth. Chinese people need to learn several thousand characters in order to read and write, but they speak with a restricted code because the social system (highly status and group oriented) dictates what can be said to whom in a given social circumstance. Restricted codes also emerge in individualistic cultures as interactants develop close relationships. Restricted codes can be found in what Bernstein calls "closed" communities, such as prison camps and criminal subgroups, but can develop within any social structure where the individuals share social identifications (e.g., spouses, co-workers, and so on). In this way, restricted codes show up in both high- and low-context cultures, although they tend to be more salient across the entire culture in a high- rather than low-context culture.[32]

With an elaborated code, speakers can choose from among a variety of linguistic options to communicate. Bernstein argues that speakers using an elaborated code are able, via the social system, to put their thoughts, intents, and goals into an explicit verbal message. Bernstein argues that elaborated codes develop in circumstances where the speakers' intents are unknown or vary widely, as in individualistic cultures. Because the individual speaker's intent is unclear, the speaker has a variety of linguistic options available from which to choose. The speaker must expand and elaborate so that his or her intentions are clearly communicated. Any language will allow the speaker to do that, but the social system regulates it. The social structure of an elaborated code user is such that considerable flexibility exists in one's role prescription. To communicate one's intent, the speaker must be given much linguistic latitude. In this way, it is very difficult to predict the vocabulary and syntax of a speaker using an elaborated code. Students in the United States, for example, may have no idea what kinds of things a new professor will say on the first day of class. Students in China, on the other hand, can probably predict quite accurately the kinds of messages their professor will send. In the United States, the culture generally uses an elaborated code, whereas in China, it is restricted.[33]

CROSS-CULTURAL COMMUNICATION STYLES

Although the capacity for language is universal, the language of a particular culture must be learned by its members. Moreover, cultures seem to have a predominant manner, fashion, or style in which they use their language. Communication theorists William Gudykunst and Stella Ting-Toomey argue that at different language acquisition stages, children learn not only the structure and lexicon of their culture's language, but also the various styles of language interaction unique to their culture. Such language style reflects the affective, moral, and aesthetic patterns of a culture. Gudykunst and Ting-Toomey describe a culture's verbal style as its tonal coloring of a message that is communicated through shades of tonal qualities. Gudykunst and Ting-Toomey describe four verbal communication styles that have been identified by intercultural theorists. The styles are direct-indirect, elaborate-succinct, personal-contextual, and instrumental-affective. Variations of these styles may exist in any culture, but typically one style tends to dominate within a culture.[34]

Direct-Indirect

According to Gudykunst and Ting-Toomey, cultures differ in the degree to which speakers disclose their intentions through precise and candid verbal communication. Persons using a direct style employ overt expressions of intention. In using a direct style, interactants assert self-face needs. Such messages clearly articulate the speaker's desires and needs. Direct styles are often used in low-context, individualistic cultures. Conversely, an indirect style, which is often seen in high-context and collectivistic cultures, is one where the speaker's intentions are hidden or only hinted at during interaction. The use of ambiguity and vagueness is characteristic of an indirect style. In high-context cultures, there is no need to articulate every message. True understanding is implicit, coming not from words but from actions in the environment. Moreover, indirect communication prevents potentially embarrassing moments that might threaten the face of either speaker.[35]

The direct style is preferred in cultures such as the United States, England, Australia, Germany, and Israel, among others. In the United States we frequently use such phrases as "for sure," "no question," "without a doubt." We value verbal precision and self-expression. Americans are encouraged to "speak their mind." We are so direct and candid that we will even announce to an entire room when we are going to use the bathroom, as in "I'll be right back, I have to use the restroom." Gudykunst and Ting-Toomey allege that Israel is also considered a direct culture, perhaps even more so than the

United States. Fedarko points out that many Israelis use the direct style of *dugri* (straight talk) that is quintessentially Israeli. Israelis value communication that is simple, direct, and honest. A speaker displaying dugri places substance before style and makes no attempt at pretense or deception. Some have referred to Israel as an "in your face" culture when it comes to interacting.[36] Germans, too, value frankness and directness in their interaction with others and are especially fond of the use of examples. Along with their direct style is an absence of small talk. Hall and Hall maintain that in their quest for direct and candid talk, Germans despise social chit-chat. Sometimes, Germans are perceived by their European counterparts as brutally frank.[37]

The use of an indirect style of language is seen in many Asian cultures. Indirectness is valued in these cultures because saving face and harmony in social relationships are highly valued. Directness threatens both of these goals. According to Gudykunst and Ting-Toomey, Japanese speakers, for example, limit themselves to implicit and even ambiguous use of words such as "maybe" and "perhaps." Children in Japan are taught not to be self-centered, and those who take the initiative are generally not rewarded. Japanese mothers typically use rhetorical questions and tone of voice and context to express disapproval. Sumiko Iwao argues that there is an unspoken belief among Japanese that verbalizing deep feelings spoils their value. To the Japanese, being understood without words is far more cherished than precise articulation. Iwao asserts that in Japan, interpersonal communication is based on a great deal of guessing and reading between the lines. Directness is disagreeable and repugnant. The ability to correctly grasp what a person thinks and feels without verbal expression is considered a sign of closeness between two persons. In marital relationships verbal communication is thought to be unnecessary. Iwao calls Japan "a culture of no words." She alleges that this may be due to the high value placed on masculinity. According to Japanese ideals, the most masculine of men is a man of few words who does not disclose personal weakness by complaints or expose his innermost thoughts and feelings, especially to his wife.[38] To a certain degree, the French are indirect. Hall and Hall argue that the French often indulge in small talk and prefer some mystery in their interaction with others. They maintain that the French will often talk around the point they wish to make.[39]

AN INTERCULTURAL CONVERSATION: DIRECT AND INDIRECT SPEAKING

To some extent direct and indirect modes of communication are universal. Indirect modes, for example, are often used out of simple politeness. But direct modes of communication are seen most often in cultures like the United

States, whereas indirect modes are seen in many Asian cultures, such as Japan, Korea, and China. The following dialogue takes place between a young couple who have been dating for a short time. The man is a U.S. student, and the woman is from an Asian culture. Note the misunderstanding that results as a consequence of the use of direct and indirect modes of communication.[40]

Jim:	*Ya know, Michiko, I really enjoy the time we spend together. I really like you. I've been so happy since we met.*
Michiko:	*Hmmm, thank you.*
Jim:	*I mean, I feel like I've learned so much about you and your culture.*
Michiko:	*Yeah, it's very interesting.*
Jim:	*I'm so glad you came to the United States. Do you like it here? What is your favorite thing about us?*
Michiko:	*Well, it's pretty big. It's very nice here.*
Jim:	*What do you think about Americans?*
Michiko:	*I don't know. Maybe I haven't been here long enough to know.*
Jim:	*You must think something!*
Michiko:	*Well, I'd probably have to think about it.*
Jim:	*I mean, do you like us?*
Michiko:	*Well, I don't really know that many Americans yet.*

In all likelihood, Jim is not going to get much of an answer from Michiko. She continues throughout the dialogue using rather general answers to Jim's very specific and direct questions about her feelings toward the United States. Michiko might believe that Jim is being far too direct and invading her privacy. Besides, the fact that she has traveled halfway around the world should be indicative of her desire to be here, right? There must be something about the United States that attracted her. Michiko cannot possibly say something critical about the United States because she would lose face, as would Jim, as a native. She relies on imprecise and indefinite answers.

Elaborate, Exacting, and Succinct Styles

According to Gudykunst and Ting-Toomey, the elaborate, exacting, or succinct communication style deals with the quantity and/or volume of talk that is preferred across cultural groups. There are three levels—an elaborate style, which emphasizes flashy and embellished language; an exacting style, where persons say no more or less than is needed; and a succinct style characterized by the use of concise statements, understatements, and even silence.[41] An elaborate style of communication can be seen in many Arab, Middle Eastern, and Afro-American cultures. Many Middle Easterners tend to use metaphors, similes, and adjectives in everyday conversation. African-Americans, too, prefer personalized, often exaggerated, spontaneous styles of interaction. Kochman writes,

> Stylistic self-expression within Black culture is characterized by dramatic self-conscious flair. . . . Black stylistic self-expression is also characterized by inventive (humorously ironic) exaggeration as in the self-promotion of demonstrably capable aspects of self ("If you've got it, flaunt it") or even by less demonstrably positive capabilities ("If you don't have it, flaunt it anyway"), which is all part of Afro-American boasting: the "making of one's noise." As Hollywood Henderson said, "I put a lot of pressure on myself to see if I can play up to my mouth." But exaggeration also serves to characterize (and neutralize the impact of) negative situations, such as poverty ("The soles on my shoes are so thin, I can step on a dime and tell you whether it's heads or tails").[42]

Americans tend to prefer an exacting style of interaction consistent with a "Just the facts" mentality popularized by the *Dragnet* television series of the 1960s.

A succinct style can be found in Japan, China, and some Native American (e.g., Apache, Navajo) cultures. These cultures value the use of concise talk and silence. To the Chinese, silence is a means to maintain social control in a situation. Stowell points out that the Chinese, in general, do not value verbal skills. In fact, speaking skills in general are considered immoral. The skilled speaker may be labeled as "having a flattering mouth," "an oil-mouth," or a "honey-mouth." Chinese children are taught to be cautious about the use of words. The Chinese say "One should use the eyes and ears, not the mouth," and "Disaster emanates from careless talk." The Chinese consider the wisest and most trustworthy person as the one who talks the least but the one who listens, watches, and restricts his or her verbal communication.[43]

The American Indian tribes of the Navajo and Apache also value the use of silence as a way to deal with ambiguity. Steven Pratt, an actively participating member of the Osage tribe, and Lawrence Weider, a professor of communication, argue,

To the real Indian, it appears that White Americans who are strangers to each other may freely engage in conversation in such places as the supermarket check-out line. Commercial airlines provide an even more intense opportunity for easy conversation between strangers. Seatmates often disclose their life histories to each other. In the culture of real Indians, these are extraordinary and improper ways to behave, especially when both parties are real Indians. When real Indians who are strangers to one another pass each other in a public space, wait in line, occupy adjoining seats, and so forth, they take it that it is proper to remain silent and to not initiate conversation. Being silent at this point is a constituent part of the real Indian's mode of communicating with others, especially other Indians.[44]

The use of an elaborated, exacting, or succinct style is closely related to Hall's high- and low-context communication and Bernstein's classification of restricted and elaborated codes. Gudykunst and Kim contend that restricted codes resemble jargon or shorthand speech in which speakers are almost telegraphic. This seems to correlate with a succinct style. Conversely, Bernstein asserts that elaborate codes rely heavily on verbal amplification for message transmission with much less emphasis on the nonverbal code or environmental cues. This seems to correspond with the elaborate style.[45]

Personal and Contextual Style

Gudykunst and Ting-Toomey define the personal communication style as one that amplifies the individual identity of the speaker. Such a style stresses and underscores "personhood." This style is often seen in individualistic cultures. A personal style relies on the use of first-person pronouns in sentence construction. Person-oriented language stresses informality and symmetrical power relationships. For example, English has only one form for the second person, that is, *you*. Regardless of whether they are speaking to someone of higher, equal, or lower status, English speakers use the same form for the second person. For example, if we were to meet the President of the United States, we might say, "It's nice to meet you." If we were to meet a new colleague or neighbor, we could say, "It's nice to meet you." If we meet our new colleague's first-grade daughter, we might say, "It's nice to meet you." The personal nature of our language does not distinguish status or rank via pronoun usage.

Moreover, in the United States, we tend to treat each other with informality and forgo the use of formal titles and strict manners. These cultural attitudes are reflected in our personal verbal style. As Condon notes, two of the most frequently used words in English are "I" and "you." He points out that for many Americans, it is difficult to talk for any length of time without using pronouns. In Japan, however, there are at least ten words that might be equivalent to the English "I."[46] In addition, Storti notes that the Thai language has twelve forms of the pronoun "you."[47]

On the other hand, assert Gudykunst and Ting-Toomey, a contextual style accentuates and highlights one's role identity and status. In cultures that employ a contextual style, the social context dictates word choice, especially personal pronouns. For example, when using Thai language, one must look carefully at the situation, including the status and intimacy level among the interactants, in order to decide what form of pronoun to use. Unlike a personal style, where pronoun usage is consistent across situations, contextual-style language varies across situations. The correct form of pronoun is contingent on the context. Storti notes that German and French, for example, have familiar and formal forms of the pronoun *you.* The decision to use one form over another is based on the context of the interactants.[48] To use the familiar form with an unfamiliar interactant would be inappropriate. Germans are well known for their formality and strict use of titles, even among friends. German neighbors who have known each other for years still use the title "Herr" when addressing each other. June Ock Yum maintains that a fundamental function of many East Asian languages is to recognize the social status, degree of intimacy, age, and sex of the interactants. These types of demographics will influence the degree of formality and the use of honorifics in the language code. Many Asian languages highlight status differences and asymmetrical power relationships. According to Samuel Martin, Korean and Japanese have what he calls two "axes of distinction"—the axis of address and the axis of reference. In the axis of address, the speaker carefully chooses language based on the status role of the speakers. With the axis of reference, the speaker chooses language based on the speaker's attitude about the subject of communication. Yum provides the example of the phrase "to eat." In English, "to eat" is "to eat" regardless of with whom one is eating (e.g., a friend, a parent, or the President of the United States). In Korean, however, there are at least three different ways to say "to eat" depending on the role of the speakers: *muka-da* (plain), *du-shin-da* (polite), and *chap-soo-shin-da* (honorific).[49]

The Japanese use a contextual style, and their language includes an elaborate system of honorifics. Honorifics are linguistic forms that communicate respect according to one's rank and the rank of those to whom one is speaking. Honorifics take the form of suffixes to nouns, adjectives, and verbs. For example, the informal form of the verb "to go," *iku,* is used when speaking with someone to whom one is intimate. If the person with whom one is interacting is a stranger or is older, then the politeness marker, *-masu,* appears, as in *iki-masu*. If the person with whom one is interacting is socially superior, then the honorific form of the verb "to go," *irassyaru*, is used.[50] Hooker notes that one cannot learn to speak Japanese without learning the honorific language forms, including syntax and grammar, for defining one's social status. According to Hooker, through most of Japanese history, learning the language meant experiencing and reinforcing the social differences that ordered society. He points out that there was a time in Japanese history when one literally could not construct a sentence without defining one's own social class and the social class to whom one was speaking. In addition, Hooker notes, Japanese honorifics are a gendered system. Women's speech tends to be filled with honorifics and a sense of deference (i.e., honor, regard) to males.[51]

AN INTERCULTURAL CONVERSATION: PERSONAL AND CONTEXTUAL STYLES

In the following interaction, Jim is a student at a local university. He was born and raised in the United States. Akira is an exchange student from Japan. Jim and Akira are eating dinner together in a local restaurant. They have known each other for only a short time. Not only is Jim's style of communication overtly personal, but he's also quite direct.

Jim: *Hey buddy, what do you think of this American restaurant? I really like it.*

Akira: *Yes, Mr. Jim. This is very nice.*

Jim: *I always prefer restaurants like this, kinda casual but good food. I come here a lot. Do you go out to eat much in Japan?*

Akira: *Japanese restaurants are nice, too.*

Jim: *Yeah, but do you go out to eat much?*

Akira: *Sure, Japanese people like restaurants.*

Jim: *Whenever I come here I usually order the same thing. It's kinda funny, but since I like it, I figure I may as well eat it. I have a lot of friends that do that.*

Akira: *Sure.*

Jim: *Yeah, I was thinking the other day that since the dorm food sucks so bad, I should go out to eat more often.*

Akira: *Yes, that's a good idea.*

Jim is trying to involve Akira in the conversation by relating to him his personal experiences and preferences. Jim uses the first person "I" no fewer than eleven times and even refers to Akira as "Buddy." Akira never refers to himself in the first person. Akira generally defers to Jim and says little, even addressing Jim as "Mr. Jim." As a foreigner, Akira probably sees Jim as socially superior and uses a formal title. Moreover, rather than talking about his personal preferences, Akira mentions that Japanese people enjoy restaurants.

Instrumental and Affective Style

Gudykunst and Ting-Toomey define an instrumental verbal style as sender-based and goal-outcome based. The instrumental speaker uses communication to achieve some goal or outcome. Instrumental messages often are constructed to persuade and influence others and to maintain one's face. Yum says that instrumental-style users believe that communication should end after some goal has been attained and outcomes can be assessed, such as friends gained, opponent defeated, or some form of self-fulfillment has been reached.[52] Julia Wood reports that men in the United States engage in an instrumental style more often than U.S. women. U.S. women, on the other hand, use collaborative and cooperative talk.[53] An affective communication style is receiver and process oriented. The affective speaker is concerned not so much with the outcome of the communication, but with the process. In cultures where an instrumental style predominates, the burden of understanding often rests with the speaker. The speaker carefully chooses and organizes his or her messages in order to be understood by the audience. In cultures where an affective style is used, the responsibility of understanding rests with both parties; that is, the speaker and the listener. Affective speakers carefully watch for the reactions of their listener. Verbal expressions are insinuated and quite subtle. Affective speakers often operate on an intuitive sense and are nonverbally expressive. Hall and Hall assert that before getting down to business, the French prefer to establish a mood or a feeling, and a certain amount of intuition is required on the part of the listener in order to discover the meaning.[54] Condon argues that where Americans like to talk about themselves, Japanese talk about each other. The Japanese are very conscious of the other person with whom they are interacting; it is an interdependent concern unlike the American concern for independence. Condon notes,

> The difference in orientations is apparent when friends who have not seen each other for a while happen to meet. Americans are likely to ask about each other and tell each other about where they

have been or what they have been doing. Who speaks first does not seem to matter very much. When Japanese friends meet, one is likely to begin by thanking the other for some previous favor or gift or letter that was sent. Most often, a reference to the last time they were together is part of this greeting. Thus, they re-establish a particular continuing relationship.[55]

Samual Martin contends that the Japanese language has a complex array of polite formulas, or stock phrases, that have a leveling effect in just about any social situation. Martin argues that foreigners traveling in Japan can increase their effectiveness if they memorize these twenty or thirty polite formulas. Martin states that, to some extent, Japanese conversation is all formula and no content.[56] Perhaps the affective style of the Japanese is best reflected in Haiku poetry. Haiku is a very short form of poetry popular in Japan. Haiku poems always deal with some aspect of the season. Japanese Haiku poets are required to communicate a vivid impression using only 17 Japanese characters. The Haiku poem is concise while simultaneously communicating a deep spiritual understanding. From the reader of Haiku, much effort is required. One of the most popular Haiku poets was Basho who lived some 300 years ago, but whose poetry is still used as the definitive model for contemporary Haiku poets.

Waterjar cracks:
I lie awake
This icy night.
Lightning:
Heron's cry
Stabs the darkness
Sick on a journey:
Over parched fields
Dreams wander on.[57]

Chinese communication is also said to be more affective than instrumental. Becker argues that Chinese people reject debate and argumentation during the process of communication.[58] June Ock Yum believes that Confucianism has a large impact on Chinese communication and asserts that the Chinese emphasize a process and receiver orientation. According to Confucian philosophy, the primary function of communication is to initiate, develop, and maintain social relationships. Yum states that in China, it is important to engage in small talk before initiating business and to communicate personalized information. The Chinese view communication as a never-ending interpretive process. During a conversation, Chinese do not calculate what they give or receive. To do so, states Yum, would be to think about immediate personal profits, which conflicts with the Confucian notion of mutual faithfulness. The Chinese are disgusted by purely business-like transactions that are carefully planned and orchestrated.[59] Echoing Yum's seminal work, Stowell contends that Chinese is a listener-responsible language, rather than a speaker-responsible language, as is English. In a listener-responsible language, the listener is required to construct the meaning based on his or her relationship with the speaker. The Chinese view communication as an interdependent process whereby both speaker and listener are active participants who, together, create meaning.[60]

AN INTERCULTURAL CONVERSATION: INSTRUMENTAL AND AFFECTIVE SPEAKING

In the following dialogue Mr. Benton has traveled to China to introduce Mr. Yeh-Ching to a new operating system. Mr. Benton is coming from a culture that values an instrumental style of speaking, so he wants to get right down to business. Mr. Yeh-Ching, on the other hand, wants to establish a relationship before discussing any business possibilities. Mr. Benton and Mr. Yeh-Ching are meeting at a local restaurant in Beijing.[61]

Mr. Benton:	*Ah, Mr. Yeh-Ching. I've been waiting awhile. Had you forgotten about our meeting?*
Mr. Yeh-Ching:	*Good morning, Jerry, it is so nice to see you.*
Mr. Benton:	*Well . . . I'm glad you're finally here. I have all the material you need to see about the new computers we're installing. Here's our plan . . .*
Mr. Yeh-Ching:	*Jerry, have you seen much of our city?*
Mr. Benton:	*Well . . . I really don't have much time for sightseeing. This isn't a vacation, ya know. Business, business, business. My boss expects me to close this deal today and be back in New York by the weekend. So, here's my idea for installation.*
Mr. Yeh-Ching:	*Our city is so beautiful and full of history. Please allow me to arrange a tour for you. We can go together.*
Mr. Benton:	*I'd love to, but ya know . . . business is business.*
Mr. Yeh-Ching:	*Can I arrange a tour for you? My staff would be delighted to get to meet you.*

Mr. Benton:	*No thanks, but I'd like to show you something. Look at these new configurations for the computers we're installing. Now . . . notice that—*
Mr. Yeh-Ching:	*Here is a menu. This restaurant has some very interesting Chinese dishes that I would like for you to try.*
Mr. Benton:	*Oh, I grabbed a bite to eat at the Hilton. Go ahead and eat, though. I can show you the production schedule.*

Chances are pretty good that Mr. Yeh-Ching will not buy Mr. Benton's new computer system. To an affective speaker like Mr. Yeh-Ching, Mr. Benton is too concerned about his business and not concerned enough about the personal side of business; that is, relationships. Affective speakers are sometimes suspicious of people who refuse to get to know each other before striking a deal.

Cross-Cultural Conflict Styles

As in any relationship, whenever two people from different cultures come together and exchange verbal and nonverbal messages, conflict can emerge. Conflict often surfaces as a result of incompatible goals, limited or inadequate resources, differing opinions on important topics, and so on. Intercultural conflict involves emotional frustrations or a clash of expectations based on cultural differences. Communication professor Stella Ting-Toomey has spent much of her professional career studying conflict and communication conflict styles across cultures. Ting-Toomey has observed that how people manage communication during conflict differs considerably across cultures. She notes that people from different cultures often use different communication styles during conflict.[62] According to Ting-Toomey, conflict style refers to a person's overall orientation toward initiating and managing conflict. Ting-Toomey maintains that a person's conflict style is based on two communication dimensions. The first dimension is the degree to which a person asserts a *self-face need;* that is, seeks to satisfy his or her own interests during conflict. The second is the degree to which a person is cooperative (i.e., *other-face need*) and seeks to incorporate the interests of the other.[63] The combination of assertiveness, or *self-face need,* and cooperativeness, or *other-face need,* defines five styles of managing conflict.

The degree to which a person asserts a high self-face need while simultaneously discounting the other-face need defines the dominating communication style. On the other hand, the person who assumes a high self-face need while also attending to the needs of the other-face takes on an integrating style. The person who tries to balance both self-face and other-face

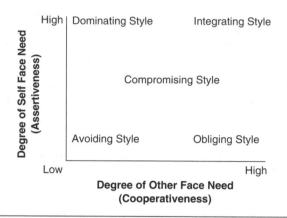

Figure 7.5

needs takes on a compromising style. The person using an avoiding style ignores both self-face need and other-face need. The person who puts the other-face need ahead of self-face need assumes an obliging style (see Figure 7.5).

Some research has shown that a culture's individualism-collectivism orientation affects the preference of conflict management style. Although the research is not conclusive, many studies have shown that persons from Asian cultures, many of which are collectivistic, generally prefer avoiding and obliging styles, especially when compared to the United States (an individualistic culture), where we see a preference for dominating and integrating styles. Related research has shown that Middle Eastern managers prefer integrating styles of conflict management over dominating and compromsing.[64]

LANGUAGE AND ETHNIC IDENTITY

As we saw in Chapter 6, a fundamental way in which groups distinguish themselves from other groups, and thereby maintain their group identity, is through the language they speak. Within groups, status and hierarchy are recognized primarily through the use of language. Often, immigrant groups maintain their cultural heritage and identity by using their native language in their host culture and by teaching it to their children. Other immigrant groups may discourage the use of their native tongue so as to establish themselves as legitimate members of their new culture. McNamara argues that immigrants entering a new culture may have to redefine their former social identity. In a study of Hebrew-speaking Israeli immigrants in Australia, McNamara found that as the Israeli immigrants changed their social identities, there was a corresponding change in their attitudes favoring English over Hebrew. The subjects in McNamara's study were considered *yordin,* a term with negative connotations referring to Israelis living abroad. Among other things, language identified the yordin as an outgroup in Australia. As with most migrant languages used in Australia, Hebrew had low status. By learning and speaking English and teaching it to their children, the yordin were able, to some extent, to manage their negative social identities in their new host culture.[65]

Patricia SanAntonio conducted research on the language practices of an American computer company based in Japan. This particular company required its employees to speak English. Because they wanted to hire native Japanese persons with business expertise and English skills, however, they had trouble attracting high-quality candidates. In order to compete with other Japanese companies, they hired new college graduates who lacked proficient English skills. The result was that they had a workforce with a great deal of English-speaking variety; that is, some were quite competent, whereas others struggled considerably. Because English was so important to the company, the ability to speak English and to interact with American managers became a real source of power within the company. SanAntonio argued that within the Japanese context, language and identity are inextricably linked, and that the ability and willingness for Japanese employees to use English identified them and their desire to become integrated into the organization. SanAntonio concluded that the English-only policy created a boundary between the Japanese and Americans such that Japanese input was reduced. The policy essentially circumvented the Japanese hierarchy and allowed the Americans to maintain control within the organization.[66]

Intraculturally, the use of language can mark a person as a member of a particular group. In their analysis, Weider and Pratt argue that among some Native Americans, being silent is fundamental in the real Indian's mode of communicating. Moreover, the topic of one's "Indianness" is forbidden; "real" Indians do not discuss it. Real Indians do not engage in casual conversation or idle chit-chat with other Indians. Weider and Pratt note that individuals who initiate small talk or openly discuss their Indianness are disqualified from the group of "real" Indians.[67] In Gerry Philipsen's seminal research on speaking "Like a Man in Teamsterville," he argued that to present oneself as a man requires an implicit understanding of the communication rules of the particular speech community of real men. "Real" men in Teamsterville engage in a variety of communicative strategies that signal their membership in the group. Real men do not rely on speech as their primary mode of self-expression. Only in situations where the interactants are equal (e.g., two "Men") is speaking allowed. Here, speaking serves as a means for solidarity. Speaking is restricted when the communicants are unequal, as in cases where a man is interacting with someone of higher status, such as a boss, or of lower status, such as a wife/girlfriend or children. Moreover, speaking is discouraged when a man must assert his power or influence over others, as in cases where he is responding to an insult to himself or his wife/girlfriend, in cases of disciplining children, and in asserting himself in political or economical discussions. In these types of contexts nonverbal communication is preferred. In some cases, men may be silent, but in others they may react physically, as in the case of responding to an insult. As Philipsen argues,

> In critical symbolic ways, as protector and as master of a house the Teamsterville man disvalues speech as a resource for male role enactment. . . . Speech is not an integral part of earning a living or other aspects of economic life. . . . For the Teamsterville man, minimal emphasis of talk in work settings is one part of a pattern of minimal talk with outsiders to the neighborhood, with persons in positions of authority who are not long-time associates, and with white collar persons, with whom there is a perceived status *difference*.[68]

Like any other group in the United States, African-Americans are identified by their use of language, specifically Ebonics. Moreover, Blacks clearly identify themselves in terms of their use of Ebonics. Smitherman estimates that 80 to 90 percent of all African-Americans use some form of Ebonics in some situations. Weber asserts that Ebonics is critical in fostering Black identity in the United States for at least three reasons. First, Weber maintains that because Blacks experience life differently from other groups, they need a language to express their unique experience. Second, Black language bridges the economic, educational, and social gap among Blacks. Weber states that Ebonics "is the language that binds, that creates community for blacks, so that the brother in the three-piece Brooks Brothers suit can go to the local corner where folks 'hang out' and say, 'hey blood, what it is?' and be one with them." Finally, Ebonics expresses a political statement that Blacks have not relinquished a vital part of themselves—that is, language—and that they can maintain control over at least one part of their lives.[69]

The controversy over Ebonics is both political and linguistic. Linguists disagree about whether Ebonics is a dialect (of English) or a language by itself. If a language is defined as a set of sounds, combined with a set of rules, for the purpose of communicating, then Ebonics should be considered a language. A dialect is typically thought of as a regional variety, or subset, of a language. Dialects are distinguished by their variations in vocabulary, grammar, and pronunciation from other regional varieties. As Smitherman notes, the labels "language" and "dialect" are equally respectable among linguists. The term *dialect* has, however, taken on negative connotations among the public.[70] Politically, the debate centers on the appropriateness of Ebonics in various social settings, such as schools. Politically, some factions argue that Ebonics is appropriate and should be taught in schools. For example, in December 1996, the Oakland, California School Board wrote,

> BE IT RESOLVED that the Board of Education officially recognizes the existence, and the cultural and historic bases of West and Niger-Congo African Language Systems, and each language as the predominantly primary language of African-American students . . . BE IT FURTHER RESOLVED that the Superintendent in conjunction with her staff shall immediately devise and implement the best possible academic program for imparting instruction to African-American students in their primary language for the combined purposes of maintaining the legitimacy and richness of . . . "Ebonics" . . . and to facilitate their acquisition and mastery of English language skills.[71]

The resolution prompted an anti-Ebonics movement spearheaded by Peter King (New York), member of the U.S. House of Representatives. On January 9, 1997, King introduced House Resolution 28, which read, in part, that no federal funds should be used to pay for or support any program that is based on the premise that Ebonics is a legitimate language.[72] Linguistic and political arguments notwithstanding, Ebonics is clearly a medium of expression for many African-Americans. Ebonics not only serves as a vehicle for communication, but also fosters a sense of identity and community among those who speak it.

Do You Speak American?

In 2004, celebrated award-winning author and journalist, Robert MacNeil traveled across the United States exploring how the English language is used throughout the various regions of the country. MacNeil wanted to answer the question, What does it mean to "speak American"? Throughout his travels, MacNeil discovered that the English used in the United States differs considerably from region to region, among ethnic and social groups, and by age and gender. In addition, MacNeil found that many people shift from one version of English to another depending on the person with whom they are speaking.[73]

Linguists often argue over the term *Standard English;* that is, the variety of English spoken in the United States that is considered correct. Some linguists argue that there is a right and a wrong way to speak English and that certain correct forms should always be used. But most linguists also recognize that different varieties of English exist in different geographical areas. As we move from region to region across the country we can hear differences in pronunciation, grammatical structures, vocabulary, and pitch. Most people think of such differences as *accents;* hence, the phrase "Southern accent" is used to describe the speech of people who live in the southern United States. Another term often used by sociolinguists (scholars who study language as it is used in various social contexts) is *dialect;* that is, a language variety associated with a particular region or social group. An accent or dialect should not be confused with *slang* or *jargon.* Slang refers to words or expressions typically used in informal communication. Slang words often do not last long, and other slang replaces them. Jargon refers to the specialized or technical vocabulary used by persons in the same group, such as doctors, lawyers, computer specialists, and so on. Many sociolinguists now use the term *language variety* to refer to the way a particular group of people uses language.[74]

Throughout the United States a debate rages over whether English should be the *official* language. An official language is one that has been specifically designated in the constitution of a country or territory. More than half the countries in the world have official languages, including Egypt, Saudi Arabia, Syria, Lebanon, Kuwait, Jordan, Palestine, and Libya, all of whom designate Arabic as their official language. The federal government of the United States does not recognize an official language, but 30 states have established English as the official state language.[75]

States with English as the Official Language

Alabama
Alaska
Arkansas
California
Colorado
Florida
Georgia
Hawaii (with Hawaiian language)
Illinois
Indiana
Iowa
Kentucky
Louisiana (with French)
Massachusetts
Mississippi

Missouri
Montana
Nebraska
New Hampshire
New Mexico (with Spanish)
North Carolina
North Dakota
Puerto Rico (with Spanish)
South Carolina
South Dakota
Tennessee
U.S. Virgin Islands
Utah
Virginia
Wyoming

Speakers of a particular dialect often believe that their language variety is the best, correct, and standard way to speak. They may even believe that their language variety is so standard that it is not even considered a dialect. Noted sociolinguist Walt Wolfram argues that everyone speaks some form of dialect. Wolfram maintains that it is not possible to speak a language without speaking a dialect of that language. Moreover, he dispels the myth that dialects result from unsuccessful attempts of people to speak the correct form of a language. Instead, Wolfram contends that speakers acquire their dialect by adopting the speech features of those around them, not by failing in their attempts to adopt standard language features. Dialects, like all language systems, are systematic and regular, and they function as any standard language variety.[76]

Estimating the number of dialects in the United States is difficult. Some linguists argue that there may be as few as only three, whereas others contend that there are as many as 25 dialects in the United States (which would include Ebonics, Spanglish, and Chicano English discussed in Chapter 3). Still others maintain that it is impossible to count the possible language varieties in the United States. A few U.S. dialects are discussed below.

Appalachian English (AE). Appalachian English (AE) is spoken by people in the Appalachian mountains from eastern Pennsylvania to North Carolina. Perhaps the most distinctive feature of AE is *a-prefixing;* that is putting an *a-* sound before words that end in *-ing,* as in, "I was a-slippin' and a-slidin' on the ice," or "What are you a-doin' here so early?" The a-prefix can only occur with verb complements, with -ing participles that function as nouns. Thus, the sentence "The man went a-sailin'," is appropriate, but the sentence "The man likes a-sailin'" is not.[77]

Cajun English. Cajun English, sometimes called Linguistic Gumbo, is the term that describes the variety of French spoken in South Louisiana. It originates in the language spoken by the French and Acadian people who settled in Louisiana in the 17th century. Five features distinguish Cajun English, including vowel pronunciation, stress changes, the lack of the /th/ phonemes, non-aspiration of /p/, /t/, and /k/, and lexical differences. Cajuns talk extremely fast, their vowels are clipped, and French terms abound in their speech.[78]

R-less or R-Dropping Dialects. Regional differences in how the *r* sound is pronounced distinguish one dialect from another. The *r* sound before a vowel (e.g., red, bread) is pronounced much the same way across the United States. But in many dialects of the East Coast (e.g., Boston, New York), the *r* sound before a consonant is dropped and speakers of such dialects lengthen the preceding vowel sound, as in "paahk the caah."[79]

California English. In recent years much attention has focused on the "Valley Girl" dialect phenomenon (e.g., "Gag me with a spoon!"). But California is very diverse ethnically, with substantial Black and Hispanic populations. Thus, the stereotypic "Valley Girl" dialect is spoken mostly by the White population. In such speech, the vowels of *hock* and *hawk, cot* and *caught,* are pronounced the same—so *awesome* rhymes with *possum.* Also, the vowels in *boot* and *boat* (called back vowels because they are pronounced in the back of the mouth) all have a tendency to move forward in the mouth, so that the vowel in *dude* or *spoon* (as in "gag me with a . . .") sounds a little like the word *you,* or the vowel in *pure* or *cute.* Also, *boat* and *loan* often sound like *bewt* and *lewn—*or *eeeeuuw.*[80]

Language has an immense impact on how individuals see themselves and others within any cultural milieu. Language is perhaps the major marker that people use to categorize and group others.

CHAPTER SUMMARY

All human languages are made up of a system of sounds, syntax, and semantics. The sole purpose of language is to communicate. Historically, linguists once believed that language was tied to race and culture. Contemporary linguists have discounted that notion in favor of the idea that languages are essentially human and are not unique to any particular race or culture. As humans, regardless of culture, we are born with a universal grammar that allows us to learn the particular language of our culture. Any individual language is simply a subset of the universal grammar that is embedded in our brains. Considerable evidence shows that children (even deaf and blind children) acquire language in the same way at about the same time.

Moreover, children are able to construct grammatically correct sentences without ever having been formally taught.

Language is a guide to social reality, helping people to observe events around them and to organize their thoughts. Moreover, language is so powerful that speakers can generate an infinite number of never-before-spoken sentences that are completely comprehensible by speakers of the same language. Although the universal grammar of all languages is similar, persons from different cultures use different styles of language, ranging from direct to indirect, personal to contextual, instrumental to affective, and elaborate to succinct. Direct-indirect style refers to how speakers reveal their intentions. The personal-contextual style refers to the degree to which speakers focus on themselves during communication or on their partner. Instrumental styles are goal-oriented, whereas affective styles are process oriented. Elaborate and succinct styles refer to the actual quantity or volume of talk that is preferred. These different styles probably reflect cultural values and beliefs.

GLOSSARY OF TERMS

Affective Style: Communication manner where the process of interaction is emphasized, placing the burden of understanding on both the speaker and the listener. Relies heavily on nonverbal cues.

Avoiding Style: During conflict, a style that ignores both self-face need and other-face need.

Compromising Style: During conflict, a style that balances both self-face and other-face needs.

Conceptual Symbols: Specific stimuli that refer to concepts that have no physical referent and exist in the mind of the user, such as "liberty" or "democracy."

Contextual Style: Role-centered mode of speaking where one's choice of messages is influenced by one's relative status in the conversation.

Dialect: A language variety associated with a particular region or social group.

Direct Style: Manner of speaking where one employs overt expressions of intention.

Dominating Style: The degree to which a person asserts a high self-face need while simultaneously discounting the other-face need.

Elaborate Style: Mode of speaking that emphasizes rich, expressive language.

Elaborated Code: A cultural context wherein the speakers of a language have a variety of linguistic options open to them in order to explicitly communicate their intent via verbal messages.

Ethnic Identity: The degree to which a person identifies, associates, and empathizes with his or her ethnic group. Often, this is accomplished and recognized via language use.

Exacting Style: Manner of speaking where persons say no more nor less than is needed to communicate a point.

Generative Grammar: The idea that from a finite set of rules, a speaker of any language can create or generate an infinite number of sentences, many of which have never before been uttered.

Iconic Semblances: Signs that visually represent their referent to some degree, as in a map or photograph.

Indirect Style: Manner of speaker wherein the intentions of the speakers are hidden or only hinted at during interaction.

Instrumental Style: Sender-focused manner of speaking that is goal and outcome oriented. Instrumental speakers use communication to achieve some goal or purpose.

Integrating Style: Assuming a high self-face need while also attending to the needs of the other-face.

Language: A systematic set of sounds, combined with a set of rules, for the sole purpose of communicating.

Language Variety: The way a particular group of people uses language.

Morpheme: Smallest meaningful unit of sound; a combination of phonemes.

Obliging Style: During conflict, asserting the other-face need ahead of self-face need.

Personal Style: Manner of speaking relying on the use of personal pronouns that stresses informality and symmetrical power relationships.

Phoneme: Smallest unit of sound, as in a consonant or vowel.

Proper Symbols: Specific stimuli that name reality; the word "cat" is a proper symbol for a specific type of animal.

Restricted Code: A cultural context wherein the speakers of a language are limited as to what they can say or do verbally. A restricted code is a status-oriented system.

Ritual Semblances: Exaggerated symptoms, such as begging or acts of submission.

Standard English: The variety of English spoken in the United States that is considered correct.

Succinct Style: Manner of very concise speaking often accompanied by silence.

Symbol: Arbitrarily selected and learned stimulus representing something else.

Symptoms: Fixed, hard-wired reactions to environmental stimuli, such as pupil dilation, blushing, or piloerection.

Syntactic Symbols: Symbols that express grammatical relationships for other symbols, such as possession or tense.

Universal Grammar: The idea that all languages share a common rule structure or grammar that is innate in human beings, regardless of culture.

REFERENCES

1. Searchinger, G. (Director & Producer). (1996). *The human language series: Part I: Colorless green ideas* [Film]. (Available from Ways of Knowing, Inc. 200 West 72nd Street, New York, NY 10023).
2. Salzmann, Z. (1993). *Language, culture, & society.* Boulder, CO: Westview.
3. Sapir, E. (1929). The status of linguistics as a science. *Language, 5,* 207–214.
4. Salzmann, *Language, culture, & society.*
5. Whorf, B. (1940). Science and linguistics. *Technology Review, 42,* 229-231, 247–248.
6. Whorf, B. (1940). Linguistics as an exact science. *Technology Review, 43,* 61–63, 80–83.
7. Salzmann, *Language, culture, & society.*
8. Carroll, J. B. (1963). Linguistic relativity, contrastive linguistics, and language learning. *International Review of Applied Linguistics in Language Teaching, 1,* 1–20.
9. Chomsky, N. (1965) *Aspects of the theory of syntax.* Cambridge: MIT Press; Goss, B., & O'Hair, D. (1988). *Communicating in interpersonal relationships.* New York: Macmillan.
10. Katzner, K. (1975). *Languages of the world.* New York: Funk & Wagnalls.
11. Tohsaku, C. K. (1997). Japanese "Kanji" [On-line] Available: http://edweb.sdsu.edu/courses/edtec670/cardboard/card/k/kanji.html
12. Liska, J. (1993). Bee dances, birdsongs, monkey calls, and cetacean sonar: Is speech unique? *Western Journal of Speech Communication, 57,* 1–26.
13. Ibid.
14. Liska, Bee dances, birdsongs, monkey calls, and cetacean sonar.
15. Chomsky, N. (1957). *Syntactic structures.* The Hague: Mouton & Company.
16. Much of this discussion of language is based on interviews with Chomsky and other linguists in Searchinger, *The human language series.*

17. Gleitman, L. P. O. (1993). A human universal: The capacity to learn language. *Modern Philology, 90,* s13-s33.

18. Searchinger, *The human language series.*

19. Gleitman, A human universal.

20. Pinker, S. (1995). Language acquisition. In L. R. Gleitman & M. Liberman (Eds.), *An invitation to cognitive science: Vol. 1: Language* (2nd ed.). Cambridge: MIT Press.

21. Gleitman, "A human universal."

22. Searchinger, *The human language series.*

23. Pinker, S., Language acquisition. Some of these examples are from an interview with Pinker in Searchinger, *The human language series.*

24. Heath, J. (1997). Super-quick overview of characteristics of the Japanese language. [Online]. Available: http://stripe.colorado.edu/-jheath/faq4.html

25. Katzner, *Languages of the world.*

26. Searchinger, *The human language series;* Kulick, D. (1992). *Language shift and cultural reproduction, socialization, self, and syncretism in a Papua, New Guinea village.* Cambridge, UK: Cambridge University Press.

27. Ibid.

28. Salzmann, *Language, culture, & society.*

29. Searchinger, *The human language series.*

30. Ibid.

31. Bernstein, B. (1966). Elaborated and restricted codes: Their social origins and some consequences. In A. G. Smith (Ed.), *Communication and culture* (pp. 427–441). New York: Holt, Rinehart and Winston.

32. Ibid.

33. Ibid.

34. Gudykunst, W. B., & Ting-Toomey, S. (1988). Verbal communication styles. In W. B. Gudykunst, & S. Ting-Toomey (Eds.), *Culture and interpersonal communication* (pp. 99–115). Newbury Park, CA: Sage.

35. Gudykunst & Ting-Toomey, Verbal communication styles.

36. Fedarko, K. (1995). Man of Israel: Rabin's stirring life story marks out the mileposts in the history of his nation. *Time, 146*(20), 68–72.

37. Hall, E. T., & Hall, M. R. (1990). *Understanding cultural differences:Germans, French, and Americans.* Yarmouth, ME: Intercultural Press.

38. Iwao, S. (1993). *The Japanese woman: Traditional image & changing reality.* Cambridge, MA: Harvard University Press.

39. Hall & Hall, *Understanding cultural differences.*

40. This dialogue is very loosely adapted from Storti, C. (1994). *Cross-cultural dialogues: 74 brief encounters with cultural difference.* Yarmouth, ME: Intercultural Press.

41. Gudykunst & Ting-Toomey, Verbal communication styles.

42. Kochman, T. (1990). Cultural pluralism: Black and White styles. In D. Carbaugh (Ed.), *Cultural communication and intercultural contact* (pp. 219–224). Hillsdale, NJ: Erlbaum.

43. Stowell, J. (1996). *The changing face of Chinese communication: A synthesis of interpersonal communication concepts.* Paper presented at the annual convention of the Speech Communication Association, San Diego, CA.

44. Weider, D. L., & Pratt, S. (1990). On being a recognizable Indian among Indians. In D. Carbaugh, (Ed.), *Cultural communication and intercultural contact,* (pp. 45–64). Hillsdale, NJ: Erlbaum.

45. Bernstein, Elaborated and restricted codes: Their social origins and some consequences; Gudykunst, W. B., & Kim, Y. Y. (1997). *Communicating with strangers: An approach to intercultural communication.* New York:McGraw-Hill.

46. Condon, J. C. (I 984). *With respect to the Japanese: A guide for Americans.* Yarmouth, ME: Intercultural Press; Gudykunst & Ting-Toomey, *Culture and interpersonal communication.*

47. Storti, C. *Cross-Cultural Dialogues: 74 Brief Encounters with Cultural Differences.* (Yarmouth, MA: Intercultural Press, 1994).

48. Ibid.

49. Yum, J. O. (1997). The impact of Confucianism on interpersonal relationships and communication patterns in East Asia. In L. A. Samovar, & R. E. Porter, (Eds.), *Intercultural communication: A Reader* (pp. 78–88), Belmont, CA: Wadsworth: Martin, S. E. (1964). Speech levels in Japan and Korea. In D. Hymes, (Ed.), *Language in culture and society* (pp. 407–415). New York: Harper and Row.

50. Miyagawa, S. *The Japanese Language.* (www.-japan.mit.edu/articles/Japanese Language.html). 8Massachusetts Institute of Technology, 1995

51. Hooker, R. *The Japanese Language* (www.wsu.edu:8080/~dee/ANCJAPAN/languagc.htm), 1999.

52. Gudykunst & Ting-Toomey, *Verbal communication styles;* Yum, *The impact of Confucianism on interpersonal relationships and communication patterns in East Asia.*

53. Wood, J. T. (1997). *Gendered lives: Communication, gender, and culture.* Belmont, CA: Wadsworth.

54. Hall & Hall, *Understanding cultural differences.*

55. Condon, *With respect to the Japanese,* (p. 50).

56. Martin, Speech levels in Japan and Korea.

57. *A haiku homepage* [On-line] Available: http://www.dmu.ac.uk/-pkal/haiku.html: *The shiki internet salon* [On-line] Available: http://mikan.cc.matsuyama.u.acjp/-shiki/

58. Becker, C. B. (1986). Reasons for the lack of argumentation and debate in the Far East. *International Journal of Intercultural Relations,* 10, 75–92.

59. Yum, The impact of Confucianism on interpersonal relationships and communication patterns in East Asia.

60. Stowell, *The changing face of Chinese communication*; Lustig, M. W., & Koester, J. (1996). *Intercultural competence: Interpersonal communication across cultures.* New York: HarperCollins.

61. This dialogue is adapted from Copeland, L. (Producer) (1983). *Managing the overseas assignment* [videorecording]. San Francisco: Copeland Griggs Productions.

62. Ting-Toomey, S., & Oetzel, J. G. (2003). Cross-cultural face concerns and conflict styles. In W. B. Gudykunst (Ed)., *Cross-cultural and intercultural communication,* (pp. 127–147). Thousand Oaks, CA: Sage.

63. The concepts of assertiveness and cooperativeness are found in a number of sources, including Thomas, K. W., & Kilmann, R. H., (1974). *Thomas-Kilmann conflict MODE instrument.* New York: XICOM, Tuxedo; Rahim, M. A., (1983). A measure of styles of handling interpersonal conflict. *Academy of Management Journal,* 26, 368–376; Ting-Toomey, S., (1988). Intercultural conflict styles: A face-negotiation theory. In Y. Y. Kim & W. B. Gudykunst (Eds.), *Theories of intercultural communication* (pp. 213–235). Newbury Park, CA: Sage.

64. Ting-Toomey & Oetzel, Cross-cultural face concerns and conflict styles.

65. McNamara, T. F. (1988). Language and social identity: Israelis abroad. In W. B. Gudykunst, (Ed.), *Language and ethnic identity,* (pp. 59–72). Clevedon, UK: Multilingual Matters, Ltd.

66. SanAntonio, P. M. (1988). Social mobility and language use in an American company in Japan. In W. B. Gudykunst, (Ed.), *Language and ethnic identity,* (pp. 35–44). Clevedon, UK: Multilingual Matters, Ltd.

67. Weider & Pratt, On being a recognizable Indian among Indians.

68. Philipsen, G. (1990). Speaking "like a man" in Teamsterville: Culture patterns of role enactment in an urban neighborhood. In D. Carbaugh (Ed.), *Cultural communication and intercultural contact,* (pp. 11–20). Hillsdale, NJ: Erlbaum, (p. 17).

69. Smitherman, G. *Talkin That Talk: Language, Culture and Education in African America,* (New York: Routledge, 2000); Weber, S. "The Need to Be: The Socio-Cultural Significance of Black Language," in *Intercultural Communication: A Reader* ed. L. A. Samovar and R. E. Porter (Belmont, Calif: Wadsworth, 1994), pp. 221–226.

70. Smitherman, G. *Talkin That Talk.*

71. Excerpt taken from Smitherman, *Talkin That Talk,* (p. xi).

72. Richardson, E. "The Anti-Ebonics Movement: 'Standard' English Only," *Journal of English Linguistics,* 26 (1998), 156–170.

73. MacNeil, R., & Cran, W. (2005). *Do you speak American?* New York: Random House; *Do you speak American?* Online source: www.pbs.org/speak.

74. MacNeil & Cran, *Do you speak American?* Online source: www.pbs.org/speak; Wolfram, W., & Schilling-Estes, N. (1998). *American English: Dialects and Variation,* Oxford, UK: Basil Blackwell.

75. List of Official Languages. (2005). *Wikipedia: The Free Encyclopedia.* Online source: http://en.wikipedia.org/wiki/List_of_official_languages.

76. Wolfram and Schilling-Estes, *American English.*

77. A-Prefixing in Appalachian English: Archaism or Innovation? *Do you speak American?* Online source: www.pbs.org/speak/seatosea/americanvarieties/a-prefixing/background.

78. Stirring the Linguistic Gumbo. *Do you speak American?* Online source: www.pbs.org/speak/seatosea/americanvarieties/cajun/

79. Fought, J., (2004). Starting with the coast. [on-line] Available: http://www.pbs.org/speak/seatosea/americanvarieties/southern/

80. Eckert, P., & Mendoza-Denton, N. (2002) Getting real in the Golden State. *Language Magazine,* 1(7), 29–30, 33–34.

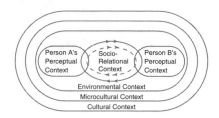

CHAPTER 8

The Nonverbal Code

Speakers of every language accompany their words with nonverbal signals that serve to mark the structure of their utterances.

—Peter Farb[1]

Chapter Objectives

After reading this chapter, you should be able to

1. Define nonverbal communication.

2. Compare and contrast verbal and nonverbal codes.

3. Define kinesics and provide examples of kinesic behavior across cultures.

4. Define paralanguage and provide cross-cultural examples of paralinguistic differences.

5. Define proxemics and provide cross-cultural examples of proxemic differences.

6. Define haptics and provide cross-cultural examples of haptic differences.

7. Define olfactics and discuss how smell is perceived across cultures.

8. Define chronemics and discuss how time is perceived across cultures.

9. Recount the fundamental assumptions of the nonverbal expectancy violation theory.

Many linguists, psychologists, and sociologists believe that human language evolved from a system of nonlinguistic (nonverbal) communication. To these scholars, language and communication are not the same. Humans possess a host of nonlinguistic ways to communicate with each other through the use of their hands, arms, face, and personal space. When we combine verbal and nonverbal language, we create an intricate communication system through which humans come to know and understand each other.[2] All animals communicate nonlinguistically—that is, nonverbally—through sight, sound, smell, or touch. Moths, for example, communicate by smell and color. Through smell, some species of male moths can detect female moths miles away. Elephants communicate with low-frequency sound waves undetectable by humans. Felines are well known for rubbing their scent on (marking) people and objects to communicate their ownership of such property. This kind of animal or nonlinguistic communication is probably innate and invariant within a particular species. Most scholars also recognize that a significant portion of our nonverbal behavior, such as the expression of emotion, is innate and varies little across cultures. Like verbal language, however, much of our nonverbal communication is learned and varies across cultures.

This chapter investigates nonverbal communication and how it differs across cultures. It begins with some definitions of nonverbal communication and a discussion of how verbal and nonverbal codes differ. The chapter then outlines the various channels of nonverbal communication and how cultures differ regarding their use. These channels are kinesics, paralanguage, proxemics, haptics, olfactics, physical appearance and dress, and chronemics. The chapter closes with a discussion of nonverbal expectancy violation theory.

DEFINITIONS OF NONVERBAL COMMUNICATION

The study of nonverbal communication focuses on the messages people send to each other that do not contain words, such as messages sent through body motions; vocal qualities; and the use of time, space, artifacts, dress, and even smell. Communication with the body, called *kinesics,* consists of the use of the hands, arms, legs, and face to send messages. *Paralanguage,* or the use of the voice, refers to vocal characteristics such as volume, pitch, rate, and so forth. Through paralanguage, people communicate their emotional state, veracity, and sincerity. Most of us can identify when speakers are confident or nervous through their vocal pitch, rate, and pace. Through *chronemics,* the use of time, people can communicate status and punctuality. We saw in Chapter 3 that cultures differ widely in their monochronic or polychronic orientation. By studying space, or *proxemics,* we can learn how people express intimacy and power. In the United States, for example, people tend to prefer an "arm's length" distance from others during communication. Through smell, called *olfactics,* a person's ethnicity, social class, and status are communicated. Many cultures establish norms for acceptable and unacceptable scents associated with the human body. To other cultures, for example, people raised in the United States seem obsessed with deodorants, perfumes, soaps, and shampoos that mask natural body odors.

Linguist Deborah Tannen estimates that as much as 90 percent of all human communication is nonverbal, although other scholars argue that the percentage is much lower.[3] During intercultural communication, verbal and nonverbal messages are sent simultaneously. Verbal communication represents the literal content of a message, whereas the nonverbal component communicates the style or how the message is to be interpreted. Hence, the nonverbal code often *complements, accents, substitutes, repeats,* or even *contradicts* the verbal message.[4] For example, a speaker might complement the verbal message "This dinner is delicious!" with a smile and increased vocal volume. Politicians often accent their speeches by pounding their fists on podiums. When asked how many minutes are left to complete an exam, the professor might simply raise five fingers to substitute for the words "five minutes." Persons often repeat their verbal message "Yes" with affirmative head nodding.

Sometimes, however, a person's verbal and nonverbal messages contradict each other. When this happens, we usually believe the nonverbal message. For example, your roommate has been very quiet and reserved for a couple of days. Finally, you ask what is wrong. Your roommate replies with a long sigh and says, "Oh . . . nothing." Which do you believe, the verbal or the nonverbal message? Most people believe the nonverbal message because, unlike the verbal message, which requires conscious effort to encode, nonverbal messages are often less conscious and therefore are perceived as more honest. Psychologist David McNeill argues that our nonverbal behavior is partly unconscious and represents a sort of visual metaphor or analogue of conscious thought. He states that gestures and other body motions are primitive forms of speech. Whereas verbal language takes thought and puts it into linear digital form—that is, a sentence—gestures and body movements show the instantaneous thought itself as an analogue of the thought.[5] This is why verbal communication is often called *digital communication* and nonverbal communication is called *analogic communication.* Because we have less control over our nonverbal behavior, it tends to be perceived as more honest than our verbal behavior.

In addition to complementing, accenting, substituting, repeating, and contradicting verbal communication, nonverbal communication also regulates and manages our conversations with others. Professors delivering lectures can monitor the reactions of their students through their eye contact, body posture, and other nonverbal behaviors (for example, yawning) and adapt their lectures accordingly. Students who raise their hands are signaling the professor that they have questions or comments. Such behavior manages the flow of communication in the classroom. Individually, we can regulate the flow and pace of a conversation by engaging in direct eye contact, affirmative head nodding, and stance, thus signaling our conversational partner to continue or stop the communication.

THE RELATIONSHIP BETWEEN VERBAL AND NONVERBAL CODES

By comparing and contrasting the human verbal and nonverbal codes, many linguists have concluded that verbal language evolved from its nonlinguistic predecessor. Noam Chomsky argues that verbal language is an advanced and refined form of an inherited nonlinguistic (nonverbal) system.[6] A key distinction between the two is that the verbal language system is based primarily on symbols, whereas the nonverbal system is signal based. The difference between a symbol and a signal is that a *symbol* is an arbitrarily selected and *learned* stimulus representing something else. A *sign,* or *signal,* however, is a natural and constituent part of that which it represents. For example, when we hear thunder in the distance, it signals us that a storm is approaching. The thunder is a sign of a storm. But the thunder is also an intrinsic part of the storm. Sweating, for example, signals that one may be hot, but sweating is a natural part of being hot, as is shivering of being cold. Humans do not learn to sweat or shiver. Unlike signals, symbols have no natural relationship with that which they represent; therefore, they are arbitrary abstractions and must be learned. For example, the symbol *cat* have no intrinsic connection with a feline animal. Speakers of any language learn to associate symbols with referents.

Another difference between the verbal and nonverbal code is that the nonverbal signal system is much more restrictive in sending capacity than the verbal code. For example, it is virtually impossible to communicate about the past or future through nonverbal communication. You might be able to signal a friend of impending danger by waving your hands, but you cannot warn your friend of danger that might occur tomorrow or recall danger that occurred yesterday with nonverbal signals. In addition, communication of negation is practically impossible with the nonverbal code system. Try communicating to a friend nonverbally that you are not going to the grocery store tomorrow. The same task is relatively easy through the linguistic system, however.[7]

Formal Versus Informal Code Systems

In Chapter 7, verbal language was defined as a systematic set of sounds combined with a set of rules for the sole purpose of communication. All verbal languages have a formal set of sounds, syntax, and semantics. The degree of formality of verbal language is not found in the nonverbal code, however. The alphabets of most verbal languages in the world represent about forty sounds. No such formalized alphabet exists for nonverbal codes. Different types of nonverbal behavior can be categorized, but these categories are much more loosely defined than in the verbal code. All verbal languages have a set of rules, called grammar or syntax, that prescribes how to combine the various sounds of the language into meaningful units, such as words and sentences. Although there are rules governing the use of nonverbal communication, a formal grammar or syntax does not exist. Nowhere is there a book or guide prescribing exactly what nonverbal behavior should be used when and where. There is no doubt that certain social contexts prescribe certain nonverbal behaviors, such as a handshake when greeting someone in the United States, but no systematic rule book on the same level of formality as an English grammar book exists for nonverbal communication. The rules for nonverbal communication are learned informally through socialization and vary considerably, even intraculturally. Finally, the verbal code, when used with the correct syntax, takes on *denotative meaning*. When using verbal language, if we hear a word that we do not understand, we can quickly go to a dictionary that will define the word for us. The dictionary tells us what the language means. No such device exists for our nonverbal communication. If someone touches us, or stands too close, or engages in prolonged eye contact, we can only surmise its meaning. Popular psychology notwithstanding, we have no dictionary for nonverbal communication. To be sure, nonverbal communication is meaningful, perhaps even more meaningful than verbal communication, but the denotative meaning of the nonverbal act must be inferred.[8]

CHANNELS OF NONVERBAL COMMUNICATION

The closest thing the nonverbal code has to an alphabet is a gross classification system of the various channels though which nonverbal communication is sent. These channels are kinesics, paralanguage, proxemics, haptics, olfactics, physical appearance and dress, and chronemics. As we will see later in this chapter, some nonverbal expressions, particularly some facial expressions of emotion, seem to be universal, but much of our nonverbal behavior is learned and is therefore culturally unique.

Kinesics

Kinesic behavior, or body movement, includes gestures, hand and arm movements, leg movements, facial expressions, eye gaze and blinking, and stance or posture. Although just about any part of the body can be used for communicating nonverbally, the face, hands, and arms are the primary kinesic channels through which nonverbal messages are sent. Relative to other body parts, they have a high sending capacity, especially the face.

The most widely recognized system for classifying kinesic channels was developed by Paul Ekman and Wallace Friesen. Together, they organized kinesic behavior into five broad categories: (1) *emblems*, (2) *illustrators*, (3) *affect displays*, (4) *regulators*, and (5) *adaptors*. The meaning behind most of these kinesic behaviors varies across cultures.[9]

Emblems and Illustrators

Emblems are primarily (though not exclusively) hand gestures that have a direct literal verbal translation. In the United States, the hand gesture used to represent "peace" is an example of a widely recognized emblem. Dane Archer asserts that emblems are a rich channel of communication. Moreover, he maintains that emblems are often subtle yet filled with precise meaning. People in different cultures use different emblems, yet within any culture there is usually a high level of agreement on a particular emblem's meaning. To a stranger, however, a culture's favorite emblem is probably meaningless.[10]

Whereas emblems are primarily hand gestures that have a direct verbal translation, *illustrators* are typically hand and arm movements that accompany speech or function to accent or complement what is being said. Pounding your fist on the podium during a speech is an illustrator. Illustrators serve a *metacommunicative function*—that is, they are messages about messages. They are nonverbal messages that tell us how to interpret verbal messages. Shaking your fist at someone while expressing anger is an illustrator.

For the most part, emblems and illustrators are not taught in school but are learned informally through a child's socialization in his or her culture. By six months, babies in all cultures begin to use gestures to communicate to their parents.

Dane Archer maintains that emblems and illustrators are at least 2,500 years old and can be seen in the ancient artwork of various cultures. Archer asserts that the systematic study of gestures began about 400 years ago, during Shakespeare's time. Although cultures differ widely in their use of emblems and illustrators, people in most cultures tend to use them for the same kinds of communication situations. For example, most cultures use emblems and illustrators during greetings and departures, to insult or to utter obscenities to others, to indicate fight or flight, and to designate friendly or romantic relationships.[11]

Greeting rituals are an important component in any person's communicative repertoire. To know the greetings of different cultures when interacting outside your own culture is a first step toward developing intercultural communication competence. In high-context and collectivistic cultures, greeting rituals often differ according to one's social status. Moreover, in some cultures, men and women have different rules for how to greet someone. Bowing is the customary greeting in Korea and other Asian cultures, such as Japan and Vietnam. When Koreans greet elders, professors, persons of power, and persons of higher status than themselves, they bow lower and longer and divert eye contact. When businesspeople or friends meet, the bow is generally shorter and quicker.[12] In Japan, the appropriate bow is with the hands sliding down toward the knees, back and neck stiff, and eyes averted (see Figure 8.1). As in other Asian cultures, bowing recognizes social stratification. Social subordinates should bow lower and longer than their superiors. Persons of equal status match bows unless one is younger, in which case the younger person should bow a shade lower and longer. The eyes should always be lowered.[13]

In addition to bowing as a greeting, Japanese businesspeople typically exchange business cards. The exchange is indispensable in order to commence formal communication with each other. The business card communicates the group to which the person belongs and the rank of the person. Great care and time should be spent examining another's card, and only when a meeting is finished can the card be put away into a shirt or coat pocket (but never into a pants pocket, as that shows disrespect). When receiving the card of a Japanese businessperson, one should take the card with both hands, as a sign of respect.[14]

Microcultural groups in the United States have unique greetings as well. Moellendorf notes that although most Amish generally will not initiate greetings with strangers or non-Amish persons, many Amish will respond to an outsider's wave by pointing their index finger toward the sky. The raised finger points to heaven and shows respect to non-Amish while revealing the Amish people's strong religious beliefs.[15]

Figure 8.1   Bowing is the customary greeting in most Asian cultures

As in the United States, the handshake is a common gesture/illustrator during a greeting in most parts of developed Kenya. In this case, however, when greeting a person of higher status, such as a teacher, the person of lower status should take the left hand (the hand not being used in the handshake) and grasp his or her own right arm somewhere in the proximity of the forearm during the shake. According to Axtell, the handshake is a common greeting in China as well. The traditional Chinese greeting is to cup one's hands (left over right), place them about chest high, and raise them while bowing.[16] According to Bishop, when greeting a holy man or priest, East Indians bow slightly or kneel with their hands pressed together palm to palm in front of their chests. This shows ultimate respect for the higher castes.[17] Harris and Moran report that when greeting male friends in Saudi Arabia, Saudi men kiss both cheeks of the friend. They prefer to get very close during the greeting. The cheek-kissing ritual is practiced in other Middle Eastern cultures as well. The Arab handshake feels loose compared with the firm handshake practiced in many Western cultures.[18] In traditional Sri Lanka greetings, the hands are placed together, palms touching at the chin level, and the person bows slightly and says "*Namaste,*" which means "I salute the Godlike qualities in you."[19]

Archer has observed that many cultures have emblems and illustrators for insulting others and for communicating obscenities. According to Archer, some cultures may have as many as six or seven obscene gestures, whereas some northern European cultures, such as the Netherlands and Norway, do not have any native obscene gestures.[20] Giving someone "the finger" (making a fist with the hand and extending the middle finger upward) is a widely recognized obscene gesture in many parts of the world, including the United States, Mexico, and much of Europe. Forming a "V" with the index finger and middle fingers with the palm facing in is vulgar in Australia and England, communicating the same intent as "the finger." Creating the very same gesture with the palm facing out is completely acceptable, however, and represents "V for victory." In the Ladino culture of Guatemala, a hand gesture called the *la mano caliente* ("the hot hand") is equivalent to "the finger" and is created by placing the thumb between the first and middle fingers then squeezing the hand to make a fist (see Figure 8.2). This gesture is considered obscene in other Central and South American cultures as well. In the Ladino culture, however, this gesture is very offensive, and anyone using it should be prepared to fight. If a person were to use the *mano caliente* to a military or police officer, the offender could expect to spend time in jail or do hard labor in the army.[21] The same hand gesture is used in Hmong culture to belittle or insult someone. In the Hmong culture, only males use this gesture.[22] In Jamaica, this gesture is called "the fig" and is considered obscene there also.[23]

In Peru, making a pistol gesture with each hand and then pointing the "pistols" at someone from about waist level is considered obscene and may provoke a fight (see Figure 8.3). In Iran, putting an open hand directly in front of and horizontal to one's face with the palm facing in and rubbing the hand down over the face from about the eyes to the chin, almost as if stroking a beard, is considered obscene and is equivalent to "Fuck you" (see Figure 8.4). An obscene gesture recognized in many European cultures, especially France, is taking either hand, palm down, and putting it on the biceps of the opposite arm while quickly raising the opposite arm and making a fist in one fluid motion (see Figure 8.5). This gesture is basically equivalent to "the finger" and to the verbal designate "Up yours" or "Fuck you."[24]

Archer points out that in addition to obscene emblems and illustrators, many cultures have gestures indicating that someone is homosexual or an

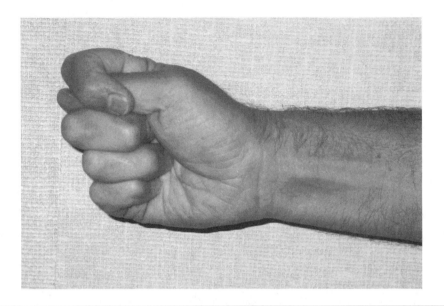

Figure 8.2   In the Latino culture of Guatemala, this gesture, called *la mano caliente,* is considered offensive

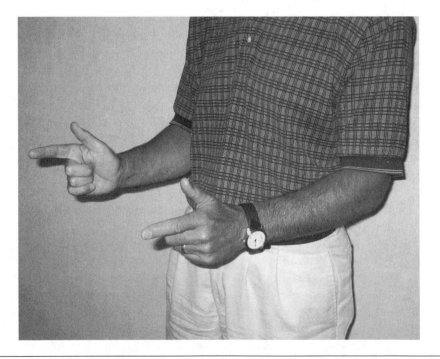

Figure 8.3   This hand gesture is highly offensive in Peru and could provoke a fight

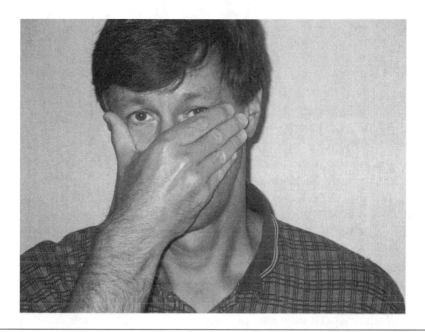

Figure 8.4   The Iranian equivalent to "the finger"

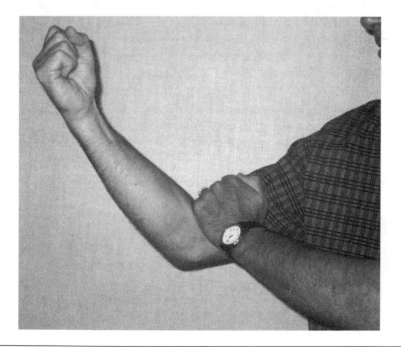

Figure 8.5   In European cultures, this gesture is similar to "the finger"

adulterer. These gestures are strongly linked to one's sex role. Most gestures indicating that someone is a homosexual almost always apply to men, whereas gestures indicating that someone is unfaithful usually apply to women. In Japan, putting the hand, palm out, against the cheek while turning the face away, almost as if to pretend to be telling a secret, is a sign that someone is homosexual. In Colombia, making a circle with the index finger and thumb (like the "OK" gesture in the United States), and then placing the circle around the nose, is a sign for homosexual. The limp-wrist gesture, or slight variations of it, for homosexual is recognized in the United States, China, Mexico, and Thailand, among other countries. In Uruguay, four or five quick claps of the hands indicates that a woman is a lesbian.[25]

Archer contends that gestures communicating "I am afraid" or "I want to fight you" (that is, fight or flight) are uncommon in the United States but occur with some regularity across cultures. In Mexico and Nepal, placing a hand with the palm up, fingers extended upward while moving in and out touching the thumb is an invitation to fight. In Japan, putting the index fingers on the temples of the head, as in making horns, is a sign that one is angry. In China, pretending to pull up one's sleeve with the hand of the opposite arm designates that one is ready to fight.[26] In Hmong culture, clapping one's hands during an argument is a signal to the opponent that it is time to fight. The gesture is usually reserved for very intense situations in which someone intends to harm the other.[27]

Most cultures use emblems and illustrators to designate friendly and/or romantic relationships. In the United States, for example, crossing the index and middle fingers of the same hand designates closeness and communicates, "We're close" or "We're tight." In China, clasping the index fingers from each hand together signals love or romance. In Thailand, pressing the palms of both hands together and placing them against a cheek (as in a "Sleeping Beauty" gesture) is indicative of romance. Tapping the tips of the index fingers together in Japan, or extending both index fingers parallel at waist level in Mexico, communicates that someone is in love.[28]

Affect Displays: Facial Expressions of Emotion

Knapp and Hall point out that perhaps more than any other part of the body, the face has the highest nonverbal sending capacity. Through facial expressions, we can communicate our personality; open and close channels of communication; complement or qualify other nonverbal behavior; and, perhaps more than anything, communicate emotional states.[29]

Many linguists believe that our verbal language evolved from a system of nonlinguistic communication that was inherited from our animal past. If this is a valid assumption, then we should expect that some forms of our nonverbal communication would be invariant across cultures. Current evidence suggests that some facial expressions of emotion, called *affect displays,* are universal. Paul Ekman alleges that humans can make more than 10,000 facial expressions, and that 2,000 to 3,000 of them have to do with emotion. Ekman is careful to point out that by studying faces, we cannot tell what people are thinking, only what they are feeling about what they are thinking.[30] Initially, Ekman believed that affect displays, like so many other forms of communication, were the result of learning and were culturally unique. He originally agreed with sociologist Ray Birdwhistell, who wrote,

> Just as there are no universal words, no sound complexes, which carry the same meaning the world over, there are no body movements, facial expressions, or gestures which provoke identical responses the world over.[31]

In contrast to Birdwhistell, other scholars hypothesized that because they were inherited, human nonverbal expressions would be similar, if not universal, the world over. The basis of this argument can be found in the writings of evolutionary scholar Charles Darwin, who wrote,

> We can thus also understand the fact that the young and the old of widely different races, both with man and animals, express the same state of mind by the same movements. . . . I have endeavoured to show in considerable detail that all the chief expressions exhibited by man are the same throughout the world. This fact is interesting, as it affords a new argument in favour of the several races being descended from a single parent-stock, which must have been almost completely human in structure, and to a large extent in mind, before the period at which the races diverged from each other.[32]

The late Harvard University professor Stephen Jay Gould, well known for his stance on evolution, agrees with Darwin and argues that although universal facial expressions may have been functional for the animals from whom we inherited them, they are not functional for us today. Take, for example, a facial expression of anger, in which a person snarls, grits his or her teeth, and displays the canine teeth (see Figure 8.6) This facial expression is remarkably similar to expressions of anger in several animal species (see Figure 8.7). The fact that there is no need for us to display our teeth in order to express anger (we can simply say how angry we are) suggests that such a gesture must have been inherited.[33]

Figure 8.6

Ekman was determined to find whether certain elements of facial behavior are universal or culturally specific. He and his colleagues believed that there may be distinctive movements of the face for the primary emotions of surprise, fear, anger, disgust, happiness, and sadness that are probably universal. They further argued that while people from divergent cultures may express emotions similarly, what stimulates the emotion and the intensity with which it is expressed is probably culturally specific. In other words, although Germans and Japanese may express fear, surprise, anger, happiness, disgust, and sadness similarly in terms of muscular facial expressions, what *elicits* fear in Germans may be different from what elicits fear in Japanese. Moreover, cultures may differ in how they manage and regulate facial expressions of emotion, particularly in the presence of others.[34]

Ekman and Friesen (among others) have conducted numerous studies testing their hypotheses. In one study, Ekman, Friesen, and a number of

Figure 8.7   A facial expression of anger in humans is remarkably similar to several animal species

their associates had more than 500 participants from ten different countries look at slides of people expressing the six emotions of fear, anger, happiness, disgust, sadness, and surprise. The participants in the study came from a variety of cultures the world over: Estonia, Italy, Germany, Japan, Hong Kong, Scotland, Sumatra, Turkey, Greece, and the United States. Participants were shown photographs of Caucasians in posed facial expressions of the six different emotions, one at a time for ten seconds each, and were instructed to indicate which of the six emotions was presented. The participants were also asked to rate the intensity of the presented emotion on a scale of 1 to 8. The results showed that in the overwhelming number of trials, the emotion rated strongest by the largest number of observers in each culture was the predicted emotion. Where cultures differed was in their ratings of intensity of the emotion. Ekman reasoned that perhaps people judge a foreigner's expressions to be less intense than expressions shown by members of their own culture, or that attributions of less intense emotions to foreigners might be due more to uncertainty about the emotional state of a person from an unfamiliar culture. In interpreting these results, Izard claims that there appears to be an evolutionary and biological relationship between facial expressions and certain emotional states, but that this connection can be uncoupled by the human capacity to exercise voluntary control over innate emotional expressions.[35]

Although Ekman's studies provide evidence that facial expressions of primary emotions appear to be universal, other data suggest that cultural influences, such as individualism and collectivism, play a role in the expression of emotion. Stephan, Stephan, and De Vargas found that persons from individualistic cultures express emotions affirming independent self-conceptions, such as self-actualized, capable, self-satisfied, and proud of oneself. They also found that persons from collectivistic cultures were less comfortable expressing negative emotions (for example, indignant, annoyed, distrustful) than persons from individualistic cultures.[36]

In related research, Schimmack found that persons from individualistic cultures are better able to recognize happiness than collectivists, and that persons from high-uncertainty-avoidant cultures were less accurate in the recognition of facial expressions of fear and sadness than persons with low uncertainty avoidance.[37] Matsumoto alleges that high-uncertainty-avoidant cultures create social institutions to deal with fear and therefore recognize this emotion less well.[38] Along similar lines, Pittam, Kroonenberg, Gallois, and Iwawaki found that Australians were rated as more expressive by Japanese, and that Japanese may conceptualize emotions as less intense.[39]

Cross-Racial Recognition of Faces. Most of us have heard statements such as "I can't tell one Japanese from another . . . they all look alike!" Although this statement smacks of racism and ignorance, scientific evidence indicates that own-race identifications tend to be more accurate, by as much as 10 percent to 15 percent, than cross-race identifications. Own-race identifications are those in which we identify someone of the same race as our own. Cross-race identifications are those in which we identify people from a race different from our own.[40] Legal scholars have expressed a concern over an own-race recognition bias in eyewitness identification for some time. In fact, Feingold argued nearly ninety years ago that it is well known that, other things being equal, individuals of a given race are distinguishable from each other in proportion to our familiarity, to our contact with the race as a whole. Thus, to the uninitiated American, all Asiatics look alike, whereas to the Asiatic, all White people look alike.[41]

Experts in the field of eyewitness memory and about half of potential jurors endorse the belief that cross-racial identifications are less reliable than same-race identifications. This presumption is based on the belief in the existence of an own-race bias—that is, that people recognize people of their own race better than people of another race. Brigham and Malpass note that the own-race recognition bias has been demonstrated among Whites, Blacks, Asians, Latinos, and Hispanics. Explanations for this phenomenon vary. Some evidence shows that persons who have close friends of the other race show less of an own-race recognition bias.[42] Moreover, Ferman and Entwistle found that children living in mixed-race environments show less of an own-race recognition bias than children living in a segregated environment.[43] Conversely, other research indicates that the own-race recognition bias is not reduced by frequent contact with the other race and that prejudiced persons are no more likely to exhibit an own-race recognition bias than nonprejudiced persons.[44] There is some evidence indicating that persons who view other-race faces tend to focus on the constituent (individual) features of the face, whereas observers of same-race faces focus on configural features of the face.[45]

Regulators

Nonverbal regulators are those behaviors and actions that govern, direct, and/or manage conversation. During conversations in the United States, for example, direct eye contact and affirmative head nodding typically communicate agreement or that a conversant understands what is being communicated. How close one stands to another during a conversation can also signal to the conversant whether to continue the communication. Rules for direct eye contact and distance during communication vary considerably across cultures. In many Asian cultures, such as South Korea, Vietnam, and Japan, direct eye contact is prohibited between persons of differing status. In these cultures, the person of lower status avoids making direct eye contact with his or her superior as a sign of respect. Direct eye contact in these cultures can communicate insolence or signal a challenge to the person of higher status. In South Korea, when people of higher status hand something to a person of lower status (for example, a professor handing something to a student), the person of lower status accepts whatever is handed with both hands, gives a slight nod of the head, and averts eye contact during the act, all as a sign of recognizing the status differential.

Communicator distance during conversation can also govern the flow of communication (see Figure 8.8). According to Almaney and Alwan, in some Middle Eastern cultures, people stand very close together during interaction to smell each other's breath. To smell one another is considered desirable. In fact, to deny someone your breath communicates shame.[46] Harris and Moran point out that in many Arab cultures, men hold hands as they converse to demonstrate their trust in each other. During conversation, a raising of the

Figure 8.8   Communicator distance during conversation can govern the flow of communication

eyebrows or a clicking of the tongue signifies a negative response and a disruption in the flow of communication.[47]

Adaptors

Adaptors are kinesic actions that satisfy physiological or psychological needs. Scratching an itch satisfies a physiological need, whereas tapping the tip of your pen on the desk while waiting for the professor to deliver a final exam satisfies a psychological need. Very little, if any, cross-cultural research on adaptors has been conducted. For the most part, adaptors are not learned and probably do not vary much across cultures.

Paralanguage

Paralanguage refers to vocal qualities that usually, though not necessarily, accompany speech. Knapp and Hall divide paralanguage into two broad categories: voice qualities and vocalizations. Paralinguistic voice qualities include pitch, rhythm, tempo, articulation, and resonance of the voice. Paralinguistic vocalizations include laughing, crying, sighing, belching, swallowing, clearing of the throat, snoring, and so forth. Other paralinguistic vocalizations are intensity and *nonfluencies,* such as "um," "ah," and "uh." Silence is also considered within the domain of paralanguage.[48]

Often, paralinguistic qualities, vocalizations, and nonfluencies reveal a speaker's emotional state and/or veracity. Audiences can discern when speakers are nervous or confident by listening to their tone of voice, rhythm, pace, and number of nonfluencies. Parents often detect a child's deception not so much by what the child says but by how it is said. Through paralanguage we can tell whether speakers are being genuine, cynical, or sarcastic. Moreover, a person's geographical origin can be determined by listening closely to his or her paralanguage.[49]

In all spoken languages, vocal sounds are carried by vowels; it is impossible to speak words without them. Consonants, on the other hand, function to stop and start sound. Linguist Peter Ladefoged has observed that although there are perhaps as many as nine hundred consonants and two hundred vowels in all the world's languages, many languages tend to use only five vowel sounds. In fact, one in five languages uses the same vowel sounds as used in Spanish and English—*a, e, i, o,* and *u*—although there are variations on their pronunciation. According to Ladefoged, although there are literally thousands of speech sounds that any human is capable of making, only a few hundred sounds have ever been observed among the world's spoken languages. The average language uses only about forty sounds, and all babies are capable of making all of them. All babies, the world over, make the same sounds during infancy. Linguists believe that these sounds are the building blocks by which infants construct mature sounds. Although infants have not yet learned the specific language of their culture and have not yet spoken a single word, they practice the sounds of all human languages. All babies regularly produce a small subset of universal syllable types that occur in all of the world's languages. This is strong evidence that human language was not invented by humans but rather evolved. To be sure, unusual sounds show up in some languages. Clicking sounds, for example, can be heard in South Africa's Zulu and Xhosa languages, and nasal sounds are heard in Eskimo languages. And although these sounds may be unique components of these languages, all human babies, regardless of culture, can be heard making them at some time prior to learning their culture's formal verbal language.[50]

Some languages, called tonal languages, rely on vocalized tones to communicate meaning. In these languages, a rising or falling tone changes the meaning of a word. Thai is a pentatonal language that uses five tones: monotone, low, falling, high, and rising. Modern Vietnamese is a monosyllabic language, meaning that all words are only one syllable long. Like the Thai language, Vietnamese is tonal, and the meaning of the syllable changes with tone. The Chinese language is tonal also. Mandarin Chinese, the most common language in China, is based on four or five tones. Every syllable in Mandarin has its definite tone. The first tone, called *yinping,* is a high-pitched tone without variation from beginning to end. The syllable is spoken with an even tone, using the highest pitch of the speaker's voice. The second tone, *yangping,* starts from a lower pitch and ends high. The syllable is spoken with a rising tone, not unlike speakers of English asking a question. The third tone, *shangsheng,* is perhaps the most difficult to master. It begins as a middle-level tone, goes down, bounds up, and ends with a relatively higher pitch. The fourth tone, *chyusheng,* is a falling tone that starts high and ends at the lowest range of the speaker's voice. The fifth tone, *chingsheng,* is often left out of descriptions of Mandarin. This tone is spoken very quickly and lightly, as if it has no tone. *Chingsheng* is often called the neutral tone.[51]

To be sure, English and other languages have inflections—that is, a change in pitch on certain words and sentences. English speakers can communicate anger or sadness by changing the pitch of their voice. Without the appropriate inflection, the meaning of an English speaker's sentence can be misinterpreted. In Chinese, however, tones completely change the meaning of a word. Take, for example, the word *ma.* In the first tone, *ma* is "mother." In the second tone, *ma* becomes "hemp" or "grass." In the third tone, *ma* becomes "horse," and in the fourth tone, *ma* becomes "to scold" or "to nag." In Mandarin Chinese, the meanings of words are strictly based on the tones, which remain constant in whispering, yelling, or even singing. Mandarin tones are relative to the natural pitch of the speaker. A deep-voiced man's high note may be much lower than the high note of a woman.[52]

As with any other form of communication, some paralinguistic devices are learned and vary across cultures. South Koreans are taught to avoid talking or laughing loudly in any situation; such behavior is seen as rude and unbecoming since it tends to draw attention. Many Koreans, especially women, cover their mouths when laughing.[53]

In their study of paralanguage, Zukerman and Miyake introduce the idea of a vocal attractiveness stereotype. They contend that, like one's physical attractiveness, individuals perceived to be vocally attractive elicit more favorable impressions than those not perceived to be vocally attractive. The results of their study indicate that attractive voices are those that are relatively loud, resonant, and articulate. Unattractive voices are squeaky, nasal, monotone, and off-pitched. Zukerman and Miyake found some sex differences in vocal attractiveness. For example, throatiness was perceived more negatively among female voices than among male voices.[54]

Silence is a part of the paralinguistic channel. Hasegawa and Gudykunst maintain that silence is the lack of verbal communication or the absence of sound. Hasegawa and Gudykunst assert that culture influences the meaning and use of style. In their research, they compared the use of silence among Japanese and Americans and found that, in the United States, silence is defined as pause, break, empty space, or lack of verbal communication.

Hasegawa and Gudykunst maintain that silence generally is not a part of Americans' everyday communication routines. They argue that although silence is acceptable among intimate others, when meeting strangers, Americans are very conscious of silence and find it quite awkward. In Japan, however, silence is a space or pause during verbal communication that has important meaning. Pauses, or silence, are to be interpreted carefully. Stylistically, Japanese are taught to be indirect and sometimes ambiguous to maintain harmony. Silence, then, can be used to avoid directness, such as bluntly saying "no" to a request.[55]

Charles Braithwaite has studied silence across cultures and argues that silence is a central nonverbal component of any speech community. He argues that some communicative functions of silence may be universal and do not vary across cultures. For example, Braithwaite maintains that among Native American groups, Japanese, Japanese-Americans in Hawaii, and people in rural Appalachia, the use of silence as a communicative act is associated with communication situations where the status of the interactants is uncertain, unpredictable, or ambiguous. In addition, Braithwaite argues that silence as a communicative act is associated with communication situations where there is a known and unequal distribution of power among interactants. In other words, when interactants consciously recognize their differential status, they consciously use silence. Braithwaite cites evidence of this in many cultures, including the Anang of southwestern Nigeria, the Wolof of Senegal, the Maori of New Zealand, the Malagasy in Madagascar, urban African-American women, amd some working-class White Americans.[56]

Proxemics

Proxemics refers to the perception and use of space, including territoriality and personal space. Territoriality refers to physical geographical space; personal space refers to perceptual or psychological space—sometimes thought of as the "bubble" of space that humans carry with them in their day-to-day activities. In cultures whose population density is high, personal space and territoriality are highly valued. Privacy in densely populated locations is often accomplished psychologically rather than physiologically. In Calcutta, India, for example, there are nearly eighty thousand persons per square mile. There is literally not enough room in the city to claim any personal space. Touching and bumping into others while walking through the streets of Calcutta is quite common and to be expected.[57]

Socioeconomic factors can also affect a culture's perception of space. Cramped and insufficient housing is common in much of Sri Lanka. In the 1980s most housing units were quite small. Thirty-three percent of the homes had only one room, 33 percent had two rooms, and only 20 percent had three rooms. Moreover, the average number of persons per home was five. (Overcrowding in Sri Lanka is declining, however, since the government initiated intensive housing programs in the 1990s).[58]

The Moroccan perception of space reflects the culture's valuing of community. Personal space during a conversation is typically less than an arm's length. In mosques, worshipers line up shoulder to shoulder to pray. Houses typically have very little space between them as well.[59] Because Kenyan culture values harmony and sharing, Kenyans tend to be less aware of personal territory than people in the United States. For example, many Kenyans do not designate specific rooms in the home for specific activities, such as a living room or a dining room. In addition, the personal space distance between interactants is much closer than in the United States.[60] Saudi Arabians, too, are known to have closer personal space than Americans. Saudis typically enjoy getting very close, face to face, and engaging in direct eye contact.[61] Many other studies support the link between culture and proxemic behavior in comparing Americans with Arabs, Latin Americans, Pakistanis, Germans, Italians, Japanese, and Venezuelans. These examples suggest that culture plays a decisive role in how spatial distances are maintained during communication. Other variables besides culture can affect proxemic distances, however, such as the age and sex of the interactants, the nature of the relationship, the environment, and ethnicity. Several studies have documented that in most cultures, the need for personal space increases with age. In addition, the use of space as influenced by sex seems to vary significantly by culture.[62]

Haptics

Haptics, or tactile communication, refers to the use of touch. Mark Knapp argues that touch may be the most primitive form of communication. In the United States, much research has been conducted to examine the impact of touching during the first few years of life.[63] Haptic communication varies widely across cultures, and the amount and kind of touch varies with the age, sex, situation, and relationship of the people involved. In his theorizing about culture and nonverbal communication, Edward Hall distinguishes between contact and noncontact cultures.[64] Contact cultures are those that tend to encourage touching and engage in touching more frequently than either moderate-contact or noncontact cultures, in which touching occurs less frequently and is generally discouraged. Many South and Central American cultures are considered contact countries, as are many southern European countries. The United States is regarded as a moderate-contact culture, whereas many Asian countries are considered noncontact. Many Asian cultures have established norms that forbid public displays of affection and intimacy that involve touch. One of the five central tenets of Confucian philosophy is the division between the sexes. Because Confucianism is so central to many Asian cultures, engaging in touch with the opposite sex is considered uncivil.[65] In their field study of touch patterns among cross-sex couples, McDaniel and Andersen observed the touch behavior of couples in airports. They found that couples from the United States touched most, followed by (in order of most to least touching) couples from Northern Europe, Caribbean/Latins, Southeast Asia, and Northeast Asia.[66] Psychologist Sidney Jourard conducted a study that counted the frequency of body contact between couples as they sat in cafés in different cities and countries. He found that the average number of touches per hour in San Juan, Puerto Rico, was 180; in Paris, 110; in Gainesville, Florida, 2; and in London, 0.[67]

Because we are often taught not to touch others, some people develop touch avoidance. These people feel uncomfortable in situations requiring touch and generally avoid touching when possible. In her study of Americans, Japanese, Puerto Ricans, and Koreans, Beth Casteel found no touch avoidance differences in same-sex dyads for the Japanese and Americans, in that both were significantly more touch-avoidant than same-sex dyads in Puerto Rico and Korea. In opposite-sex dyads, however, Japanese and Koreans showed much higher levels of touch avoidance than Americans and Puerto Ricans. Casteel concluded that the Japanese and Americans allow women to touch other women, but men should not touch men. Koreans and Puerto Ricans are just the reverse.[68]

In their comparison of high-contact cultures of southern Europe and low-contact cultures of northern Europe, psychologists Remland, Jones, and Brinkman found that more touch was observed among Italian and Greek dyads than among English, French, and Dutch dyads.[69] The people of northern Italy have few inhibitions about personal space and touch. Heterosexual men are often seen kissing each other on both cheeks and walking together arm in arm, as are women. East Indians are very expressive with touch. To touch the feet of elders is a sign of respect. Indians demonstrate their trust for one another by holding hands briefly during a conversation or religious activity. When a Hindu priest blesses others at religious gatherings, he gently touches the palms of their outstretched hands.[70] Saudi Arabians tend to value touching also. Saudi businessmen often hold hands as a sign of trust, a form of touch behavior that some Americans often misunderstand. Saudi women, however, are never to be touched in public.[71]

Most cultures prohibit some forms of touch. Harris and Moran observe that in Thailand, Sri Lanka, and some other cultures, the head is considered sacred and should not be touched by others. Americans sometimes make the mistake of patting children of other cultures on the top of the head as a sign of affection or endearment. In some cultures, this is seen as a serious breach of etiquette.[72]

In many African and Middle Eastern cultures, the use of the left hand is forbidden in certain social situations. In Kenya, Indonesia, and Pakistan, for example, the left hand should not be used in eating or serving food. Harris and Moran report that in Kenya, the left hand is considered weak and unimportant. Sometimes, Kenyans intentionally use the left hand when serving food to someone they disrespect. In other cultures, such as Iraq and Iran, the left hand is used for cleaning and bodily functions and should never be used to give or receive gifts or other objects.[73]

Like proxemics, the nature of touch is often mediated by more than culture. The relationship between the interactants, the location and duration of touch, the relative pressure of the touch, the environment in which the touch occurs (public or private), and whether the touch is intentional or accidental influence touch across cultures.

Olfactics

Probably the least understood, yet most fascinating, of all human sensations is olfactics—that is, our sense of smell. Our lack of understanding is certainly not because we lack a sense of smell. According to Gibbons, humans can detect as many as ten thousand different compounds by smell. Moreover, approximately 1 percent of our genes are devoted to detecting odors. Although this may not seem like much, humans have more olfactory genes than any other type of gene identified in human and mammalian DNA. Gibbons suggests that our lack of understanding may be because we lack a vocabulary for smell and are discouraged from talking about smell. Particularly in the United States, we have become obsessed with masking certain smells, especially those of the human body. According to Gibbons, the biggest users of fragrance in the world are U.S.-based companies like Procter & Gamble, Lever Bros., and Colgate. Some brands of soap use more than 2 million pounds of fragrance a year. In many Western cultures, body odor is regarded as unpleasant and distasteful, and we go to great efforts to mask or remove it.[74]

David Stoddart asserts that in addition to their ability to detect odors, humans are even more adept at producing odors. According to Stoddart, evidence from anatomy, chemistry, and psychology indicates that humans are the most highly scented of all the apes. Human scent comes from two types of glands that lie beneath the skin, the sebaceous glands and the apocrine glands. Sebaceous glands are all over the body wherever there are hair follicles. They produce an odorous oily fluid whose original purpose was to protect hair. The apocrine glands are a type of sweat gland. They are most dense in our armpits but are also found in the pubic and anal regions, the face, the scalp, and the umbilical region of the abdomen (the belly button). Women appear to have more apocrine glands than men, but some evidence suggests that their glands are less active than those in men. The most distasteful odors come from the apocrine glands, which are activated when we are frightened, excited, or aroused. Human saliva and urine also produce human scent.[75]

According to Kohl and Francoeur, research has repeatedly shown that women perceive odors differently at various phases of their menstrual cycles. They tend to be the most sensitive to odors during ovulation. Other studies indicate that when in close proximity to each other over time, as in dormitory living, women synchronize their menstrual cycles. Scientists believe that axillary organ secretions function as odor cues to stimulate their cycles. On a related note, studies have shown that vaginal secretions during ovulation are minimally unpleasant, whereas such secretions before and after ovulation are described as distinctly unpleasant.[76]

Kohl and Francoeur suggest that although preferences for certain smells seem to vary across cultures, there appears to be a universal preference for some kinds of scents that may have biological and evolutionary roots. These preferences are probably mediated by culture to some extent, however. For example, the finest perfumes in the world contain olfactory hints of urine. Scientists allege that these scents function as sex attractants. We know, for example, that sex-attractant pheromones are expelled from the body in urine. These two kinds of smell may mirror those of our humanoid ancestors and unconsciously stimulate the deepest parts of the brain.[77]

In addition to functioning as a sex attractant, smell is also used politically for marking social class distinctions. Classen, Howes, and Synnott contend that smell plays a signficant role in the construction of power relations in many societies.[78] Le Guerer comments, for example, that idiomatic expressions often employ smell-related terms to voice antagonism and repugnance toward others. People refer to persons they dislike as "stinkers." When we are suspicious of someone, we say we "smell a rat." When something seems wrong or amiss, we comment that "it doesn't smell right" or "smells fishy." Dishonest politicians may "reek of hypocrisy."[79]

Anthony Synnott claims that odor is often used to categorize groups of people into status, power, and moral classes. To be sure, the smells themselves are not intrinsically moral or immoral, but the qualities or thoughts attributed to the specific scents are what give them their moral significance. Synott argues that a person's scent is not only an individual emission and a moral statement, but also a perceived social attribute that is significant especially for members of subordinate groups, who are often labeled "smelly." Such labels often foster racial, ethnic, and religious preju- dice and hatred. Subordinate and microcultural groups are often described as possessing negative olfactory characteristics. In fact, Synnott argues that perceived foul odors legitimize inequalities and are one of the criteria by which a negative identity is imposed on a particular class or race.[80] Many cul- tures establish norms for acceptable and unacceptable scents associated with the human body. When individuals or groups of people fail to fit into the realm of acceptability, their odor signals that something is "wrong" with them, either physically or mentally. Kohl and Francoeur note that the American Puritan tradition of "cleanliness is next to godliness" may explain the American obsession with deodorants, perfumes, soaps, and shampoos.[81] Muslims believe that cleanliness of the body and purity of the soul are related. Muslim women are told to purify themselves after menstruation. Cleanliness is prescribed before and after meals. The Koran specifies that all five daily prayers must be preceded by washing of the hands, arms, and feet.[82]

Social class distinctions based on smells are the cultural product of edu- cation, religion, parenting, and social pressure from peers. With the excep- tion of those scents that appeal to everyone, people are conditioned to find certain scents attractive and others dirty or foul. Moreover, such distinctions sustain social barriers between groups and even justify a dominant group's persecution of subordinate groups.[83] In the Middle Ages, wealthy people bought perfumes to diminish the scent of the lower classes. Nineteenth- century Japanese described European traders as *bata-kusai*—"stinks of but- ter."[84] Adolf Hitler's hatred of Jews was based partially on olfactics; he claimed that their foul odor was representative of their "moral mildew" and reflected their outer and inner foulness, and therefore their immorality.[85] Gibbons reports that during World Wars I and II, German and English sol- diers claimed they could identify the enemy by their smell. Similar claims have been made by North Vietnamese and U.S. troops.[86] Baker reports that in U.S. history, Thomas Jefferson is purported to have said that Blacks have "a very strong and disagreeable odour."[87] Dollard claims that many White racists used the "disagreeable scent" of Blacks as a final proof of the impos- sibility of close association between the races.[88] In 1912, sociologist Georg Simmel wrote, "It would appear impossible for the Negro ever to be accepted into high society in North America because of his bodily odor."[89] Indeed, Simmel concluded that "the moral ideal of harmony and equality between the different classes and races runs up against the brick wall of an invincible disgust inspired by the sense of smell."[90]

Classen, Howes, and Synnott maintain that more than any other group, women are stereotyped and classified by their scent. Historically, in many cultures, women were considered the fragrant sex, unless they were prostitutes or suffragettes or challenged the male-dominated social order. The role of fragrance was primarily to entice men. In general, the Western cultural axiom has been that, unless perfumed, women stink. Jonathan Swift's poem *The Lady's Dressing Room* expresses this belief:

> His foul imagination links
> Each Dame he sees with all her Stinks:
> And, if unsav'ry Odours fly,
> Conceives a Lady standing by.[91]

Although it may be the least studied of all the senses, social scientists are discovering that olfactory sensation is a potent influence on social interaction. Survey data indicate that a significant percentage of adults are conscious of and influenced by smells in their environment. In their poll of more than 350 American adults, the Olfactory Research Fund found that 64 percent of respondents indicated that smell greatly influenced the quality of their lives. Specifically, 76 percent of the respondents reported that the sense of smell was "very important" in their daily relationships with persons of the opposite sex, and 20 percent indicated that it was "somewhat important." Seventy-four percent indicated that smell was "very important," and 22 percent said that it was "somewhat important" in their relationships with their spouses. Although the percentages dropped somewhat, 36 percent of the respondents indicated that smell was "important" in their relationships with friends, and 40 percent agreed that smell was "very important" in their relationships with co-workers. Eighty percent of the respondents reported using environmental fragrances, such as potpourri, room sprays, and scented candles. Well over 60 percent of respondents believed that particular aromas enhance the quality of life, relieve stress, and help retrieve memories. Of those respondents who used cologne, perfume, or aftershave, 83 percent said they did so because they liked the scent, 68 percent said it made them feel better about themselves, 56 percent said it enhanced their sense of well-being, 51 percent said they used fragrances to make themselves more romantically attractive to others, and 46 percent said they used fragrances to make a fashion statement.[92]

This emphasis on smell is often motivated by the pivotal role olfactics play in the maintenance of social relationships. Todrank, Byrnes, Wrzesniewski, and Rozin assert that most cultures assign meaning to odors that is often displaced onto the people wearing them.[93] This is especially evident in relationships with members of the opposite sex. Although it is widely recognized that odors play a determinant role in the mating practices of many animal species, Kohl and Francoeur argue that odors are also an important ingredient in human mating and bonding and cite empirical evidence showing that odors hasten puberty, mediate women's menstrual cycles, and even influence sexual orientation.[94] Extant research indicates that odors help people identify their family members, facilitate the bond between parents and children, and influence how often and with whom individuals mate.

Kate Fox is a social anthropologist and the Director of the Social Issues Research Center in Oxford, England. Fox has studied cultural differences in olfactics, with a special emphasis on non-Western cultures. Fox maintains that, unlike most Western cultures, smell is "the emperor of the senses" in many cultures. For example, Fox describes the importance of smell among the Ongee people of the Andaman Islands, a group of islands off the southeast coast of India. According to Fox, much of Ongee cultural life revolves around smell. For example, their calendar is based on the smell of flowers that bloom at different times of the year. One's personal identity is defined by smell. Fox writes that to refer to oneself, an Ongee touches the tip of his or her nose, which is a gesture meaning both "me" and "my smell." Fox also reports that during greetings, Ongee routinely ask "How is your nose?" rather than "How are you?" Ongee etiquette prescribes that if a person responds that he or she feels "heavy with smell," the greeter should inhale deeply to remove the excess smell. Conversely, if the greeted person indicates that he or she is short of smell energy, Ongee etiquette prescribes that the greeter contribute some extra scent by blowing on him or her.[95]

Fox also describes smell rituals among the Bororo peoples of Brazil and the Serer Ndut of Senegal (Western Africa). Among the Bororo, personal body smell indicates the life force of the individual, whereas one's breath odor indicates the state of one's soul. The Ndut believe that individuals possess a physical smell, defined by one's body and breath odor, and a spiritual smell. The spiritual smell is thought to be a reincarnated smell. For example, the Ndut can tell which ancestor has been reincarnated by associating the smell of a child to that of a deceased person.[96]

In her olfactic research, Fox has discovered that among those cultures where smell is so closely associated with one's personal identity, the exchange or mixing of odors among people is carefully prescribed. For example, among the Amazonian Desana, members of a particular tribal group are thought to share a similar odor. Marriage is only allowed between people of different odors; that is, between members of different tribal groups. Similarly, among the Batek Negrito of the Malay Peninsula, people of similar odor groups are prohibited from engaging in sexual intercourse and even sitting too close to one another. The Batek Negrito believe that the prolonged mixing of similar odors causes illness in the people themselves and any children they may conceive.[97]

Fox also writes that Western smell preferences are not universal. For example, the Dassanetch, a tribal cattle-raising group in Ethiopia, believe that the smell of cows is the most pleasing of all smells. Dassanetch men routinely wash their hands in cattle urine and smear their bodies with cattle manure. Such smells are associated with status and fertility. The Dogon people of Mali find the scent of onions very attractive, especially for young men and women, who rub fried onions all over their bodies.[98]

SELF-ASSESSMENT 8.1

Personal Report of Olfactory Perception and Sensitivity (PROPS)
The following instrument is designed to assess your level of olfactory perception and sensitivity. On a scale of 1 to 7, indicate the degree to which each statement applies to you.

1 = strongly disagree, 2 = disagree, 3 = slightly disagree, 4 = undecided, 5 = slightly agree, 6 = agree, and 7 = strongly agree.

_6_ 1. When interacting with a stranger of the opposite sex, I am typically conscious of the scent of his or her breath.

_6_ 2. When interacting with a stranger of the opposite sex, I am typically conscious of the scent of his or her body.

_6_ 3. When interacting with a stranger of the opposite sex, I am typically conscious of the scent of his or her cologne or perfume.

_6_ 4. When interacting with a stranger of the same sex, I am typically conscious of the scent of his or her breath.

_4_ 5. When interacting with a stranger of the same sex, I am typically conscious of the scent of his or her body.

_5_ 6. When interacting with a stranger of the same sex, I am typically conscious of the scent of his or her cologne or perfume.

_6_ 7. When interacting with a close friend of the opposite sex, I am typically conscious of the scent of his or her breath.

_6_ 8. When interacting with a close friend of the opposite sex, I am typically conscious of the scent of his or her body.

_6_ 9. When interacting with a close friend of the opposite sex, I am typically conscious of the scent of his or her cologne or perfume.

_6_ 10. When interacting with a close friend of the same sex, I am typically conscious of the scent of his or her breath.

_4_ 11. When interacting with a close friend of the same sex, I am typically conscious of the scent of his or her body.

_5_ 12. When interacting with a close friend of the same sex, I am typically conscious of the scent of his or her cologne or perfume.

_1_ 13. When interacting with a stranger of the opposite sex, I am typically conscious of the scent of my breath.

_6_ 14. When interacting with a stranger of the opposite sex, I am typically conscious of the scent of my body.

_5_ 15. When interacting with a stranger of the opposite sex, I am typically conscious of the scent of my cologne or perfume.

_7_ 16. When interacting with a stranger of the same sex, I am typically conscious of the scent of my breath.

_3_ 17. When interacting with a stranger of the same sex, I am typically conscious of the scent of my body.

_2_ 18. When interacting with a stranger of the same sex, I am typically conscious of the scent of my cologne or perfume.

_7_ 19. When interacting with a close friend of the opposite sex, I am typically conscious of the scent of my breath.

_5_ 20. When interacting with a close friend of the opposite sex, I am typically conscious of the scent of my body.

_4_ 21. When interacting with a close friend of the opposite sex, I am typically conscious of the scent of my cologne or perfume.

_6_ 22. When interacting with a close friend of the same sex, I am typically conscious of the scent of my breath.

_2_ 23. When interacting with a close friend of the same sex, I am typically conscious of the scent of my body.

_1_ 24. When interacting with a close friend of the same sex, I am typically conscious of the scent of my cologne or perfume.

_6_ 25. When interacting with someone from a different culture or ethnicity, I am typically conscious of the scent of his or her breath.

_5_ 26. When interacting with someone from a different culture or ethnicity, I am typically conscious of the scent of his or her cologne or perfume.

_6_ 27. When interacting with someone from a different culture or ethnicity, I am typically conscious of the scent of his or her body.

28. When interacting with someone in a private environment, I am typically conscious of the scent of the immediate surroundings.

 29. When interacting with someone in a private environment, I am typically conscious of the scent of the furniture.

 30. When interacting with someone in a public environment, I am typically conscious of the scent of the immediate surroundings.

To calculate your PROPS score, sum your responses as follows:

1. Perception and sensitivity to others: add Items 1–12 (range = 12–84).
2. Perception and sensitivity to self: add Items 13–24 (range = 12–84).
3. Perception and sensitivity to different cultures: add Items 25–27 (range = 3–21).
4. Perception and sensitivity to environment: add Items 28–30 (range = 3–21).

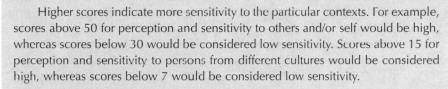

Higher scores indicate more sensitivity to the particular contexts. For example, scores above 50 for perception and sensitivity to others and/or self would be high, whereas scores below 30 would be considered low sensitivity. Scores above 15 for perception and sensitivity to persons from different cultures would be considered high, whereas scores below 7 would be considered low sensitivity.

Source: J. W. Neuliep and E. L. Groshkopf, *Toward a Communication Theory of Olfactics: Explication, Development of the Personal Report of Olfactic Perception and Sensation and Some Initial Tests.* Paper presented at the 2001 annual convention of the National Communication Association, Atlanta, GA.

Physical Appearance and Dress

Often, we can identify a person's culture by his or her physical appearance and dress. Communication with another is often preceded by visual observations of the other's physical appearance. Moreover, in most cultures, people consciously manipulate their physical appearance to communicate their identity. Most cultures have strict rules for how their members should present themselves. To violate a culture's prescriptions for appearance may result in negative sanctions. In many cultures, a person's physical appearance and dress communicate the person's age, sex, and status within the culture.

In virtually every culture, men and women dress differently, and in many cultures, the differences begin at birth. In the United States, for example, male infants are traditionally dressed in blue and female infants are dressed in pink. In the Masai culture of Kenya, the distinction between young girls and women is communicated through body artifacts. According to Vandehey, Buerger, and Krueger, Masai women wear specific necklaces and earrings to designate their marital status. For a married woman to be seen without her earrings may bring harsh physical punishment from her husband. Masai men wear earrings and arm rings that designate social status. The specific earring distinguishes the man as an elder or warrior. Other body ornaments communicate whether a Masai (male or female) has been circumcised.[99]

In most Islamic cultures, Muslim women are often easily recognized by their headscarves, or turbans, which are important symbols of religious faith among Muslims. Smucker maintains that the scarves are often perceived by Westerners as a sign of male subjugation of women. In Turkey, however, many young Muslim women believe that rather than being a symbol of subservience to men, the headscarf, or veil, serves as a guard against the eyes of men and as a symbol of women's allegiance to God, rather than to their husbands or fathers.[100] Harris and Moran note that in many Middle Eastern cultures, such as Saudi Arabia, Islamic law decrees that women dress conservatively and cover their hair in public. Although women are not required to wear the traditional full-length *abaya* (black cloak) over their clothing, they are encouraged to wear a knee-length tunic/dress over slacks and a scarf on their heads. Moreover, they should avoid explicit makeup in the presence of Saudi men. The idea behind these dictates is to avoid sexually arousing men. Saudi men may wear either Saudi dress or their normal Western dress but should not wear shorts or open shirts. Long hair for men is discouraged.[101]

Harris and Moran observe that in India, businessmen wear a *dhoti,* a single piece of white cloth about five yards long and three feet wide that wraps around their lower body. Long shirts are worn on the upper part of the body. Most Indian women wear a *sari* and blouse. A *sari* consists of several yards of lightweight cloth draped so that one end forms a skirt and the other a head and shoulder covering. It is not acceptable for women to show skin above the knees or a large portion of the back. Wearing clothes that are in any way revealing is discouraged because it may unintentionally communicate "a loose woman."[102]

In Japan, the kimono—a long robe with wide sleeves—is the traditional clothing for both men and women; it is traditionally worn with a broad sash, or *obi,* as an outer garment. The specific design of the kimono varies according to one's sex, age, marital status, the time of year, and the occasion. In the ancient past, there was no distinction between a man's and a woman's kimono. Today, there are several types of kimonos worn by men, women, and children. Men typically wear kimonos of blue, black, brown, gray, or white. Women's kimonos are the most elaborate and varied in style and design. The fabric, cut, color, sleeve length, and the details of the *obi* vary according to a woman's age, social status, marital status, and the season. During the summer months, women wear *yukatas,* or lightweight cotton kimonos. Many Japanese hotels provide *yukatas* for guests to wear in their rooms. In Japan, on "7–5–3 Day" (November 15), boys who are three or five years old and girls who are three or seven years old dress up in kimonos to pray at the temples. There is also a special day for all girls and all boys to go to the temple: March 3 is Girls' Day and May 5 is Boys' Day. Kimonos are worn on these days as well.[103]

Chronemics

Chronemics refers to the nonverbal channel of time. Recall (from Chapter 4) Hall's description of monochronic and polychronic time-oriented cultures. According to Hall, monochronic (M-time) orientations emphasize schedules and the compartmentalization and segmentation of measurable units of time. Many M-time cultures are low context, including the United States, Germany, Scandinavia, Canada, France, and most of northern Europe. Conversely, polychronic (P-time) orientations see time as much less tangible and stress multiple activities with little emphasis on scheduling. P-time cultures stress involvement of people and the completion of tasks as opposed to a strict adherence to schedules. Many P-time cultures are high context, including southern Europe, Latin America, and many African and Middle Eastern countries.[104]

The primary system for organizing time, in just about every culture, is the calendar. According to L. E. Doggett, one of the world's leading authorities on calendars, cultures create and use calendars as a way of organizing units of time to satisfy the needs of the society. Doggett maintains that calendars give people a sense that they can control time. Calendars also provide a link between people and the cosmos, or the supernatural. Doggett asserts that, in many cultures, calendars are considered nearly sacred and serve as a source of social order and cultural identity. In many ways, calendars dictate human communication patterns. When people eat, work, celebrate, worship, engage in leisure, attend school, hunt, rest, and fight wars is often prescribed by the calendar. Social contracts of just about every kind are typically determined by calendars. For example, marriages are deemed successful by the number of years they have lasted. Prison terms are defined in terms of months or years. In most cultures, an individual's age, which is measured by a calendar, is the primary criterion for social and cultural privileges and responsibilities.[105]

According to Doggett, there are about forty calendars used in the world today. Most of these calendars are astronomically based. The primary astronomical cycles include the day, month, and year. Days are defined by the rotation of the earth on its axis. The month is based on the revolution of the moon around the earth. The year is based on the revolution of earth around the sun.

Most cultures use either a solar, lunar, or lunisolar calendar. Many Western cultures, such as the United States, use a solar calendar. Islamic cultures use a lunar calendar. The Hebrew and Chinese use a lunisolar calendar.[106]

Doggett points out that the Gregorian calendar (a solar calendar) serves as the international standard. The United States functions under the Gregorian calendar. A common year is 365 days, with leap years of 366 days. Months are either 30 or 31 days, except for February, which has 28 or 29 days depending on whether or not the year is a leap year. The Hebrew calendar is lunisolar and is the official calendar of Israel. Each year consists of either 12 or 13 months. Months consist of either 29 or 30 days. The beginning of each month is determined by a new moon. Traditionally, days of the week are designated by number, except for the seventh day, the Sabbath. Days begin and end at sunset. In the Islamic calendar months correspond to the lunar cycle. Based on religious principles, Muslims begin each month upon the first visibility of the moon's crescent. Like the Hebrew calendar, days begin at sunset. In China, the Gregorian calendar is used for governmental purposes, but the traditional Chinese calendar is used for scheduling cultural festivals and for timing agricultural activities. The Chinese calendar is lunisolar, where months are either 29 or 30 days.[107]

Hall has pointed out that perceptions of time differ considerably across cultures. In the United States, for example, time is tangible (i.e., concrete, perceptible). Hall notes that to Americans, time can be bought, sold, saved, spent, wasted, lost, made up, and measured. Americans are also future-oriented, in that we take great efforts to plan and schedule what we expect (or want) to happen. Conversely, to many Arabs, a person who tries to look into the future is regarded as either irreligious or insane. To many Arabs, only God can decree what will or will not occur. Hall also notes that duration is an important component to one's perception of time. According to Hall, duration is what happens between two points. Most Americans view time in this manner and carefully schedule and evaluate cultural events according to their duration (e.g., minutes, hours, days) as in "Oh, that movie was way too long," "This won't take but a minute," "When will you get here?" To some Native American groups, time is not thought of as measurable. Time is a sequence of events that differs for each set of circumstances.[108]

NONVERBAL COMMUNICATION AND DIMENSIONS OF CULTURAL VARIABILITY

Throughout this book several dimensions of cultural variability have been discussed, including individualism-collectivism, power distance, and high-low context. Each of these dimensions can help explain cultural differences in nonverbal communication across cultures.

Individualism-Collectivism

In Chapter 2, individualism was defined as a cultural orientation where individuals precede groups. In individualistic cultures, emphasis is placed on individuals' goals over group goals, and social behavior is guided by personal goals, perhaps at the expense of other types of goals. Individualistic cultures stress values that benefit the individual person. The self is promoted because each person is viewed as uniquely endowed and possessing distinctive talent and potential.

In collectivistic cultures, on the other hand, group goals have precedence over individual goals. Collectivistic cultures stress values that serve the ingroup by subordinating personal goals for the sake of preserving the ingroup. Collectivistic societies are characterized by extended primary groups such as the family, neighborhood, or occupational group in which members have diffuse mutual obligations and expectations based on their status or rank. In collectivistic cultures people are not seen as isolated individuals but as *interdependent* with others (e.g., their ingroup), where responsibility is shared and accountability is collective. A person is seen not as an individual, but as a member of a group.

In their review of nonverbal communication in individualistic and collectivistic cultures, Andersen, Hecht, Hoobler, and Smallwood note that persons in individualistic cultures tend to be distant proximally whereas persons in collectivistic cultures tend to work, play, live, and sleep in close proximity. In addition, body movements tend to be more synchronized in collectivistic cultures than in individualistic cultures. Facial behaviors (i.e., affect displays) differ as well. Persons in individualistic cultures tend to smile more than persons in collectivistic cultures. Andersen and his colleagues reason that people in collectivistic cultures are more likely to suppress their emotional displays because maintaining group harmony is primary. Finally, individualistic cultures are more nonverbally affiliative (i.e., nonverbal behaviors that bring people closer together physically and psychologically) than collectivistic cultures.[109]

Power Distance

A culture's power distance (i.e., large vs. small) may account for nonverbal differences across cultures. Power distance refers to the extent to which less powerful members of a culture expect and accept that power is distributed unequally. Cultures with a smaller power distance emphasize that inequalities among people should be minimized and that there should be interdependence between less and more powerful people. In cultures with a larger power distance, inequalities among people are both expected and desired. Less powerful people should be dependent on more powerful people. In high power distant cultures, interaction between persons of low and high power may be very restricted, thus limiting the amount of nonverbal interaction. Andersen and his colleagues point out that in large power distant cultures, people without power are expected to express only positive emotional displays when interacting with those of higher power (e.g., smile more).[110]

Power distance also affects paralinguistic cues. Persons in small power distance cultures are generally less aware of their vocalics (e.g., volume, intensity) than persons in large power distance cultures. Andersen and his colleagues mention that North Americans (small power distance) are often perceived as noisy, exaggerated, and childlike.[111]

Occulesics are also affected by power distance. In large power distance cultures, subordinates are taught to avert direct eye contact often as a sign of respect for those in superior roles. For example, in large power distant cultures, students rarely give teachers direct eye contact. Direct eye gaze can be interpreted as a threat or a challenge to the person of higher power.

High and Low Context

Recall from Chapter 2 that high and low context refers to the degree to which interactants focus on the physical, social, and psychological (i.e., the nonverbal) context for information. Persons in high-context cultures are especially sensitive to the nonverbal context. Persons in low-context cultures focus less on the social or physical context and more on the explicit verbal code. Persons from low-context cultures are perceived as very direct and talkative, whereas persons from high-context cultures are perceived as quiet, shy, and perhaps even sneaky.

Persons in high-context cultures tend to pay a great deal of attention to nonverbal behavior during interaction. Thus, facial expressions, touch, distance, and eye contact serve as important cues. Subtle body movements that may be missed by a low-context person may take on special meaning to the high-context person.

Nonverbal Expectancy Violations Theory

Judee Burgoon has formalized a theory of nonverbal communication called the nonverbal expectancy violation theory (NEV).[112] The basic premise of the theory is that people hold expectancies about the appropriateness of the nonverbal behaviors of others. These expectations are learned and culturally driven. For example, in the United States, people expect to shake hands when they are introduced to someone. Burgoon posits that occasionally people violate nonverbal expectations. When this happens, the violation produces arousal, which can be physiological or cognitive and either positive

Table 8.1   Fundamental Assumptions of the Nonverbal Expectancy Violations Theory

Assumption 1: Humans have two competing needs, a need for affiliation and a need for personal space (or distance). These two needs cannot be satisfied at once.

Assumption 2: The desire for affiliation may be elicited or magnified by the presence of rewards in the communication context. The rewards may be biological or social.

Assumption 3: The greater the degree to which a person or situation is defined as rewarding, the greater the tendency for others to approach that person or situation; the greater the degree to which a person or situation is defined as punishing, the greater the tendency for others to avoid that person or situation.

Assumption 4: Humans are able to perceive gradations in distance.

Assumption 5: Human interaction patterns, including personal space or distance patterns, are normative.

Assumption 6: Humans may develop idiosyncratic behavior patterns that differ from the social norms.

Assumption 7: In any communication context, the norms are a function of three classes of factors: (a) characteristics of the interactants, (b) features of the interaction itself, and (c) features of the immediate physical environment.

Assumption 8: Interactants develop expectations about the communication behavior of others. Consequently, they are able to recognize or at least respond differently to normative versus deviant behaviors on the part of others.

Assumption 9: Deviations from expectations have arousal value.

Assumption 10: Interactants make evaluations of others.

Assumption 11: Evaluations are influenced by the degree to which the other is perceived as rewarding such that a positively valued message is only rewarding if the source is highly regarded and a negatively valued message is only punishing if the source is not highly regarded.

Source: Reprinted from Burgoon, J. K., A Communication Model of Personal Space Violations: Explication and an Initial Test, in *Human Communication Research*, 4, 1978, pp. 129-142. Reproduced with permission of Oxford University Press, Inc. via Copyright Clearance Center.

or negative. Burgoon maintains that once a violation has been committed and arousal is triggered, the recipient evaluates the violation and the violator. Violations initiated by highly attractive sources may be evaluated positively, whereas those initiated by unattractive sources may be evaluated negatively.[113] The very same violation may produce very different evaluations, depending on who committed it. The evaluation of the violation depends on (1) the evaluation of the communicator, (2) implicit messages associated with the violation, and (3) evaluations of the act itself. In presenting the theory, Burgoon outlines several key assumptions (see Table 8.1).

Burgoon bases Assumption 1 on literature from anthropology, sociology, and psychology, indicating that humans are a social species with a biological/survival instinct to be with other humans. Conversely, humans cannot tolerate extended physical contact with, or excessive closeness with, others; that is, humans have a basic need to insulate themselves from others and a need for privacy. Although this first assumption appears to be universal, the degree to which a person feels the need to be with others or insulated from them is probably culturally driven. Individualists may be more comfortable alone in the same situations in which a collectivist feels uncomfortable. Moreover, the way in which a person satisfies the need for privacy or affiliation certainly varies across cultures. In the United States and Germany, for example, privacy is often satisfied by physical separation from others (for example, closed doors), whereas in densely populated cultures such as India, privacy may be fulfilled psychologically.

Assumption 2 indicates that affiliation for others is triggered by rewards within the communicative context. These rewards may be biological (food, sex, safety) or social (belonging, esteem, status). Biological needs are no doubt universal, but social needs are often learned and vary across cultures. Belonging needs are felt much more strongly in collectivistic cultures than in individualistic ones. Conversely, esteem needs are more strongly felt in individualistic cultures than in collectivistic ones. Assumption 3 extends Assumption 2 by stating that humans are attracted to rewarding situations and repelled by punishing situations. This phenomenon is probably universal, but it should be noted that what people deem rewarding and punishing varies across cultures.

Assumption 4 asserts that humans have the perceptual ability to discern differences in spatial relationships. We can tell when someone is standing close to us or far away from us. Assumption 5 deals with the establishment of normative nonverbal behaviors. Normative behavior is that which is usual or typical, or that follows a regular pattern. For example, the lecture style of your professor is probably consistent day after day. The professor has established a normative way of delivering his or her material. Many normative behaviors are established by society and culture. In the United States, for example, saying "good-bye" is a normative way of terminating a telephone conversation.

Assumption 6 recognizes that even though most of us follow similar normative rules and regulations for our verbal and nonverbal behavior, we also develop our own personal style of interaction that is unique in some way. Assumption 7 states that norms operate as a function of the interactants, the interaction, and the environment. Characteristics of the interactants might include their sex, age, personality, and race. Characteristics of the interaction itself might include status differences or degree of intimacy between the interactants. Finally, characteristics of the environment may include the physical features of the setting, such as furniture arrangement, lighting, or even temperature.

Assumption 8 deals with the notion of expectancies, a key element of the theory. Burgoon argues that during interaction, interactants develop expectancies and preferences about the behaviors of others. These expectancies are anticipations of others' behavior that are perceived to be appropriate for the situation. Typically, expectancies are based on a combination of societal and cultural norms. For example, students expect that their professors will behave in an appropriate and consistent manner. In certain cases, however, students might expect idiosyncratic deviations from the norms for particular professors (for example, a certain professor frequently tells jokes in class).

Assumption 9 focuses on two other key ingredients in the theory, violation of expectancies and arousal. Burgoon subscribes to the notion that when a person's nonverbal expectancies are violated, the person becomes aroused. The violation tends to stimulate the receiver/communicator's attention and to arouse either adaptive or defensive reactions. For example, we learned earlier in this chapter that in some cultures (for example, Korea), touching the top of a child's head is prohibited. To do so would be a violation of expectancy, and the child or the parents might respond negatively or defensively. In some situations, however, some violations are perceived positively. A shaman may be allowed to touch the top of a child's head, and such behavior may be perceived positively.

Assumption 10 states that people make value judgments about others. Assumption 11 extends this notion by specifying how evaluations are made. Burgoon contends that the first factor influencing the positive or negative evaluation of a violation is the communicator reward valence—that is, how much the violator is perceived as someone with whom it is desirable to interact. Thus, communicator reward valence is based on communicator and relationship characteristics (age, sex, personality, status, reputation, anticipated future interaction) and interactional behaviors (style, positive feedback). Communicator reward valence influences how one will evaluate the violation of expectancies. Burgoon's theory holds that more favorable evaluations will be given when the violation is committed by a high-reward person than when it is committed by a low-reward person. If someone to whom you are attracted stands very close to you at a party, much closer than is normative, you may interpret this violation positively as a sign of mutual attraction or affiliation. Conversely, if someone by whom you are repulsed stands too close to you at a party, you may evaluate this violation quite negatively.

Burgoon asserts that positively evaluated violations produce favorable communication patterns and consequences, whereas negatively evaluated violations produce unfavorable communication patterns. In addition, Burgoon contends that even extreme violations, if committed by a high-reward person, can be evaluated positively and produce reciprocal communication patterns. Although a significant number of studies support the assumptions of Burgoon's theory, very few, if any, have investigated its cross-cultural applicability.

Cultural Contexts and Nonverbal Expectancies

As we have seen throughout this book, the cultures of Japan and the United States differ significantly. Japan is a collectivistic, high-context culture, whereas the United States is an individualistic, low-context culture. Individualistic cultures stress the importance of an individual's unique identity. Emphasis is placed on individual goals over group goals. From an early age, American children are taught that they are individuals with unique abilities and talents. People are rewarded for being "the best," "the one and only," and "number one" in whatever they do. The goal of Americans is to be the best that they can be and to strive for the top. A well-known cliché in the United States states that "the squeaky wheel gets the grease," meaning that in order to get attention or to have one's needs met, one must draw attention to oneself.

In contrast, collectivistic cultures place precedence on group goals over individual goals. Collectivist cultures emphasize values that serve the ingroup by subordinating personal goals for the sake of the ingroup. Group activities are dominant and pervasive. Responsibility is shared, and accountability is collective.[114] Japan has an unofficial motto that reads, *"Deru kugi wa utareru,"* or "The tallest nail gets hammered down." Children are taught at a young age that their identity is based on their relationship within the group (family or business). Group leadership, rather than individual initiative, is valued. However, especially among Japanese youth, a new sense of individualism is growing in Japan.[115]

A high-context culture, such as Japan, is one whose members are highly sensitive to the perceptual, socio-relational, and environmental contexts for information. High-context cultures have a restricted code system (language). Members do not rely on verbal communication as their main source of information. Silence and nonverbal behavior are most informative. Statements or actions of affection are rare. Members are quite adept at decoding nonverbal behavior. Japanese, for example, expect others (that is, Japanese) to understand the unarticulated communication. Cultural members are expected to know how to perform in various situations where the guidelines are implicit.[116]

Members of a low-context culture, such as the United States, are less sensitive to the perceptual, socio-relational, and environmental contexts. That is not to say that they ignore the environment—they are simply less aware of it than are members of a high-context culture. A low-context communication is one in which the mass of information is found in the explicit code. Hence, low-context cultures have an elaborated code system. Verbal messages are extremely important when information to be shared with others is coded in the verbal message. Members of low-context cultures do not perceive the environment as a source of information. Guidelines and expectations are frequently explained explicitly.[117] In addition to high-context/low-context distinctions between the two countries, Japan is considered a low-contact culture, whereas the United States is considered a moderate contact culture.

Many of the communicative behaviors of high/low context, individualistic/collectivistic, and high-/low-contact cultures are different, and the interactants will inevitably violate each other's expectations regarding appropriate nonverbal behavior.

AN INTERCULTURAL CONVERSATION: VIOLATION OF NONVERBAL EXPECTANCIES

In the following two scenarios, Jim, Akira, and Mitsuko interact. Akira and Mitsuko are exchange students from Japan who are spending a semester studying at an American college. Jim is an American student at the same college. Notice how each violates the others' expectations without realizing it. When reading the scenes, keep in mind the different cultural orientations and the assumptions of nonverbal expectancy violation theory.

Jim and Akira are at a party.

1. **Jim:** (Nudges Akira and says loudly) *This is a great party, eh?*

2. **Akira:** (Is startled—stands back—tries to put some distance between himself and Jim) *Yes, thank you.*

3. **Jim:** (Leaning forward toward Akira, with direct eye contact) *If you want to meet some girls, I could introduce you.*

4. **Akira:** (Shocked by such an offer, he backs away) *But I don't know them. They might be upset.*

5. **Jim:** *Well, how else are you going to meet them?*

6. **Akira:** (Uncomfortable) *Maybe during a class or something*

Mitsuko, another Japanese exchange student, approaches Jim and Akira. She knows Akira, but not Jim.

7. **Mitsuko:** *Hello, Akira.* (Bows slightly and looks down)

8. **Akira:** *Ah, Mitsuko, this is my friend Jim.*

9. **Jim:** *Hi!* (Forward leaning into her space)

10. **Mitsuko:** *Hi, Jim.* (Bows slightly and does not make direct eye contact)

11. **Jim:** *Are you two friends?* (Wonders why she won't look at him, thinks to himself, "Well, I'm not one of them. She probably thinks I'm ugly.")

12. **Akira:** *Yes, we know each other.*

A long pause ensues.

13. **Jim:** (Thinks to himself, "This is going nowhere—I've got to think of something to say." He speaks rather loudly) *Great party, hey guys?*

Akira and Mitsuko both jump back.

14. **Akira:** (Thinks to himself, "This guy is too weird") *Yeah, this is fun.*

During this scenario, Jim violates Akira's kinesic, proxemic, paralinguistic, and haptic expectations. Several of the axioms and propositions from Burgoon's NEV theory can be applied to this interaction. Notice in Lines 1 through 4 that Akira perceives that Jim is standing too close, talking too loud, and thus backs away. From Akira's point of view, Jim violated his proxemic and paralinguistic expectations. In Line 1 Jim touches Akira, which probably violated Akira's nonverbal expectations regarding haptics. From Jim's vantage point, Akira violated his expectations as well, by not looking at him and not responding to his offer that he introduce him to women.

According to NEV theory, violations have arousal value (Assumption 9). Throughout the dialogue we can see how Akira and Jim became aroused (shocked, uncomfortable, startled, annoyed) by each other's violations. Both Mitsuko and Akira jump when Jim yells, "Great party, hey guys?" In Lines 13 and 14 we can see how Burgoon's Assumption 10 applies in that the arousal leads to evaluations ("This is going nowhere," "This guy is too weird"). In this case, the evaluations are negative.

According to the theory, the greater the degree to which a person is perceived as rewarding, the greater the tendency for others to approach that person. Likewise, the greater the degree to which a person is perceived as punishing, the greater the tendency for others to avoid that person. Unfortunately for Akira, because he is in a "foreign" country, he will be the more likely of the two to change his behavior to conform to the expectations of others.

CHAPTER SUMMARY

Many social scientists believe that our verbal language evolved from a system of nonlinguistic communication that we inherited from our animal predecessors. As humans we possess a host of nonlinguistic ways to communicate with each other through the use of kinesics, proxemics, paralanguage, haptics, olfactics, and physical appearance. Our nonverbal communication, when combined with verbal language, creates a very complicated communication system through which humans come to know and understand each other.

Our nonverbal behavior is innate and learned. Many of our unconscious behaviors, such as the expression of emotions, are universal. People from all cultures express anger, happiness, and sadness the very same way. Yet other forms of nonverbal communication, such as gestures, are unique manifestations of our culture's distinctive cosmos. We learn how to communicate with our bodies (kinesics) through the use of space (proxemics), by touching others (haptics), with our voice (paralanguage), with smell (olfactics), and through the way we dress and present ourselves. Sometimes, our nonverbal behaviors violate the expectations of others. Sometimes, we stand too close or touch too much. When this happens, the other person evaluates the violation as positive or negative depending on whether we are perceived as attractive or unattractive. If we are thought of as attractive, our violation may be welcome. If we are perceived as unattractive, the same violation may be evaluated quite negatively.

GLOSSARY OF TERMS

Adaptors: Mostly unconscious nonverbal actions that satisfy physiological or psychological needs, such as scratching an itch.

Affect displays: Nonverbal presentations of emotion, primarily communicated through facial expressions.

Analogic communication: Nonverbal communication.

Chronemics: The use of time.

Denotative meaning: The literal meaning of a word; the dictionary meaning.

Digital communication: Verbal communication.

Emblems: Primarily hand gestures that have a direct verbal translation. Can be used to repeat or to substitute for verbal communication.

Haptics: Nonverbal communication through physical contact or touch.

Illustrators: Primarily hand and arm movements that function to accent or complement speech.

Kinesics: General category of body motion, including emblems, illustrators, affect displays, and adaptors.

Nonverbal expectancy violation theory: Theory that posits that people hold expectations about the nonverbal behavior of others. When these expectations are violated, people evaluate the violation positively or negatively, depending on the source of the violation.

Olfactics: The perception and use of smell, scent, and odor.

Paralanguage: Characteristics of the voice, such as pitch, rhythm, intensity, volume, and rate.

Proxemics: The perception and use of space, including territoriality and personal space.

Regulators: Nonverbal acts that manage and govern communication between people, such as stance, distance, and eye contact.

REFERENCES

1. Farb, P. *Word Play: What Happens When People Talk* (New York: Bantam, 1973), p. 234.
2. Searchinger, G. director and producer, *The Human Language Series: Part III: With and Without Words* [film] (1996; available from Ways of Knowing, Inc., 200 West 72nd Street, New York, NY 10023).
3. Ibid.
4. Knapp, M. L., & Hall, J. A. *Nonverbal Communication in Human Interaction,* 3d ed. (Fort Worth, TX: Holt, Rinehart and Winston, 1992).
5. Searchinger, *The Human Language Series.*
6. Ibid.
7. Ibid.
8. Littlejohn, S. W. *Theories of Human Communication,* 5th ed. (Belmont, Calif.: Wadsworth, 1996); Condon, J. C. & Yousef, F. *An Approach to Intercultural Communication* (Indianapolis: Bobbs-Merrill, 1975).
9. Ekman, P., & Friesen, W. V. "The Repertoire of Nonverbal Behavior: Categories, Origins, Usage, and Coding," *Semiotica,* 1 (1969), 49–98.

10. Archer, D., producer, & Silver, J., director, *A World of Gestures: Culture and Nonverbal Communication* [film] (1991; available from University of California Extension, Center for Media and Independent Learning, 2000 Center Street, Fourth Floor, Berkeley, CA 94704).

11. Ibid.

12. Choi, M. "Cultural Profile of South Korea" (unpublished student manuscript, St. Norbert College, De Pere, Wisc., 1995).

13. Harris, P. R., & Moran, R. T. *Managing Cultural Differences,* 4th ed. (Houston: Gulf Publishing, 1996).

14. Schug, D., & Sturino, M. "The Japanese Cultural Profile" (unpublished student manuscript, St. Norbert College, De Pere, Wisc., 1995).

15. Moellendorf, S., Warsh, H., & Yoshimaru, K. "The Amish Culture: A Closer Look at the People of Lancaster County" (unpublished manuscript, St. Norbert College, De Pere, Wisc., 1996).

16. Axtell, R. E. *Gestures: The Do's and Taboos of Gestures and Body Language Around the World* (New York: Wiley, 1991).

17. Bishop, R. J. "Cultural Profile, Examination of Value Orientations and Sociocultural Influences, and Verbal and Nonverbal Language Aspects of the East Indian Culture" (unpublished student manuscript, St. Norbert College, De Pere, Wisc., 1995).

18. Harris and Moran, *Managing Cultural Differences;* A. Wolter, "Saudi Arabia and Its Culture" (unpublished manuscript, St. Norbert College, De Pere, Wisc., 1994).

19. Rieck S., & Ogura, M. "Sri Lanka: The Pearl of the Indian Ocean" (unpublished manuscript, St. Norbert College, De Pere, Wisc., 1996).

20. Archer and Silver, *A World of Gestures.*

21. Keberlein, M. C. "A Cultural Profile of the Guatemalan Ladinos" (unpublished manuscript, St. Norbert College, De Pere, Wisc., 1993).

22. Thao, K. "The Hmong Culture" (unpublished student manuscript, St. Norbert College, De Pere, Wisc., 1995).

23. Penasa, A. G., Peters, M., & Smits, S. "Jamaica: Out of Many, One People" (unpublished manuscript, St. Norbert College, De Pere, Wisc., 1996).

24. These examples are shown in Archer and Silver, *A World of Gestures.*

25. Ibid.

26. Ibid.

27. Thao, K. "The Hmong Culture."

28. Archer and Silver, *A World of Gestures.*

29. Knapp and Hall, *Nonverbal Communication in Human Interaction.*

30. Searchinger, *The Human Language Series.*

31. Birdwhistell, R. L. *Kinesics and Context: Essays on Body Motion Communication* (New York: Ballantine, 1970), p. 42.

32. Darwin, C. *The Expression of the Emotions in Man and Animals* (London: J. Murray, 1872), p. 361.

33. Searchinger, *The Human Language Series.*

34. Ekman, P., Friesen, W., O'Sullivan, M. et al., "Universals and Cultural Differences in the Judgment of Facial Expressions of Emotions," *Journal of Personality and Social Psychology,* 53 (1987), 712–717.

35. Izard, C. E. "Innate and Universal Facial Expressions: Evidence from Developmental and Cross-Cultural Research," *Psychological Bulletin,* 115 (1994), 288–299.

36. Stephan, W. G., Stephan, C. W., & DeVargas, M. C. "Emotional Expressions in Costa Rica and the United States," *Journal of Cross-Cultural Psychology,* 27 (1996), 147–160.

37. Schimmack, U. "Cultural Influences on the Recognition of Emotion by Facial Expressions," *Journal of Cross-Cultural Psychology,* 27 (1996), 37–51.

38. Matsumoto, D. "Cultural Influences on the Perception of Emotion," *Journal of Cross-Cultural Psychology,* 20 (1989), 92–105.

39. Pittan, J., Kroonenberg, P., Gallois, C., & Iwawaki, S. "Australian and Japanese Concepts of Expressive Behavior," *Journal of Cross-Cultural Psychology,* 26 (1995), 451–464.

40. Bothwell, R. K., Brigham, J. C., & Malpass, R. S. "Cross-Racial Identification," *Personality and Psychology Bulletin,* 15 (1989), 19–25; Malpass, R. S., & Kravitz, J. "Recognition for Faces of Own and Other Race," *Journal of Personality and Social Psychology,* 13 (1969), 330–354.

41. Feingold, C. A. "The Influence of Environment on Identification of Persons and Things," *Journal of Criminal Law and Police Science,* 5 (1914), 50.

42. Brigham, J. C., & Malpass, R. S. "The Role of Experience and Contact in the Recognition of Faces of Own- and Other-Race Persons," *Journal of Social Issues,* 41 (1985), 139–155.

43. Ferman, S., & Entwistle, D. R. "Children's Ability to Recognize Other Children's Faces," *Child Development,* 47 (1976), 506–510.

44. Brigham, J. C., & Barkowitz, P. "Do They All Look Alike? The Effect of Race, Sex, Experience, and Attitudes on the Ability to Recognize Faces," *Journal of Applied Social Psychology,* 8 (1978), 306–318; Malpass & Kravitz, "Recognition for Faces of Own and Other Race"; Teitelbaum, S., & Geiselman, R. E. "Observer Mood and Cross-Racial Recognition of Faces," *Journal of Cross-Cultural Psychology,* 28 (1997), 93–106.

45. Rhodes, G., Tan, S., Brake, S., & Taylor, K. "Expertise and Configural Coding in Face Recognition," *British Journal of Psychology,* 80 (1989), 313–331.

46. Almaney, A., & Alwan, A. *Communicating with the Arabs* (Prospect Heights, IL: Waveland, 1982).

47. Harris and Moran, *Managing Cultural Differences.*

48. Knapp and Hall, *Nonverbal Communication in Human Interaction.*

49. Ibid.

50. Searchinger, *The Human Language Series.*

51. Hsin-Yun, Y. "The Four Tones in Mandarin Chinese" (1998) (www.wellgot.ca/english-fm.html); "Mandarin Tones," *QI: The Journal of Traditional Eastern Health and Fitness* (www.qi-journal.com/tones.html).

52. Ibid.

53. Choi, "Cultural Profile of South Korea."

54. Zuckerman, M., & Miyake, K. "The Attractive Voice: What Makes It So?" *Journal of Nonverbal Behavior,* 17 (1993), 119–135.

55. Hasegawa, T., & Gudykunst, W. B. "Silence in Japan and the United States," *Journal of Cross-Cultural Psychology,* 29 (1998), 668–684.

56. Braithwaite, C. A. "Cultural Uses and Interpretations of Silence," in *The Nonverbal Communication Reader,* 2nd ed., ed Guerrero, L. K., DeVito, J. A., & Hecht, M. L. (Prospect Heights, IL: Waveland, 1999), pp. 163–172.

57. Bishop, "Cultural Profile, Examination of Value Orientations and Sociocultural Influences, and Verbal and Nonverbal Language Aspects of the East Indian Culture."

58. Rieck and Ogura, "Sri Lanka: The Pearl of the Indian Ocean."

59. Hesselink, R. C., Mullen, R. T., & Rouse, J. M. "Moroccan Culture: An In-Depth Study" (unpublished manuscript, St. Norbert College, De Pere, Wisc., 1996).

60. Ishikawa, Y., & Hashimoto, M. "The Kenyan Culture" (unpublished student manuscript, St. Norbert College, De Pere, Wisc., 1996).

61. Wolter, "Saudi Arabia and Its Culture"; Argyle, M. *Bodily Communication* (New York: International Universities Press, 1975).

62. Dolphin, C. Z. "Variables in the Use of Personal Space in Intercultural Transactions," in *Intercultural Communication: A Reader,* 8th ed., ed. Samovar, L. A., & Porter, R. E. (Belmont, Calif.: Wadsworth, 1997), pp. 266–276.

63. Knapp and Hall, *Nonverbal Communication in Human Interaction.*

64. Hall, E. T. "A System for the Notation of Proxemic Behavior," *American Anthropologist,* 65 (1963), 1003–1026.

65. Kim, M. S. "A Comparative Analysis of Nonverbal Expressions as Portrayed by Korean and American Print-Media Advertising," in *Readings in Cultural Contexts,* ed. J. N. Martin, T. K. Nakayama, and L. A. Flores (Mountain View, Calif.: Mayfield, 1998), pp. 206–216.

66. McDaniel, E., & Andersen, P. A. "International Patterns of Interpersonal Tactile Communication: A Field Study," *Journal of Nonverbal Behavior,* 22 (1998), 59–76.

67. Jourard, S. M. "An Exploratory Study of Body Accessibility," *British Journal of Social and Clinical Psychology,* 5 (1966), 221–231.

68. Casteel, B. "A Cross-Cultural Study of Touch Avoidance" (unpublished master's thesis, West Virginia University, cited in D. W. Klopf, *Intercultural Encounters: The Fundamentals of Intercultural Communication* (Englewood, Colo.: Morton, 1995).

69. Remland, M. S., Jones, T. S., & Brinkman, H. "Interpersonal Distance, Body Orientation, and Touch: Effects of Culture, Gender, and Age," *Journal of Social Psychology,* 135 (1995), 281–298.

70. Bishop, "Cultural Profile, Examination of Value Orientations and Sociocultural Influences, and Verbal and Nonverbal Language Aspects of the East Indian Culture."

71. Wolter, "Saudi Arabia and Its Culture."

72. Harris and Moran, *Managing Cultural Differences.*

73. Ibid.

74. Gibbons, B. "The Intimate Sense of Smell,4" *National Geographic,* 170 (1987), 324–361.

75. Stoddart, D. M. *The Scented Ape: The Biology and Culture of Human Odour* (Cambridge: Cambridge University Press, 1990).

76. Kohl, J. V. & Francoeur, R. T. *The Scent of Eros* (New York: Continuum, 1995).

77. Ibid.

78. Classen, C., Howes, D., & Synnott, A. *Aroma: The Cultural History of Smell* (New York: Routledge, 1994).

79. Le Guerer, A. *Scent: The Mysterious and Essential Powers of Smell* (New York: Turtle Bay Books, 1992).

80. Synnott, A. "A Sociology of Smell," *Canadian Review of Sociology and Anthropology,* 28, no. 4 (1996), 437–460; Howes, D., Synnott, A., & Classen, C., "The Anthropology of Odour," in *Compendium of Olfactory Research,* ed. A. N. Gilbert (Dubuque, Iowa: Kendall-Hunt, 1995), pp. 111–116.

81. Kohl and Francoeur, *The Scent of Eros.*

82. Fernea, E., & Fernea, R. "Cleanliness and Culture," in *Psychology and Culture,* ed. Lonner, W. J., & Malpass, R. (Boston: Allyn and Bacon, 1994), pp. 65–70.

83. Classen, Howes, and Synnott, *Aroma: The Cultural History of Smell.*

84. Gibbons, "The Intimate Sense of Smell."

85. Synnott, "A Sociology of Smell."

86. Gibbons, "The Intimate Sense of Smell."

87. Baker, R. L. *Race* (New York: Oxford University Press, 1974).

88. Dollard, J. *Caste and Class in a Southern Town* (New York: Doubleday, 1957); Classen, Howes, and Synnott, *Aroma: The Cultural History of Smell.*

89. Simmel, G. *Mélanges de philosophie relativiste* (Paris: F. Alcon, 1912), p. 12; Classen, Howes, and Synnott, *Aroma: The Cultural History of Smell;* A. LeGuerer, *Scent: The Mysterious and Essential Powers of Smell.*

90. Simmel, G. *Mélanges de philosophie relativiste,* p. 34; Classen, Howes, and Synnott, *Aroma: The Cultural History of Smell;* A. LeGuerer, *Scent: The Mysterious and Essential Powers of Smell.*

91. This poem was cited in Classen, Howes, and Synnott, *Aroma: The Cultural History of Smell.* The original source is H. Williams, *The Poems of Jonathan Swift,* vol. 2 (Oxford, UK: Clarendon Press, 1937), p. 529.

92. Olfactory Research Fund, "Enthusiastic Response to Website Sense of Smell Survey" (1996–1997) (www.olfactory.org/response.html).

93. Todrank, J., Byrnes, D., Wrzesniewski, A., & Rozin, P. "Odors Can Change Preferences for People in Photographs: A Cross-Modal Evaluative Conditioning Study With Olfactory USs and Visual CSs," *Learning and Motivation,* 26 (1995), 116–140.

94. Kohl and Francoeur, *The Scent of Eros.*

95. Fox, K. *The Smell Report* (Oxford, UK: Social Issues Research Centre, 2001).

96. Ibid.

97. Ibid.

98. Ibid.

99. Vandehey, K., Buerger, C., & Krueger, K. "Traditional Aspects and Struggles of the Masai Culture" (unpublished manuscript, St. Norbert College, De Pere, Wisc., 1996).

100. Smucker, P. G. "The Meaning of a Scarf: Turkish Students Fight to Wear Islamic Head Coverings," *US News & World Report* (March 16, 1998), pp. 31–33.

101. Harris and Moran, *Managing Cultural Differences;* Batarfi, K. M. "Welcome to Saudi Arabia: The Land of Islam" (1998) (http://darkwing.uroegon.edu/~kbatarfi/saudi.html).

102. Harris and Moran, *Managing Cultural Differences;* "Recreational Travel Guide to India" (1993) (www.solutions.mb.ca/rec-traqvel/asia/india/india-guide.html).

103. "A History of Kimono" (www.japan.mit.edu/kimono/intro.html). This site is a part of the Japanese Language and Culture Network.

104. Hall, E. T. *The Silent Language* (New York: Doubleday, 1959).

105. Doggett, L. E. "Calendars" in *Explanatory Supplement to the Astronomical Almanac,* ed. P. K. Seidelmann (Sausalito, CA: University Science Books, 1992).

106. Ibid.

107. Ibid.

108. Hall, *The Silent Language.*

109. Andersen, P. A., Hecht, M. L., Hoobler, G. D., & Smallwood, M. (2003). Nonverbal communication across cultures. In W. B. Gudykunst (Ed.), *Cross-Cultural and Intercultural Communication* (pp. 73–90). Thousand Oaks, CA: Sage.

110. Ibid.

111. Ibid.

112. Burgoon, J. K. "A Communication Model of Personal Space Violations: Explication and an Initial Test," *Human Communication Research,* 4 (1978), 129–142; Burgoon J. K., & Jones, S. B. "Toward a Theory of Personal Space Expectations and Their Violations," *Human Communication Research,* 2 (1976), 131–146.

113. An excellent review of research associated with NEV can be found in Burgoon, J. K., & Hale, J. L. "Nonverbal Expectancy Violations: Model Elaboration and Application to Immediacy Behaviors," *Communication Monographs,* 55 (1988), 58–79.

114. Schwartz, S. H. "Individualism-Collectivism: Critique and Proposed Refinements," *Journal of Cross-Cultural Psychology,* 21 (1990), 139–157.

115. Harris and Moran, *Managing Cultural Differences.*

116. Schwartz, "Individualism-Collectivism."

117. Gudykunst, W. B. ed., *Intercultural Communication Theory: Current Perspectives* (Beverly Hills, CA: Sage, 1983).

CHAPTER 9

Developing Intercultural Relationships

Without others, there is no self.

—Kenneth J. Gergen[1]

Chapter Objectives

After reading this chapter, you should be able to

1. Recount the fundamental assumptions of the Uncertainty Reduction Theory.
2. Discuss the relationship between uncertainty reduction and intercultural communication apprehension.
3. Cogently discuss the fundamental assumptions of Anxiety Uncertainty Management Theory.
4. Identify assertive and responsive sociocommunicative styles.
5. Define relational empathy and third-culture building.
6. Compare ratings of relational intimacy across cultures.
7. Describe differences in relationships between Eastern and Western cultures.
8. Compare marital types across cultures.
9. Compare divorce rates across cultures.

Initiating and maintaining relationships with others is one of the most necessary and challenging functions of human survival. Our self-concept and self-esteem are sustained largely by the substance of our relationships with others. From our relational partners we receive feedback that we use to assess ourselves. In essence, the only way we know ourselves is through our relationships with others. Our existence is relative to other people. Take a moment and think of three terms that describe you. Perhaps you see yourself as a good student, a loyal good friend, and a fast runner. How do you know that these descriptors are accurate? For example, if you describe yourself as a "good student," the only way you know that is because of your relationships with teachers who have provided you with feedback. If you describe yourself as a "fast runner," the only way you know that is by comparing your running with that of other runners. You can describe yourself only in relation to others. A person cannot be tall unless someone else is short. A person cannot be fast unless someone else is slow. As the quote at the beginning of the chapter states, without others, there is no self.

Regardless of one's cultural origins, relationships provide the substance of life. Several variables affect the initiation and maintenance of personal relationships. Much of our communication behavior during the first stage of a relationship is designed to reduce uncertainty about our relational partner. One factor that affects our ability to do that is the degree to which we experience intercultural communication apprehension. Another variable that affects the uncertainty process is our sociocommunicative style—that is, the extent to which we are assertive and responsive with our relational partners. Two other variables that affect our relations with others are the degree to which we can empathize with others and how similar we perceive ourselves to be to the other. Uncertainty reduction, intercultural communication apprehension, sociocommunicative style, empathy, and similarity are experienced differently by each interactant in a relationship. The relationship established by any two people is the result of a complex combination of these factors, as is depicted in Figure 9.1.

This chapter explores a variety of topics associated with relationships. The first section deals with uncertainty reduction and factors that affect how people go about reducing uncertainty, including intercultural communication apprehension and sociocommunicative style. The next part of the chapter focuses on empathy, third-culture building, and similarity. The third part of the chapter examines how perceptions about relationships vary across cultures, with particular emphasis on how relationships are perceived in Eastern and Western cultures. The final part of the chapter looks

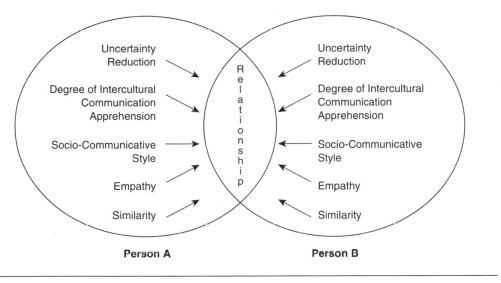

Figure 9.1

at marital relationships, including mate selection across cultures, arranged marriages, and divorce.

COMMUNICATION AND UNCERTAINTY

All relationships must begin somewhere. The people with whom we are now intimate were at one time strangers. Initiating communication with a stranger, particularly a person from a different culture, can be frightening. Many people experience anxiety when interacting with others for the first time. Moreover, interacting with a person from a different culture may be even more anxiety producing. In an attempt to explain our communication behavior during initial communication encounters with others, Charles Berger and Richard Calabrese have developed a communication theory called the Uncertainty Reduction Theory (URT). The major premise of this theory is that when strangers first meet, their primary goal is to reduce uncertainty and increase predictability in their own and the other person's behavior.[2]

According to the theory, uncertainty can be both a proactive and a retroactive process. That is, we can experience and reduce uncertainty both before and after interacting with someone. We can proactively reduce uncertainty when we weigh alternative behavioral options prior to interacting with another. We try to figure out ways the other might interact and then select our own communication strategies on the basis of this prediction. For example, if you are about to interact with a person from a different culture, you might anticipate that the other person does not speak English and adjust your speech accordingly. Retroactively, uncertainty is reduced by attempting to explain behavior after it has been enacted. For example, having interacted with a South Korean, we may be able to explain why the person did not engage in direct eye contact.

In their original theory, Berger and Calabrese posited seven axioms outlining the fundamental assumptions of their theory.

The Seven Axioms of Uncertainty Reduction Theory

Axiom 1: Given the high level of uncertainty present at the onset of the entry phase, as the amount of verbal communication between strangers increases, the level of uncertainty for each interactant in the relationship will decrease. As uncertainty is further reduced, the amount of verbal communication will increase.

Axiom 2: As nonverbal affiliative expressiveness increases, uncertainty levels will decrease in an initial interaction situation. In addition, decreases in uncertainty level will cause increases in nonverbal affiliative expressiveness.

Axiom 3: High levels of uncertainty cause increases in information-seeking behavior. As uncertainty levels decline, information-seeking behavior decreases.

Axiom 4: High levels of uncertainty in a relationship cause decreases in the intimacy level of communication content. Low levels of uncertainty produce high levels of intimacy.

Axiom 5: High levels of uncertainty produce high rates of reciprocity. Low levels of uncertainty produce low reciprocity rates.

Axiom 6: Similarities between persons reduce uncertainty, whereas dissimilarities produce increases in uncertainty.

Axiom 7: Increases in uncertainty level produce decreases in liking; decreases in uncertainty level produce increases in liking.

Source: C. R. Berger and R. J. Calabrese, "Some Explorations in Initial Interaction and Beyond: Toward a Developmental Theory of Interpersonal Communication," *Human Communication Research,* 1 (1975), 99–112. Reproduced with permission of Oxford University Press, Inc. via Copyright Clearance Center.

Although people in any culture seek to reduce uncertainty, Berger and Calabrese's seven axioms are based on communication patterns of people in the United States and may not be generalizable across cultures. Many researchers believe that the verbal and nonverbal communication strategies people use to reduce uncertainty vary from culture to culture. For example, William Gudykunst and his associates have begun a research program investigating cross-cultural differences in uncertainty reduction communication. Gudykunst maintains that people may be more motivated to reduce uncertainty during initial intercultural communication than during communication with someone who is familiar.[3] He argues that several factors may influence the amount of uncertainty experienced by people during an intercultural encounter, including the interactants' expectations about communicating, individual social identities, the degree of similarity between interactants, shared communication networks, and the interpersonal salience of the contact with strangers. For example, Gudykunst points out that, like others, people from high-context cultures try to reduce uncertainty in initial encounters, but the nature of the information they seek seems to be different from that sought by persons from low-context cultures. Because much of the information resides in the context as opposed to the individual, persons from high-context cultures are more cautious concerning what they talk about with strangers. In addition, certain types of information are more important sources of uncertainty to persons in high-context cultures than to people in low-context cultures, including the other's social background, knowing whether others will behave in a socially appropriate manner, knowing that others understand individuals' feelings, knowing what others mean when they communicate, and knowing whether others will make allowances for individuals when they communicate.[4] So when interacting together for the first time, people from high- and low-context cultures are each trying to reduce uncertainty, but they use different kinds of communication. The low-context person asks a lot of questions, whereas the high-context person focuses on nonverbal aspects.

Axioms 1 and 2 deal with the quantity of verbal and nonverbal communication and its effect on uncertainty—that is, as communication increases, uncertainty decreases. Gudykunst and Nishida found that the frequency of communication predicts uncertainty reduction in individualistic, low-context cultures but not in collectivistic, high-context cultures.[5] In Axiom 2, "nonverbal affiliative expressiveness" refers to nonverbal behaviors that reduce the physiological and psychological distance between interactants. In the United States, eye contact, pleasantness of vocal expressions, affirmative head nods, head and arm gestures per minute, and closer physical distance between interactants are considered affiliative. In other cultures, these same behaviors may actually increase uncertainty and anxiety. In

South Korea, for example, children and people of lower status do not engage in direct eye contact with parents or people of higher status because to do so communicates a challenge. Sanders and Wiseman found that positive nonverbal expressiveness predicts uncertainty reduction for Whites, Hispanics, and Asian-Americans, but not for African-Americans.[6] These studies indicate that the specific nonverbal behaviors that constitute affiliative expressiveness may vary across cultures.

Axiom 3 is closely related to the first two insofar as information-seeking behavior is defined as the number of questions asked by each interactant. In the United States, people seek information from others by asking questions. In other cultures, particularly high-context cultures, people may seek information through nonverbal means, perhaps through silence or by observing the other's cultural and socio-relational background. In fact, Gudykunst, Sodetani, and Sonoda suggest that question asking as a form of uncertainty reduction may be limited to Whites.[7]

Axiom 4 refers not to the quantity of communication, as in the case of the preceding axioms, but to the quality of communication. In this case, the lower the level of uncertainty, the more intimate the communication. Intimate communication may be defined as interaction based on issues related to the interactants' attitudes, beliefs, motivations, and dispositions. There is limited cross-cultural research in this area.

Axiom 5 deals with the concept of communication reciprocity, or the mutual exchange of information between interactants. Berger and Calabrese contend that at early stages in a relationship, the interactants are compelled to ask for and give the same kinds of information at the same rate so that neither person gains information power over the other. As the relationship develops, and uncertainty is reduced, there is less felt need to reciprocate because the interactants are more comfortable with the relationship.[8] To date, there is little or no cross-cultural research that has examined this hypothesis outside the United States.

Axiom 6 centers around the notion of similarity. Berger and Calabrese argue that as similarity between interactants increases, uncertainty decreases. Likewise, the more dissimilarity, the more uncertainty. Berger and Calabrese assert that knowledge of dissimilar attitudes leads to a greater number of attributions about why another may hold such attitudes, thus increasing uncertainty about the other.[9] Cross-cultural research about Germany, Norway, Canada, and Japan seems to validate this axiom. There are a number of ways people can be similar to one another. Two people may share race, language, age, sex, or occupation. Linguistic similarity is of particular importance here. Uncertainty can be very difficult to reduce if two people speak different languages and have little knowledge of the other's linguistic code.[10]

Finally, Axiom 7 focuses on the concept of liking. This axiom is based on research that indicates a positive relationship between similarity and liking— that is, the more similar two people are, the more they tend to like each other. Thus, if similarity decreases uncertainty, it is likely to increase liking simultaneously. The research on this axiom, even within the United States, is mixed. In some cases, the more we know about another, the less we may like the person.

In many of the communication studies reported above, uncertainty is assessed using some form of variation of an instrument called the CL7 (a seven-item scale designed to measure confidence level—hence, CL7).[11]

SELF-ASSESSMENT 9.1

Assessing Attributional Confidence (CL7)

Please answer the following questions with respect to your ability to predict selected aspects of the behavior of the person with whom you have just interacted. Answer each question using a scale from zero (0) to one hundred (100). If you have to make a total guess about the person's behavior or feelings, you should answer "0"; if you have total certainty about the other person's behavior, your answer should be "100." Feel free to use any number between 0 and 100.

1. How confident are you in your general ability to predict how he or she will behave? _____ %

2. How confident are you that he or she likes you? _____ %

3. How accurate are you at predicting his or her attitudes? _____ %

4. How accurate are you at predicting the values he or she holds? _____ %

5. How well can you predict his or her feelings? _____ %

6. How much can you empathize with (share) the way he or she feels about himself or herself? _____ %

7. How well do you know him or her? _____ %

8. How certain are you of his or her background? _____ %

9. How certain are you that he or she will behave in a socially appropriate way when this is important? _____ %

10. How certain are you that he or she can understand your feelings when you do not verbally express them? _____ %

11. How certain are you that you understand what this person means when you communicate? _____ %

12. How confident are you that this person will make allowances for you when you communicate? _____ %

Scoring: Sum the percentages and divide by 12. This is your average confidence level, by which comparisons with others can be made.

Source: Reprinted from Gudykunst, W. B., & Nishida, T., The influence of cultural variability on perceptions of communication behavior associated with relationship terms, in *Human Communication Research,* 13 (1986), 147–166. Reproduced with permission of Oxford University Press, Inc. via Copyright Clearance Center.

The scale is designed to assess the degree of attributional confidence (that is, how much uncertainty) a person has about another person after initial interactions. In a typical cross-cultural communication study, participants are asked to interact with (or think about) someone from another culture and then complete the CL7 instrument. Other variables play a role in many of these studies. For example, people from high- and low-context cultures might be asked to interact for a few minutes, then complete the CL7. Researchers then compare the scores on the CL7 across the two cultures. Other researchers may have participants from individualistic and collectivistic cultures engage in certain types of uncertainty reduction behaviors (for example, nonverbal affiliative gestures or verbal information seeking) to see how CL7 scores are affected. There are a variety of ways in which this scale can be used in cross-cultural communication research. Think about the last time you interacted with someone for the first time, then complete the attributional confidence assessment in the box. The scale is designed to assess how much uncertainty you experienced during that initial encounter.

ANXIETY UNCERTAINTY MANAGEMENT (AUM) THEORY OF EFFECTIVE COMMUNICATION

Over the past 20 years, William Gudykunst has been developing a theory, called Anxiety Uncertainty Management Theory (AUM), to explain the interrelationships among uncertainty, anxiety, mindfulness, and communication effectiveness.[12] According to AUM, the general processes underlying communication between people from different cultures or ethnicities are the same processes underlying communication between people from the same culture. Gudykunst refers to these common properties as *communicating with strangers.* According to AUM, a stranger is someone who is physically near and conceptually distant simultaneously. Thus, interacting with strangers is replete with uncertainty and anxiety.

AUM and Uncertainty Reduction Theory (URT) are similar in that each theory focuses on the effects of uncertainty and anxiety on communication. But AUM is different from URT. According to URT, the primary motive of interactants is the reduction of uncertainty. The axioms of URT point out the specific communicative strategies people use to reduce uncertainty. AUM shifts the focus from uncertainty and anxiety reduction to uncertainty and anxiety *management.* AUM also incorporates the concepts of mindfulness and communication effectiveness. Gudykunst maintains that the focus of AUM is toward effective communication; that is, to the extent that interactants can manage uncertainty and anxiety, and be mindful, effective communication can be achieved.[13]

According to AUM, uncertainty is a cognitive phenomenon. Uncertainty affects the way people *think* about communication and involves our ability, or inability, to predict a stranger's attitudes, beliefs, values, and behaviors. People experience more uncertainty when interacting with strangers. Anxiety is the affective equivalent of uncertainty. Anxiety affects the way people *feel* about interacting with someone else and includes a sense of uneasiness, apprehensiveness, worry, and so on. Uncertainty and anxiety are related in that as uncertainty increases, people experience anxiety. Anxiety affects one's motivation to approach or avoid communication.[14]

AUM stipulates that people have minimum and maximum thresholds for uncertainty and anxiety. The maximum threshold is the highest amount of uncertainty or anxiety individuals can experience and still believe they can predict a stranger's attitudes, beliefs, values, and so on and remain comfortable communicating. An individual's minimum threshold of uncertainty or anxiety is the lowest amount of uncertainty a person can experience before becoming unmotivated or overconfident about predicting the stranger's behavior about interacting. If our uncertainty is above the maximum or below the minimum thresholds, we cannot communicate effectively. Communicating effectively requires that uncertainty and anxiety are between the minimum and maximum thresholds. Gudykunst also points out that minimum and maximum thresholds vary considerably across cultures.[15]

In addition to uncertainty and anxiety, AUM incorporates the concepts of mindfulness and communication effectiveness. Mindfulness refers to the idea that most of the time, people are not acutely aware of their behavior and operate on a kind of automatic pilot. To be sure, many communicative acts are routine or habitual and do not require intense cognitive attention. For example, the automatic cognitive process of categorizing and stereo-typing strangers was discussed in Chapter 5. Mindfulness, on the other hand, refers to a person's conscious attention to incoming information. A mindful communicator is open to new information and the processing of new categories. Mindful communicators perceive aspects of the self and others that mindless communicators miss. Gudykunst points out that to be mindful, people must recognize that strangers may use different perspec-tives to understand or explain interaction. When we are mindless, we tend to assume that strangers interpret our messages the same way as we do. Mindfulness, on the other hand, means to *negotiate* meaning with strangers. Communication effectiveness refers to the idea that a person receiving and interpreting a message attaches a meaning to the message that is relatively similar to what was intended by the person transmitting it. The result of communication effectiveness is maximum understanding among commu-nicators. Gudykunst maintains that the majority of the time when people are not mindful, communication is ineffective.[16]

In his theory of AUM, Gudykunst identifies seven superficial causes that mediate one's ability to manage uncertainty and anxiety. To the extent that one can mediate uncertainty and anxiety, and be mindful, communication effectiveness can be achieved. Gudykunst's schematic of AUM appears in Figure 9.2.[17]

According to the schematic, the degree of communication effectiveness achieved is based on the degree to which uncertainty and anxiety are man-aged, plus one's degree of mindfulness. Mindfulness can either increase or decrease uncertainty and anxiety during interaction. Mindfulness decreases uncertainty and anxiety in cases where we try to understand the perspec-tives of strangers. But mindfulness can sometimes increase uncertainty and anxiety because it heightens our awareness of the differences between us and strangers.

In the model, the seven superficial causes are those factors that can either facilitate or hinder the management of uncertainty and anxiety. For example, regarding the self-concept, Gudykunst maintains that an increase in the degree to which our social identities, personal identities, and self-esteem guide our interactions with strangers will produce a decrease in uncertainty and anxiety and increase our ability to predict their behavior, but *only when we are not mindful;* when we are mindful, we choose how to communicate and our behavior is not determined by such internal characteristics as social or personal identities. Our self-concept also affects our motivation to interact with strangers. An increase in our need for group inclusion and to sustain our self-concept increases our anxiety when interacting with strangers, but only

Figure 9.2 Model of Anxiety Uncertainty Management

when we are not mindful. Yet an increase in the degree to which strangers confirm our self-concept produces decreases in our anxiety. How we react to strangers also affects our communication effectiveness. To the extent that we can empathize and are tolerant of ambiguity, our uncertainty and anxiety will decrease. Moreover, if we maintain rigid and inflexible social categories and stereotypes of strangers, our uncertainty and anxiety will increase. The context (i.e., situational processes) in which we interact and our connection with strangers also affect our levels of uncertainty and anxiety. If we are engaged in cooperative work tasks that require interdependence with strangers (i.e., team efforts where everyone has a specific but related role to play), our levels of uncertainty and anxiety will decrease. In such tasks, as the quality and quantity of interaction with strangers increases, our levels of uncertainty and anxiety will also decrease.

Finally, if we can maintain our own self-dignity and respect strangers' differences, our uncertainty and anxiety will decrease. [18]

UNCERTAINTY REDUCTION AND INTERCULTURAL COMMUNICATION APPREHENSION

Persons from different cultures reduce uncertainty during initial interaction in various ways. One factor that may affect how persons reduce uncertainty is whether they experience intercultural communication apprehension. Communication researchers Jim Neuliep and Dan Ryan investigated the relationship between intercultural communication apprehension and uncertainty reduction during initial cross-cultural interaction. Imagine that you have just been introduced to someone from a different culture. You have never met this person before and know very little about his or her culture. Chances are good that you will experience a bit of anxiety and apprehension. This is a very common response, and you need not feel bad about yourself for having felt it. Neuliep and Ryan argue that because intercultural communication is loaded with novelty and dissimilarity, people may experience inordinate amounts of anxiety, which inhibit the ability to reduce uncertainty.[19] Mark Leary argues that anxiety is typically experienced as an unpleasant emotional state marked by feelings of tension, apprehension, and worry regarding potentially negative outcomes.[20] Many people, regardless of culture, experience anxiety when communicating, or when they anticipate communicating, with persons from different cultures or ethnic groups. Often, we tend to avoid those situations that make us feel anxious. In this case, if intercultural communication causes us to feel anxious, we may avoid initiating interaction with people from different cultures. However, unless we interact, we cannot reduce much uncertainty, and therefore, our anxiety levels remain high.

In their theory of uncertainty reduction, Berger and Calabrese maintain that the principal way people reduce uncertainty during initial interaction is through verbal and nonverbal communication.[21] To the extent that people can reduce uncertainty and anxiety during communication, they can increase their communication effectiveness. In their study, Neuliep and Ryan found a direct relationship between intercultural communication apprehension (ICA) and uncertainty reduction. Specifically, they found that during initial intercultural communication, people who experienced high ICA also experienced high uncertainty. Neuliep and Ryan reasoned that because persons with high ICA may avoid or withdraw from communication with persons from different cultures, they are less likely to engage in communication tactics that reduce uncertainty. Persons who generally do not experience apprehension interacting with persons from other cultures communicate comfortably, thereby facilitating uncertainty reduction. A lesson here is that by increasing our interaction with persons from different cultures we can reduce our uncertainty about them and reduce our anxiety. In fact, in related research, Neuliep and Grohskopf found that as individuals reduce uncertainty, their satisfaction with communication increases. Hence, by engaging in intercultural communication, we can reduce uncertainty, which will reduce anxiety and result in more satisfying communication with others. It is a "win-win" situation![22]

Although an individual may be faced with large amounts of uncertainty and anxiety during initial intercultural communication, Neuliep and Ryan reasoned that the person's communication style may enable him or her to effectively reduce uncertainty. Jim McCroskey and Virginia Richmond have outlined two types of communication style—what they call *sociocommunicative orientation*—that affect how one communicates in different situations: (1) assertiveness and (2) responsiveness.[23] Assertiveness refers to one's ability to make requests; actively disagree; express positive or negative personal rights and feelings; initiate, sustain, and terminate conversations; and defend oneself without attacking others. Responsiveness refers to one's ability to be sensitive to the communication of others, be a good listener, engage in comforting communication, and recognize the needs and wants of relevant others. McCroskey and Richmond note that assertiveness and responsiveness are inversely related to communication apprehension. In other words, persons high in communication apprehension are not likely to engage in assertive or responsive communication behaviors. Because apprehensive persons tend to avoid communication, they are not likely to initiate conversation or advance their position on a topic of communication during a conversation.[24] Likewise, a responsive communicator is one who invites others to engage in conversation. In their research, Neuliep and Ryan argued that these tendencies may be highlighted during initial intercultural interaction, in which situational novelty, unfamiliarity, and dissimilarity are prominent. Indeed, in their study, Neuliep and Ryan found that people who were assertive and responsive reported experiencing less intercultural communication apprehension.[25]

Neuliep and Ryan contend that the fundamental components of assertiveness and responsiveness are consistent with those behaviors associated with reduced uncertainty. For example, a characteristic of assertiveness is the ability to make requests. In Axiom 3, Berger and Calabrese point out that as information-seeking behavior (question asking) increases, uncertainty decreases. In addition, assertiveness is associated with initiation and maintenance of conversations. In Axiom 1, Berger and Calabrese maintain that as verbal communication increases, uncertainty decreases. Responsive communicators invite others to interact, thus increasing verbal communication. Likewise, responsive communicators are nonverbally sensitive to others. Responsiveness is communicated through eye contact, smiling, forward leaning, and touching. Axiom 2 states that as nonverbal affiliative expressiveness increases, uncertainty decreases. From the association of assertiveness and responsiveness with behaviors designed to reduce uncertainty, Neuliep and Ryan predicted that assertive and responsive communicators may be better able to reduce uncertainty. Their results supported their prediction. Persons scoring high on assertiveness and responsiveness instruments reported experiencing less uncertainty during initial cross-cultural interaction.[26]

AN INTERCULTURAL CONVERSATION: UNCERTAINTY REDUCTION AND SOCIOCOMMUNICATIVE STYLE

In the following intercultural conversations, we see how an individual's sociocommunicative style affects uncertainty reduction during initial intercultural communication. In the first conversation, we see Dan, who is from the United States, interacting with Natasha, who is from Ukraine. Dan seems unassertive and unresponsive. In the second conversation, we see Jim, who is from the United States, interacting with Foday, who is from Sierra Leone. In comparison to Dan, Jim seems assertive and responsive. Jim's assertiveness and responsiveness help him reduce uncertainty about Foday and Sierra Leone.

Natasha:	*Hi, I'm Natasha.*
Dan:	*Oh, hi.*
Natasha:	*What's your name?*
Dan:	*Dan.*
Natasha:	*Hi, Dan.*
Dan:	*Hi.*
Natasha:	*I'm not from here. I'm from Ukraine.*

Dan:	*Oh.*
Natasha:	*You've heard of it?*
Dan:	*Ah, yeah, I think so.*
Natasha:	*Ukraine is in Eastern Europe, between Poland and Russia.*
Dan:	*Oh.*
Natasha:	*Yeah. Have you ever been to Europe?*
Dan:	*Yeah, but I was pretty young.*
Natasha:	*It must have been quite an experience, though.*
Dan:	*Ah . . . do you know what time it is?*
Natasha:	*It's about 3 o'clock.*
Dan:	*I have to go now. Bye.*
Natasha:	*Bye, Dan, nice meeting you.*
Jim:	*Hi, I'm Jim. I don't believe we've met.*
Foday:	*Hello, Jim, I'm Foday.*
Jim:	*Hi, Foday, where are you from?*
Foday:	*I'm from Sierra Leone.*
Jim:	*Oh really? Where is Sierra Leone? I know it's on the African continent, but I'm not sure where.*
Foday:	*It's on the western coast between Guinea and Liberia.*
Jim:	*Oh, toward the north? How big is it?*
Foday:	*Yes, that's right. We're about the size of your South Carolina.*
Jim:	*That's interesting. What kind of government do you have in Sierra Leone?*
Foday:	*We have a constitutional democracy.*
Jim:	*Is that based on English law?*
Foday:	*Yes.*
Jim:	*Who's the president, and how long a term does he serve?*
Foday:	*His name is Ahmad Tejan Kabbah. He is elected for a five-year term.*
Jim:	*Oh yeah . . . I think I've heard of him. By the way, you speak English very well. Is that your official language?*

> **Foday:** *English is the official language of my country, but it is spoken only by a literate minority of about 20 percent of the population.*
>
> **Jim:** *Really? What language does the other 80 percent speak?*
>
> **Foday:** *People in the north speak a vernacular language called Temme, whereas those in the south speak Mende.*
>
> **Jim:** *That's fascinating. I suspect that most citizens are Muslim?*
>
> **Foday:** *About 60 percent are Muslim, with about 20 percent Christian. The other 20 percent or so vary.*
>
> **Jim:** *I understand that mining is a major industry in Sierra Leone. I hear you mine diamonds.*
>
> **Foday:** *Yes, they are a big export. But many people live by simple subsistence farming, like my father.*
>
> **Jim:** *Foday, it has been really nice meeting you. I'd like to introduce you to my wife. She's over there.*
>
> **Foday:** *Thank you, I'd like to meet her.*

In comparing the two conversations, notice how much more uncertainty Jim reduces in his short conversation with Foday than Dan does with Natasha. Jim is assertive in initiating conversation with Foday and asking him questions about his country. Jim also appears responsive to Foday, using such comments as "That's interesting." Dan, on the other hand, says very little, even when prompted by Natasha. Natasha is probably more uncertain about Dan after the conversation than before. His lack of assertiveness and responsiveness probably leaves a negative impression with her.

Assessing Sociocommunicative Orientation/Style

In their study of uncertainty reduction during initial intercultural communication, Neuliep and Ryan measured assertiveness and responsiveness using scales developed by McCroskey and Richmond. These scales have been used successfully in other cultures, including China, Finland, Japan, Korea, and Russia. Note, however, that these scales were designed to measure assertiveness and responsiveness as defined in the United States and may not be generalizable across all cultures. In fact, studies examining assertiveness and responsiveness across cultures have reported differences. American men and women, for example, score higher on the assertiveness dimension than Finnish and Japanese men and women. Generally, American women score higher on the responsiveness scale than men and women from other cultures. Within most cultures, however, men generally score higher on the assertiveness scale, whereas women score higher on the responsiveness scale.[27]

SELF-ASSESSMENT 9.2

The Sociocommunicative Orientation/Style Instrument

The following questionnaire lists twenty personality traits. Indicate the degree to which you believe each of these characteristics applies to you, as you normally communicate with others, by marking whether you (5) strongly agree that it applies, (4) agree that it applies, (3) are undecided, (2) disagree that it applies, or (1) strongly disagree that it applies. There are no right or wrong answers. Work quickly; record your first impression.

_____ 1. Helpful

_____ 2. Defends own beliefs

_____ 3. Independent

_____ 4. Responsive to others

_____ 5. Forceful

_____ 6. Has strong personality

_____ 7. Sympathetic

_____ 8. Compassionate

_____ 9. Assertive

_____ 10. Sensitive to the needs of others

_____ 11. Dominant

_____ 12. Sincere

_____ 13. Gentle

_____ 14. Willing to take a stand

_____ 15. Warm

_____ 16. Tender

_____ 17. Friendly

_____ 18. Acts as a leader

_____ 19. Aggressive

_____ 20. Competitive

Scoring: Items 2, 3, 5, 6, 9, 11, 14, 18, 19, and 20 measure assertiveness. Add the scores on these items to get your assertiveness score. Scores above 40 indicate that you see yourself as assertive. Items 1, 4, 7, 8, 10, 12, 13, 15, 16, and 17 measure responsiveness. Add the scores on these items to get your responsiveness score. Scores above 40 suggest that you see yourself as responsive. Being assertive and responsive is not necessarily "good" or "bad." Your sociocommunicative style is a barometer of how you interact with others, not whether you are a good or bad person.

Source: From McCroskey, J. C., & Richmond, V. P., *Fundamentals of Human Communication: An Interpersonal Perspective.* Copyright © 1996. Reprinted by permission of Waveland Press, Inc. All rights reserved.

EMPATHY AND SIMILARITY IN RELATIONSHIP DEVELOPMENT

The majority of uncertainty reduction occurs during the initial stages of a relationship. To the extent that relational partners are able to reduce uncertainty, they learn more about each other and can further develop their relationship. Two factors (among others) that have a significant influence on communication and relational development are empathy and similarity. Empathy and similarity are important in any relationship, but they take on added importance in intercultural relationships. Due to their cultural differences, persons in intercultural relationships may find it difficult to empathize with their relational partners because they are dissimilar.

Empathy

As uncertainty is reduced, people get to know each other more and can work on developing their relationship. The ability to empathize with someone is a crucial ingredient in any relationship. Empathy takes on added importance in intercultural relationships, however. Because persons from other cultures are different from us, it may be difficult for us to empathize with them, their ideas, and their style of communication. In these types of relationships, reducing uncertainty becomes essential. In fact, some communication scholars maintain that empathy may be impossible in intercultural communication. However, in general, communication scholars believe that because empathy motivates communication behavior, it is an essential ingredient in effective interpersonal communication.[28]

Empathy is often defined as the degree to which we can accurately infer another's thoughts or feelings. Benjamin Broome contends that this definition is inadequate for the study of intercultural communication and offers what he calls a model of *relational empathy* (see Figure 9.3).[29]

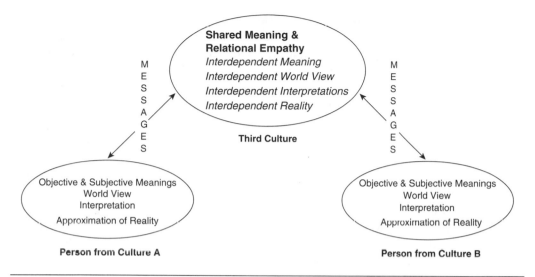

Figure 9.3

Broome argues that because our thoughts and perceptions are based on our unique personal, cultural, sociocultural, and individual past experiences, we can never completely comprehend or directly know what another is thinking or feeling. As Broome argues, "While we can never become another person, it is possible to erect a structure within the framework of which the other's interpretation of the world or us takes shape or assumes meaning."[30] The model of relational empathy is based on the idea that whenever two people come together and interact, they create a *third culture* of shared meaning and relational empathy.[31] Broome argues that mutual understanding and shared meaning are a product of the meeting between individuals. Relational empathy is conceptualized not as the ability to accurately reproduce another's perceptions or emotions, but rather that which is created by two people interacting. This third culture of relational empathy and shared meaning is the outcome or harmonization of communication in which unique values, beliefs, norms, and symbols are shared by the interactants. Broome asserts that the third culture emerges when the interactants are open and willing to communicate with others and expose themselves to new meanings.

According to the model, persons cannot possess direct, firsthand knowledge of the emotional states or cognitive processes of another person. Instead, people possess objective and subjective meanings. Objective meaning, according to Broome, is one's interpretation of one's own personal experiences to oneself. For example, your interpretation of what it meant to grow up in your hometown with your family is a part of your own objective meaning. Subjective meaning, on the other hand, is one's interpretation of the other person's experiences in relation to one's own. For example, a friend's description of what it meant to grow up in his or her hometown and of his or her family experiences would be a part of your subjective meaning.

When two people come together and interact, a product of the third culture is interdependent meaning—that is, new meaning based on the combining of each individual's objective and subjective meanings. People also bring with them a personal worldview largely based on cultural orientation. Hence, a Japanese person brings a collectivistic, high-context worldview, and an American brings an individualistic, low-context worldview. In a relationship, these two different worldviews merge into an interdependent worldview. Because of the individuals' objective and subjective knowledge and worldviews, they have different interpretations of what is real. Through the establishment of relational empathy, an interdependent interpretation and approximation of reality materializes.

Broome asserts that similarity among individuals is not necessary to achieve relational empathy and shared meaning. Instead, Broome's model assumes that the emergence of a third culture creates a medium in which the interactants can relate and one in which similarity becomes moot. Because a third culture has evolved through the verbal and nonverbal messages of the interactants, each is an active participant in its creation. Hence, neither person has to re-create anything because each is an integral part of its existence.[32]

Intercultural researcher Donald Klopf maintains that we can approach empathy with others by developing empathic listening skills. Empathic listening means listening more to the meanings than to the words of another person. According to Klopf, empathic listening involves (1) *paraphrasing,* the rewording of what the other person has said; (2) *reflecting feelings,* relating back to the other the feelings we believe the other is experiencing; (3) *reflecting meanings,* the restating of what we heard to confirm its meaning; and (4) *summarizing,* briefly restating the major topics the other has communicated. [33]

Although complete empathy cannot be experienced by anyone, taking Broome's model of relational empathy and Klopf's prescription for empathic listening into account and practice, we can develop and enhance our relationships with persons from cultures different from our own.

Similarity

Although Broome's model of relational empathy discounts the importance of similarity, a great deal of research (mostly conducted in the United

States) has demonstrated that similarity plays a key role in the establishment and development of relationships. As communication researcher Steve Duck states, "All communication and all relationships are likewise founded on a necessary base of similarity of understanding or similarity of meaning that facilitates the development of each."[34] This topic is important for communication researchers because of the belief that we are attracted to those people we perceive as similar to ourselves. Intercultural researchers have found that the more we perceive another as similar to ourselves, the more we are able to reduce uncertainty about the person and to form accurate categories of him or her. Thus, similarity may be particularly important during initial encounters with another person.

One of the pioneers in the study of similarity is Donn Byrne. Although similarity may come in many forms, Byrne's efforts have focused mainly on attitude similarity and attraction. Byrne's fundamental postulate is that attitude similarity between persons leads to positive affect, which in turn leads to attraction (see Figure 9.4).[35] Byrne has become well known for his "bogus stranger" experiments, which have relevance for intercultural communication. In these experiments, Byrne asks research participants to indicate their attitudes on a variety of topics and issues. The participants are then paired with a "stranger," who is portrayed as a research participant whose attitudes on the same topics and issues were assessed at an earlier time. Prior to the pairing of the research participants and the stranger, the research participants are shown the stranger's attitude responses. In actuality, however, the stranger is "bogus" because his or her attitude responses are manufactured to either match or conflict with the research participants' attitude responses. After interacting with the stranger, the research participants then rate the stranger's level of attractiveness. Consistently, those research participants paired with an attitudinally similar stranger provide higher attractiveness ratings than those paired with an attitudinally dissimilar stranger. Yet in each case, the stranger is the same person.[36]

Attitude similarity is only one way in which people label themselves as like or unlike others. A White student once commented that similarity was not a factor in her relationship with her boyfriend, explaining that her boyfriend was Black. Upon further questioning, it was discovered that she and her boyfriend were the same age, were studying at the same college, were pursuing the same major, enjoyed similar tastes in music and food, and had very similar attitudes on a variety of topics. The point here is that although we may have dissimilarities with others, the people with whom we develop and maintain interpersonal relationships are typically very much like ourselves. Perceived similarity, sometimes called perceived homophilly, is perhaps the most dominant force in our motivations to interact with

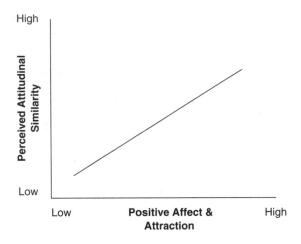

Figure 9.4

others. But similarity can come in many shapes and sizes. We can be similar to others culturally, attitudinally, linguistically, racially, behaviorally, affectively, and/or physically. The more we find ourselves like someone else, the more likely we are to initiate and sustain communication with that person. Although it facilitates interaction and attraction, cultural similarity (which is only one kind of similarity) may not be a necessary ingredient in forming meaningful and lasting relationships. Two persons from radically different cultures may find a great deal of similarity with each other.

PERCEPTIONS OF RELATIONAL INTIMACY ACROSS CULTURES

Although the same types of relationships exist across cultures, the level of intimacy varies considerably. In other words, what it means to be a student in your culture is probably not the same as what it means to be a student in another culture. Moreover, the relationship between student and teacher varies widely across cultures. In the United States, for example, student/teacher relationships at the college level might be perceived as relatively informal and personal compared with student/teacher relationships in China or Korea. William Gudykunst and Tsukasa Nishida studied the influence of culture on perceptions of intimacy and communication behavior in the United States and Japan.[37] In each culture, students were asked to rate the level of intimacy (on a scale of 1 to 9, where 1 = intimate, 9 = nonintimate) for thirty different relationships. Gudykunst and Nishida reasoned that because of their collectivistic tendencies, the Japanese students would perceive ingroup relationships as more intimate than would the American students, who are individualistic. Gudykunst and Nishida also maintained that because Japan is considered a masculine-oriented culture in which sex roles are clearly differentiated, male/female relationships (lover, spouse, boy/girlfriend) would be perceived as less intimate than in the United States. Gudykunst and Nishida argue that in cultures such as Japan, where sex roles are strictly distinguished, there is not much informal interaction between males and females. Moreover, when interaction does occur, the content of it is relatively superficial. The results of their survey are shown in Table 9.1.

When comparing the ratings, American students are often surprised to see that Japanese students rate close friend and best friend as the most intimate of their relationships. In Japan, even classmates are rated as more intimate than spouses. These results confirm the notion that when you travel to cultures different from your own, your relationships in that culture (as student, friend, employee) could be perceived very differently from when you occupy the same role in the United States.

Eastern and Western Cultures and Relationships

As demonstrated by Gudykunst and Nishida, perceptions of relationships differ widely across cultures. In individualistic cultures such as the United States, relationships are typically viewed from the perspective of the self. As June Ock Yum asserts, individualists see themselves as distinct individuals who participate in relationships to maximize their own self-interests.[38] In many collectivistic cultures, like China, relationships are guided by Confucianism. According to Yum, the fundamental theme of Confucianism is that proper relationships form the cornerstone of society. Moreover, an individual's conduct in society should be guided by four principles: (1) *humanism:* treating others as one wishes to be treated; (2) *faithfulness:* loyalty rather than personal interest or profit; (3) *propriety:* social decorum and etiquette; and (4) *wisdom.*[39] Yum points out that three of these four principles have direct implications for how relationships are perceived in East Asian cultures like China, as compared with Western cultures like the United States. First, in contrasting Eastern and Western relationships, Yum alleges that many East Asian cultures practice *particularism*—that is, the belief that there are particular or unique rules and guidelines that apply to each individual relationship. Relational partners are to be sensitive to differences in such things as status when interacting with others. Most East Asian cultures believe in strict and well-defined social hierarchies in which people are perceived as higher or lower. In contrast, persons in Western cultures

Table 9.1

Relationship Type	U.S.*	Japan*
Family		
Spouse (*haigusha*)	1.33	4.32
Father (*chichioya*)	2.75	2.57
Mother (*hahaoya*)	2.35	2.06
Son (*musuko*)	2.59	4.76
Daughter (*musume*)	2.55	4.87
Brother (*kyodai*)	3.12	3.51
Sister (*shimai*)	2.88	3.78
Aunt (*oba*)	4.53	4.99
Cousin (*itoko*)	4.67	4.66
Grandparent (*sofubo*)	3.75	4.15
Uncle (*oji*)	4.55	5.21
Social		
Fiancé (*konyakusha*)	1.29	4.32
Lover (*koibito*)	1.25	2.81
Boy/Girlfriend (*otoko/onna tomodachi*)	1.70	3.32
Best friend (*ichiban no shinyu*)	2.51	1.73
Mate (*tsureai*)	1.75	4.45
Steady (*kosai shiteiru hito*)	2.27	2.92
Close friend (*shinyu*)	2.85	1.83
Friend (*tomo*)	3.67	3.42
Date (*detonoaite*)	4.02	3.48
Companion (*tomodachi*)	3.08	3.05
Neighbor (*kinjo no hito*)	5.72	5.92
Acquaintance (*chijin*)	6.79	4.95
Professional/Work		
Cohort (*nakama*)	5.40	2.85
Coworker (*shigato-makama*)	5.76	5.27
Employer (*koyosha*)	6.39	6.86
Colleague (*doryo*)	5.33	4.76
Roommate (*doshukusha*)	3.85	4.88
Classmate (*dokyusei*)	5.72	3.84
Other		
Stranger (*shiranai hito*)	8.35	7.99

*In each culture, students were asked to rate the level of intimacy for thirty different relationships on a scale of 1 to 9 (1 = intimate; 9 = nonintimate). Lower scores represent more perceived intimacy.

Source: Gudykunst, W. B. & Nishida, T. "The Influence of Cultural Variability on Perceptions of Communication Behavior Associated with Relationship Terms," *Human Communication Research*, 13 (1986), 147–166. Reprinted by permission of Oxford University Press, Inc. via Copyright Clearance Center.

practice what Yum calls a *universalistic orientation* to relationships. Yum alleges that most Westerners try to treat others as equally as possible, regardless of status or intimacy level of the partners.[40]

Yum also contends that relational partners in Eastern cultures engage in *long-term and asymmetrical reciprocity.* You may recall from Chapter 3 that reciprocity refers to the give and take or mutual exchange in interpersonal encounters. According to Yum, in Confucian philosophy, dependency on others is an inevitable and accepted part of relations with others. People will always be indebted to others who help or assist them in some way. Yum states that "under this system of reciprocity, the individual does not calculate what he or she gives and receives. To calculate would be to think about immediate personal profits, which is the opposite of the principle of faithfulness."[41] Western relationships, on the other hand, are characterized by short-term and symmetrical reciprocity or even contractual reciprocity. In the United States, for example, some marital relationships begin with premarital legal agreements that carefully spell out expectations, possessions, and obligations that are to be followed.

Another difference between Eastern and Western relationships is that in many Eastern cultures, there is a clear difference between who is and is not a member of the ingroup or the outgroup. Yum maintains that Confucian philosophy prescribes that people associate and identify with relatively few, yet very cohesive, groups. Moreover, one's affiliation with ingroups is long-lived, perhaps even lifelong. Group associations in most Western cultures are, for the most part, optional and voluntary. Many of the groups with whom one associates in the United States, for example, are designed to somehow facilitate one's individual development (for example, "self-help" groups), and one's association with the group lasts only as long as one benefits from membership.[42]

A fourth difference between relationships in Eastern and Western cultures is the use of intermediaries (go-betweens). For the most part, persons in Western cultures prefer direct, face-to-face contact in interpersonal relationships, including with business associates. In the United States, for example, the use of intermediaries is typically reserved for very formal and/or legal situations and is usually contractual (as with lawyers or realtors). Yum points out that in Eastern cultures, because the distinctions between ingroups and outgroups are so well defined, intermediaries are essential and are used even in informal situations, such as introductions, dating, marital arrangements, and even relatively small business transactions. The principle behind the use of intermediaries is to save face.[43]

A fifth difference in interpersonal relations in Eastern and Western cultures, according to Yum, is that Confucianism's emphasis on faithfulness and loyalty in relationships leads to blending of personal and public relationships. In the United States, people can maintain "strictly business" relationships, whereas many Eastern cultures prefer to do business with trusted associates with whom they have established a strong interpersonal bond. Many U.S. businesses would be well served by initiating frequent contact, establishing mutual interests, and developing shared experiences with their Eastern culture counterparts.[44]

MARITAL RELATIONSHIPS

Marital relationships exist in virtually every culture. According to anthropologist Michael Howard, the most common type of marriage practice in the United States and most Western industrialized nations is monogamy—that is, marriage between one man and one woman.

In most cases, monogamy is prescribed legally, and acquiring multiple spouses is illegal. In cultures in which marriage is governed legally, people are allowed, by law, to enter into and leave marriages—that is, people can marry, divorce, and marry again. This is called *serial monogamy.* Howard asserts that most cultures prefer not to limit the number of spouses available to a person. These cultures practice *polygamy*—that is, marriage to more than one spouse. Contrary to popular belief, polygamy is not the practice of a husband's having multiple wives. Actually, there are two types of polygamy: *polygyny,* in which a man has multiple wives, and *polyandry,* in which a woman has more than one husband. According to Howard, polygyny is permitted in the majority of societies.[45] Indeed, in their study of cross-cultural differences in family and sexual life among sixty-eight cultures, Becker and Posner report that only two cultures did not practice polygyny.[46]

Intercultural and Interracial Marriages

Although the number of intercultural and/or interracial marriages is growing, according to the U.S. Census Bureau, more than 97 percent of married couples in the United States are of the same race. Nearly 95 percent of unmarried couples living together are of the same race. Interracial couples account for nearly 2 percent of the population of married couples and just over 4 percent of unmarried couples living together.[47] It is important to note, however, that these percentages take into account only interracial marriages and couples living together. The number of intercultural, or cross-cultural, marriages may be much higher.

In addition to the growing number of cross-cultural marriages, American attitudes about these relationships are changing. A recent national survey conducted by *The Washington Post,* the Henry J. Kaiser Family Foundation, and Harvard University found that 86 percent of Black respondents said their families would welcome a White, Asian, or Hispanic person to their family. Among Whites, 66 percent would accept Hispanics or Asians, but only 55 percent would accept a Black person. Among Hispanics, 86 percent would accept Whites, 79 percent would accept Asians, and 74 percent would accept Blacks. Among Asians, 77 percent would accept Whites, 71 percent would accept Hispanics, and 66 percent would accept Blacks.

Although the percentage of cross-cultural marriages is growing, and the attitudes about such relationships are improving, cross-cultural (i.e., racial or ethnic) relationships are susceptible to pressures and strains not experienced in same-race or same-ethnicity marriages or relationships. For example, results from the same survey reported above indicate that 65 percent of White-Black couples said they experienced problems within their families at the start of their relationship, and 24 percent of White-Asian or White-Hispanic couples reported problems.[48]

Communication plays a principal role in marriage. Depending on the type of marriage, communication within marriages can vary considerably, however. For example, Howard notes that jealousy and rivalry among wives is common in cultures that practice polygyny. Sororal polygyny, in which a man marries sisters, is one way of getting around the interpersonal problems associated with polygyny. Another is restricting the communication among wives—for example, housing each wife in a separate dwelling, as is practiced by the Plauteau Tonga. Rationing communication is another strategy: the Tanala people of Madagascar require that a husband must spend one day with each of his wives in succession. In the Lacandon culture of southern Mexico, wives are assigned hierarchical positions in which senior-ranking wives have more privileges than junior-ranking wives.[49]

Australian researchers Halford, Hahlweg, and Dunne argue that communication skills consistently differentiate distressed from nondistressed marital couples across countries. They note, however, that specific types of communication skills may vary across cultures. In their research Halford, Hahweg, and Dunne coded the communication behaviors of happy and unhappy German and Australian couples. Their results showed that, across both cultures, unhappy couples engaged in higher rates of negative verbal and nonverbal behaviors and were more likely to engage in coercive escalation; that is, a sequence of negative responses that increases as the length of interaction increases. They also observed cultural differences in couples' reactions to negative responses. Happy Australian couples typically accepted or agreed with negative responses, whereas unhappy and happy German couples and unhappy Australian couples typically counterrefused.[50]

Although the Koran permits polygyny, polygyny is not widely practiced in Muslim countries, contrary to popular belief. The Koran permits polygyny only under certain circumstances. For example, a Muslim man may have up to four wives but he must be "perfectly equitable" with each wife. If married to more than one wife, he must spend absolutely the same amount of time with each of his wives and treat each wife exactly the same. He is not allowed the slightest preference for one wife over another. Most Muslims believe that no man can fulfill the Koran's requirement of complete and total impartiality, and so most do not engage in the practice of multiple wives.[51]

Polyandry, the practice of having multiple husbands, is observed less frequently than polygyny. Howard reports that polyandry is practiced on a regular basis in Tibet and in some parts of India, Nepal, and Sri Lanka. Howard also reports that the most common form of polyandry is fraternal polyandry—that is, a woman's marrying brothers.[52]

Mate Selection Across Cultures

When you think about getting married, what are the characteristics you look for in a potential mate? Are you looking for someone who is good looking? Educated? Has a sense of humor? Wealthy? David Buss has been interested in the answers to these questions and has investigated mate preferences across cultures for decades. Before looking at his findings, take a moment to complete the survey on page 364.

For more than ten years, Buss has led the International Mate Selection Project, consisting of forty-nine research collaborators from thirty-three countries located on six continents and five islands.[53] The focus of Buss's work has been to identify people's preferences in choosing a mate. According to Buss, scholars from myriad academic fields are interested in mating practices and mate selection. Evolutionary biologists, for example, believe that mate preference is a central evolutionary force. Sociologists study mating practices because they affect the distribution of wealth in society (for example, when the rich prefer to mate with the rich). Geneticists understand that mate preferences can affect genetic inheritability estimates. Social psychologists see mate preference as a psychological phenomenon related to interpersonal attraction. Yet despite all of the interest, Buss alleges that very little is known about the types of characteristics people value in potential mates and how these values might vary across cultures. Hence, Buss initiated the International Mate Selection Project. The purpose of his research was to identify (1) which characteristics individuals value in potential mates, (2) similarities and differences among countries in their values, (3) clusters of countries that are similar to each other, and (4) sex differences in the degree of variation in mate selection within each country. Buss and his research collaborators surveyed more than 10,000 people from thirty-three different countries. In Africa, subjects were from Nigeria, South Africa, and Zambia. Asian countries sampled were China, India, Japan, and Taiwan. In the Middle East, Jewish and Palestinian Israel and Iran were surveyed. European countries studied were Belgium, Bulgaria, Estonia, Finland, France, Germany, Great Britain, Greece, Ireland, Italy, the Netherlands, Norway, Poland, Spain, Sweden, and the former Yugoslavia. In North America, the United States (including Hawaii) and Canada were sampled. South American countries surveyed were Brazil, Colombia, and Venezuela. Oceanic countries were Australia and New Zealand. Participants from Indonesia were also sampled.[54]

SELF-ASSESSMENT 9.3

Selecting a Mate: Factors in Choosing a Mate

Below are 18 characteristics of people that you may find either desirable or undesirable. On a scale of 0 to 3, rate each of the characteristics on how important or desirable it is in choosing a mate. A score of 0 = irrelevant or unimportant, 1 = somewhat important, 2 = important, and 3 = indispensable.

1. _____ Sociability
2. _____ Similar education
3. _____ Pleasing disposition
4. _____ Refinement, neatness
5. _____ Similar religious background
6. _____ Good looks
7. _____ Education and intelligence
8. _____ Mutual attraction—love
9. _____ Good cook and housekeeper
10. _____ Good financial prospect
11. _____ Desire for home and children
12. _____ Chastity (no previous experience in sexual intercourse)
13. _____ Dependable character
14. _____ Good health
15. _____ Favorable social status or rating
16. _____ Similar political background
17. _____ Emotional stability and maturity
18. _____ Ambitious and industrious

Preferences Concerning Potential Mates

Below is a set of 13 characteristics. Please rank them on their desirability in someone you might marry. Give a "1" to the most desirable characteristic in a potential mate; a "2" to the second most desirable characteristic in a potential mate; a "3" to the third most desirable characteristic in a potential mate, and so on until you have ranked all 13 characteristics. No characteristic can receive the same ranking as another.

1. _____ Easygoing

2. _____ Healthy

3. _____ Physically attractive

4. _____ Good heredity

5. _____ College graduate

6. _____ Exciting personality

7. _____ Intelligent

8. _____ Creative and artistic

9. _____ Good housekeeper

10. _____ Good earning capacity

11. _____ Religious

12. _____ Wants children

13. _____ Kind and understanding

Sources: D. M. Buss, "Mate Preferences in Thirty-Seven Cultures," in *Psychology and Culture*, ed. W. J. Lonner and R. Malpass (Boston: Allyn & Bacon, 1994), pp. 197–202; D. M. Buss, "Sex Differences in Human Mate Preference: Evolutionary Hypotheses Tested in Thirty-Seven Cultures," *Behavioral and Brain Sciences* 12 (1989), 1–49.

In the study, individuals were asked to complete the "Factors in Choosing a Mate" and the "Preferences Concerning Potential Mates" instruments (see box). After analyzing the completed surveys, Buss found that in spite of the unique cultural variability associated with each sample, there were substantial commonalities among all the samples. Table 9.2 outlines the top-four-rated variables.

Some of the least preferred characteristics from the rating instruments were chastity, similar religious background, similar political background, and favorable social status. The lowest-ranked characteristics were college graduate, good earning capacity, and religion. Buss noted that although there

Table 9.2 Universally Preferred Characteristics

Universally Preferred Characteristics: Ranking Instrument = Preferences Concerning Potential Mates

1. Kind and understanding
2. Intelligent
3. Exciting personality
4. Healthy

Universally Preferred Characteristics: Rating Instrument = Factors in Choosing a Mate

1. Mutual attraction-love
2. Emotional stability and maturity
3. Good health
4. Pleasing disposition

Source: D. M. Buss, "Mate Preferences in Thirty-Seven Cultures," in *Psychology and Culture*, ed. W. J. Lonner and R. Malpass (Boston: Allyn & Bacon, 1994), pp. 197–202; D. M. Buss, "Sex Differences in Human Mate Preference: Evolutionary Hypotheses Tested in Thirty-Seven Cultures," *Behavioral and Brain Sciences*, 12 (1989), 1–49.

were some overall commonalities among the cultures, each country displayed some unique mate preferences. For example, the highest-rated characteristic for Iranian men and women was refinement and neatness. On the other hand, Chinese men rated good health as most important. Chinese women chose emotional stability as their top-rated characteristic. Nigerian men rated good health the highest, whereas Nigerian women rated emotional stability the highest. Buss reported that the largest effect of culture was seen in the variable of chastity. China, India, Indonesia, Iran, Taiwan, and Palestinian Israel placed the most importance on this characteristic, whereas Sweden, Finland, Norway, the Netherlands, and West Germany gave it the least importance.[55]

Probably the greatest difference among cultures occurred between men and women. In some countries, the sexes differed little in their rankings, whereas in others, the sexes differed greatly. The two countries with the highest degree of sexual dimorphism, Nigeria and Zambia, were also the two that practice polygyny. Moreover, there was more similarity between men and women from the same culture than between men and men or women and women from different cultures. The largest sex difference occurred for the variables of "good financial prospect" and "good earning capacity." Women generally valued these traits more than men. Men across the globe valued physical attractiveness in marriage partners more than women. Buss states,

Figure 9.5   Culture exerts substantial effects on mate preferences

The importance of good looks is not limited to Western Europe or North America; nor is it limited to cultures saturated with visual media such as television, movies, and videos; nor is it limited to particular racial, ethnic, religious, or political groups. In all known cultures worldwide, from the inner-continental tribal societies of Africa and South America to the big cities of Madrid, London, and Paris, men place a premium on the physical appearance of a potential mate.[56]

Women, on the other hand, place somewhat greater value than do men on "emotional stability and maturity," "favorable social status," "education and intelligence," and "college graduate." In another sex difference, men, worldwide, prefer wives who are younger than themselves. In polygynic cultures such as Zambia and Nigeria, where men may have multiple wives, men prefer brides who are much younger than themselves. Conversely, women prefer men who are older. In his conclusion, Buss notes that culture appears to exert substantial effects on mate preferences, and that, in general, the effects of sex on mate preferences are small compared with those of culture (see Figure 9.5).[57]

Arranged Marriages

In some cultures, an individual's preference in selecting a mate becomes moot because marriage is arranged by parents or a trusted family friend and/or mediator. In many instances, the bride and groom of an arranged marriage do not even meet until the day of the wedding. In many cultures, a bride price similar to that of a dowry is an essential ingredient of the arranged marriage. Although not as common as they once were, arranged marriages are still practiced in a variety of cultures and within some microcultural groups in the United States, such as the Hmong. Many young persons in the United States find the prospect of an arranged marriage quite frightening and unnerving. Yet Katie Thao, a Hmong woman who emigrated from Laos to the United States when she was young, indicates that the arranged marriage in which she participated was one of the most satisfying events of her life.[58] To Katie, the time and effort associated with searching for a mate represented considerable uncertainty and anxiety. In traditional Hmong culture, arranged marriages are negotiated by the parents. Because Katie had faith and trust in her parents to select for her the ideal spouse, she had little to worry about and very little uncertainty. Although she admits to being nervous on her wedding day, Thao says she very much loves the man she married, and they have three children. Although it happens only infrequently, the woman can reject the match. As Lor notes, however, there are certain situations in which the match cannot be refused. According to Lor, if the groom's family clan has high status, is unusually wealthy, or is related to the bride's family in some way, the match is essentially permanent.[59]

Jill Hoffman estimates that as many as 95 percent of marriages in India are arranged. As in other cultures with arranged marriages, in India there is a certain amount of bargaining and negotiation. Hoffman notes that family status and wealth play key roles in the process. Although it is illegal, in southern India, according to Hoffman, the groom's family often pays a bride price, especially if the bride is exceptionally beautiful or if the groom himself is flawed or impaired in some way. In most cases, the bride and groom do not meet before the wedding.[60] In her analysis of marriage in Iran, Kelly Pretty found that in traditional Iranian families, a marriage is arranged by the parents and a bride price is negotiated. In some instances, arranged marriages are between cousins, although this trend is changing.[61] In traditional Pakistani families, marriages are arranged by the fathers. According to Rebecca Sinnen, Pakistanis place a great deal of importance on status and wealth and so are careful to arrange marriages between a bride and groom of the same caste. Typically, the fathers negotiate through intermediaries. Sinnen notes that parents consider this the most important of all parental duties.[62] In Japan, as many as 25 percent of all marriages are arranged through an intermediary called a *pro nakodo*. The pro nakodo serves as a kind of dating service in that he interacts with other nakodos in order to find an appropriate match. Prospective brides and grooms begin the procedure by completing a lengthy registration process. Their applications are then kept on file and can be reviewed by other pro nakodos looking for a match. When a possible match is made, the clients meet to become acquainted. If the match is successful, the pro nakodo receives a substantial payment for his services. Another payment is then made to the bride's family. For the groom's family, the process can be very expensive. Renkens notes that the success rate is rather low at about 20 percent.[63]

In China, a grotesque form of arranged marriage has been rekindled: bride trafficking. *Newsweek* correspondent Dorinda Elliot reports that in many of the rural communities of China, crooked marriage brokers offer kidnapped women and girls for sale to prospective buyers. According to Elliot, from 1991 through 1996, Chinese authorities freed almost 100,000 kidnapped women and children and arrested almost 150,000 bride traffickers for participating in what she calls a virtual slave trade. Ironically, writes Elliot, local Chinese peasants sympathize with men who buy their wives, believing that if a woman takes the bride price and sends it to her parents, the man deserves to have her as his wife.[64]

Marital Dissolution and Divorce Across Cultures

A fact of life for all of us is that some of our relationships will end. Like marriage practices, divorce customs vary across cultures. Although it is relatively easy to calculate the divorce rate in any given culture, to understand why people divorce is a much more difficult task. In many cultures, social and economic issues often play a role in divorce decisions. Factors such as income, sexual dissatisfaction, childlessness, women's equality issues, religion, and the ease with which one can obtain a divorce all vary across cultures. In general, monogamy is correlated with lower divorce rates than polygyny.[65] Although the reasons for divorce vary, one trend that seems to be consistent across most cultures is that the overall divorce rate is on the rise. For example, since the passage of legislative reforms in the early 1980s, divorce has become much simpler in China, and divorce rates are soaring. In urban areas, such as Beijing, the divorce rate increased from 2 percent in 1981 to almost 20 percent of all marriages in 1992.[66] Similarly, Hall reports that in Canada, both cohabitation and divorce rates have increased considerably in the past quarter century. Approximately 30 percent of Canadian marriages now end in divorce.[67] Great Britain has the second highest divorce rate in Europe (Denmark's is the highest), with two out of five new marriages ending in divorce. The rise in Britain's divorce rates correlates with the rise of married women's employment.[68] Avner Gidron of the *World Press Review* reports that more than twenty years of civil war are partially responsible for the rise in divorce in Lebanon. Not only has divorce risen some 30 percent since the outbreak of civil war, but the marriage rate has fallen 25 percent. According to Gidron, between 30 and 40 percent of Christian marriages now end in divorce. The divorce rate among Shiite Moslems has risen about 26 percent.[69] Citing increased opportunities for women, the *Women's International Network News* reports that the divorce rate in Russia is rising quickly. Because they are able to find new apartments and support themselves financially, more and more Russian women are seeking divorce. The divorce rate in Russia has plateaued at about 40 percent.[70]

Although there is an upward trend, Japan has a relatively low divorce rate. According to sociologist Steve Stack, Japan is characterized by a low divorce rate, high family integration, cultural conformism, and low couple-centeredness. Stack argues that Japan's low divorce rate may be attributable to the degree of role segregation in Japan. Japanese women tend to remain in marriages because of their financial dependence on their husbands. Furthermore, asserts Stack, Japan emphasizes cultural conformity, in which the individual is subordinate to larger cultural institutions, such as marriage.[71] Ho writes that divorce in traditional Asian cultures, such as Japan, is discouraged because it disrupts familial harmony.[72] Sweden, too, has a relatively low divorce rate although it is higher than most European cultures. Part of the reason for the declining divorce rate in Sweden is that the rate of cohabitation is rising significantly. According to David Popenoe, about 15 percent of all couples in Sweden are cohabitating (compared with about 5 percent in the United States). Hence, more than 50 percent of all Swedish children are born out of wedlock, the highest percentage in the industrialized world. As Popenoe points out, "In order to divorce, one must marry, and that is precisely what Swedes in large numbers are not doing."[73]

As most people know, the United States has the highest divorce rate in the world, at about 48 percent. The number of U.S. citizens who are currently divorced has quadrupled since 1970 and now numbers at about 17 million. Divorced persons make up nearly 40 percent of the adult population.[74] Although they have the lowest outgroup interracial marriage rate (that is, exogamy) of any microcultural group, Blacks have the highest divorce rate of any microcultural group in America. Research by Oggins, Veroff, and Leber suggests that there may be more affective intensity in African-American marriages than in Caucasian marriages, which can lead to more open, direct interaction and is therefore more likely to erupt in marital difficulties.[75]

CHAPTER SUMMARY

People across the world, in all cultures, initiate, maintain, and dissolve relationships. Reducing uncertainty is a major part of initiating relationships, and one's level of intercultural communication apprehension and one's sociocommunicative style affect this process. Empathy and similarity are important in maintaining relationships. Perceptions of relationships differ significantly across cultures, particularly between Eastern and Western cultures. Perhaps the most important of all relationships, marriage varies across cultures in terms of the different types of marriage, mate selection, arranged marriage, and marital dissolution.

GLOSSARY OF TERMS

Arranged marriages: Marriages that are initiated and negotiated by a third party rather than by the bride and groom.

Assertiveness: An individual's ability to make requests, actively disagree, and express positive or negative personal rights and feelings.

Polyandry: The practice of having multiple husbands.

Polygamy: The practice of having multiple spouses.

Polygyny: The practice of having multiple wives.

Relational empathy: Shared meaning and harmonization that is the result of the interaction of two people.

Responsiveness: An individual's ability to be sensitive to the communication of others, including providing feedback, comforting communication, and listening.

Sociocommunicative style: Degree of assertiveness and responsiveness during communication.

Third culture: That which is created when a dyad consisting of persons from different cultures come together and establish relational empathy.

Uncertainty: The amount of predictability in a communication situation.

Uncertainty reduction theory: Theory whose major premise is that when strangers first meet, their primary goal is to reduce uncertainty.

REFERENCES

1. Gergen, K. J. *The Saturated Self: Dilemmas of Identity in Contemporary Life* (New York: Basic Books, 1991). Quote on page 178.
2. Berger, C. R. & Calabrese, R. J. "Some Explorations in Initial Interaction and Beyond: Toward a Developmental Theory of Interpersonal Communication," *Human Communication Research* 1 (1975), 99–112.
3. Gudykunst, W. B., & Kim, Y. Y. *Communicating with Strangers: An Approach to Intercultural Communication* (New York: McGraw-Hill, 1997).
4. Gudykunst, W. B. "Uncertainty Reduction and Predictability of Behavior in Low- and High-Context Cultures," *Communication Quarterly* 31 (1983), 49–55; ibid., "Uncertainty and Anxiety," in *Theories of Intercultural Communication,* ed. Kim, Y. Y. & Gudykunst, W. B. (Newbury Park, Calif.: Sage, 1988), pp. 123–156; ibid., "Anxiety/Uncertainty Management (AUM) Theory," in *Intercultural Communication Theory,* ed. R. Wiseman (Thousand Oaks, Calif.: Sage, 1995), pp. 8–58.
5. Gudykunst, W. B., & Nishida, T. "Individual and Cultural Influences on Uncertainty Reduction," *Communication Monographs* 51 (1984), 23–36.
6. Sanders, J., & Wiseman, R. "Uncertainty Reduction Among Ethnicities in the United States" (paper presented at the annual convention of the International Communication Association, Chicago, Ill., 1991).
7. Gudykunst, W. B., Sodetani, L. L., & Sonoda, K. T. "Uncertainty Reduction in Japanese-American-Caucasian Relationships in Hawaii," *Western Journal of Speech Communication* 51 (1987), 256–278.
8. Berger and Calabrese, "Some Explorations in Initial Interaction and Beyond," 99–112.
9. Ibid.
10. Gudykunst and Kim, *Communicating with Strangers.*
11. Clatterbuck, G. W. "Attributional Confidence and Uncertainty in Initial Interaction," *Human Communication Research* 5 (1979), 147–157.
12. Gudykunst, W. B. (2005). An anxiety/uncertainty management (AUM) theory of effective communication: Making the mesh of the net finer. In W. B. Gudykunst (Ed.), *Theorizing about intercultural communication* (pp. 281–322). Thousand Oaks, CA: Sage.
13. Ibid.
14. Ibid.
15. Ibid.
16. Ibid.
17. Ibid.
18. Ibid.
19. Neuliep, J. W., & Ryan, D. J. "The Influence of Intercultural Communication Apprehension and Socio-Communicative Orientation on Uncertainty Reduction During Initial Cross-Cultural Interaction," *Communication Quarterly* 46 (1998), 88–99.

20. Leary, M. "Anxiety, Cognition, and Behavior: In Search of a Broader Perspective." Pp. 39–44 in "Communication, Cognition, and Anxiety," ed. M. Booth-Butterfield, [special issue] *Journal of Social Behavior and Personality* 5 (1990).

21. Berger and Calabrese, "Some Explorations in Initial Interaction and Beyond."

22. Neuliep and Ryan, "The Influence of Intercultural Communication Apprehension and Socio-Communicative Orientation on Uncertainty Reduction During Initial Cross-Cultural Interaction." Neuliep, J. W., & Grohskopf, E. L., "Uncertainty Reduction and Communication Satisfaction during Initial Interaction: An Initial Test and Replication of a New Axiom," *Communication Reports* 13 (2000), 67–78.

23. McCroskey, J. C., & Richmond, V. P. *Fundamentals of Human Communication* (Prospect Heights, Ill.: Waveland, 1996).

24. Ibid.

25. Neuliep and Ryan, "The Influence of Intercultural Communication Apprehension and Socio-Communicative Orientation on Uncertainty Reduction During Initial Cross-Cultural Interaction."

26. Ibid.; Berger and Calabrese, "Some Explorations in Initial Interaction and Beyond."

27. Anderson, C. M., Martin, M. M., Zhong, M., & West, D. "Reliability, Separation of Factors, and Sex Difference on the Assertiveness-Responsiveness Measure: A Chinese Sample" (paper presented at the annual convention of the International Communication Association, Montreal, Quebec, Canada, 1997); Thompson, C. A., & Klopf, D. W. "An Analysis of Social Style Among Disparate Cultures," *Communication Research Reports* 8 (1991), 65–72; Thompson, C. A., Ishii, S., & Klopf, D. W. "Japanese and Americans Compared on Assertiveness/Responsiveness," *Psychological Reports* 66 (1990), 829–830.

28. Broome, B. J. "Building Shared Meaning: Implications of a Relational Approach to Empathy for Teaching Intercultural Communication," *Communication Education* 40 (1991), 235–249.

29. Ibid., p. 240.

30. Ibid., p. 241.

31. The concept of third-culture building was initially articulated by Fred Casmir. Broome's approach is based on Casmir's work in this area.

32. Broome, "Building Shared Meaning."

33. Klopf, D. W. *Intercultural Encounters: The Fundamentals of Intercultural Communication* (Englewood, Colo.: Morton, 1998).

34. Duck, S., & Barnes, M. K. "Disagreeing About Agreement: Reconciling Differences About Similarity," *Communication Monographs* 59 (1992), 199–208.

35. Byrne, D. "The Transition from Controlled Laboratory Experimentation to Less Controlled Settings: Surprise! Additional Variables Are Operative," *Communication Monographs* 59 (1992), 190–198.

36. Ibid.

37. Gudykunst, W. B. & Nishida, T. "The Influence of Cultural Variability on Perceptions of Communication Behavior Associated with Relationship Terms," *Human Communication Research* 13 (1986), 147–166.

38. Yum, J. O. "The Impact of Confucianism on Interpersonal Relationships and Communication Patterns in East Asia," in *Intercultural Communication: A Reader,* 8th ed., ed. L. A. Samovar and R. E. Porter (Belmont, Calif.: Wadsworth, 1997), pp. 78–88.

39. Ibid.

40. Ibid.

41. Ibid., p. 81.

42. Ibid.

43. Ibid.

44. Ibid.

45. Howard, M. C. *Contemporary Cultural Anthropology* (Glenview, Ill.: Scott, Foresman, 1989).

46. Becker, G. S. & Posner, R. A. "Cross-Cultural Differences in Family and Sexual Life," *Rationality and Society* 5 (1993), 421–432.

47. Fields, J., & Casper, L.M. "American Families and Living Arrangements: March 2000." Current Population Reports, U.S. Census Bureau, Washington, DC.

48. Race and Ethnicity in 2001: Attitudes, Perceptions, and Experience. The Henry J. Kaiser Foundation, Menlo Park, CA. [Available: www.kff.org]

49. Howard, *Contemporary Cultural Anthropology.*

50. Halford, W. K., Hahlweg, K., & Dunne, M. "The Cross-Cultural Consistency of Marital Communication Associated with Marital Distress," *Journal of Marriage and the Family* 52, (1990), 487–501.

51. "Polygamy: The Truth" (www.moslem.org/polygamy/htm); K. Armstrong, "Polygamy in Islam" (1998) (twf.org/Library/Polygamy.html).

52. Howard, *Contemporary Cultural Anthropology.*

53. Buss, D. M. "Mate Preferences in Thirty-Seven Cultures," in *Psychology and Culture,* ed. W. J. Lonner and R. Malpass (Boston: Allyn & Bacon, 1994), pp. 197–202; Buss, D. M. "Sex Differences in Human Mate Preference: Evolutionary Hypotheses Tested in Thirty-Seven Cultures," *Behavioral and Brain Sciences* 12 (1989), 1–49.

54. Ibid.

55. Ibid.

56. Ibid., p. 200.

57. Ibid.

58. The account was provided by Katie Thao in a personal communication in the summer of 1995.

59. Lor, H. "The Hmong" (unpublished student manuscript, St. Norbert College, De Pere, Wisc., 1997).

60. Hoffman, J. "Arranged Marriage in India: Rules Governing the Process" (unpublished student manuscript, St. Norbert College, De Pere, Wisc., 1997).

61. Pretty, K. "Marriage in Iran: A Changing Way of Life" (unpublished student manuscript, St. Norbert College, De Pere, Wisc., 1997).

62. Sinnen, R. "Arranged Marriages in Traditional Pakistani Culture" (unpublished student manuscript, St. Norbert College, De Pere, Wisc., 1997).

63. Renkens, S. "Pro Nakodo Arranged Marriages" (unpublished student manuscript, St. Norbert College, De Pere, Wisc., 1997).

64. Elliot, D. "Trying to Stand on Two Feet," *Newsweek* 313 (1998), 48–50.

65. Gage-Brandon, A. J. "The Polygyny-Divorce Relationship: A Case Study of Nigeria," *Journal of Marriage and the Family* 54 (1992), 285–293.

66. "China: Divorce Increase and Change Affect Women," *Women's International Network News* 20 (1994), 59.

67. Hall, D. R. "Marriage as a Pure Relationship: Exploring the Link between Premarital Cohabitation and Divorce in Canada," *Journal of Comparative Family Studies* 27 (1996), 1–12.

68. "Not Such a Family Affair," *The Economist* 321 (1991), 69–71.

69. Gidron, A. "War on Families," *World Press Review* 40 (1993), 35.

70. "Russian Business Women Are Moving Up Slowly," *Women's International Network News* 24 (1998), 75.

71. Stack, S. "The Effect of Divorce on Suicide in Japan: A Time Series Analysis, 1950–1980," *Journal of Marriage and the Family* 54 (1992), 327–335.

72. Ho, M. K. *Family Therapy with Ethnic Minorities* (Beverly Hills, Calif.: Sage, 1987).

73. Popenoe, D. "Family Decline in the Swedish Welfare State," *Public Interest* 102 (1991), 65–78.

74. Grier, P. "New Census Bureau Portrait of the American Landscape," *Christian Science Monitor* 88 (1996, March 6), 69.

75. Oggins, J., Veroff, J., & Leber, D. "Perceptions of Marital Interaction Among Black and White Newlyweds," *Journal of Personality and Social Psychology* 65 (1993), 494–511.

CHAPTER 10

Intercultural Communication in Organizations

However objective and uniform we try to make organizations, they will not have the same meaning for individuals from different cultures.

—Fons Trompenaars[1]

Chapter Objectives

After reading this chapter, you should be able to

1. Discuss how dimensions of the cultural context affect organizations across cultures.

2. Identify how the environmental context affects doing business in other cultures.

3. Identify variables in the perceptual context and how they influence business with other cultures.

4. Compare and contrast socio-relational contexts on the job across cultures.

5. Discuss some verbal and nonverbal differences across cultures.

6. Compare managerial styles of Japanese, Germans, Mexicans, and Arabs.

7. Describe differences in manager-subordinate relationships in Japan, Germany, Mexico, and Arab countries.

Coordinating and managing people from different cultures within an organizational context represents one of the greatest challenges for the corporate world in the new millennium. Businesses and organizations from virtually every culture have entered into the global marketplace. In the United States, our top export partners include (in order) Canada, Mexico, Japan, United Kingdom, and China. In early 1994, the United States, Canada, and Mexico set in motion the North American Free Trade Agreement (NAFTA), which generated the largest free-trade area in the world. Although NAFTA will not be fully implemented until the year 2008, in 2004, U.S. trade with Canada and Mexico represented 31 percent of all U.S. foreign trade.[2]

Within our borders as well, the face of U.S. business is becoming more and more intercultural. In 1997, there were three million minority-owned businesses in the United States, employing 4.5 million people and generating nearly 600 billion dollars in revenues. These firms made up 15 percent of the nation's 21 million nonfarm businesses, employed four percent of its workers, and generated three percent of its receipts. Of these firms, Hispanics or Latinos owned 1.2 million (40%), more than any other group. Their firms generated 190 billion dollars in revenues. Asians and Pacific Islanders owned just over 900,000 businesses, accounting for revenues of 300 billion dollars, which led all groups in revenues. African Americans were owners of 823,000 businesses that generated 70 billion dollars in revenues.[3]

Given the dramatic cultural transformation in today's marketplace, the relevance of intercultural communication competence cannot be overstated. To compete in the global and U.S. markets, today's managers must possess the skills to interact with people who are different from themselves.

INTERCULTURAL MANAGEMENT

The purpose of this chapter is to introduce some of the salient issues affecting intercultural management. This chapter will take the components of the model of intercultural communication introduced in Chapter 1 and apply them to intercultural management. First, the cultural context within organizations will be explored prior to a discussion of the environmental context. Next, the chapter will identify the variables in the perceptual context and how they affect business in other cultures. The chapter will then compare and contrast socio-relational job contexts across cultures, along with some verbal and nonverbal differences. Finally, the chapter examines managerial practices among Japanese, German, Mexican, and Arab managers. The chapter concludes with a model of intercultural conflict.

Table 10.1   Top Three Organizational Success Factors

Japan	*Germany*	*United States*
1. Product Development (54)	Work Force Skills (63)	Customer Service (52)
2. Management (41)	Problem Solving (47)	Product Quality (40)
3. Product Quality (36)	Management (44)	Technology (36)

There is no culture-free theory of management. Managing other people is the responsibility of people who, like everyone else, have been enculturated and socialized into a cultural set of values and beliefs that governs their thinking, emotions, and behaviors. Like communication, management is culture bound. Moreover, managerial perceptions regarding the factors that lead to organizational success vary across cultures. For example, in her survey of more than 12,000 managers, Rosabeth Moss Kanter asked them to rate factors they considered important for their organization's success. The top-rated factors varied considerably across cultures. Table 10.1 shows ratings by managers in the United States, Japan, and Germany. The numbers in parentheses refer to the percentage of managers checking that particular factor.[4]

Unfortunately, many U.S. managers are ill equipped to handle overseas assignments. For example, 20 percent of U.S. managers sent abroad are asked to return home because of poor performance. Moreover, only 11 percent of managers receive promotions after completion of an overseas assignment, and nearly 80 percent are demoted. Although fostering competent intercultural communication managerial skills represents an enormous challenge, the rewards of successful international commerce are extraordinary. Managers are receiving a different message than they did only a few years ago; now, to be promoted to top levels of the organization, an overseas assignment is virtually a prerequisite. Gayle Kosterman, a vice president for S. C. Johnson & Son (makers of Pledge and Windex), states that the top managers must have a sense of the global marketplace, particularly of how it differs from the U.S. market. Each year Johnson selects its best new employees and devises for them a five-year career plan that includes a one- or two-year overseas assignment. Many corporations simply expect that to advance in the ranks, one must have international experience. Seventy-five percent of Citicorp's top officers have completed assignments outside the United States. Major businesses such as AT&T, GE Medical Systems, and Motorola have initiated cross-cultural development programs for their overseas managers. The managers, along with their families, engage in intense cultural and language programs designed to increase the probability of success.[5]

Professor Philip Rosenzweig of Harvard University argues that successful cross-cultural management depends on the abilities of managers to communicate effectively. Rosenzweig points out that communication is especially important during the initial stages of a business relationship. Depending on the culture, the process of building trust among business partners may take days, weeks, or even months. Moreover, Rosenzweig asserts, this process cannot be accelerated. Rosenzweig recognizes that many American managers prefer to "get down to business" without spending much time getting to know their business partners. In fact, according to Rosenzweig, many American managers view such relationship building as a waste of valuable time. Rosenzweig argues that investing the time and energy in building trust and developing relationships may pay huge benefits in terms of confidence and trust.[6]

Perceptions of time and timing are also important considerations in cross-cultural business exchanges. Rosenzweig recommends that American managers allow the pace of negotiations to develop on its own. He cautions managers not to impose artificial deadlines for the sake of efficiency. How agreement and disagreement are communicated is another important factor during cross-cultural negotiations. Rosenzweig points out that American managers tend to favor forthrightness during negotiations. In many other cultures, such directness may be seen as rude and discourteous. Finally, Rosenzweig points out that the specificity with which a contract is written may vary considerably across cultures. In the United States, we tend to favor explicit contracts that include a great deal of precise wording covering all aspects of the agreement. In some cultures this may be interpreted as a sign of distrust. Many cultures prefer very general contracts. Such cultures place significance on trust and mutual obligation rather than on formalized agreement.[7]

Most of what you have been exposed to in this textbook can be applied to your role in organizational settings across cultures. The topics and issues discussed in each chapter can guide you in becoming a successful intercultural manager. Most businesses and organizations can be thought of as mini-cultures, each representing a pattern of values held by a recognizable group of people with a common goal pursued by means of a collective verbal and nonverbal symbol system. Like cultures themselves, organizations possess value systems, exist in some environmental context, process information with a unique perceptual perspective, develop socio-relations with others, and communicate using distinctive verbal and nonverbal codes. As you prepare to conduct business with persons in organizations from different cultures or microcultures, you cannot assume that your business practices will be understood or accepted by your counterpart. Figure 10.1 outlines some of the more salient issues that affect the development of organizational culture in any culture.

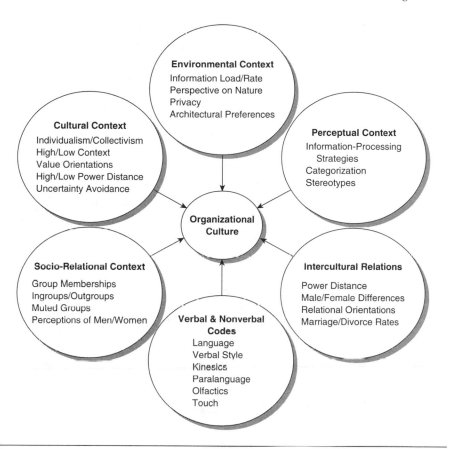

Figure 10.1

Prior to entering into a business transaction with an organization from a different culture or microculture, you should conduct an extensive organizational analysis. This model can help. In your analysis, take into account your foreign partner's cultural, environmental, perceptual, and socio-relational contexts as well as the verbal and nonverbal code system and the nature of the relationships you are about to initiate.

The Cultural Context

First, consider the cultural context of an organization. Organizational culture often parallels country culture. Hence, if values differ significantly across cultures, then the management practices of those cultures are also likely to differ. In their study of twelve countries, Bass and Burger found that cultural differences accounted for differences in managers' goals, risk taking, pragmatism, interpersonal competence, emotional stability, and leadership style. In similar research Adler, Campbell, and Laurent found that cultural values, beliefs, and norms affected managers' leadership style and organizational strategies.[8]

When managing people from other cultures, try to ascertain where on the individualism/collectivism continuum an organization falls. Organizations in collectivistic cultures are more likely to emphasize group harmony and teamwork. For example, Mitsui Group of Japan, one of the largest cross-ownership companies in Japan, with nearly one thousand subsidiaries and associates worldwide, including Toyota and Toshiba, employs almost eight thousand people and lists group harmony as its number one corporate value. Similarly, Apple Computer workers in Singapore listed teamwork and reserve as their number one and two (respectively) corporate values. However, these same employees indicated that individualism was the number one value of Apple Computer workers in the United States.[9]

AN INTERCULTURAL CONVERSATION: CLASHING CULTURAL CONCEPTS ON THE JOB

In the following conversation, American businessman Jim Neumouth is applying for a job in Japanese businessman Kietaro Matsumoto's corporation, located in Kyoto, Japan.

Kietaro:	*So, Mr. Neumouth, why would you like to work for our corporation?*
Jim:	*I believe I have the necessary skills and experience for this position. I'm very independent, I set very high goals for myself, and I believe your company will allow me to pursue them.*
Kietaro:	*What do you mean by "goals"?*
Jim:	*I have very high sales objectives. I try to reach the top in whatever I do. One of my goals is to become your leading salesperson. For example, I had the highest percentage of sales of anyone in the company I worked for in the United States. I was named salesperson of the year in 2005.*
Kietaro:	*I see, that's very impressive.*
Jim:	*Thanks. Now I'd like to expand into an international market, and I'd like to bring my experience and motivation to your company. I think I can be the best here, too.*

In the above conversation, Mr. Neumouth does a good job of expressing his talents and experience. In the United States, he might appear like the ideal candidate. However, to Mr. Matsumoto, he does not appear to be a team player because he may disrupt the harmony of his sales teams.

Therefore, when doing business with companies in collective cultures, it may be wise to formulate strategies that are consistent with group unity. Strategies that are perceived to promote the individual within the organization may be frowned upon (see page 380). Also keep in mind that reaching a decision in collectivistic organizations sometimes takes much longer than in individualistic organizations. Often, collectivists go to great pains to win everyone over in order to achieve consensus.

Power distance is another important cultural influence to assess when dealing with organizations across cultures. Recall from Chapter 2 that Malaysia ranked at the top of the power distance index (indicating high power distance). A recent survey indicated that the highest-rated values of middle-level managers of Petronas Corporation, the Malaysian state-owned oil company, included status consciousness (position, degree); top-down communication; and welfare of the employees. Petronas owns Petronas Towers, which in 1996 became the world's tallest office building, surpassing Chicago's Sears Tower, which had held that record since 1974. Hence, when planning business with Petronas or other Malaysian companies, be prepared to treat your counterpart with more humility and formality than you might expect from your U.S. partners.[10]

Uncertainty avoidance is another important consideration. Because the United States is a low-uncertainty-avoidant culture, the U.S. marketplace is associated with a great deal of risk. In fact, middle-line managers at Advanced Micro Devices, a U.S.-based company, indicate that aggressiveness and risk taking are the top two values guiding their company. Risky business propositions are likely to be rejected by cultures high in uncertainty avoidance, however.[11]

Detelin Elenkov has investigated cultural differences between Russia and the United States. He argues that Russia is more collectivistic and has a higher power distance and higher uncertainty avoidance than the United States. In his comparison of managers and business students from Russia and the United States, Elenkov found that the Russians scored higher than the persons from the United States on measures of collectivism, power distance, and uncertainty avoidance. In discussing his research, Elenkov argues that the results of his study support the contention that managerial values closely parallel cultural values.[12]

The Environmental Context

Consider the following scenario:

You have traveled to Korea to meet with your Korean counterpart, whom you have never met in person but with whom you have communicated through letters, e-mail, and so forth. You arrive at his office building at the appointed time. The weather in Seoul today is incredibly hot and humid. As you enter the floor of your partner's office, you notice that there are no walls separating the various desks. The scene appears very relaxed to you. Most of the men are sitting around in their undershirts. When you locate your partner, you find him sitting with his feet up on the desk, in his undershirt, fanning himself. When you introduce yourself, your Korean partner acts as if nothing has happened and puts on a shirt, tie, and jacket in a very matter-of-fact way. Your meeting now begins.

In addition to assessing an organization's cultural context, it is important to assess its perspective on the environment, including such issues as information load, privacy, and the company's overall orientation to nature. Recall from Chapter 4 that some cultures believe they can master nature, whereas others attempt to live in harmony with it, and still others believe they are subjugated by it. International business expert Fons Trompenaars suggests that a culture's perspective on nature often translates into its organizational practices. Paralleling their culture's attitude toward nature, some organizations believe they can control market forces and create new markets where none exists. Others attempt a balancing act with the market, sometimes trying to influence and at other times adjusting to its fluctuations. Still others believe that the market is in control, and they simply react to it. Trompenaars points to Indonesia as a culture that sees itself as controlled by external forces (e.g., nature, the marketplace). In Indonesia, incentive programs designed to motivate employees may fail because they consider market changes to be natural and arbitrary. To them it makes no sense to attribute blame or lack of incentive to those who are caught in a market downturn. Moreover, it makes even less sense to reward those who have the fortune of being in a market upturn. As Trompenaars notes, to either blame or reward may deplete the morale of the team by simply adding to the randomness of events.[13]

A culture's tolerance of, and comfort with, varying information rates should also be ascertained. In cultures such as the United States, managers often prefer to have as much factual information as possible before making decisions. Statistics, sales projections, historical trends, and so forth all help them with decision making. In some Arab cultures, however, decision making is fairly inexact and rests on the manager's personal position in the organization, his intuition, and his religious beliefs.[14]

Assumptions about privacy are also important considerations to take into account. In collectivistic cultures, for example, in which group harmony is paramount, employees may prefer to work together in the same physical location, not isolated by office walls and doors. Many U.S. corporations have borrowed the Japanese model of an open working environment devoid of private offices. Imagine what the reaction might be if a U.S. corporation hired a group of Japanese managers and put each in his or her own private office, or if a U.S. manager in Japan requested a private space. The scenario presented at the beginning of this section is based on a fascinating discussion of privacy in Korea by Philip Harris and Robert Moran. They report that in Korea, privacy is a luxury that few possess or can afford. Because privacy may be impossible to obtain physically, Koreans build imaginary and/or psychological walls around themselves. A client calling on a Korean on a typically hot and humid day may actually find this person in his undershirt with his feet on his desk, fanning himself. Because there are no physical walls, the informed visitor coughs to announce his arrival. Harris and Moran allege that although the person he has come to visit is in clear view, the visitor pretends not to "see" him. Moreover, the Korean does not "see" the visitor. Only after he has risen and put on his shirt, coat, and tie and adjusted himself, do they "see" each other and introduce themselves. According to Harris and Moran, in order to secure some level of privacy, Koreans retreat behind a psychological curtain and do what they have to do, not being seen by those who are in plain view. To violate the screen of privacy once it has been created is rude and discourteous.[15]

The Perceptual Context

The perceptual context of the individual, learned through enculturation, is often manifest in the organization. Understanding how the organization processes information is crucial to establishing and maintaining effective communication. One information-processing strategy in which people from all cultures engage is categorizing and stereotyping. Before embarking on a business venture with a foreign culture, it may be useful to know of the culture's stereotypes of U.S. business practices. Harris and Moran surveyed what Arab business managers thought of U.S. managers working in the Middle East. The results shed light on why so many U.S. managers have difficulty working in Arab countries.[16] Arab managers believe that

1. Americans think they are superior.

2. Americans take credit for everything, even in joint efforts.

3. Americans do not adjust to or respect the local customs.

4. Americans refuse to work through normal administrative channels.

5. Americans lose their democratic ways when working in foreign cultures.

Most Americans have been brought up to think in very logical, linear, and rational terms. We prefer to make decisions on the basis of empirical (verifiable through direct observation) data. Many of our business decisions are based on the logic that the shortest distance between two points is a straight line. Such thinking permeates our business transactions. Asian employers, however, may be guided by their intuition and base their decisions on trial and error. They may get sidetracked or take multiple paths to get to the same point. Chinese, for example, are known to be very patient and to take their time in making decisions, a characteristic that sometimes frustrates their American business counterparts. Remember, the way a person processes information is very much influenced by his or her enculturation.

The Socio-Relational Context

An organization's emphasis on group membership is clearly something that U.S. managers should know about their foreign counterparts. As mentioned in Chapter 6, all people of all cultures belong to groups. One of the primary groups to which all people belong is the family. Recall that Chapter 6 profiled family life across a variety of cultures. Trompenaars employs a family metaphor in describing a particular type of ideal corporate culture seen often in Turkey, Venezuela, Hong Kong, Malaysia, India, Singapore, and Spain. This does not mean that all corporations in these countries are family-like; it simply means that this prototype is seen more frequently in these cultures than in others.

According to Trompenaars, the family corporation culture is simultaneously personal, with close face-to-face relationships, and hierarchical in the sense that everyone knows his or her place in the rank order. At the top of the hierarchy are the parents (the chief executives), who are regarded as caring and as knowing better than the children (the subordinates). The power at the top is perceived not as threatening, but as intimate and benign. The philosophy of the employees is to do more than is required contractually to please the older brother or father (the person of higher rank). Trompenaars notes that the primary reason for working hard and performing well in this type of corporate culture is the pleasure derived from familial relations. To please one's elders is reward in itself. The main sanction for poor performance is loss of affection and place in the family. In the family corporate culture, pressures to perform are moral and social rather than financial and/or legal.

Trompenaars argues that family corporate cultures sometimes experience difficulty with project-group organization, in which authority is divided. Moreover, U.S. businesses dealing with family-oriented cultures often see

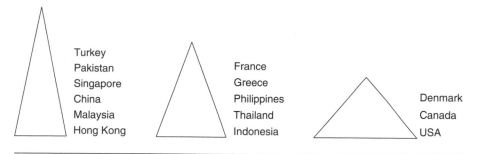

Figure 10.2

Source: Adapted from F. Trompenaars, *Riding the Waves of Culture: Understanding Diversity in Global Business* (Burr Ridge, Ill.: Irwin, 1994).

them as nepotistic (that is, as practicing favoritism or patronage, usually with family members). In many instances, such corporations literally hire and promote bona fide family members over other candidates who may be more qualified. Trompenaars notes that the strict hierarchy in family corporations is akin (metaphorically) to the gradient angle of a triangle. The steeper the angle, the stricter the hierarchy. The hierarchy in the family-oriented corporation *is* analogous to the steep triangles depicted in Figure 10.2.[17]

Verbal and Nonverbal Codes

Obviously, understanding the verbal and nonverbal codes of your foreign counterpart is an essential part of a successful business venture. Although it is true that most of your foreign business partners will speak some English, your knowledge and use of their language demonstrates your willingness to meet them halfway and will be very much appreciated. International business expert Roger Axtell argues that although most of the representatives of international corporations speak English, the English spoken in the United States is of such a type that it is not understood by foreigners. In a survey of persons doing business overseas with a foreign corporation, Axtell found that 80 percent had difficulties interacting with foreigners because of the latter's misunderstanding of American English. However, the same respondents reported that the problem lay with them, not their foreign counterparts. The type of English spoken in the United States is so laden with jargon, colloquialisms, and slang that English-speaking foreigners have a very difficult time understanding us. Most foreigners learn "standard" English and are unfamiliar with how Americans actually use the language. As Axtell notes, American business is perhaps the worst offender in language proliferation. Axtell points out what he calls the "seven deadliest sins" of international misunderstanding:

local color, jargon, slang, officialese, humor, vocabulary, and grammar.[18] When conducting business with your foreign counterpart, be very conscious of terms and phrases that may be well understood within your corporation but may be misunderstood by an outsider. At St. Norbert College, for example, women's groups such as sororities annually select an "Ugly Man" to represent their group in homecoming activities. An "Ugly Man" is analogous to a homecoming king. Imagine how a foreigner might respond to seeing "Ugly Man" on a potential client's resume! Axtell recalls a U.S. firm that lost an international client by using the phrase "This is a whole new ballgame" during sensitive renegotiations of a contract. Apparently the client did not consider the negotiations a "game" and terminated their relationship. Consider the slang, jargon, and colloquialisms listed in the box on the next page and how they might be misinterpreted across cultures.

Axtell recommends that when verbally communicating with your foreign host, you should not speak too quickly or too slowly. Fast is difficult to comprehend, whereas slow is offensive and condescending. Finally, Axtell remembers a piece of advice given to him by a well-traveled vice president, who recommended talking with your foreign host as if answering a somewhat hard-of-hearing, wealthy old aunt who just asked you how much money to leave you in her will.[19]

Another important consideration here is the use of a mediator. Unlike U.S. businesspeople, who enjoy face-to-face encounters and direct bargaining, some Asian cultures, such as China, save face by negotiating through the use of a mediator. In addition, because of their emphasis on the group, the overuse of personal pronouns, for example, is perceived negatively.

AN INTERCULTURAL CONVERSATION: MISINTERPRETATION OF COMMON U.S. PHRASES

American Phrase	Foreign Interpretation
"See ya later."	*To schedule a definite future contact.*
"Y'all come for another visit."	*Bring more people next time. "Y'all" interpreted to mean "more."*
"You're on a roll."	*I look like a hot dog or hamburger?*
"Let's use a shotgun approach."	*Shoot our competition?*

"Let's organize this like a Chinese menu."	*Very offensive to Chinese counterparts.*
"Send me your response ASAP."	*Have no idea what you're talking about.*
"I have to find a bathroom."	*You're going to take a bath now?*
"It'll take me the better part of the day to finish this report."	*Which is the better part? Morning, midday, or evening?*
"We need to cover all the bases."	*Do we need a blanket?*

One's verbal style is of utmost importance in situations where managers need to resolve conflicts with coworkers from different cultures. For example, American managers often misinterpret silence used by their Asian (e.g., Chinese, Japanese, Korean) coworkers. Asians characteristically express objection with silence. U.S. managers often interpret the silence as an expression of consent. Similarly, many Asian managers misread U.S. managers' directness in communication. Asians often see directness as unreasonable and disrespectful. Morris and his colleagues point out that Asian managers typically use an avoiding style of conflict resolution characterized as low levels of assertiveness and cooperativeness. The avoiding manager tends to evade conflict. Conversely, U.S. managers favor a competing style of conflict resolution, characterized as high levels of assertiveness and low levels of cooperativeness. The competing manager confronts conflict directly and forcefully.[20]

Although your knowing your foreign partner's language (and his or her knowing yours) is certainly an advantage, there are other communication considerations, independent of verbal language, that can affect your business propositions—most notably nonverbal communication. As discussed in Chapter 8, nonverbal communication varies a great deal across cultures. One's kinesic, paralinguistic, olfactory, haptic, and proxemic behaviors can be interpreted differently depending on with whom one is interacting. For example, greetings occur in all cultures and are typically ritualized to that culture. In the United States, businesspersons typically greet each other with a firm handshake and direct eye contact. In the Middle East, however, a limp handshake is preferred. Moreover, many Middle Eastern men will hold hands with their male counterparts as a display of trust in the business deal. Most U.S. businessmen would find such behavior disquieting, to say the least. Direct eye contact should also be avoided during greetings in many Asian cultures, where it is interpreted as a challenge or as an instigation of conflict. In what

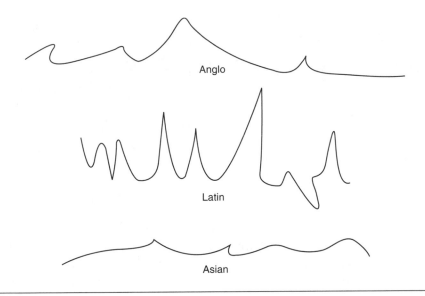

Anglo

Latin

Asian

Figure 10.3

Source: Adapted from F. Trompenaars, *Riding the Waves of Culture: Understanding Diversity in Global Business* (Burr Ridge, Ill.: Irwin, 1994).

may seem like unusual rituals, some East African tribesmen greet each other by spitting at each other's feet, and Tibetan men greet each other by sticking out their tongues.[21]

In addition to kinesics, Trompenaars notes that one's tone of voice may prove crucial during cross-cultural business transactions. Tone of voice can communicate much about the person speaking. Figure 10.3 shows characteristic paralinguistic patterns for Anglo, Latin, and Asian cultures.

Trompenaars suggests that fluctuations and variations in vocal pitch carry different meanings across cultures. For example, in Latin-American cultures, exaggerated ups and downs in pitch communicate that the individual is actively involved in what is being said. Many Asian cultures, however, prefer a more monotonous style, which communicates self-control and respect for the person with whom one is communicating. Most Anglo speakers are in between the Latin and Asian models. Trompenaars recalls the story of a British manager in Nigeria who raised his voice during meetings and presentations. The Nigerians perceived his way of speaking as positive and as demonstrative of his concern for the issues. The same manager was relocated to Malaysia, where he employed the same vocal style, but in Malaysia he was perceived negatively and was quickly transferred out.[22]

Other channels of nonverbal communication are equally important in the cross-cultural business exchange but are often overlooked—for example, olfactics, or smell. Most Americans are taught to bathe frequently and to mask as much of the natural odor of the human body as possible. To other cultures we smell antiseptic. Koreans, for example, have been known to call American businesspersons "butter-breath." Apparently our use of dairy products is evident in our breath.

INTERCULTURAL RELATIONS

As mentioned throughout this textbook, especially in Chapters 6 and 9, perceptions of relationships vary dramatically across cultures. Especially important are male/female relations within corporations. Although women have made great strides in the U.S. corporate world, in many cultures women still occupy a subordinate role and are treated as second-class citizens. Because of this situation, more than half (54 percent) of multinational corporations in North America say they are hesitant to send female managers abroad for fear that the host culture's perspective on women will have a negative impact on their effectiveness. According to Nancy Adler, many countries simply do not promote women into management positions. In Japan, reports Adler, women are encouraged to obtain the level of education that will enable them to *marry* managers rather than attain management positions for themselves. In fact, according to Adler, many large Japanese corporations encourage female employees to marry male employees, then use the company's antinepotism policies to force the women to retire. Moreover, one-third of Japanese companies indicate that they will not promote female college graduates even if they are as qualified as their male counterparts. Even in Europe, reports Adler, opposition to women in high-level management is quite strong. In one survey, nearly 70 percent of British managers said they preferred male applicants for executive positions. Likewise, two-thirds of Italian managers said they did not want to receive orders from female managers. In Germany, nearly 95 percent of job advertisements for top executives use the masculine noun form, thereby discouraging women from even applying for the position. There are encouraging signs, however, especially for American women entering the international market. According to Adler, in many cultures, foreign women (for example, Americans) are much better received in management positions than local women. Moreover, many women managing abroad have achieved excellent results, thereby encouraging U.S. corporations to continue sending women abroad. In addition, the success of U.S. women abroad encourages the local community to hire more of their own women into management positions.[23]

As more and more U.S. businesses enter the intensely competitive global marketplace, they will be confronted with myriad management styles, especially within those cultures with whom we do much business. In 2004, three of the United States' top five trading partners were Mexico, Japan, and the Federal Republic of Germany. Because Mexico, Japan, and Germany represent such important trading partners, their cultures and management practices will be profiled next. Then, a discussion about doing business in the Middle East will follow.

Japanese Management Practices

Japan is a country of nearly 130 million people, including a work force of 64 million. According to the U.S. Department of State, per capita income is just over $25,000 a year. Japan is considered an urban culture because only about 7 percent of the work force is engaged in agriculture. Japan's $4.7 trillion economy is the second largest in the world. After maintaining one of the highest economic growth rates in the world from the 1960s through the 1980s, the Japanese economy slowed significantly in the 1990s. According to the U.S. State Department, the economic relationship between Japan and the United States is quite healthy. Although it has taken time and patience, American businesses are competing successfully in Japanese markets.[24]

As American/Japanese business relationships continue to develop, managers and workers from both countries will be expected to communicate with each other. In so doing, they may find very different work ethics and managerial styles. First, the Japanese corporation is very paternalistic (i.e., fatherly, patriarchal). Most Japanese corporations furnish their workers with a host of services and social activities designed to foster allegiance and group harmony. A typical Japanese worker may spend as many as four hours a day commuting to and from work in Tokyo. It is not at all uncommon for a Japanese worker to spend as many as fifteen hours a day on the job. He (they are mostly men) is expected to be at work early and to remain there until late at night, six days a week. Many Japanese work groups begin their day by exercising together, called *taiso*. Interestingly, the primary purpose of the *taiso* is not for physical benefits, but to get the group members engaging in coordinated activity. After the day's work is finished, businesses encourage their employees to eat and drink together to maintain harmonious group relationships. Though it may appear that such activity is for purely social reasons, the underlying motivation is to continue work. According to Brown, Lubove, and Kwalwasser, the typical Japanese worker spends more than 2,500 hours on the job every year, compared with about 1,900 hours for the typical U.S. worker. In their interviews of Japanese managers, Brown, Lubove, and Kwalwasser found that because many Japanese workers spend their entire working careers with one company, maintaining harmony with their colleagues is considered a prime motive. Brown and his colleagues also found that, on average, Japanese managers are less than satisfied with their jobs, perhaps because of the stress of long hours.[25]

Robert Bolda of the University of Michigan asked Japanese and American managers to list the skills, behaviors, traits, or other attributes that they thought were characteristic of productive supervisors. Although there was a broad range of agreement between the Japanese and American managers, there were some interesting disagreements (see box).

Traits Characteristic of Productive Supervisors

Traits Endorsed by Japanese and American Managers	Traits Endorsed by American Managers	Traits Endorsed by Japanese Managers
Prioritizes tasks	Works well with people	Open to innovation
Motivates employees	Delegates	Good listener
Communicates clearly	Considers alternatives	Puts right person in right job
Leadership	States expectations	Thinks in future tense
Makes good use of resources	Good speaker	Thinks about the "big picture"
Decision-making ability	Can shift attention	Helps other departments get job done
	Knowledgeable of company	Monitors employee progress

Traits Where Japanese and American Managers Differed the Most

Believes in his or her ability to get job done (Americans agreed/ Japanese disagreed)

Helps other departments get their job done (Americans disagreed/ Japanese agreed)

Delegates (Americans agreed/Japanese disagreed)

Reprimands and disciplines employees (Americans agreed/Japanese disagreed)

Monitors employees (Americans disagreed/Japanese agreed)

Source: Data from R. A. Bolda, "Correlates of Personal Productivity of Supervisors: Perceptions of American and Japanese Managers," *Current Psychology* 9 (1990), 339–346.

In reviewing the results of this survey, Bolda concluded that Japanese managers endorsed behaviors that were other-oriented and principle-oriented. For example, Japanese managers preferred traits that dealt with innovations, employee selection, and performance monitoring. The American managers, on the other hand, supported behaviors that were more instrumental—that is, goal-oriented—such as individual supervisory skills, belief in one's own ability, and decision making.[26] Although the Japanese and American managers in Bolda's survey agreed on many of the traits that constitute good management, the differences expressed by the two groups of managers may lead to communication problems on the job. Neil Abramson and his colleagues maintain that contract negotiations between Japanese and American firms are often difficult and frustrating. Abramson points out that the American preference for individualistic, rational decision making often clashes with the Japanese tendency toward relationships and group harmony. Moreover, Abramson points out that American and Japanese managers may require different kinds of information to solve problems or negotiate contracts. Americans, for example, tend to negotiate by exchanging information with the expectation that the other side will reciprocate. Furthermore, Americans have a tendency to focus on efficiency and quick closure to negotiations by pinpointing disagreements and attempting to resolve them promptly. Additionally, Americans do not highly value interpersonal relationships with their negotiation partners, instead allowing legal contracts to define future alliances. On the other hand, contends Abramson, Japanese negotiate by trying to foster steady relationships with their partners with the ultimate goal of consensus. Whereas Americans negotiate a contractual agreement, Japanese think of it as negotiating a relationship. During initial stages of a negotiation, Japanese are more interested in interpersonal attraction and deference toward their partner (as opposed to clearly identifying any disagreements). Instead of quickly reaching closure, Japanese prefer to take their time in order to establish relationships built on trust and deliberate negotiations.

In their comparison of North American and Japanese management students, Abramson and his colleagues found that the North Americans preferred a thinking-based cognitive style that is logical, impersonal, and objective. Abramson claims that such a style may lead to quick, impersonal, and analytically based decisions. In such cases, there may be a tendency to subordinate human relationships by discounting some kinds of information (for example, affiliation with partner) in favor of theoretically based models of decision making. The Japanese management students, on the other hand, preferred a feeling-based cognitive style that emphasizes the human element in decision making. Such a style, according to Abramson, expresses a concern for group harmony and a preference for friendly relations with one's partner. In decision making and in contract negotiations, Japanese may resist fast decisions and remain open to new information.[27]

Negotiating with the Japanese

A recent edition *of Manager's Intelligence Report* listed several recommendations for negotiating with the Japanese. The recommendations are based on case study analyses of a variety of U.S. firms doing business in Japan.

1. **Stay in the game.** Be prepared for long negotiations. The Japanese take their time to get to know you and your business. They want to establish a relationship before signing any deal.

2. **Understand the "need" principle.** The Japanese will try to create and count on the idea that you "need" their deal. Once you start believing that you might lose the much-needed deal, you lose face to them.

3. **Communicate with their top decision makers.** Too much time is wasted interacting with people who can't and won't make decisions.

4. **Suspend assumptions and expectations.** The deal isn't done until it's done. Do not assume that once you have an agreement it's a done deal.

5. **Focus on the Japanese rather than yourself.** Attend to what the Japanese need from you and demonstrate how you can accommodate them.

6. **Instead of telling them, let the Japanese discover what you want.** Negotiations in the United States are often characterized by one side explicitly telling the other side what it wants and needs. But to the Japanese the skill of negotiating is to allow your position to surface on its own.

Source: "What You Can Learn from Japanese Negotiation," *Manager's Intelligence Report,* (1996), 8–10.

In related research, Brett and Okumura studied the negotiation styles of U.S. and Japanese managers. They reasoned that because U.S. culture is individualistic and egalitarian and Japanese culture is collectivistic and hierarchical, managers from the two cultures would exercise different styles of negotiation. Their results showed that Japanese negotiators paid significantly more attention to power during negotiations than did U.S. negotiators. Brett and Okumura also found a difference in the two cultures' focus on self-interest during negotiations. The American negotiators were much more focused on self-interest than were the Japanese. The two researchers also found that joint gains in negotiations were significantly higher in intracultural negotiations than in intercultural ones. In other words, when U.S. managers negotiated with other U.S. managers, there were higher gains than when U.S. managers negotiated with Japanese managers. The same result was found among Japanese managers.[28]

In most organizations across cultures, managers are in positions of power and influence. As such, managers engage in a variety of behavioral strategies to influence the attitudes and behaviors of their subordinates. In a recent study, Rao, Hashimoto, and Rao surveyed Japanese managers regarding their preferences for a variety of influence strategies. Although some of the Japanese managers preferred influence tactics similar to those preferred by U.S. managers, Rao, Hashimoto, and Rao identified several strategies that appear to be unique to the Japanese. One strategy is labeled *firm's authority*. In contrast to American managers, who may appeal to "higher-ups" to influence their employees, Japanese managers do not appeal to a specific person in the organizational hierarchy, but to the entire organization itself, independent of their superiors. This strategy is probably linked to the Japanese concept of business organization as a family. A second type of strategy, called *personal development,* occurs when a Japanese manager convinces his (most managers are men) employees to comply with a request to enhance their careers within the organization. This tactic may be effective because many Japanese remain with a single company for their entire lives. American managers, on the other hand, convince employees that by complying with a request, the employees will develop skills they can take with them when they leave the organization.

Another strategy is labeled *socializing.* With this strategy, Japanese managers ask to spend time with their employees after hours. According to Rao, Hashimoto, and Rao, such a strategy allows for informal interaction between managers and subordinates that is impossible in the context of the formal work environment. Interestingly, Rao, Hashimoto, and Rao report that Japanese managers in Canada were disappointed when their subordinates rejected their requests to socialize after work. The Japanese managers felt that this severely limited their influence potential and had to resort to using assertive tactics on the job. Rao, Hashimoto, and Rao report that Japanese managers use a variety of tactics outside the work environment to influence their subordinates.

In general, Rao, Hashimoto, and Rao indicate that, compared with American managers, Japanese managers use influence tactics that are subtle and indirect. For example, if a Japanese manager wants a subordinate to focus on the Canadian market for a specific product, the manager, rather than telling him directly, might funnel information about that market to the employee, hoping that the employee would sense his intent. In addition, Japanese managers use strategies that rely on the influence of the organization and group harmony. Such strategies are associated with the three main principles of Japanese management practices: (1) lifetime employment, (2) promotion through seniority, and (3) consensus decision making.[29] The promotion system in Japanese companies is based almost exclusively on seniority. In contrast to the norm in many U.S. companies, the older employees get, the more enthused they become about their corporation and the more effectively they communicate their enthusiasm to the other employees. According to William Drake and Associates, work attitudes within an organization evolve from the senior members of the organization, who are ensured promotion and lifetime employment. One reason the older employees are so satisfied with their jobs is that they know that they are secure; they do not have to worry about the younger, more energetic employees jeopardizing their jobs.[30]

While interacting with Japanese businesspersons, Americans often notice behaviors that are widely misunderstood by non-Japanese (see Table 10.2). To be sure, the Japanese businessperson has perceptions of American behavior that may be misinterpreted as well. For example, Japanese are astonished by the typical American's informality and spontaneity. The quick pace of conversation and what are perceived to be ostentatious—that is, flashy or showy—nonverbal mannerisms are off-putting to most Japanese. In fact, many Japanese believe that Americans are inclined to make mistakes because of the fast pace with which they conduct business dealings. The "don't take it personally—it's just business" attitude portrayed by most American businesspersons intimidates Japanese because to them it disrupts the harmony of the business relationship. The Japanese tend to view conversations and negotiations as formalized rituals rather than as a meeting of minds.[31]

German Management Practices

Although there have been fluctuations in the German economy since reunification, in 1997 the German economy was slowly growing at a rate of about 2.5 percent; it is now the fourth largest economy in the world. The U.S. Department of State maintains that the German market, the largest in Europe, is attractive to many U.S. businesses. Germans are attracted to innovative products that display high quality and contemporary styling. They are especially interested in high-tech products, particularly those that assist them in entering the age of the Internet.[32]

Table 10.2

American Perception	Japanese Reality
1. The Japanese are really shy.	1. As a high-context culture, the Japanese do not feel a need to talk. They are comfortable with silence.
2. Japanese fall asleep a lot during class or presentations.	2. Many Japanese close their eyes when they are deeply concentrating.
3. Japanese say yes even when they mean no. Why can't they just say what they mean?	3. To save face (yours and theirs), Japanese will agree with you in principle.
4. It takes Japanese forever to make decisions or even to respond to a fax or written correspondence.	4. Japanese will not make a decision without first consulting relevant others to reach a consensus.
5. Japanese will never look you in the eye.	5. Indirect eye contact is a sign of deference in Japan.
6. When Japanese talk, they seem so ambiguous. I never know what they're trying to say or what they really mean.	6. Japanese language is vague. But even more, to the Japanese, communication is a two-way process. The burden of understanding rests with the speaker and the listener. Often, the speaker will only hint at what is meant. The listener must be an active participant.

Source: Table adapted from pages 410-412 of *When Cultures Collide* by R. D. Lewis. Copyright © 2000 Nicholas Brealey Publishing. Used by permission. (London: Nicholas Brealey, 1997).

Like the United States and Europe in general, Germany is a decentralized collection of states and regions. Many are quite diverse, with unique customs and conventions. The northern and the southern regions are particularly different, so generalizing about Germany is difficult and should be approached with some degree of caution. According to intercultural consultants William Drake and Associates, most Germans believe that people are controlled by their own actions, that facts are more important than face (in sharp contrast to the Japanese), and that factual honesty is more important than politeness (again, clashing with Japanese conventions). According to Drake, German children are taught that useless people amount to nothing, and that they are to be quiet and respectful. Children are also taught to "save for a rainy day."[33]

Focusing their analysis primarily on West Germans, anthropologists Edward and Mildred Hall contend that compartmentalization is the most prominent structural feature of German culture—that is, that Germans have a tendency to isolate and divide many aspects of their lives into discrete, independent units. Germans are known to compartmentalize their daily schedules, educational system, office buildings, corporations, homes, and even lines of communication. In fact, Hall and Hall argue that on the job, Germans will not share information with others except within their own working groups. Hall and Hall maintain that such a restricted flow of information may be the biggest obstacle in doing business with the Germans. One result of German compartmentalization is a culture in which significant events and changes can take place without people knowing about them. Even informal information networks that connect public and private organizational boundaries are rare in Germany.[34] Given this condition, U.S. companies wishing to do business in Germany would be wise to understand that they may not be able to operate out of a centralized location. Instead, they may have to set up multiple sites from which to conduct commerce.

German emphasis on compartmentalization manifests itself in many areas of German life and business, particularly with respect to privacy and specialization. Germans are a very private (and formal) people. Most German managers isolate themselves in their offices behind closed doors, contrasting sharply with open-door policies exercised by American managers. Doors are an important cultural symbol to the Germans. According to Hall and Hall, doors provide a protective shield between the individual and outsiders. When encountering a closed door in German businesses or homes, an "intruder" should always knock. As Hall and Hall note, closed doors uphold the honor of the space; afford a boundary between people; and eliminate the possibility of eavesdropping, interruptions, and accidental intrusions. Moreover, according to Hall and Hall, within corporations, the closed door indicates that a manager respects the privacy of subordinates and is not looking over their shoulders.[35]

German compartmentalization can also be seen in the overall market strategy of many very successful German corporations. Unlike many U.S. or Japanese corporate conglomerates whose global market success is attributable to diversification, many German firms concentrate on specialization—that is, doing one thing and doing it right. German corporations with large shares of specialized markets can focus on design, quality, and service rather than on competing with price. Such corporations manufacture a smaller and narrower class of products, sell to fewer consumers, and contract with fewer suppliers than their less successful competition. To be sure, many of these exclusive products are expensive. But the Germans believe that specialization leads to quality and profit. German products are known worldwide for their high caliber and workmanship (for example, Mercedes, BMW). Steiner Optik maintains 80 percent of the global market for military field glasses. Krones manufactures over 70 percent of the world's bottle labeling machines. The Germans seem to be teaching the rest of the world that, at least for them, specialization works.[36]

Like the United States, Germany is considered a low-context, monochrome culture, except even more so. According to Hall and Hall, the German language is quite literal, individual German words having exact and precise meaning. For example, the Germans have no fewer than eight words for "comfort," each reflecting a slightly different type of comfort. Having been conditioned by their language, Germans are fairly formal, nitpicky about precision, punctual, and fanatic about facts. All of these characteristics carry over into their business relations. On the job and in business dealings, Germans are absolutely obsessed with facts and precision. Lines of authority are carefully observed. Interactions between business partners and friends are reserved and formalized. Germans are very conscious of rank and will always refer to someone by the person's appropriate title. Even neighbors who may have lived next door to one another for years address each other with their last names, as in "Herr (Mr.) Schmidt." If a person also carries a degree, such as a Ph.D. or an M.D., he will be called "Herr Doktor Neulieb," and so forth.[37] Women, however, are typically addressed with their first names, as in "Frau Batina Neulieb."

Even in social situations, Germans often appear unfriendly. They generally will not smile during a greeting and are intolerant of small talk. On the job, German workers expect that their managers will respect their privacy and that procedures will be executed precisely. Table 10.3 outlines some features of doing business with the Germans that may help Americans transacting business in Germany.

Although to many Americans the outward appearance and demeanor of the typical German is aloof, intense, humorless, and quite formal and rigid, on the inside, Germans desire meaningful interpersonal relationships. As intercultural expert Richard Lewis asserts,

> Anglo-Saxons do not always see the way towards making quick friends with them, but when they succeed in entering into the somewhat complicated structure of a German friendship, they find rich rewards. A German is generally a loyal and true friend of incredible durability. Outwardly glum and cautious, they are inwardly desperate for affection and popularity. They want to be cherished just as the rest of us do. . . . A German friendship is indeed a very worthwhile investment.[38]

Table 10.3 Interacting Effectively with Germans

1. Be prepared. In business, the Germans will be very informed and will expect that you are too.

2. Engage in only minimal small talk.

3. Be informed about, and use, appropriate titles.

4. Avoid emotional appeals. Emphasize facts and figures. Germans respect quantitative reports.

5. Observe hierarchical seating and order of speaking.

6. Organize your presentation in compartments, and have your specialists present their own areas separately and as distinct parts of the presentation.

7. Be very punctual; start and stop as you planned. Follow your agenda closely.

8. Avoid humor. Be frank, direct, and honest. Demonstrate that you have done your homework.

Source: Based on E. T. Hall and M. R. Hall, *Understanding Cultural Differences* (Yarmouth, Maine: Intercultural Press, 1990); William Drake and Associates, "Managing Business Relationships in Germany" (1997) (wmv.culture-bank.com/demo/dernogermany/sld001.htm); R. D. Lewis, *When Cultures Collide* (London: Nicholas Brealey, 1997); P. R. Harris and R. T. Moran, *Managing Cultural Differences*, 4th ed. (Houston: Gulf Publishing, 1996).

Mexican Management Practices

In 1994, Canada, Mexico, and the United States entered into the North American Free Trade Agreement (NAFTA). In 2001, the United States accounted for more than 80 percent of Mexico's total trade. Mexico is the United States' second most important trading partner following Canada. In 2001, the Mexican peso was one of the strongest currencies in the world against the U.S. dollar. In addition to its economic development, the Mexican political climate has improved dramatically too. Elections have become more free and fair, and in 2000, the National Action Party won the presidency, the first opposition party to win in years. Many U.S. government officials believe that Mexico's stabilizing political system and economic development represent a unique opportunity for U.S. businesses.[39]

As mentioned earlier, a country's cultural orientation and values are typically reflected in the business practices of that culture. Three dimensions of cultural variability discussed in Chapter 2 are closely associated with Mexican business practices: individualism-collectivism, power distance, and uncertainty avoidance. Generally, in comparison with the United States, Mexico is more collectivistic, and is considered a large power distance and high-uncertainty-avoidant culture.[40]

Crouch points out that Mexicans are unusually group-oriented. He maintains that Mexicans are exceptionally concerned about any behavior that would upset the harmony of their household, their church, or their workplace. In fact, Crouch argues that on a scale of individual- versus group-oriented work styles, Mexicans and Americans would fall at opposite ends of the continuum. Mexican workers assume that working together is the ideal, because people who work better in solidarity with others, valuing loyalty to the group above individual effort, will prosper in a group-oriented work environment. Generally, Mexican organizations do not emphasize self-determination on the job. Unlike workers in the United States, Mexicans usually are not rewarded for initiative. Pelled and Xin point out that Mexicans see work as a "necessary evil." To many Mexicans, work is required to appreciate the more important things in life, such as family and friends. Crouch cautions American managers working in Mexico not to reward individuals within work groups. Generally, Mexican workers do not wish to call attention to themselves for outperforming a coworker and may be ashamed and embarrassed if recognized above others. In Mexico, individual effort and self-starting are met with suspicion. Even arriving early to work requires an explanation to coworkers because they will think you are trying to get ahead by showing off. Crouch points out that for a worker to leave his or her workstation to talk to the supervisor about mundane, work-related issues is disquieting to others in the group, unless the employee has explained his or her need to communicate to the supervisor beforehand. Moreover, Crouch asserts that the Mexican worker's attitude toward the boss is virtually never confrontational. Mexican workers value harmony above all else. A manager expressing favoritism to an individual Mexican worker will upset the harmony and shatter the team spirit.[41]

In the United States, people often change jobs and switch organizations in order to get ahead and be promoted. U.S. workers are generally in charge of their own careers and strive to succeed individually. Schuler and his colleagues argue that under Mexican law, Mexican organizations are responsible for the life, health, and dignity of their workers. In this way, Mexican organizations are considered paternalistic. Consistent with a collectivistic orientation, Mexican workers value harmonious relations between union and management. Conversely, in the United States, union and management interactions are often antagonistic. De Forest points out that traditional Mexican ideals stress employee/employer interdependence, mutual responsibilities, loyalty between superiors and subordinates, belongingness, cooperation (rather than competition), and not exceeding boundaries. According to De Forest, Mexican employers rebuff employees who criticize others to higher authorities and are competitive on the job. Such behaviors disrupt the harmony of the organization.[42]

Mexico is considered a large power distance culture. Recall that in large power distance cultures, people expect and accept that the power within the culture and its institutions will be distributed unequally. De Forest contends that Mexico's high power distance can be seen in the government, in the church, and throughout Mexican society. According to De Forest, most Mexican businesses have a rigid hierarchy where the power is centralized in the person or people at the top. Often, the top positions are not gained through hard work and initiative but are inherited or acquired through friendships or mutual favors. De Forest has observed that Mexican managers reward submission, taking direction, and loyalty to the person with power. Crouch explains that, historically, Mexicans have never known a world without hierarchy. For example, the Spanish had kings and queens, and the Aztecs had powerful *caciques* (warrior chiefs). To be sure, Spanish language is replete with words and phrases that communicate hierarchy (e.g., proper titles, salutations, and honorifics) and emphasize the idea that some people hold superior positions over others. Crouch asserts that Mexicans hold to traditional hierarchical roles based on family, education, age, and position. According to Crouch, Mexicans are puzzled and offended by Americans' casual and informal communication style. He maintains that Mexicans find the relaxed and easy communication between people of different hierarchical levels off-putting. The Mexican distinction between superior and subordinate is part of a deeply rooted pattern dating back to Aztec divisions among priest, prince, and peasant, and among Spanish queen, soldier, and citizen. For the low power distance Americans, the implications of superior and inferior status that accompany this pattern are unacceptable.[43]

Relationships among Mexican managers and their subordinates are generally distant and communication is rather formal. For example, managers and subordinates are usually not on a first-name basis. Unlike U.S. manager/subordinate communication, interactive strategies that promote equality, participative decision making, open communication, and employee ownership are not considered necessary—or even desirable—in Mexican organizations. When interacting with Mexican employees, managers need not explain the reasoning behind a decision because employees may perceive this as a sign of weakness. In fact, Mexican workers expect to be given orders. They accept their unequal status and prefer that those in power protect their interests, give clear direction, and treat them with civility. Communication channels should follow the hierarchical structure of the business.[44]

In low- (or weak) uncertainty-avoidant cultures like the United States, employees are encouraged to innovate and take risks. In high- (or strong) uncertainty-avoidant cultures like Mexico, innovative or risk-taking behavior is inappropriate. Mexican workers generally prefer close supervision. Likewise, compensation based on incentive is eschewed. Mexican workers prefer to know exactly what they are supposed to do, and they want to be rewarded for doing it.

De Forest maintains that one of the most frustrating aspects for Americans doing business in Mexico is the Mexican perception of time. American managers should be advised to be patient. According to De Forest, life is simply slower in Mexico than in the United States. She points out that in Mexico, time does not advance; it tends to be either right now or some other time. American managers should be prepared for delays. De Forest says that phone service may take months to be installed or repaired; obtaining a post office box can take weeks or months; people frequently show up late for meetings; businesses and government offices open and close at all hours, as if at random; electricity shuts down for no apparent reason and may be off for days.[45]

Since the start of NAFTA, the United States and Mexico have become active trading partners. If American managers can adjust to the culturally influenced business environment in Mexico, they can make great strides. The key to being successful in Mexico is adjusting and adapting to the cultural environment.

Commerce in the Middle East

To many Americans, the Middle East is a place of great mystery riddled with intrigue, hostility, and contradiction. Most Americans are uninformed of the history, geography, and culture of the Middle East. After World War II, many Arab countries, which had been subjected to European colonial rule, won independence. Along with independence came many new challenges. Unfortunately, few Arab countries had experienced leaders able to cope with their novel circumstances. Of the many tests facing the Arab world, national development is in the vanguard. Many Arab countries have spent immense amounts of financial and human resources in an attempt to improve the capabilities and performance of their national economies and toward generating change in their political systems and innovations in technology. Today, however, most Arab states are ruled by authoritarian political regimes that do not encourage, or allow, public participation in decision making. The determination of war, investment strategies, military armaments, and national budgetary allocations are ultimately decreed by one person. There is virtually no free press or free expression, and the citizenry is essentially insulated from any governmental practices. To make matters worse, corruption is so prevalent that most public officials deem it a natural part of doing business.[46]

Members of the Arab League

Algeria
Bahrain
Comoros
Djibouti
Egypt
Iraq
Jordan
Kuwait
Lebanon
Libya
Mauritania
Morocco
Oman
Palestine
Qatar
Saudi Arabia
Somalia
Sudan
Syria
Tunisia
United Arab Emirates
Yemen

Abbas J. Ali, Professor of Business Policy and International Management at Indiana University, has written extensively about the Arab world. According to Ali, some of the contradictions Americans see in the Middle East are rooted in religion. Most countries in the Middle East (excluding Israel) are Moslem. More than anything else, Islam has united Arabs as a single dynamic entity. Yet, in what appears to be an obvious paradox to many Americans, Arabs who staunchly believe in the ideals of Islamic principles consistently disobey them in practice. For example, Islam functions as law in Saudi Arabia. One of the principles of Islamic teaching is to trust God over kings and rulers. In addition, Islam teaches Muslims never to use such titles as Majesty, Highness, Royal, and so on. Moreover, Muslim scholars contend that Islamic law is egalitarian, where rulers should be elected, and that authority should rest on the consent of the people. Of course, in direct contradiction to such teachings, Saudi Arabia functions as a kingdom with an absolute monarchy. This is only one example, but according to Ali, Arabia depicts a condition where the ideals of Islam are officially sanctioned but persistently violated.[47]

According to Jamil Jreisat of the Department of Government and International Affairs at the University of Southern Florida, the Arab world is replete with diversity and conflicting attributes. Dramatic changes have occurred in the Arab world in just the past 80 years. Take population, for example. In 1914, the entire population of the Arab world was 35–40 million persons. Due to advances in health care and a decreasing death rate, within twenty years it approached nearly 60 million, and by 1990 reached 215 million. The Arab world's population is projected to increase from 280 million in 2005 to more than 400 million in 2020. Egypt, for example, is expected to double its population in the next 20 years. The U.S. Arab population totaled 1.19 million people in 2000, up from 610,000 in 1980 and 860,000 in 1990 and making up about 0.42 percent of the country's 281.4 million people. In addition, the Arab world has a very youthful population, with high levels of poverty and unemployment. In the Arab world as a whole, 40 percent of the population is under the age of 14. In 2005, more than 60 percent of the Arab population earned less than US$1,000 annually. Illiteracy is also problematic. In Egypt, nearly half of the people are illiterate.[48]

National development seems to be the top priority among most Middle Eastern Arab countries. Following their independence, Arab governments became the instant owners and operators of public utilities, banks, railways, airlines, mass transit systems, telephones, water, gas, and electricity. Most of the governments simply lacked the technological and human resources to manage. Coupled with national development, a push toward industrialization has generated immense pressures in many Arab countries. Ali contends that the existing infrastructures (e.g., roads, ports, distribution centers, and so on) have been unable to keep pace with the rapid growth of most Arab countries. Moreover, asserts Ali, a severe shortage of skilled managers in the new government and private institutions has forced many organizations to hire foreign experts and workers. Finally, writes Ali, most Arab countries suffer from "cultural discontinuity." For more than 500 years the Arab world has been under the influence of numerous foreign powers. Generations of Arabs have lost their attachments to their cultural roots and cultural values. In fact, explains Ali, formal education systems did not exist in Arabia until the beginning of this century.[49]

Although faced with problems, the growth of many Arab economies has been rapid, and the United States has played an active role. For example, according to the U.S. Department of State, the United States is Saudi Arabia's leading trade and joint venture partner. In 1996 alone, U.S. exports to Saudi Arabia increased from $6 to $7 billion dollars. U.S. direct investment in joint ventures in 1997 totaled nearly $7 billion dollars. There are more than 200 U.S. companies in Saudi Arabia. In Kuwait, the United States is the largest supplier of goods and services. Economic relations between the United States and Saudi Arabia, its main trade partner in the Middle East have been greatly damaged in the period following the attacks of September 11, 2001, against the United States. The volume of American exports, according to the statistics, decreased during the first four months of 2002 by 43 percent, reaching $1.3 billion in comparison to $2.3 billion for the same period in 2001. U.S. corporations are the source of nearly 40 percent of Kuwait's import market. Moreover, U.S. exports to Kuwait are estimated at about $2 billion dollars annually. Qatar, one of the smallest yet wealthiest Arab countries, has become an active trading partner with the United States. In 2003, U.S. exports to Qatar amounted to $408 million, while Qatari exports to the United States reached $331 million.[50]

Because of their lack of knowledge and sensitivity, many American managers are unable to conduct business successfully in Arabia. Even Arab names, for example, are so confusing to most Americans that they give up trying to understand. An Arab man's name could be Ali bin Ahmed bin Saleh Al-Fulani. His first name is Ali, and he is probably called that by his friends. His family name is Al-Fulani. The word "bin" means "son of." So Ali bin Ahmed bin Saleh means that he is the son of Ahmed, who is the son of Saleh. Many Arabs give their ancestors' names for at least five or six generations. Women's names are handled a bit differently. From the example above, say Ali has a sister. Her name might be Nura bint Ahmed bin Saleh Al-Fulani. "Bint" means "daughter of." She is Nura, the daughter of Ahmed, who is the son of Saleh. Her family name is Al-Fulani. When an Arab woman marries, she does not change her name, although her children take their father's name.[51]

AN INTERCULTURAL CONVERSATION: BUSINESS COMMUNICATION IN THE MIDDLE EAST

Names notwithstanding, many Americans are completely ignorant of subtle Arab conventions that can define the success or failure of a business deal. Consider the following exchange between Arab businessman Hashim Abdu Hashim and his American counterpart, Steve Jones.[52]

The Scene: Mr. Jones is sitting (on the floor) in the hallway of a building in Saudi Arabia, waiting to meet with his Saudi counterpart, Hashim Abdu Hashim. The hallway is noisy, cluttered with people moving quickly from room to room. Mr. Jones arrived in Saudi Arabia two days earlier for a scheduled meeting. Since then, his meeting has been postponed and rescheduled several times. After several hours of waiting in the hallway, Mr. Jones is called into Hashim's office. The office has no chairs, but instead elaborate and ornate pillows on the floor. The walls are draped with embellished afghans. Mr. Jones enters.

> **Jones:** *Hello, Hashim, gosh, I finally get to see you. I've been waiting for two days!*
>
> **Hashim:** *Ah, hello, Mr. Jones. It is good to see you.*
>
> **Jones:** *Thanks. It's good to see you also. How's Mrs. Hashim?*
>
> **Hashim:** *Was your trip to our country all right?*
>
> **Jones:** *Yes, everything is fine.* (At this point, the two are interrupted by a servant pouring tea. Jones refuses.) *No . . . no . . . thanks, I've had enough tea. So . . . Hashim. I came all the way over here to see if I could get you to speed things up with our order. See, our supplies have been sitting in some dock along the coast for two weeks. I was wondering if you could sign this petition* (hands it to Hashim using his left hand) *to hurry up the process.*
>
> **Hashim:** *Hmmm . . . this is a problem?*
>
> **Jones:** *Yes, gosh Hashim, I understand that sometimes supplies sit on ships for weeks at a time! Your people could really use these computers you've ordered. I need to have them released to your custody as soon as possible.*
>
> **Hashim:** *I see. Well . . . we have been without computers for thousands of years. Waiting is no problem.*

Mr. Jones commits five cultural blunders that severely jeopardize any possible future contract with Hashim. First, he mentions that he's been waiting for two days to see Hashim. Jones has not recognized the polychronic nature of Saudi Arabia. Business gets done on its own time. Second, he refuses the tea that has been offered to him in hospitality. Then, in a gross error of etiquette, he inquires about Hashim's wife. In Saudi Arabia, a man's wife is for his eyes only. Continuing on his blundering way, Jones hands Hashim the contract with his left hand. In many Muslim cultures, the left hand is the "dirty" hand; that is, it is used for cleaning the body and handling of waste, and so on. Finally, Jones demonstrates the urgency of his mission and getting the computers off the supply ship. His emphasis on schedules and deadlines communicates to Hashim that he is either insane or irreligious. Many Arabs believe literally in the phrase "Insha Allah," meaning "God Willing." To them, the nature of things, especially time, is controlled by God. Events, meetings, and happenings are completed only if God wills them.[53]

According to Ali, one of the problems facing expatriates in the Middle East is the lack of any coherent Arab management profession or theory. Ali contends that Arab societies moved too rapidly toward industrialization without establishing the foundations necessary for dealing with the challenges of modern institutions. This, according to Ali, has led to inefficient operations, lack of clear direction, displacement of the traditional labor force, and dramatic shifts in social structures. Specifically, asserts Ali, Arab management reflects the political and social instability of the region, which serves only the powerful political elites.[54]

In the absence of an Arab management theory, Ali points to several societal qualities in Arab cultures that have management implications in Arab organizations. Arab idealism and hopefulness are necessary elements in Arab society. Hence, organizational development can be introduced without resentment as long as the changes conform to the ideal. Arab infatuation with ideal forms means that new and modern management practices can be used. Unlike the Germans, who are persuaded only by facts and figures, the typical Arab resorts to personal relationships, emotional appeals, and intuitiveness in decision making. Ali labels this phenomenon "non decision-making." Yet Arab reliance on intuition can speed up the decision-making process through flexibility and tolerance for ambiguity. Arabs also tend to avoid public conflict and criticism. Hence, mediation is sometimes necessary in conducting business. Dimensions of Islamic teaching also enter into the management picture. Hard work is a virtue to Muslims, thus commitment to organizational goals can be sustained. Islam also preaches that religion is known in the way of dealing with other people as equals. Within the organization, equity issues are salient where a horizontal (rather than vertical) line of authority is preferred. In fact, directives from the top are often received negatively. In this sense, maintains Ali, communication with formal and informal leaders is necessary to achieve organizational goals. Courage is also an Islamic virtue. Workers are willing to confront managers and will express their concerns openly.[55]

Given the extreme diversity in literacy rates, health care systems, educational institutions, technological advancement, management techniques, and forms of government, it is difficult to offer generalizations about managing people in Arab countries. The list below, however, offers some broad guidelines for doing business in the Middle East that most Americans would be wise to consider.[56]

Interacting with Arabs

Arabs have a tendency to use elaborate and ritualized forms of communication, especially during greetings. Even in markets, loud and boisterous bargaining is accepted and expected and accompanied with wide gestures and animated facial expressions. Many Americans are unnerved by this.

Arab women's bodies are not to be seen. American women should dress with their arms and legs covered.

As a sign of trust and friendship, Arab men may be seen holding hands. During greetings, men kiss on the cheeks.

Generally, Arabs have a smaller personal space than most Americans. They tend to stand very close while interacting, sometimes in order to smell their partner's breath. They expect intense eye contact.

During negotiations, Arabs will personalize arguments and appeal to emotions.

In general, Arabs are less private than Americans. Visiting and long conversations are expected.

Do not hesitate to praise an Arab's country, food, and art. But do not make comments of any kind about Arab women, especially an Arab's wife. Do not appear detached or reluctant to accept favors.

Unlike the Japanese, Arabs enjoy verbal interaction and expect it from others. Silence will be perceived as a sign that something is wrong.

CONFLICT IN ORGANIZATIONS

Conflict is an inevitable part of life. Attempts to eliminate conflict are futile. Conflict can, however, be reduced and managed. In fact, effective conflict management can have many positive outcomes. As U.S. businesses increase their interactions with different cultures, intercultural conflict will be inescapable. Young Kim has developed a model of intercultural conflict that points out several variables that facilitate or promote conflict.[57] According to Kim, there are three levels of intercultural conflict: individual, intermediary, and societal levels. At each level are factors that increase the probability that conflict will ignite.

Factors Facilitating Intercultural Conflict

Individual Level	Intermediary Level	Societal Level
Cognitive simplicity/ rigidity	Segregation/contact	History of subjugation
Ingroup bias	Intergroup salience	Ideological/structural inequalities
Insecurity	Status discrepancy	Minority group strength

The *individual* level of intercultural conflict refers to factors that the individual personally brings to the interaction. An individual's attitudes, dispositions, and beliefs are included here. Cognitive simplicity/rigidity refers to the degree of inflexibility in the way that the individual thinks about people from different cultures. Rigid, simplistic thinking would include gross stereotyping (e.g., all Blacks are lazy; all Whites are rich; all Japanese are sneaky). Ingroup bias refers to the degree to which the individual is ethnocentric. (Recall from Chapter 1 that ethnocentrism is defined as viewing one's own group as at the center of everything and using the standards of one's own group to measure or gauge the worth of all other groups.) Insecurity/frustration refers to the degree to which the individual has a high level of uncertainty about, and fear of, outgroup members. Divergent behavior refers to the behavioral patterns of the individual that clearly *differentiate* and distance him or her from outgroup members. For example, obviously different speech patterns or accents may ostensibly separate groups from one another. Sometimes people even exaggerate their mannerisms and speech to accentuate their differences from outgroups. Imagine two employees working together, each from a different culture, who have gross stereotypes of each other, are both ethnocentric, fear each other, and have highly divergent behavioral patterns. The model predicts that such a situation is likely to engender conflict.

The *intermediary* level of intercultural conflict refers to the actual location and context of the interaction. Some business environments may be more likely than others to facilitate conflict. Segregation and contact refer to the extent to which the cultural groups of the individuals interact on a daily basis. Perhaps the most basic condition for intercultural conflict is contact between diverse cultures or ethnicities on a day-to-day basis. Segregated workplaces do not allow for much interaction, and components at the individual level (e.g., cognitive rigidity, ingroup bias, and so on) tend to escalate to intolerable levels that facilitate intercultural conflict. Intergroup salience refers to the observable physical and social differences between the conflicting individuals. Such cultural markers include distinct physical and behavioral differences, such as race, language, and speech patterns. As Kim notes, to the extent that the groups are culturally distinct, the communicative skills of the less powerful cultural group will clash with those of the majority group members. The majority group's symbol system is dominant. Status discrepancy refers to the degree to which conflicting parties differ in status along cultural lines. For example, Blacks often argue that American culture practices an asymmetrical power structure. Blacks may feel that the American corporate culture reflects the same asymmetry. On the job, managers and supervisors have more power than workers. If all the managers in a business are

White and all the workers are Black (or Hispanic, etc.), then the status discrepancy is heightened.

The *societal* level of intercultural conflict includes factors that probably are out of the control of the interactants. These conditions include any history of subjugation, ideological/structural inequality, and minority group strength. The history of subjugation of one group by another is a key environmental factor in many intercultural conflicts. For example, Blacks have long been subjugated by Whites in America. Historically, African Americans were slaves. Even upon emancipation, they were not allowed to vote. As late as the 1960s, restaurants in the South had separate bathrooms, seating areas, and drinking fountains for Blacks and Whites. Often, the tensions expressed today are rooted in the history of the subjugation of one group over another. Ideological and structural inequity refers to societal differences regarding power, prestige, and economic reward. Historically, in the United States, Whites have held most of the power positions and gained most of the economic reward. Hence, there is a vast ideological and structural difference between Whites and other groups. Blacks and Hispanics have much higher levels of unemployment, for example. Minority (i.e., microcultural) group strength refers to the amount of power (e.g., legal, political, economic) a particular group possesses. Microcultural groups vary in their ability to rally their members against structural inequalities. Minority group strength varies as a function of the status of the group's language within the society, the sheer numbers of members in the group, and forms of societal support (e.g., governmental services designed specifically for the group). Relative to other microcultural groups, Blacks, for example, are economically and politically quite powerful. Political scientists argue, for instance, that presidential elections are swung by the African-American voting block. According to Kim, the greater the ethnic group strength, the more likely will the individual take action in intercultural conflict situations.[58]

CHAPTER SUMMARY

Doing business and managing people in a culture other than one's own is a daunting task indeed. This chapter has discussed how the principles presented throughout the text can be applied to the business world across cultures. An understanding of the cultural, microcultural, environmental, perceptual, socio-relational, verbal, nonverbal, and relational contexts of the host culture increases the probability of being an effective and productive manager across cultures. Four diverse cultures—Japan, Germany, Mexico, and the Middle East—are active participants in the global marketplace, each with its own unique way of doing business. The Japanese are subtle and indirect, Germans forthright and direct, Arabs expressive and intuitive, and Mexicans collectivistic and hierarchical. Managers who understand the contexts of these cultures are in a much better position to do business. Finally, we have seen that several factors affect and facilitate intercultural conflict. Although conflict can never be eliminated, identifying these factors can help us reduce and manage conflict in our professional lives.

GLOSSARY OF TERMS

Cultural context: An accumulated pattern of values, beliefs, and behavior held by an identifiable group of people with a common verbal and nonverbal symbol system.

Environmental context: The geographical and psychological location of communication within some cultural context.

Organizational culture: An organized pattern of values, beliefs, behaviors, and communication channels held by the members of an organization.

Perceptual context: The cognitive process by which persons gather, store, and retrieve information.

Power distance: The extent to which less powerful members of a particular culture accept and expect that power within the culture will be distributed unequally.

Socio-relational context: The roles that one assumes within a culture; roles are defined by verbal and nonverbal messages.

REFERENCES

1. Trompenaars, F. *Riding the Waves of Culture: Understanding Diversity in Global Business* (Burr Ridge, Ill.: Irwin, 1994), p. 14.
2. Foreign Trade Division, U.S. Census Bureau, Washington, D.C.; Office of Consumer Affairs, and the U.S. Department of Commerce International Trade Administration, Office of NAFTA, The North American Free Trade Agreement (1997) (www.doc.gov/oca/nafta.htm).
3. *Minority-Owned Businesses: 1997 Census Brief: Survey of Minority-Owned Business Enterprises.* U.S. Census Bureau, Washington, D.C.
4. Kanter, R. M. (1991). Transcending business boundaries: 12,000 world managers view change. *Harvard Business Review,* 69(3), 151–164.

5. Hannon, K. "The Fast Track Now Leads Overseas," *U.S. News & World Report,* 117 (1994), 92–96.

6. Rosenzweig, P. M. "National Culture and Management," (Teaching Note 9–394–177, Harvard Business School, Boston, 1994).

7. Ibid.

8. Bass, B. M., & Burger, P. C. *Assessment of Managers: An International Comparison* (New York: Free Press, 1979); Adler, N. J., Campbell, N., & Laurent, A. "In Search of Appropriate Methodology: From Outside the People's Republic of China Looking In," *Journal of International Business Studies* 20 (1989), 61–74.

9. Elashmawi, F., & Harris, R. R. *Multicultural Management: New Skills for Global Success* (Houston: Gulf Publishing, 1993).

10. Ibid.

11. Ibid.

12. Elenkov, D. S. "Differences and Similarities in Managerial Values Between U.S. and Russian Managers," *International Studies of Management & Organization* 27 (1997), 85–107.

13. Trompenaars, *Riding the Waves of Culture.*

14. Elashmawi and Harris, *Multicultural Management.*

15. Harris, P. R., & Moran, R. T. *Managing Cultural Differences* (Houston: Gulf Publishing, 1991).

16. Ibid.

17. Trompenaars, *Riding the Waves of Culture.*

18. Axtell, R. E. ed. *Do's and Taboos Around the World: A Guide to International Behavior* (New York: Wiley, 1985).

19. Ibid.

20. Morris, M. W., Williams, K. Y., Leung, K., Larrick, R., Mendoza, M. T., Bhatnagar, D., Li, J., Kondo, M., Luo, J., & Hu, J. "Conflict Management Style: Accounting for Cross-National Differences," *Journal of International Business Studies* 29 (1998), 729–748.

21. Some of these examples are from R. E. Axtell, *Gestures: The Do's and Taboos of Body Language Around the World* (New York: Wiley, 1991).

22. Trompenaars, *Riding the Waves of Culture.*

23. Adler, N. J., "Competitive Frontiers: Women Managers in the Triad," *International Studies of Management and Organization* 23 (1993), 3–24.

24. *Top Ten Countries with Which the U.S. Trades* (Washington, D.C.: United States Bureau of the Census, 2000) (www.census.gov/foreign-trade/top/dst/current/balance.html); United States Department of State, *Background Notes: Japan* (Washington, D.C.: Bureau of Public Affairs, 2001).

25. Brown, W. S., Lubove, R. E., & Kwalwasser, J. "Karoshi: Alternative Perspectives of Japanese Management Styles," *Business Horizons* 37 (1994), 58–61.

26. Bolda, R. A. "Correlates of Personal Productivity of Supervisors: Perceptions of American and Japanese Managers," *Current Psychology* 9 (1990), 339–346.

27. Abramson, N. R., Lane, H. W., Nagai, H., & Takagi, H. "A Comparison of Canadian and Japanese Cognitive Styles: Implications for Management Interaction," *Journal of International Business Studies* 24 (1993), 575–588.

28. Brett, J. M., & Okumura, T. "Inter- and Intracultural Negotiation: U.S. and Japanese Negotiators," *Academy of Management Journal* 41 (1998), 495–510.

29. Rao, A., Hashimoto, K., & Rao, A. "Universal and Culturally Specific Aspects of Influence: A Study of Japanese Managers," *The Leadership Quarterly* 8 (1997), 295–313.

30. William Drake & Associates, "The Japanese Seniority System" (1997) (www.culturebank.com/jpn043.html).

31. William Drake & Associates, "Japanese and Americans: Sources of Mutual Misunderstandings" (1997) (www.culturebank.com/jpn027.html).

32. United States Department of Commerce, "Country Commercial Guide: Germany Fiscal Year 1998" (1997) (www.ita.doc.gov/uscs/ccg98/ccgogerm.html).

33. William Drake and Associates, "Managing Business Relationships in Germany" (1997) (www.culturebank.com/dcmo/demogermany/sld00l.htm).

34. Hall, E. T., & Hall, M. R. *Understanding Cultural Differences* (Yarmouth, Maine: Intercultural Press, 1990).

35. Ibid.

36. "German Lessons," *The Economist* 340 (1996), 59.

37. Ibid.; Drake and Associates, "Managing Business Relationships in Germany."

38. Lewis, R. D. *When Cultures Collide* (London: Nicholas Brealey, 1997), p. 212.

39. "Mexico: Country Commercial Guide" (Washington, D.C.: United States & Foreign Commercial Service and the United States Department of State, 2001).

40. Schuler, R. S., Jackson, S. E., Jackofsky, E., & Slocum, J. W. "Managing Human Resources in Mexico: A Cultural Understanding," *Business Horizons* 39 (1996), 55–62; Pelled, L. H., & Xin, K. R. "Work Values and the Human Resource Management Implications: A Theoretical Comparison of China, Mexico, and the United States," *Journal of Applied Management Studies* 6 (1997), 185–199.

41. Crouch, E. C. (2004). *Mexicans and Americans : Cracking the Cultural Code.* Yarmouth, ME: Intercultural Press; Pelled & Xin, "Work Values and the Human Resource Management Implications."

42. Ibid.; M. E. De Forest, "Hecho en Mexico: Tips for Success," *Apparel Industry* 59 (1998), 98–104.

43. Ibid.; Crouch, *Mexicans and Americans: Cracking the Cultural Code.*

44. Schuler, Jackson, Jackofsky, and Slocum, "Managing Human Resources in Mexico"; De Forest, "Hecho en Mexico."

45. De Forest, "Hecho en Mexico."

46. Jreisat, J. E. "Managing National Development in the Arab States," *Arab Studies Quarterly* 14 (1992), 1–17.

47. Ali, A. J. "Cultural Discontinuity and Arab Management Thought," *International Studies of Management and Organization* 25 (1995), 7–31; Ali, A. J. "Decision-Making Style, Individualism, and Attitudes Toward Risk of Arab Executives," *International Studies of Management and Organization* 23 (1993), 53–74.

48. Jreisat, "Managing National Development in the Arab States;" Wetzel, H., *Egypt Country Commercial Guide FY 2004.* U.S. Department of State, Washington, D.C.

49. Ali, "Cultural Discontinuity and Arab Management Thought"; "Decision-Making Style, Individualism, and Attitudes Toward Risk of Arab Executives."

50. U.S. Department of State, *Country Commercial Guide: Saudi Arabia Fiscal Year 1998* (1997) (www.ita.doc.gov/uscs/ccg98/ccgosaud.html); U.S. Department of State, *Country Commercial Guide: State of Qatar Fiscal Year 1998* (1997) (www.ita.doc.gov/uscs/ccg98/ccgoqata.html); U.S. Department of State, *Country Commercial Guide: United Arab Emirate Fiscal Year 1998* (1997) (www.ita.doc.gov/uscs/ccg98/ccgouae.html); Wallace, D., *Consider Qatar,* Supplement to the Qatar 2005 Country Commercial Guide; U.S. Department of State; *Doing Business in: Kuwait, 2005; Commercial Guide for U.S. Companies.* U.S. Department of Commerce & The Department of State: Washington DC.

51. Arab Names (www.arab.net/arabnames).

52. This dialogue is adapted from a scene in Copeland, L. (Producer). *Managing the Overseas Assignment* [videorecording], San Francisco, CA: Copeland Griggs Productions, 1983.

53. Harris & Moran, *Managing Cultural Differences.*

54. Ali, "Cultural Discontinuity and Arab Management Thought"; "Decision-Making Style, Individualism, and Attitudes Toward Risk of Arab Executives."

55. Ibid.

56. This figure is adapted from Harris and Moran, *Managing Cultural Differences*; Lewis, *When Cultures Collide.*

57. Kim, Y. Y. "Interethnic Conflict: An Interdisciplinary Overview," in *Annual Review of Conflict Knowledge and Conflict Resolution,* vol. 1, ed. J. B. Gittler (New York: Garland, 1989); Y. Y. Kim, "Explaining Interethnic Conflict: An Interdisciplinary Overview" (paper presented at the annual convention of the Speech Communication Association, Chicago, Ill., 1990).

58. Ibid.

CHAPTER 11

Acculturation and Culture Shock

Nothing so sensitizes us to our own culture as living outside it and then trying to return.

—John Condon and Fathi Yousef[1]

Chapter Objectives

After reading this chapter, you should be able to

1. Define acculturation.
2. Identify and discuss the factors that facilitate or hinder acculturation.
3. Define culture shock.
4. Identify and name the stages of culture shock.
5. Recognize and discuss the causes of culture shock.
6. Identify and discuss strategies for managing culture shock.
7. Assess your level of culture shock.

Having read the previous ten chapters of this book, you may well be motivated to go out and interact with people from different cultures. Perhaps you are even ready to travel abroad! In either case, remember that intercultural communication assumes the principle of difference. Not all intercultural communication is successful. This chapter focuses on two important features associated with intercultural communication as they relate to traveling abroad to foreign cultures: (1) acculturation and (2) culture shock. *Acculturation* is the process whereby you adapt to a new culture by adopting its values, attitudes, and practices. *Culture shock* is a multifaceted experience resulting from the stress associated with entering a new culture. Each of these variables affects the success rate of your intercultural communication experiences.

When individuals or groups of individuals enter a new culture, they are faced with a different set of values, different behavioral patterns, and a different verbal and nonverbal communication system. In most (perhaps all) cases, such people are affected by their new cultural surroundings. *Acculturation* is the term used to describe what happens when people from one culture enter a different culture. Acculturation was defined by Redfield, Linton, and Herskovits as "those phenomena which result when groups of individuals having different cultures come into continuous first-hand contact with subsequent changes in the original culture pattern of either or both groups."[2] John Berry, well known for his work on acculturation, argues that in practice, when two different cultural groups engage in continuous contact, one of the two groups will induce more change than the other. For example, when immigrants enter the United States, they are probably going to experience more change than the people already living here. Berry also distinguishes between acculturation at the group level and acculturation at the individual level. He contends that the distinction is important because not all members of the group experience the same levels of acculturation.[3]

According to Berry, in pluralistic, diverse societies like the United States, there are three factors that bring cultural groups together: mobility, voluntariness, and permanence. For example, regarding mobility, some groups experience acculturation because they have moved into a new culture, as do immigrants and refugees like the Hmong people of Laos, who came to the United States. Other groups experience acculturation because they have had a new culture thrust upon them, as did indigenous peoples like Native Americans. Some groups enter acculturation voluntarily, such as Mexican immigrants entering the United States, whereas others experience acculturation involuntarily, as did African slaves brought to the United States. Finally, some groups will experience a relatively permanent acculturation change, as African Americans and Mexican Americans have, whereas others face only temporary acculturation, as do exchange students studying abroad or expatriates in temporary job transfers. Berry maintains that despite the sometimes dramatic differences in the circumstances of acculturating groups, the overall acculturation process is universal across groups.[4]

Acculturative Stress

Most people experience a degree of stress and strain when they enter a culture different from their own. Acculturation is often marked by physical and psychological changes that occur as a result of the adaptation required to function in a new and different cultural context. People adapting to new cultures face changes in their diet; climate; housing; communication; role prescriptions; media consumption; and the myriad rules, norms, and values of a new and (relatively) dissimilar culture. Moreover, such persons are isolated from familiar social networks and may experience problems with language, unemployment, and discrimination. The stress associated with such changes, known as *acculturative stress,* is marked by a reduction in one's physical and mental health.[5]

Many immigrant groups in the United States experience acculturative stress. A rather substantial body of research has documented the effects of acculturative stress on America's largest microcultural group, Hispanics. Miranda and Matheny point out that among Hispanics, acculturative stress is related to decreased self-efficacy expectations, decreased career aspirations, depression, and suicidal ideation (especially in Hispanic adolescents).[6] In their work with Hispanics, Julie and David Smart have observed that acculturative stress is associated with fatalistic thinking. Smart and Smart argue that acculturative stress has a lifelong effect on Hispanics' psychological well-being, decision-making abilities, occupational effectiveness, and physical health. Smart and Smart contend that for Hispanic immigrants, the most significant aspect of acculturative stress is the loss of social support from the family. They maintain that the loss of social support is particularly intense for Hispanics because of their collectivistic orientation. In fact, Hispanic women may be more likely than men to suffer from acculturative stress because in their native culture their roles were very clearly prescribed. In the United States, an individualistic, equality-based society, women's roles are more open and unspecified.[7] In his work, Hovey found that family dysfunction, separation from family, negative expectations for the future, and low income levels were significantly related to higher levels of acculturative stress.[8]

In an interesting line of research, Nwadiora and McAdoo investigated acculturative stress among Amerasian refugees in the United States. Amerasians are individuals born of American servicemen and Vietnamese or Cambodian women during the Vietnam War. Because of their mixed racial background, these children were considered half-breeds and social outcasts in their homeland. In 1987, Congress passed the Amerasian Homecoming Act, permitting all Amerasians and their immediate families (including wives, half-siblings, and mothers) to immigrate to the United States. Nwadiora and

McAdoo report that Amerasians have faced pervasive prejudice in the United States, often by Asian, European, and especially African Americans. In their research they found that the Amerasians experienced acculturative stress in the areas of spoken English, employment, and limited formal education. They also report that gender and race had no significant impact on acculturative stress.[9]

In addition to the above factors, Berry argues that the degree of acculturative stress experienced by people adapting to new cultures varies according to the similarities and dissimilarities between the host culture and the native culture of the immigrants. To the extent that the cultures are more similar than different, less stress is experienced. Individual personal traits also play a role in the manifestation of acculturative stress. Berry notes that such characteristics as the amount of exposure one has had to the new culture; one's level of education; one's sex, age, language, race, and income; and one's psychological and spiritual strength all affect acculturative stress.[10] A well-educated woman from the United States may experience more acculturative stress than a well-educated man from the United States when entering a culture that does not recognize sexual equality (either socially or legally).

A MODEL OF ACCULTURATION

Acculturation is not unilateral; it is an interactive process between a culture and groups of people. When individuals or groups of individuals enter a new culture, they are often changed by the culture, but they also have an impact on the culture. For example, although Mexican immigrants face challenges imposed on them by the dominant culture, their presence has changed the United States' cultural milieu, especially in places such as Texas and California. Young Kim's model of cultural adaptation takes into account both individual and cultural factors that affect acculturation. Kim argues that acculturation is not a linear, one-way process; rather, there is an interaction between the stranger and the host culture. Kim argues that the role of communication, the role of the host environment, and the role of predisposition best explain the acculturation process.[11]

Factors Affecting Cultural Adaptation and Acculturation		
Communication	**Environment**	**Predisposition**
Personal Communication	Host Receptivity	Preparedness
Social Communication	Host Conformity Pressure	Ethnicity
Ethnic Group Strength	Personality	

In terms of the role of communication, personal communication refers to the individual's host communication competence—that is, the degree to which the newcomer can encode and decode verbal and nonverbal messages within the host environment. Kim argues that natives acquire this competence early in life, so it comes to them automatically. Host communication competence also refers to the degree to which the newcomer understands the host's language rules and norms, understands effective and appropriate conflict resolution strategies, and is motivated to initiate and develop host culture relationships. Social communication refers to the actual interaction between the newcomer and host persons. Participating in relationships, engaging in conflict resolution, and exposing oneself to the mass communication of the host culture can enhance and facilitate the acculturation process.[12]

Kim argues that the environment plays a key role in the acculturation process. The degree to which the host culture is receptive to strangers is important. Certain factions in the United States, for example, believe the country should close its borders to immigrants. Given the tensions in the Middle East, Americans sometimes face hostilities when they enter certain countries. Host conformity pressure is another factor. The extent to which natives within the host culture exert pressure on newcomers to conform to their culture's values, beliefs, and practices can facilitate or alienate the newcomers. In the United States, for example, people expect that newcomers will speak English. In fact, some members of the U.S. Congress have introduced legislation that would make English the official language of the United States. Ethnic group strength refers to the amount of influence the newcomer's group wields in the host culture. Clearly, some ethnic groups are more powerful politically, economically, and socially than others. Because of their numbers, Blacks and Hispanics have become powerful ethnic groups in the United States. Kim notes that as ethnic group strength increases, members of the ethnic group may encourage newcomers to maintain their native ethnic heritage and pressure them not to conform to the host culture. Hence, newcomers may feel pressure from the host culture to adapt while simultaneously facing pressure from their native ethnic group to preserve their ethnic heritage.[13]

Predisposition factors also affect acculturation. Kim argues that newcomers enter into their new culture with varying degrees of readiness. How much people know about their new culture, their ability to speak the language, the probability of employment, and their understanding of the cultural institutions will have a dramatic effect on their acculturation process. Newcomers' ethnicity will also play a role in the pace of their acculturation. Kim uses the term *ethnicity* to refer to the inherited characteristics that newcomers have as members of distinct ethnic groups. Such characteristics include race and language. For example, because of their ethnicity, Japanese may have a more difficult time acculturating to the United States than a person from Great Britain. Finally, Kim argues that there are certain personality characteristics that affect the individual's acculturation process. Age, for example, has been shown to affect acculturation. Generally, young persons adapt more quickly to new and different modes of behavior than do older persons, who may be set in their ways. Karmela Liebkind found that among Vietnamese refugees in Finland, younger generations maintained much more positive attitudes about acculturation than did older generations. Liebkind explains that the Finnish values and practices of gender equality and egalitarian parent/child relationships contrasted sharply with Southeast Asian values of hierarchical familial relationships and filial piety. In the traditional Southeast Asian family, children are taught to be loyal. They are obligated to show respect and obedience to their parents. Wives are expected to rear the children and serve their husbands. Not having been completely enculturated into Vietnamese society, the younger generations of the refugee Vietnamese families found it much easier than their parents to acculturate into Finnish society.[14]

Modes of Acculturation

In order for acculturation to occur, there must be contact between the members of the host culture and the newcomers. Berry argues that such contact needs to be continuous and direct. He maintains that short-term accidental contact does not generally lead to much acculturation. Moreover, the purpose of contact between the two groups is an important consideration. Berry points out that acculturation effects may vary according to whether the purpose of contact is colonization, enslavement, trade, military control, evangelization, or education. The length of contact is also a factor, as are the social or political policies of the mainstream culture as they relate to the immigrant group (that is, political representation, citizenship criteria, language requirements, employment opportunities, and so forth).[15]

Berry points out that an individual's level of acculturation depends in part on two independent processes: the degree to which the person approaches or avoids interaction with the host culture (that is, outgroup contact and relations), and the degree to which the individual maintains or relinquishes his or her native culture's attributes (ingroup identity and maintenance). On the basis of these two factors, Berry has identified four modes of acculturation: (1) *assimiliation,* (2) *integration,* (3) *separation,* and (4) *marginalization* (see Figure 11.1).

To the extent that the individual desires contact with the host culture (and the various microcultures) while not necessarily maintaining an

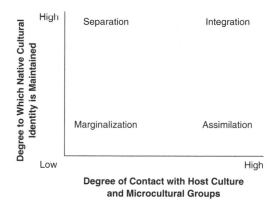

Figure 11.1

identity with his or her native culture, *assimilation* occurs. In this case, the individual loses his or her original cultural identity as he or she acquires a new identity in the host culture. During assimilation, the individual takes on the behaviors and language habits and practices the basic rules and norms of the host culture. There is an ongoing effort to approach the dominant culture while discontinuing the values, beliefs, and behaviors associated with the native culture. The defining property of the assimilation mode is that the individual endeavors to acquire the values and beliefs of a single cultural group with the ultimate goal of becoming indistinguishable from other members of the host culture. The individual will seek interaction with members of the host culture and build social networks with them.[16]

On the other hand, some people desire a high level of interaction with the host culture while maintaining identity with their native culture. This kind of acculturation is called *integration.* In this mode, the individual develops a kind of bicultural orientation that successfully blends and synthesizes cultural dimensions from both groups while maintaining an identity in each group. People practicing this mode of acculturation take part in activities that allow individuals from different groups to interact without the obstacle of social hierarchies. Presumably, integration is associated with less acculturative stress and conflict. To be sure, an individual's successful integration of cultural skills and norms does not mean that the person relinquishes his or her native cultural identity. In fact, many researchers contend that it is the development of the bicultural identity that leads to a successful life in a bicultural context. In other models of acculturation, this mode is called *pluralism* and/or *multiculturalism.* This mode of acculturation guides many of the social and legislative efforts in the United States' educational and affirmative action statutes.[17]

When individuals prefer low levels of interaction with the host culture and associated microcultural groups while desiring a close connection with, and reaffirmation of, their native culture, the mode of acculturation is called *separation.* Here the individual resists acculturation with the dominant culture and chooses not to identify with the host cultural group. At the same time, the person retains his or her native cultural identity. People choosing separation may harbor animosity toward the host culture as a result of social or historical factors. Such persons generally focus on the perceived incompatibility between their native culture and the host culture. Although the values and beliefs of the host culture are eschewed, the individual may take on selected behaviors of the host culture for purely functional reasons (such as to get a job). Separated persons communicate almost exclusively with their own group while actively avoiding participation in situations with members of the host culture. Some African-Americans and Native Americans, for example, prefer not to identify with the dominant White culture because of past racism and the country's history of slavery. In some models, the separation mode is labeled the segregation mode.[18]

The fourth type of acculturation is *marginalization.* Marginalization occurs when the individual chooses not to identify with his or her native culture or with the host culture. In many instances, marginalized people give up their native culture only to find that they are not accepted by the host culture, to which they would choose to acculturate if given the opportunity. These persons experience alienation from both cultures. Often they feel a sense of abandonment. Dysfunctional behaviors (for example, alcoholism or drug abuse) are often seen in marginalized people. African-Americans, Asian-Americans, and Hispanic-Americans often feel marginalized in U.S. culture. Acculturative stress is often found among marginalized groups.[19]

Another possible acculturation mode, articulated by Richard Mendoza, is *cultural transmutation.* In this mode, the individual chooses to identify with a third cultural group (microculture) that materializes out of the native and host cultural groups. For example, a youth may choose to join a gang or some other kind of microcultural outlet. Although similar to separation, cultural transmutation is different in that a new cultural identity is created. In other models of acculturation, this is called *fusion.* Gay and lesbian groups are a good example of the cultural transmutation mode of acculturation. In this mode, individuals have left their native heterosexual groups and have immigrated into homosexual contexts. Religious groups are another example of acculturative transmutation. Many religious communities merge the values, beliefs, and behaviors of diverse religions into a new religion.[20]

Figure 11.2 The two largest ethnic populations in the United States are Hispanics and Blacks

ACCULTURATION IN THE UNITED STATES

The two largest ethnic populations in the United States are Hispanics and Blacks. For these groups, acculturation refers to the degree to which they participate in the cultural traditions, values, beliefs, and norms of the dominant White society, remain immersed in their own unique cultural customs and conventions, or participate in both. As Hope Landrine comments, some microcultural groups remain highly traditional, whereas others are highly acculturated. Highly traditional Hispanics and Blacks differ significantly from Whites in a variety of values and behaviors, whereas highly acculturated Hispanics and Blacks do not (see Figure 11.2).[21]

Social scientists are beginning to understand that the degree of acculturation for microcultural groups within the United States is associated with a variety of social and medical problems, such as alcoholism; cigarette smoking; drug abuse; and HIV/AIDS-related knowledge, attitudes, and behaviors.[22] Moreover, microcultural group acculturation is associated with methods of conflict resolution (for example, belligerent behaviors), willingness to use counseling, career development and work habits, and educational achievement—that is, increased absences, lower grades. The more marginalized or segregated the group, the more likely they are to experience physical and mental health problems and the less likely they are to seek out appropriate avenues to handle them. Landrine maintains that ethnic differences observed in the United States might be better understood as degrees of acculturation. According to Landrine, understanding a microcultural group's level of acculturation has the potential to diminish racist beliefs about ethnic differences and to increase our knowledge of such differences as a symptom and/or an exhibition of culture.[23]

In an effort to better understand maladaptive attitudes and behaviors among the various microcultural groups in the United States, researchers have devoted considerable effort to assessing levels of acculturation. The Acculturation Rating Scale for Mexican-Americans (ARSMA) was first published in 1980.[24] The scale was recently revised and is designed to assess Mexican-American acculturation according to Berry's four modes of acculturation—namely, integration, assimilation, separation, and marginalization.[25] It is designed to be completed by persons of Mexican or Hispanic origin.

Approximately 13 percent of the population in the United States is African-American. As with other microcultural groups, some African-Americans are more acculturated than others. Hope Landrine and Elizabeth Klonoff have developed an instrument designed to measure levels of African-American acculturation. Landrine and Klonoff argue that within the microcultural context, acculturation refers to the degree to which microcultural groups (for example, African-Americans, Asian-Americans, Native Americans) participate in the traditional values, beliefs, and practices of the dominant White culture, remain immersed in their own cultural traditions, or blend the two traditions.[26]

SELF-ASSESSMENT 11.1

Acculturation Rating Scale for Mexican-Americans II

In the blank space to the left of each item, place a number between 1 and 5 that best applies to you. 1 = not at all, 2 = very little or not very often, 3 = moderately, 4 = much or very often, and 5 = extremely often or almost always.

1. _____ I speak Spanish.
2. _____ I speak English.
3. _____ I enjoy speaking Spanish.
4. _____ I associate with Anglos.

5. _____ I associate with Mexicans and/or Mexican-Americans.

6. _____ I enjoy listening to Spanish music.

7. _____ I enjoy listening to English-language music.

8. _____ I enjoy Spanish-language TV.

9. _____ I enjoy English-language TV.

10. _____ I enjoy English-language movies.

11. _____ I enjoy Spanish-language movies.

12. _____ I enjoy reading books in Spanish.

13. _____ I enjoy reading books in English.

14. _____ I write letters in Spanish.

15. _____ I write letters in English.

16. _____ My thinking is done in English.

17. _____ My thinking is done in Spanish.

18. _____ My contact with Mexico has been . . .

19. _____ My contact with the U.S.A. has been . . .

20. _____ My father identifies or identified himself as "Mexicano."

21. _____ My mother identifies or identified herself as "Mexicana."

22. _____ My friends while I was growing up were of Mexican origin.

23. _____ My friends while I was growing up were of Anglo origin.

24. _____ My family cooks Mexican food.

25. _____ My friends now are of Anglo origin.

26. _____ My friends now are of Mexican origin.

27. _____ I like to identify myself as an Anglo.

28. _____ I like to identify myself as a Mexican-American.

29. _____ I like to identify myself as a Mexican.

30. _____ I like to identify myself as an American.

31. _____ I have difficulty accepting some ideas held by Anglos.

32. _____ I have difficulty accepting certain attitudes held by Anglos.

33. _____ I have difficulty accepting some behaviors exhibited by Anglos.

34. _____ I have difficulty accepting some values held by some Anglos.

35. _____ I have difficulty accepting certain practices and customs commonly found in some Anglos.

36. _____ I have, or think I would have, difficulty accepting Anglos as close personal friends.

37. _____ I have difficulty accepting some ideas held by some Mexicans.

38. _____ I have difficulty accepting certain attitudes held by Mexicans.

39. _____ I have difficulty accepting some behaviors exhibited by Mexicans.

40. _____ I have difficulty accepting some values held by some Mexicans.

41. _____ I have difficulty accepting certain practices and customs commonly found in some Mexicans.

42. _____ I have, or think I would have, difficulty accepting Mexicans as close personal friends.

43. _____ I have difficulty accepting ideas held by some Mexican-Americans.

44. _____ I have difficulty accepting certain attitudes held by Mexican-Americans.

45. _____ I have difficulty accepting some behaviors exhibited by Mexican-Americans.

46. _____ I have difficulty accepting some values held by Mexican-Americans.

47. _____ I have difficulty accepting certain practices and customs commonly found in some Mexican-Americans.

48. _____ I have, or think I would have, difficulty accepting Mexican-Americans as close personal friends.

Scoring:

1. Sum your responses to the following items: 2, 4, 7, 9, 10, 13, 15, 16, 19, 23, 25, 27, and 30. Divide the sum by 13. This is your Anglo Orientation Score (AOS).

2. Sum your responses to the following items: 1, 3, 5, 6, 8, 11, 12, 14, 17, 18, 20, 21, 22, 24, 26, 28, and 29. Divide the sum by 17. This is your Mexican Orientation Score (MOS).

3. Sum your responses to the following items: 31, 32, 33, 34, 35, and 36. This is your Anglo Marginality (ANGMAR).

4. Sum your responses to the following items: 37, 38, 39, 40, 41, and 42. This is your Mexican Marginality (MEXMAR).

5. Sum your responses to the following items: 43, 44, 45, 46, 47, and 48. This is your Mexican-American Marginality (MAMARG).

Acculturative Types Generated by ARSMA-II
Traditional Mexican = MOS scores ≥ 3.7 and AOS scores ≤ 3.24.
Integrated = AOS ≥ 3.5 and MOS ≥ 2.8.
Marginal = ANGMAR ≥ 17.34, MEXMAR ≥ 17, and MAMARG ≥ 15.
Separation = MEXMAR ≤ 11, ANGMAR ≥ 15, and MAMARG ≥ 15.
Assimilated = MOS ≤ 2.4 and AOS ≥ 4.

Source: Acculturation Scale for Mexican-Americans II from I. Cuellas et al., "Acculturation Rating Scale for Mexican-Americans," *Hispanic Journal of Behavioral Sciences,* Vol. 17, 1995, pp. 274–305. Copyright © 1995 Sage Publications. Used by permission of the publisher.

African-Americans who complete the instrument are asked to indicate their preference for things African-American, their religious beliefs and practices, their experience with traditional African-American foods, childhood experiences, superstitions, interracial attitudes and cultural mistrust of the White majority, "falling out," traditional African-American games, Black family values, and family practices. This scale is designed for African-Americans in the United States and is not applicable to other microcultural groups.

The two scales discussed here are valid indices of acculturation for Hispanics and African-Americans and indicate that cultural diversity can be measured reliably. Such measurements give us a better understanding of an individual's perceptual context. The more we know about a person's individual level of acculturation, the better able we are to provide culturally competent services to him or her.

SELF-ASSESSMENT 11.2

African-American Acculturation Scale

On a scale ranging from 1 to 7, indicate the extent to which you agree or disagree with the statement. 1 = totally disagree, 2 = disagree, 3 = slightly disagree, 4 = don't know, 5 = slightly agree, 6 = agree, and 7 = totally agree.

1. _____ Most of the music I listen to is by black artists.
2. _____ I like black music more than white music.
3. _____ The person I admire most is black.
4. _____ I listen to black radio stations.
5. _____ I try to watch all the black shows on TV.
6. _____ Most of my friends are black.
7. _____ I believe in the Holy Ghost.
8. _____ I believe in heaven and hell.
9. _____ I like gospel music.
10. _____ I am currently a member of a black church.
11. _____ Prayer can cure disease.
12. _____ The church is the heart of the black community.
13. _____ I know how to cook chitlins.
14. _____ I eat chitlins once in a while.
15. _____ Sometimes I cook ham hocks.
16. _____ I know how long you're supposed to cook collard greens.
17. _____ I went to a mostly black elementary school.

18. _____ I went (or go) to a mostly black high school.

19. _____ I grew up in a mostly black neighborhood.

20. _____ I avoid splitting a pole.

21. _____ When the palm of your hand itches, you'll receive some money.

22. _____ There's some truth to many old superstitions.

23. _____ IQ tests were set up purposefully to discriminate against black people.

24. _____ Most tests (like the SAT and tests to get a job) are set up to make sure blacks don't get high scores on them.

25. _____ Deep in their hearts, most white people are racists.

26. _____ I have seen people "fall out." I know what "falling out" means.

27. _____ When I was a child, I used to play tonk. I know how to play bid whist.

28. _____ It's better to move your whole family ahead in this world than it is to be out for only yourself.

29. _____ Old people are wise.

30. _____ When I was young, my parent(s) sent me to stay with a relative (aunt, uncle, grandmother) for a few days or weeks, and then I went back home again.

31. _____ When I was young, I took a bath with my sister, brother, or some other relative.

Scoring: Sum your responses to the above 33 items. Your score must range between 33 and 231.

Scores 33–60 = Acculturated.

Scores 66–85 = Mostly acculturated.

Scores 99–130 = Bicultural (slightly acculturated).

Scores 165–185 = Bicultural (slightly traditional).

Scores 198–200 = Mostly traditional.

Scores 200–231 = Traditional.

Source: "The African American Acculturation Scale II" from H. Landrine & E. A. Klonoff, "The African American Acculturation Scale II," *Journal of Black Psychology,* Vol. 21, 1995, pp. 124–153. Copyright © 1995 Association of Black Psychologists. Used by permission of Sage Publications.

CULTURE SHOCK

When people move to a new culture, they take with them the values, beliefs, customs, and behaviors of their old culture. Often, depending on the degree of similarity between the old and the new culture, the values, beliefs, customs, and behaviors of the native culture clash with those of the new culture. This can result in disorientation, misunderstandings, conflict, stress, and anxiety. Researchers call this phenomenon *culture shock.* Winkelman defines culture shock as a multifaceted experience that results from the numerous stressors that occur when coming into contact with a different culture.[27] Anyone can experience culture shock, although some are more prone to it than others. Winkelman maintains that culture shock can occur with immigrant groups, such as foreign students and refugees, international business exchanges, Peace Corps volunteers, and social workers entering new communities during crises, as well as for members of microcultural groups within their own culture and society. Expatriate professors teaching abroad often describe their experiences using the term *education shock.*

Anthropologist Kalervo Oberg was the first to apply the term *culture shock* to the effects associated with the tension and anxiety of entering into a new culture combined with the sensations of loss, confusion, and powerlessness resulting from the forfeiture of cultural norms and social rituals.[28] Likewise, Winkelman points out that culture shock stems from the challenges associated with new cultural surroundings in addition to the loss of a familiar cultural environment.[29]

Culture shock appears to be a psychological and social process that progresses in stages, usually lasting as long as a year. Most models of culture shock include four stages. The first model of culture shock, developed by Oberg nearly fifty years ago, incorporates a medical metaphor and terminology, beginning with the incubation stage, followed by crisis, leading to recovery, and finishing with full recovery.[30] Smalley's model begins with a fascination stage, then hostility, adjustment, and biculturalism. Richardson's four-stage model includes elation, depression, recovery, and acculturation. Kealey's model incorporates exploration, frustration, coping, and adjustment phases[31] (see Table 11.1).

Most models of culture shock describe the process curvilinearly, or by what Lysgaard called the "U curve hypothesis."[32] Elaborating on the "U curve," Professor Kim Zapf asserts that culture shock begins with feelings of optimism and even elation that eventually give way to frustration, tension, and anxiety as individuals are unable to interact effectively with their new environment. As they develop strategies for resolving conflict, people begin to restore their confidence and eventually recover and reach some level of acculturation.[33]

Table 11.1   Culture Shock Models

Oberg (1954)	Smalley(1963J	Richardson (1974)	Kealey(1978)
1. Incubation	1. Fascination	1. Elation	1. Exploration
2. Crisis	2. Hostility	2. Depression	2. Frustration
3. Recovery	3. Adjustment	3. Recovery	3. Coping
4. Full recovery	4. Biculturalism	4. Acculturation	4. Adjustment

The initial stage of culture shock, usually called something like the *tourist* or *honeymoon stage,* is characterized by intense excitement and euphoria associated with being somewhere different and unusual (see Figure 11.3). Winkelman asserts that this stage is typical of that experienced by people who enter other cultures temporarily during honeymoons, vacations, or brief business trips.[34] The stresses associated with cultural differences are tolerated and may even seem fun and humorous. During the tourist phase, the newcomers' primary interaction with their new cultural environment is through major cultural institutions, such as museums, hotels, Western restaurants, and so forth. This phase may last weeks or months but is temporary. In some instances, the tourist phase may be very short, as when newcomers are confronted with drastic changes in climate or hostile political environments.

Eventually, the fun and excitement associated with the tourist phase gives way to frustration and real stress, or active *culture shock.* Failure events once considered minor and funny are now perceived as stressful. Winkelman maintains that culture shock is partially based on the simultaneous effects of cognitive overload and behavioral inadequacy that are rooted in the psychological and physical stresses associated with confronting a new environment. The new environment requires a great deal of conscious energy that was not required in the old environrnent, which leads to cognitive overload and fatigue. People also experience role shock in that the behaviors associated with their role in their native culture may be dramatically different in the new culture. Finally, people may experience personal shock in the form of a loss of intimacy with interpersonal partners. In describing the second phase of culture shock, Winkelman notes,

> Things start to go wrong, minor issues become major problems, and cultural differences become irritating. Excessive preoccupation with cleanliness of food, drinking water, bedding, and surroundings begins. One experiences increasing disappointments, frustrations, impatience, and tension. Life does not make sense and one may feel helpless, confused, disliked by others, or treated like a child.[35]

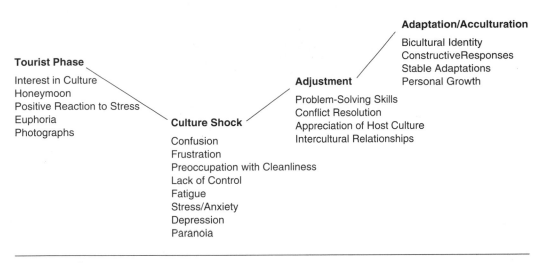

Adaptation/Acculturation

Bicultural Identity
ConstructiveResponses
Stable Adaptations
Personal Growth

Tourist Phase

Interest in Culture
Honeymoon
Positive Reaction to Stress
Euphoria
Photographs

Adjustment

Problem-Solving Skills
Conflict Resolution
Appreciation of Host Culture
Intercultural Relationships

Culture Shock

Confusion
Frustration
Preoccupation with Cleanliness
Lack of Control
Fatigue
Stress/Anxiety
Depression
Paranoia

Figure 11.3

Rinesmith notes that during the culture shock phase, people feel help-less, isolated, and depressed. Paranoia—in which newcomers are convinced that their troubles are deliberate attempts by the natives to disrupt their lives—is also a typical response to culture shock. In this phase, people may develop irrational fears of being cheated, robbed, or even assaulted.[36]

The degree to which one experiences culture shock varies from person to person. Walt Lonner has identified six factors that affect the nature of culture shock experienced: (1) control factors, (2) interpersonal factors, (3) organismic/biological factors, (4) intrapersonal factors, (5) spatial/temporal factors, and (6) geopolitical factors. Churchman and Mitrani have added three additional factors: (1) the degree of similarity between one's native and new culture, including the physical environment; (2) the degree and quality of information about the new environment, and (3) the host culture's attitude and policies toward immigrants (see Figure 11.4).[37]

Some people never recuperate from the crisis stage of culture shock and return home or isolate themselves from the host culture by restricting their interaction with it, such as by fostering only intracultural relationships (for example, in a military base or university setting). When the lines of communication with the host culture are severed, there is little hope of acculturation or recovery from the crisis stage.

The third phase of culture shock is typically called the *adjustment or reorientation phase.* Here people eventually realize that the problems associated with the host culture are due not to deliberate attempts by the natives, but to a real difference in values, beliefs, and behaviors. At this stage, people actively seek out effective problem-solving and conflict resolution

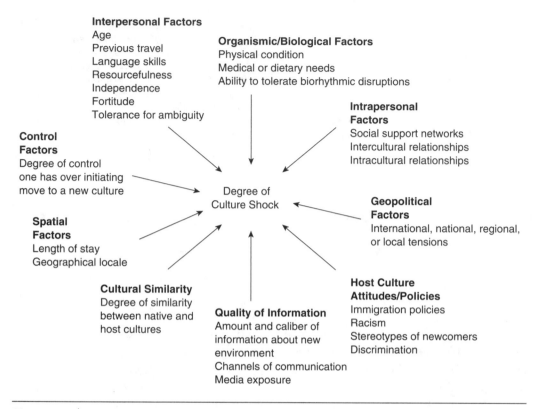

Interpersonal Factors
Age
Previous travel
Language skills
Resourcefulness
Independence
Fortitude
Tolerance for ambiguity

Organismic/Biological Factors
Physical condition
Medical or dietary needs
Ability to tolerate biorhythmic disruptions

Intrapersonal Factors
Social support networks
Intercultural relationships
Intracultural relationships

Control Factors
Degree of control one has over initiating move to a new culture

Spatial Factors
Length of stay
Geographical locale

Degree of Culture Shock

Geopolitical Factors
International, national, regional, or local tensions

Cultural Similarity
Degree of similarity between native and host cultures

Quality of Information
Amount and caliber of information about new environment
Channels of communication
Media exposure

Host Culture Attitudes/Policies
Immigration policies
Racism
Stereotypes of newcomers
Discrimination

Figure 11.4

strategies. They begin to develop a positive attitude about solving their problems. As Winkelman notes, the host culture begins to make sense, and pessimistic reactions and responses to it are lessened as people recognize that their problems are due largely to their inability to understand, accept, and adapt.[38] Typically the adjustment phase is gradual and slow, and often people relapse into minicrisis stages.

The final stage of culture shock is labeled the *adaptation or acculturation stage*. At this point, individuals actively engage the culture with their new problem-solving and conflict resolution tools with some degree of success. Young Kim argues that to the extent that people acculturate to their new culture, they experience cultural transformation. They possess a degree of functional fitness in which the external demands of the host culture are met with appropriate and consistent internal responses. Moreover, they develop a level of competency in communicating with the natives. As a result of their successes, people also acquire psychological health, take on an intercultural identity, and foster a sense of integration with their host environment.[39]

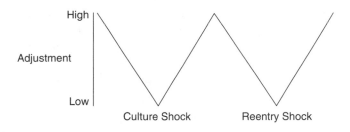

Figure 11.5

W Curve Models of Reentry Culture Shock

As mentioned above, most models of culture shock contain four phases in the "U curve" tradition. But many people who have lived outside of their native culture argue that they experience a kind of reentry shock when they return to their native culture. Furnham and Bochner's "W curve" model of culture shock contains two "U curves"—the initial culture shock experienced when the traveler enters a new culture, and a reentry shock "U curve" (see Figure 11.5). In other words, when people return home after an extended stay in a foreign culture, they experience another round of culture shock, this time in their native culture.

Furnham and Bochner note that students returning from study abroad often report a reentry shock phenomenon. Some students fear that they will be treated differently by their "stay-at-home" peers, friends, and parents when they return. In addition, because they have successfully acculturated themselves to a foreign culture, they essentially have to reacculturate to their native culture. Students frequently report that the nature of long-term international travel transforms them. When they return home, they are different and have taken on new perspectives and see the world with a different outlook. Students lament that communicating their experiences abroad to their friends and families is often very difficult.

Strategies for Managing Culture Shock

If you are traveling to a new culture for the first time, it is likely that you will experience some kind of culture shock. The level of intensity you experience will vary. In addition, the duration of your culture shock will depend on your ability to manage it. Probably the best piece of commonsense advice is to do your homework and be prepared.

Successful management of culture shock depends on an awareness of its symptoms and the degree of its severity. Winkelman maintains that sometimes people falsely attribute their problems to sources other than culture shock. He argues that there is a tendency to deny that one is experiencing it. His advice is that one should accept the fact that virtually all atypical problems that occur during acculturation are caused by or exacerbated by culture shock.[40] Professor Kim Zapf has developed a questionnaire, called the Culture Shock Profile, that is designed to assess the intensity of culture shock you are experiencing.

Please keep in mind that everyone experiences some degree of culture shock when entering a new culture for some length of time. Zapf recommends that the Culture Shock Profile should be taken several times during the first year of your move—specifically, after the first month, then sometime during about your fourth or fifth month, and then after one year. If managed appropriately, most culture shock is significantly reduced after a year.[41]

Study the Host Culture. Read about your new culture, attend seminars, rent films, and socialize with host nationals about their culture. Popular "Hollywood" films may distort the reality of the culture, so be careful interpreting them. Most embassies have Web pages that include information about the geography, population, climate, government, and education system of their country. If possible, interview friends or colleagues who have traveled or lived in the culture.

Study the Local Environment. In addition to studying about the general culture, try to learn as much as you can about the local environment in which you will live—such as where to buy favorite foods, where to find physicians trained in the United States, where schools are located, how public transportation operates (if there is any), or how to fill prescriptions. Taken-for-granted operations that we unconsciously perform in our day-to-day lives will be different in your host culture.

Learn Basic Verbal and Nonverbal Language Skills. If you are not fluent in the language of your host culture, or even if its members speak English, it is a good idea to familiarize yourself with their verbal and nonverbal language. Attach labels to the various items of your home in the language of the host culture. Practice functional and frequently used phrases that will help you perform basic survival tactics. Keep in mind that common verbal colloquialisms can be wildly misinterpreted across cultures. Find out nonverbal mannerisms and expectations for personal space, time, paralanguage, kinesics, haptics, and so forth. Learn some appropriate verbal and nonverbal formalities of greeting rituals.

Develop Intercultural Relationships. A common mistake made by many expatriates is remaining within a network of intracultural relationships. The best way to get to know and understand another culture is to establish relationships with host nationals. You will learn more about another culture by initiating and developing relationships with host nationals in your own country than you will by traveling to their country and staying in Western hotels and seeing the countryside on a tour bus with a translator. Host nationals know the norms and subtleties of their culture and can be of immense help in assisting you to learn and understand them.

Maintain an Intimate Social Network. Although this may sound contradictory to the above recommendation, if possible, maintain your intimate intracultural relational network. Close interpersonal relations can provide positive feedback on matters related to one's self-esteem and emotional needs. Venting your problems to understanding and empathetic others can be an effective outlet for stress and frustration.

Assume the Principle of Difference/Remember Your Perceptual Context. Try to understand that things are simply going to be different in your new culture and that the way you are accustomed to doing things is not the only way. Remember that your perceptual context is biased in favor of your culture and your ingroup. How you perceive your host culture is not objective or neutral. All of the verbal and nonverbal messages encoded and decoded are filtered through your cultural, microcultural, environmental, socio-relational, and perceptual filters. These filters bias and color your expectations, which will certainly be violated as you interact with your host culture.

Anticipate Failure Events. Regardless of how well you prepare for your journey, there will be moments when you are unsuccessful at accomplishing your goals. Before you depart, anticipate failure events. No doubt you will engage in acts that are unintentional, intentionally performed but inappropriate for the situation, or incorrectly executed.

SELF-ASSESSMENT 11.3

Culture Shock Profile

Below is a list of 33 terms that may or may not describe how you feel about your experiences in your new culture. On a scale of 0 to 3, indicate the frequency with which you experience the feeling. 0 = none, 1 = slight, 2 = moderate, and 3 = great.

I feel:

1. _____Enthusiastic

2. _____Impatient/irritable

3. _____A desire to resign

4. _____Happy/content

5. _____Energetic

6. _____Rejected

7. _____Purposeful/directed

8. _____Pessimistic/hopeless

9. _____Contemptuous of others (natives)

10. _____Angry/resentful

11. _____A need to complain

12. _____Creative

13. _____Confident/self-assured

14. _____Ready to cry

15. _____Challenged

16. _____Cynical

17. _____A sense of discovery

18. _____Helpless/vulnerable

19. _____Optimistic/hopeful

20. _____Inadequate/self-doubt

21. _____Isolated/homesick

22. _____Physically ill

23. _____I need to "get out"

24. _____Confused /disoriented

25. _____Excited/stimulated

26. _____Accepted

27. _____A sense of loss

28. _____Overwhelmed/bewildered

29. _____Afraid/panic

30. _____Depressed/withdrawn

31. _____Frustrated/thwarted

32. _____Exhausted/sleep difficulty

33. _____Apathetic/"I don't care"

Scoring: To determine your level of culture shock, reverse your score for items 1, 4, 5, 7, 12, 13, 17, 19, 25, and 26. If your original score was a 0, reverse it to a 3. If your original score was a 1, reverse it to a 2. If your original score was a 2, reverse it to a 1, and if your original score was a 3, reverse it to a 0. After reversing the score for those 10 items, sum the entire 33 items. Scores must range from 0 to 99. The higher your score, the more culture shock you are experiencing, and you should engage in some of the strategies listed in this section.

Source: M. K. Zapf, "Remote Practice and Culture Shock: Social Workers Moving to Isolated Northern Regions," *Social Work* 38 (1993), 694–705.

CHAPTER SUMMARY

Leaving your native culture for a new one can be one of the most rewarding yet challenging experiences of a lifetime. Having relocated to a new culture, everyone goes through a process of acculturation—that is, a process of cultural change that results from ongoing contact between two or more culturally different groups. For some, this process can be particularly difficult, whereas for others it is relatively easy. Acculturation is in large part a function of how much interaction one chooses to have with members of the new culture and how much of the old culture one desires to maintain.

Virtually everyone experiences some degree of culture shock when entering a new culture for an extended period of time. Culture shock results in feelings of disorientation, misunderstandings, conflict, stress, and anxiety. Often the very same feelings are experienced when a traveler returns home. In addition to discussing its causes and symptoms, this chapter has offered several strategies for assessing and managing culture shock. Although culture shock sounds awful, having an understanding of its causes, symptoms, and effects is the first step in alleviating the severity you might experience. Generally speaking, most students who travel abroad experience only minor levels of culture shock.

GLOSSARY OF TERMS

Acculturation: The process of cultural change that results from ongoing contact between two or more culturally different groups.

Acculturative stress: The anxiety and tension associated with acculturation.

Adjustment phase: Third stage of culture shock, in which people actively seek out effective problem-solving and conflict resolution strategies.

Assimilation: The degree to which an individual takes on the behaviors and language habits and practices the basic rules and norms of the host culture while relinquishing ties with the native culture.

Cultural transmutation: Mode of acculturation in which the individual chooses to identify with a third cultural group (microculture) that materializes out of the native and host cultural groups.

Culture shock: The effects associated with the tension and anxiety of entering a new culture, combined with the sensations of loss, confusion, and powerlessness resulting from the forfeiture of cultural norms and social rituals.

Integration: Mode of acculturation in which the individual develops a kind of bicultural orientation that successfully blends and synthesizes cultural dimensions from both groups while maintaining an identity in each group.

Reentry Shock: The effects associated with the tension and anxiety of returning to one's native culture after an extended stay in a foreign culture.

REFERENCES

1. Condon, J. C., & Yousef, F. *An Introduction to Intercultural Communication* (Indianapolis, Ind.: Bobbs-Merrill, 1975). (Quote on page 270.)

2. Redfield, R., Linton, R., & Herskovits, M. "Memorandum on the Study of Acculturation," *American Anthropologist* 38 (1936), 149–152.

3. Berry, J. W., & Sam, D. T. "Acculturation and Adaptation," in *Handbook of Cross-Cultural Psychology: Social Behavior and Applications,* vol. 3, ed. Berry, J. W., Segall, M. H., & Kagitcibasa, C. (Boston: Allyn & Bacon, 1997), 291–326.

4. Ibid.

5. Nwadiora, E., & McAdoo, H. "Acculturative Stress Among Amerasian Refugees: Gender and Racial Differences," *Adolescence* 31 (1996), 477–488.

6. Miranda, A. O., & Matheny, K. B. "Socio-Psychological Predictors and Acculturative Stress Among Latino Adults," *Journal of Mental Health Counseling* 22 (2000), 306–318.

7. Smart, J. F., & Smart, D. W. "Acculturative Stress of Hispanics: Loss and Challenge," *Journal of Counseling & Development* 73 (1995), 390–397; D. Hovey, "Psychosocial Predictors of Acculturative Stress in Mexican Immigrants," *Journal of Psychology* 134 (2000), 490–502.

8. Hovey, J. D. "Psychological Predictors of Acculturative Stress in Mexican Immigrants." *Journal of Psychology* 134, (2000), 490–502.

9. Nwadiora, E., & McAdoo, H. "Acculturative Stress Among Amerasian Refugees."

10. Berry, J. W. "Understanding the Process of Acculturation for Primary Intervention" (unpublished manuscript, Department of Psychology, Queen's College, Kingston, Ontario, 1987), cited in Nwadiora and McAdoo, "Acculturative Stress Among Amerasian Refugees."

11. Kim, Y. Y. "Adapting to a New Culture," in *Intercultural Communication: A Reader,* 8th ed., ed. L. A. Samovar and R. E. Porter (Belmont, Calif.: Wadsworth, 1997), pp. 404–417.

12. Ibid.

13. Ibid.

14. Liebkind, K. "Acculturation and Stress: Vietnamese Refugees in Finland," *Journal of Cross-Cultural Psychology* 27 (1996), 161–180.

15. Berry, J. W. "Psychology of Acculturation," in *Nebraska Symposium on Motivation 1989,* ed. R. A. Dienstbier (Lincoln: University of Nebraska Press, 1990), pp. 201–234.

16. Berry, "Psychology of Acculturation"; H. L. K. Coleman, "Strategies for Coping with Cultural Diversity," *Counseling Psychology* 23 (1995), 722–741.

17. Coleman, "Strategies for Coping with Cultural Diversity"; Cuellar, L., Arnold, B., & Maldonado, R. "Acculturation Rating Scale for Mexican-Americans II: A Revision of

the Original ARSMA," *Hispanic Journal of Behavioral Sciences* 17 (1995), 275–305.

18. Ibid.

19. Cuellar, Arnold, and Maldonado, "Acculturation Rating Scale for Mexican-Americans II."

20. Mendoza, R. H. "An Empirical Scale to Measure Type and Degree of Acculturation in Mexican-American Adolescents and Adults," *Journal of Cross-Cultural Psychology* 20 (1989), 372–385; Cuellar, Arnold, and Maldonado, "Acculturation Rating Scale for Mexican-Americans II"; Coleman, "Strategies for Coping with Cultural Diversity."

21. Landrine, H., & Klonoff, E. A. "The African-American Acculturation Scale II: Cross Validation and Short Form," *Journal of Black Psychology* 21 (1995), 124–153.

22. DeLeon, B., & Mendez, S. "Factorial Structure of a Measure of Acculturation in a Puerto Rican Population," *Educational and Psychological Measurement* 56 (1996), 155–166.

23. Landrine and Klonoff, "The African-American Acculturation Scale II."

24. Cuellar, L., Harris, C., & Jasso, R. "An Acculturation Scale for Mexican-Americans: Normal and Clinical Populations," *Hispanic Journal of Behavioral Sciences* 2 (1980), 199–217.

25. Cuellar, Arnold, and Maldonado, "Acculturation Rating Scale for Mexican-Americans II."

26. Landrine and Klonoff, "The African-American Acculturation Scale II."

27. Winkelman, M. "Cultural Shock and Adaptation," *Journal of Counseling and Development* 73 (1994), 121–127.

28. Oberg, K. *Culture Shock,* Bobbs-Merrill Series in Social Science, A-329 (Indianapolis: Bobbs-Merrill, 1954); K. Oberg, "Culture Shock: Adjustments to New Cultural Environments," *Practical Anthropology* 4 (1960), 177–182.

29. Winkelman, "Cultural Shock and Adaptation."

30. Oberg, *Culture Shock;* Oberg, "Culture Shock: Adjustments to New Cultural Environments."

31. These models are briefly reviewed in M. K. Zapf, "Remote Practice and Culture Shock: Social Workers Moving to Isolated Northern Regions," *SocialWork* 38 (1993), 694–705; see also W. A. Smalley, "Culture Shock, Language Shock, and the Shock of Self-Discovery," *Practical Anthropology* 10 (1963), 49–56; A. Richardson, *British Immigrants and Australia: A Psycho-Social Inquiry* (Canberra: Australian National University Press, 1974); D. J. Kealey, "Adaptation to a New Environment," in *Pre-Departure Documentation Kit,* ed. Canadian International Development Agency (Hull, Quebec: CIDA Briefing Centre, 1978), pp. 48–55.

32. Lysgaard, S. "Adjustment in a Foreign Society: Norwegian Fulbright Grantees Visiting the United States," *International Social Science Bulletin* 7 (1995), 45–51.

33. Zapf, "Remote Practice and Culture Shock."

34. Winkelman, "Cultural Shock and Adaptation."

35. Ibid.

36. Rhinesmith, S. *Bringing Home the World* (New York: Walsh and Co., 1985).

37. W. Lonner, "Foreword," in *Culture Shock: Psychological Reactions to Unfamiliar Environments,* ed. Furnham, A., & Bochner, S. (London; Methuen, 1986), pp. xv-xx; A. Churchman and M. Mitrani, "The Role of the Physical Environment in Culture Shock," *Environment and Behavior* 29 (1997), 64–87.

38. Winkelman, "Cultural Shock and Adaptation."

39. Kim, "Adapting to a New Culture."

40. Winkelman, "Cultural Shock and Adaptation."

41. Zapf, "Remote Practice and Culture Shock."

CHAPTER 12

Intercultural Competence

All human beings are captives of their culture.

—Edward Hall[1]

Chapter Objectives

After reading this chapter, you should be able to

1. Identify the four fundamental components of intercultural communication competence.
2. Identify and discuss the elements of the knowledge component of intercultural competence.
3. Assess your general cultural awareness.
4. Identify and discuss the elements of the affective component of intercultural competence.
5. Assess your intercultural willingness to communicate.
6. Identify and discuss the elements of the psychomotor component of intercultural competence.
7. Identify and discuss the elements of the situational features that affect intercultural competence.
8. Prepare an intercultural training seminar.

One of the fundamental goals of this book is to help you become a competent intercultural communicator. This final chapter is devoted to *intercultural communication competence,* which is defined as the degree to which you effectively adapt your verbal and nonverbal messages to the appropriate cultural context. When you communicate with someone from a different culture, in order to be interculturally competent, you will have to adjust and modify the kinds of verbal and nonverbal messages you send. This process requires that you have some *knowledge* about the person with whom you are communicating, that you are *motivated* to communicate with him or her, and that you have the appropriate verbal and nonverbal *skills* in order to encode and decode messages.

Interculturally competent people successfully and effectively adapt their verbal and nonverbal messages to the appropriate cultural context. For the most part, competence is something that is perceived about another person, rather than something an individual inherently possesses. In other words, an individual may appear competent to one person but not to another. Moreover, intercultural competence varies from situation to situation. That is, a particular American may be quite competent while interacting with Chinese people and relatively incompetent when interacting with Germans.

Verbal and nonverbal appropriateness and effectiveness are two important qualities of intercultural competence. According to Brian Spitzberg, appropriate behaviors conform to the rules, norms, and expectancies of the cultural context.[2] For example, when greeting a Japanese person in Japan, you are expected to bow. The rules associated with bowing are determined by one's status (e.g., age, sex, occupation, education). The person of lower status bows lower and longer than the person with higher status and typically does not make direct eye contact. Effective behaviors are those that successfully perform and accomplish the rules and norms.[3] For example, to the extent to which you are able to bow correctly, your behavior will be perceived as effective and competent. As we have seen throughout this book, the appropriateness and effectiveness of verbal and nonverbal messages varies considerably across cultures. Behaviors considered appropriate in one culture may not be wholly appropriate in another culture.

AN INTERCULTURAL CONVERSATION: BUSINESS COMMUNICATION

Consider the exchange between Arab businessman Hashim Abdu Hashim and his American counterpart Steve Jones.[4]

The scene: Mr. Jones is sitting (on the floor) in the hallway of a building in Saudi Arabia, waiting to meet with his Saudi counterpart, Hashim Abdu Hashim. The hallway is noisy, cluttered with people moving quickly from room to room. Mr. Jones arrived in Saudi Arabia two days earlier for a scheduled meeting. Since then his meeting has been postponed and rescheduled several times. After several hours of waiting in the hallway,

Mr. Jones is called into Hashim's office. The office has no chairs, but instead, elaborate and ornate pillows on the floor. The walls are draped with embellished afghans. Mr. Jones enters.

Jones: *Hello, Hashim. Gosh, I finally get to see you. I've been waiting for two days!*

Hashim: *Hello, Mr. Jones. It is good to see you.*

Jones: *Thanks. It's good to see you also. How's Mrs. Hashim?*

Hashim: *Was your trip to our country all right?*

Jones: *Yes, everything is fine.* (At this point the two are interrupted by a servant pouring tea. Jones refuses . . . then reluctantly accepts) *No . . . no . . . thanks, I've had enough tea. Well . . . OK, thanks. So . . . Hashim, I came all the way over here to see if I could get you to speed things up with our order. See, our supplies have been sitting at some dock along the coast for two weeks. I was wondering if you could sign this petition* (hands it to Hashim using his left hand) *to hurry up the process.*

Hashim: *Hmmm . . . this is a problem?*

Jones: *Yes. Gosh, Hashim, I understand that sometimes supplies sit on ships for weeks at a time! Your people could really use these computers you've ordered. I need to have them released to your custody as soon as possible.*

Hashim: *I see. Well . . . we have been without computers for thousands of years. Waiting is no problem.*

Source: Adapted from L. Copeland, *Managing the Overseas Assignment* (San Francisco: Copeland Griggs Productions, 1983.)

Do you think Mr. Hashim perceived Mr. Jones as competent? Do you think Mr. Hashim perceived Mr. Jones's behaviors as appropriate and effective? Probably not. Mr. Jones commits at least five cultural blunders that severely jeopardize any possible future contract with Hashim. First, he mentions that he's been waiting for two days to see Hashim. Jones has not recognized the polychronic nature of Saudi Arabia. Business gets done on its own time. Second, Jones refuses the tea that has been offered to him in hospitality. Then, in a gross error of etiquette, he inquires about Hashim's wife. In Saudi, a man's wife is for his eyes only. Continuing on his blundering way, Jones hands Hashim the contract with his left hand. In many Muslim

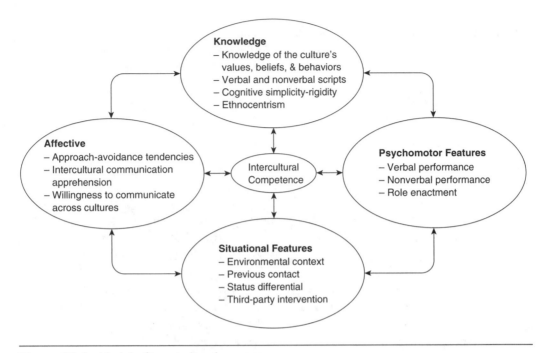

Figure 12.1 Model of intercultural competence

cultures the left hand is the "dirty" hand—that is, used for cleaning the body and handling waste. Finally, Jones demonstrates the urgency of his mission and getting the computers off the supply ship. His emphasis on schedules and deadlines communicates to Hashim that he is either insane or irreligious. Many Arabs believe literally in the phrase "Insha Allah," meaning "God willing." To them, the nature of things, especially time, is controlled by God. Events, meetings, and happenings are completed only if God wills them. Mr. Jones's behavior was neither appropriate nor effective. Mr. Hashim was probably offended and may never do business with Mr. Jones again.[5]

A MODEL OF INTERCULTURAL COMPETENCE

Brian Spitzberg and his colleague Bill Cupach argue that there are three necessary and interdependent ingredients of communication competence: (1) knowledge, (2) motivation, and (3) behavior.[6] The model of *intercultural competence* presented in this text includes these three dimensions along with a fourth component, situational features (see Figure 12.1). In this model, intercultural competence is the potential outcome of four interdependent components of the intercultural communication encounter. Each component influences and is influenced by the other three.

The Knowledge Component

The *knowledge component* of intercultural competence consists of how much one knows about the culture of the person with whom one is interacting. To the extent that people have knowledge about other cultures, they are more likely to be perceived as competent (although there is no guarantee!). Consider your own general cultural awareness. Below is a self-report instrument designed to assess your level of cultural awareness.[7]

SELF-ASSESSMENT 12.1

Cross-Cultural Awareness

The scale consists of 15 items about what you know or don't know about other cultures. Respond to each item on a scale of 1 to 5. 1 = definitely no, 2 = not likely, 3 = not sure, 4 = likely, and 5 = definitely yes. Be as honest with yourself as possible in completing the scale.

1. __3__ I can accurately list three countries that are considered collectivistic.
2. __4__ I can accurately identify three countries that have high power distance.
3. __2__ I can conduct business in a language other than my own.
4. __4__ I know the appropriate distance at which to stand when interacting with people in at least two other cultures.
5. __4__ I know the appropriate touch rules in at least two other cultures.
6. __2__ I know in what countries I can use first names when conducting business.
7. __1__ I can name the (political/governmental) leaders of four other countries.
8. __2__ I understand and can practice appropriate gift-giving in three other countries.
9. __2__ I can identify some gestures appropriate in the U.S.A. that are considered obscene in other countries.
10. __2/3__ I understand sex-role differences in at least two other countries.
11. __3__ I can name three countries that are considered polychronic.
12. __1__ I understand the proper protocol for exchanging business cards in at least two other countries.
13. __4__ I understand the business philosophies of Japan and China.
14. __3__ I can name the United States' top three trading partners.
15. __5__ I can name the currencies in four other countries.

Scoring: Sum the 15 responses. Scores must range from 15 to 75. The higher your score, the more culturally aware you are. Scores at or above 50 indicate a relatively healthy degree of cultural awareness.

In order to be perceived as culturally knowledgeable, minimally one should have some comprehension of the other person's dominant cultural values and beliefs. In addition, one should know whether the person is from an individualistic or collectivistic, high- or low-context, high or low power distance, or high- or low-uncertainty-avoidant culture. In the model of intercultural competence, *verbal and nonverbal scripts* are also a part of the knowledge component. Communication theorist Charles Berger argues that verbal and nonverbal scripts (or plans) guide communication action. Scripts are like blueprints for communication that provide people with expectations about future communicative encounters with others. Berger has argued that knowledgeable communicators develop and maintain a repertoire of scripts that enable them to comprehend and predict the actions of themselves and others. Berger has demonstrated that people store scripts in long-term memory. According to Berger, when anticipating interaction with others, communicators establish goals. They search their long-term memory for instances when they have tried to accomplish similar goals and then access a script or plan that was successful in achieving these goals in the past. The frequency and similarity with which a particular script has been used facilitates access to it. In never-before-encountered situations people may possess vicariously based scripts. Perhaps one witnessed a similar event by watching a film or by reading a comparable account.[8] The more plans one has, the better equipped one is to enact them.

Cognitive simplicity and rigidity refers to the degree to which individuals process information about persons from different cultures in a simplistic and rigid manner. Young Kim includes this dimension in her model of intercultural conflict. According to Kim, people with simplistic and rigid cognitive systems tend to engage in gross stereotyping. Moreover, such individuals may have very narrowly defined and inflexible categories. Narrow categorizers tend to make more negative and more confident judgments about other people, particularly those from other cultures. Such persons probably think dogmatically (are narrow minded). Metaphorically, a person with a simple and rigid cognitive system sees the world with blinders on, like a racehorse. Obviously, the competent communicator would possess an open and flexible cognitive system. The person with a simple and rigid system would not be perceived as competent.[9]

As discussed in Chapter 5, *ethnocentrism* is the extent to which one perceives one's own group as the center of everything and judges other groups with reference to it. Ethnocentrics tend to create and reinforce negative attitudes and behaviors toward outgroups. Judgments about ingroups and outgroups almost always are biased in favor of the ingroup at the expense of the outgroup. Furthermore, ethnocentric groups see themselves as righteous and exceptional and view their own standards as universal and moral. Outgroups are seen as immoral, subordinate, and impotent. Ethnocentrism is clearly an obstacle to intercultural communication competence. The ethnocentric person most likely possesses narrow categories and a simple and rigid cognitive system.[10] In his research, Rich Wiseman found that ethnocentrism was the strongest predictor of general cultural understanding. That is, higher levels of ethnocentrism were associated with less general cultural understanding. Higher levels of ethnocentrism were also related to less positive regard for other cultures.[11]

The Affective Component

The *affective component* of intercultural communication is the degree to which one approaches or avoids intercultural communication; that is, one's motivation to interact with others from different cultures. A central feature here is intercultural communication apprehension (ICA). ICA is defined by Neuliep and McCroskey as the fear or anxiety associated with either real or anticipated interaction with persons from different cultures. Persons high in ICA tend to avoid interacting with others from different cultures.[12] As mentioned in Chapter 1, because they are seen as strangers, people from different cultures may seem unusual and novel. This difference can create tension and anxiety, which, in turn, can lead to avoidance. On the other hand, some people may be positively predisposed to initiate intercultural interactions even when they are completely free to choose whether or not to communicate. This predisposition, labeled by Jeffrey Kassing, is called *intercultural willingness to communicate*.[13] You can assess your individual level of intercultural willingness to communicate by completing the Intercultural Willingness to Communicate Scale in Self-Assessment 12.2.

SELF-ASSESSMENT 12.2

Intercultural Willingness to Communicate Scale

Below are six situations in which a person might choose to communicate or not to communicate. Assume that you have *completely free choice*. Indicate the percentages of times you would choose to communicate in each type of situation. Keep in mind that you are reporting not the likelihood that you would have an opportunity to talk in these instances, but rather the percentage of times you would talk when the opportunity presented itself. Indicate in the space to the left what percentage of time you would choose to communicate. 0 = never, 100 = always.

1. _____ Talk with someone I perceive to be different from me.

2. _____ Talk with someone from another country.

3. _____ Talk with someone from a culture I know very little about.

4. _____ Talk with someone from a different race than mine.

5. _____ Talk with someone from a different culture.

6. _____ Talk with someone who speaks English as a second language.

Scoring: Your score must range from 0 to 600. Scores below 300 indicate a general unwillingness to communicate interculturally. Scores above 350 indicate a slight willingness to communicate interculturally. Scores above 400 indicate a moderate level, and scores above 500 indicate a high willingness to communicate interculturally.

Source: Adapted from J. W. Kassing, "Development of the Intercultural Willingness to Communicate Scale," *Communication Research Reports* 14 (1997), 399–407.

Young Kim has argued that one's ability to cope with stress also affects one's approach/avoidance tendencies. Because of the potentially inordinate uncertainty of intercultural communication, anxiety levels may be high as well, leading to increased stress. Some people handle stress well, whereas others do not. Gudykunst and Kim maintain that to be an effective intercultural communicator, one needs to tolerate ambiguity to a certain degree. The more that one is able to manage stress and endure ambivalence, the more likely one is to initiate intercultural communication and to be an effective and competent intercultural communicator.[14]

The knowledge component and the affective component of intercultural competence are interdependent in that the more knowledge one has, the more likely one is to approach situations involving intercultural communication. The increase in knowledge generally leads to an increase in motivation. Likewise, the more motivation one has, the more likely one is to pursue interaction with people from different cultures, thereby learning more about them and their culture and increasing one's knowledge.

The Psychomotor Component

The psychomotor component of intercultural communication is the actual enactment of the knowledge and affective components. The elements of the psychomotor component are (1) verbal and nonverbal performance and (2) role enactment. Verbal performance is how people use language. A person may know a great deal about the language of the host culture but not be able to engage in a conversation. Many foreign exchange students in the United States come here not to learn more about English but to practice using it in actual conversations. An American student who recently returned from a year's stay in Japan reported that she had been paid handsomely for hourly conversations with Japanese.

People would come to her apartment and pay her simply to converse in English about trivial subjects for sixty minutes. These Japanese had all the knowledge they needed about English but wanted to sharpen their performance skills. Knowing and being able to use a second language certainly increases one's perceived competence when interacting interculturally. Language scripts and plans that reduce uncertainty are of particular importance. The psychomotor function is where one puts the scripts and plans into action. If one does not speak the language of the host culture, then at the very least one should know some of the basic greetings, requests, and routines used frequently in that language.

Nonverbal performance is also an important part of the psychomotor component. Here the individual needs to pay close attention to the nuances of the kinesic, paralinguistic, haptic, olfactic, and proxemic codes of the other culture. As with verbal knowledge and performance, one may have knowledge of a particular culture's nonverbal mannerisms but may not be able to execute them. Hence, before traveling to a foreign country, it might be wise to polish and refine your repertoire of nonverbal skills. For example, before traveling to Japan, you might practice bowing with family members or friends. Keep in mind also that how you smell will affect how others perceive you. Many cultures feel that Americans tend to smell antiseptic because of our frequent use of soaps, perfumes, and so forth. As mentioned in Chapter 8, we have a tendency to mask the natural odor of the human body, and to many other cultures this custom seems strange and odd.

Role enactment refers to how well one executes the appropriate verbal and nonverbal messages according to one's relative position and role in the host culture. The behaviors that professors in the United States enact in the classroom may be misinterpreted or seen as improper in classrooms in other cultures. Managers must be particularly careful about the types of strategies they employ across cultures. Men and women should know how their sex roles vary across cultures. American women returning from abroad frequently comment on how badly they were treated. The freedoms U.S. women have gained throughout this century are not shared by women across the globe. A female student who had recently returned from a semester of study in southern Italy recounted her experience:

I couldn't believe how the men acted toward me and my friends. When we would walk through town, they would whistle and hiss at us. They would try to touch us and acted like all we wanted to do was sleep with them. It was simply expected. Everyone told us that this was how they treated women and to just get used to it.

As we have seen throughout this text, the verbal and nonverbal behaviors expected for sex and occupation roles vary considerably across cultures. In particular, understanding these two role positions is key to becoming interculturally competent.

Situational Features

The fourth component of intercultural competence is the actual situation in which intercultural communication occurs. Remember that a person may be perceived as competent in one situation and not in another. Perceived competence varies with the situation. Some of the situational features that may affect competence include, but are not limited to, the *environmental context, previous contact, status differential,* and *third-party interventions.* Recall from Chapter 4 the influence of the environment on communication. Some situations may have higher information loads than others, which may affect your motivation and ability to enact appropriate verbal and nonverbal behaviors. Highly loaded situations may increase anxiety and reduce your motivation to approach another. In addition, you should have some knowledge of the host culture's perception of time and space. If you are lucky enough to be invited into someone's home, keep in mind that the use of space in homes varies dramatically across cultures.

In some of her work, Young Kim discusses the importance of previous contact and status differences.[15] Because of the dynamic nature of competence, any previous contact you may have had with a person from another culture may enhance your perception of competence. Competence and trust take time to establish and build, and your competence will grow as you interact more with the people of your host culture. Conversations with persons from other cultures provide a particularly rich source of data for you. The more contact you can have with these people, the more likely you are to learn about them (knowledge) and feel comfortable (affective) interacting with them, thus enabling you to master your verbal and nonverbal skills (psychomotor).

Although you may have sufficient knowledge about another culture and be motivated to interact, status differences may require you to take on multiple modes of behavior. Certain verbal and nonverbal strategies may be more or less appropriate depending on whether you are interacting with someone of lower, equal, or higher status. In the United States, we have a tendency to minimize status differences. In other cultures, as we learned in Chapter 2, one's status determines the order of speakers and the types of codes to use in a given situation. Because your status may be high in one situation and low in another, you should be mindful in understanding how the communication will vary accordingly.[16]

The addition of a third party may noticeably change the dynamics of the situation, and hence your competence. All of a sudden your status may go up or down, as might the status of the person with whom you are interacting. The sex of the third party may also alter the situational features. Topics that were just a moment ago appropriate may now be unfit for discussion. The competent communicator keeps a sharp eye on the changing characteristics of the situation and adapts his or her verbal and nonverbal communication accordingly.

The model of intercultural competence given in Figure 12.1 depicts the knowledge, affective, psychomotor, and situational features as interdependent. This means that as one component changes, the others are affected as well. Generally, as knowledge increases, one's motivation to approach increases. As motivation increases, one is more likely to engage in behaviors. If the behaviors are successful, one learns more about intercultural communication, which serves to further increase motivation. And the cycle continues.

INTERCULTURAL TRAINING PROGRAMS

Throughout the United States communication practitioners offer workshops, seminars, and training programs designed to introduce people to culture and to assist them in becoming interculturally competent. Because of the near reality of the "global village" concept, people from all walks of life, including business owners, managers, teachers, government officials, and family members of expatriates (i.e., persons from the United States living and working abroad) need the knowledge and skills to interact with people from different cultures. Cross-cultural training programs vary in content, but are typically designed to accomplish four goals: (1) assist people in overcoming cultural obstacles that might interfere with their enjoyment of their intercultural experiences, (2) teach people how to initiate and develop relationships with people from other cultures, (3) help people accomplish job-oriented tasks in intercultural assignments, and (4) assist people in learning how to deal with the stress that often accompanies intercultural communication.[17]

The content of cross-cultural training programs varies, of course, but most contain a combination of lecture/discussion, self-assessment instruments, case studies, simulation role-plays, videos, and a variety of homework assignments. The most traditional format of cross-cultural training workshops involves the lecture/discussion format. According to Gudykunst and his colleagues, in this type of format trainers assume that a cognitive understanding of a culture is necessary to be effective in communication. In the lecture/discussion format, the trainer presents and discusses the similarities and differences between cultures. This format is analogous to the college classroom context, where the primary mode of instruction is a professor lecturing to students. The lecture/discussion format is designed to strengthen the knowledge component of the intercultural competence model.[18] Brislin and Yoshida point out that many cross-cultural training programs contain self-assessment exercises.

Virtually every chapter in this textbook offers self-assessment instruments. In Chapter 1, for example, students can measure their level of ethnocentrism. In Chapter 2, scales designed to measure individualism/collectivism, high/low context, high/low power distance, and weak/strong uncertainty avoidance are presented. In this chapter, a cross-cultural awareness scale and an intercultural willingness to communicate scale are presented. Many of the same instruments presented throughout this book are used in cross-cultural training programs. These instruments, if completed honestly, present a reliable and valid index of the individual's relative position on the concept being measured.[19] Self-assessment instruments are useful because trainees can use them to discover dimensions of the knowledge component and the affective component of the intercultural competence model.

Case studies are stories or narratives that have an educational message. In cross-cultural training programs, case studies are either real or hypothetical stories dealing with people in intercultural situations where something has gone wrong or miscommunication occurs. The specific cases are chosen because they serve to illustrate general principles and practices of intercultural communication. They typically have correct answers. Case studies are useful because they tap into the knowledge and affective components of intercultural competence. Moreover, case studies allow trainees to indirectly observe intercultural communication and empathize with the people involved. Virtually every chapter in this text includes intercultural conversations depicting people in intercultural communication situations. These conversations are similar to case studies because they allow you to see how the concepts discussed in the text (e.g., individualism/collectivism) are evident in human intercultural communication. In cross-cultural training programs, trainees are presented with a case study, are asked to discuss it, and may be asked a series of questions.

AN INTERCULTURAL CONVERSATION: PRACTICE IN THE REAL WORLD

Jim Neuman works in the sales division of General Kitchen Appliances. Jim sells kitchen equipment to industrial-sized kitchens (e.g., for hotels, restaurants). In the United States, Jim has been very successful. Last year he was named General Kitchen's salesperson of the year, surpassing all of his sales goals. Jim has decided that he would like to expand into international markets. He has been granted a job interview by Sonado Corporation, a major kitchen equipment manufacturer in Japan. Sonado is about to expand into European markets. Here's part of Jim's interview with Mr. Kietaro, head of sales at Sonado.

Mr. Kietaro:	*Mr. Neuman, why would you like to work for Sonado?*
Jim Neuman:	*I believe I have the necessary skills and experience for this position. I'm independent and I set very high goals for myself. I believe your company will give me the opportunity to pursue them.*
Mr. Kietaro:	*I see. What kind of goals do you have?*
Jim Neuman:	*I have very high sales objectives. I try to reach the top in whatever I do. One of my goals is to become your leading salesperson. For example, I had the highest percentage of sales of anyone at General Kitchen. I was salesperson of the year last year.*
Mr. Kietaro:	*I see. That's very impressive.*
Jim Neuman:	*I'm a self-starter and self-motivator. Now I'd like to expand into an international market, I'd like to bring my experience and motivation to your company. I can be the best at Sonado, too.*

In the end, Jim Neuman was not offered a position at Sonada. In his letter to Jim, Mr. Kietaro was very complimentary about Jim's performance at General Kitchen and explained that although Jim certainly had experience, he was not sure Jim would fit into the Sonado corporate culture.

Did Jim make any mistakes in his interview?

Characterize Jim's answers to Mr. Kietaro's questions.

What did Mr. Kietaro mean when he said Jim might not "fit into" Sonada's corporate culture?

What dimension of cultural variability (as discussed in Chapter 2) might have played a role in Mr. Kietero's decision to not hire Jim?

Some cross-cultural trainers will incorporate simulation role-play exercises into their workshops. This approach is based on experiential learning (i.e., learning from experience). Role-play exercises typically have trainees actually engage in intercultural communication. For example, trainees might be asked to interview someone from a different culture. Other role-playing exercises might have trainees engage in a communicative situation designed to simulate the types of situations they are likely to face in another culture. For instance, in many countries during shopping, bargaining and negotiation are expected. Shoppers are encouraged to bargain with shop owners. In some countries, bargaining may be intense and loud. To the uninitiated American, this may seem very unusual and could be misinterpreted. Role-playing exercises that simulate such bargaining behavior could be very useful. Role-play simulations are valuable because they tap into the knowledge, affective, and psychomotor components of intercultural competence. In addition, role-play simulations can be modified to reflect the various situational features that affect intercultural communication. Careful attention should be paid to the construction of role-plays because trainees can experience intense affective reactions (e.g., apprehension, anxiety) to them.

In addition to lecture/discussions, self-assessment instruments, case studies, and simulation role-plays, videos and homework assignments are often used in cross-cultural training programs. Videos allow the trainee to "witness" intercultural communication situations and perhaps empathize with the people in the video. Homework assignments often include some type of journaling, in which trainees are asked to write their thoughts and reactions to the knowledge, emotions, and skills they are learning.

SAMPLE INTERCULTURAL TRAINING PROSPECTUS

Below is a sample of an intercultural awareness seminar program used by the author of this book.

Workshop Goals

Superordinate Goal: To increase cultural awareness at Acme National.
Subordinate Goal: To increase intercultural communication competence in the workplace.
Knowledge: Our awareness and understanding of culture's impact on behavior, including a consciousness of cultural differences and similarities.
Motivation: Our emotional reaction to the knowledge we acquire and the degree to which we approach or avoid others from different cultures.
Action: Engaging in appropriate verbal and nonverbal communication.

Workshop Overview

This workshop focuses on cross-cultural awareness and intercultural communication and provides insight into a culture's system of values, attitudes, and beliefs. Cultural background has an immense impact on how people approach their personal and business affairs. Culture teaches us how to think, conditions us how to feel, and instructs us how to act. Culture provides people with an implicit theory about how to behave and how to interpret the behavior of others. People from different cultures learn different implicit theories.

Benefits of Cross-Cultural Awareness and Intercultural Communication

Although the challenges of an increasingly diverse world are great, the benefits are even greater. Understanding cultural differences and communicating and establishing relationships with people from different cultures can lead to a whole host of benefits, including healthier communities and organizations; increased international, national, and local commerce; reduced conflict; and personal growth through increased tolerance.

A genuine organizational community is a condition of togetherness where people have lowered their defenses and learned to accept and celebrate their differences. The successful organization values differences with others whether they be about culture, race, gender, ethnicity, or even occupation or professional discipline.

Healthy organizations consist of individuals working collectively for the benefit of everyone. Through cultural awareness and open and honest intercultural communication, people can work together to achieve goals that benefit everyone, regardless of group or cultural orientation.

Our ability to interact with persons from different cultures both from within and outside our borders has immense economic benefits. According to the U.S. Department of Commerce, the markets that hold the greatest potential for dramatic increases in U.S. exports are Argentina, Brazil, China, India, Mexico, Poland, South Africa, South Korea, Turkey, and ASEAN (The Association of Southeast Asian Nations, which includes Brunei, Indonesia, Malaysia, the Philippines, Singapore, Thailand, and Vietnam). India, for example, is the fifth largest economy in the world (ranking above France, Italy, the United Kingdom, and Russia), and one of the few world markets that offers immense prospects for growth and earning potential in practically all areas of business, especially for small- and medium-sized businesses. Only through successful intercultural communication can such business potentials be realized.

Within any organization, conflict is inevitable; we will never be able to erase it. However, through cultural awareness and cooperative intercultural communication, we can reduce and manage conflict. Conflict often stems from our inability to see another person's point of view, especially if that person is from a different culture. We develop blatant generalizations about them (which are often incorrect) and mistrust them. Such feelings lead to defensive behavior, which fosters conflict. If we can learn to think and act cooperatively by engaging in assertive (not aggressive) and responsive intercultural communication, we can effectively manage and reduce conflict with others.

As you communicate with people from different cultures you learn more about them and their way of life, including their values, history, habits, and the substance of their personality. As your relationship develops you start to understand them better, perhaps even empathizing with them. One of the things you will learn (eventually) is that although your cultures are different, you have much in common. As humans we all have the same basic desires and needs, we just have different ways of achieving them. As we learn that our way is not the only way, we develop a tolerance for difference. This can be accomplished only when we initiate relationships with people who are different from ourselves.

Workshop Features

The information provided in this workshop features a balance between specific cultural information and general theories of culture. In the end, the workshop provides participants with lifelong learning skills that can be applied in their personal and professional lives. By learning about other cultures, participants learn much about their own culture and its impact on their attitudes, beliefs, and behaviors.

The workshop is designed for active participation from participants and utilizes a variety of active learning tools, such as the following:

- Self-assessment exercises that allow participants to discover what they know or what their attitudes are so that they can identify aspects of their intercultural awareness and relationships that need attention.
- Case studies that allow participants to see theory in practice and to empathize with people experiencing problems in intercultural situations.
- Depictions of cross-cultural conversations that allow the participants to see how cultural differences are manifest in verbal and nonverbal communication.

- Video presentations of people (i.e., managers) engaged in intercultural communication in the diverse workplace.
- Presentation of key concepts and theories that enable the participants to broaden their knowledge base and awareness of other cultures.

Workshop Objectives

By the end of this workshop, participants should be able to

- define communication, especially intercultural communication
- cogently discuss the nature of intercultural communication within a variety of contexts, including interpersonal and organizational contexts
- identify, compare, and contrast cultural variability and its impact on intercultural communication
- identify, compare, and contrast group membership variability and its impact on intercultural communication
- recognize and identify universal and culturally specific aspects of intercultural communication
- compare and contrast verbal communication styles and patterns of various cultures
- compare and contrast nonverbal communication styles and patterns of various cultures

Workshop Education Modules

The workshop is organized into six 3-hour education modules.

Education Module 1

This module provides introductory material about the nature of communication and how it is affected by culture. Topics include

- The nature of communication
- The challenges of effective communication
- Fear of communication (communication apprehension)
- Models of the communication process
- What culture adds to the communication process
- Models of intercultural communication

Education Module 2

This module provides theoretical and practical information about the essence of culture. The major focus of this module is on four dimensions of cultural variability:

Individualism/Collectivism—in some cultures persons are viewed as independent entities, whereas in others they are seen as dependent on others.

High/Low Context—some cultures emphasize verbal communication, whereas many others rely heavily on nonverbal messages.

Power Distance—the extent to which less powerful members of institutions and organizations expect and accept that power is distributed unequally varies considerably across cultures.

Uncertainty Avoidance—the extent to which members of a culture tolerate uncertainty and unpredictability varies from culture to culture and affects how they conduct business.

Education Module 3

This module is a continuation and extension of Module #2 and includes information about cross-cultural comparison of values, cross-cultural perceptions of time (people in other cultures have very different perceptions of time), and cross-cultural perceptions of sex roles (how men and women are perceived varies dramatically across cultures).

Education Module 4

This module focuses on verbal communication across cultures and includes such topics as

- Relationship between language and culture (culture has an immense impact on the use of language)
- Communication styles across cultures (direct/indirect, personal/contextual, instrumental/affective, succinct/elaborate)
- Forms of address
- Greeting rituals and business protocols across cultures

Education Module 5

The module addresses nonverbal communication across cultures, such as

- Cross-cultural perceptions of body language (What does it mean if I sit or stand in a certain way?)
- Cross-cultural perceptions of space (How close should we stand or sit next to one another?)
- Cross-cultural perceptions of touch (Is it acceptable to touch each other?)
- Cross-cultural perceptions of smell (why do some cultures think Americans smell of butter or antiseptic?)

Education Module 6

This module addresses information about communicating effectively across cultures, such as

- Managing cross-cultural conflict (factors that foster conflict)
- Cultural adaptation (factors that affect how one adapts to a new culture)

CHAPTER SUMMARY

One of the foremost goals of this book is to help you become a competent intercultural communicator. As defined in this chapter, *intercultural communication competence* is the degree to which you effectively adapt your verbal and nonverbal messages to the appropriate cultural context. This chapter has presented a model of intercultural competence that includes knowledge, affective, psychomotor, and situational components. In order to be a competent communicator, you must have some *knowledge* about the person with whom you are communicating. In order to be a competent intercultural communicator, you need to be *motivated* to communicate with people who are different from you. You need to engage in appropriate and effective verbal and nonverbal *skills* in order to encode and decode messages. And you need to be sensitive to the situational features that influence the verbal and nonverbal messages you send. It is to be hoped that having read this text, you are more knowledgeable about culture, are more motivated to enter into new cultures and establish relationships with persons from different cultures, and have gained some communication skills. Although challenging, intercultural communication is one of the most rewarding life experiences you will ever have.

GLOSSARY OF TERMS

Affective component: Approach-avoidance tendencies during intercultural communication. The extent to which one experiences intercultural communication apprehension and one's willingness to communicate.

Intercultural competence: The ability to adapt one's verbal and nonverbal messages to the appropriate cultural context.

Intercultural willingness to communicate: Predisposition to initiate intercultural interaction with persons from different cultures even when completely free to choose whether or not to communicate.

Knowledge component: The extent of one's awareness of another culture's values, and so forth. Also the extent to which one is cognitively simple, rigid, and ethnocentric.

Psychomotor component: The extent to which one can translate cultural knowledge into verbal and nonverbal performance and role enactment.

Situational features: The extent to which the environmental context, previous contact, status differential, and third-party intervention affect one's competence during intercultural communication.

REFERENCES

1. Hall, E. T., & Hall, E. "How Cultures Collide," *Psychology Today* 10 (1976). (Quote on page 66.)
2. Spitzberg, B. H. "A Model of Intercultural Competence," in *Intercultural Communication Reader,* 8th ed., ed. L. A. Samovar and R. E. Porter (Belmont, Calif.: Wadsworth, 1997), pp. 379–391.
3. Spitzberg, "A Model of Intercultural Competence."
4. This dialogue is loosely adapted from a scene in L. Copeland (Producer) *Managing the Overseas Assignment* [videorecording] (San Francisco: Copeland Griggs Productions, 1983.)
5. Harris, P. R., & Moran, R. T. *Managing Cultural Differences* (Houston, TX: Gulf Publishing, 1991).
6. Spitzberg, B. H., & Cupach, W. R. *Interpersonal Communication Competence* (Beverly Hills, Calif.: Sage, 1984).
7. This scale is loosely adapted from Goodman, N. R. "Cross-Cultural Training for the Global Executive," in *Improving Intercultural Interaction: Models for Cross-Cultural Training Programs,* ed. Brislin, R. W., & Yoshida, T. (Thousand Oaks, Calif.: Sage, 1994), pp. 34–54.
8. Berger, C. R., & Jordan, J. "Planning Sources, Planning Difficulty, and Verbal Fluency," *Communication Monographs* 59 (1992), 130–149.
9. Kim, Y. Y. "Explaining Interethnic Conflict: An Interdisciplinary Overview" (paper presented at the annual convention of the Speech Communication Association, Chicago, Ill., 1990).
10. See, for example, W. G. Sumner, *Folkways* (Boston: Ginn, 1906); Segall, M. H. *Cross-Cultural Psychology: Human Behavior in Global Perspective* (Monterey, Calif.: Brooks/Cole, 1979); Hewstone, M., & Ward, C. X. "Ethnocentrism and Causal Attribution in Southeast Asia," *Journal of Personality and Social Psychology* 48 (1985), 614–623; Islam, M. R., & Hewstone, M. "Intergroup Attribution and Affective Consequences in Majority and Minority Groups," *Journal of Personality and Social Psychology* 64, (1993) 936–950.
11. Wiseman, R. L., Hammer, M. R., & Nishida, H. "Predictors of Intercultural Communication Competence," *International Journal of Intercultural Relations* 13, (1989), 349–370.

12. Neuliep, J. W., & McCroskey, J. C. "The Development of Intercultural and Interethnic Communication Apprehension Scales," *Communication Research Reports* 14, (1997), 145–156.

13. Kassing, J. W. "Development of the Intercultural Willingness to Communicate Scale," *Communication Research Reports* 14, (1997), 399–407.

14. Kim, Y. Y. "Intercultural Communication Competence: A Systems-Theoretic View." In *Cross-Cultural Interpersonal Communication,* ed. Ting-Toomey, S. & Korzenny, F. (Newbury Park, Calif.: Sage, 1991), pp. 259–275; Gudykunst, W. B., & Kim, Y. Y. *Communicating with Strangers: An Approach to Intercultural Communication* (New York: McGraw-Hill, 1997).

15. Kim, "Explaining Interethnic Conflict."

16. Ibid.; Gudykunst and Kim, *Communicating with Strangers.*

17. Brislin, R. W., & Yoshida, T. "The Content of Cross-Cultural Training: An Introduction." In *Improving Intercultural Interactions: Modules of Cross-Cultural Training Programs,* ed. Brislin, R. W,. & Yoshida, T. (Thousand Oaks, Calif.: Sage, 1994), pp. 1–16.

18. Gudykunst, W. B., Guzley, R. M., & Hammer, M. R. "Designing Intercultural Training." In *Handbook of Intercultural Training,* ed. Landis, D., & Bhagat, R. S. (Thousand Oaks, Calif.: Sage, 1996), pp. 61–80.

19. Brislin and Yoshida, "The Content of Cross-Cultural Training."

Author Index

Subject Index

About the Author

James W. Neuliep (PhD, University of Oklahoma) conducts research and teaches courses in interpersonal communication, small group communication, intercultural communication, communication theory, communication apprehension, ethnocentrism, and research methods. Along with Jim McCroskey, he has developed a number of assessment scales used throughout the discipline. In addition to his introductory intercultural communication textbook, he has also written an introductory communication theory textbook (*Human Communication Theory: Applications and Case Studies*, Allyn & Bacon), and his research has appeared in the following journals: *Communication Research Reports, Journal of Intercultural Communication Research, Communication Reports, Journal of Social Behavior and Personality, Communication Education, Communication Quarterly,* and *Human Communication Research.* He is the editor of the *Journal of Intercultural Communication Research* and has served on the editorial boards of *Communication Studies, Journal of Communication, Journal of Applied Communication Research, Journal of Social Behavior and Personality,* and *Communication Quarterly.*